FILM GENRE READER III

FILM GENRE READER III

Edited by Barry Keith Grant

 University of Texas Press • Austin

Requests for permission to reproduce material from this work should
be sent to Permissions, University of Texas Press, P.O. Box 7819,
Austin, TX 78713-7819.

♾ The paper used in this book meets the minimum requirements of
ANSI/NISO Z39.48-1992 (R1997) (Permanence of Paper).

Library of Congress Cataloging-in-Publication Data

Film genre reader III / edited by Barry Keith Grant.
     p.   cm.
Includes bibliographical references and index.
   ISBN 0-292-70184-5 (hardcover : alk. paper) —
   ISBN 0-292-70185-3 (pbk. : alk. paper)
   1. Motion picture plays—History and criticism.   2. Film genres.
I. Grant, Barry Keith, 1947–
   PN1995.F45793   2003
   791.43′6—dc21
2003002794

ACKNOWLEDGMENTS

RICK ALTMAN. "A Semantic/Syntactic Approach to Film Genre," appeared originally in a slightly different form in *Cinema Journal* 23, no. 3 (Spring 1984): 6–18. Copyright © 1984 by *Cinema Journal*. Reprinted by permission.

JEAN-LOUP BOURGET. "Social Implications in the Hollywood Genres," from *Journal of Modern Literature* 3, no. 2 (April 1973): 191–200. Copyright © 1973 by *Journal of Modern Literature*. Reprinted by permission of *Journal of Modern Literature*.

EDWARD BUSCOMBE. "The Idea of Genre in the American Cinema," from *Screen* 11, no. 2 (March–April 1970): 33–45. Copyright © 1970 by *Screen*. Reprinted by permission.

JOHN G. CAWELTI. "*Chinatown* and Generic Transformation in Recent American Films," from *Film Theory and Criticism,* 2d ed., edited by Gerald Mast and Marshall Cohen (New York: Oxford University Press, 1979), 559–579. Copyright © 1979 by John G. Cawelti. Reprinted by permission of the author.

DAVID DESSER. "Global Noir: Genre Film in the Age of Transnationalism." Copyright © 2002 by David Desser. Used with permission of the author.

THOMAS ELSAESSER. "Tales of Sound and Fury: Observations on the Family Melodrama," from *Monogram,* no. 4 (1973): 2–15. Copyright © 1985 by the British Film Institute. Reprinted by permission of the author and the British Film Institute.

JANE FEUER. "The Self-Reflexive Musical and the Myth of Entertainment," from *Quarterly Review of Film Studies* 2, no. 3 (August 1977):

DAVID R. SHUMWAY. "Screwball Comedies: Constructing Romance, Mystifying Marriage," from *Cinema Journal* 30, no. 4 (Summer 1991): 7–23. Copyright © 1991 by Board of Trustees of the University of Illinois. Reprinted by permission of The University of Texas Press and the author.

THOMAS SOBCHACK. "Genre Films: A Classical Experience," from *Literature/Film Quarterly* 3, no. 3 (Summer 1975): 196–204. Copyright © 1975 by *Literature/Film Quarterly*. Reprinted by permission.

VIVIAN SOBCHACK. "'Surge and Splendor': A Phenomenology of the Hollywood Historical Epic," appeared originally in a slightly different form in *Representations*, no. 29 (Winter 1990): 24–49. Copyright © 1990 by the Regents of the University of California. Reprinted by permission of the Regents and the author.

JANET STAIGER. "Hybrid or Inbred: The Purity Hypothesis and Hollywood Genre History" appeared originally in *Film Criticism* 22, no. 1 (Fall 1997): 5–20 and was reprinted in Staiger, *Perverse Spectators: The Practices of Film Reception* (New York: New York University Press, 2000), pp. 61–76. Copyright © 2000 by New York University Press. Reprinted by permission of the author, *Film Criticism,* and New York University Press.

CHRIS STRAAYER. "Redressing the 'Natural': The Temporary Transvestite Film," from *Wide Angle* 14, no. 1 (January 1992): 36–55. Copyright © 1992 by Chris Straayer. Reprinted by permission of The Johns Hopkins University Press and the author.

MARGARET TARRATT. "Monsters from the Id," from *Films and Filming* 17, no. 3 (December 1970): 38–42, and no. 4 (January 1971): 40–42. Copyright © 1970 by Margaret Tarratt. Reprinted by permission.

ANDREW TUDOR. "Genre," from *Theories of Film* (New York: Viking Press, 1973), 131–150. Copyright © 1973 by Andrew Tudor. Reprinted by permission of the Viking Press and Martin Secker & Warburg Ltd.

LINDA WILLIAMS. "Film Bodies: Gender, Genre, and Excess," appeared originally in a slightly different form in *Film Quarterly* 44, no. 4 (Summer 1991): 2–13. Copyright © 1991 by the Regents of the University of California. Reprinted by permission of the Regents and the author.

For Genevieve again, with love

Contents

Preface to the Third Edition

The first edition of *Film Genre Reader* was published by the University of Texas Press in 1986, and the second in 1995. To my great satisfaction, the book has continued to remain of value to film scholars and students. Because *Film Genre Reader* has enjoyed such success over the years, and because of the limitations dictated by the practical constraints of space, this third edition includes just three new essays. But together they address important genres and directions in genre study not covered in the two preceding editions. The bibliography has been thoroughly updated to include relevant work published in English since 1995.

Thanks to my former students Melissa Charlesworth and Cat Velasco for their help with parts of the bibliography. Once again I would like to express my gratitude to all those colleagues and students who have used the earlier editions and provided me with their insights, impressions, and responses regarding genre films, film genres, and this book. And above all, many thanks to Jim Burr at the University of Texas Press for his support for this third edition of *Film Genre Reader,* and to Carolyn Cates Wylie for once again seeing the manuscript through the publication process.

B.K.G.

Introduction

Stated simply, genre movies are those commercial feature films which, through repetition and variation, tell familiar stories with familiar characters in familiar situations. They also encourage expectations and experiences similar to those of similar films we have already seen. Genre movies have comprised the bulk of film practice, the iceberg of film history beneath the visible tip that in the past has commonly been understood as film art. They have been exceptionally significant as well in establishing the popular sense of cinema as a cultural and economic institution, particularly in the United States, where Hollywood studios early on adopted an industrial model based on mass production. Traditionally, Hollywood movies have been produced in a profit-motivated studio system which, as the result of sound business practice, has sought to guarantee acceptance at the box office by the exploitation and variation of commercially successful formulas. In this system, praised for the "genius" of its efficiency by André Bazin, genre movies are the Model Ts or the Colt revolvers of film, with interchangeable parts.

Yet despite this central place of genre in the cinema, critical recognition of its importance is a relatively recent development. The first significant essays of film genre criticism, Robert Warshow's articles on the gangster film and the western (originally published in the *Partisan Review* in 1948 and 1954, respectively) and Bazin's two pieces on the western from the early fifties, were all written within a few years of each other. Chronologically, genre criticism thus narrowly predates the early work of auteurism, but it developed more slowly because it failed to enjoy the popularization that heralded the arrival of director-oriented "theory," first in Great Britain—primarily in the journal *Movie*—and then in North America through the writings of Andrew Sarris. Valorizing the artist responsible for the dubious art of film, auteur criticism proved at the time more amenable to the serious discussion of cinema.

It is not surprising that Warshow and Bazin focused on westerns and gangster films, since these have been perhaps the two most durable of

American film genres, beginning with *The Great Train Robbery* (Edwin S. Porter, 1903) and *The Musketeers of Pig Alley* (D. W. Griffith, 1912). Today it seems clear that these essays suffer from an impressionism and prescriptiveness that, while unfortunate, is also not uncharacteristic of later genre criticism. Yet their flaws are readily understandable, given that these first essays were unprecedented and were written at a time when genres were undergoing radical change after a period of relative stability. Indeed, despite their problems, they have also pointed the way for many of the concerns of later critics. For example, Warshow was extremely perceptive in the essay on gangster films about the essential dynamics of the genre and the satisfactions it typically provides the viewer; thus he anticipated one of the central topics of more sophisticated contemporary film theory—the positioning or construction of the spectating subject. His cogent observation that "the real city . . . produces only criminals; the imaginary city produces the gangster" reveals that in some way he understood genre as a system of conventions structured according to cultural values, an idea not dissimilar to what structuralists would later call the "deep structure" of myth. Warshow's distinction initiated the now generally accepted separation of historical verisimilitude (but not history) from the analysis of genre, which is the way it had most often been discussed before. In addition, his acknowledgment of a difference between actual social restraints ("the real city") and the structures of the imaginative escape from it ("the imaginary city") adumbrates the project of much later work in deconstructing the processes—what Roland Barthes calls the mythologies—by which ideology contains and reinforces itself.

While the works of these two critics may be seen as crucial to the development of a more rigorous genre criticism, however, in another sense they were only attempts at articulating concepts already implicitly understood by filmmakers and viewers alike. Well before their articles were first published, the idea of genre circulated in public thinking, if not in critical discourse. Films were loosely typed by producers, audiences, and even reviewers: a movie was a "western" or a "war movie" or a "musical," and such descriptive labels came to signal information to prospective consumers about the story and the kind of pleasure it was likely to offer. Only after this circuit of economic and aesthetic relations was firmly established was it possible for critics to realize that if those handy descriptive tags actually referred to true traditions of film practice, then they might be worth identifying, analyzing, and theorizing about. *Genre* thus became a critical term as well as a collection of popular categories, and it has since proved to be a useful conceptual tool for understanding popular film as both art and artifact.

As film study developed in the 1970s, interest in the narrative film, nurtured a decade earlier by auteurism's enthusiasm for popular American movies, began to wane in favor of more formal concerns. Critical interest shifted from the signified of films to the practice of signification, from what a film "means" to how it produces meaning. Accordingly, both non-narrative, experimental films and those that somehow broke with the seamless, "classical" construction of Hollywood narrative (what Noel Burch has called the "institutional mode of representation") received an increasing degree of critical attention. At the same time, a heightened concern with the operation of ideology in art, stimulated by the importation to film of theoretical work by John Berger, Louis Althusser, Brecht, Freud, and others, shattered the operating assumption that an understanding of a film's director and his or her oeuvre would provide the key to interpretation. Rather, meaning was now seen to arise from the conjunction of various discursive codes at work in the film text, of which the directorial code was only one. Fuller, Hawks, and Hitchcock became, in the famous formulation by Peter Wollen in the revised edition of *Signs and Meaning in the Cinema* (1972), "Fuller," "Hawks," and "Hitchcock"—that is, filmic structures designated by the name appearing on the director's credit. As Barthes had shown, writing degree zero, a discourse that exists outside ideology, is impossible.

Eventually, this emphasis on signification and ideology brought about a renewed interest in the classical narrative film, and genre films in particular became an important site of inquiry. The general view of popular film now was that it was little more than bourgeois illusionism, essentially conservative in both style and theme. Genres therefore existed primarily as mythic edifices to be deconstructed. They were valuable for study because generic analysis could easily involve the consideration of economic and historical contexts (conditions of production and consumption), conventions and mythic functions (semiotic codes and structural patterns), and the place of particular filmmakers within genres (tradition and the individual auteur).

Thus genre criticism has been able to accommodate the interests of newer approaches to film, and in fact may be seen as a locus of the overlapping but often separate concerns of auteurism, Marxism, semiology, structuralism, and feminism. Similarly, the more contemporary interest in issues of gender, race, class, and sexuality, and in audience reception in cinema also finds much ground for analysis in the fertile fields of genre. If, in the eighties, leftist critics were able to shift away from the view of genre as necessarily mythic embodiments of the dominant ideology—for example, a convincing case was made for reading many horror films as critiques of American society rather than as endorsements of its fears and repressions—so, more recently, previously marginalized voices have been finding spaces from which to speak within the discourse on genre, as in the case of queer readings of popular films. While it is true that genre movies tell familiar stories with familiar characters in familiar situations, it by no means follows that they do so in ways that are completely familiar.

Film Genre Reader III, like the first two editions, gathers together some of the best writing on genre, balancing more recent work with a sense of historical development. The book has two sections, the first concentrating on theory and the second on criticism. As the essays in Part One were generally written earlier than those in the second section, and because they raise a number of issues crucial to the understanding of any particular genre(s), it is recommended that this part be read first. However, at the same time it should be noted that the anthology was not conceived as a definitive history of genre criticism. A number of historically important essays, such as those by Warshow and Bazin as well as Susan Sontag's important 1965 article on science fiction movies, have not been included for the practical reason that they are all readily available elsewhere. Nor are the essays here presented in a strict chronological arrangement; rather, they proceed in a manner that should help the reader to achieve a progressive understanding of film genre. (One further stylistic note: the first mention in each essay of a film is followed parenthetically by the name of the director and the year of release. This is motivated less by an auteurist bias than by a desire to suggest the extent to which certain directors have worked within a particular genre or genres.)

Part One begins with Andrew Tudor's consideration of some of the problems arising in the very attempt to delineate individual genres. Edward Buscombe next offers a partial solution to Tudor's dilemma by theorizing a distinction, adapted from literary criticism, between a film's "outer forms" (iconography) and its "inner forms" (themes) and by discussing their relationship. Rick Altman suggests a way to approach the range of works within individual genres by introducing concepts borrowed from linguistics. The social and political implications of genres and of individual genre films are discussed by both Judith Hess Wright and Jean-Loup Bourget, who present almost diametrically opposed arguments. For Wright, genre films act as conservative reaffirmations of dominant values because they are grounded in the predictability of conventions, while Bourget sees them as possessing the ability to become subversive statements for precisely the same reason. Robin Wood considers this issue in relation to the place of the auteur by contrasting some of the genre work of Alfred Hitchcock and Frank Capra. The political issues raised by Wright, Bourget, and Wood are then placed by Barbara Klinger within the influential theoretical framework for categorizing the relation of all narrative films to ideology originally proposed by Jean-Louis Comolli and Jean Narboni. Next, Thomas Schatz offers an overview of the ways in which structuralism has been applied to film genre, and the experiential nature of genre films is discussed in Thomas Sobchack's essay as well as in my own. Richard de Cordova discusses aspects of performance in relation to genre, an element of cinema largely ignored by scholarly writing. Linda Williams rethinks traditional generic distinctions by offering some provocative points of comparison between three of what she calls "body genres," and Steve Neale usefully summarizes several important issues examined in much recent genre theory, as well as suggesting some directions for future work. The section concludes with Janet Staiger's lucid unpacking of the debate regarding genre hybridity.

Together the essays in Part One introduce a range of approaches to film genre, many of which are applied in the second section. Each of the selections in Part Two treats a particular genre from a somewhat different perspective, and together they provide a comprehensive overview of applied genre criticism. Since the western has been central to American popular culture and subjected to the most sustained critical analyses over the years, Part Two begins with a discussion of this genre by Douglas Pye, employing the concept of modes as outlined in the work of Northrop Frye. Next, the history and social myths that contributed to the development of the gangster film, a genre that shares many elements with the western, are examined by Edward Mitchell. Paul Schrader discusses film noir primarily from a stylistic perspective, and although he begins by asserting that film noir is actually not a genre, it would seem that his analysis, and the work of later critics, has demonstrated that it may indeed be considered one. John G. Cawelti and Tag Gallagher both address the question of generic alteration or "evolution," and once again there is a marked difference of opinion: Cawelti identifies distinct modes of change in recent genre films, but Gallagher seriously challenges the accuracy of the commonly held evolutionary view. Maurice Yacowar's essay on the disaster film seeks to define a typology of that genre, while Vivian Sobchack examines the relations between the form of the epic film and the spectator's viewing experience. Bruce Kawin offers a useful distinction between horror and science fiction, two closely related and overlapping genres. In the following essay, Margaret Tarratt discusses some of these movies from a Freudian perspective, an approach also found in the analysis of melodrama offered by Thomas Elsaesser. Next, the ideology of romance offered by the screwball comedy is examined by David Shumway. A similar concern with gender and desire informs Chris Straayer's identification of what she dubs the "temporary transvestite film," and Susan Jeffords's consideration of both women characters in and the spectating subject of Vietnam War films. Jane Feuer analyzes the mythic strategies by which the classic musical valorizes itself. Mark Reid considers the representation of race in his discussion of black gangster films, and Timothy Shary outlines the parameters and permutations of the teen film, a genre uniquely defined in terms of the age group represented in the narrative.

As one might expect, genre criticism has concentrated on (mainstream) American cinema, and the essays collected in this volume are no exception. But such questions as the relation of genre to ideology have ramifications beyond Hollywood. From Japanese samurai films to Italian westerns to French gangster films to Hong Kong action movies, almost all national cinemas have been influenced to some degree by American genre movies. In the concluding essay of Part Two, David Desser considers the international dimensions of commercial filmmaking in the context of what he calls "global noir."

The essays in this collection may of course be read in the order presented, or in groups concerned with similar issues. For example, an examination of genre and ideology would include, among others, the essays by Wright, Bourget, Wood, Klinger, Feuer, and Jeffords. The relation between genre and auteur is examined in the selections by Bourget, Wood, Cawelti, and Gallagher. The complexities of genre and the viewing experience connect the essays by Thomas Sobchack, Williams, Kawin, Vivian Sobchack, Straayer, Jeffords, and Grant. Issues of representation and difference unite such otherwise different essays as those by Straayer, Jeffords, Reid, Shary, and Desser. Other groupings are certainly possible, and however one chooses to use the book, it should provide both the general reader and the student of film with a comprehensive view of film genre. The marked difference of opinion among many of these essays indicates less the lack of an editorial position than the attempt to generate lively debate of the issues.

Part One: THEORY

1. Genre

ANDREW TUDOR

Auteur originated in film criticism of the recent past; *genre* had a lengthy pedigree in literary criticism long before the advent of the cinema. Hence the meaning and uses of the latter term vary considerably, and it is very difficult to identify even a tenuous school of thought on the subject. For years it provided a crudely useful way of delineating the American cinema. The literature abounds with references to the western, the gangster movie, or the horror film, all of which are loosely thought of as genres. On occasion it becomes almost the end point of the critical process to fit a film into such a category, much as it once made a film "intelligible" to fit it into, say, the French "nouvelle vague." To call a film a western is thought of as somehow saying something interesting or important about it. To fit it into a class of films suggests we presumably have some general knowledge about it. To say a film is a western is immediately to say that it shares some indefinable "*X*" with other films we call westerns. In addition, it provides us with a body of films to which our film can be usefully compared—sometimes the only body of films. The most extreme, and clearly ridiculous, application might be to argue that it is necessarily more illuminating to compare, say, *The Man Who Shot Liberty Valance* (John Ford, 1962) with a Roy Rogers short than with *The Last Hurrah* (Ford, 1958). It is not that the first comparison might not be instructive; merely that it is not necessarily the case. Extreme genre imperialism leads in this direction.

Now almost everyone uses terms like "western," the neurotic critic as much as the undisturbed cinemagoer. The difference, and the source of difficulty, lies in how the critic seeks to use the term. What is normally a thumbnail classification for everyday purposes is now being asked to carry rather more weight. The fact that there is a special term, *genre*, for these categories suggests that the critic's conception of "western" is more

Note: This chapter is excerpted from a longer essay published previously.

complex than is the case in everyday discourse; if not, why the special term? But in what way critical usage is more complex is not entirely clear. In some cases it involves the idea that if a film is a western it somehow draws on a tradition—in particular, on a set of conventions. That is, westerns have in common certain themes, certain typical actions, certain characteristic mannerisms; to experience a western is to operate within this previously defined world. Jim Kitses tries to isolate characteristics in this way by defining *genre* in terms of such attributes: " . . . a varied and flexible structure, a thematically fertile and ambiguous world of historical material shot through with archetypal elements which are themselves ever in flux." [1] But other usages, such as "horror" films, might also mean films displaying certain themes, actions, and so on, or, just as often, films that have in common the *intention* to horrify. Instead of defining the genre by attributes, it is defined by intentions. Likewise with the distinction between "gangster" movies and "thrillers."

Both these uses display serious problems. The second (and for all practical purposes least important) suffers from the notorious difficulties of isolating intentions. In the first and more common case the special genre term is frequently entirely redundant. Imagine a definition of a western as a film set in the western United States between 1860 and 1900 and involving as its central theme the contrast between garden and desert. Any film fulfilling these requirements is a western, and a western is only a film fulfilling these requirements. By multiplying such categories it is possible to divide all films into groups, though not necessarily mutually exclusive groups. The usefulness of this (and classification can only be justified by its use) depends on what it is meant to achieve. But what is certain is that just as the critic determines the criteria on which the classification is based, so he or she also determines the name given to the resultant groups of films. Our group might just as well be called "type 1482/9a" as "westerns."

Evidently there are areas in which such individually defined categories might be of some use: a sort of bibliographic classification of the history of film, for instance, or even an abstract exploration of the cyclical recurrence of certain themes. The films would be simply defined in terms of the presence or absence of the themes in question. But this is not the way in which the term is usually employed. On the contrary, most writers tend to assume that there is some body of films we can safely call the western and then move on to the real work—the analysis of the crucial characteristics of the already recognized genre. Hence Kitses' set of thematic antinomies and four sorts of genre conventions. Or Bazin's distinction between classic and "sur-western," assuming, as it does, that there is some independently established essence of the western that is distilled into *Stagecoach* (Ford, 1939).[2] These writers, and almost all writers using the term *genre,* are caught in a dilemma. They are defining a western on the basis of analyzing a body of films that cannot possibly be said to be westerns until after the analysis. If Kitses' themes and conventions are the defining characteristic of the western, then this is the previously discussed case of arbitrary definition—the category becomes redundant. But these themes and conventions are arrived at by analyzing films *already distinguished from other films by virtue of being "westerns."* To take a genre such as a western, analyze it, and list its principal characteristics is to beg the question that we must first isolate the body of films that are westerns. But they can only be isolated on the basis of the "principal characteristics," which can only be discovered from the films themselves after they have been isolated. That is, we are caught in a circle that first requires that the films be isolated, for which purposes a criterion is necessary, but the criterion is, in turn, meant to emerge from the empirically established common characteristics of the films. This "empiricist dilemma" has two solutions. One is to classify films according to a priori criteria depending on the critical purpose. This leads back to the earlier position in which the special genre term is redundant. The second is to lean on a common cultural consensus as to what constitutes a western and then go on to analyze it in detail.

This latter is clearly the root of most uses of genre. It is this usage that leads to, for example, the notion of conventions in a genre. The western, it is said, has certain crucial established conventions—ritualistic gunfights, black and white clothing corresponding to good and bad distinctions, revenge themes, typed villains, and many, many more. The best evidence for the widespread recognition of these conventions is to be found in those films that pointedly set out to invoke them. *Shane* (George Stevens, 1953), for example, plays very much on the stereotyped imagery, contrasting the stooping, black-clad, sallow, gloved Palance with the tall (by dint of careful camera angles), straight, white-buckskinned, fair, white-horsed Ladd. The power of this imagery is such that the sequence in which Shane rides to the showdown elevates him to a classically heroic posture. The point is reinforced by comparing Stevens's visualization of his characters with the very different descriptions offered in Schaefer's novel. The film "converts" the images to its own conventional language. Other obvious examples are provided by the series of Italian westerns. The use of Lee Van Cleef in leading roles depends very much on the image he has acquired over two decades of bit-part villains. Actors in the series—Van Cleef, Clint Eastwood, Eli Wallach, Jack Elam, Woody Strode, Henry Fonda, Charles Bronson—perpetually verge on self-parody. The most peculiar of the films, *Once upon a Time in the West* (Sergio Leone, 1969), is a fairy-tale collection of western conventions, verging on self-parody and culminating in what must be the most extended face-off ever

1. *Shane:* The classically heroic posture of Shane (Alan Ladd).

filmed. Indeed, the most telling suggestions as to the importance of conventions are to be found in the gentle parodies *Cat Ballou* (Elliott Silverstein, 1965), *Support Your Local Sheriff* (Burt Kennedy, 1969), and *The Good Guys and the Bad Guys* (Kennedy, 1969). Without clear, shared conceptions of what is to be expected from a western, such humor is not possible. One of the best sequences in *Cat Ballou* encapsulates the importance of the imagery, the sequence in which Lee Marvin is changed from drunken wreck to classic gunfighter. Starting very humorously with Marvin struggling into a corset, the transformation not only alters him but brings out a response in us as piece by piece the stereotyped image appears.

In short, to talk about the western is (arbitrary definitions apart) to appeal to a common set of meanings in our culture. From a very early age most of us have built up a picture of a western. We feel that we know a western when we see one, though the edges may be rather blurred. Thus in calling a film a western the critic is implying more than the simple state-

2. *Cat Ballou:* Lee Marvin as the drunken ex-gunfighter.

ment "This film is a member of a class of films (westerns) having in common *x, y,* and *z.*" The critic is also suggesting that such a film would be universally recognized as such in our culture. In other words, the crucial factors that distinguish a genre are not only characteristics inherent in the films themselves; they also depend on the particular culture within which we are operating. And unless there is world consensus on the subject (which is an empirical question), there is no basis for assuming that a western will be conceived in the same way in every culture. The way in which the genre term is applied can quite conceivably vary from case to case. Genre notions—except the special case of arbitrary definition—are not critics' classifications made for special purposes; they are sets of cultural conventions. Genre is what we collectively believe it to be.

It is for precisely this reason that notions about genre are potentially so interesting—but more for the exploration of the psychological and sociological interplay between filmmaker, film, and audience than for the immediate purposes of film criticism. (Given that it is not entirely possible to draw a clear line between the two, this is really an argument for using a concept in one area rather than another.) Until we have a clear, if speculative, notion of the connotations of a genre class, it is difficult to see how critics, already besieged by imponderables, could usefully apply the term, certainly not as a special term at the root of their analyses. To use the concept in any stronger sense it becomes necessary to establish clearly what filmmakers mean when they conceive themselves as making a western; what limits such a choice may impose on them; in effect, what relationship exists between *auteur* and *genre*. But specific answers to such questions must tap the conceptions held by particular filmmakers and industries. To methodically analyze the way in which a filmmaker utilizes a genre for his or her own purposes (at present a popular critical pursuit) requires that we clearly establish the principal components of that filmmaker's conception of the genre. But this is not all. The notion that someone utilizes a genre suggests something about audience response. It implies that any given film works in a particular way because the audience has certain expectations of the genre. We can meaningfully talk of, for instance, an auteur breaking the rules of a genre only if we know what these rules are. And, of course, such rule-breaking has no consequence unless the audience knows as well. Now, as I have suggested, *Shane* may well take on its almost "epic" quality because Stevens for the most part sticks to the rules. In a similar way, *Two Rode Together* (Ford, 1961) and *Cheyenne Autumn* (Ford, 1964) are slightly disconcerting because they break the rules, particularly vis-à-vis the relation between Indian and white man. And, most obviously in recent years, Peckinpah's westerns use such elements to disturb the conventional universe of this genre—the much-remarked opening scene of *Ride the High Country* (1962) with its policeman and motor cars; the cavalry charging the French army in *Major Dundee* (1965); the car in *The Wild Bunch* (1969). Now you, the reader, may agree that these are cases of deliberate rule-breaking, and such agreement reflects that there is, in America and in Europe as well, some considerable consensus of what constitutes the characteristic "language" of a western. But this could well be a special case. To infer from it that all genre terms are thus easily employed is hardly justified.

This is not to suggest that genre terms are totally useless but merely that to employ them requires a much more methodical understanding of the working of film. And this in turn requires that we specify a set of sociological and psychological context assumptions and construct explicit genre models within them. If we imagine a general model of the workings of film language, genre directs our attention to sublanguages within it. Less centrally, however, the genre concept is indispensable in more strictly social and psychological terms as a way of formulating the interplay between culture, audience, films, and filmmakers. For example, there is a class of films thought of by a relatively highly educated middle-class group of filmgoers as "art movies." Now for present purposes genre is a conception existing in the culture of any particular group or society; it is not a way in which a critic classifies films for methodological purposes, but the much looser way in which an audience classifies its films. According to this meaning of the term, "art movies" is a genre. If a culture includes such notions of genre, then over a period of time and in a complicated way certain conventions become established as to what can be expected from an "art movie" as compared to some other category. The critics (the "posh" critics, in this case) are mediating factors in such developments. But once such conventions develop, they can in turn affect a filmmaker's conception of what he or she is doing. Hence the "art movie" category is commercially played up.

Let me take an impressionistic example, bearing in mind that much more extensive work would be needed to establish this in anything more than an intuitive way. At the beginning of the 1960s the general conception of an art movie revolved around the films of a group of European directors. Bergman was already established with, in particular, *The Seventh Seal* (1956) and *Wild Strawberries* (1957). The first year of the new decade had seen Antonioni's *L'Avventura* (1960), Resnais' *Hiroshima Mon Amour* (1959), and Fellini's *La Dolce Vita* (1959). These four directors—though perhaps Resnais less than the others—served to define the "conventions" of the developing art movie genre: deliberately and obviously intellectual (there is nothing more deliberate than the final scene of *La Dolce Vita*), with extremely visible individual stylistic characteristics. Bergman's silhouettes, puritan obsessiveness, and grunting Dark Age meals; Antonioni's minimal dialogue, grey photography, and carefully bleak compositions; and Fellini's self-indulgent surrealistic imagery, partly in *La Dolce Vita* but much more clearly in *8½* (1962), circumscribed what was expected of an art movie. Increasingly, European films, whether "deliberate" copies (a sub-Antonioni example is Giuseppi Patroni Griffi's 1963 film *Il Mare*) or later films made by the original directors, were based on the conventions that the earlier films had established. Antonioni's *Il Deserto Rosso* (1964), Fellini's *Juliet of the Spirits* (1965), and Bergman's *Winter Light* (1963) and *The Silence* (1963) are almost stylistic parodies of each director's earlier films. *Juliet of the Spirits* becomes the ultimate in color-supplement art movies, a combination of the earlier films and the newly established conventions of the genre.

This should serve to illustrate the way in which notions of genre might constructively be used in tapping the sociopsychological dynamics of film, although it is not designed to convince anyone of the particular case of "art movies." To properly establish such an argument would require detailed research on the changing expectations of art-movie audiences (perhaps via analysis of the "posh" critics), on the genre conceptions (and self-conceptions) held by individuals and groups in various film industries, and on the films themselves. Now there does not seem to me to be any crucial difference between the most commonly employed genre term —the western—and the art-movie category that I have been discussing. They are both conceptions held by certain groups about certain films. Many of the theoretical problems of using genre terms have, however, been overlooked in the case of the western. It has become so much a part of our cultural patterning that film criticism has tended to use it as if it were possible to assume common agreement in all the respects on which research would be necessary in the art-movie case. It may be that there is such common agreement on the western; but it does not follow that this would be true of all genre categories. Anyway, it is not at all clear that there is that much consensus on the western. It seems likely that for many people the most western of westerns (certainly the most popular, if revivals are any indicator) is John Sturges's *The Magnificent Seven* (1960). On the other hand, in the 1940s the same position might be filled by *My Darling Clementine* (Ford, 1946), in the 1950s by *High Noon* (Fred Zinneman, 1952). Conventions change, often for reasons entirely out of the control of filmmakers and film critics.

In sum, then, genre terms seem best employed in the analysis of the relation between groups of films, the cultures in which they are made, and the cultures in which they are exhibited. That is, it is a term that can be usefully employed in relation to a body of knowledge and theory about the social and psychological context of film. Any assertion we might make about a director's use of genre conventions—Peckinpah uses the contrast between our expectations and actual images to reinforce the "end of an era" element in *Ride the High Country* and *The Wild Bunch*—assumes, wrongly, the existence of this body of knowledge. To labor the point, it assumes (1) we know what Peckinpah thinks; (2) we know what the audience thinks about the films in question and about westerns; (3) Peckinpah knows what the audience thinks; and so on. Most uses of genre effectively invent answers to such questions by implicitly claiming to tap some archetypal characteristic of the genre, some universal human response. This depends on the particular context of the assumptions employed and on a more general notion of film language. To leap in with genre immediately is to put the cart before the horse.

Notes

1. Jim Kitses, *Horizons West* (Bloomington and London: Indiana University Press, 1970), p. 19.

2. André Bazin, "Evolution du Western," *Cahiers du Cinéma* 9, no. 54 (December 1955), reprinted in André Bazin, *Cinéma et sociologie,* vol. 3 of *Qu'est-ce que le cinéma?* (Paris: Editions du Cerf, 1961). This essay is available in English in André Bazin, *What Is Cinema?* edited and translated by Hugh Gray (Berkeley: University of California Press, 1971), 2:149–157.

2. The Idea of Genre in the American Cinema

EDWARD BUSCOMBE

Genre is a term much employed in film criticism at the moment, yet there is little agreement on what exactly it means or whether the term has any use at all. There appear to be three sorts of questions one could profitably ask: first, do genres in the cinema really exist, and if so, can they be defined? second, what are the functions they fulfill? and third, how do specific genres originate or what causes them?

It seems sensible to start with a brief review of the history of genre criticism in literature, since it is in this context that certain problems first arise. The notion that there are different kinds of literature, with different techniques and subjects, was first developed by Aristotle; in his *Poetics* he tried to separate what he called poetry—what we simply call literature—into a number of categories such as tragedy, epic, lyric, and so forth. His purpose was to decide what were the particular qualities of each distinctive kind, and what each kind could be expected to do and not do. He then tried to establish their relative importance, and after much debate concluded that tragedy was the highest kind of poetry.

During the Renaissance Aristotle's ideas were taken up and erected into a rigid system of rules so that certain precise styles and forms were prescribed for each kind (the three dramatic unities are the most notorious example). Such codification was extended in the neoclassical period of the seventeenth and eighteenth centuries, when literature was divided into more and more categories, or "species," as they were called, each with its own proper tone, form, and subject matter. As a result of this rather mechanical and dictatorial approach, the theory of literary kinds gradually became discredited. Even the classical Dr. Johnson was moved to exclaim: "There is therefore scarcely any species of writing, of which we can tell what is its essence, and what are its constituents; every new genius produces some new innovation, which, when invented and approved subverts the rules which the practice of foregoing authors had established." [1]

Under the impact of the romantic revolt against rules and traditions of all kinds, the idea of literary species, or genres, as they later came to be called, suffered greatly. Artists were to be free to write in any manner to which the spirit moved them. It was not until the rise in the late 1930s and early 1940s of a Chicago-based school of criticism known as the neo-Aristotelians that much attention was paid to the influence on the artist of already existing forms and conventions. The neo-Aristotelians were consciously reacting against the so-called New Criticism, which had expressly repudiated any kind of historical approach to literature. The famous catch phrase "a poem is a poem is a poem" sums up their attitude: that a work of literature exists by itself and relies upon no reference to any external reality, whether contemporary or historical.

The neo-Aristotelians were concerned with rescuing literature from such self-imposed isolation, and in attempting to do so they partially resurrected the theory of genres. But they did not always avoid what has often been a source of confusion; Aristotle had spoken of literary kinds in two senses: first, as a number of different groups of conventions that had grown up historically and developed into particular forms such as satire, lyric, and tragedy; and second, as a more fundamental division of literature, into drama, epic, and lyric, corresponding to major differences in the relation between artist, subject matter, and audience.

More time, in fact, was spent in assessing the natures and possibilities of these three modes of literature than in exploring the historical genres. As a result, not much of the work is relevant to the cinema, for these three modes (which correspond approximately to drama, fiction, and poetry) appear to be equally present in the cinema. And, on the other hand, such work as has been done on the development of particular genres like the Gothic novel or Victorian melodrama has not ventured far beyond the mere recording of lists of examples.

Nevertheless, some profit is to be gained from the literary critics, even if only a warning. Many people wish to avoid the whole question of genre because it is held that it will lead to the laying down of rules and regulations that will arbitrarily restrict the freedom of artists to create what they like, or the freedom of critics to talk about anything they want to. But if the theory of genres in literature has usually been restrictive and normative, it need not necessarily be so. One does not have to set up a Platonic ideal, to which all particular examples try vainly to aspire, nor even to say that the closer any individual film comes to incorporating all the different elements of the definition, the more fully it will be a western, or gangster picture, or musical. Aristotle's original intention was descriptive, not prescriptive.

Some positive assistance is afforded by Wellek and Warren in their *Theory of Literature.* They neatly state the crux of the problem: "The dilemma of genre history is the dilemma of all history: i.e., in order to discover the scheme of reference (in this case, the genre) we must study the history; but we cannot study the history without having in mind some scheme of selection." [2]

As they recognize, the problem is only another aspect of the wider philosophical problem of universals. With regard to the cinema, we may state it thus: if we want to know what a western is, we must look at certain kinds of films. But how do we know which films to look at until we know what a western is?

For some people the futility of many of the arguments that arise out of this dilemma—such as whether a film like, say, *Lonely Are the Brave* (David Miller, 1962) is a western or not—is so obvious that they give up in despair. But having posed the problem in such apparently insoluble terms, Wellek and Warren offer a way out. To begin with, common sense suggests that it is possible to draw up a list of elements found in films that, for the purposes of the argument, are called westerns and to say that any film with one or more of these elements is thereby held to be a western, though not therefore necessarily identical to other examples of the form. Wellek and Warren go further, however: "Genre should be conceived, we think, as a grouping of literary works based, theoretically, upon both outer form (specific metre or structure) and also upon inner form (attitude, tone, purpose—more crudely, subject and audience). The ostensible basis may be one or the other (e.g., 'pastoral' and 'satire' for the inner form: dipodic verse and Pindaric ode for the outer); but the critical problem will then be to find the *other* dimension, to complete the diagram." [3]

This idea of both inner and outer form seems essential, for if we require only the former, in terms of subject matter, then our concept will be too loose to be of much value; and if only the latter, then the genre will be ultimately meaningless, since devoid of any content.

What, then, are the cinematic equivalents of, first, outer form? Not rhythm, clearly. To the extent to which a film can be said to have rhythm, this depends not upon the conventions of the genre within which it is made, but upon the artistic personalities of the director and editor (except perhaps the rapid montage sequences of many gangster films). Nor does the notion of structure open up many possibilities. It seems extremely difficult to argue that there is any significant similarity between the plots of different westerns, for example. There are, of course, a number of plot structures that reappear in film after film. There is the one in which a bigoted and usually disciplinarian cavalry officer is narrowly prevented from starting a "full-scale Indian war." Or, again, there is the one in which a reformed gunfighter (or ex-marshal) is reluctantly persuaded to accept responsibility for cleaning up the town. But to use such structures as a basis for defining the genre would mean ending up not with one genre called "the western," but an almost infinite number of subgenres. Some may wish to argue that this is the best that can be done. Yet it does seem that these films have something more in common, something that makes the two kinds of story mentioned above part of the same genre.

Since we are dealing with a visual medium we ought surely to look for our defining criteria in what we actually see on the screen. It is immediately apparent that there before our eyes is a whole range of "outer forms." There is, first of all, the setting, the chief glory of many of the films. Often it is outdoors, in very particular kinds of country: deserts, mountains, plains, woods. Or it is indoors—but again, special kinds of indoors: saloons, jails, courtrooms, ranch houses, hotels, riverboats, brothels—all places frequented by those who live an outdoor and/or wandering kind of life.

Then there are the clothes: wide-brimmed hats, open-neck shirts with scarves, tight jeans (which have become steadily tighter as the years have gone by), sometimes worn with leather chaps and almost always with spurs and high-heeled boots; or, alternatively, army uniforms or the wide but carefully distinguished variety of Indian costume. There are also certain clothes for specialist occupations. There are bootlace ties for gamblers and black gloves for psychopathic hired guns; a man who wears a watch chain is often a judge; and a black hat can denote a preacher; a bowler, a newspaperman. For women there are usually only two sorts of clothes: wide, full skirts and tight bodices or the more tomboyish jeans and shirt. (There is a third costume usually reserved for the Mexican girl or prostitute—often synonymous—in which the bodice is looser and the neckline appreciably lower.)

Third, there are the various tools of the trade, principally weapons, and of these, principally guns. They are usually specifically identified: Colt 45's, Winchester and Springfield rifles, shotguns for certain situations (such as robbing banks or facing a numerically superior enemy), and, in westerns of an earlier period, single-shot, muzzle-loading muskets. Such care in the choice of weapons is not mere pedantry nor dictated purely by considerations of historical accuracy, for an incredible variety of arms were in use. The weapons employed in the films are there for largely stylistic reasons; consider, for example, the significant difference in the style of movement required to cock a Winchester and a Lee-Enfield 303. Other weapons have their place: knives, often the murderous looking Bowie type, whips (used by women or bullies), sometimes cannon for the military, and assorted Indian hardware, notably the bow and arrow. Again, there are specialist weapons. The man who wears a bootlace tie should be watched carefully in case he produces a Derringer.

Next in importance come horses, also used in formally differentiated ways. Indians ride barebacked or with only a blanket, a sign perhaps of their closeness to the animal world. White and black horses have frequently a symbolic function, and if a woman does not ride sidesaddle she is no lady, though not always the worse for that. Doctors and judges ride in a buggy, unless, like Doc Holliday, they have ceased to practice. We know, too, what kind of people travel in stagecoaches: in descending order of their entitlement to respect, women, gamblers, corset salesmen, and Easterners.

Fourth, there is a large group of miscellaneous physical objects that recur and thereby take on a formal function. Trains are invariably of the same kind, with cowcatchers in front of the engine, carriages with a railed open platform at the back (useful for fights), and seats either side of a central aisle. Mines, general stores, and forts also feature largely, representing the corruption of money, the virtue of honest industry, and an oasis of strength in a hostile land. Indians, too, in spite of the more liberal attitudes of the last few years, are still primarily important not as people in their own right but as part of the setting.

All these things operate as formal elements. That is to say, the films are not "about" them any more than a sonnet is about fourteen lines in a certain meter. For example, *Winchester 73* (Anthony Mann, 1950) is not about the gun, which is a mere connecting device to hold the story together. The film, like all films, is about people. Obviously the formal structure is looser than that of a sonnet; not all the elements need be present. But if we say that a western is a film that includes at least one of them (and of course the list is by no means exhaustive), then we are saying something both intelligible and useful. The visual conventions provide a framework within which the story can be told.

But what is more important is that they also affect what kind of story it will be. Just as the nature of the sonnet makes it more likely you will be successful in writing a love poem of a very personal kind rather than something else, and has so grown up as a genre with both outer and inner form, so too what kind of film a western is, is largely determined by the nature of its conventions. One can put this more forcefully in a negative way: it is unlikely you will produce a good poem on a large-scale historical theme such as the Trojan War if you choose the sonnet form. So, too, if you are going to make a western, you will tend not to consider certain themes or subjects (unless, as in *High Noon* [Fred Zinneman, 1952], you are consciously trying to adapt the form to your purpose in an arbitrary way).

In trying to be more specific here, one is inevitably on dangerous ground, for unless one has seen all the westerns ever made (or, to be absolutely logical, all the westerns that ever could be made), there cannot be any certainty that generalizations will hold. Since the object is to stimulate discussion, not end it, however, a start can be made by saying that because of the physical setting, a western is likely to deal successfully with stories about the opposition between man and nature and about the establishment of civilization. As Jim Kitses points out in his book *Horizons West,* such oppositions are seen from two points of view: for nature or for civilization. If, on the other hand, you want to deal with the sense of fear, isolation, and excitement engendered by great cities, you won't do it very well within the framework of the western.

This much perhaps is obvious. But it is possible to go further. The men in westerns wear clothes that are aggressively masculine, sexy in a virile sort of way. (As if to underline this, the gambler, whose clothes are flashier, is invariably a ladies' man.) This in turn determines the character of the hero—taciturn, tough, uncomplicated, self-sufficient. It is surely no accident that the most famous western heroes are not, by conventional standards, good-looking. John Wayne, Randolph Scott, James Stewart, Gary Cooper, and Kirk Douglas all have their attractions, but they are not, like Cary Grant, at home in a drawing room. Likewise, the clothes of the women determine that they will be either very feminine or very masculine. Part of the interest comes from feminine clothes hiding a masculine character—Angie Dickinson in *Rio Bravo* (Howard Hawks, 1959)— or vice versa, as with characters like Calamity Jane, who usually turn out to be pining for a home and children.

But either way, because the men are so aggressively masculine and lead wandering lives and the women are forced either to stay at home or become the equivalents of men, few westerns have a strong love interest. The formal elements of the genre make it hard to deal with subjects that presuppose in the characters an interest in, and a time for, the heart's affections.

It is also likely that, given the arsenal of weapons on view in the films, violence will play a crucial part in the stories. This is not to say that there could not be pacifist westerns, though they are significantly less common than pacifist war films, because the kind of weapons used makes the violence less immediate and unpleasant. But it is hard to think of a western in which there is at least no threat of violence. Thus the world of the West is different from that of a Henry James novel, where no hand is ever raised in anger. Because the guns are there as part of the formal structure, there will be, characteristically, a dilemma that either can only be resolved by violence or in which the violence would be a solution, though a wrong one. The characters will be of a kind whose virtue resides not so much in subtlety of intellect, or sensitivity, or imagination, as in their willingness and ability to stand up for themselves, to be in some sense, not necessarily physical, strong.

One could go on. But it might already be objected that it is the subject matter that determines the outer form, not the other way round; that the things a director wants to say will decide the form he or she uses. Not enough is known about how most westerns are conceived in the minds of

3. Femininity and masculinity in *Rio Bravo* (John Wayne and Angie Dickinson).

directors and writers to say whether this is the actual process of creation. One may be forgiven for suspecting, however, that the worst way to make a western is to think of a theme and then try to transpose it into western form.

If one looks at a cinematic genre in this way, as being composed of an outer form consisting of a certain number of visual conventions that are, in a sense, arbitrary (in the same way that a tragedy has five acts), then certain problems are on the way to being solved. First, we are not bound to make any very close connections between the western genre and historical reality. Of course there are connections. But too many discussions of these problems fall down over this point because it is usually assumed that the relationship must be a direct one; that since in fact there was a West, westerns must be essentially concerned with it. Kitses, for instance, states that "the basic convention of the genre is that films in Western guise are about America's past."[4] This is simply not true of many of the films, including several of the ones he discusses, for only Peckinpah of his three directors is at all preoccupied with historical themes. In some of his films Mann includes such material, though that is not where the central interest lies; and Boetticher appears quite oblivious to any such considerations. To be fair, Kitses is aware of other elements in the genre. He summarizes what he calls "interrelated aspects of the genre" under the headings of "history," "themes," "archetypes," and "icons" (which are equivalent to what I have called visual conventions).[5] But he fails to show in what their interrelation consists; nor, ultimately, does this first chapter have much to do with his discussion of particular directors, and for the reason I have suggested, that history, to which Kitses devotes most of his attention, is a relatively unimportant part of many westerns.

There are several reasons why it is necessary to resist the temptation to talk about westerns largely in terms of history. First, one usually ends up by talking about Ford, who is, clearly, more concerned with it than most. But Ford is not the western. Second, if this is what westerns chiefly present, it is hard to see why half the world's population should spend its time watching them. Third and most serious, to define westerns as films about a certain period of America's past is to misunderstand the nature and meaning of genres and how they work.

Before going on to deal with this, however, two more points should be made. Although the western seems to me the most important of the genres, the one in which the largest body of good work has been done, there are obviously others. The same approach could be applied to them; namely, to inquire into the outer form, the visual and other conventions, and to see whether there is the same relation between form and content, whether it could be shown that the subject matter dealt with is determined by a series of formal and given patterns. The gangster movie[6] is an obvious subject of inquiry, though one problem is that it shades off into the thriller, so that at one end of the spectrum we have, say, *White Heat* (Raoul Walsh, 1949) and at the other, Hitchcock. Musicals, too, would repay attention. Nor need visual elements be the only defining ones, for film is not only a visual art. For example, it is (or used to be) understood that in Hollywood's romantic comedies people do not sleep together unless they are married. Clearly this is a convention—it never was actually true. And it cannot be explained merely by referring to the Hays Code, for that would make it simply a restriction. Although it does limit the kind of subject that can be dealt with, in the same way that it does in the Victorian novel, a lot of mileage can be got out of it. The famous scene in *It Happened One Night* (Frank Capra, 1934) where Clark Gable and Claudette Colbert share a room together uses the convention as the basis of its humor. All the same, the major defining characteristics of genre will be visual: guns, cars, clothes in the gangster film; clothes and dancing in the musical (apart from the music, of course!); castles, coffins, and teeth in horror movies.

The second point is that while it is possible to talk of themes and archetypes in genres, as Kitses does in his book, it doesn't in the end help very much. He cites archetypes such as "the journey and the quest, the ceremonies of love and marriage, food and drink, the rhythms of waking and sleeping, life and death."[7] Not only do these appear in other genres besides the western; they exist in films that can scarcely be classified into any genres, and what is more, they occur in other forms of art besides the cinema. What we need is a way of looking at a genre that can make clear what is distinctive about it and how its outer and inner forms relate.

But what functions does genre perform? Or, in other words, why bother to talk about it at all? Can't we get along just as well with our present director-oriented theories, while admitting that some films are like others? The trouble is that our present theories are so extreme. They assume that the auteur (who need not necessarily be the director, of course) is personally responsible for everything that appears in the film—or that someone is responsible, if only a heavy-handed producer. This form of overcompensation, a reaction to the critical Dark Ages when American cinema was dismissed as repetitive rubbish, mass-produced to a formula (unfortunately all too successful) in the factories of Hollywood, has led to a situation in which American films are held to be wholly the expressions of the artistic personalities of their highly original creators.

There may well be several reasons for this, apart from the swing of the pendulum. There is a kind of critical snobbery which assumes that you cannot really appreciate a film unless you have seen all its director's other films and which leads to the more bizarre forms of auteur-hunting.[8] For if an individual film is good, then it must have an auteur behind it, and if he or she is an auteur, it follows that this person's other works will be good—or at least interesting. And yet there are films which are totally successful and which derive their power from the traditions of a genre rather than from any distinctive directorial contribution. *Casablanca* (Michael Curtiz, 1942) is such a one, as Andrew Sarris recognizes in *The American Cinema*. It doesn't help much to have seen other Curtiz films, but one's enjoyment is enormously enriched by having seen Humphrey Bogart and the rest in other films of the period. It may be objected that strictly speaking this has nothing to do with genre, since the qualities that actors can bring to a film cut across genres. Yet is it not a fact that Bogart's battered face instantly communicates a blend of cynicism and honesty, weariness and generosity, that is genuinely part of a tradition of the

4. *Psycho:* Obvious relations to the horror genre.

American film noir? What he represents in the film owes little to Michael Curtiz, much to the other films he played in.

But the chief justification of the genre is not that it allows merely competent directors to produce good films (though one is grateful enough for that). Rather, it is that it allows good directors to be better. And the main reason why this has not been more generally recognized is that the auteur theory is not very well equipped to deal with popular art. Even in its less extreme forms, it cannot really make room for the contribution of the tradition in which a film was made. Thus in order to appreciate *Casablanca,* we must do more than simply accept Curtiz as an auteur (which is what Higham and Greenberg want us to do in *Hollywood in the Forties*).[9] When we are faced with genuinely distinctive artists, we too often consider them apart from the genre background they work in. Robin Wood's book on Hitchcock is an excellent piece of criticism. But in his discussion of *Psycho* (1960) he says nothing of the film's obvious relation to the horror genre. Surely our sense of fear depends at least in part on our built-in response to certain stock symbols that Hitchcock employs. People rarely take Hitchcock seriously when he talks about his pictures; yet at the head of the section on *Psycho* Wood has this quotation: "The process through which we take the audience [is it not significant that he so often says 'we,' not 'I'?], you see, it's rather like taking them through the haunted house at the fairground. . . ." [10] The house itself, with its vague suggestion of Victorian Gothic, is straight out of any number of horror films. And when at the end Vera Miles goes down to the cellar, we are terrified, not just because we have heard Norman say he is taking his mother down there (we don't know yet that his mother is a corpse, though of course we suspect all is not well); our certainty that something unpleasant will be found comes from our knowledge that nasty things come out of cellars in this kind of film. This is not to deny Wood's ascription of Freudian overtones to the cellar; but the trouble with Freudian overtones is that you aren't supposed to be aware of them. It seems more likely that our conscious reaction to the scene owes more to our having assimilated them through an exposure to the tradition of the genre.

Most people see films this way. No one would suggest that we must be bound by the aesthetic criteria of the man in the street. Yet anyone who is at all concerned with education must be worried at the distance between much of the criticism now written and the way the average audience reacts to a film. For them it is not a new Hawks or Ford or Peckinpah; it is a new western. And to sympathize with this view is not to deny the claims of these directors to be artists. Popular art does not condemn its creators to a subsidiary role. Instead it emphasizes the relation between the artist and the material, on the one hand, and the material and the audience on the other. The artist brings to the genre his or her own concerns, techniques, and capacities—in the widest sense, a style—but receives from the genre a formal pattern that directs and disciplines the work. In a sense this imposes limitations, as I have suggested. Certain themes and treatments are, if not ruled out, unlikely to be successful if they work too hard against the genre. But the benefits are considerable. Constant exposure to a previous succession of films has led the audience to recognize certain formal elements as charged with an accretion of meaning. Some of these I have tried to isolate, and in some cases their meaning has been suggested. Some critics like to refer to them as "icons."

All too often, however, discussion has ceased there. But it is vital to see not how icons relate to the cinema in general but to genres in particular, and how in the popular cinema they may be reconciled to our natural desire to see films as the expression of an artistic personality.

This can best be done through the notion that a genre film depends on a combination of novelty and familiarity. The conventions of the genre are known and recognized by the audience, and such recognition is in itself a pleasure. Popular art, in fact, has always depended on this; one might argue that the modern idea of novelty (or "originality") as a major, even *the* major, quality to be desired in a work of art dates from the romantic period. And, as Raymond Williams shows in *Culture and Society,* it is during this period that art began to move away from its contact with a large, roughly homogeneous audience. We have there the beginnings of the present-day division between "mass" and "highbrow" culture. All too easily this originality degenerates into eccentricity, and communication is sacrificed in the interests of self-expression. It is one of the chief merits of the American cinema that this has, on the whole, not yet happened; and because this is so, the popular cinema (which is almost, though not quite, synonymous with the American cinema) offers one of the richest sources of material for those teaching liberal studies to the culturally unsophisticated. Those who are unconvinced by this might wish to argue that the opposite of eccentricity is the cliché. It is true that if a director slavishly copies the conventions rather than uses them, then we get a film which is just what Hollywood is so often, even now, held to have produced exclusively: a thoroughly predictable string of stock situations and images. However, this article is not primarily intended as propaganda for Hollywood. That battle, if not won, is at least being fought by increasing numbers of people on ever widening fronts. Rather, the intention is to argue that it is a mistake to base the argument for popular cinema exclusively on a case for the auteur.

One of the best examples of the way in which genre actually works is in Peckinpah's *Guns in the Afternoon* [in the United States released as *Ride the High Country,* 1962—Ed.]. Knowing the period and location, we expect at the beginning to find a familiar western town. In fact, the first minutes of the film brilliantly disturb our expectations. As the camera roves around the town we discover a policeman in uniform, a car, a camel, and Randolph Scott dressed up as Buffalo Bill. Each of these images performs a function. The figure of the policeman conveys that the law has become institutionalized; the rough and ready frontier days are over. The car suggests, as in *The Wild Bunch* (Peckinpah, 1969), that the West is no longer isolated from modern technology and its implications. Significantly, the camel is racing against a horse; such a grotesque juxtaposition is painful. A horse in a western is not just an animal but a symbol of dignity, grace, and power. These qualities are mocked by having it compete with a camel; and to add insult to injury, the camel wins.

Randolph Scott is not just an actor. It is enough to have seen two or three of his films to know that he represents a quiet, cheerful kind of integrity. Peckinpah uses this screen image by having him play against it all through the film; but the initial shock of seeing him in a wig, running a crooked booth at the fair, does more than upset our expectations about

5. The opening race in *Ride the High Country*.

his role in the film. It calls into question our whole attitude to the heroes of western legend. Scott dressed up as Buffalo Bill is an image that relies not only on Scott's screen personality, but also on the audience's stock response to Buffalo Bill, for he too is debased by this grotesque impersonation. This, Peckinpah is saying, is the state that things have come to, that heroes are exploited for money.

Clearly, then, although Peckinpah is working against the conventions, he could not do this unless he and the audience had a tradition in common. He needs the outer form, though in many ways he is making an antiwestern. What is especially interesting is the relation between this and the inner form. Here I am obliged to take issue again with Jim Kitses. He believes that Peckinpah's films are essentially about a search for personal identity. While not wishing to deny that some such concern may be traced in the pictures, one must protest that this rather tends to ignore the most obvious fact about them: that they are westerns. Personal identity can be sought for anywhere, anytime. But the essential theme of *Guns in the Afternoon* is one that, while it could be put into other forms, is ideally suited to the one chosen. The film describes the situation of men who have outlived their time. Used to a world where issues were decided simply, on a test of strength, they now find this way of life threatened by complications and developments they do not understand. Since they cannot, or will not, adapt, all that remains to them is a tragic and bitter heroism.

The cluster of images and conventions that we call the western genre is used by Peckinpah to define and embody this situation, in such a way that we know what the West was and what it has become. The first is communicated through images that are familiar, the second through those that are strange. And together they condition his subject matter. Most obviously, because the film is a western, the theme is worked out in terms of violent action. If it were a musical, the theme might be similar in some ways, but because the conventions would be different, it would probably not involve violence (or if it did, the violence might well be highly stylized and so quite different in effect). And if it were a gangster picture, it seems unlikely that the effect of the film's ending, its beautifully elegiac background of autumn leaves, would be reproduced, suggesting as it does that the dead Judd is at one with nature, that nature which seems at the beginning of the film to have been overtaken by "civilization."

Much of what has been said has been expressed in other ways by recent writers, occasionally more esoterically. What needs to be done now is to put to work our increasing understanding of how important semiology is, to explore the precise relation between the artist and his or her given material, in order to explain our intuitive feeling that a genre is not a mere collection of dead images waiting for a director to animate it, but a tradition with a life of its own. We return to the third question asked at the beginning of this article. Genres predate great directors. The western was going along happily under its own steam well before John Ford, or even James Cruze, came upon it. We need much more work on the early history of these various forms if we are to fully comprehend their strange power and the exact process by which they grew rich enough to attract the talents they did. Last, the question of the relation between the western and history, which I have argued is by no means simple, and not always central, can only be answered with certainty when we know how the form began. It's usually assumed that it sprang, fully armed, from pulp fiction, and yet so much of it is visual that it is hard to believe this is quite true. And if the western originates in history and is a response to it, what about the musical? Or the horror film? Can we possibly evolve a theory to fit them all?

Notes

1. Samuel Johnson, *The Rambler,* no. 125, in *The Yale Edition of the Works of Samuel Johnson* (New Haven and London: Yale University Press, 1969), 4:300.

2. René Wellek and Austin Warren, *Theory of Literature,* 3d ed. (New York: Harcourt, Brace & World, 1956), p. 260.

3. Ibid., p. 231.

4. Jim Kitses, *Horizons West* (Bloomington and London: Indiana University Press, 1970), p. 24.

5. Ibid., pp. 24–25.

6. See Colin McArthur, "Genre and Iconography," paper delivered at a British Film Institute seminar.

7. Kitses, *Horizons West,* p. 20.

8. I use the term loosely, to mean the artist awarded credit for a film's succession: the distinction between *auteur* and *metteur-en-scène* has no importance here.

9. Charles Higham and Joel Greenberg, *Hollywood in the Forties* (London: A. Zwemmer; New York: A. S. Barnes, 1968), p. 19.

10. Robin Wood, *Hitchcock's Films* (London: Zwemmer; New York: Barnes, 1965).

3. A Semantic/Syntactic Approach to Film Genre

RICK ALTMAN

What is a genre? Which films are genre films? How do we know to which genre they belong? As fundamental as these questions may seem, they are almost never asked—let alone answered—in the field of cinema studies. Most comfortable in the seemingly uncomplicated world of Hollywood classics, genre critics have felt little need to reflect openly on the assumptions underlying their work. Everything seems so clear. Why bother to theorize, American pragmatism asks, when there are no problems to solve? We all know a genre when we see one. Scratch only where it itches. According to this view, genre theory would be called for only in the unlikely event that knowledgeable genre critics disagreed on basic issues. The task of the theorist is then to adjudicate among conflicting approaches, not so much by dismissing unsatisfactory positions but by constructing a model that reveals the relationship between differing critical claims and their function within a broader cultural context. Whereas the French clearly view theory as a first principle, we Americans tend to see it as a last resort, something to turn to when all else fails.

Even in this limited, pragmatic view, whereby theory is to be avoided at all costs, the time for theory is nevertheless upon us. The clock has struck thirteen; we had best call in the theoreticians. The more genre criticism I read, the more uncertainty I note in the choice or extent of essential critical terms. Often what appears as hesitation in the terminology of a single critic will turn into a clear contradiction when studies by two or more critics are compared. Now, it would be one thing if these contradictions were simply a matter of fact. On the contrary, however, I suggest that these are not temporary problems, bound to disappear as soon as we have more information or better analysts. Instead, these uncertainties reflect constitutive weaknesses of current notions of genre. Three contradictions in particular seem worthy of a good scratch.

When we establish the corpus of a genre we generally tend to do two things at once, and thus establish two alternate groups of texts, each corresponding to a different notion of corpus. On the one hand, we have an unwieldy list of texts corresponding to a simple, tautological definition of the genre (e.g., western = film that takes place in the American West, or musical = film with diegetic music). This *inclusive* list is the kind that gets consecrated by generic encyclopedias or checklists. On the other hand, we find critics, theoreticians, and other arbiters of taste sticking to a familiar canon that has little to do with the broad, tautological definition. Here the same films are mentioned again and again, not only because they are well known or particularly well made, but because they somehow seem to represent the genre more fully and faithfully than other apparently more tangential films. This *exclusive* list of films generally occurs not in a dictionary context, but instead in connection with attempts to arrive at the overall meaning or structure of a genre. The relative status of these alternate approaches to the constitution of a generic corpus may easily be sensed from the following typical conversation:

> "I mean, what do you do with Elvis Presley films? You can hardly call them musicals."

> "Why not? They're loaded with songs and they've got a narrative that ties the numbers together, don't they?"

> "Yeah, I suppose. I guess you'd have to call *Fun in Acapulco* a musical, but it's sure no *Singin' in the Rain*. Now there's a real musical."

When is a musical not a musical? When it has Elvis Presley in it. What may at first have seemed no more than an uncertainty on the part of the critical community now clearly appears as a contradiction. Because there are two competing notions of generic corpus on our critical scene, it is perfectly possible for a film to be simultaneously included in a particular generic corpus and excluded from that same corpus.

A second uncertainty is associated with the relative status of theory and history in genre studies. Before semiotics came along, generic titles and definitions were largely borrowed from the industry itself; what little generic theory there was tended therefore to be confused with historical analysis. With the heavy influence of semiotics on generic theory over the last two decades, self-conscious *critical* vocabulary came to be systematically preferred to the now-suspect *user* vocabulary. The contributions of Propp, Lévi-Strauss, Frye, and Todorov to genre studies have not been uniformly productive, however, because of the special place reserved for genre study within the semiotic project. If structuralist critics systematically chose as the object of their analysis large groups of popular texts, it was in order to cover a basic flaw in the semiotic understanding of textual analysis. Now, one of the most striking aspects of Saussure's theory of language is his emphasis on the inability of any single individual to effect change within that language.[1] The fixity of the linguistic community thus serves as justification for Saussure's fundamentally synchronic approach to language. When literary semioticians applied this linguistic model to problems of textual analysis, they never fully addressed the notion of interpretive community implied by Saussure's linguistic community. Preferring narrative to narration, system to process, and *histoire* to *discours,* the first semiotics ran headlong into a set of restrictions and contradictions that eventually spawned the more process-oriented second semiotics. It is in this context that we must see the resolutely synchronic attempts of Propp, Lévi-Strauss, Todorov, and many another influential genre analyst.[2] Unwilling to compromise their systems by the historical notion of linguistic community, these theoreticians instead substituted the generic context for the linguistic community, as if the weight of numerous "similar" texts were sufficient to locate the meaning of a text independently of a specific audience. Far from being sensitive to concerns of history, semiotic genre analysis was by definition and from the start devoted to bypassing history. Treating genres as neutral constructs, semioticians of the sixties and early seventies blinded us to the discursive power of generic formations. Because they treated genres as the interpretive community, they were unable to perceive the important role of genres in exercising influence on the interpretive community. Instead of reflecting openly on the way in which Hollywood uses its genres to short-circuit the normal interpretive process, structuralist critics plunged head-long into the trap, taking Hollywood's ideological effect for a natural ahistorical cause.

Genres were always—and continue to be—treated as if they spring full-blown from the head of Zeus. It is thus not surprising to find that even the most advanced of current genre theories, those that see generic texts as negotiating a relationship between a specific production system and a given audience, still hold to a notion of genre that is fundamentally ahistorical in nature.[3] More and more, however, as scholars come to know the full range of individual Hollywood genres, we are finding that genres are far from exhibiting the homogeneity that this synchronic approach posits. Whereas one Hollywood genre may be borrowed with little change from another medium, a second genre may develop slowly, change constantly, and surge recognizably before settling into a familiar pattern, while a third may go through an extended series of paradigms, none of which may be claimed as dominant. As long as Hollywood genres are conceived as Platonic categories, existing outside the flow of time, it will be impossible to reconcile *genre theory,* which has always accepted as given the timelessness of a characteristic structure, and *genre history,* which has concentrated on chronicling the development, deployment, and disappearance of this same structure.

A third contradiction looms larger still, for it involves the two general directions taken by genre criticism as a whole over the last decade or two.

Following Lévi-Strauss, a growing number of critics throughout the seventies dwelled on the mythical qualities of Hollywood genres and thus on the audience's ritual relationship to genre film. The film industry's desire to please and its need to attract consumers were viewed as the mechanism whereby spectators were actually able to designate the kind of films they wanted to see. By choosing the films it would patronize, the audience revealed its preferences and its beliefs, thus inducing Hollywood studios to produce films reflecting its desires. Participation in the genre film experience thus reinforces spectator expectations and desires. Far from being limited to mere entertainment, filmgoing offers a satisfaction more akin to that associated with established religion. Most openly championed by John Cawelti, this ritual approach appears as well in books by Leo Braudy, Frank McConnell, Michael Wood, Will Wright, and Tom Schatz.[4] It has the merit not only of accounting for the intensity of identification typical of American genre film audiences, but it also encourages the placing of genre film narratives into an appropriately wider context of narrative analysis.

Curiously, however, while the ritual approach was attributing ultimate authorship to the audience, with the studios simply serving, for a price, the national will, a parallel ideological approach was demonstrating how audiences are manipulated by the business and political interests of Hollywood. Starting with *Cahiers du Cinéma* and moving rapidly to *Screen, Jump Cut,* and a growing number of journals, this view has recently joined hands with a more general critique of the mass media offered by the Frankfurt School.[5] Looked at in this way, genres are simply the generalized, identifiable structures through which Hollywood's rhetoric flows. Far more attentive to discursive concerns than the ritual approach, which remains faithful to Lévi-Strauss in emphasizing narrative systems, the ideological approach stresses questions of representation and identification previously left aside. Simplifying a bit, we might say that it characterizes each individual genre as a specific type of lie, an untruth whose most characteristic feature is its ability to masquerade as truth. Whereas the ritual approach sees Hollywood as responding to societal pressure and thus expressing audience desires, the ideological approach claims that Hollywood takes advantage of spectator energy and psychic investment in order to lure the audience into Hollywood's own positions. The two are irreducibly opposed, yet these irreconcilable arguments continue to represent the most interesting and well defended of recent approaches to Hollywood genre film.

Here we have three problems that I take to be not limited to a single school of criticism or of a single genre but implicit in every major field of current genre analysis. In nearly every argument about the limits of a generic corpus, the opposition of an inclusive list to an exclusive canon surfaces. Wherever genres are discussed, the divergent concerns of theorists and historians are increasingly obvious. And even when the topic is limited to genre theory alone, no agreement can be found between those who propose a ritual function for film genres and those who champion an ideological purpose. We find ourselves desperately in need of a theory which, without dismissing any of these widely held positions, would explain the circumstances underlying their existence, thus paving the way for a critical methodology that encompasses and indeed thrives on their inherent contradictions. If we have learned anything from poststructuralist criticism, we have learned not to fear logical contradictions but instead to respect the extraordinary energy generated by the play of contradictory forces within a field. What we need now is a new critical strategy enabling us simultaneously to understand and to capitalize on the tensions existing in current generic criticism.

In assessing theories of genre, critics have often labeled them according to a particular theory's most salient features or the type of activity to which it devotes its most concentrated attention. Paul Hernadi, for example, recognizes four general classes of genre theory: expressive, pragmatic, structural, and mimetic.[6] In his extremely influential introduction to *The Fantastic*, Tzvetan Todorov opposes historical to theoretical genres, as well as elementary genres to their complex counterparts.[7] Others, like Fredric Jameson, have followed Todorov and other French semioticians in distinguishing between semantic and syntactic approaches to genre.[8] While there is anything but general agreement on the exact frontier separating semantic from syntactic views, we can as a whole distinguish between generic definitions that depend on a list of common traits, attitudes, characters, shots, locations, sets, and the like—thus stressing the semantic elements that make up the genre—and definitions that play up instead certain constitutive relationships between undesignated and variable placeholders—relationships that might be called the genre's fundamental syntax. The semantic approach thus stresses the genre's building blocks, while the syntactic view privileges the structures into which they are arranged.

The difference between semantic and syntactic definitions is perhaps most apparent in familiar approaches to the western. Jean Mitry provides us with a clear example of the most common definition. The western, Mitry proposes, is a "film whose action, situated in the American West, is consistent with the atmosphere, the values, and the conditions of existence in the Far West between 1840 and 1900."[9] Based on the presence or absence of easily identifiable elements, Mitry's nearly tautological definition implies a broad, undifferentiated generic corpus. Marc Vernet's more detailed list is more sensitive to cinematic concerns, yet overall it follows the same semantic model. Vernet outlines general atmosphere

6. *Red River:* The Texas western.

("emphasis on basic elements, such as earth, dust, water, and leather"), stock characters ("the tough/soft cowboy, the lonely sheriff, the faithful or treacherous Indian, and the strong but tender woman"), as well as technical elements ("use of fast tracking and crane shots").[10] An entirely different solution is suggested by Jim Kitses, who emphasizes not the vocabulary of the western but the relationships linking lexical elements. For Kitses the western grows out of a dialectic between the West as garden and as desert (between culture and nature, community and individual, future and past).[11] The western's vocabulary is thus generated by this syntactic relationship, and not vice versa. John Cawelti attempts to systematize the western in a similar fashion: the western is always set on or near a frontier, where man encounters his uncivilized double. The western thus takes place on the border between two lands, between two eras, and with a hero who remains divided between two value systems (for he combines the town's morals with the outlaw's skills).[12]

In passing we might well note the divergent qualities associated with these two approaches. While the semantic approach has little explanatory power, it is applicable to a larger number of films. Conversely, the syntactic approach surrenders broad applicability in return for the ability

7. *Drums along the Mohawk:* The "Pennsylvania" western.

to isolate a genre's specific meaning-bearing structures. This alternative seemingly leaves the genre analyst in a quandary: choose the semantic view and you give up *explanatory power;* choose the syntactic approach and you do without *broad applicability.* In terms of the western, the problem of the so-called "Pennsylvania western" is instructive here. To most observers it seems quite clear that films like *High, Wide and Handsome* (Rouben Mamoulian, 1937), *Drums along the Mohawk* (John Ford, 1939), and *Unconquered* (Cecil B. DeMille, 1947) have definite affinities with the western. Employing familiar characters set in relationships similar to their counterparts west of the Mississippi, these films construct plots and develop a frontier structure clearly derived from decades of western novels and films. But they do it in Pennsylvania, and in the wrong century. Are these films westerns because they share the syntax of hundreds of films we call westerns? Or are they not westerns, because they don't fit Mitry's definition?

In fact, the "Pennsylvania western" (like the urban, spaghetti, and sci-fi varieties) represents a quandary only because critics have insisted on dismissing one type of definition and approach in favor of another. As a rule, semantic and syntactic approaches to genre have been proposed,

analyzed, evaluated, and disseminated separately, in spite of the comple-
mentarity implied by their names. Indeed, many arguments centering on
generic problems have arisen only when semantic and syntactic theoreticians have simply talked past each other, each unaware of the other's divergent orientation. I maintain that these two categories of generic analysis are complementary, that they can be combined, and in fact that some
of the most important questions of genre study can be asked only when
they *are* combined. In short, I propose a semantic/syntactic approach to
genre study.

Now, in order to discover whether the proposed semantic/syntactic approach provides any new understanding, let us return to the three contradictions delineated earlier. First, there is the split corpus that characterizes current genre study—on the one side an inclusive list, on the other
an exclusive pantheon. It should now be quite clear that each corpus corresponds to a different approach to generic analysis and definition. Tautological semantic definitions, with their goal of broad applicability, outline a large genre of semantically similar texts, while syntactic definitions,
intent as they are on explaining the genre, stress a narrow range of texts
that privilege specific syntactic relationships. To insist on one of these approaches to the exclusion of the other is to turn a blind eye on the necessarily dual nature of any generic corpus. For every film that participates
actively in the elaboration of a genre's syntax there are numerous others
content to deploy in no particular relationship the elements traditionally
associated with the genre. We need to recognize that not all genre films
relate to their genre in the same way or to the same extent. By simultaneously accepting semantic and syntactic notions of genre we avail ourselves of a possible way to deal critically with differing levels of "genericity." In addition, a dual approach permits a far more accurate description
of the numerous intergeneric connections typically suppressed by single-
minded approaches. It is simply not possible to describe Hollywood cinema accurately without the ability to account for the numerous films
that innovate by combining the syntax of one genre with the semantics
of another. In fact, it is only when we begin to take up problems of genre
history that the full value of the semantic/syntactic approach becomes
obvious.

As I pointed out earlier, most genre theoreticians have followed the
semiotic model and steered clear of historical considerations. Even in the
relatively few cases where problems of generic history have been addressed, as in the attempts of Metz and Wright to periodize the western,
history has been conceptualized as nothing more than a discontinuous
succession of discrete moments, each characterized by a different basic
version of the genre—that is, by a different syntactic pattern that the
genre adopts.[13] In short, genre theory has up to now aimed almost exclu-

sively at the elaboration of a synchronic model approximating the syntactic operation of a specific genre. Now, quite obviously, no major genre remains unchanged over the many decades of its existence. In order to mask the scandal of applying synchronic analysis to an evolving form, critics have been extremely clever in their creation of categories designed to negate the notion of change and to imply the perpetual self-identity of each genre. Westerns and horror films are often referred to as "classic," the musical is defined in terms of the so-called "Platonic ideal" of integration, the critical corpus of the melodrama has largely been restricted to the postwar efforts of Sirk and Minnelli, and so on. Lacking a workable hypothesis regarding the historical dimension of generic syntax, we have insulated that syntax, along with the genre theory that studies it, from the flow of time.

As a working hypothesis, I suggest that genres arise in one of two fundamental ways: either a relatively stable set of semantic givens is developed through syntactic experimentation into a coherent and durable syntax, or an already existing syntax adopts a new set of semantic elements. In the first case, the genre's characteristic semantic configuration is identifiable long before a syntactic pattern has become stabilized, thus justifying the previously mentioned duality of the generic corpus. In cases of this first type, description of the way in which a set of semantic givens develops into a henceforth relatively stable syntax constitutes the history of the genre while at the same time identifying the structures on which genre theory depends. In dealing with the early development of the musical, for example, we might well follow the attempts during the 1927–1930 period to build a backstage or night-club semantics into a melodramatic syntax, with music regularly reflecting the sorrow of death or parting. After the slack years of 1931–1932, however, the musical began to grow in a new direction; while maintaining substantially the same semantic materials, the genre increasingly related the energy of music-making to the joy of coupling, the strength of the community, and the pleasures of entertainment. Far from being exiled from history, the musical's characteristic syntax can be shown by the generic historian to grow out of the linking of specific semantic elements at identifiable points. A measure of continuity is thus developed between the task of the historian and that of the theoretician, for the tasks of both are now redefined as the study of the interrelationships between semantic elements and syntactic bonds.

This continuity between history and theory is operative as well in the second type of generic development posited earlier. When we analyze the large variety of wartime films that portray the Japanese or Germans as villains, we tend to have recourse to extrafilmic events in order to explain particular characterizations. We thus miss the extent to which films like *All through the Night* (Vincent Sherman, 1942), *Sherlock Holmes and the*

Voice of Terror (John Rawlins, 1942), or the serial *The Winslow Boy* (Anthony Asquith, 1948) simply transfer to a new set of semantic elements the righteous cops-punish-criminals syntax that the gangster genre of the early thirties had turned to starting with *G-Men* (William Keighley, 1935). Again, it is the interplay of syntax and semantics that provides grist for both the historical and the theoretical mill. Or take the development of the science fiction film. At first defined only by a relatively stable science fiction semantics, the genre first began borrowing the syntactic relationships previously established by the horror film, only to move in recent years increasingly toward the syntax of the western. By maintaining simultaneous descriptions according to both parameters, we are not likely to fall into the trap of equating *Star Wars* (George Lucas, 1977) with the western (as numerous recent critics have done), even though it shares certain syntactic patterns with that genre. In short, by taking seriously the multiple connections between semantics and syntax, we establish a new continuity, relating film analysis, genre theory, and genre history.

But what is it that energizes the transformation of a borrowed semantics into a uniquely Hollywood syntax? Or what is it that justifies the intrusion of a new semantics into a well-defined syntactic situation? Far from postulating a uniquely internal, formal progression, I would propose that the relationship between the semantic and the syntactic constitutes the very site of negotiation between Hollywood and its audience, and thus between ritual and ideological uses of genre. Often, when critics of opposing persuasions disagree over a major issue, it is because they have established within the same general corpus two separate and opposed canons, each supporting one point of view. Thus, when Catholics and Protestants or liberals and conservatives quote the Bible, they are rarely quoting the same passages. The striking fact about ritual and ideological genre theoreticians, however, is that they regularly stress the same canon, that small group of texts most clearly reflecting a genre's stable syntax. The films of John Ford, for example, have played a major role in the development of ritual and ideological approaches alike. From Sarris and Bogdanovich to Schatz and Wright, champions of Ford's understanding and transparent expression of American values have stressed the communitarian side of his films, while others, starting with the influential *Cahiers du Cinéma* study of *Young Mr. Lincoln* (1939), have shown how a call to community can be used to lure spectators into a carefully chosen, ideologically determined subject position. A similar situation obtains in the musical, where a growing body of ritual analyses of the Astaire-Rogers and postwar MGM Freed unit films is matched by an increasing number of studies demonstrating the ideological investment of those very same films.[14] The corpus of nearly every major genre has developed in the same way, with critics of both camps gravitating toward and eventually basing their arguments on the same narrow range of films. Just as Minnelli and Sirk dominate the criticism of melodrama, Hitchcock has become nearly synonymous with the thriller. Of all major genres, only the film noir has failed to attract critics of both sides to a shared corpus of major texts—no doubt because of the general inability of ritual critics to accommodate the genre's anticommunitarian stance.

This general agreement on a canon stems, I would claim, from the fundamentally bivalent nature of any relatively stable generic syntax. If it takes a long time to establish a generic syntax and if many seemingly promising formulas or successful films never spawn a genre, it is because only certain types of structure, within a particular semantic environment, are suited to the special bilingualism required of a durable genre. The structures of Hollywood cinema, like those of American popular mythology as a whole, serve to mask the very distinction between ritual and ideological functions. Hollywood does not simply lend its voice to the public's desires, nor does it simply manipulate the audience. On the contrary, most genres go through a period of accommodation during which the public's desires are fitted to Hollywood's priorities (and vice versa). Because the public doesn't want to know that it is being manipulated, the successful ritual/ideological "fit" is almost always one that disguises Hollywood's potential for manipulation while playing up its capacity for entertainment.

Whenever a lasting fit is obtained—which it is whenever a semantic genre becomes a syntactic one—it is because a common ground has been found, a region where the audience's ritual values coincide with Hollywood's ideological ones. The development of a specific syntax within a given semantic context thus serves a double function: it binds element to element in a logical order, at the same time accommodating audience desires to studio concerns. The successful genre owes its success not alone to its reflection of an audience ideal, nor solely to its status as apology for the Hollywood enterprise, but to its ability to carry out both functions simultaneously. It is this sleight of hand, this strategic overdetermination, that most clearly characterizes American film production during the studio years.

The approach to genre sketched out in this article of course raises some questions of its own. Just where, for example, do we locate the exact border between the semantic and the syntactic? And how are these two categories related? Each of these questions constitutes an essential area of inquiry, one that is far too complex to permit full treatment here. Nevertheless, a few remarks may be in order. A reasonable observer might well ask why my approach attributes such importance to the seemingly banal distinction between a text's materials and the structures into which they are arranged. Why this distinction rather than, for example, the more

cinematic division between diegetic elements and the technical means deployed in representing them? The answer to these questions lies in a general theory of textual signification that I have expounded elsewhere.[15]
Briefly, that theory distinguishes between the primary, linguistic meaning
of a text's component parts and the secondary or textual meaning that
those parts acquire through a structuring process internal to the text or
to the genre. Within a single text, therefore, the same phenomenon may
have more than one meaning depending on whether we consider it at the
linguistic or textual level. In the western, for example, the horse is an animal that serves as a method of locomotion. This primary level of meaning, corresponding to the normal extent of the concept "horse" within the
language, is matched by a series of other meanings derived from the structures into which the western sets the horse. Opposition of the horse to the
automobile or locomotive ("iron horse") reinforces the organic, nonme-
chanical sense of the term "horse" already implicit in the language, thus
transferring that concept from the paradigm "method of locomotion" to
the paradigm "soon-to-be-outmoded preindustrial carry-over."

In the same way, horror films borrow from a nineteenth-century literary tradition their dependence on the presence of a monster. In doing so,
they clearly perpetuate the linguistic meaning of the monster as "threatening inhuman being," but at the same time, by developing new syntac-
ticities, they generate an important new set of textual meanings. For the
nineteenth century, the appearance of the monster is invariably tied to a
romantic overreaching, the attempt of some human scientist to tamper
with the divine order. In texts like Mary Shelley's *Frankenstein,* Balzac's
La Recherche de l'absolu, or Stevenson's *Dr. Jekyll and Mr. Hyde,* a studied syntax equates man and monster, attributing to both the monstrosity
of being outside nature as defined by established religion and science.
With the horror film, a different syntax rapidly equates monstrosity not
with the overactive nineteenth-century mind, but with an equally overactive twentieth-century body. Again and again, the monster is identified
with his human counterpart's unsatisfied sexual appetite, thus establishing with the same primary "linguistic" materials (the monster, fear, the
chase, death) entirely new textual meanings, phallic rather than scientific
in nature.

The distinction between the semantic and the syntactic, in the way I
have defined it here, thus corresponds to a distinction between the primary, linguistic elements of which all texts are made and the secondary, textual meanings that are sometimes constructed by virtue of the syntactic bonds established between primary elements. This distinction is
stressed in the approach to genre presented here not because it is convenient nor because it corresponds to a modish theory of the relation be-

tween language and narrative, but because the semantic/syntactic distinction is fundamental to a theory of how meaning of one kind contributes to and eventually establishes meaning of another. Just as individual texts establish new meanings for familiar terms only by subjecting well-known semantic units to a syntactic redetermination, so generic meaning comes into being only through the repeated deployment of substantially the same syntactic strategies. It is in this way, for example, that making music—at the linguistic level primarily a way of making a living—becomes in the musical a figure for making love—a textual meaning essential to the constitution of that syntactic genre.

We must of course remember that, while each individual text clearly has a syntax of its own, the syntax implied here is that of the genre, which does not appear as *generic* syntax unless it is reinforced numerous times by the syntactic patterns of individual texts. The Hollywood genres that have proven the most durable are precisely those that have established the most coherent syntax (the western, the musical); those that disappear the quickest depend entirely on recurring semantic elements, never developing a stable syntax (reporter, catastrophe, and big-caper films, to name but a few). If I locate the border between the semantic and the syntactic at the dividing line between the linguistic and the textual, it is thus in response not just to the theoretical but also to the historical dimension of generic functioning.

In proposing such a model, however, I may leave too much room for one particular type of misunderstanding. It has been a cliché of the last two decades to insist that structure carries meaning, while the choice of structured elements is largely negligible in the process of signification. This position, most openly championed by Lévi-Strauss in his cross-cultural methodology for studying myth, may seem to be implied by my model, but is in fact not borne out by my research.[16] Spectator response, I believe, is heavily conditioned by the choice of semantic elements and atmosphere, because a given semantics used in a specific cultural situation will recall to an actual interpretive community the particular syntax with which that semantics has traditionally been associated in other texts. This *syntactic expectation,* set up by a *semantic signal,* is matched by a parallel tendency to expect specific syntactic signals to lead to predetermined semantic fields (e.g., in western texts, regular alternation between male and female characters creates expectation of the semantic elements implied by romance, while alternation between two males throughout a text has implied—at least until recently—confrontation and the semantics of the duel). This interpenetration of the semantic and the syntactic through the agency of the spectator clearly deserves further study. Suffice it to say for the present that linguistic meanings (and thus the import of semantic elements) are in large part derived from the textual meanings of previous texts. There is thus a constant circulation in both directions between the semantic and the syntactic, between the linguistic and the textual.

Still other questions, such as the general problem of the "evolution" of genres through semantic or syntactic shifts, deserve far more attention than I have given them here. In time, I believe, this new model for the understanding of genre will provide answers for many of the questions traditional to genre study. Perhaps more important still, the semantic/syntactic approach to genre raises numerous questions for which other theories have created no space.

Notes

1. Ferdinand de Saussure, *Course in General Linguistics*, edited by Charles Bally and Albert Sechehaye, translated by Wade Baskin (New York: McGraw-Hill, 1959), pp. 14–17.

2. Especially in Vladimir Propp, *Morphology of the Folktale* (Bloomington: Indiana Research Center in Anthropology, 1958); Claude Lévi-Strauss, "The Structural Study of Myths," in *Structural Anthropology*, trans. Claire Jacobson and Brooke Grundfest Schoepf (New York: Basic Books, 1963), pp. 206–231; Tzvetan Todorov, *Grammaire du Décaméron* (The Hague: Mouton, 1969); and Tzvetan Todorov, *The Fantastic*, translated by Richard Howard (Ithaca: Cornell University Press, 1975).

3. Even Stephen Neale's recent discursively oriented study falls prey to this problem. See *Genre* (London: British Film Institute, 1980).

4. John Cawelti, *The Six-Gun Mystique* (Bowling Green: Bowling Green University Popular Press, [1970]), and John Cawelti, *Adventure, Mystery and Romance* (Chicago: University of Chicago Press, 1976); Leo Braudy, *The World in a Frame: What We See in Films* (Garden City: Anchor Books, 1977); Frank McConnell, *The Spoken Seen: Film and the Romantic Imagination* (Baltimore: Johns Hopkins University Press, 1975); Michael Wood, *America in the Movies, or Santa Maria, It Had Slipped My Mind* (New York: Delta, 1975); Will Wright, *Sixguns and Society: A Structural Study of the Western* (Berkeley: University of California Press, 1975); Thomas Schatz, *Hollywood Genres: Formulas, Film-making, and the Studio System* (New York: Random House, 1981).

5. See especially the collective text "*Young Mr. Lincoln* de John Ford," *Cahiers du Cinéma*, no. 223 (August 1970): 29–47, translated in *Screen* 14, no. 3 (Autumn 1973): 29–43; and Jean-Louis Comolli's six-part article "Technique et ideologie," *Cahiers du Cinéma*, nos. 229–241 (1971–1972). The entire *Screen* project has been usefully summarized, with extensive bibliographical notes, by Philip Rosen, "*Screen* and the Marxist Project in Film Criticism," *Quarterly Review of Film Studies* 2, no. 3 (August 1977): 273–287; on *Screen*'s approach to ideology, see also Stephen Heath, "On Screen, in Frame: Film and Ideology," *Quarterly Review of Film Studies* I, no. 3 (August 1976): 251–265. The most important influence on all these positions is Louis Althusser, "Ideology and Ideo-

logical State Apparatuses," in *Lenin and Philosophy and Other Essays,* translated by Ben Brewster (New York: Monthly Review Press, 1971), pp. 127–186.

6. Paul Hernadi, *Beyond Genre: New Directions in Literary Classification* (Ithaca: Cornell University Press, 1972).

7. Todorov, *The Fantastic.*

8. Fredric Jameson, "Magical Narratives: Romance as Genre," *New Literary History* 7 (1975): 135–163. It should be noted here that my use of the term "semantic" differs from Jameson's. Whereas he stresses the overall semantic input of a text, I am dealing with the individual semantic units of the text. His term thus approximates the sense of "global meaning," while mine is closer to "lexical choices."

9. Jean Mitry, *Dictionnaire du cinéma* (Paris: Larousse, 1963), p. 276.

10. Marc Vernet, *Lectures du film* (Paris: Albatros, 1976), pp. 111–112.

11. Jim Kitses, *Horizons West* (Bloomington: Indiana University Press, 1969), pp. 10–14.

12. Cawelti, *The Six-Gun Mystique.*

13. See, for example, Christian Metz, *Language and Cinema* (The Hague: Mouton, 1974), pp. 148–161; and Wright, *Sixguns and Society,* passim.

14. This relationship is especially interesting in the work of Richard Dyer and Jane Feuer, both of whom attempt to confront the interdependence of ritual and ideological components. See in particular Richard Dyer, "Entertainment and Utopia," in *Genre: The Musical,* edited by Rick Altman (London and Boston: Routledge and Kegan Paul, 1981), pp. 175–189; and Jane Feuer, *The Hollywood Musical* (Bloomington: Indiana University Press, 1982).

15. Charles F. Altman, "Intratextual Rewriting: Textuality as Language Formation," in *The Sign in Music and Literature,* edited by Wendy Steiner (Austin: University of Texas Press, 1981), pp. 39–51.

16. The most straightforward statement of Lévi-Strauss's position is in "The Structural Study of Myths." For a useful elucidation of that position, see Edmund Leach, *Claude Lévi-Strauss* (New York: Viking Press, 1970).

4. Genre Films and the Status Quo

JUDITH HESS WRIGHT

The ideas of order that [the culture industry] inculcates are always those of the status quo. . . . Pretending to be the guide for the helpless and deceitfully presenting to them conflicts that they must perforce confuse with their own, the culture industry does not resolve these conflicts except in appearance—its "solutions" would be impossible for them to use to resolve their conflicts in their own lives. —T. W. ADORNO, The Culture Industry[1]

American genre films—the western, the science fiction film, the horror film, the gangster film—have been the most popular (and thus the most lucrative) products ever to emerge from the machinery of the American film industry. Critics have long pondered the genre film's success and have attempted to ferret out the reasons for the public's appreciation of even the most undistinguished "singing cowboy" westerns. In general, critics have examined these films as isolated phenomena—as found objects—instead of considering genre films in relation to the society that created them. Genre films have been defined as pure myth, as well-made plays, and as psychodramas bearing within themselves the working out of unconscious anxieties inherent in the psychological makeup of us all. Certainly any and all of these explanations contain some truth; however, none of them explains why American genre films grew to become our most numerous, if not most artistically significant, film productions.

I think that we may see what genre films are by examining what they do. These films came into being and were financially successful because they temporarily relieved the fears aroused by a recognition of social and political conflicts; they helped to discourage any action that might otherwise follow upon the pressure generated by living with these conflicts. Genre films produce satisfaction rather than action, pity and fear rather than revolt. They serve the interests of the ruling class by assisting in the maintenance of the status quo, and they throw a sop to oppressed groups who, because they are unorganized and therefore afraid to act, eagerly accept the genre film's absurd solutions to economic and social conflicts. When we return to the complexities of the society in which we live, the same conflicts assert themselves, so we return to genre films for easy comfort and solace—hence their popularity.

Genre films address these conflicts and resolve them in a simplistic and reactionary way. Genre films have three significant characteristics that make such resolutions seem possible and even logical. First, these films never deal directly with present social and political problems; second, all of them are set in the nonpresent. Westerns and horror films take place in the past; science fiction films, by definition, take place in a future time. The gangster film takes place in a social structure so separate from the contemporary structure in which it appears to be taking place that its actual time and place become irrelevant. Third, the society in which the action takes place is very simple and does not function as a dramatic force in the films—it exists as a backdrop against which the few actors work out the central problem the film presents. As Robert Warshow points out in *The Immediate Experience*,[2] the westerner exists in isolation. We have no idea where he gets his money or where he washes. His trials and confrontations take place in utter isolation (the desert or mountains) or in the setting of a tiny, uncomplicated western town. Horror films present an isolated group of people who live in a tiny village or meet in a castle or island that they do not leave until the end of the movie, if at all. Many science fiction films show professionals moving away from society—to an island, an experimental station of some sort, the South Pole, outer space—to cope with alien intruders. Although some science fiction films are set in modern cities, the cities are weirdly empty and serve as labyrinths through which the protagonists thread their ways. The gangster lives in a very limited world populated by a few other gangsters and their molls.

All of these genre films, science fiction included, present a greatly simplified social structure. However frequently this kind of very limited social structure may have existed in the past, it no longer exists in the present. Thus, genre films are nostalgic; their social structure posits some sort of movement backward to a simpler world. And in this simple structure, problems that haunt us because of our inability to resolve them are solved in ways not possible today. Genre films reject the present and ignore any likely future.

The genre films focus on four major conflicts. The western centers on the violent act and ascertains when, if ever, it becomes morally right. The horror film attempts to resolve the disparities between two contradictory ways of problem solving—one based on rationality, the other based on faith, an irrational commitment to certain traditional beliefs. The science fiction film provides a solution to the problems presented by intrusion—that is, they tell us how to deal with what may be called "the other." Gangster films resolve the contradictory feelings of fear and desire that are aroused by attempts to achieve financial and social success.

The problems posed by these contradictions are solved simply. The western decrees that the violent act can become morally right when it occurs within the confines of a code that allows for executions, revenge killings, and killings in defense of one's life and property. In the microcosmic western society everyone's code is the same; thus absolute guilt and innocence are possible because social and moral goodness are the same. Horror films present human beings as fallen, prey to uncontrollable evil impulses. Only by reliance on traditional beliefs and the domination of a well-defined upper class can we be saved from doom and perdition. The science fiction film's answer to the problem of the intruder is sheerest isolationism. No possible advance in knowledge gained from communication could possibly outweigh the dangers it presents—the only sane response is to eradicate it. The gangster film, by implication, opts for happy anonymity. To be successful is to become vulnerable; the successful ones become the foes of all who wish to take their place. Gangster films show the fearful results of attempting to rise within a hierarchical society and thus defend class lines. These simplistic solutions—the adherence to a well-defined, unchanging code, the advocacy of methods of problem solving based on tradition and faith, the advocacy of isolationism, and the warning to stay within one's station to survive—all militate against progressive social change.

In order to flesh out these assertions it is necessary to examine each of the genres in some detail. The western male is dominated by a code of honor that prescribes his every action; violence by lynching or shooting, amorous advances, or friendships are determined by some fixed rule. One lynches cattle rustlers but not petty thieves—one runs them out of town. One sleeps only with bar girls, not eastern schoolteachers. One never shoots a man in the back; one is utterly loyal to one's friends, defending them physically and verbally at every possible opportunity. At a certain mystical point in the interaction between two opposing forces, the western version of the duel becomes morally acceptable; both the villain and the hero know immediately when this point comes, as they do not exist as psychological entities apart from the code—rather, they embody the code. The earliest westerns afford the clearest expression of the workings of this code. In these movies the heroes and villains are like chess pieces moved about to depict the code's intricacies. In a great many westerns we can note the eerie occurrence of two phrases that are as far as these movies go toward positing motivation: "I have to . . ." and "All I know is . . ." These phrases express how the code provides motivation, not the persons themselves. Westerners act together in absolute, unthinking accord. Westerns examine those aspects of the code that determine the westerner's response to situations demanding violence. The compartmentalizations of the code—one treats bank robbers one way and friends another—allow for situations involving contradictory responses. What happens, for example, in *The Virginian* (Victor Fleming, 1929), a movie that Robert Warshow calls "archetypal," when a captured rustler is at the same time a friend? Gary Cooper, a chess-piece representation of the code, is caught on the horns of a moral and social dilemma. Although he must bow to the will of the other members of the posse, for whom the situation is not complicated (the rustler is not their friend), and assist in the lynching and see his friend exonerate him, Cooper must work within the code to redeem himself—to rid himself of guilt by balancing the books.

And there is a single, simple solution. His friend has been drawn into rustling by the film's real villain, Trampas. Cooper must wipe him out, at the same time showing the restraint demanded of the westerner. He must wait for that mystical point in time at which the showdown becomes morally and socially right. And Trampas, because he is a villain and thus cannot act in any other way, provides Cooper with sufficient injury and insult, and is thus shot in a fair fight. Several violent actions are condoned in the movie: traditionally sanctioned violence demanded by the group (Cooper never questions the lynching; he suffers only because he is forced to abandon his friend); violence brought about by repeated attacks on one's character (Trampas indicates that Cooper is a coward); and violence that redeems the violence Cooper has been forced to commit against his friend. These acts of violence have complete social sanction. Only Cooper's eastern schoolmarm girlfriend fails to condone Cooper's actions; she has not as yet been assimilated into western society.

In the western every man who operates solely with reference to this strict code lives and dies redeemed. He has retained his social and moral honor. The code provides justification; thus it allows for a guiltless existence. On the other hand, we do not know ourselves when, if ever, violence is justifiable. We have great difficulty in forming a personal code and we cannot be sure that this code will conform in any way to the large, impersonal legal code set up to regulate our unwieldy, decaying economic structure. The westerner's code is at once personal and social—if a man lives by it he both conforms to social norms and retains his personal integrity. The source of the satisfaction we get from the western is evident. Momentarily we understand the peace that comes from acting in accord with a coherent moral and social code and forget our fragmented selves. Many critics have seen the western as a glorification of traditional American individualism. On the contrary, the western preaches integration and assimilation and absolute obedience to the laws of the land.

The horror film deals with the conflict between rational or scientific and traditional ways of problem solving. In *Dracula* (Tod Browning, 1931), *Frankenstein* (James Whale, 1931), *The Mummy* (Karl Freund, 1932), and *The Wolf Man* (George Waggner, 1948), the monsters are the embodiment of human evil. They are three-dimensional representations of our uncontrollable will to evil; we must conquer them if society is to survive. Lawrence Talbot ignores the gypsy's warnings, is tainted by a wolf bite, and becomes dominated by evil desires—he kills those he cares for. Dracula, the incarnation of unbridled sensuality, attracts his victims,

8. *Dracula:* The vampire (Bela Lugosi) as the incarnation of unbridled sensuality.

sucks them dry, and condemns them to becoming like him. Before becoming a mummy, an Egyptian prince has unsuccessfully pitted himself against the will of the gods. He, too, represents unbridled sensual appetite, the naked id. Dr. Frankenstein's poor maimed creation is a projection of his own overwhelming will to power and knowledge beyond that granted by God. Because he relies totally on scientific means to ends, he becomes a monster himself—he is redeemed by suffering and by his complete rejection of his heretical drive to uncover the secrets of life and death.

Various groups attempt to overcome the monsters. "Ignorant peasants" (for example, the Egyptian workers or the Carpathian peasants), who believe in the reality of evil but who belong to a traditionally oppressed class, are overcome, or, at best, live out a miserable existence under the monster's sway. The masses are shown to be without sufficient moral strength to overcome the monster themselves. These monsters are at some point opposed by enlightened scientists who, because they believe only in the ability of science to defeat social and physical ills and in rational, demonstrable means to ends, disregard tradition and thus threaten the existing social order. Because these scientists refuse to believe in the power of the irrational will to evil, the monster annihilates them. The monster is finally defeated by members of the upper class who abandon scientific training in favor of belief in the traditional ways in which others before them have overcome evil forces. Dr. Van Helsing, once he realizes that medical science cannot save Dracula's victims, does research, finds what traditionally has been used against Dracula (beheading, garlic, a stake through the heart), and employs these means. The wolfman is killed by a silver-headed cane; the mummy is destroyed by an appeal to the ancient Egyptian gods. Van Helsing makes the required return to tradition with a commitment to articles of faith, as do all those who defeat the evil.

The message is clear: science must not be allowed to replace traditional values and beliefs. Otherwise, chaos will result, as humans cannot control their own evil tendencies or those of the people around them without suprarational help. The social order out of which these monsters spring is posited as good—it must remain unchanged. Only by the benevolent dictatorship of the hereditary aristocracy can these monsters be kept at bay; the existing class structure prevents chaos. Like the German expressionist horror films that preceded them, American horror films (the first and best of which appeared in the early thirties) may be seen as a reaction to a period of economic and social upheaval—the films are, in effect, a plea to go back to older methods of coping. This solution works in the horror film's oversimplified world.

The science fiction film, which developed during the forties and fifties, may be seen as a dramatization of those fears and desires aroused by the cold war. "The other," however strange and alien, has at least some significant relation to those massed hordes of Communists foisted on the American people by such venomous Red-baiters as Joseph McCarthy, Richard Nixon, and Billy Graham. Confronted by "the other," according to these films, there is only one possible response. We must use every scientific means at our disposal to destroy the invader.

As in the horror film, the social order that exists previous to the coming of the aliens is posited as good. The aliens, who are scientifically advanced but who lack emotions (that is, they do not share our values), invade in frightening machines. Often nonviolent communication is established between a few scientists and the aliens. However, these scientists invariably learn that these beings aim to take our bodies, as in *Invasion of the Body Snatchers* (Don Siegel, 1956) or to assume social and political control, as in *Earth vs. the Flying Saucers* (Fred F. Sears, 1956), or to suck our blood, as in *The Thing* (Christian Nyby, 1951). The uneasiness Americans feel about scientific advance and intellectuals in general is evident in many of these films—often a wild-haired scientist is

9. *Invasion of the Body Snatchers* (1956): The "other" invades the home.

willing to hand over the country to the invaders in order to learn more about the secrets of the universe. He is either annihilated by the very invaders he has tried to protect, or he regroups when confronted by the invaders' lack of concern with our traditional values and social structures. Usually, however, the scientists (often they are allied with the military) are the first to recognize the extent of the aliens' ill will and band together to defeat them. Great ingenuity and immediate scientific advance are required to win the fight, but the scientists discover the necessary materials in the nick of time and save the world. Although a few films like *20 Million Miles to Earth* (Nathan Juran, 1957) and *The Day the Earth Stood Still* (Robert Wise, 1951) question the absolute evil of the aliens, these films were not well received. It was those films that gave a single, unequivocal answer to the problem of "the other" which were the most successful. The message of these films was that "the other" will do only evil, no matter what blandishments disguise its true intent. The only recourse is to destroy it utterly. And, so say these films, we can. These films build on fears of the intrusive and the overpowering and thereby promote isolationism. They also imply that science is good only inasmuch as it serves to support the existing class structure.

The best beginning to a discussion of the gangster film is Robert Warshow's description of our reactions to it:

> The gangster is doomed because he is under obligation to succeed, not because the means he employs are unlawful. In the deeper layers of the modern consciousness, *all* means are unlawful, every attempt to succeed is an act of aggression, leaving one alone and guilty and defenseless among enemies: one is *punished* for success. This is our intolerable dilemma: that failure is a kind of death and success is evil and dangerous and—ultimately—impossible. The effect of the gangster film is to embody this dilemma in the person of the gangster and resolve it by his death. The dilemma is resolved because it is his death, not ours. We are safe; for the moment we can acquiesce in our failure, we can choose to fail.[3]

The world of the gangster is made up of a pyramidal hierarchy. Only one man can be the top dog. We follow a single man as he makes his way up the various ranks of the structure. In *The Public Enemy* (William Wellman, 1931), he starts out as a petty thief who sells his loot to a fence a few steps higher up in the system. He quickly graduates to stealing liquor supplies and, finally, to the rank of boss. Unlike Scarface and Little Caesar, who make it all the way, Cagney is undone by his own temper and arrogance before he becomes much more than small-time. However, he is intrepid enough to attempt to revenge another gang's decimation of his own hierarchy, and is killed as a warning to others who might attempt to meddle with the strong. These men are rebels and renegades, but only within the confines of the existing order. They do not wish to establish a different kind of structure, but to fight their way to the top of an existing one. This pyramid is a microcosm of the capitalist structure. We have a very ambivalent response to the competition necessary to survive in our own competitive society. We know that we must defeat other people to succeed ourselves. And because we have reached some worthwhile position through aggression, we are left vulnerable to any competitor who covets our position. We are left with the choice of fighting with all comers—and we know we cannot do that successfully forever—or else failing. As Warshow states, we can exist with our own economic and social failure as we watch the gangster's death. For a moment it becomes acceptable to survive, even at the price of economic anonymity. A gangster film would never suggest that a different sort of social and political structure might allow for more humane possibilities. In fact, the gangster film implicitly upholds capitalism by making the gangster an essentially tragic figure. The insolubility of his problem is not traced to its social cause; rather the problem is presented as growing out of the gangster's character. His tragic flaw is ambition; his stature is determined by the degree to which he rises in the hierarchy. We are led to believe that he makes choices, not that he is victimized by the world in which he finds himself. The gangster film retains its appeal because our economic structure does not change—we must commit aggressive acts to survive within the confines of our capitalistic structure. And, as Warshow implies, when we see a gangster film—be it *Little Caesar* (Mervyn LeRoy, 1930) or *The Godfather* (Francis Ford Coppola, 1971)—we are moved not to struggle out of our class to question our hierarchical social structure, but to subside and survive.

We may trace the amazing survival and proliferation of the genre films to their function. They assist in the maintenance of the existing political structure. The solutions these films give to the conflicts inherent in capitalism require obeisance to the ruling class and cause viewers to yearn for not less but greater freedom in the face of the insoluble ambiguities surrounding them. Viewers are encouraged to cease examining themselves and their surroundings, and to take refuge in fantasy from their only real alternative—to rise up against the injustices perpetrated by the present system upon its members.

Notes

1. T. W. Adorno, "The Culture Industry," trans. Rafael Cook, *Cinéaste* 5, no. 1, 8–11.

2. Robert Warshow, "Movie Chronicle: The Westerner," in *The Immediate Experience* (New York: Atheneum, 1971), pp. 135–154.

3. Ibid., p. 133.

5. Social Implications in the Hollywood Genres

JEAN-LOUP BOURGET

From the outset, the cinema has been characterized by a certain tension, even a certain conflict, between an apparent content, derived from popular literature, and a number of autonomous stylistic devices (the various uses of actors, sets, camera movements, montage). Strictures traditionally passed on the Hollywood film fail to take into account the basic fact that its conventionality is the very paradoxical reason for its creativity. Conventions inherited from literature have added themselves to social pressures, such as the necessity for self-censorship, and to commercial imperatives, and may well have badly hampered the explicit content and meaning of movies—plot and characterization frequently tending to become stereotyped. But in many instances the newness of the medium made it possible, even mandatory, to resort to a language both visual and aural, whose implicit meaning was far removed from what the mere script might convey. Here are two brief examples. In Griffith's films, we find a tension between the conventional Victorian moralizing of the plot and titles, and the much more subtle meanings of sets, lighting, close-ups of actresses' faces, camera movements, and editing. In Josef von Sternberg's films, there is an open, unresolved conflict between the stereotypes of the plot and dialogue and the "pure poetry" of the visual elements.

Another point that should be borne in mind is that, whenever an art form is highly conventional, the opportunity for subtle irony or distanciation presents itself all the more readily. The director's (that is to say, the camera's) point of view need not coincide with the hero's point of view; or again, and more generally, since a film represents a superposition of texts, it is not surprising that large segments of an audience (notably including literary-minded critics) should decipher only one of these texts and therefore misread the sum total of the various texts. European directors working in Hollywood developed a technique for telling stories with implicit ironical meanings. For example, Ernst Lubitsch's *Trouble in Paradise* (1932) presents a coherent view of contemporary society under the neat gloss of the sophisticated comedy: thieves are capitalists; capitalists are thieves. Similarly, *To Be or Not to Be* (Lubitsch, 1942) is not just a farce: it makes the not altogether frivolous point that the historical Nazis were worse actors than the fictitious bad actors of the Polish underground. The point was completely missed by the contemporary audience, who regarded the film as being in very bad taste. The same remark applies to most of Douglas Sirk's American films. Thus *All That Heaven Allows* (1956) is not a "weepie," but a sharp satire of small-town America; *Written on the Wind* (1957) is not about the glamor of American high society, but about its corruption; *Imitation of Life* (1959) is superficially naïve and optimistic, but profoundly bitter and antiracist.

The conflict between the movie's pre-text (the script, the source of the adaptation) and its text (all the evidence on the screen and sound track) provides us with an analytic tool, because it allows for a reconciliation of two apparently antagonistic approaches: the auteur theory, which claims that a film is the work of one creative individual, and the iconological approach, which assumes that a film is a sequence of images whose real meaning may well be unconscious on the part of its makers. Elsewhere I have tried to show that the original version of *Back Street* (John M. Stahl, 1932), while apparently describing a woman's noble and sad sacrifice, is in fact a melodrama with profound social and feministic implications.[1] I also stated that "melodrama" in its traditional sense was born at the time of the French Revolution and reflected social unrest in a troubled historical period. In the context of the description of society, we may therefore distinguish between melodramas such as *Back Street,* which express a certain state of society, depicting its relative stability and the occasions of potential conflict, and melodramas such as *Orphans of the Storm* (D. W. Griffith, 1922) and *Anthony Adverse* (Mervyn LeRoy, 1936), which comment on actual turmoil. It would probably be possible to give a survey of other popular genres in search of similar examples of these alternative approaches: description of an operative system, description of the breaking up of a given structure.

In the first category—films describing how a given social structure operates—we find many movies belonging to genres that are often dismissed as escapist and alienating. While this may well be true in a majority of cases, it nevertheless remains that escapism can also be used as a device for criticizing reality and the present state of society. A utopian world that calls itself a utopia is not escapist in the derogatory sense of the word; rather, it calls the viewer's attention to the fact that his or her own society is far removed from such an ideal condition. Many films by such Rousseauistic directors as Allan Dwan and Delmer Daves belong to this category; they might best be described as "South Seas adventure dramas"—see Allan Dwan's adaptation of Melville's *Typee* (*Enchanted Island,* 1958) and Delmer Daves's *Bird of Paradise* (1951), *Treasure of the Golden*

Condor (1953), and his western *Broken Arrow* (1950). Some of these films suffer from a stylistic incompetence that somewhat forces the implicit meaning back out of the film itself, into the director's generous but unrealized intentions. More to the point are perhaps two films by John Ford, *The Hurricane* (1937) and *Donovan's Reef* (1963). The first film implicitly contrasts Raymond Massey, who embodies the oppressive law, with the Lincoln of other John Ford films, Lincoln being an incarnation of the law which gives life and freedom. In *Donovan's Reef*, a brief scene located in Boston supplies the key to implicit meaning as we are allowed to glimpse a caricatural reality of America opposed to the idealized vision of the Pacific island.

In contradistinction to the legend that in all traditional westerns "the only good Indian is a dead Indian," a closer look at early Hollywood westerns reveals surprising conflicts between explicit and implicit meanings. Thus in DeMille's *The Squawman*, a subject obviously dear to him since he treated it on three different occasions (1913, 1918, 1931), an Englishman who has settled in America is seduced by the "primitive" and therefore "immoral" beauty of an Indian woman drying her naked body by the fire. He lives with her without marrying her, and she bears him a child. Years later, the Englishman's relatives look him up and insist on taking his child to England in order to give him a proper education. Because of her "primitive" mind (as the man puts it), the Indian woman does not understand why her son should be taken away from her, and she commits suicide. Earlier on, she had already been rejected by the child, who had preferred an electric train to the crude wooden horse that she had carved for him. In its treatment of the story, DeMille's point of view is sympathetic to the Indian woman rather than to the Europeans. To him, she is morally superior. This is made clear less by the plot than by the lyricism of the sequences devoted to Lupe Velez "seducing" the Englishman or carving the wooden toy. At the same time, because of its tragic conclusion, the film could hardly be accused of being escapist or naively optimistic. In a much more subtle way, the indictment of white pseudo-civilization is as harsh as in Arthur Penn's *Little Big Man* of 1970. But these cultural tensions remain implicit and unresolved. Obviously, the "deconstruction" of ironical analysis is not synonymous with "destruction." Is this failure to resolve tensions due to weakness in the creative act or rather to the capitalistic mode of film production? In Hollywood, the director's work, however conscious it may be of social alienation, is bound by the same alienation.

Ironical implications of a social breakdown can be embedded in the most highly conventional and least realistic films. Such a movie is *Heidi* (Allan Dwan, 1937), starring Shirley Temple, where kitsch, as is usual, verges on parody. Only in a kitsch film or in a comedy could servants be emblematically described as holding a feather duster. The kitsch movie is often located in Central Europe, and the ideal society it tends to refer to is that of the Hapsburg Empire. There we find a static hierarchical society where everybody is defined by a social function rather than by individual traits. But the providential architecture of this social system is so exaggerated that (whether consciously or unconsciously on the part of the film-makers) the effect produced is, in the last analysis, satirical. Stylistically, social functions are indicated by emblems (folkloric costumes, pointed helmets, plumes), which look slightly ridiculous. For example, in *Zoo in Budapest* (Rowland V. Lee, 1933), society is neatly divided between the haves and the have-nots, between those with some parcel of authority and those without any. On the one hand, we find certain aristocratic visitors to the zoo and a multitude of characters in quasi-military uniforms: wardens, policemen, bus drivers. On the other hand, we have the peasant visitors in colorful garb, the girls from an orphanage, and the unsociable hero who seeks the company of animals rather than that of men. This amounts to the description of a society so alienated that, in order to be free, one has to live behind bars in a zoo! The last part of the film bursts into nightmare, as all the wild beasts escape from their cages—a suggestion that this neatly organized society is no less prone to explosions and revolutions, notwithstanding the literally incredible ending, which claims to reconcile the feudal system and the individual's happiness.[2]

Similarly, a turn-of-the-century setting seems to be very popular in a variety of genres, from the literary adaptation (*The Picture of Dorian Gray*, Albert Lewin, 1945) to the horror film (*Hangover Square*, John Brahm, 1945), from the romantic drama (*Letter from an Unknown Woman*, Max Ophuls, 1948) to the musical (*Meet Me in St. Louis*, Vincente Minnelli, 1944; *Gigi*, Minnelli, 1958; *My Fair Lady*, George Cukor, 1964). There are probably two reasons for this popularity. For one thing, such a setting has stylistic qualities that readily lend themselves to artistic effects. For another thing, it refers to Western society—usually but not necessarily European—at its most sophisticated, on the eve of the First World War and of the economic collapse of Europe. This presumably accounts for the success of the Viennese film, a genre that has often been wrongly explained in naively biographical and nostalgic terms. The satirical element that is obvious in von Stroheim's films is implicit in the works of other European directors. Josef von Sternberg's *Dishonored* (1931) contrasts Marlene Dietrich's *amour fou* with the sense of decadence and the collapse of empires, Austrian and Russian. In Anatole Litvak's *Mayerling* (1936), the lovers are doomed, not by fate but by the ominous sign of the Hapsburg Empire, the oppressive Eagle of *raison d'état*: the ball scene in particular opens with the camera seemingly tracking through a glass eagle and ends with the same movement in reverse. In many "Viennese" films, both European and American, Ophüls uses the device of a duel, which points out the way in which a particular class of society goes about solving its private problems when they cannot be kept private any longer.

Such films therefore enable us to put forward a tentative definition of melodrama as opposed to tragedy: in melodrama, fate is not metaphysical but rather social or political. Thus melodrama is bourgeois tragedy, dependent upon an awareness of the existence of society. This echoes Benjamin Constant's own definition of the new tragedy: "Social order, the action of society on the individual, in different phases and at different epochs, this network of institutions and conventions in which we are caught from our birth and which does not break until we die, these are the mainsprings of tragedy. One only has to know how to use them. They are absolutely equivalent to the Fatum of the Ancients." [3]

In several respects, the musical is close to the cinematic melodrama, both having developed from forms of spectacle associated with the conventions of the popular stage. In order to express an implicit meaning, they both have to rely almost exclusively on stylization, at once visual and musical (melodrama is etymologically "drama with music"), for they are both removed from the convention of realism.[4] In the hands of creative individual directors, musicals therefore lend themselves to statements that will pass unnoticed by the majority of the entertainment-seeking audience and by critics who judge the explicit content. Unsurprisingly, some directors have excelled in both genres—above all, Minnelli. *Brigadoon* (1954) is an excellent example of what is meant here: the musical is set against the motif of bustling New York, and the meaning of the supposedly escapist part of the movie can only be induced from the satirized madness of the everyday setting toward the end of the film.

An allegory frequent in the musical is that of Pygmalion, of a member of respectable society raising a girl of the lower classes to his own level of civilized sophistication. It is the particular failure of *My Fair Lady* (George Cukor, 1964) to have used Audrey Hepburn in such a part, because the actress is evidently an extremely sophisticated one. Thus the parable rings false; in order to make it convincing, Cukor should have used an actress of a completely different type, Shirley MacLaine, for example, and have her look like a lady by the end of the film. For the implication should be that there is nothing in high society that a good actor or dancer should not be capable of achieving through imitation. Again, it should suggest a reversal of the apparent roles and functions similar to the one found in Lubitsch's *Trouble in Paradise:* if dancers are ladies, ladies cannot be far different from dancers. The whole oeuvre of such directors as Minnelli and Cukor is based on this underlying assumption, which, hidden behind a playful guise, is both a satire of actual social solidity and an indication of possible social fluidity (see Cukor's films starring Judy Holliday and Minnelli's films starring Judy Garland).

Easter Parade (Charles Walters, 1948) tells a story similar to that of *My Fair Lady,* with Fred Astaire and Judy Garland in roles similar to those of Rex Harrison and Audrey Hepburn. But there the allegory works, and goes farther, because it has serious bearings on woman's status in society. At the end of the film, Judy Garland, tired of waiting to be proposed to, decides that there is no reason why she should not in fact woo Fred Astaire. She adopts the man's traditional role, sends numerous gifts to the object of her thoughts, and compliments him on his beautiful clothes. The musical, like a court jester, is allowed a saturnalian freedom because it is not a "serious" genre. Its self-eulogy ("Be a Clown" in Minnelli's *The Pirate,* 1948; "Make 'Em Laugh" in Donen and Kelly's *Singin' in the Rain,* 1952; and "That's Entertainment" in Minnelli's *The Band Wagon,* 1953) shows its understandable reluctance to part with such a liberty.

Another category of films is not content with describing a system, but portrays its collapse. (Screwball comedies and Busby Berkeley musicals, connected with the Depression, can be mentioned in passing.)[5] The implicit meaning may be more difficult to assert in historical films and epics because they often refer to revolutions or civil wars whose pattern is given as fact and thus not susceptible to an interpretation. Yet a coherent explanation is sometimes to be found hidden behind the historical or adventurous plot. *Anthony Adverse,* referred to earlier, is located in the time of the French Revolution and of the First Empire. It is critical of both the former aristocracy and of the new classes, depicted as a ruthless mob aping the former nobility. The only solution is found in leaving a doomed continent and sailing for the new land and the democratic society of America. A somewhat similar point of view is expressed in *A Tale of Two Cities* (Jack Conway, 1935), where the French Revolution must be shown as almost simultaneously profoundly justified and profoundly unjust. This is achieved in a very interesting way. The first part of the film is, despite a few hints, rather sympathetic to the idea of a revolution, which is shown as inevitable. Even more committed are the sequences of the revolution proper (the storming of the Bastille), which were directed by a different team—Jacques Tourneur and Val Lewton. They are absolutely Eisensteinlike in their depiction of blatant injustice and spontaneous union, Sovietlike, of people and army. From there on, it is impossible to think of any adequate transition; the trick consists in skipping over the transition, in reverting to a title, a pre-text, which claims that the spirit of liberty had been betrayed even before it had triumphed. But such is not the evidence on the screen, and the film embodies a strange, unresolved discrepancy between the sequences directed by Jack Conway (pleasant but traditional in style, faithful to the source of the adaptation) and those by Jacques Tourneur, formally very original, unambiguous in their meaning, and telling a tale of their own.

Conversely, a perfectly coherent film about the French Revolution is *Marie Antoinette* (Woody S. Van Dyke, 1937)—coherent, that is, from a reactionary point of view. Yet, even in this case, we see a tension at work between the explicit argument of the film as signified by the title (a woman's picture, the sad, dignified story of Marie Antoinette) and the implicit political message, according to which the hero/victim is King Louis XVI rather than Marie Antoinette. In the light of the film, she is not much more than a pleasure-loving girl, but he is portrayed as a man of good will who was betrayed by a conspiracy of Freemasons and the Duke of Orleans.

A subgenre of the adventure film that almost inevitably acclaims a pattern of social unrest and revolution (always successful in this case, because it is far removed in time and space, and therefore with no apparent direct bearings on present society) is the swashbuckler, the pirate film. The most "democratic" examples of the genre include two films by Michael Curtiz, *Captain Blood* (1935) and *The Sea Hawk* (1940). In both, an apolitical man is charged with sedition and actually becomes a rebel (cf. a similar parable in John Ford's *Prisoner of Shark Island,* 1936). Both films describe the way a colonial system rests on political oppression, slavery, and torture; they both advocate violent revolution as the only means of destroying such a system. The evidence of the genre therefore conflicts with the evidence of colonial films set in the twentieth century—for example, in British India or in French North Africa—where it is the outlaw who is supposedly guilty of savagery. It might be illuminating to show to what extent a contemporary, politically committed film-maker like Gillo Pontecorvo has relied on the traditional Hollywood and Cinecittà genre of the pirate film in his 1968 film *Quemada* (*Burn!* in English).

As pointed out before, the danger of certain explicit statements about Robin Hood and pirate figures in distant times or remote places is that the remoteness can be emphasized rather than played down. In historical films about outlaws, the viewer is allowed to walk out with a clear conscience and a dim consciousness. This danger was realized and pointed out by directors more sophisticated than Michael Curtiz. In *Sullivan's Travels* (1942), Preston Sturges satirized the conventions of the social-problem genre that had flourished at Warners under the guidance of Mervyn LeRoy, among others. The bittersweet conclusion of Sturges's film was that directors should not go beyond the camera, that they should not make social statements when they have but the vaguest notions about the condition of society, and should rather devote their time and energy to the making of comedies. But his own film showed that he could somehow do both at the same time: entertain and make valid comments. Similarly, Minnelli's *The Pirate* underlines the conventions of the swashbuckler. It adds another dimension to the meaning of the pirate film. Judy Garland, the governor's daughter, falls in love with Gene Kelly, an actor who parades as Macoco, the fierce pirate. The point is, first, that to make a "revolutionary" and "democratic" pirate film is partly to base the argument on Errol Flynn's—or Gene Kelly's—sex appeal. But this is only the first layer of meaning. The actor, not the pirate, turns out to be the "revolutionary" individual who is going to achieve social change, for he unmasks Walter Slezak (Judy Garland's fiancé), the real Macoco who parades as a respectable citizen. The lesson is therefore that piracy can be identified with respectable bourgeois society, and that the artist (whether an actor or a Hollywood director) emerges as the one person with both a sense of individual freedom and the refusal to oppress others.

Thus the freedom of Hollywood directors is not measured by what they can openly do within the Hollywood system, but rather by what they can imply about American society in general and about the Hollywood system in particular. They can describe in extensive detail how a given social structure operates, but cannot do so openly unless the society in question is remote in time or space; if they describe the breakdown of a social system, they must somehow end on a hopeful note and show that both order and happiness are eventually restored. However, the interplay of implicit meanings, either subtly different from or actually clashing with the conventional self-gratification, allows the Hollywood director to make valid comments about contemporary American society in an indirect way, by "bending" the explicit meaning (Sirk's phrase). Genre conventions can be either used as an alibi (the implicit meaning is to be found elsewhere in the film) or turned upside down (irony underlines the conventionality of the convention). The implicit subtext of genre films makes it possible for the director to ask the inevitable (but unanswerable) question: Must American society be like this? Must the Hollywood system function like this?

Notes

1. Jean-Loup Bourget, "Aspects du mélodrame américain," *Positif,* no. 131 (October 1971): 31–43; for the English version, see "*Back Street* (Reconsidered)," *Take One* 3, no. 2 (November–December 1970): 33–34. The implicit significance of Stahl's *Back Street* is due not to the Fannie Hurst story itself, but to its treatment by Stahl. A confirmation will be found in a comparison with the latest version of the same story (retold by David Miller in 1961), where the meaning is altered, reduced both to its mawkish pretext and to very few fulgurant images listlessly "borrowed" from films by Douglas Sirk.

2. In *Zoo in Budapest,* Gene Raymond and Loretta Young first find happiness in a bear's den overlooking the town, the outside world. Their situation recalls that of Borzage's heroes in *Seventh Heaven* (1927): the "little man" lives in a garret, close to the stars, which allows him symbolic "overlooking" of a world that crushes him in every other way.

3. Benjamin Constant, *Oeuvres* (Paris: Bibl. de la Pléiade, 1957), p. 952, translation mine. Obviously, many cinematic melodramas still pretend to rely on the device of superhuman fate; it is only an analysis of their implicit meanings, of their subtext, which makes it possible to unmask such fate and give it its actual name of social necessity.

4. In fact, what is variously termed "romantic drama," "soap opera," "sudser," "woman's film," etc., spans all the gamut from the operatic formalism of Dietrich's films and Garbo's *Queen Christina* (Rouben Mamoulian, 1933) to the drab realism of the kitchen-sink drama. There are some successful examples of fairly "realistic" melodramas, notably John Cromwell's *Made for Each Other* and *In Name Only* (both 1939). Nevertheless, even such films are highly unrealistic in their catastrophic situations and providential endings. The impression of realism is largely due to the actors (Carole Lombard as opposed to, say, Joan Crawford) rather than to the verisimilitude of plot and setting. As a rule, both the musical and the melodrama are more openly formalized and ritualized than the realistic guise normally allows. This is due to their common theatrical origin and to their disregard of subtle, novelistic psychological analysis.

5. See Jean-Loup Bourget, "Capra et la screwball comedy," *Positif,* no. 133 (December 1971): 47–53.

6. Ideology, Genre, Auteur

ROBIN WOOD

The truth lies not in one dream but in many.
—Arabian Nights (PIER PAOLO PASOLINI, 1974)

Each theory of film so far has insisted on its own particular polarization. Montage theory enthrones editing as the essential creative act at the expense of other aspects of film; Bazin's realist theory, seeking to right the balance, merely substitutes its own imbalance, downgrading montage and artifice; the revolutionary theory centered in Britain in *Screen* (but today very widespread) rejects—or at any rate seeks to "deconstruct"—realist art in favor of the so-called open text. Auteur theory, in its heyday, concentrated attention exclusively on the fingerprints, thematic or stylistic, of the individual artist; recent attempts to discuss the complete "filmic text" have tended to throw out ideas of personal authorship altogether. Each theory has, given its underlying position, its own validity—the validity being dependent upon and restricted by the position. Each can offer insights into different areas of cinema and different aspects of a single film.

I have suggested elsewhere[1] the desirability for critics—whose aim should always be to see the work as wholly as possible, as it is—to be able to draw on the discoveries and particular perceptions of each theory, each position, without committing themselves exclusively to any one. The ideal will not be easy to attain, and even the attempt raises all kinds of problems, the chief of which is the validity of evaluative criteria that are not supported by a particular system. For what, then, *do* they receive support? No critic, obviously, can be free from a structure of values, nor can he or she afford to withdraw from the struggles and tensions of living to some position of "aesthetic" contemplation. Every critic who is worth reading has been, on the contrary, very much caught up in the effort to define values beyond purely aesthetic ones (if indeed such things exist). Yet to "live historically" need not entail commitment to a system or a cause; rather, it can involve being alive to the opposing pulls, the tensions, of one's world.

The past two decades have seen a number of advances in terms of the opening up of critical possibilities, of areas of relevance, especially with regard to Hollywood: the elaboration of auteur theory in its various man-

ifestations; the interest in genre; the interest in ideology. I want here ten-
tatively to explore some of the ways in which these disparate approaches
to Hollywood movies might interpenetrate, producing the kind of synthetic criticism I have suggested might now be practicable.

In order to create a context within which to discuss *It's a Wonderful
Life* (Frank Capra, 1946) and *Shadow of a Doubt* (Alfred Hitchcock,
1943), I want to attempt (at risk of obviousness) a definition of what we
mean by American capitalist ideology—or, more specifically, the values
and assumptions so insistently embodied in and reinforced by the classical Hollywood cinema. The following list of components is not intended
to be exhaustive or profound, but simply to make conscious, prior to a
discussion of the films, concepts with which we are all perfectly familiar:

1. Capitalism, the right of ownership, private enterprise, personal initiative; the settling of the land.

2. The work ethic: the notion that "honest toil" is in itself and for itself morally admirable, this and concept I both validating and reinforcing each other. The moral excellence of work is also bound up with the
necessary subjugation or sublimation of the libido: "the Devil finds work
for idle hands." The relationship is beautifully epitomized in the zoo-
cleaner's song in *Cat People* (Jacques Tourneur, 1942):

> Nothing else to do,
> Nothing else to do,
> I strayed, went a-courting
> 'cause I'd nothing else to do.

3. Marriage (legalized heterosexual monogamy) and family—at once
the further validation of concepts 1 and 2 (the homestead is built for the
woman, whose function is to embody civilized values and guarantee their
continuance through her children) and an extension of the ownership
principle to personal relationships ("*My* house, *my* wife, *my* children") in
a male-dominated society.

4a. Nature as agrarianism; the virgin land as Garden of Eden. A concept into which, in the western, concept 3 tends to become curiously assimilated (ideology's function being to "naturalize" cultural assumptions):
e.g., the treatment of the family in *Drums along the Mohawk* (John Ford,
1939).

4b. Nature as the wilderness, the Indians, on whose subjugation civilization is built; hence by extension the libido, of which in many westerns
the Indians seem an extension or embodiment, as in *The Searchers* (Ford,
1956).

5. Progress, technology, the city ("New York, New York, it's a wonderful town").

6. Success and wealth—a value of which Hollywood ideology is also deeply ashamed, so that, while hundreds of films play on its allure, very few can allow themselves openly to extol it. Thus its ideological "shadow" is produced.

7. The Rosebud syndrome. Money isn't everything; money corrupts; the poor are happier. A very convenient assumption for capitalist ideology; the more oppressed you are, the happier you are, as exemplified by the singing "darkies" of *A Day at the Races* (Sam Wood, 1937).

8. America as the land where everyone is or can be happy; hence the land where all problems are solvable within the existing system (which may need a bit of reform here and there but no *radical* change). Subversive systems are assimilated wherever possible to serve the dominant ideology. Andrew Britton, in a characteristically brilliant article on Hitchcock's *Spellbound* (1945), argues that there even Freudian psychoanalysis becomes an instrument of ideological repression.[2] Above all, this assumption gives us that most striking and persistent of all classical Hollywood phenomena, the happy ending: often a mere "emergency exit" (Sirk's phrase)[3] for the spectator, a barely plausible pretense that the problems the film has raised are now resolved. *Hilda Crane* (Philip Dunne, 1950) offers a suitably blatant example among the hundreds possible.

Out of this list logically emerge two ideal figures:

9. The ideal male: the virile adventurer, the potent, untrammelled man of action.

10. The ideal female: wife and mother, perfect companion, the endlessly dependable mainstay of hearth and home.

Since these combine into an ideal couple of quite staggering incompatibility, each has his or her shadow:

11. The settled husband/father, dependable but dull.

12. The erotic woman (adventuress, gambling lady, saloon "entertainer"), fascinating but dangerous, liable to betray the hero or turn into a black panther.

The most striking fact about this list is that it presents an ideology that, far from being monolithic, is *inherently* riddled with hopeless contradictions and unresolvable tensions. The work that has been done so far on genre has tended to take the various genres as "given" and discrete, defining them in terms of motifs, iconography, conventions, and themes. What we need to ask, if genre theory is ever to be productive, is less *what* than *why*. We are so used to the genres that the peculiarity of the phenomenon itself has been too little noted. The idea I wish to put forward is that the development of the genres is rooted in the sort of ideological contradictions my list of concepts suggests. One impulse may be the attempt to deny such contradiction by eliminating one of the opposed terms, or at least by a process of simplification.

Robert Warshow's seminal essays on the gangster hero and the westerner (still fruitfully suggestive, despite the obvious objection that he took too little into account) might be adduced here. The opposition of gangster film and western is only one of many possibilities. *All* the genres can be profitably examined in terms of ideological oppositions, forming a complex interlocking pattern: small-town family comedy/sophisticated city comedy; city comedy/film noir; film noir/small-town comedy, and so on. It is probable that a genre is ideologically "pure" (i.e., safe) only in its simplest, most archetypal, most aesthetically deprived and intellectually contemptible form—such as the Hopalong Cassidy films or Andy Hardy comedies.

The Hopalong Cassidy films (in which Indians, always a potentially disruptive force in ideological as well as dramatic terms, are, in general, significantly absent), for example, seem to depend on two strategies for their perfect ideological security: the strict division of characters into good and evil, with no "grays"; and Hoppy's sexlessness (he never becomes emotionally entangled). Hence the possibility of evading all the wandering/settling tensions on which aesthetically interesting westerns are generally structured. (An intriguing alternative: the ideal American family of Roy Rogers/Dale Evans/Trigger.) *Shane* (George Stevens, 1953) is especially interesting in this connection. A deliberate attempt to create an "archetypal" western, it also represents an effort to resolve the major ideological tensions harmoniously.

One of the greatest obstacles to any fruitful theory of genre has been the tendency to treat the genres as discrete. An ideological approach might suggest why they can't be, however hard they may appear to try: at best, they represent different strategies for dealing with the same ideological tensions. For example, the small-town movie with a contemporary setting should never be divorced from its historical correlative, the western. In the classical Hollywood cinema motifs cross repeatedly from genre to genre, as can be made clear by a few examples. The home/wandering opposition that Peter Wollen rightly sees as central to Ford[4] is not central only to Ford or even to the western; it structures a remarkably large number of American films covering all genres, from *Out of the Past* (Tourneur, 1947) to *There's No Business Like Show Business* (Walter Lang, 1954). The explicit comparison of women to cats connects screwball comedy (*Bringing Up Baby,* Howard Hawks, 1938), horror film (*Cat People*), melodrama (*Rampage,* Phil Karlson, 1963), and psychological thriller (*Marnie,* Hitchcock, 1964). Another example brings us to this essay's specific topic: notice the way in which the potent male adventurer, when he enters the family circle, immediately displaces his "shadow," the settled husband/father, in both *The Searchers* and *Shadow of a Doubt*.

Before we attempt to apply these ideas to specific films, however, one more point needs to be especially emphasized: the presence of ideological tensions in a movie, though it may give it an interest beyond Hopalong Cassidy, is not in itself a reliable evaluative criterion. It seems probable that artistic value has always been dependent on the presence—somewhere, at some stage—of an individual artist, whatever the function of art in the particular society and even when (as with the Chartres cathedral) one no longer knows who the individual artists were. It is only through the medium of the individual that ideological tensions come into particular focus, hence become of aesthetic as well as sociological interest. It can perhaps be argued that works are of especial interest when the defined particularities of an auteur interact with specific ideological tensions and when the film is fed from more than one generic source.

The same basic ideological tensions operate in both *It's a Wonderful Life* and *Shadow of a Doubt*. They furnish further reminders that the home/wandering antinomy is by no means the exclusive preserve of the western. Bedford Falls and Santa Rosa can be seen as the frontier town seventy or so years on; they embody the development of the civilization whose establishment was celebrated around the same time by Ford in *My Darling Clementine* (1946). With this relationship to the western in the background (but in Capra's film made succinctly explicit), the central tension in both films can be described in terms of genre: the disturbing influx of film noir into the world of small-town domestic comedy. (It is a tension clearly present in *Clementine* as well: the opposition between the daytime and nighttime Tombstones.)

The strong contrast presented by the two films testifies to the decisive effect of the intervention of a clearly defined artistic personality in an ideological-generic structure. Both films have as a central ideological project the reaffirmation of family and small-town values that the action has called into question. In Capra's film this reaffirmation is magnificently convincing (but with full acknowledgment of the suppressions on which it depends and, consequently, of its precariousness); in Hitchcock's it is completely hollow. The very different emotional effects of the films—the satisfying catharsis and emotional fullness of Capra's, the "bitter taste" (on which so many have commented) of Hitchcock's—are very deeply rooted not only in our response to two opposed directorial personalities but in our own ideological structuring.

One of the main ideological and thematic tensions of *It's a Wonderful Life* is beautifully encapsulated in the scene in which George Bailey (James Stewart) and Mary (Donna Reed) smash windows in a derelict house as a preface to making wishes. George's wish is to get the money to leave Bedford Falls, which he sees as humdrum and constricting, and travel about the world; Mary's wish (not expressed in words, but in its subsequent fulfillment—confirming her belief that wishes don't come true if you speak them) is that she and George will marry, settle down, and raise a family in the same derelict house, a ruined shell that marriage-and-family restores to life.

This tension is developed through the extended sequence in which George is manipulated into marrying Mary. His brother's return home with a wife and a new job traps George into staying in Bedford Falls to take over the family business. With the homecoming celebrations continuing inside the house in the background, George sits disconsolately on the front porch; we hear an off-screen train whistle, to which he reacts. His mother (the indispensable Beulah Bondi) comes out and begins "suggesting" that he visit Mary; he appears to go off in her direction, physically pointed that way by his mother, then reappears and walks away past the mother—in the opposite direction.

This leads him, with perfect ideological/generic logic, to Violet (Gloria Grahame). The Violet/Mary opposition is an archetypally clear rendering of that central Hollywood female opposition that crosses all generic boundaries—as with Susan (Katharine Hepburn) and Alice (Virginia Walker) in *Bringing Up Baby,* Irene (Simone Simon) and Alice (Jane Randolph) in *Cat People,* Chihuahua (Linda Darnell) and Clementine (Cathy Downs) in *My Darling Clementine,* Debby (Gloria Grahame) and Katie (Jocelyn Brando) in *The Big Heat* (Fritz Lang, 1953). But Violet (in front of an amused audience) rejects his poetic invitation to a barefoot ramble over the hills in the moonlight; the good-time gal offers no more solution to the hero's wanderlust than the wife-mother figure.

So back to Mary, whom he brings to the window by beating a stick aggressively against the fence of the neat, enclosed front garden—a beautifully precise expression of his ambivalent state of mind: desire to attract Mary's attention warring with bitter resentment of his growing entrapment in domesticity. Mary is expecting him; his mother has phoned her, knowing that George would end up at her house. Two ideological premises combine here: the notion that the "good" mother always knows, precisely and with absolute certitude, the workings of her son's mind; and the notion that the female principle is central to the continuity of civilization, that the "weaker sex" is compensated with a sacred rightness.

Indoors, Mary shows George a cartoon she has drawn of George, in cowboy denims, lassoing the moon. The moment is rich in contradictory connotations. It explicitly evokes the western and the figure of the adventurer-hero to which George aspires. Earlier, it was for Mary that George wanted to "lasso the moon," the adventurer's exploits motivated by a desire to make happy the woman who will finally entrap him in domesticity.

From Mary's point of view, the picture is at once affectionate (acknowledging the hero's aspirations), mocking (reducing them to caricature), and possessive (reducing George to an image she creates and holds within her hands).

The most overtly presented of the film's structural oppositions is that between the two faces of capitalism, benign and malignant. On the one hand, there are the Baileys (father and son) and their building and loan company, its business practice based on a sense of human needs and a belief in human goodness; on the other, there is Potter (Lionel Barrymore), described explicitly as a spider, motivated by greed, egotism, and miserliness, with no faith in human nature. Potter belongs to a very deeply rooted tradition. He derives most obviously from Dickens's Scrooge (the film is set at Christmas)—a Scrooge disturbingly unrepentant and irredeemable—but his more distant antecedents are in the ogres of fairy tales.

The opposition gives us not only two attitudes to money and property but two father images (Bailey, Sr., and Potter), each of whom gives his name to the land (Bailey Park, in small-town Bedford Falls, and Pottersville, the town's dark alternative). Most interestingly, the two figures (representing American choices, American tendencies) find their vivid ideological extensions in Hollywood genres: the happy, sunny world of small-town comedy (Bedford Falls is seen mostly in the daytime) and the world of film noir, the dark underside of Hollywood ideology.

Pottersville—the vision of the town as it would have been if George had never existed, shown him by his guardian angel (Henry Travers)—is just as "real" as (or no more stylized than) Bedford Falls. The iconography of small-town comedy is exchanged, unmistakably, for that of film noir, with police sirens, shooting in the streets, darkness, vicious dives, alcoholism, burlesque shows, strip clubs, and the glitter and shadows of noir lighting. George's mother, embittered and malevolent, runs a seedy boarding-house; the good-time gal/wife-mother opposition, translated into noir terms, becomes an opposition of prostitute and repressed spinster-librarian. The towns emerge as equally valid images of America—validated by their generic familiarity.

Beside *Shadow of a Doubt, It's a Wonderful Life* manages a convincing and moving affirmation of the values (and value) of bourgeois family life. Yet what is revealed, when disaster releases George's suppressed tensions, is the intensity of his resentment of the family and desire to destroy it—and with it, in significant relationship, his work (his culminating action is furiously to overthrow the drawing board with his plans for more small-town houses). The film recognizes explicitly that behind every Bedford Falls lurks a Pottersville, and implicitly that within every George Bailey lurks an Ethan Edwards of *The Searchers*. Potter, tempting George, is given the devil's insights into his suppressed desires. His remark, "You

10. *It's a Wonderful Life:* The happy world of small-town comedy.

once called me a warped, frustrated old man—now you're a warped, frustrated *young* man," is amply supported by the evidence the film supplies. What is finally striking about the film's affirmation is the extreme precariousness of its basis; and Potter survives without remorse, his crime unexposed and unpunished. It may well be Capra's masterpiece, but it is more than that. Like all the greatest American films—fed by a complex generic tradition and, beyond that, by the fears and aspirations of a whole culture—it at once transcends its director and would be inconceivable without him.

Shadow of a Doubt has always been among the most popular of Hitchcock's middle-period films, with critics and public alike, but it has been perceived in very different, almost diametrically opposed ways. On its appearance it was greeted by British critics as the film marking Hitchcock's coming to terms with America; his British films were praised for their humor and "social criticism" as much as for their suspense, and the early American films, notably *Rebecca* (1940) and *Suspicion* (1941), seemed like attempts artificially to reconstruct England in Hollywood. In *Shadow of a Doubt* Hitchcock (with the aid of Thornton Wilder and Sally Benson)

11. *It's a Wonderful Life:* The disturbing influx of film noir.

at last brought to American middle-class society the shrewd, satirical, affectionate gaze previously bestowed on the British. A later generation of
French critics (notably Rohmer and Chabrol in their Hitchcock book)
praised the film for very different reasons, establishing its strict formalism (Truffaut's "un film fondé sur le chiffre 2") and seeing it as one of
the keys to a consistent Catholic interpretation of Hitchcock, a rigorous
working out of themes of original sin, the loss of innocence, the fallen
world, the exchange (or interchangeability) of guilt.[5] The French noted
the family comedy beloved of British critics, if at all, as a mildly annoying
distraction.

That both these views correspond to important elements in the film and
throw light on certain aspects of it is beyond doubt; both, however, now
appear false and partial, dependent upon the abstracting of elements from
the whole. If the film is, in a sense, completely dominated by Hitchcock
(nothing in it is unmarked by his artistic personality), a complete reading
would need to see the small-town-family elements and the Catholic elements as threads weaving through a complex fabric in which, again, ideological and generic determinants are crucial.

The kind of "synthetic" analysis I have suggested (going beyond an interest in the individual auteur) reveals *It's a Wonderful Life* as a far more potentially subversive film than has been generally recognized, but its subversive elements are, in the end, successfully contained. In *Shadow of a Doubt* the Hollywood ideology I have sketched is shattered beyond convincing recuperation. One can, however, trace through the film its attempts to impose itself and render things "safe." What is in jeopardy is above all the family—but, given the family's central ideological significance, once that is in jeopardy, everything is. The small town (still rooted in the agrarian dream, in ideals of the virgin land as a garden of innocence) and the united happy family are regarded as the real sound heart of American civilization; the ideological project is to acknowledge the existence of sickness and evil but preserve the family from their contamination.

A number of strategies can be discerned here: the attempt to insist on a separation of Uncle Charlie from Santa Rosa; his death at the end of the film as the definitive purging of evil; the production of the young detective (the healthy, wholesome, small-town male) as a marriage partner for Young Charlie so that the family may be perpetuated; above all, the attribution of Uncle Charlie's sexual pathology to a childhood accident as a means of exonerating the family of the charge of producing a monster, a possibility the American popular cinema, with the contemporary overturning of traditional values, can now envisage—e.g., *It's Alive* (Larry Cohen, 1974).

The famous opening, with its parallel introductions of Uncle Charlie and Young Charlie, insists on the city and the small town as *opposed,* sickness and evil being of the city. As with Bedford Falls/Pottersville, the film draws lavishly on the iconography of usually discrete genres. Six shots (with all movement and direction—the bridges, the panning, the editing—consistently rightward) leading up to the first interior of Uncle Charlie's room give us urban technology, wreckage both human (the down-and-outs) and material (the dumped cars by the sign "No Dumping Allowed"), children playing in the street, the number 13 on the lodging-house door. Six shots (movement and direction consistently left) leading to the first interior of Young Charlie's room give us sunny streets with no street games (Santa Rosa evidently has parks), an orderly town with a smiling, paternal policeman presiding over traffic and pedestrians.

In Catholic terms, this is the fallen world against a world of apparent prelapsarian innocence; but it is just as valid to interpret the images, as in *It's a Wonderful Life,* in terms of the two faces of American capitalism. Uncle Charlie has money (the fruits of his crimes and his aberrant sexuality) littered in disorder over table and floor; the Santa Rosa policeman has behind him the Bank of America. The detailed paralleling of uncle and niece can of course be read as comparison as much as contrast, and

12. Young Charlie (Teresa Wright), Uncle Charlie (Joseph Cotton), and Louise the waitress (Janet Shaw) in *Shadow of a Doubt*.

the opposition that of two sides of the same coin. The point is clearest in that crucial, profoundly disturbing scene where film noir erupts into Santa Rosa itself: the visit to the Til Two bar, where Young Charlie is confronted with her alter ego Louise the waitress, her former classmate. The scene equally invites Catholic and Marxist commentaries; its force arises from the revelation of the fallen world/capitalist-corruption-and-deprivation at the heart of the American small town. The close juxtaposition of genres has implications that reach throughout the whole generic structure of the classical Hollywood cinema.

The subversion of ideology within the film is everywhere traceable to Hitchcock's presence, to the skepticism and nihilism that lurk just behind the jocular facade of his public image. His Catholicism is in reality the lingering on in his work of the darker aspects of Catholic mythology: hell without heaven. The traces are clear enough. Young Charlie wants a "miracle"; she thinks of her uncle as "the one who can save us" (and her mother immediately asks, "What do you mean, *save* us?"); when she finds his telegram, in the very act of sending hers, her reaction is an ecstatic

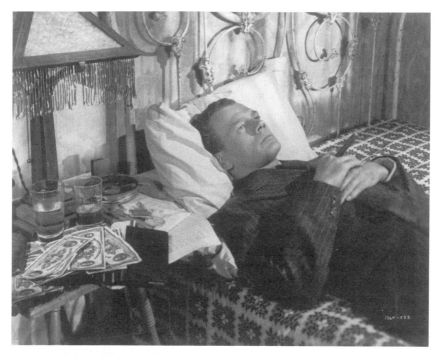

13. Uncle Charlie in repose (*Shadow of a Doubt*).

"He heard me, he heard me!" Hitchcock cuts at once to a low-angle shot of Uncle Charlie's train rushing toward Santa Rosa, underlining the effect with an ominous crashing chord on the sound track.

Uncle Charlie is one of the supreme embodiments of the key Hitchcock figure: ambiguously devil and lost soul. When he reaches Santa Rosa, the image is blackened by its smoke. From his first appearance, Charlie is associated consistently with a cigar (its phallic connotations evident from the outset, in the scene with the landlady) and repeatedly shown with a wreath of smoke curling around his head (no one else in the film smokes except Joe, the displaced father, who has a paternal pipe, usually unlit). Several incidents (the escape from the policemen at the beginning, the garage door slammed as by remote control) invest him with a quasi-supernatural power. Rather than restrict the film to a Catholic reading, it seems logical to connect these marks with others: the thread of superstition that runs through the film (the number 13; the hat on the bed; "Sing at table and you'll marry a crazy husband"; the irrational dread of the utterance, however innocent, of the forbidden words "Merry Widow") and the telepathy motif (the telegrams, the tune "jumping from head to head")—the whole Hitchcockian sense of life at the mercy of terrible, unpredictable forces that have to be kept down.

The Hitchcockian dread of repressed forces is characteristically accompanied by a sense of the emptiness of the surface world that represses them, and this crucially affects the presentation of the American small-town family in *Shadow of a Doubt*. The warmth and togetherness, the mutual responsiveness and affection that Capra so beautifully creates in the Bailey families, senior and junior, of *It's a Wonderful Life* are here almost entirely lacking—and this despite the fact, in itself of great ideological interest, that the treatment of the family in *Shadow of a Doubt* has generally been perceived (even, one guesses, by Hitchcock himself) as affectionate.

The most striking characteristic of the Spencers is the separateness of each member; the recurring point of the celebrated overlapping dialogue is that no one ever listens to what anyone else is saying. Each is locked in a separate fantasy world: Emmy in the past, Joe in crime, Anne in books that are read apparently less for pleasure than as a means of amassing knowledge with which she has little emotional contact (though she also believes that everything she reads is "true"). The parents are trapped in a petty materialism (both respond to Young Charlie's dissatisfaction with the assumption that she's talking about money) and reliance on "honest toil" as the means of using up energies. In *Shadow of a Doubt* the ideological image of the small-town happy family becomes the flimsiest facade. That so many are nonetheless deceived by it testifies only to the strength of the ideology—one of whose functions is of course to inhibit the imagining of radical alternatives.

I have argued elsewhere that the key to Hitchcock's films is less suspense than sexuality (or, alternatively, that his "suspense" always carries a sexual charge in ways sometimes obvious, sometimes esoteric); and that sexual relationships in his work are inevitably based on power, the obsession with power and dread of impotence being as central to his method as to his thematic. In *Shadow of a Doubt* it is above all sexuality that cracks apart the family facade. As far as the Hays Code permitted, a double incest theme runs through the film: Uncle Charlie and Emmy, Uncle Charlie and Young Charlie. Necessarily, this is expressed through images and motifs, never becoming verbally explicit; certain of the images depend on a suppressed verbal play for their significance.

For the reunion of brother and sister, Hitchcock gives us an image (Emmy poised left of screen, arrested in mid-movement, Charlie right, under trees and sunshine) that iconographically evokes the reunion of lovers (Charlie wants to see Emmy again as she was when she was "the prettiest girl on the block"). And Emmy's breakdown, in front of her embarrassed friends and neighbors, at the news of Charlie's imminent departure is eloquent. As for uncle and niece, they are introduced symmetrically lying on beds, Uncle Charlie fondling his phallic cigar, Young Charlie, prone, hands behind head. When Uncle Charlie gets off the train he is bent over a stick, pretending to be ill; as soon as he sees Young Charlie, he "comes erect," flourishing the stick. One of his first actions on taking over her bedroom is to pluck a rose for his buttonhole ("deflowering"). More obviously, there is the business with the ring, which, as a symbolic token of engagement, not only links Charlie sexually with her uncle, but also links her, through its previous ownership, to his succession of merry widows. The film shows sexual pathology at the heart of the American family, the necessary product of its repressions and sublimations.

As for the "accident"—that old critical stumbling block—it presents no problem at all, provided one is ready to acknowledge the validity of a psychoanalytical reading of movies. Indeed, it provides a rather beautiful example of the way in which ideology, in seeking to impose itself, succeeds merely in confirming its own subversion. The "accident" (Charlie was "riding a bicycle" for the first time, which resulted in a "collision") can be read as an elementary Freudian metaphor for the trauma of premature sexual awakening (after which Charlie was "never the same again"). The smothering sexual/possessive devotion of a doting older sister may be felt to provide a clue to the sexual motivation behind the merry-widow murders; Charlie isn't interested in money. Indeed, Emmy is connected to the merry widows by an associative chain in which important links are her own practical widowhood (her ineffectual husband is largely ignored), her ladies' club, and its leading light, Mrs. Potter, Uncle Charlie's potential next-in-line.

A fuller analysis would need to dwell on the limitations of Hitchcock's vision, nearer the nihilistic than the tragic; on his inability to conceive of repressed energies as other than evil and the surface world that represses them as other than shallow and unfulfilling. This explains why there can be no heaven corresponding to Hitchcock's hell, for every vision of heaven that is not merely negative is rooted in a concept of the liberation of the instincts, the resurrection of the body, which Hitchcock must always deny. But my final stress is less on the evaluation of a particular film or director than on the implications for a criticism of the Hollywood cinema of the notions of interaction and multiple determinacy I have been employing. Its roots in the Hollywood genres, and in the very ideological structure it so disturbingly subverts, make *Shadow of a Doubt* so much more suggestive and significant a work than Hitchcock the bourgeois entertainer could ever have guessed.

Notes

1. Robin Wood, "Old Wine, New Bottles: Structuralism or Humanism?" *Film Comment* 12, no. 6 (November–December 1976): 22–25.

2. Andrew Britton, "Hitchcock's *Spellbound:* Text and Counter-Text," *Cine-Action!* no. 3/4 (January 1986): 72–83.

3. See *Sirk on Sirk,* edited by Jon Halliday (London: Secker & Warburg/British Film Institute, 1971).

4. Peter Wollen, *Signs and Meaning in the Cinema,* 3d. ed. (Bloomington and London: Indiana University Press, 1972), pp. 94–101.

5. See Eric Rohmer and Claude Chabrol, *Hitchcock: The First Forty-Four Films,* translated by Stanley Hochman (New York: Ungar, 1979), p. 72.

7. "Cinema/Ideology/Criticism" Revisited: The Progressive Genre

BARBARA KLINGER

Since the publication of the Jean-Louis Comolli and Jean Narboni editorial "Cinema/Ideology/Criticism" in *Cahiers du Cinéma* in 1969, there has been strong theoretical and critical attention devoted to the elaboration of the particular relation between cinematic text and ideology as a central aspect of the overall post-1968 concern with the area of cultural production. The terms of this elaboration—advanced fundamentally through a Marxist/feminist perspective that employs, variably, a quartet of textual theories drawn from formalism, structuralism, semiotics, and psychoanalysis—have been as diverse as the textual objects addressed, which range from classic Hollywood cinema to the work of the experimental avant-garde. Vital to and constant within this primarily textual focus of the cinema/ideology inquiry are the twin interrogatives of what constitutes dominant cinematic practices and then what deconstitutes them. These concerns have led to a full-scale critical expedition into the Hollywood cinema as a particularly compelling site for the analysis of dominant aesthetic/cultural production, resulting in the development of a refined set of analytical procedures that designate and differentiate the ideological contours of specific textual practices within this only apparently monolithic mainstream.

Though the pursuit of a "countercinema" has defined encounters with all manner of texts, the subdivision I wish to reconsider here is that which has addressed differing textual "politics" within Hollywood cinema. Part of this work on the signification practices of dominant cinema has involved the critical identification of a series of "rebel" texts within the Hollywood empire. These texts, while firmly entrenched within the system, display certain features that are critically deemed as combative to the conventions governing the "typical" classic text. Ideological criticism, which has so entertained the variability of textual politics within mainstream production, has distinguished a category of films referred to as "progressive" or "subversive."

While this classification has influenced and contributed to developments in both auteur and genre studies, my explanatory emphasis primarily concerns film genre. It is important to note, however, that ideological genre criticism is quite substantially inflected by questions of auteur; within each specific critical argument engaged with defining the progressive coordinates of certain generic periods, auteurist considerations are frequently instrumental. Among film groups that have been of interest to ideological criticism are film noir, the woman's film, the forties and fifties melodrama, the seventies horror film, and the exploitation and B film.[1] This list is by no means exhaustive of the criticism that has addressed the notion of "progressivity," but simply suggestive of the expanse of work that has consistently taken up and elaborated the parameters of the progressive film. What follows is both a reconsideration and reevaluation of the theoretical genealogy and critical terms through which this substantial current in film studies has developed.

NEO-MARXIST AESTHETIC THEORY

The theoretical formulation that underwrites the critical constitution of the "progressive" text originates with the work of Louis Althusser. Though his essays expressly on art—"A Letter on Art in Reply to André Daspre" and "Cremonini, Painter of the Abstract"[2]—are not voluminous meditations on a Marxist theory of the artistic text, they do furnish the basis from which such a theory and its adjacent conceptualization of a critical praxis for film were constructed.

Briefly, the focus of discussion in these essays is on an elaboration of art's specific relation to ideology. For Althusser, the most emphatic aspect of art to be addressed within this inquiry is its essential, definitive epistemology. Art, here, is neither "knowledge in the strictest sense" or unadulterated ideology; rather, it provides a particularly valuable epistemological halfway house between the two. According to Althusser, "What art makes us *see,* and therefore give us in the forms of '*seeing,*' '*perceiving*' and '*feeling*' . . . is the ideology from which it is born, in which it bathes, from which it detaches itself as art, and to which it alludes."[3] Art is a special perceptual agency that performs a quasiepistemic function: it literally makes a spectacle of ideology, and in so doing, elucidates, even materially objectifies, the presence and activity of ideology. Further, in this distinction of the epistemological contours of art, certain artists' works are singled out (Balzac, Cremonini) as they exhibit an exceptionally revelatory view of the ideology in which they "bathe." This view, in Althusser's words, "presupposes a *retreat,* an *internal distanciation,* from the very ideology from which their [work] emerged." Similarly, these texts make us "perceive. . . in some sense from the *inside,* by an *internal distance,* that ideology in which they are held."[4] This commentary implies a class of texts with a slightly superior epistemology; that is, it suggests the existence of a textual practice that amplifies the "basic" epistemological dynamics of the aesthetic text, to the point where the text not only objectifies the ideological, but effects a more emphatic distance from it—a "break"—which, in turn, forces the ideological into conspicuous view.

Central to Althusser's discussion of an aesthetic epistemology is the definition of a corresponding, distinctly Marxist critical practice, the function of which is to compose a knowledge of art. This knowledge of art, like all knowledge for Althusser, "presupposes a preliminary *rupture* with the language of *ideological spontaneity*," and constructs "a body of scientific concepts to replace it."[5] The mission of criticism here is not, as in some traditions, to act in complicity with the aesthetic facade of the text, so as to bolster its consumption, but rather to realize and quantify the internal textual objectification of ideology produced by art's peculiar epistemological character.

Summarily, this theorization of the artistic text and consonant specification of a critical practice of reading promote a strong, explicitly textual focus to questions of the relation of art and ideology. The text is characterized as a site upon which the significant relations of representation and ideology are distilled, almost in bilateral configuration. The language of Althusser's aesthetic epistemology used to describe the text/ideology relation—rupture, break, internal distanciation, deformation—foster this sense of the reflexive, formal geography of the text, which, by critical extension, can be viewed as internally empowered to engineer an "autocritique" of the ideology in which it is held. The potential of this perspective on the artistic text is elaborated within film studies to produce a critical and aesthetic category of films designated generally as "progressive."

FILM THEORY/CRITICISM: THE PROGRESSIVE FORMULATION

The mobilization of Althusser's precepts into active critical service in film, via the Comolli/Narboni editorial, provides the means through which film texts were purposefully scrutinized anew expressly to ascertain their "textual politics." The overall project of the Comolli/Narboni essay, to differentiate the text's specific relation to the ideology it produces in form and content, results in a seven-category classification of film types, wherein films are appraised according to how they adhere to or depart from predominant expressions of ideology.

The categories most pertinent for discussion here, categories "a" and "e," feature films within the tradition of classical Hollywood cinema— that tradition recognized as both forming the basis for and exemplifying dominant representational concerns and practices. In this critical scheme, category "a" (the one most populated) typified a "zero degree" state of textual politics; these films act only as conduits for and perpetuators of existing ideological norms, both in content (for instance, as they salute the institutions and premises that define "the American way") and in form (accepting the conventional system of depiction in the cinema). An "e" film, on the other hand, though appearing supportive of the ideology that conditions its existence, hampers the straightforward expression of it through the production of a formally impelled rupture with the veneer of its own premises. The cinematic framework of "e" films "lets us see [the operative ideology] but also shows it up and denounces it," producing "an internal criticism. . . which cracks the film apart. . . [creating] an internal tension . . . simply not there in an ideologically innocuous film." Here Comolli and Narboni identify a textual practice, which while fully integrated within dominant cinema "ends up by partially dismantling the system from within."[6] The "e" category, then, fits the description of the more epistemologically ambitious text outlined by Althusser, which produces ideological critique.

The importance of these particular classifications to the identification of a body of texts as progressive lies in their critical provision for a differential typology of textual politics within dominant cinema, and, crucially, in the essential systemic relationship through which that difference is established. "E" films achieve their preferential "politic" status through their reflexive, deconstructive relation to what is recognized as the standard classic text. This relational distinction, proposed by Comolli and Narboni, informs subsequent and more extensive elaborations of the specific textual parameters of the progressive text and genre. This discrimination is clear in one of the bedrock propositions regulating the critical establishment of progressive textual practice: that the progressive work must exhibit textual characteristics which are strategically reactive to commonplace "classicism." In general, the strong critical investment in designating and elucidating countercinema or progressive cinema is financed through a staunch conception of classic textuality, against which progressive practice relies for its very definition.

PROFILE OF THE PROGRESSIVE GENRE

As Kaplan notes, "The 'classic text' (applicable to genre and nongenre films) describes a *dominant mode of production,* which masks its own operation . . . in terms of covering over ideological tension and contradiction . . . which [then] represents the Truth *vis-à-vis* the film's content and meaning; or in terms of giving the impression that it gives access to the 'real world.'"[7] The classic form subscribes to an ideology of representation—the achievement of the "impression of reality"—and, in so doing, unproblematically broadcasts dominant cultural ideas. A distinguishing mark of the progressive film is its operational refusal of the overall ambition of the classic form toward concealment and transparency, the chief attributes of realism. This formal dynamic embodies a challenge to the conventional means of representing reality in the cinema in such a way as to expose those means as practice, as a product of ideology, and not as a manifest replication of reality. The progressive generic text is, in this sense, antirealist, as it rattles the perfect illusionism transmitted by a major sector of classic cinema. Assessments of progressive texts/genres generally establish the features of departure from convention in this way and subsequently endow those features with the edifying effects of "rupture."

Pam Cook's essay on exploitation and B films, for example, presents the logic of the progressive genre argument based on the reaction against certain tactics of classic Hollywood cinema. She recommends a critical reappraisal of these previously considered "low-life" films, because of the way in which they "lay bare" the underlying suppositions and operative principles of Hollywood films with higher production values. Exploitation films almost contradictorily (given their capitalistic fervor) crystallize, exaggerate, and expose the "ground rules" from which mainstream films are built. Cook defends exploitation and B films in this way as less objectionable in their representation of women than sophisticated Hollywood or European art films; images of women in the former are obviously stereotyped, display themselves as such, and so resist the sort of naturalization process Cook believes classic films of "good taste" excel in. In the "better-quality" film, the myth of the star persona (Bette Davis, Katharine Hepburn, etc.) and/or the density of character traits, which seem to construct fuller, more real characters, do nothing more than camouflage the normative function and actual stereotyped status of the female character in question. Here, then, a film like *Student Nurses* (Stephanie Rothman, 1970) fares better than *An Unmarried Woman* (Paul Mazursky, 1978).

Though the critics engaged in distinguishing progressive genres are not at all homogeneous in methodology (all do not draw explicitly from Althusser; some arguments are more heavily inflected by auteurism than others), the terms in which they identify the requisite characteristics of progressive genres are strikingly similar. The consistent conceptual basis for this constitution involves an exclamation of the genre's reactive difference from what is "classic" in classic Hollywood fare, as well as the establishment of the generic period's insurgent inventional qualities within the diachronic structures that govern its entire system.

Robin Wood, for instance, in his writings on horror films, sets the genre off from Hollywood films in general, because horror films seem to have a special pipeline to the unconscious. They possess the potential, that is, to exhibit as explicit content what most other films soundly repress (the

14. *Psycho:* The locus of horror is specifically familial.

repressiveness of the family vs. the insistent celebration or sentimental-
ization of family solidarity). This characteristic, according to Wood, gives
the horror film a revelatory rather than a complacent relation to ideology.
In addition, because horror films have a marginal and disreputable status
within Hollywood production, they are "capable of being more radical
and subversive in their social criticism, since works of conscious social
criticism . . . must always concern themselves with the possibility of re-
forming aspects of a social system whose basic rightness must not be challenged." [8] Horror films are not obliged in this way; their relentless critique
can remain, ultimately, unredemptive. Aside from establishing the "anti-
classicism" of the horror film, there is also in Wood's argument an internal set of distinctions produced from a consideration of the genre's con-
ventional/historic trajectory that results in a choice of a specific period
therein—the horror of the seventies. *Psycho* (Alfred Hitchcock, 1960) is
the film that transforms the genre's formula and instigates the progres-
sive/subversive character of horror films of the seventies like *The Texas
Chainsaw Massacre* (Tobe Hooper, 1974), *The Hills Have Eyes* (Wes
Craven, 1977), and *Night of the Living Dead* (George Romero, 1968).

The formula for the genre, "normality threatened by the monster," which represents the conventional core of narrative/thematic oppositions, is in horror films preceding *Psycho* usually dramatized less problematically: that is, the monster is always foreign, exotic, radically other than the family it threatens, as in the thirties with *Dracula* (Tod Browning, 1931) or *King Kong* (Merian C. Cooper and Ernest B. Schoedsack, 1933) or in the fifties with its proliferation of giant, mutant insects. The strategic importance of *Psycho* within this trajectory is in revealing the locus of horror as specifically familial, as being produced from within the family institution itself; this is a "truth" Wood finds always lurking but repressed in earlier films.

Wood's work on horror is representative of the fundamental operative tenets implicitly required to establish generic "progressivity." Difference from the environment of conventions within which these films exist, then, is a paramount feature of their progressive status, and the rationale by which they are accorded a radical valence. The diverse critical positions that address film noir, the woman's film, the sophisticated family melodrama of the forties and fifties, the horror film of the seventies, and the exploitation and B film are united in particular by an emphasis on the identity of these film groups as alternative or "countercinemas" within the province of dominant cinematic practice. These generic propositions are not forged exclusively on the basis of genre considerations alone, however, but are usually substantially articulated through specific auteurs and films—evidence the preference of Sirk and Minnelli melodramas over those of Curtiz or Mankiewicz, Wes Craven's horror films over David Cronenberg's, and the emphasis on the woman's films of Dorothy Arzner and Stephanie Rothman. But even given the myriad areas of emphasis within ideological-generic criticism, the ideological "aesthetics" employed in each argument are implicitly dictated through the presence or nonpresence of certain textual attributes necessary to the architecture of the progressive category. What follows is a selective, synthetic exposition of the characteristics that describe the progressive class of films. These traits do not by any means exhaust each individual critical argument but rather display in schematic form the consistent means through which the "progressive" is critically constructed.

A "Pessimistic World View"

Instead of the optimism that characterizes the typical celebratory or complacent view of the American way of life in the classic text, such as *The Bells of St. Mary's* (Leo McCarey, 1945), the overall atmosphere of these films is bleak, cynical, apocalyptic, and/or highly ironic—as in *Kiss Me Deadly* (Robert Aldrich, 1955), *It's Alive* (Larry Cohen, 1974), *All That*

Heaven Allows (Douglas Sirk, 1956)—in such a way as to disturb or disable an unproblematic transmission or affirmative ideology. Thus Sylvia Harvey writes of film noir that it "captures and magnifies the rumbles that shift the hidden foundations of a society and . . . begins the displacement of its characteristic and dominant system of values and beliefs"; Robin Wood writes of seventies horror that it gives "the sense of civilization condemning itself . . . a negativity . . . not recuperable into the dominant ideology, but constituting the recognition of that ideology's disintegration, its untenability"; and Thomas Elsaesser comments on the way in which fifties melodramas portray the "demise of the affirmative culture." [9]

Themes

Associated with this world view, the themes of the progressive film dramatize the demolition of values positively propounded in dominant cinema's characterization of the role and nature of social institutions—such beliefs as the inviolability and/or ultimate benevolence of the law, and the family as an institution of social and sexual "salvation" for the individual members of a couple, especially women. The law and the family are two institutions that come consistently under the remonstrative gun in these films, mainly through an hysterical exaggeration of and attack on their repressive and deforming principles, as in *Shadow of a Doubt* (Hitchcock, 1943), *Mildred Pierce* (Michael Curtiz, 1945), *Home from the Hill* (Vincente Minnelli, 1960), *The Texas Chainsaw Massacre*, and *Jackson County Jail* (Michael Miller, 1976). In film noir, the law is depicted as corrupt and/or ineffectual, and the family, as Harvey indicates, is absent, depicted in either a too-sunny glow of banality or as sterile and monstrous. In the melodrama, the psychic destructiveness of social institutions, often centering on the heterosexual couple, results in a rampant representation of ambition and of romantic love, disquieted through expressions of nymphomania, impotency, suicidal tendencies, obsessions with paternity, and the like (Sirk's 1957 film *Written on the Wind* is an especially rich example of these psychodynamics). There is, in short, no longer any restful identity to be found in the family in these films; the center of hope in most narratives, the romantic couple, is shown as either cloyingly insipid or deranged, two spectral expressions of the same impulse to denaturalize and explode the myth of the happy, unproblematic founding unit of the family.

Narrative Form

It is in the narrative and stylistic elements of progressive films that their dual critique of classic form/classic ideology is substantially generated. There are several structural components that are essential to this critique.

First, the overall narrative structure is refined toward an exposure— rather than a suppression, as in the classic text—of ideological contra- dictions and tensions. The progressive structure can work, for instance, to conflate oppositions within the dramatic conflict, which usually act to segregate good (that which upholds the existing order) from evil (that which threatens it). So structural correspondences may be drawn between hero and villain and the respective systems they represent. This char- acteristic is very important to Robin Wood's distinction between Cap- ra's *It's a Wonderful Life* (1946) and Hitchcock's *Shadow of a Doubt*,[10] and to his discussion of seventies horror films like *The Hills Have Eyes*. The concept of structurally impelled contradiction figures prominently in Elsaesser's discussion of cinematic counterpoint in melodrama and in Gledhill's analysis of point-of-view structures in film noir. The parallels wrought by the structural complexity of these films create ambiguity that prevents both easy identification and separation of systems of "good" and "evil."

Most important, the narrative form of the ideologically complex film departs from perceived demands of the classical Hollywood form. The principles of this latter type of construction require a general effect of leg- ibility and transparency, qualities obtained through a well-defined chain of cause and effect ending in satisfying closure. Conventional rules of con- struction promote the invisibility of the mechanisms at work and the ex- pulsion of any feature that would distract from the hegemony of the nar- rative line. The progressive film genre conversely departs from the letter of the classical system by either paring it down to its barest essentials (as does the exploitation film) so that cause and effect exist, but merely as the most minimal acknowledgment of that system of construction more than as a systematic illumination of the narrative flow; or by maximizing and exaggerating its principles (as in the structure of reversal in melodrama or the circuitous jungle of cause and effect in film noir), so that the logic of the system is overdetermined in such a way as to stretch its credibility and legibility. Through these distinct mutations of classic narrative rules, rep- resented in such films as *Terminal Island* (Rothman, 1973), *Imitation of Life* (Sirk, 1959), or *The Locket* (John Brahm, 1946), the system is both reflexively exposed and countered.

The issue of closure here is also crucial. The progressive film must es- cape the compromising forces inherent in the conventional procedure of closure. Whereas closure usually signals the ultimate containment of mat- ters brought out in the narrative—the network of cause and effect is re- solved, and the narrative returned to a final state of equilibrium—pro- gressive films end in such a way as to "refuse" closure. The "progressive" critics claim that such an ending cannot contain the excess of meaning produced in the course of the film, cannot solve all the conflicts. Of film noir narratives Harvey writes that "narrative resolutions cannot recuperate their subversive significance." [11] Wood similarly posits that, in contradistinction to "works of conscious social criticism," the finale of the seventies horror film remains ultimately unredemptive. The violence and destructiveness centered upon the social institutions are not adequately resolved merely through the conventional appearance of the device of closure. The circumvention of this process is fostered through the use of certain textual strategies. For example, in the melodrama with the happy ending (especially when that most stalwart of Hollywood conventions is used by Douglas Sirk), there is a veneer of optimism present that is not only unconvincing, but countered by a system of meaning produced stylistically, which imbues the conclusion with unmistakable irony, as in *Written on the Wind* or *Magnificent Obsession* (Sirk, 1954).[12] A combination of "excessive" narrative problems encountered during the film and the manner in which elements of the mise-en-scène undercut the affirmative ending conspire to disturb the harmonizing tendencies of closure. The strong sense of irony or desolation that frequently characterizes these generic endings questions the achievement of "containing" closure and imparts a rather hollow victory to this convention. The terms "excess" and "irony" are central then to the issue of closure, as they wrench the intentions of conventional form to unilaterally resolve contradiction.

Visual Style

These films are basically characterized by stylistic self-consciousness and formal excess, which are seen in varying degrees of specificity as supporting or implementing a vital part of their subversive commentary. This is in contrast to films that do not actively use their visual register to produce meaning—what Elsaesser calls "liberal films of sophistication," such as those of Fred Zinnemann, which "do nothing in terms of visual elaboration to compensate for their verbal explicitness." [13] In the progressive film, there is a foregrounding of visual style, which is manifested so forcefully as to contend with the dominance of the narrative line: in exploitation and B films, the visual register calls attention to itself through its sheer bargain-basement look; in film noir and horror, it is the use of expressionistic chiaroscuro and camera angles; and in melodrama, there is a similar "baroque" foregrounding of the formal aspects of mise-en-scène and camera—all of which are seen as intensifying the text's internal structure of distanciation.

Character

Rather than the humane, dimensional characters who populate films of "good taste," the excessive sexual stereotyping of genre films is critically

15. *Home from the Hill:* Robert Mitchum's den.

preferred, and, again, endowed with a revelatory salience; the stereotype is considered to foreground rather than camouflage the representational basis through which codes of "masculinity" and "femininity" are constructed in the cinema (see Robert Mitchum's den in *Home from the Hill*). Especially evident in the dynamics of gender representation is an intense focus on both the threat and enigma of female sexuality, in all of its psychoanalytic complexity, as in *Psycho, Written on the Wind, Gun Crazy* (Joseph H. Lewis, 1949), and *Caged Heat* (Jonathan Demme, 1974).

THE VALUATION OF "ANTICLASSICAL" DIFFERENCE

The identification of the progressive genre film depends heavily on the critical leverage imparted to the intrinsic inventional characteristics described above, which serve to distinguish these films from the dominant classic cinema and, often, from within their own generic categories as well. So film noir is "recognizably different from other films"; it "stands out as a phase in the development of the gangster/thriller [because of] . . . certain highly foregrounded inflections of plot, character, and visual style which dominated at the expense of narrative coherence and the comprehensible solution of the crime, the usual goal of the thriller."[14] The major

16. *Gun Crazy:* The threat and enigma of female sexuality.

axis upon which the progressive argument revolves is this valuation of inventional signifiers, wherein "difference" is conferred with deconstructive capabilities and a subversive effectivity. In addition, the assessment of "textual politics" based on systemic/textual attributes is not consistently considered solely as the product of critical computations derived from a certain reading position, but tends to introject the progressive features as intrinsic, effectual properties of the texts themselves; hence, texts can be labeled "reactionary" or "progressive" according to their internal subscription to or rejection of the classic paradigm and its imputed ideology. The ideological effects of a text come to be identified and ratified through the espoused critical reading.

That the cinema/ideology inquiry has become strongly situated within the province of textual reading is indicated especially in the logic and tenets of the progressive-text argument, wherein specific textual features embody that relation. This emphasis is true even in those genre studies that do attend to the external social/ideological environments that house the production of a given cycle of films. In the descriptions of the historical conditions circumscribing film noir or melodrama, the brunt of the relational analysis tends to spotlight the activity of the textual features as they respond to these conditions. This can assume a one-to-one correlation between social formation and representation, where, for instance, the economic and psychic preoccupations of postwar or corporate capitalist America are seen as both crystallized in and "disturbed" by the mise-en-scène of film noir or melodrama.

While the critical readings of Hollywood films developed from Marxist and feminist film theory have produced invaluable critical perspectives and tools with which to differentiate textual articulations of ideology—an absolutely necessary advance, historically, to ward off competing and reductive theories of Hollywood cinema forwarded by "monolithmongers" (such as the writers of *Cinéthique* circa 1969), who asserted the basic monolithic ideology of all Hollywood films—there is a strong impulse to overestimate the effectiveness of textual signifiers in determining the text/ideology relation. The central issue here, then, is not a dispute with criticism tuned toward the definition of textual variation as significant in producing a cultural symptomatology, but simply with the prescription of a political value to those differences within a system of representation that is so absolutely based on a univocal, textual-centric consideration of the cinema/ideology relation. In the transit from Althusser's explication of an aesthetic epistemology to the parallel formulation in film studies, there is a marked tendency toward a sort of "textual isolationism," an intrinsic formalization of the cinema/ideology inquiry. In progressive text and genre criticism, this results in an overvaluation and overestimation of inventive, "reactive," textual elements—a phenomenon that bears further and alternative commentary.

GENRE THEORY: "DIFFERENCE" IN CONTEXT

The designation of text and genres as "progressive," which is dependent on a radical valorization of inventional qualities, provokes at least two theoretical problems, which arise directly from other systemic theories as they account for the phenomenon of difference. The valuation of invention in progressive-text criticism enables a disturbance of the system to be felt sheerly through the intervention of invention without sufficient deliberation of how the elements of difference figure within the overall dynamics of the system of representational history or within the system of narrative itself. Indeed, classical narrative is often considered almost nothing more than a backdrop against which the inventions and departures of the progressive text move and have effect. The excesses that mark these genre films are theorized as they distinguish their systemic exceptionalness, not as they may characterize the very mainstays of their mother systems. The overvaluation of invention in these arguments, then, underplays any sense of systemic context for these works that might qualify the progressive assertion. Specifically, when examining the coordinates of the progressive/subversive genre, it seems quite necessary to consider the attributes of the diachronic systems they, as microsystems, inhabit. This emphasis poses both the question of generic/systemic evolution and of genre's relation to classical narrative.

In defining the place of genre within its systemic history, theories emanating from Russian formalist and semiotic accounts of literary evolution are particularly germane. Semiotician Maria Corti, aided and abetted by formalist theories of literary evolution, addresses herself specifically to the question of innovation within the generic system. She writes: "The process of transformation inside a literary genre . . . has regulative power. In every hypersign of strong individuality the program of the literary genre matures and is modified as it becomes a constitutive law of the work itself. . . . From the moment in which such a process takes place, the transformation which was an individual event, becomes another link in the chain that is the path of the literary genre." [15] This view of the literary system parallels the normative evaluation of violation within literary evolution forwarded by such formalists as Jury Tynyanov and Roman Jakobson. The terms "deviation," "deformation," and "defamiliarization," which are fueled with subversive implications in some ideological criticism, are used in formalism to define the normative dynamics of literary evolution; [16] innovations in the system do not entail sudden and complete renovations, but are mutations that genetically engineer the modifications necessary to the maintenance and perseverance of the system. The chiaroscuro lighting schemes in film noir, for instance, which are critically observed as cuing the disequilibrium and subversive disturbances to the norm, have ancestral ties to German expressionist lighting tactics and, as well, generically extend lighting codes that characteristically signified criminal environments in crime films of the thirties. In short, no film genre is an island. The individual work itself intrinsically reflects and modifies the diachronic characteristics of the system; as Roman Jakobson remarked, "This simultaneous presentation of tradition and breaking away from tradition . . . form the essence of every new work of art." [17] Here, the notion of difference, even a staunchly innovative one, seems firmly entrenched within the vicissitudes of the system.

The relation of genre to narrative system results in a parallel minimization of the autonomy of difference. The explicit relation of genre to the literary system, theorized by Corti, defines genre as a type of literary process reproducing "like a microcosm those functional variations that generate the very movement of literature." [18] Similarly, rather than privileging overtly inventional genres as "escapees" from the regulations of the classical narrative system, one can argue that they instead be regarded as instances of the system's requisite operation. The "rupture thesis" as it has been developed in the branch of ideological criticism considered here relies on a very restricted formulation of classical narrative, which enables a deviation from the identified principles to be readily gauged as challenging the entire foundation of the system.

In theories of classical Hollywood narrative the work of Stephen Heath, among others, has stressed a less petrified formula for the classic text via a consideration of its principles of structuration and process.[19] Stephen Neale's monograph on genre redefines genre through a Heathian perspective on the operations of the classic narrative. In his view, genre is an instance of the classical Hollywood system par excellence: genres are "modes of this narrative system, regulated orders of its potentiality."[20] This theory of classical narrative relieves the rigidity of definition drawn by the term "classic text" and offers instead the notion of a classical textual system, which is produced from a volatile combination of disequilibrium (excess, difference) and equilibrium (containment, repetition). Neale, like Corti, recognizes disequilibrium/difference not as a partisan component of the subversive text, but as an essential functioning element of the overall system—here, the classic textual system. Genres play an essential role in demonstrating and supporting the principles of this system, which "allow for (regulated) forms of excess, and (regulated) forms of display of its process: part of the very function of genres is precisely to display a variety of possibilities of the semiotic processes of mainstream narrative cinema while containing them simultaneously as genre. Hence the musical with its systematic freedom of space . . . , its shifting balance of narrative and spectacle . . . ; or the film noir, with its display of the possibilities of chiaroscuro lighting, frequently unmotivated, diegetically impossible. . . ."[21] Genre, then, is an exigent permutation of this system which thrives on a play of variation and regulation. Genres provide what Neale calls "regularized variety" and so are directly related to the textual economy of the system in that they "systematize its regime of difference and repetition," providing an "economy of variation, rather than rupture. . . ."[22]

What these contextual perspectives provide is a less inflammatory reading of the impact of moments of textual difference, by projecting the dynamics of difference/innovation as system-descriptive rather than system-subversive. The question of the nature and processes of both systemic-historic evolution and classical narrativity does not efface the cogent results of textually oriented ideological analyses, but qualifies contentions about the ideological effectivity of texts that are presumed "rupturous." In the case of progressive-text criticism, "textual isolationism" invites an assessment of textual politics based on a rather rigid sense of both what "makes" and "breaks" the system. This streamlining critical position seems especially difficult to maintain, logically, in the face of the overall phenomenon of generic textuality—which is so explicitly heterogeneous due to the "pluralizing" forces of both diachronic and synchronic factors that impinge upon the internal contours and reception/consumption of the genre film. The critical assumptions that measure the subversiveness of a genre, based on its anticlassical formal attributes, selectively overstate the radical valency of inventional signifiers and underestimate the means through which supervising systems negotiate a normative function for even the most excessive, foregrounded, deformative textual tendencies.

Notes

1. Among such pieces involving mainstream productions are Christine Gledhill, "*Klute:* A Contemporary Film Noir and Feminist Criticism," and Sylvia Harvey, "Woman's Place: The Absent Family of Film Noir," in *Women in Film Noir,* edited by E. Ann Kaplan (London: British Film Institute, 1978), pp. 6–21 and 22–33, respectively; Claire Johnston, "Women's Cinema as Counter Cinema," in *Sexual Stratagems,* edited by Patricia Erens (New York: Horizon Press, 1979), pp. 133–143; Claire Johnston, ed., *The Work of Dorothy Arzner: Towards a Feminist Cinema* (London: British Film Institute, 1975); Thomas Elsaesser, "Tales of Sound and Fury: Observations on the Family Melodrama," *Monogram,* no. 4 (1973): 2–15 (reprinted in this volume); Robin Wood, "Ideology, Genre, Auteur," *Film Comment* 13, no. 1 (January–February 1977): 46–51 (reprinted in this volume); *The American Nightmare,* edited by Robin Wood and Richard Lippe (Toronto: Festival of Festivals, 1979); and Pam Cook, "Exploitation Films and Feminism," *Screen* 17, no. 2 (1976): 122–127.

2. Louis Althusser, *Lenin and Philosophy and Other Essays,* translated by Ben Brewster (New York: Monthly Review Press, 1971), pp. 221–227, 228–242.

3. Ibid., p. 222.

4. Ibid., p. 241.

5. Ibid.

6. Jean-Louis Comolli and Jean Narboni, "Cinema/Ideology/Criticism," *Screen* 12, no. 1 (Spring 1971): 27–36.

7. Kaplan, "Introduction," in *Women in Film Noir,* p. 2.

8. Robin Wood, "Introduction," in *The American Nightmare,* p. 13.

9. Harvey, "Woman's Place," in *Women in Film Noir,* p. 22; Wood, *The American Nightmare,* p. 22; Elsaesser, "Tales of Sound and Fury," p. 15.

10. See Wood, "Ideology, Genre, Auteur."

11. Harvey, "Woman's Place," p. 33.

12. Elsaesser, "Tales of Sound and Fury," p. 6.

13. Ibid., p. 8.

14. *Women in Film Noir,* pp. 2, 13–14.

15. Maria Corti, *An Introduction to Literary Semiotics,* translated by Margherita Bogat and Allen Mandelbaum (Bloomington: Indiana University Press, 1978), p. 16.

16. A more extensive discussion of this point can be found in Tony Bennett, *Formalism and Marxism* (London: Methuen, 1979).

17. Roman Jacobson, "The Dominant," in *Readings in Russian Poetics*, edited by L. Matejka and K. Pomorska (Cambridge: MIT Press, 1971), pp. 76–77.

18. Corti, *Literary Semiotics*, p. 134.

19. Stephen Heath, "Film and System," *Screen* 16, no. 1 (Spring 1975): 7–77, and no. 2 (Summer 1975): 91–113.

20. Stephen Neale, *Genre* (London: British Film Institute, 1980), p. 20.

21. Ibid., p. 31.

22. Ibid.

8. The Structural Influence: New Directions in Film Genre Study

THOMAS SCHATZ

There has been in recent years a rather dramatic upsurge of scholarly interest in the Hollywood film—particularly the genre film—as a "product" of a conventionalized production system. One might suggest a number of reasons for this interest: the overwhelming auteurism of the 1960s, the influence of such critical methodologies as structuralism and semiotics, and also our natural inclination to perform an autopsy on the studio system now that its death has been verified by the New Hollywood. Aside from the issue of its motivation, however, this broadened perspective would seem to indicate an increased consideration in film study for the Hollywood movie as an industrial and cultural document as well as an autonomous aesthetic artifact.

Perhaps the most evident manifestation of this concern for the conventionalized nature of American movies and their production is in the burgeoning field of popular culture, which itself is founded on something of a structuralist concept in its basic assumption that members of a mass-mediated society develop and participate in complex systems of unexamined beliefs. This culturally responsive perspective already has been evident in structuralist film theory—whether semiological or psychoanalytic—which seeks to delineate the various signification systems that inform virtually all Hollywood films. More recently, this perspective has influenced film history and criticism as well, and further promises to delimit or at least clarify the generally artificial boundaries that traditionally have distinguished the study of film history, theory, and criticism. Such historical studies as Robert Sklar's *Movie-Made America* (1976) and Michael Wood's *America in the Movies* (1976) as well as genre studies like Stuart Kaminsky's *American Film Genres* (1974), Will Wright's *Sixguns and Society* (1975), and Stanley Solomon's *Beyond Formula* (1976) all rely for their conceptual thrust upon some degree of sensitivity to the Hollywood film's industrial and cultural context.

Both Sklar's and Wood's studies represent efforts to treat the complex relationship between the Hollywood cinema and American culture (or what a decade ago might have been termed American ideology) by examining the virtual "world" that the studios projected onto neighborhood movie screens throughout this century. Sklar, whose book is subtitled *A Cultural History of the Movies,* assumes a rather traditional historical approach, treating chronologically the patterns of American thought as reflected in its national cinema, whereas Wood is much more eclectic in his effort to trace the "fragments of myth" incorporated in the Hollywood films of the 1940s and 1950s.

Sklar's study marks a considerable advance over Arthur Knight's and Gerald Mast's historical surveys, although Sklar ultimately offers only tentative suggestions as to precisely how America has been "moviemade." It is Wood's study, despite its conversational tone and general disdain for scholarly discipline, that is of special interest here. His conception of American movie production as a mythmaking process in which both the Hollywood studios and the mass audience reciprocally participate is an idea that promises to redefine the study of Hollywood film genres. In his effort to examine the "classic" Hollywood era (which Wood defines, somewhat arbitrarily, as spanning the late thirties to the early sixties), he in fact does develop an extended generic analysis, identifying various cinematic forms and conventions in terms of the myths—or "clusters of worries"—that characterize them. So even though Wood views the Hollywood cinema from a personalized and often somewhat self-indulgent perspective, it would seem that there are certain methodological and conceptual aspects of his work that are directly applicable to recent developments in film genre study.

Regarding genre study, the most significant implication of Wood's cultural history is that we can begin finally to confront film genres as something other than individual, isolated narrative formulae. In each of the genre studies cited above, for example, there is an effort—even if only a marginal one—to treat the notion of genre per se, to address the "genreness" of repetitive cinematic forms and the reasons why only certain forms have been refined into genres. But while both Kaminsky and Solomon examine several genres, ranging from screwball comedy to science fiction, only in their suggestive but ultimately underdeveloped introductions do they consider what these varied forms might have in common beyond their being termed film genres. After prefatory comments regarding cultural and narrative patterns, both analysts proceed to deal with each genre as a distinct and unique conventionalized system, as a bundle of formalized elements that individual filmmakers animate in the course of production. Consequently, these studies recall both Jim Kitses's introduction to *Horizons West* and Colin McArthur's opening chapters to *Underworld USA,* which presented litanies of generic conventions manipulated by cinematic auteurs whose films somehow "transcended" the genres in which they worked. Despite their initial allusions to the role of genre films in contemporary culture, each of these analysts displays an overt traditionalist bias in emphasizing the distinctive aesthetic value as opposed to the shared ritualistic value of Hollywood genre films.

It is somewhat ironic that Will Wright's *Sixguns and Society,* a perceptive but limited structural study of the western, finally comes closest to tapping that form's broad appeal as cultural ritual and hence its relationship to other generic forms. His synthesis of the seminal ideas of Claude Lévi-Strauss, Vladimir Propp, and Kenneth Burke in their respective studies of mythic, narrative, and symbolic form proves to be both enlightening and unwieldy when applied to the western genre. But more important, it does indicate the sort of conceptual perspective from which we might consider the fundamental popular appeal and cultural value of seemingly disparate cinematic forms. As such, Wright's work is something of a watershed in the general study of Hollywood film genres, even though he deals only with the western genre. One comes away from Wright's rather tedious analysis of scores of westerns wishing he had broadened his inquiry to consider other generic forms as well, a project that seems most appropriate to his methodological approach.

As Wright's work indicates, recent developments not only in cultural studies but also in such varied fields as structural anthropology, mythology, and linguistics suggest the vital importance of both cultural and formal conventions in every commercial cinematic product. The importance of these conventions is most pronounced, of course, in genre films, in those westerns and musicals and gangster films in which a tacit "contract" has been established through the reciprocal studio-audience relationship. From the audience's viewpoint, this contract represents a distinct cluster of narrative, thematic, and iconographic patterns that have been refined through exposure and familiarity into systems of reasonably well-defined expectations. I would suggest that it is this high degree of audience familiarity with the Hollywood generic product, and thus the audience's active but indirect participation in that product's creation, that provides the basis for whatever claims might be made for the genre film as a form of cultural ritual and for its status as contemporary myth.

I accept the fact, somewhat grudgingly, that the elitist biases implicit in most traditional film study have done a great deal to promote both popular and scholarly interest in the Hollywood cinema, but not until we examine the genre film in its ritualistic capacity will we fully appreciate its cultural and aesthetic value. We might recall in this context an observation by André Bazin, whose cultural sensibilities generally have been underrated, that "the cinema's existence precedes its essence." [1] Neither Bazin nor I would wish to minimize the commercial cinema's status as a contemporary art form. There clearly is a need, however, for those very attributes of the commercial cinema which have been considered its short-comings—its popularity with a mass audience, its obvious marketability, its system of production—to be reconsidered in a broader cultural perspective. This perspective should encourage new approaches to the study of American film, redirecting at least a portion of our critical and theoretical energies away from the traditionalist aesthetics that have inhibited certain areas of film study.

As I indicated earlier, a number of genre analysts have noted its ritualistic and socially functional character, although few have pursued it beyond the level of casual observation. In his brief but illuminating essay on film genre, Thomas Sobchack describes this process in classical terms, stating that "the cathartic potentials of the genre film can be seen in the way in which the tensions of cultural and social paradoxes inherent in human experience can be resolved."[2] John G. Cawelti assumes a more direct approach in his analysis of the western entitled *The Six-Gun Mystique.* Cawelti observes that an important dimension of the western "is social and cultural ritual,"[3] and he later defines ritual as "a means of affirming certain basic cultural values, resolving tension and establishing a sense of continuity between present and past."[4]

This view of the genre film as a contemporary folktale leads us even further into an area of investigation that genre analysts have consistently recognized as important and yet have never profitably developed—the relationship of the genre film to myth. In his introduction to *American Film Genres,* Kaminsky offers an insight that he regrettably does not pursue, stating that "on one level one can argue that the genre films, television, and literature have to a great extent replaced more formal versions of mythic response to existence such as religion and folk tale."[5] John Fell follows this line of reasoning when he suggests that "the conjunction of the terms 'popular culture' and 'myth' poses a central issue of genre study."[6] Fell pursues this central issue for only a single paragraph, concluding that the genre film incorporates a "corrupted form" of myth, a notion clearly borrowed from Northrop Frye.

More detailed and influential genre studies, especially those of Cawelti and Kitses, have also demonstrated a recognition of the importance of ritual and myth in the popular arts generally, and particularly in the Hollywood genre film. But due once again to an admitted allegiance to the position of literary genre analyst Northrop Frye, they both assume an aesthetically oriented definition of myth. Consequently, Kitses concludes that the idea of myth, "ever in the air when the [western] form is discussed, clouds the issue completely."[7] Cawelti's position is similar, as he opts for the term "formula" rather than "genre" specifically to avoid the issue of myth. "For Frye myths are universal patterns of action," observes Cawelti, and he argues that as such they cannot exist within a medium that is essentially culturally specific in terms of both imagery and ideology.[8]

These arguments are derived from a definition of myth which, for these analysts as well as for Frye, is dependent upon a classical conception of myth as a formal vehicle for sacred or pantheistic narrative content. Kitses's stance, for example, is indicative of that assumed by the majority of genre theorists when confronted with the issue of myth and ritual. According to Kitses, "In strict classical terms of definition myth has to do with the activity of the gods and as such the western has no myth."[9] It is interesting that Kitses's analysis of the structure of the western brings him quite close to some recently developed ideas about mythic structure, but his allegiance to Frye's classical position prevents him from making that connection. On the one hand, he cites the presence of a functional or dualistic—in his words a "dialectical"—structure of the western, but when confronted with the concept of myth in the generic sense, he defines it in terms of narrative content rather than structure or function.

As numerous mythologists and also cultural and structural anthropologists have recently observed, however, a ritualized form, whether religious or secular, does not *have* a myth; it *is* a myth—or rather it serves a mythic function. Myth is not defined by the repetition of some classical content or universal narrative; it is defined according to its function as a unique conceptual system that embodies elements specific to the culture which realizes it. Bronislav Malinowski, one of the fathers of modern anthropology, observes that myth fulfills "an indispensable function; it expresses, enhances, and codifies belief; it safeguards and enforces morality; it vouches for the efficiency and contains practical rules for the guidance of man."[10]

In describing Ernst Cassirer's reflections on myth, anthropologist David Bidney states that "according to Cassirer, mythical thinking is a unitary form of consciousness with its specific and characteristic features. There is no unity of *object* in myth but only a unity of function expressed in a unique mode of experience."[11] In *The Myth of the State,* Cassirer contends that the function of myth is not that of explanation but is, instead, practical and social, to promote a feeling of unity and harmony between the members of a society and also with the whole of nature or life.[12]

This view of myth recalls both Sobchack's earlier premises that genre films resolve the "tensions of cultural and social paradoxes" and also Cawelti's view of the western film as "cultural and social ritual." As a ritualization of collective ideals, the genre film necessarily treats the relationship between the individual and the community, thereby considering the value of that community within the natural world of which the individual is sensually and emotionally a part. Sobchack finds these conflicts— "between the individual and the group, between self-realization and communal conformity"—to be the seminal characteristics of the genre film. He also contends that because of the specific nature of the ritualized form, "the resolution of the tension between the two poles will always be in favor of the community."[13]

This conception of the genre film as a unique functional structure is closely akin to the work of Claude Lévi-Strauss in his structural analyses of myth. Lévi-Strauss defines mythical thought as "a whole system of references which operates by means of a pair of cultural contrasts: between the general and the particular on the one hand and nature and culture on the other."[14] Lévi-Strauss, along with linguist Roman Jakobson, argues that myth as a functional structure is analogous to language in that we do not define it by the content of its sentences but rather by its syntax, by the rules governing the sentences' construction. As Lévi-Strauss states: "If there is meaning to be found in mythology, this cannot reside in the isolated elements which enter into the composition of a myth, but only in the way the elements are combined."[15] This observation is itself indebted to Ferdinand de Saussure's insight distinguishing *langue* from *parole* in verbal language. Saussure held that the speakers' and listeners' shared knowledge of the rules of grammar comprising the language system (*langue*) enables them to develop and understand a virtually unlimited and even grammatically incorrect range of individual utterances (*parole*).[16]

Like language and myth, the film genre as a textual system represents a set of rules of construction that are utilized to accomplish a specific communicative function. In his metaphor describing the variation of individual folktales that constitute a mythic structure, Lévi-Strauss might just as easily be describing the individual films within a genre:

> Thus, a myth exhibits a "slated" structure which seeps to the surface, if one may say so, through the repetition process. However, the slates are not absolutely identical to each other. And since the purpose of myth is to provide a logical model capable of overcoming a contradiction, . . . a theoretically infinite number of slates will be generated, each one slightly different from the others.[17]

The concept of genre as a filmic system must be characterized, like that of myth, by its function; its value is determined not according to what it is, but rather according to what it does. In its ritualistic capacity, a film genre transforms certain fundamental cultural contradictions and conflicts into a unique conceptual structure that is familiar and accessible to the mass audience. The issue of cultural specificity, a cinematic characteristic that encouraged Cawelti to avoid altogether the concepts of genre and myth in dealing with the western, is actually vital to any mythic structure. Edmund Leach, in his study of the works of Lévi-Strauss, holds that myth is "the expression of unobservable realities in terms of observable phenomena." [18] Lévi-Strauss himself points out that different cultures "express their different originalities by manipulating the resources of a dialectical system of contrasts and correlations within the framework of a common conceptual world." [19]

Thus, a mythic structure must indeed be incorporated within a culturally specific context, or else it would be unrecognizable or meaningless to the members of the culture who experience it. When Cawelti argues that cinematic formulas "relate to culture rather than to the generic nature of man," he is in fact addressing two sides of the same mythic coin. [20] The mythic ritual of the folktale is, to paraphrase Lévi-Strauss, a society collectively speaking to itself, confronting basic human issues in a familiar context. The "generic nature of man" that Cawelti refers to is precisely that mythmaking faculty by which individuals deal with the culturally specific in order to make palatable certain truths about the human condition that people have always found it difficult to contemplate. [21]

When we assume this view of the genre film functioning as a form of contemporary mythic ritual, we establish a basis for examining genres not only as individual, isolated forms, but also as related systems that exhibit fundamentally similar characteristics. In this context, we can begin to treat two vitally important questions regarding the study of film genre that thus far have gone unanswered: first, why only certain narrative-thematic structures have been refined into genres in the American cinema; second, what cultural appeal and conceptual basis endows these forms with their generic identity, with their "genre-ness," as it were.

Considering the genre film as a popular folktale assigns to it a mythic function that generates its unique structure, whose function is the ritualization of collective ideals, the celebration of temporarily resolved social and cultural conflicts, and the concealment of disturbing cultural conflicts behind the guise of entertainment, behind what Michael Wood terms "the semitransparent mask of a contradiction." [22] By assuming this mythic perspective when analyzing the genre film, we must necessarily consider the collective audience's participation in the studio system of production, which further substantiates the role of that production system in the contemporary mythmaking process. This role has been suggested by various analysts, but it generally has been done without initially delineating the interaction of the studio system with the audience and thereby recognizing the audience's collective participation in the generation and development of film genres. [23] This reciprocal studio-audience relationship provides the cultural context in which the genre film has been produced, endowing that film with its distinctive ritualistic character and providing the foundation for any theoretical approach that treats the genre film in terms of its mythic function.

In treating the Hollywood genre film as a form of mythic expression within a popular art form, we should not fail to consider certain basic qualifications imposed by the nature of the commercial cinematic medium that necessarily affect the narrative and thematic composition of that expression. That is, there are a number of general cinematic codes indigenous to the Hollywood production system that influence (and ultimately characterize) all of its products, including genre films. Beyond the obvious consideration of the cinema's incorporating an audiovisual as opposed to an oral or written mode of mythic expression, we might also consider Hollywood's penchant for narrative as opposed to documentary or abstract films, its "closed" economic system that made independent feature film production virtually impossible in America until the 1960s, its nurturing of the star system, and other related aspects of production. Whereas these considerations by no means undercut the notion of genre films representing an idealized cultural self-image in a ritualized form—indeed, the deification of such stars as John Wayne and Fred Astaire seem to underscore it—they do testify to the fact that the Hollywood cinema's mode of production provides a unique context for mythic expression.

Perhaps the characteristic of the commercial cinema that marks its most significant departure from traditional forms of ritual is the tendency, even within the conservative Hollywood system, toward rapid evolution of certain aspects of its popular narrative forms. Films within a genre represent variations on a theme, so to speak; the theme itself, as a manifestation of fundamental cultural preoccupations, may remain essentially consistent, but without variation the form necessarily will stagnate. The widespread exposure of genre films to the audience and the demand that filmmakers sustain audience interest in popular forms encourage continued manipulation of generic conventions if the genre is to maintain its vitality and cultural significance. As Robert Warshow has observed in his study of the western: "We do not want to see the same movie over and over again, only the same form."[24]

The western genre, for example, has enjoyed a life span roughly equivalent to that of the commercial American cinema itself, and throughout that span it has dealt with the basic oppositions of social order and anarchy as manifested in various dualities (East versus West, town versus wilderness, garden versus desert, group versus individual, and so on). While consistently focusing upon these oppositions, the genre has undergone considerable evolutionary development, both in terms of its historical depiction of the western environment and its casting of the western hero, who has tended in more recent films to be aligned with the forces of anarchy rather than those of social order.

In his structural study of the western, sociologist Will Wright views this evolutionary development in terms of extracinematic social and economic change. Wright suggests that "the narrative structure varies in accordance with the changing social actions and institutions. The oppositions, on the other hand, create images of social types that are fundamental in the consciousness of the society."[25] From his sociological perspective, Wright tends to minimize the creative input of the Hollywood production system. I would complement Wright's position with the suggestion that once the generic conventions have been established (which may take several decades, as with the western, or only a few years, as with the gangster film), filmmakers are stimulated, either by economic or aesthetic impulse, to take considerable liberties with the basic forms that are readily comprehensible in the context of audience familiarity and expectations. Thus, the "psychological" westerns of the early 1950s or the more recent celebration of the western outlaw should seem to the mass audience a reasonable extension of the genre's conventional ritualization of the forces of social order, progress, and individual freedom.

Our consideration of the genre film, then, is qualified by something of a dual perspective. It is, on the one hand, a product of a commercial, highly conventionalized popular art form and subject to certain demands imposed by both the audience and the cinematic system itself. On the other hand, the genre film represents a distinct manifestation of contemporary society's basic mythic impulse, its desire to confront elemental conflicts inherent in modern culture while at the same time participating in the projection of an idealized collective self-image. Having suggested the value of this perspective, I would like to close with a brief comment on what seem to be certain dangers inherent in this approach. As Wood's cultural study of the Hollywood film indicates, we might extend the previously elaborated methodological inquiry to yet a "higher" level, considering the Hollywood product generally as a contemporary manifestation of the human being's mythic impulse. But while there is certainly a degree to which virtually every mass-mediated cultural artifact can be examined from such a perspective, there appears to be a point at which we tend to lose sight of the initial object of inquiry.

Symptomatic of this brand of scholarly myopia—and again Wood's study is perhaps the most appropriate example—is the propensity either to expound generalizations about popular culture of such breadth and scope as to be essentially meaningless, or else to lapse into highly personal, impressionistic recollections of preadolescent Saturday afternoons spent with the Duke or Garbo or Godzilla. If we avoid overextending its reach, it would seem that the ultimate value of the form of analysis outlined here is that it enables students of the Hollywood genre film to broaden their analytical perspective without violating the integrity of the individual films or the genres in which they participate. Consequently, we can consider the genre film and the film genre in the same analytical context, examining westerns and musicals, screwball comedies and war films, from a culturally responsive perspective that acknowledges their shared as well as their distinctive individual qualities.

Notes

1. André Bazin, "In Defense of Mixed Cinema," in *What Is Cinema?* edited and translated by Hugh Gray (Berkeley: University of California Press, 1971), 1:71.

2. Thomas Sobchack, "Genre Film: A Classical Experience," *Literature/Film Quarterly* 3, no. 3 (Summer 1975): 201. Reprinted in this volume.

3. John G. Cawelti, *The Six-Gun Mystique* (Bowling Green, Ohio: Bowling Green University Popular Press, [1970]), p. 32.

4. Ibid., p. 73.

5. Stuart M. Kaminsky, *American Film Genres: Approaches to a Critical Theory of Popular Film* (Chicago: Pflaum, 1974), p. 3.

6. John C. Fell, *Film: An Introduction* (New York: Praeger, 1975), p. 116.

7. Jim Kitses, *Horizons West* (Bloomington: Indiana University Press, 1969), p. 13.

8. Cawelti, *Six-Gun Mystique*, p. 30. This issue of "cultural specificity" provides the basis for much recent discussion concerning the viability of myth in various cultures. As I intend to elaborate throughout this essay, the denial by Cawelti, Kitses, and Frye that a culturally specific narrative form *itself* can be mythic is in direct opposition to recent studies in mythology and structural anthropology.

9. Kitses, *Horizons West*, p. 13.

10. Bronislav Malinowski, *Myth in Primitive Psychology* (New York: W. W. Norton, 1926), p. 13.

11. David Bidney, "Myth, Symbolism, and Truth," *Journal of American Folklore 68*, no. 270 (October–December 1955): 381.

12. Ibid., p. 384.

13. Sobchack, "Genre Film," p. 201.

14. Claude Lévi-Strauss, *The Savage Mind* (Chicago: University of Chicago Press, 1966), p. 135.

15. Claude Lévi-Strauss, "A Structural Study of Myth," in *The Structuralists*, edited by Richard T. DeGeorge and Fernande M. DeGeorge (Garden City: Doubleday, 1972), p. 105.

16. Ferdinand de Saussure, *A Course in General Linguistics* (Paris: Bally and Sechehaye, 1972), p. 16.

17. Lévi-Strauss, "Structural Study of Myth," p. 109.

18. Edmund Leach, *Claude Lévi-Strauss* (New York: Viking, 1970), p. 58.

19. Claude Lévi-Strauss, *The Raw and the Cooked: Introduction to a Science of Mythology* (Evanston, Ill.: Harper and Row, 1969), p. 8.

20. Cawelti, *Six-Gun Mystique*, p. 31.

21. Robert Scholes, *Structuralism in Literature: An Introduction* (New Haven: Yale University Press, 1974), p. 68.

22. Michael Wood, *America in the Movies* (New York: Basic Books, 1975), p. 80.

23. See, for example, Will Wright's *Sixguns and Society: A Structural Study of the Western* (Berkeley: University of California Press, 1975), an entire volume devoted to the western film genre that does not once mention the studio system or the influence of the audience in the generation and development of the form.

24. Robert Warshow, "The Westerner," in *The Immediate Experience* (Garden City: Doubleday, 1962), p. 147.

25. Wright, *Sixguns and Society*, p. 27.

9. Genre Film: A Classical Experience

THOMAS SOBCHACK

In *An Illustrated Glossary of Film Terms,* Harry M. Geduld and Ronald Gottesman define *genre* as a "category, kind, or form of film distinguished by subject matter, theme, or techniques." [1] They list more than seventy-five genres of film, both fiction and nonfiction. There are categories within categories and categories which overlap and are not mutually exclusive. In light of the difficulty of accurately defining the individual genres, I would rather sidestep the problem by considering the fictional genre film as a single category that includes all that is commonly held to be genre film—i.e., the western, the horror film, the musical, the science fiction film, the swashbuckler—in order to show that all of these films have a common origin and basic form. Bound by a strict set of conventions, tacitly agreed upon by filmmaker and audience, the genre film provides the experience of an ordered world and is an essentially classical structure predicated upon the principles of the classical world view in general and indebted to the *Poetics* of Aristotle in particular; in the genre film the plot is fixed, the characters defined, the ending satisfyingly predictable.

Because the genre film is not realistic, because it is so blatantly dramatic, it has been condescendingly treated by many critics for its failure to be relevant to contemporary issues, philosophies, and aesthetics. Yet the truth of the matter is that the genre film lives up to the guiding principle of its classical origins: "there is nothing new under the sun," and truth with a capital T is to be found in imitating the past. The contemporary and the particular are inimical to the prevailing idea in classical thought that knowledge is found in the general conclusions that have stood the test of time. Thus originality, unique subject matter, and a resemblance to actual life are denigrated as values, while conformity, adherence to previous models, and a preoccupation with stylistic and formal matters are held to be the criteria for artistic excellence.

The subject matter of a genre film is a story. It is not about something that matters outside the film, even if it inadvertently tells us something about the time and place of its creation. Its sole justification for existence is to make concrete and perceivable the configurations inherent in its ideal form. That the various genres have changed or gone through cycles of popularity does not alter the fact that the basic underlying coordinates of a genre are maintained time after time. From *The Great Train Robbery* (Edwin S. Porter, 1902) to *The Cowboys* (Mark Rydell, 1972) or *True Grit* (Henry Hathaway, 1968), the western has maintained a consistency of basic content; the motifs, plots, settings, and characters remain the same. What is true of the western is also true of the adventure film, the fantasy film, the crime film, and the musical, or any fictional genre one can identify. Any particular film of any definable group is only recognizable as part of that group if it is, in fact, an imitation of that which came before. It is only because we have seen other films that strongly resemble the particular film at hand that we can say it is a horror film or a thriller or a swashbuckler. Consciously or unconsciously, both the genre filmmaker and the genre audiences are aware of the prior films and the way in which each of these concrete examples is an attempt to embody once again the essence of a well-known story.

This use of well-known stories is clearly a classical practice. Homer, the Greek dramatists, Racine, Pope, Samuel Johnson, and all the other great figures of the classical and neoclassical periods used prior sources for their stories. The formative principle behind the creation of classical art has always been the known and the familiar. The Greeks knew the stories of the gods and the Trojan War in the same way we know about hoodlums and gangsters and G-men and the taming of the frontier and the never-ceasing struggle of the light of reason and the cross with the powers of darkness, not through first-hand experience but through the media. For them it was tales told around the hearth and the yearly ritual of plays; for us it is the newspapers, television, and the movies themselves.

The body of stories is, to use Balazs's terms, the "material" out of which the "content" of a genre film can be made. And it is a strictly delimited area: other films may have the whole of life experience to choose from, but the genre film must be made from certain well-known and immediately recognizable plots—plots usually dealing with melodramatic incidents in which obvious villains and heroes portray the basic conflict of good versus evil. No matter how complicated the plot of a genre film may be, we always know who the good guys and the bad guys are; we always know whom to identify with and for just how long. Sam Spade may be considered by real-life standards to be a man of dubious moral character, but in the world of *The Maltese Falcon* (John Huston, 1941) he is clearly the hero akin to Odysseus threading his way through the obstacles of a hostile universe, using lies and deceit if necessary to complete his task.

Aristotle used the word *mimesis* to describe what a play is about. Supposedly it means imitation. Aristotle goes on to say that a plot is an imitation of a human action, and there are those who see in this definition the prescription for a kind of literal realism, holding the mirror up to life. But Greek drama, from which Aristotle drew his conclusions, was never that at all. Very few people in fifth-century Athens killed their fathers and slept with their mothers. The story of Oedipus, no matter how rife with Freudian implications for us today, was after all simply a story, albeit a kind of horror tale of its time, as were most of the stories upon which Greek writing was based. In practical terms Greek writings are imitations of prior stories, redone, reshaped, given dramatic form or epic form as the case may be, but nevertheless imitations of fictions.

Genre films operate on the same principle. They are made in imitation not of life but of other films. True, there must be the first instance in a series or cycle, yet most cases of the first examples of various film genres can be traced to literary sources, primarily pulp literature. Even the gangster films of the thirties derive not from life itself but from newspaper stories; the musical film, from the musical stage. And once the initial film is made, it has entered the pool of common knowledge known by film-maker and film audience alike. Imitations and descendants—the long line of "sons of," "brides of," and "the return of"—begin.

One of the paradoxes of a classical approach to form is aptly demonstrated in the genre film's unrelenting pursuit of imitation. Classical theory insists upon the primacy of the original. It is that which must be imitated, and the basic and fundamental elements must not be changed. Therefore, to avoid an exact duplicate, subsequent imitations can merely embroider and decorate, which in most cases destroys the elegance and simplicity of the original design. The Doric column came first, simple, balanced, proportioned, direct. As the years passed, the Doric gave way to the Ionic, and the Ionic to the Corinthian, the last column so cluttered and intricate that it diluted the original idea. Classical painting and architecture give way to the rococo and the baroque. The decorations increase; the power and the purity of the original are somehow dissipated.

We can see the same process at work in the genre film, and it explains why so often the original version or the "classic" version seems so much better than any of its followers. The original Draculas, silent and sound, *Little Caesar* (Mervyn LeRoy, 1930) and *The Public Enemy* (William Wellman, 1931), *The Iron Horse* (John Ford, 1924) and *The Covered Wagon* (James Cruze, 1923), Busby Berkeley musicals, *The Maltese Falcon*—not only were they progenitors of their kind and therefore to be venerated as examples from the Golden Age, but seen today they have a sparseness and an economy of means that put most of the recent remakes to shame. Christopher Lee cannot compare to Bela Lugosi, and full-color blood cannot make up for the spectral mysteriousness of F. W. Murnau's *Nosferatu* (1922).

A genre film, no matter how baroque it may become, however, still differs fundamentally from other films by virtue of its reliance on preordained forms, known plots, recognizable characters, and obvious iconographies; it is still capable of creating the classical experience because of this insistence on the familiar. It is what we expect in a genre film and what we get. Other fiction films are not genre films precisely because they do the opposite; they go out of their way to be original, unique, and novel. They appear more realistic, more true to life. Their characters are more highly individualized, their actions physically and psychologically more believable, and the events of the plot, employing random events and inconsequential details, well within the realm of possibility.

There are grey areas, of course—films that seem to be closer to genre than others depending on the total effect of the film, the way in which the realistic elements are emphasized or deemphasized, the way in which generic elements are used or abused. Yet for most films the issue is more clear-cut. The ideas and attitudes informing genre films are diametrically opposed to the other kind of fiction film. Although there is a detective (the reporter) and a mystery (what's Rosebud?), it would be difficult to make a case for *Citizen Kane* (Orson Welles, 1941) as a detective or mystery genre film. Though it has certain generic elements, they are not prominent, nor are they the sole justification for the creation of the film. On the other hand, Sherlock Holmes films, the Thin Man series, Charlie Chan movies, and others exist primarily to flesh out the idea of the detective story on film. They exist as variations on the motif of sleuthing. "Who dun it?" is the primary question raised and answered by these movies. No matter how rich a gold mine of interpretation one may find in *The Maltese Falcon,* for example, the basic question dealt with is still "Who dun it?" and not "Who am I?" or "What is the discrepancy between what a man appears to be and what he really is?" This is not to say that something of the latter question is not raised by Sam Spade's character, but certainly the film does not invite the general audience to take the question seriously, even if critics do.

One of the most important characteristics of the classical complex is a concern with form. Genre films, as suggested, are invariably more involved with formal matters both in content and in style, since they begin in imitation of other formal objects and not in imitation of life. In keeping with this notion, the form of a genre film will display a profound respect for Aristotelian dramatic values. There is always a definite sense of beginning, middle, and end, of closure, and of a frame. The film begins with "Once upon a time . . ." and ends only after all the strings have been neatly tied, all major conflicts resolved. It is a closed world. There is little room in the genre film for ambiguity anywhere—in characters, plots, or iconography. But even when seeming ambiguities arise in the course of a film, they must be either deemphasized or taken care of by the end of the film.

The most important single aspect of the genre film that gives it this compact sense of shape is the plot. It's what happens that is most important, not why. Incident crowding on incident, reversal after reversal, all strung out like beads on a string (or a rosary), to be counted one after another until the final shoot-out, the burning of the castle, the destruction of the fiend, the payment of the mortgage on the Big Top, or the return of the spacecraft to earth. Inherent and implicit in the beginning of any genre plot is the end; the elements presented in the exposition at the beginning are all clearly involved with the inevitable conclusion. Nothing extraneous to the plot can be introduced at random, somewhere in the middle. The best genre films always seem shorter than they really are. The classical virtue of economy of means may have been forced upon the genre film because of its usually low production budget, but it has maximized this possible defect. Only those scenes that advance the plot are permitted. Only that dialogue which will keep things moving is allowed. The adage attributed apocryphally to Hitchcock, that you should never use dialogue when you can show it in pictures, is often reversed in the genre film— even in Hitchcock's films. Whenever it takes too long to show it, say it instead. Do anything and everything to keep the plot moving, to create the sense of gathering momentum, of inevitable causality.

To further speed comprehension of the plot, genre films employ visual codes, called iconographies, in order to eliminate the need for excessive verbal or pictorial exposition. Strictly speaking, beyond the use of masks, there is nothing in Greek drama comparable to the iconography of the genre film, for as Aristotle pointed out, "spectacle"—what we see—is the least important element of a play, while it is obviously a primary aspect of film. A more appropriate analogy can be found in the Greek narrative art—the epic poems. Homer is an exceptionally visual poet, particularly when he is describing the armor and weapons of his heroes in *The Iliad;* *The Odyssey,* too, pictorializes costumes, metamorphoses, monsters, and settings in a way that brings to mind the vividness of the modern equivalent—the genre film.

Iconography consists of certain photographed objects, costumes, and places composing the visible surface of a genre film that creates economically the context and milieu, the field of action on which the plot will unravel itself. Over a period of use in many films, these visual elements have become encrusted with shared meanings, so that dialogue and camera can concentrate on revealing the twists and turns of the plot. Iconography, like familiar plot situations and stereotypical characters, provides a short-hand of mutually recognizable communications that neither film-maker nor audience need ponder: the jungle is treacherous, the castle that towers darkly over the village is sinister, the flat horizon of the desert is unyielding. Capes and evening clothes create threatening figures unless they are in a musical; laboratories with bubbling liquids are occupied by men tampering with things no human being should.

Like the epithet—a descriptive, characterizing tag line in the epic poems (the "wine-dark sea," the "bronze-shot arrows," the "cunning Odysseus")—the icons of genre films serve to remind the viewer of the internal consistency and familiarity of the characters and places in the film. These places and characters do not change in the course of a film, and very little from film to film. The visual appearance of a western town in one film is just about the same as in other films. The landscape in a sci-fi picture can be depended upon. The world of the musical is always a glittering unreality poised somewhere between our doughty old world and heaven, whether it is set backstage at the Broadway Theater or high in the Swiss Alps.

As indicated above, characterization in a genre film often uses the shorthand of iconography. We know a person by what he wears as opposed to what he says and does. And once known, the character cannot change except in the most limited ways. Curiously enough, the Greek word for *character* as applied to human beings was the same as that applied to a letter of the alphabet. That is, the root word means the "stamp" that imprints the letter on the paper, or the stamp that imprints the character onto the person. Right up until the end of the classical era—and the neoclassical—in the eighteenth century, the prevailing opinion was that human character was imprinted at birth and that it did not develop or change. Though the subsequent revolutions of thought in the nineteenth and twentieth centuries have all but wiped out this idea, the genre film continues to employ this extremely classical concept.

Frequently generalized and known by their vocation, genre characters are conveyed through iconographical means—costumes, tools, settings, and so on. The man who wears a star, whether he is a figure in the crowd or a major character, has a limited range of responses to situations. The same is the case with men who wear lab coats, carry sawed-off shotguns, or drink their whiskey straight. These men are their functions in the plot. Revealed to us through costume, dialogue, or physiognomy, they remind us of other sheriffs, private eyes, and mad scientists from other movies we've seen. Typecasting in the genre film is a bonus, not a debit. It is just one more way of establishing character quickly and efficiently. John Wayne is the character type John Wayne, his face no more expressive than the painted masks used in ancient times by the Greeks. Other performers like

Bela Lugosi, Peter Lorre, and Vincent Price are instantly "knowable" as genre figures.

In addition to establishing character with speed and directness, the use of less individualized characters sets up the basis for the existence of Aristotelian catharsis by allowing for an increase in empathy by the audience. Being so much their exteriors, genre characters allow us to easily assume their roles. The fact that we know that they are not realistic, not part of our real world, lets us slip into their trench coats or boots with ease. We can identify so strongly and safely with their roles that we leave the theater walking a little bow-legged or pulling up the collar of a nonexistent trench coat to ward off the wind. Genre characters, because they are so unrealistic and without depth, because they are so consistent and unwavering in their purpose, because they are never forced to come to terms with themselves—they have no "self" in one sense—invite identification with the role or type; that identification releases us from the ordinary and mundane realism of our own lives. We can say, "I wish I were like him"— so tough, so hard-boiled, so ruthless, so lucky, so pure, so wonderfully one-dimensional, so bent on destruction or revenge, or on saving the world that eating and sleeping and other everyday occurrences and responsibilities can never interfere. While we may all live quiet lives of desperation, genre characters do not. We are all Walter Mittys, and for a few short hours we can be lifted out of our inconsequential existences into a world of heroic action.

This difference in level between our world and the world of the genre film I would regard as fulfilling Aristotle's dictum that the characters of drama be elevated. Genre characters are certainly far superior to us in what they can do; they may be limited as ordinary human beings, but they are unlimited as far as action. They can do what we would like to be able to do. They can pinpoint the evil in their lives as resident in a monster or a villain, and they can go out and triumph over it. We, on the other hand, are in a muddle. We know things aren't quite right, but we are not sure if it is a conspiracy among corporations, the world situation, politicians, our neighbors down the street, our boss, our spouse; but whatever it is, we can't call it out of the saloon for a shoot-out or round up the villagers and hunt it down. Genre characters inhabit a world that is better than ours, a world in which problems can be solved directly, emotionally, in action. It is in a sense an ideal plane, a utopia, as far removed from our world as was the world of kings and nobles and Olympian gods from the lives of the Athenians who attended the plays and heard the epics.

That we desire to witness such worlds and to experience classical catharsis is demonstrated by the current phenomenal attendance at martial arts films, the newest of film genres; it would be impossible to count the number of people who partake of such experiences through the older genres as offered on their television screens, both in reruns of theatrical films and the made-for-TV variety. The emotional involvement and subsequent release that Aristotle called catharsis is an obviously desired tonic in our postromantic modern world. Critics, sociologists, psychologists, and politicians may argue over the social impact of literature and films that depict violent action—are they only a reflection of the times or are they a cause of the violence in our culture?—but Aristotle's position is quite clear: there is a social benefit, a point at which art and the good of the community come together. If spectators identify strongly with the figures of the drama, feeling pity and fear as drawn out by the activities going on before their eyes and ears, then, when properly concluded, given the appropriate ending, these emotions are dissipated, leaving viewers in a state of calm, a state of stasis in which they can think rationally and clearly. Properly conceived and executed, the genre film can produce this effect.

The cathartic potentials of the genre film can also be seen as a way in which the tension of cultural and social paradoxes inherent in a human experience can be resolved. Freud in *Civilization and Its Discontents* and Nietzsche in *The Birth of Tragedy* discuss the issue at length. Nietzsche identifies the two poles of human behavior as the Apollonian and the Dionysian. The Apollonian is the urge to individuate the self from others and the Dionysian is the urge to submerge the self into a group, mob, clan, family, or chorus.

Since the conflict between the individual and the group, between self-realization and communal conformity, between the anxiety and loneliness engendered by the freeing of the self and the security of passive identification with the crowd, is so all-pervasive an element of human life, it is not surprising to find this tension between individual needs and community needs metaphorically represented in genre films, not only in gangster films, as Warshow has suggested, or in western films, as Cawelti has stated, but in all genre films. This tension, being so universal, may appear in other films as well, but because of the classical nature of the genre film, the resolution of the tension between these two poles will always be in favor of the community. The human being is after all a social animal. Thus, in classical thought, anything that can relieve or diffuse conflicting emotions and purge them from the individual can only be seen as a social good. Group values must be continually reinforced in the individual; in the old days religion did the job, but in post-Reformation times the burden has moved elsewhere. Patriotic nationalism and world communism have sought to pick up the standard in real life, but the only twentieth-century art that has consistently reenacted the ritual of reaffirmation of group values has been the genre film. Simply enough, it is the form of the genre film, its repetitive quality, its familiarity, and violent plotting that has made this work. During the course of a genre film we can vicariously play out our desire for individuation by identifying with the protagonist free from the anxiety of group censure. Personal fears of actually acting out our fantasies of sex and power are eliminated because we know it is only a movie. There are no penalties to pay, as there are in real life, for being either hero or villain. A short survey of several plot structures found in various genres will serve to show how genre plots are the key to the dispersal of the tension between individual and group.

In the war film, for example, the most popular plot involves a group of men, individuals thrown together from disparate backgrounds, who must be welded together to become a well-oiled fighting machine. During the course of the film, the rough edges of the ornery and the cantankerous, the nonjoiners, the loners, like John Garfield in Hawks's *Air Force* (1943), must be smoothed down to make them fit. They must all hang together or all hang separately. The emphasis is on the team. And, of course, for the war film the end goal of the fighting is always the even larger group, the nation. Or peace in the world, to protect us all from some peculiarly successful individuals—Hitler or Hirohito or the kaiser. The hero's primary function is to mold the group and personally oppose the idea of individualism whenever it rears its head in its own cause and not that of the group effort. What better metaphor than the coward—the man interested only in saving his own skin, who somehow or other must be forced into changing his attitude or else destroyed before he infects the rest of the group. The hero, not just in the war film but in all genre films, is always in the service of the group, of law and order, of stability, of survival, not of himself but of the organization or the institution, no matter how individual his activities, while a villain could be defined as a man who ruthlessly looks after his own needs first and who works for and will sacrifice himself for no one or nothing but himself.

In the swashbuckler, the Errol Flynn character must restore the true social order, and though he may appear to be an outlaw now (which allows him to do all sorts of antisocial actions like killing and robbing), by the end of the film his crimes against the crown have been pardoned since they were all done in a good cause. He kneels to his liege lord and marries the girl (marriage traditionally having connotations of responsibility to the social order).

The police or detective film follows the same general pattern. The cops can do violent antisocial acts (acts which all of us would like to do) with impunity, for they are fulfilling their primary function to catch the guilty party and restore order. At first glance the private-eye film doesn't seem to fit this pattern, but it does. Sam Spade and the police are really on the same side, protecting the mindless masses (who seldom play a central role in the films) from evil. True, the police may be corrupt or stupid or slow to figure things out, yet the end goal is the same. The ideal of commitment to square dealing and presumably to a community of square dealers is demonstrated in the moral integrity of the private eye who can't be bought. Hence we may understand that in the particular social order shown, the police may be stupid or even corrupt, but that there is somewhere a moral order of community and group benefit as opposed to personal and material benefit, an ideal vindicated by the private eye's sending to prison the girl he's fallen in love with.

Horror films and monster films need no elaboration on this point, nor do science fiction films. Though the latter may leave us slightly wondering if the community shown in the film will survive in the future, there is the implicit assertion that there is no survival without the group. Science, that corporate analytical endeavor, will save us if anything can—not any individual. Westerns are also clearly involved with the eventual triumph of the forces of civilization, law and order, even as they are tinged with melancholy for the loss of individual freedom.

The musical will often end with a wedding or the promise of one as the boy and girl come together after overcoming all obstacles—a perfect example of a socially regenerative action, as Northrop Frye has pointed out in his discussion of New Comedy in *The Anatomy of Criticism*. In those musicals in which a star is born, in which it seems as though an individual is rising to the heights of individual achievement, it usually turns out that the star must go on despite personal tragedy, again emphasizing the group—the Broadway show, the production, standing as a metaphor for society.

Any brief rundown of basic plots should serve to demonstrate that the catharsis engendered in genre films is a basic element of their structure. The internal tension between the opposing impulses of personal individuation and submission to the group, which normally is held in check by the real pressures of everyday living, is released in the course of a genre film as the audience vicariously lives out its individual dreams of glory or terror, as it identifies with the stereotyped characters of fantasy life. But in the end those impulses to antisocial behavior (acts of individuation no matter how innocuous or permissible are still tinged with an element of the antisocial) are siphoned off as we accept the inevitable justice of the social order: the group is always right, and we know in our hearts that it is wrong to think otherwise.

In recent years it has become the fashion for some directors to use the elements of the genre film—the plots, characters, and iconographies—to create an antigenre film. That is, they will use everything according to the normal pattern, but simply change the ending so as not to satisfy the audience's expectations of a conventional group-oriented conclusion. If the detective finally gives in and takes the money and the girl, if the crook gets away with it, if an individual solves his problems so as to enhance his position vis-à-vis the world, that is, to increase the distance between his values and the values of the group—then the film has turned its back on the idea of genre. It violates the basic principle of the genre film: the restoration of the social order. Instead of justifying the status quo, these films intend the opposite. They suggest that individuals can succeed in individual schemes, that separation from the group can be had without consequences. In this sense they are not classical but romantic in their tenor.

The genre film is a structure that embodies the idea of form and the strict adherence to form that is opposed to experimentation, novelty, or tampering with the given order of things. The genre film, like all classical art, is basically conservative, both aesthetically and politically. To embody a radical tenor or romantic temper in a classical form is to violate that form at its heart. One can parody the conventions, one can work against the conventions, one can use the conventions with great subtlety and irony. To hold up individual ideals as superior to group ideals, however, changes the whole frame of reference. When a seeming genre film merely changes the ending in a final reversal, catharsis is restricted. The audience is unprepared by what has come before. There is no release of tensions, since the inevitable conclusion for which the audience has come and which would send them back into the real world smiling has not taken place. Rather than stasis, such endings produce agitation, discomfort, a vague anxiety. The guilt of having identified with the scoundrel or hero is never dissipated and viewers must bear the responsibility for their individual desires all alone.

In *Charlie Varrick* (Don Siegel, 1973), an otherwise conventional caper movie, the title character gets away with a million dollars scot-free at the end, which denies the audience the opportunity of saying, "That's the way it is. Nobody gets away with fighting against the mob or syndicate." His escape from just punishment for daring to wrest something of value from the Olympians of today, the banks, the corporations, the Mafia, makes him a Prometheus figure who doesn't get caught. It induces in the audience a kind of irrational radicalism as opposed to a reasonable conformism: "If he can do it, then maybe I, too, can fight the system, the institutions, and win." This is not what ordinary people—fated to a life in society in which they are relatively powerless to change the course of things—like to comfort themselves with and not what a true genre film provides.

For the time that genre characters play out their lives upon the screen we can safely identify with them, confident that the group will assert its overwhelming force in the end—like the chorus in a Greek play, always having the last word, reminding us that "That's the way it is. If you reach beyond your grasp, you will fall." We need not feel guilty; our surrogates will take the blame. We will switch allegiance by the end and become a member of the chorus. Our split personality is no longer split. Crime doesn't pay. True love wins out. The monster is destroyed. The forces of evil and darkness are vanquished by faith and reason. All is for the best in this best of all possible worlds. We have achieved the stasis that Aristotle mentions as the product of catharsis—a quiet calm. This is not to say that this feeling lasts long after we leave the theater, but at least we have been internally refreshed by our brief sojourn in a realm of cosmos, not chaos. If nothing else, the genre film is a paradigm of ritual and order.

The genre film is a classical mode in which imitation not of life but of conventions is of paramount importance. Just as in the classical dramas of Greece, the stories are well known. Though there may be some charm in the particular arrangement of formula variables in the most current example of a genre, the audience seeks the solid and familiar referents of that genre, expecting and usually receiving a large measure of the known as opposed to the novel. Elevated and removed from everyday life, freed from the straitjacket of mere representationalism, genre films are pure emotional articulation, fictional constructs of the imagination, growing essentially out of group interests and values. Character takes a second place to plot, in agreement with Aristotle's descriptions of drama. And it is this emphasis on the plot that makes genre films the most cinematic of all films, for it is what happens in them, what actions take place before our eyes that are most important. They move; they are the movies.

Note

1. Harry M. Geduld and Ronald Gottesman, *An Illustrated Glossary of Film Terms* (New York: Holt, Rinehart and Winston, 1973), p. 73.

10. Experience and Meaning in Genre Films

BARRY KEITH GRANT

It is an essential quality of the cinematic medium (with the exception, perhaps, of certain structuralist films) that the spectator is engaged during the viewing experience. In fact, it would seem that this engagement is consistently more intense, more complete, with film than with any other art. The technological requirement that the projector gears grab the sprocket holes of the celluloid to move it through the gate thus provides an apt metaphor for the way we commonly relate to movies. While viewing a film one is able simultaneously to say something to the effect of "It's only a movie," yet also have distinct physiological responses—sweating palms, for instance, or an unsettled stomach in a sequence like the car chase through the sloping streets of San Francisco in *Bullitt* (Peter Yates, 1968) —a phenomenon observed at least fifty years ago by the aesthetician and psychologist Rudolf Arnheim.[1]

Of course the very perception of a *motion* picture begins with the synthesis by the spectator's eye of the individual still frames. But movies also engage us in more complex ways. The viewer's willing suspension of disbelief and propensity for character identification, for example, are especially encouraged in the cinema, where one experiences images and sounds larger and louder than life. (It is just this ability of cinema to "magnify" reality that explains the medium's apparent affinity for the melodramatic, the fantastic, and the spectacular—modes that tend to magnify reality in different ways.) In fact, the cinema's greatest artists in one manner or another have all been concerned with the nature of film experience. The films of directors who exploit the viewer's emotions, such as Alfred Hitchcock, Claude Chabrol, or Francois Truffaut, for example, take as their recurrent theme the psychological/sociological dimension of the viewing experience, and often are structured in such a way as to depend upon audience identification and involvement for their meaning. Similarly, more intellectual and politically committed filmmakers such as Sergei Eisenstein, Jean-Luc Godard, and Rainer Werner Fassbinder construct their films in ways that comment upon the ideological implications of the viewing experience. Even the so-called "closed" cinema of Fritz Lang derives both its effect and meaning from audience involvement no less than the "open," participatory cinema of Jean Renoir: the former encourages judgments in the viewer that are subsequently exposed as morally corrupt, the latter invites suspension of judgment.[2] Other directors— Luis Buñuel, Federico Fellini, and Jean Cocteau, for instance—exploit the cinema's special contiguity with fantasy and the dream; their film practice illustrates well Suzanne Langer's contention that "cinema is 'like' dream in the mode of its presentation: it creates a virtual present, an order of direct apparition."[3] In short, whether directors consider emotional or intellectual involvement of paramount importance, they all mobilize elements of the viewing experience as an essential structural element of their film work.

Although generally acknowledged in film criticism, however, the qualities of the cinematic experience have implications that for the most part have remained unexplored; rather, analysis has tended to focus on film texts as discrete objects—as expressions of a director's personality and vision or as a network of signifying practices. I would like to suggest that while the exploration of the viewing experience is always relevant to film, it is of central importance to a consideration of those movies that can be subsumed under generic categories. The idea of genre includes two essential elements: the function of generic works as secular myth and the assumed "contract" between filmmaker and film viewer that allows for their existence—their system of production, distribution, and consumption— in the first place. Genre criticism has concentrated primarily on the former aspect, enumerating the conventions, iconography, plots, themes, and characters that distinguish the various genres and carry their mythic meanings. However, it would seem impossible to appreciate in any meaningful way individual genre films without considering the special manner in which we experience them. Because a genre, as Andrew Tudor reminds us, is "what we collectively believe it to be"[4] and because what we believe a genre to be sets up expectations that condition our responses to a genre film from the very first shot—indeed, often even before the lights in the cinema are dimmed—an analysis of the generic contract in operation, its actual dynamics, becomes crucial.

Commonly invoking the work of such anthropologists as Bronislav Malinowski and Claude Lévi-Strauss, genre criticism has viewed both film genres and genre films—that is, both a tradition of common works and individual instances of that tradition—as contemporary versions of social myth.[5] Indeed, genre films are directly related to lived experience, their traditions clearly connected to communal values. While most filmgoers do not go to the literal extreme of attempting to live generic conventions directly, as do both the Jean-Paul Belmondo character in *A bout de souffle* (Jean-Luc Godard, 1959) and the Dennis Christopher character in the more recent *Fade to Black* (Vernon Zimmerman, 1980), audiences do model their values and behavior to a significant degree according to those conventions.

For example, the resurgence in the early seventies of the outlaw-couple cycle of gangster films—*Bonnie and Clyde* (Arthur Penn, 1967), *Badlands* (Terrence Malick, 1973), *Thieves Like Us* (Robert Altman, 1974), *Aloha Bobby and Rose* (Floyd Mutrux, 1975), and *The Sugarland Express* (Steven Spielberg, 1974), to mention the most notable—can be seen as an expression of that period's youthful disaffection with the Establishment. These films, with their young romantic couple on the fringes of society pursued by an unyielding authority, invite a reading relevant to the contemporary zeitgeist. This attitude influenced not only popular film but also popular music (for example, Georgie Fame's hit song "The Ballad of Bonnie and Clyde" and Bob Dylan's numerous ballads about outlaws and outsiders), politics (Tom Hayden and Jane Fonda), and fashion (the nostalgic return to the styles of the thirties—particularly, for some reason, in the decor of aspiring upscale restaurants). Then, as a sense of political disaffection deepened during the trauma of the Nixon administration and spread to other social groups, the outlaw-couple films were replaced by a resurgence of both political conspiracy films (*The Parallax View*, Alan J. Pakula, 1974; *Executive Action*, David Miller, 1973; *All the President's Men*, Pakula, 1976) and disaster films, with their equally obvious metaphors. *The Towering Inferno* (John Guillerman, 1974), for example, depicted the dangers of corruption in the capitalist edifice, while *Earthquake* (Mark Robson, 1974) rocked the very foundations of American society. The shared convention of these films, wherein a cross section of social types is faced with the same crisis and the good seem to perish indiscriminately along with the evil, blunts the clear moral polarization of the outlaw-couple film but pointedly expresses the increasingly prevalent social dis-ease of the time. *The Poseidon Adventure* (Ronald Neame, 1972) literally inverts society by turning the microcosmic ship upside down, forcing isolated groups of individuals to struggle to escape by ascending to the bottom of the ship in a Dantesque vision of contemporary society as hell.

Surely one of our basic ways of understanding film genres, and of explaining their evolution and changing fortunes of popularity and production, is as collective expressions of contemporary life that strike a particularly resonant chord with audiences. It is virtually a given in genre criticism that, for example, the thirties musicals are on one level "explained" as an escapist Depression fantasy; that film noir in the forties expressed first the social and sexual dislocations brought about by World War II and then the disillusionment when it ended; and that the innumerable science fiction films of the fifties embodied cold-war tensions and nuclear anxiety new to that decade. In short, it can be said that because they are so integral to our cultural consciousness, genre films provide us with what John Dewey in *Art as Experience* considers to be true aesthetic experience—for such movies are indeed "a product, one might almost say a by-product, of continuous and cumulative interaction of the organic self with the world" in which "the conventions themselves live in the life of the community." [6] Of course, such a description may apply as well to many nongenre films, from popular movies like *Casablanca* to the more art-house allegories of Ingmar Bergman; but it is their reliance on communally shared conventions that brings genre films so close so often to our continual negotiations between the world and the self.

The conventional nature of genre films has been cited most frequently to support the argument that genres have become the contemporary equivalent of tribal ritual and myth for mass-mediated society. But it equally well supports the claim for genre films as art (if, indeed, such an argument any longer needs to be made) primarily because of their potential richness as experience (by contrast, a relatively novel argument), if we understand works of art, again, in the sense that Dewey does. For him, the phrase "work of art" implies an action, an interaction with the text, an aesthetic experience rather than object. As Dewey says, "Art is the quality of doing and of what is done. Only outwardly, then, can it be designated by a noun substantive. . . . The product of art—temple, painting, statue, poem—is not the *work* of art. The work takes place when a human being cooperates with the product so that the outcome is an experience that is enjoyed because of its liberating and ordered properties." [7] This is something substantially different from the claim for genre films as art either because of their characteristic economy of expression (a concentrated use of conventions) or because of their individual variation (unusual inflections of conventions).

To take an obvious but vivid example, consider how the meaning of *Psycho* (Alfred Hitchcock, 1960) would be severely reduced if we did not take into account our relation to it, our interaction with it—particularly the manner in which we first identify with the character of Marion Crane (Janet Leigh) and then, when that is frustrated by her sudden death, how we shift our identification to Norman Bates (Anthony Perkins). Robin Wood convincingly points out the many stylistic and narrative devices Hitchcock uses in the first part of the film to encourage the viewer's identification with Marion, and how this affects our response to what follows. [8] The viewer's intense identification with Marion is even further strengthened when, after meeting Norman, she decides to return the money she has stolen.

This apparent moral redemption, visually underscored by the cleansing shower, promises us the expected, typical generic pleasure of having it both ways—here, specifically, the invitation to identify with a character engaging in antisocial actions and at the same time to remain free of the burden of guilt. The film until this point has concentrated on Marion's crime, the robbery of $40,000, and is therefore likely to invoke further expectations raised by the gangster film, which operates according to a very similar dynamic. In that genre, however, gangsters conventionally pay for their flamboyant denial of social restraint, which the audience has experienced vicariously, by being obligatorily gunned down in the closing minutes. Thus the death of Marion in *Psycho* is all the more shocking and our strategic shift of point of view to Norman that much more necessary because the criminal/protagonist here dies at an unexpected (unconventional) moment in the narrative.

It is true that *Psycho* encourages viewer identification with Marion only to transfer it later to Norman; but it is also true that the profoundly disturbing and frightening quality of this experience (and hence of the film's essential meaning) depends largely upon generic expectations: the horror icon of the Victorian (in California?) house on the hill as opposed to the clean, modern motel room; the unexpected death of the protagonist; and so on. Such a response is deepened by both our past experience of thrillers and horror films and by Hollywood cinema itself as an institution, with certain seemingly inviolable rules entrenched across genres. One of these primary rules is that the protagonist/hero does not die, especially after being redeemed by a correct moral choice. The notable exception to this is, of course, the war film, but in this case we are already prepared for such a possibility by generic category. The essential concern of the war film (until recently, at least) is to show the importance of a group working together to achieve a common goal; individuals must be welded together into a unit, a platoon, in which each works for the good of all and a clear, mutually accepted hierarchy is established.

The narrative turn of Marion's death in *Psycho* was virtually unprecedented in previous thrillers or horror films; but this in no way reduces this sequence to a mere shock effect, for it becomes thematically functional in the manner in which it implicates the viewer in the immoral desires of the characters (the $40,000 going to waste, the momentary halt of the car as Norman sinks it in the swamp, the emphasis on voyeurism). Robin Wood of course understands this, emphasizing that the film is a particularly salient example of what he calls Hitchcock's therapeutic theme: "*Psycho* is Hitchcock's ultimate achievement to date in the techniques of audience-participation. . . . The characters of *Psycho* are *one* character, and that character, thanks to the identification the film evokes, is us."[9] But while Wood's analysis convincingly emphasizes the importance of viewer response more than most film criticism, he does not go far enough in identifying the nature of this response, the extent to which it is generically influenced.

In his book *The Basis of Criticism in the Arts,* which takes as its project the organization of all possible critical approaches and methods within four basic categories, the aesthetician Stephen C. Pepper coined the term *contextualism* to describe that type of critical practice that acknowledges and places value upon experience in formulating aesthetic judgments. Although Pepper nowhere in the book specifically addresses the film medium, his notion of aesthetic experience seems particularly germane to the cinema. According to Pepper, contextualism views as positive aesthetic value the work of art's instrumentality in achieving what he describes as "the intensification and clarification of experience." [10] For contextualism, the pleasure of an aesthetic experience, while not disregarded, is secondary to its force: "*The more vivid the aesthetic experience and the more extensive and rich its quality,*" Pepper declares, "*the greater its aesthetic value.*" [11] He adds that the specific nature or "quality" of this experience —"the character, the mood, and you might almost say, the personality" of it—becomes the central focus of the contextualist approach. [12] Thus contextualism, as Pepper notes, is the only aesthetic theory that can account adequately for the pleasures involved in the experience of classical tragedy—and, by extension, melodrama and horror. As D. L. White has written, a horror film is more than simply a bundle of conventions and icons; it is "not just a sequence of certain events . . . but the unity of a certain kind of action." [13] More precisely, as the exemplary case of *Psycho* reveals, it is a certain kind of *inter*action that characterizes the horror film; and this dynamic, the degree to which our experience of horror is examined or exploited may also serve, as Bruce Kawin has shown, to distinguish the aesthetically better horror films from the rest. [14] In Dewey's terms, it is precisely this interaction which marks the crucial difference between a product of art and a work of art, between a thesis and a demonstration.

Now, it may at first seem odd to attempt to fit contextualist theory to film genre, primarily since most genre films are, quite simply, conventional. They are by definition predictable: classically, they resolve conflicts in favor of the status quo, and therefore apparently they cannot engage the viewer in any significant way. It is for this reason that Morris Dickstein has claimed that the horror film "washes over us without really reaching us," that such works are a vicarious experience, no more challenging than a ride on a roller coaster or a parachute jump. [15] In this sense horror films may be seen as paradigmatic examples of the limitations many critics view as integral to all of popular culture. As Abraham Kaplan puts it, popular art is "never a discovery, only a reaffirmation," and, so to speak, it merely "tosses baby in the air a very little way and quickly catches him again." [16] Pepper himself is quite careful to point out that "habit," which he defines as "convention, tradition, and the like," reduces aesthetic value because it "simply dulls experience and reduces it to routine." [17] In terms of contemporary film theory, this view of popular culture and its genres is one that sees the spectating subject as "positioned" by generic conventions, themselves determined by the dominant ideology, so as to contain desire and structure perception to reinforce itself.

But if this view of genre films were in fact correct, then contextualist aesthetics would necessarily devalue them. Pepper's notion of habit, I think, applies primarily to those movies that are, in Robin Wood's phrase, "pure" genre films [18]—that is, ones that are full of their generic elements but lack an interpretive perspective upon them or that present them in ways that they have commonly been presented before. For Wood, then, a genre film is truly interesting only insofar as it is filtered through the consciousness of an auteur, whose concerns provide a "tension" with the basic generic material. If the richer genre films do indeed result from such a tension, then contextualist aesthetics actually proves itself particularly relevant here. Pepper would substitute the term "conflict" for "tension": while there is of course aesthetic virtue to be found in the formal unity of a work (or rather, a *product*) of art, he asserts that "it is something new in aesthetic theory to discover the aesthetic value of conflict. This side of his theory is what a contextualist should exploit. The integration he should stress is an integration of conflicts." [19] Pepper's main example of the positive value of conflict consists of a detailed analysis of a Shakespearean sonnet, in which the conflict between the poem's theme (sadness) and its form (the accentuation of "brightness" implied by the tone of the final rhymed couplet) is said to increase its aesthetic value, as the reader is enlivened by this tension.[20] In the general context of film genre, conflict may be seen to exist inherently in the shifting ideological relationships between mainstream American cinema as an institution; its forms of expression (genres); those social and economic forces that encourage generic modification; the auteurs who, working within or against this system, animate these forms; and the audience viewing the generic work.

The "pure" genre movie falls into that group of films that Jean-Louis Comolli and Jean Narboni, in their discussion of the possible ways films relate to ideology, label category "a": "those films which are imbued through and through with the dominant ideology in pure and unadulterated form, and give no indication that their makers were even aware of the fact." [21] Such films constitute the largest and most common category of both genre and nongenre films. However, many films embody ideological tensions, either intentionally or inadvertently, stylistically or thematically, or by a combination of both (categories "b," "c," and "e"). It is these films that are said to reveal "cracks" or "fissures" in their narrative and in their articulation of what is normally presented as the seamless, calm surface of bourgeois illusionism. The genre films that work in this manner gain considerably from their very nature as generic instances, from their position within a clear tradition, for it is precisely their conventionally conservative generic qualities that "anchor" the potentially subversive elements.[22]

For example, the context of genre is perhaps the most significant factor in determining a star's persona or iconographical meaning. As Maurice Yacowar has said, "The film actor is all image, hence all fluid associative potential, so his performance is continuous over a number of roles."[23] This is especially true of genre films, in which actors are typecast (see Eisenstein's notion of *typage*)[24] from film to film within the same genre. The character actors and supporting players who populate genre films provide the firmament for the stars to shine. Fred Astaire, John Wayne, and Edward G. Robinson have been in films that were not musicals, westerns, or gangster films, respectively; but their significance as "fluid associative potential" would be virtually nil if not for their work in those genres. For example, the moral authority and rugged independence of Wayne, as depicted in his films with John Ford, deepen our experience of his roles in the westerns of Howard Hawks, particularly *Red River* (1948), when the western code of behavior as embodied in Wayne's Ringo Kid from *Stagecoach* (1939) is revealed as a monomania in his portrayal of Dunson.

In the case of Robinson, his roles in crime films such as *Little Caesar* (Mervyn LeRoy, 1930) inform not only his performance as a meek clerk with a gangster double in Ford's *The Whole Town's Talking* (1935), but also his henpecked husband with apron and kitchen knife in *Scarlet Street* (Fritz Lang, 1945). In this film the viewer is signaled from the beginning by the appearance of a number of icons of the gangster genre, including the presence of the actor Robinson, to expect the character he plays, Christopher Cross, to stab his wife one evening as he is subjected to one of her shrill harangues while slicing bread. Lang teasingly raises the viewer's expectation here, then thwarts it, as nothing happens, only to fulfill it later when Cross wildly hacks to death the woman he has loved with an ice pick. In this way the film has suggested not only that the most abject and repressed of men may reveal themselves as little Caesars and that it may happen suddenly and unexpectedly, but also that this is true for us, too—for we have been implicated in imagining (even hoping) that Cross will murder his wife. The casting of Henry Fonda as the brutal villain in Sergio Leone's *Once upon a Time in the West* (1969) or the appearance of John Wayne in *The Fighting Seabees* (Edward Ludwig, 1944)

17. Edward G. Robinson as Caesar Enrico Bandello in *Little Caesar*.

are two more of many possible examples in which meaning is generated by generic association of actors—the former another instance of generic subversion through casting.

Just as a genre film possesses the capability to play upon an actor's image, so it may play with the conventional diegetic structures of genre. George Romero's *Night of the Living Dead* (1968), which predates but inspired the rise of the dreadful "slice and dice" films, may serve as a particularly vivid example. With *Psycho* and *Scarlet Street* it shares the theme of the monster within us, although it is significant for the boldness and originality with which it locates the monster, in a movie overpopulated by monsters, within society. Romero's films have not yet received their critical due, and so in order to explain fully the contextualistic complexity of *Night of the Living Dead,* the discussion below temporarily shifts into the first person.

When I viewed the film for the first time, two years after its original release, I immediately noticed that the film was shot in black and white, and so assumed it was made on a low budget. Thus I quickly formed the expectation that the film would be something like the classic black and white horror films, the Universal films of the thirties or Val Lewton's RKO cycle in the forties—movies that elicited horror by suggestion rather than through graphic presentation. I reasoned to myself that this movie, with-

18. Robinson as Christopher Cross in the opening dinner scene in *Scarlet Street*.

out color, would not be as graphic as the more recent British Hammer Studio horror films (aside from Roger Corman's Poe cycle, the only group of horror films photographed in color). Yet within minutes I found myself struggling to adapt to each of its generic alterations and violations: the black hero (something never commented on by the other characters, even the despicable Harry Cooper, but nonetheless charged with meaning at the time of the film's release in 1968); the disorganized and unheroic military; the graphic depiction of entrails; the death of the teenage romantic couple. The film also consistently eliminates the conventional means of such narratives for dealing with monsters, since both religion and reason ultimately prove ineffective in halting the threat of the living dead.

Most disturbing of all was that, unlike most horror films up to that point, *Night of the Living Dead* withholds any explanations for its bizarre events until it is almost half over. And then, when we are given an explanation, it is difficult to hear because the television newsman who offers the long-awaited explanation is periodically drowned out by the protagonist's noisy construction of defensive barriers and by the govern-

19. Christopher Cross, the henpecked husband in *Scarlet Street*.

ment's evasive responses to the reporter's pressing questions (and by extension, ours). And so a tension is created as Ben's immediate concern for survival conflicts with and thwarts our generically reinforced desire either to find the *cause* of the living dead or, on an intellectual level, to know what they *mean*—and so make them manageable and safe. However, I renewed my "contractual" faith in the text by remembering that it is only a horror film, after all; I looked forward to the traditional resolution that I was now hoping, but no longer securely assuming, would come. And, sure enough, it didn't. When the long night seemed over and survival finally achieved, the film shook my complacency irretrievably: for with the arrival of the sheriff and his vigilante posse, the resourceful and morally admirable Ben is shot from a distance, insensitively mistaken for one of the living dead he has been fighting so hard against.

The ending, while certainly constituting a considerable shock at the time, is in fact consistent with the theme of the film. For even then I thought of the events of the Democratic National Convention in Chicago in 1968, the same year as the film's release, and I began to understand,

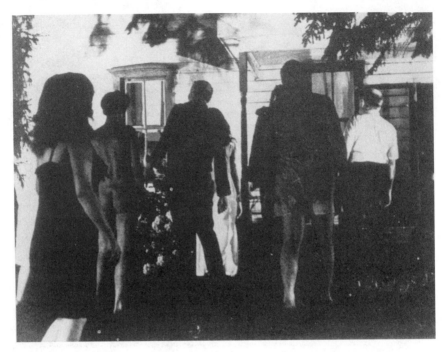

20. *Night of the Living Dead:* The zombies look like average folk.

first, that the night of the living dead is not the evening of the film's narrative but the darkness in the human spirit brought about by the absence of compassion and understanding; and, second, who the living dead really are—not the lurching zombies but average folk like Harry Cooper, the sheriff and his men, and, ultimately, myself. The film didn't preach this to me, but was instrumental in providing me with an experience with which I had to admit this truth; for I remembered that, given a choice in the resolution of the tension concerning my wish to have the zombies explained and Ben's frenzy to secure his position in the farmhouse, I would have, in effect, "sacrificed" Ben, even as I identified with him, to satisfy that wish. Like the repulsive Harry Cooper, I was instinctively looking out for Number One, an attitude that the film suggests is analogous to the desensitized state of the zombies.

D. H. Lawrence once referred to those people who did not fully embrace what he perceived as the life principle as the "living dead," saying that they were both angels and devils, at once vibrant and corrupt.[25] *Night of the Living Dead* similarly forces us to acknowledge that we have the capacity to be both Ben and Harry, however repugnant this notion might be. From other approaches, *Night of the Living Dead* may seem like cheap exploitation filmmaking; but when one is open to it as potential experience, it is a rich film indeed.

One of the key characteristics of aesthetic experience, according to Pepper, is the possibility of repeated interactions with the art object. Pepper calls this "funding," the building and enriching of aesthetic experience through subsequent encounters with the physical work of art, each instance of which is likely to be different in quality. In its simplest form, funding occurs when, say, we reread a poem and in this subsequent reading discover new linguistic potential previously unnoticed. Of course this is a common enough experience. But it assumes special relevance in the context of genre, where there exists not only the possibility of funding one's experience of a particular work by seeing it again, but also, because of our generic expectations of the text, the inevitability of instantly funding our experience by the composite sum of all the other films of that genre we have seen. A similar idea informs T. S. Eliot's description of an artistic tradition as an "existing order which is complete before the new work arrives"; but with the appearance of this new work "the relations, proportions, values of each work of art toward the whole are readjusted"—a point that Eliot insists is "a principle of aesthetic, not merely historical criticism." [26] And since our relationship to genre films is synchronic rather than diachronic, these "new works" need not necessarily be experienced in chronological sequence. Just as *Red River* funds our experience of earlier westerns, so too does *The Godfather* fund our experience of earlier gangster films and *Pennies from Heaven* (Herbert Ross, 1981) our experience of preceding musicals. In this sense the experience of funding is similar to the way we understand the films of auteurs, since the later films often shed light on the earlier ones. So our experience of, say, Ford's *Stagecoach* or *Wagon Master* (1950) is made richer by already knowing the later *Cheyenne Autumn* (1964) or *The Man Who Shot Liberty Valance* (1962). And any of these westerns by Ford gains not only from a knowledge of earlier westerns by, for example, Griffith, but also from later westerns by Hawks or Peckinpah.

Subsequent viewings of genre films help not only to sort through the medium's inherent encouragement of emotional response, but also to clarify that considerable part of aesthetic experience that is ideologically determined. Obviously, the more one studies something, the better one understands how it works. But with those genre films that incorporate generic expectations into their meaning, the result can be an experience that illuminates the nature of genre itself and thus its function within ideology. If, for example, we acknowledge the monstrous within ourselves in certain horror films, enjoy a Sirk melodrama, or laugh at the indignities inflicted on solid citizens by wacky protagonists in screwball comedies, we are in some way forced to deal with the cultural construction of social values. The collapse of the brontosaurus skeleton at the end of *Bringing Up Baby* (Howard Hawks, 1938), for instance, is a vivid image for the social implications of laughing at the many frustrations experienced by the rational Cary Grant in his research and, by extension, of the genre of screwball comedy itself.

Nowhere in his discussion of experience and contextualism does Pepper acknowledge the shaping power of ideology. For him the spectator would seem to exist apart from ideology, an "ideal" subject. Yet this omission, crucial as it is, does not diminish the value of the approach. On the contrary, given film criticism's recently renewed interest in the spectating subject, it is now particularly appropriate. Even the scientific semioticians have acknowledged the importance of experience. In the lovely words of Christian Metz, "I am at the cinema, attending a film show. ATTENDING. Like a midwife who attends at a birth, and thereby also helps the woman, I am present to the film in two (inseparable) ways: witness and helper; I watch, and I aid. In watching the film I help it to be born, I help it to live, since it is in me that it will live and it was made for that. . . ."[27]

Genre criticism of course should continue to map out, to describe, generic structures, their differences, and—more recently—their similarities. But it must address more directly the nature of the audience contract and generic experience as well as the connections between them. Pepper says of subjective response that it is most often "explained away . . . called merely subjective," but that it in fact cannot be, because it is an undeniable aspect of aesthetics, and "one cannot explain an ultimate fact."[28] Genre criticism may indeed be past the point where it is necessary for it to remain detached, "objective," simply descriptive, in the manner of Northrop Frye. Yet if most genre films fail the contextualist criterion of value, they are all of considerable interest as ideological constructs. And the aspects of myth and ritual so central to genre films require us to understand not only the logic behind their construction but our individual and collective responses to them as well.

Notes

1. Rudolf Arnheim, "Selections Adapted from *Film*," in *Film as Art* (Berkeley: University of California Press, 1971), pp. 8–160.

2. This distinction is persuasively examined by Leo Braudy in *The World in a Frame* (Garden City: Anchor, 1977).

3. Suzanne K. Langer, "A Note on the Film," in *Feeling and Form: A Theory of Art* (New York: Macmillan, 1953), p. 412.

4. Andrew Tudor, *Theories of Film* (New York: Viking Press, 1973), p. 139.

5. See, for example, Will Wright, *Sixguns and Society* (Berkeley and Los Angeles: University of California Press, 1975), and Thomas Schatz, *Hollywood Genres* (New York: Random House, 1981). See also Thomas Schatz, "The Structural Influence: New Directions in Film Genre Study," *Quarterly Review of Film Studies* 2, no. 3 (August 1977): 302–311; reprinted in this volume.

6. John Dewey, *Art as Experience* (New York: Capricorn, 1958), pp. 220, 152.

7. Ibid., p. 214.

8. Robin Wood, *Hitchcock's Films* (London and New York: Zwemmer/Barnes, 1965), pp. 114–124.

9. Ibid., p. 119.

10. Stephen C. Pepper, *The Basis of Criticism in the Arts* (Cambridge: Harvard University Press, 1965), p. 57.

11. Ibid. Italics in the original.

12. Ibid., p. 59.

13. Dennis L. White, "The Poetics of Horror," in *Film Genre: Theory and Criticism,* edited by Barry K. Grant (Metuchen, N.J.: Scarecrow Press, 1977), p. 130.

14. See Kawin's "Children of the Light" in Part Two of this volume.

15. Morris Dickstein, "The Aesthetics of Fright," *American Film* 5, no. 10 (September 1980): 35; reprinted in *Planks of Reason: Essays on the Horror Film,* edited by Barry K. Grant (Metuchen, N.J.: Scarecrow Press, 1984), pp. 65–78.

16. Abraham Kaplan, "The Aesthetics of the Popular Arts," *Journal of Aesthetics and Art Criticism* 24, no. 3 (Spring 1966): 354–355.

17. Pepper, *Basis of Criticism,* p. 65.

18. Robin Wood, "Ideology, Genre, Auteur," *Film Comment* 13, no. 1 (January–February 1977): 47–48; reprinted in this volume.

19. Pepper, *Basis of Criticism,* p. 66.

20. Ibid., pp. 120–123.

21. Jean-Louis Comolli and Jean Narboni, "Cinema/Ideology/Criticism (1)," in *Screen Reader 1: Cinema/Ideology/Politics* (London: SEFT, 1977), p. 5.

22. This is demonstrated in a somewhat different context in Jean-Loup Bourget, "Social Implications in the Hollywood Genres," reprinted in this volume.

23. Maurice Yacowar, "An Aesthetic Defense of the Star System in Films," *Quarterly Review of Film Studies* 4, no. 1 (Winter 1979): 41.

24. See Sergei M. Eisenstein, "Form and Content: Practice," in *The Film Sense,* translated and edited by Jay Leyda (New York: Harcourt, Brace & World, 1947), p. 172.

25. D. H. Lawrence, "The Reality of Peace," in *Phoenix: The Posthumous Papers of D. H. Lawrence,* edited by Edward D. McDonald (New York: Viking Press, 1968), p. 677.

26. T. S. Eliot, "Tradition and the Individual Talent," in *Selected Essays of T. S. Eliot* (New York: Harcourt, Brace and World, 1960), pp. 4–5.

27. Christian Metz, "History/Discourse: A Note on Two Voyeurisms," in *Theories of Authorship,* edited by John Caughie (London and Boston: Routledge and Kegan Paul/British Film Institute, 1981), p. 227.

28. Pepper, *Basis of Criticism,* p. 63.

11. Genre and Performance: An Overview

RICHARD DE CORDOVA

Although performance has been central to the definition of a couple of genres, it has had a fairly marginal place in most genre studies. One explanation for this is that genres have been defined largely in terms of their most pertinent features. Thus, work on the musical has quite naturally assigned a central position to performance, while discussions of other genres have focused on other features—visual style, narrative structure, and thematic oppositions. What this explanation fails to explain, however, is why performance is so readily excluded from the field of pertinence in these discussions. Performance is an important part of our experience of such genres as the western, film noir, and the melodrama, and each, it can be argued, renders performance according to genre-specific rules.

The reason for this exclusion undoubtedly lies in the difficulty of the notion of performance itself. Other aspects of film seem to lend themselves to conceptualization in a way that performance does not. Once we have accepted a particular model of narrative structure, for instance, we have little trouble applying it to a wide range of genres. It is not clear that a model of performance exists that affords this kind of generality, however.[1] In fact, performance manifests itself so differently in different genres that it seems to call into question the coherence of the concept itself. Can we talk about acting in melodrama in the same terms that we talk about an Astaire dance number or a Keaton gag? Perhaps, but the diversity of these forms and traditions of performance poses an obstacle to such efforts.

Our notion of performance lacks a certain coherence largely because of the differential existence of these performances in a system of genre. The examination of the ways that different genres circumscribe the form and position of performance in film is an important and underdeveloped area of genre studies. The work to be done in this area must be accompanied by a more general reflection on film performance, however, if performance is to be extricated from its status as a catchall category and emerge as an object of theory.

The following overview of the way in which performance has entered into the definitions of the musical, historical fiction, film noir, and melodrama is offered with this in mind. I am interested in examining both the conceptualization that performance has received in the work on these different genres as well as the claims that have been made in this work concerning the generic specificity of certain forms of performance. Finally, I want to consider the question of whether a more coherent, general account of film performance can be gleaned from the somewhat prismatic treatment it has received in these various genre studies. The musical has prompted the most serious and sustained discussions of film performance.[2] There are at least four different levels at which performance has been figured in these discussions. The first, which appears most explicitly in the work of Jim Collins and Jane Feuer, views performance insofar as it incorporates a specific mode of address, one that distinguishes it both from performances in nonmusicals and nonperformances within the musical itself. This mode of address proceeds through a number of the features of the musical number—the lyrics of the song, the performer's glance into the camera, the proscenium space, and so on. The general argument is that the musical performance involves a more direct mode of address than other cinematic forms. This notion of address is informed by the work of the French linguist Emile Benveniste.[3] In many ways, his distinction between *histoire* and *discours* and the subsequent descriptions of the cinema as *histoire* provided the impetus for the examination of the discursive characteristics of the musical.[4] The musical places an obvious and extraordinary emphasis on the relations it establishes with the spectator, and it does this through performance. The performer seems to address the spectator quite directly.

Performance in the musical has also been approached in terms of its syntagmatic specificity.[5] It not only involves an appeal to the spectator; it also has an identifiable beginning and end and therefore a kind of integrity as a segment. Of course this integrity is particularly overdetermined in the musical—by the length of the song and dance; by the general opposition between singing and dancing, on the one hand, and walking and talking, on the other; and by the specific form of address sustained throughout the performance and discontinued at its end. Thus, the syntagmatic parameters of performance are more clearly marked in the musical than in other genres.

A third level of inquiry concerns the way in which performance fits into the structure and the strategy of the film as a whole. This involves, in part, an examination of the relation between the performance and the narrative sequences surrounding it. The question here typically concerns the form and degree of the performance's motivation within the narrative. This varies within the genre and even within individual films. The song

21. *The Band Wagon:* Performers in musicals seem to address the spectator directly.

may be part of a show, or it may comment indirectly on the fictional situation. Or it may fulfill a narrative function, almost in the Proppian sense, assuming a crucial role in furthering the narrative. The seduction, for instance, is quite frequently articulated through performance in the musical. Above, a number of aspects were noted that separate and distinguish the performance segments of the musical from the narrative. Here we can see a more global strategy that works to integrate these segments back into the narrative's linear movement.

The examination of the way in which performance fits into the strategy of the film as a whole cannot be restricted to these purely linear relations, however. Broader structural and thematic oppositions are articulated through performance in the musical. In films that pose popular entertainment against high art, for instance, the song or dance accrues a symbolic weight through its opposition with other performances within the film. Performance enters quite explicitly into the thematics of the musical as it is taken up in a system of differences that gives it a stable meaning.

The significance of the musical number extends beyond the strategy of the individual film, of course. It has an institutional or ideological function as well, and this constitutes a fourth level at which performance has been considered. Jane Feuer's work[6] has given the most comprehensive view of this function. For her, the musical number is the site at which a whole series of oppositions is negotiated. These oppositions may or may not be figured directly in the fiction. Their importance lies in the way they set efforts to depict film as a folk art against the evidence that film is in fact a carefully engineered, mechanically reproduced product of capitalism. Thus, a kind of disavowal proceeds through the musical performance, which has as its object this capitalistic aspect of the cinema as institution. The song or dance, typically put forward as the spontaneous creation of amateurs, becomes a misleading but extremely malleable metaphor for the cinema as a whole.

This is, of course, a very schematic summary of the considerable work that has been done on performance in the musical. What should be noted here are the different aspects of performance that have been dealt with in this work and how, taken together, they form a fairly comprehensive view of the functioning of performance in the musical. One can note, by contrast, how little work of this sort has been done on other genres.

In fact, my attention to the historical fiction is not due to the existence of any kind of general account of performance in the genre but rather to a few restricted comments that Jean-Louis Comolli makes in his article "Historical Fiction: A Body Too Much."[7] As the title indicates, Comolli is interested in the inscription of the body within the genre. He argues that two bodies potentially coexist in any fiction film—the body acting and the body acted (actor and character). In most films, he claims, there is a fairly unproblematical fit between the two, largely because the character, being fictional, has no existence *outside* of the actor's body. The situation is somewhat more complicated in the historical film, however; the character has a real historical referent, and thus a clear disjunction between the two bodies is evident from the start.

Comolli's emphasis is on the effect this has on structuring the spectator's belief. In any fiction film the spectator knows very well that the actor and character are not the same, yet at the same time must believe that they are for the film to work.[8] This denegation proceeds with a special difficulty in the historical fiction since the historical character can never be fully embodied by the actor. However, what results is not a failure of belief but rather a more direct play upon it.

The importance of Comolli's article lies both in its identification of the split between actor and character and in its conceptualization of the mechanisms of belief that this split sets in motion. Comolli's claim that historical fiction involves particular difficulties in the negotiation of the split between character and actor is well founded. However, his assumption that the split is resolved more simply in other films is somewhat misguided. The problem is that Comolli generally stresses the presence of the body to the exclusion of its activity. Here, a distinction must be made between casting (something which remains constant in a film) and performance (something which vacillates in a film and is emphasized only at certain points). The two are obviously related. But Comolli's emphasis is on the effect that Pierre Renoir has in *La Marseillaise* (Jean Renoir, 1938) solely by virtue of his *appearance* as Louis XVI. Further attention to the presence of the body, in the context of genre studies, might lead to an investigation of the way in which certain actors appear as icons of specific genres. John Wayne's association with the western is among the clearest examples of this. However, although this emphasis on casting is certainly a legitimate one, it stops short of the question of performance, which is a matter not so much of the presence of the body as its activity. In fact, it is along these lines that we can see the split between character and actor assert itself in films other than historical fictions. In those moments in films in which acting comes to the fore and is noticed, there is a split between actor and character as agents of two different actions. At the end of *Dark Victory* (Edmund Goulding, 1936), for instance, the spectator's recognition and appreciation of the performance depends on the simultaneous existence of the actions of two figures. The actor (Bette Davis) acts while the character (Judith Traherne) responds to the fictional situation, telling her friend Ann to leave her to her death. The body that appears on the screen is not at odds with another historical body in this case (Judith is fictional, without historical referent); rather, these two agents are disjoined within the same body. This splitting of agency at particular moments in a film involves more complex mechanisms of belief than Comolli allows for.

The problem of performance in film noir has not been dealt with by anyone in any detail. However, many of the aspects that have been prominent in the description of the genre have a direct bearing on it. The voice-over, for instance, though it has been approached largely in terms of its narrational function, plays a crucial role in structuring performance.[9] Categories that have entered into the discussion of performance in other genres, such as address, are applicable to the voice-over in film noir. The voice-over, like the musical number, involves a direct address to the spectator. Whether it is motivated within the fiction, such as the confession to a coworker, for example, in *Double Indemnity* (Billy Wilder, 1944) or not, the voice-over always exceeds the bounds of *histoire* as described by Benveniste and Metz. It may comment on a chronology of actions, but it is never reducible to one. The voice-over is defined, in fact, by its discur-

22. *Sunset Boulevard:* The voice-over is by the dead Joe Gillis (William Holden).

sive characteristics; it is put forward as a performance for someone—implicitly, at least, the spectator.

A second area of inquiry follows from Comolli's work and concerns the way the body is inscribed in film noir. The voice-over in film noir works to problematize the body by introducing a variety of disjunctions between the bodily image and the voice.[10] One result of this is an added emphasis on the performative aspects of the voice as it is freed from its supposedly realistic link with the image and assigned a more active role in relation to it. A particularly self-conscious example of the possibilities of disjoining voice and body occurs in *Sunset Boulevard* (Wilder, 1950): the voice-over is ascribed to a man we see floating dead in a swimming pool at the beginning of the film.

This brings up another major issue that has not yet been touched upon: the relation between performance and specific features of the cinematic apparatus. In film noir it is clear that performance functions, in part, through the split between sound and image. However, one can also note in this and other genres instances in which such devices as lighting, framing, camera movement, and the close-up ally themselves with the body of the actor and work to produce effects of performance. These forms of alliance need to be described more carefully and their generic features delineated.

The voice-over is only one site at which performance manifests itself in film noir. Performance has a more general function in the fictional strategy of these films, one that relates to the problem of verisimilitude and the negotiation of the spectator's belief. In his work on the detective novel, Todorov argues that the production of any discourse involves relations of verisimilitude, but that the detective novel specifically treats verisimilitude as its object and theme.[11] This theme is articulated particularly strongly through performance in the detective film (and more generally in film noir). We have noted that a certain problem of belief is inherent in the split between actor and character in the fiction film; at the level of enunciation it is taken up by the fiction as well in film noir.

The dynamics of this can be seen in the example of *The Maltese Falcon* (John Huston, 1941). When O'Shaughnessy first appears in Spade's office, she gives a performance that, if we recognize it as such (by calling into play the aesthetic category of acting), we must attribute to the actor, Mary Astor. Later, however, we find out that it was not Astor's performance but rather that of the character O'Shaughnessy, as she tried to deceive both Archer and Spade. We can see a fairly active play on the division between actor and character here, but the performance is finally grounded in the character. The problems of verisimilitude and belief at the level of the enunciation become couched in the fiction in a series of questions that bear upon the movement of truth in the film. Is the character lying or not lying, performing or not performing? Performance, as it is given a place in the diegesis of film noir, essentially follows a model of dissimulation.

This dissimulation would have little force in film noir if it was not read against another model of performance: that of performance as expression. If this model of performance is not properly melodramatic, then it at least receives its fullest rendering within the melodrama. The genre places an overriding emphasis on the inner emotional states of the characters, and it works to represent them through elements of the mise-en-scène. The scenic excesses that often arise in this effort have been the object of a great deal of interest. For example, Geoffrey Nowell-Smith has attempted to explain these excesses through an analogy with Freud's notion of conversion hysteria.[12] He claims that the emotional material that cannot be expressed in the actions of the character finds its expression in the body of the film. What has not been sufficiently explored in this regard is the relation between the body of the film in this sense and the body within the film. This latter body, as has been noted elsewhere, belongs

23. *The Maltese Falcon:* Is Brigid O'Shaughnessy (Mary Astor) lying or telling the truth, performing or being?

ambiguously to both character and actor. As character, this body is what the mise-en-scène acts upon, the focus of the represented emotion; as actor, however, it is an active part of the mise-en-scène which works in alliance with such features as decor and music to produce the other, fictional body. The split between these two bodies and their relation to other features of the cinematic language is not fixed at the beginning of the film but rather put in process throughout it. It is primarily at those moments of the melodrama when the performative dimension comes to the fore that the body of the actor becomes an issue in the film, and, at those moments, the spectator is involved in a particularly complex play of identification and belief.

This results in a specific textual effect, but it also relates to the broader institutional functioning of performance in the melodrama. Performance is perhaps the principal critical standard by which audiences have judged films, and there is little doubt that the melodrama, in its emphasis on acting as expression, has provided the ideal object for the application of such a standard. The melodrama has, in fact, been central to the cinema's

24. *Bigger Than Life:* Madness in the melodrama is strongly marked as performance.

claim for aesthetic legitimacy because it has supported, more than any other genre, the claim that film incorporates the art of acting.[13]

Another question that seems important to note here concerns the fictional conditions under which performance manifests itself in the melodrama. It is clear that certain melodramatic scenes are written as showcases for performance. What is striking is how often these scenes engage the same types of fictional material. Suffering, hysteria, and madness not only become topics of melodrama; they also mark out a highly conventionalized space within which the scene of performance can unfold. *Bigger than Life* (Nicholas Ray, 1956), *Splendor in the Grass* (Elia Kazan, 1961), and *Possessed* (Curtis Bernhardt, 1947) are good examples of this. In each, a character's mental disturbance in the fiction is accompanied, at the level of the enunciation, by the placement of the actor in a number of strongly marked scenes of performance.

The subject of enunciation in the cinema is not a coherent, unitary position. The sites at which one might locate an organizing productivity within a given film are multiple, and the negotiation of these different sites becomes crucial both for the strategy of the individual film and the institution of the cinema at large. The question of performance specifically concerns the way in which the actor enters into the enunciative apparatus of the cinema as subject—under what conditions and within what kind of process.

Genre studies, insofar as they have dealt with this problem, have extended discussions of performance beyond the question of the talent of the individual performer and have attempted to outline broader generic conventions that determine the place of the performer as subject within a film. Unfortunately, as we have seen, these attempts have been too fleeting and unfocused to provide a general account of performance and its role within an economy of genres. If such an account is to be arrived at, at least two lines of inquiry must be pursued. First, there must be a close analysis of the way in which performance is structured within particular films and particular genres. The kind of detail that textual analysis has brought to discussions of the narrative structure of films needs to be brought to discussions of performance as well. Second, a more comparative approach to the problem of genre and performance needs to be taken. As it stands, the work in this area exists as a number of isolated and unnecessarily circumscribed claims. The concept of performance needs to be rescued from this dispersed existence and given to a common field of questions. For instance, does performance generally involve a shift in address, and, if so, how does address function in genres other than the musical? How does the musical negotiate the shift between actor and character that Comolli describes in his work on historical fiction? The answers to these and other questions suggested by this overview should give us a much more precise sense not only of performance but of genre as well.

Notes

1. A body of analytical work on performance has begun to appear recently, however. The special issue of *Cinema Journal 20*, no. 1 (Fall 1980), is of particular note. See also Charles Affron, *Star Acting: Gish, Garbo and Davis* (New York: E. P. Dutton, 1977), and Virginia Wright Wexman, "Kinesics and Film Acting: Humphrey Bogart in *The Maltese Falcon* and *The Big Sleep*," *Journal of Popular Film and Television 7*, no. 1 (1978): 42–55.

2. See, for instance, Jim Collins, "Toward Defining a Matrix of the Musical Comedy: The Place of the Spectator within the Textual Mechanisms," in *Genre: The Musical,* edited by Rick Altman (London: Routledge and Kegan Paul, 1981), pp. 134–146; Jane Feuer, *The Hollywood Musical* (Bloomington: Indiana University Press, 1982); Patricia Mellencamp, "Spectacle and Spectator: Looking through the American Musical Comedy," *Ciné-Tracts* I (Summer 1977): 28–35; and Dana B. Polan, "It Could Be Oedipus Rex: Denial and Difference in *The Band*

Wagon, or the American Musical as American Gothic," *Ciné-Tracts,* no. 14 (Summer 1981): 15–26.

3. Emile Benveniste, *Problems in General Linguistics* (Miami: University of Miami Press, 1971).

4. Benveniste argues that *discours* (discourse) contains a number of formal markings that stake out the position of its producer (the "I") and its receiver (the "you"). *Discours* is therefore characterized by a clearly marked system of address. *Histoire* (story, history), on the other hand, effaces all of the marks that would point to the conditions of its own production. As Benveniste says, "There is . . . no longer even a narrator. The events are set forth chronologically, as they occurred. No one speaks here; the events seem to narrate themselves" (p. 208). Christian Metz has argued that the classical cinema functions as *histoire.* See "Story/Discourse (A Note on Two Kinds of Voyeurism)," in *The Imaginary Signifier* (Bloomington: Indiana University Press, 1982), pp. 89–98.

5. See, for instance, Mellencamp, "Spectacle and Spectator."

6. See Feuer, *The Hollywood Musical.*

7. Jean-Louis Comolli, "Historical Fiction: A Body Too Much," *Screen 19,* no. 2 (Summer 1978): 41–53.

8. Comolli's work on the negotiation of the spectator's belief (and the work of Metz before him) draws heavily on O. Mannoni, *Clefs pour l'imaginaire ou l'autre scène* (Paris: Editions de Seuil, 1969).

9. For an excellent account of the general functioning of the voice-over, see Mary Ann Doane, "The Voice in the Cinema: The Articulation of Body and Space," *Yale French Studies 60* (1980): 33–50.

10. Alan Williams has noted the importance of a different kind of disjunction between voice and image in "The Musical Film and Recorded Popular Music," in *Genre: The Musical,* pp. 147–158.

11. Tzvetan Todorov, "Du vraisemblable que l'on ne saurait éviter," *Communications 11* (1968): 145–147.

12. Geoffrey Nowell-Smith, "Minnelli and Melodrama," *Screen 18,* no. 2 (Summer 1977): 113–118.

13. For an account of the role of acting in establishing the cinema's aesthetic legitimacy after 1907, see Richard de Cordova, "The Emergence of the Star System in America," *Wide Angle 6,* no. 4 (Winter 1984): 4–13.

12. Film Bodies: Gender, Genre, and Excess

LINDA WILLIAMS

When my seven-year-old son and I go to the movies, we often select from among categories of films that promise to be sensational to give our bodies an actual physical jolt. He calls these movies that seem to grab and wrench our bodies "gross." My son and I agree that the fun of "gross" movies is in their display of sensations that are on the edge of respectable. Where we disagree—and where we as a culture often disagree, along lines of gender, age, or sexual orientation—is in which movies are over the edge, too "gross."

To my son, the good "gross" movies are those with scary monsters like Freddy Krueger (of the *Nightmare on Elm Street* series) who rip apart teenagers, especially teenage girls. These movies both fascinate and scare him. I have noticed that he is actually more interested in talking about than seeing them. A second category, one that I like and my son doesn't, is that of sad movies that make you cry. These are gross in their focus on unseemly emotions—emotions that may remind him too acutely of his own powerlessness as a child but that I admit to enjoying in a guilty, perverse sort of way. A third category, of both intense interest and disgust to my son (he makes the puke sign when speaking of it), he can only describe euphemistically as "the *K* word." *K* is for kissing. To a seven-year-old boy, nothing is more obscene than kissing.

There is no accounting for taste, especially in the realm of the "gross." As a culture, we most often invoke the term to designate excesses that we wish to exclude; to say, for example, which of the Robert Mapplethorpe photos we draw the line at but not to say what form and structure and function operate within the representations deemed excessive. Because so much attention goes to determining where to draw the line, discussions of the gross are often a highly confused hodgepodge of different categories of excess. For example, pornography is today more often deemed excessive for its violence than for its sex, while horror films are excessive in their displacements of sex into violence. In contrast, melodramas are deemed excessive for their gender and sex-linked pathos, for their naked displays of emotion. Ann Douglas once referred to the genre of romance fiction as "soft-core emotional porn for women." [1]

Alone or in combination, heavy doses of sex, violence, and emotion are dismissed by one faction or another as having no logic or reason for existence beyond their power to excite. Gratuitous sex, gratuitous violence and terror, gratuitous emotion are frequent epithets hurled at the phenomenon of the "sensational" in pornography, horror, and melodrama. This essay explores the notion that there may be some value in thinking about the form, function, and system of seemingly gratuitous excesses in these three genres. For if, as it seems, sex, violence, and emotion are fundamental elements of the sensational effects of these three types of films, the designation "gratuitous" is itself gratuitous. My hope, therefore, is that by thinking comparatively about all three "gross" and sensational film body genres, we might be able to get beyond the mere fact of sensation to explore its system and structure as well as their effects on the bodies of spectators.

BODY GENRES

The repetitive formulas and spectacles of film genres are often defined by their differences from the classical realist style of narrative cinema. These classical films have been characterized as efficient, action-centered, goal-oriented linear narratives driven by the desire of a single protagonist, involving one or two lines of action, and leading to definitive closure. In their influential study of the classical Hollywood cinema, Bordwell, Thompson, and Staiger call this the Classical Hollywood style.[2]

As Rick Altman has noted in a recent article, both genre study and the study of the somewhat more nebulous category of melodrama have long been hampered by assumptions about the classical nature of the dominant narrative to which melodrama and some individual genres have been opposed.[3] Altman argues that Bordwell, Thompson, and Staiger, who locate the Classical Hollywood style in the linear, progressive form of the Hollywood narrative, cannot accommodate "melodramatic" attributes like spectacle, episodic presentation, or dependence on coincidence except as limited exceptions, or "play," within the dominant linear causality of the classical.

Altman writes, "Unmotivated events, rhythmic montage, highlighted parallelism, overlong spectacles—these are the excesses in the classical narrative system that alert us to the existence of a competing logic, a second voice." [4] Altman, whose own work on the movie musical has necessarily relied upon analyses of seemingly "excessive" spectacles and parallel constructions, thus makes a strong case for the need to recognize the possibility that excess may itself be organized as a system. Yet analyses of systems of excess have been much slower to emerge in the genres whose nonlinear spectacles have centered more directly upon the gross display of the human body. Pornography and horror films are two such systems of excess. Pornography is the lowest in cultural esteem, gross-out horror is next to lowest.

Melodrama, however, refers to a much broader category of films and a much larger system of excess. It would not be unreasonable, in fact, to consider all three of these genres under the extended rubric of melodrama, considered as a filmic mode of stylistic and emotional excess that stands in contrast to more "dominant" modes of realistic, goal-oriented narrative. In this extended sense, melodrama can encompass a broad range of films marked by "lapses" in realism, by "excesses" of spectacle and displays of primal, even infantile, emotions, and by narratives that seem circular and repetitive. Much of the interest of melodrama to film scholars over the last fifteen years originates in the sense that the form exceeds the normative system of much narrative cinema. I shall limit my focus here, however, to a narrower sense of melodrama, leaving the broader category of the sensational to encompass the three genres I wish to consider. Thus, partly for purposes of contrast with pornography, the melodrama I will consider here will consist of the form that has most interested feminist critics—that of "the woman's film," or "weepie." These are films addressed to women in their traditional status under patriarchy—as wives, mothers, abandoned lovers—or in their traditional status as bodily hysteria or excess, as in the frequent case of the woman "afflicted" with a deadly or debilitating disease.[5]

What are the pertinent features of bodily excess shared by these three "gross" genres? First, there is the spectacle of a body caught in the grips of intense sensation or emotion. Carol J. Clover, speaking primarily of horror films and pornography, has called films that privilege the sensational "body genres."[6] I am expanding Clover's notion of low body genres to include the sensation of overwhelming pathos in the "weepie." The body spectacle is featured most sensationally in pornography's portrayal of orgasm, in horror's portrayal of violence and terror, and in melodrama's portrayal of weeping. I propose that an investigation of the visual and narrative pleasures found in the portrayal of these three types of excess could be important to a new direction in genre criticism that would take as its point of departure—rather than as an unexamined assumption —questions of gender construction as well as gender address in relation to basic sexual fantasies.

Another pertinent feature shared by these body genres is the focus on what could probably best be called a form of ecstasy. While the classical meaning of the original Greek word is insanity and bewilderment, more contemporary meanings suggest components of direct or indirect sexual excitement and rapture, a rapture that informs even the pathos of melodrama.

Visually, each of these ecstatic excesses could be said to share a quality of uncontrollable convulsion or spasm—of the body "beside itself" in the grips of sexual pleasure, fear and terror, and overpowering sadness. Aurally, excess is marked by recourse not to the coded articulations of language but to inarticulate cries—of pleasure in porn, screams of fear in horror, sobs of anguish in melodrama.

Looking, and listening, to these bodily ecstasies, we can also notice something else that these genres seem to share: though quite differently gendered with respect to their targeted audiences—with pornography aimed, presumably, at active men and melodramatic weepies aimed, presumably, at passive women, and with contemporary gross-out horror aimed at adolescents careening wildly between the two masculine and feminine poles—in each of these genres the bodies of women figured on the screen have functioned traditionally as the primary *embodiments* of pleasure, fear, and pain.

In other words, even when the pleasure of viewing has traditionally been constructed for masculine spectators, as in most traditional, heterosexual pornography, it is the female body in the grips of an out-of-control ecstasy that has offered the most sensational sight. So the bodies of women have tended to function, ever since the eighteenth-century origins of these genres in the Marquis de Sade, Gothic fiction, and the novels of Richardson, as both the *moved* and the *moving*. It is thus through what Foucault has called the sexual saturation of the female body that audiences of all sorts have received some of their most powerful sensations.[7]

There are, of course, other film genres that both portray and affect the sensational body—e.g., thrillers, musicals, comedies. I suggest, however, that the film genres with especially low cultural status—which have seemed to exist as excesses to the system of even the popular genres—are not simply those that sensationally display bodies on the screen and register effects in the bodies of spectators. Rather, what may especially mark these body genres as low is the perception that the body of the spectator is caught up in an almost involuntary mimicry of the emotion or sensation of the body on the screen, along with the fact that the body displayed is female. An example of another "body genre" that, despite its concern with all manner of gross activities and body functions, has not been deemed gratuitously excessive is physical clown comedy—probably because the reaction of the audience does not mimic the sensations experienced by the central clown. Indeed, it is almost a rule that the audience's physical reaction of laughter does not coincide with the often deadpan reactions of the clown.

In the body genres I am isolating here, however, the success of these

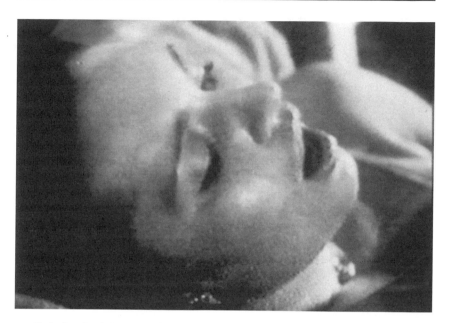

25. *Babylon Pink* (1979): The pornographic stereotype of the sexually ecstatic woman.

genres often seems to be measured by the degree to which the audience sensation mimics what is seen on the screen. Whether this mimicry is exact—e.g., whether the spectator at the porn film actually experiences orgasm, whether the spectator at the horror film actually shudders in fear, whether the spectator of the melodrama actually dissolves in tears—the success of these genres seems a self-evident matter of measuring bodily response. Examples of such measurement can be readily observed: in the "peter meter" capsule reviews in *Hustler* magazine, which measure the power of a porn film in degrees of erection of little cartoon penises; in horror films that are measured in terms of screams, fainting, and heart attacks in the audience (consider the career of horror-producer William Castle and such films as his 1959 *The Tingler*); and in the longstanding tradition of measuring women's films in terms of one-, two-, or three-handkerchief movies.

What seems to bracket these particular genres from others is an apparent lack of proper aesthetic distance, a sense of overinvolvement in sensation and emotion. We feel manipulated by these texts, an impression that the very colloquialisms "tearjerker" and "fearjerker" express—and to which we could add pornography's even cruder sense as texts to which some people might be inclined to "jerk off." The rhetoric of violence of the jerk suggests the extent to which viewers feel too directly, too viscerally, manipulated by the text in specifically gendered ways. Mary Ann Doane, for example, writing about the most genteel of these jerkers—the maternal melodrama—equates the violence of this emotion to a kind of "textual rape" of the targeted female viewer, who is "feminized through pathos." [8]

Feminist critics of pornography often evoke similar figures of sexual/ textual violence when describing the operation of this genre. Robin Morgan's famous slogan "Pornography is the theory, and rape is the practice" is well known.[9] Implicit in this slogan is the notion that women are the objectified victims of pornographic representations, that the image of the sexually ecstatic woman so important to the genre is a celebration of female victimization and a prelude to female victimization in real life.

Less well known, but related, is the observation of the critic of horror films, James Twitchell, who notices that the Latin *horrere* means "to bristle." He describes the way the nape hair stands on end during moments of shivering excitement. The aptly named Twitchell thus describes a kind of erection of the hair founded in the conflicting desires of "fight and flight."[10] While male victims in horror films may shudder and scream as well, it has long been a dictum of the genre that women make the best victims. "Torture the women!" was the famous advice given by Alfred Hitchcock.[11]

In the classic horror film the terror of the female victim shares the spectacle along with the monster. Fay Wray and the mechanized monster that made her scream in *King Kong* (Merian C. Cooper and Ernest B. Schoedsack, 1933) is a familiar example of the classic form. Janet Leigh in the shower in *Psycho* (Alfred Hitchcock, 1960) is a familiar example of a transition to a more sexually explicit form of the tortured and terrorized woman. And her daughter, Jamie Lee Curtis in *Halloween* (John Carpenter, 1978), can serve as the more contemporary version of the terrorized woman victim. In both of these later films the spectacle of the monster seems to take second billing to the increasingly numerous victims slashed by the sexually disturbed but entirely human monsters.

In the woman's film a well-known classic is the long-suffering mother of the two early versions of *Stella Dallas* (Henry King, 1925; King Vidor, 1937) who sacrifices herself for her daughter's upward mobility. Contemporary filmgoers could recently see Bette Midler going through the same sacrifice and loss in the film *Stella* (John Erman, 1990). Debra Winger in *Terms of Endearment* (James L. Brooks, 1983) is another familiar example of this maternal pathos.

With these genre stereotypes in mind we should now ask about the status of bodily excess in each of these genres. Is it simply the unseemly, "gra-

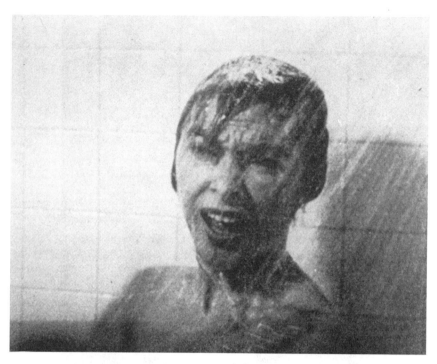

26. *Psycho:* Horror offers the female victim as spectacle.

tuitous" presence of the sexually ecstatic woman, the tortured woman, the weeping woman—and the accompanying presence of the sexual fluids, the blood and the tears that flow from her body and that are presumably mimicked by spectators—that marks the excess of each type of film? How shall we think of these bodily displays in relation to one another as a system of excess in the popular film? And, finally, how excessive are they really?

The psychoanalytic system of analysis that has been so influential to film study in general and to feminist film theory and criticism in particular has been remarkably ambivalent about the status of excess in its major tools of analysis. The categories of fetishism, voyeurism, and sadism and masochism frequently invoked to describe the pleasures of film spectatorship are, by definition, perversions. Perversions are usually defined as gratuitous sexual excesses, specifically as excesses that result when "proper" end goals are deflected onto substitute goals or objects— fetishes instead of genitals, looking instead of touching, and so forth. Yet the perverse pleasures of film viewing are hardly gratuitous. They have

27. *Stella Dallas:* Stella (Barbara Stanwyck) transcendent in self-sacrifice.

been considered so basic that they have often been presented as norms. What is a film, after all, without voyeurism? Yet, at the same time, feminist critics have asked, what is the position of women within this pleasure geared to a presumably sadistic "male gaze"?[12] To what extent is she its victim? Is the orgasmic woman of pornography and the tortured woman of horror merely in the service of the sadistic male gaze? And is the weeping woman of melodrama appealing to the abnormal perversions of masochism in female viewers?

These questions point to the ambiguity of the terms of perversion used to describe the normal pleasures of film viewing. Without attempting to go into any of the complexities of this discussion here—a discussion that must ultimately relate to the status of the term "perversion" in theories of sexuality themselves—let me simply suggest the value of not invoking the perversions as terms of condemnation. As even the most cursory reading of Freud shows, sexuality is, by definition, perverse. The "aims" and "objects" of sexual desire are often obscure and inherently substitutive. Unless we are willing to see reproduction as the common goal of the sexual drive, then we have to admit, as Jonathan Dollimore has put it, that we are all perverts. Dollimore's goal of retrieving the "concept of perversion as a category of cultural analysis," as a structure intrinsic to all sexuality rather than extrinsic to it, is crucial to any attempt to understand cultural forms—such as our three body genres—in which fantasy predominates.[13]

STRUCTURES OF PERVERSION IN THE "FEMALE BODY GENRES"

Each of the three body genres I have isolated hinges on the spectacle of a "sexually saturated" female body, and each offers what many feminist critics would agree to be spectacles of feminine victimization. But this victimization is very different in each type of film and cannot be accounted for simply by pointing to the sadistic power and pleasure of masculine subjects punishing or dominating feminine objects.

Many feminists have pointed to the victimization of the woman performers of pornography who must actually do the acts depicted in the film as well as to the victimization of characters within the films.[14] Pornography, in this view, is fundamentally sadistic. In weepies, on the other hand, feminists have pointed to the spectacles of intense suffering and loss as masochistic.

While feminists have often pointed to the women victims in horror films who suffer simulated torture and mutilation as victims of sadism,[15] more recent feminist work has suggested that the horror film may present an interesting, and perhaps instructive, case of oscillation between masochistic and sadistic poles. This argument, advanced by Clover, has suggested that pleasure, for a masculine-identified viewer, oscillates between identifying with the initial passive powerlessness of the abject and terrorized girl-victim of horror and her later, active empowerment.

This argument holds that when the girl-victim of a film like *Halloween* finally grabs the phallic knife, or ax, or chain saw to turn the tables on the monster-killer, viewer identification shifts from an "abject terror gendered feminine" to an active power with bisexual components. A gender-confused monster is foiled, often symbolically castrated by an "androgynous final girl."[16] In slasher films, identification with victimization is a roller-coaster ride of sadomasochistic thrills.

We could thus initially schematize the perverse pleasures of these genres in the following way: pornography's appeal to its presumed male viewers would be characterized as sadistic, horror films' appeal to the emerging sexual identities of its (frequently adolescent) spectators would be sadomasochistic, and women's films' appeal to presumed female viewers would be masochistic.

The masochistic component of viewing pleasure for women has been the most problematic term of perversion for feminist critics. It is interesting, for example, that most of our important studies of masochism—for example, those by Gilles Deleuze, Kaja Silverman, and Gaylyn Studlar—have all focused on the exoticism of masculine masochism rather than the familiarity of female masochism. Masochistic pleasure for women has paradoxically seemed either too normal—too much the normal yet intolerable condition of women—or too perverse to be taken seriously as pleasure.[17]

There is thus a real need to be clearer than we have been about what is in masochism for women—how power and pleasure operate in fantasies of domination that appeal to women. There is an equal need to be clearer than we have been about what is in sadism for men. Here the initial opposition between these two most gendered genres—women's weepies and male heterosexual pornography—needs to be complicated. I have argued elsewhere, for example, that pornography has been allied too simplistically with a purely sadistic fantasy structure. Indeed, those troubling films and videos that deploy instruments of torture on the bodies of women have been allied so completely with masculine viewing pleasures that we have not paid enough attention to their appeal to women, except to condemn such appeal as false consciousness.[18]

One important complication of the initial schema I have outlined would thus be to take a lesson from Clover's more bisexual model of viewer identification in horror film and stress the sadomasochistic component of each of these body genres through their various appropriations of melodramatic fantasies that are, in fact, basic to each. All of these genres could, for example, be said to offer highly melodramatic enactments of sexually charged, if not sexually explicit, relations. The subgenre of sadomasochistic pornography, with its suspension of pleasure over the course of prolonged sessions of dramatic suffering, offers a particularly intense, almost parodic, enactment of the classic melodramatic scenario of the passive and innocent female victim suffering at the hands of a leering villain. We can also see in horror films of tortured women a similar melodramatization of the innocent victim. An important difference, of course, lies in the component of the victim's overt sexual pleasure in the scenario of domination.

But even in the most extreme displays of feminine masochistic suffering, there is always a component of either power or pleasure for the woman victim. We have seen how identification in slasher horror films seems to oscillate between powerlessness and power. In sadomasochistic pornography and in melodramatic weepies, feminine subject positions appear to be constructed in ways that achieve a modicum of power and pleasure within the given limits of patriarchal constraints on women. It is worth noting as well that *non*sadomasochistic pornography has historically been one of the few types of popular film that has not punished women for actively pursuing their sexual pleasure.

In the subgenre of sadomasochistic pornography, however, the female masochist in the scenario must be devious in her pursuit of pleasure. She plays the part of passive sufferer in order to obtain pleasure. Under a patriarchal double standard that has rigorously separated the sexually passive "good girl" from the sexually active "bad girl," masochistic role play offers a way out of this dichotomy by combining the good girl with the bad: the passive "good girl" can prove to her witnesses (the superego who is her torturer) that she does not will the pleasure that she receives. Yet the sexually active "bad girl" enjoys this pleasure and has knowingly arranged to endure the pain that earns it. The cultural law that decides some girls are good and others are bad is not defeated, but within its terms pleasure has been negotiated and "paid for" with a pain that conditions it. The "bad girl" is punished, but in return she receives pleasure.[19]

In contrast, the sadomasochistic teen horror film kills off the sexually active "bad girls," allowing only the nonsexual "good girls" to survive. But these good girls are, as if in compensation, remarkably active, to the point of appropriating phallic power to themselves. It is as if this phallic power is granted so long as it is rigorously separated from phallic or any other sort of pleasure. For these pleasures spell sure death in this genre.

In the melodramatic woman's film we might think to encounter a purer form of masochism on the part of female viewers. Yet even here the female viewer does not seem to be invited to identify wholly with the sacrificing good woman, but rather with a variety of different subject positions, including those which empathically look on at her own suffering. While I would not argue that there is a very strong sadistic component to these films, I do argue that there is a strong mixture of passivity and activity—and a bisexual oscillation between the poles of each—in even this genre.

For example, the woman viewer of a maternal melodrama such as *Terms of Endearment* or *Steel Magnolias* (Herbert Ross, 1989) does not simply identify with the suffering and dying heroines of each. She may equally identify with the powerful matriarchs, the surviving mothers who preside over the deaths of their daughters, experiencing the exhilaration and triumph of survival. The point is simply that identification is neither fixed nor entirely passive.

While there are certainly masculine and feminine, active and passive,

An Anatomy of Film Bodies

Genre	Pornography	Horror	Melodrama
Bodily excess	Sex	Violence	Emotion
Ecstasy —shown by	Ecstatic sex Orgasm Ejaculation	Ecstatic violence Shudders Blood	Ecstatic woe Sobs Tears
Presumed audience	Men (active)	Adolescent boys (active/passive)	Girls, women (passive)
Perversion	Sadism	Sadomasochism	Masochism
Originary fantasy	Seduction	Castration	Origin
Temporality of fantasy	On time!	Too early!	Too late!
Genre cycles "Classic"	Stag films (1920s– 1940s): *The Casting Couch*	"Classic" horror: *Dracula* *Frankenstein* *Dr. Jekyll and Mr. Hyde* *King Kong*	"Classic" women's films Maternal melodrama: *Stella Dallas* *Mildred Pierce* Romance: *Back Street* *Letter from an Unknown Woman*
Contemporary	Feature-length hard-core porn: *Deep Throat* *The Punishment of Anne* Femme Productions *Bisexual* *Trisexual*	Post-*Psycho*: *The Texas Chainsaw Massacre* *Halloween* *Dressed to Kill* *Videodrome*	Male and female "weepies": *Steel Magnolias* *Stella* *Dad*

poles to the left and right of the positions that we might assign to these three genres (see accompanying table), the subject positions that appear to be constructed by each of the genres are not as gender-linked and as gender-fixed as has often been supposed. This is especially true today as hard-core pornography gains appeal with women viewers. Perhaps the most recent proof in this genre of the breakdown of rigid dichotomies of masculine and feminine, active and passive, is the creation of an alternative, oscillating category of address to viewers. In addition to the well-known heterosexual hard core, which once addressed itself exclusively to heterosexual men and now has begun to address itself to heterosexual couples and women as well, and in addition to homosexual hard core, which has addressed itself to gay and (to a lesser extent) lesbian viewers, there is now a new category of video called bisexual. In these videos men do it with women, women do it with women, men do it with men, and then all do it with one another—in the process breaking down a fundamental taboo against male-to-male sex.[20]

A related interpenetration of the formerly more separate categories of masculine and feminine is seen in what has come to be known in some quarters as the "male weepie." These are mainstream melodramas engaged in the activation of the previously repressed emotions of men and in breaking the taboos against male-to-male hugs and embraces. The father-son embrace that concludes *Ordinary People* (Robert Redford, 1980) is exemplary. More recently, paternal weepies have begun to compete with the maternal—such as the conventional *Dad* (David Goldberg, 1989) or the less conventional *Twin Peaks* (David Lynch, 1990–1991), with its wild paternal displays.

The point is certainly not to admire the "sexual freedom" of this new fluidity and oscillation—the new femininity of men who hug and the new masculinity of women who leer—as if it represented any ultimate defeat of phallic power. Rather, the more useful lesson might be to see what this new fluidity and oscillation permits in the construction of feminine viewing pleasures once thought not to exist at all. (It is instructive, for example, that women characters in the new bisexual pornography are shown verbally articulating their visual pleasure as they watch men perform sex with men.)

The deployment of sex, violence, and emotion would thus seem to have very precise functions in these body genres. Like all popular genres, they address persistent problems in our culture, in our sexualities, in our very identities. The deployment of sex, violence, and emotion is thus in no way gratuitous and in no way strictly limited to each of these genres. Each deployment of sex, violence, and emotion is a cultural form of problem solving; each draws upon related sensations to address its problems. As I have argued in *Hard Core,* pornographic films now tend to present sex as a problem, and the performance of more, different, or better sex is posed as the solution.[21] In horror a violence related to sexual difference is the problem; more violence related to sexual difference is also the solution. In women's films the pathos of loss is the problem; repetitions and variations of this loss are the generic solution.

STRUCTURES OF FANTASY

All of these problems are linked to gender identity and might be usefully explored as genres of gender fantasy. It is appropriate to ask, then, not only about the structures of perversion but also about the structures of fantasy in each of these genres. In doing so, we need to be clear about the nature of fantasy itself. For fantasies are not, as is sometimes thought, wish-fulfilling linear narratives of mastery and control leading to closure and the attainment of desire. They are marked, rather, by the prolongation of desire and by the lack of fixed position with respect to the objects and events fantasized.

In their classic essay "Fantasy and the Origins of Sexuality," Jean Laplanche and J. B. Pontalis argue that fantasy is not so much a narrative that enacts the quest for an object of desire as it is a setting for desire, a place where conscious and unconscious, self and other, part and whole meet. Fantasy is the place where "desubjectified" subjectivities oscillate between self and other, occupying no fixed place in the scenario.[22]

In the three body genres discussed here, this fantasy component has probably been better understood in horror film, a genre often understood as belonging to the "fantastic." However, it has been less well understood in pornography and melodrama. Because these genres display fewer fantastic special effects and because they rely on certain conventions of realism—e.g., the activation of social problems in melodrama; the representation of real sexual acts in pornography—they seem less obviously fantastic. Yet the usual criticisms—that these forms are improbable, that they lack psychological complexity and narrative closure, and that they are repetitious—become moot as evaluation if they are considered intrinsic to their engagement with fantasy.

There is a link, in other words, between the appeal of these forms and their ability to address, if never really to "solve," basic problems related to sexual identity. Here I would like to forge a connection between Laplanche and Pontalis's structural understanding of fantasies as myths of origin that try to cover the discrepancy between two moments in time and the distinctive temporal structure of these particular genres. Laplanche and Pontalis argue that fantasies which are myths of origin address the insoluble problem of the discrepancy between an irrecoverable original experience presumed to have actually taken place—as in the case of the historical primal scene—and the uncertainty of its hallucinatory revival. The discrepancy exists, in other words, between the actual existence of the lost object and the sign that evokes both this existence and its absence.

Laplanche and Pontalis maintain that the most basic fantasies are located at the juncture of an irrecoverable real event that took place somewhere in the past and a totally imaginary event that never took place. The "event" whose temporal and spatial existence can never be fixed is thus ultimately that of "the origin of the subject"—an origin that psychoanalysts tell us cannot be separated from the discovery of sexual difference.[23]

It is this contradictory temporal structure of being situated somewhere between the "too early" and the "too late" of the knowledge of difference that generates desire that is most characteristic of fantasy. Freud introduced the concept of "original fantasy" to explain the mythic function of fantasies that seem to offer repetitions of and "solutions" to major enigmas confronting the child.[24] These enigmas are located in three areas: the enigma of the origin of sexual desire, an enigma that is "solved," so to speak, by the fantasy of seduction; the enigma of sexual difference, "solved" by the fantasy of castration; and, finally, the enigma of the origin of self, "solved" by the fantasy of family romance or return to one's origin.[25]

Each of the three body genres I have been describing could be seen to correspond in important ways to one of these original fantasies. Pornography, for example, is the genre that has seemed to endlessly repeat the fantasies of primal seduction, of meeting the other, seducing or being seduced by the other in an ideal "pornotopia" where, as Steven Marcus has noted, it is always bedtime.[26] Horror is the genre that seems to endlessly repeat the trauma of castration, as if to "explain," by repetitious mastery, the original problem of sexual difference. And melodramatic weepie is the genre that seems to endlessly repeat our melancholic sense of the loss of origin, the impossible hope of returning to an earlier state that is perhaps most fundamentally represented by the body of the mother.

Of course, each of these genres has a history and does not simply "endlessly repeat." The fantasies activated by these genres are repetitious, but not fixed and eternal. If traced back to origin, each could probably be shown to have emerged with the formation of the bourgeois subject and the intensifying importance to this subject of specified sexualities.

But the importance of repetition in each genre should not blind us to the very different temporal structure of repetition in each fantasy. It could be, in fact, that these different temporal structures constitute the different utopian component of problem solving in each form. Thus the typical (nonsadomasochistic) pornographic fantasies of seduction operate to "solve" the problem of the origin of desire. Attempting to answer the insoluble question of whether desire is imposed from without through the seduction of the parent or whether it originates within the self, pornography answers this question by typically positing a fantasy of desire coming from within the subject *and* from without. Nonsadomasochistic pornography attempts to posit the utopian fantasy of perfect temporal coincidence: a subject and object (or seducer and seduced) who meet one another "on time!" and "now!" in shared moments of mutual pleasure that it is the special challenge of the genre to portray.

In contrast to pornography, the fantasy of recent teen horror corresponds to a temporal structure that suggests the anxiety of not being ready, the problem, in effect, of "too early!" Some of the most violent and terrifying moments of the horror film occur when the female victim meets the psycho-killer-monster unexpectedly, before she is ready. The female victims who are not ready for the attack die. This surprise encounter, too early, often takes place at a moment of sexual anticipation when the female victim thinks she is about to meet her boyfriend or lover. The monster's violent attack on the female victims vividly enacts a symbolic castration that often functions as a kind of punishment for an ill-timed exhibition of sexual desire. These victims are taken by surprise in the violent attacks that are then deeply felt by spectators (especially the adolescent male spectators drawn to the slasher subgenre) as linked to the knowledge of sexual difference. Again the key to the fantasy is timing—the way the knowledge of sexual difference too suddenly overtakes both characters and viewers, offering a knowledge for which we are never prepared.

Finally, in contrast to pornography's meeting "on time!" and horror's unexpected meeting "too early!" we can identify melodrama's pathos of the "too late!" In these fantasies the quest to return to and discover the origin of the self is manifest in the form of the child's fantasy of possessing ideal parents in the Freudian family romance, in the parental fantasy of possessing the child in maternal or paternal melodrama, and even in the lovers' fantasy of possessing one another in romantic weepies. In these fantasies the quest for connection is always tinged with the melancholy of loss. Origins are already lost; the encounters always take place too late, on deathbeds or over coffins.[27]

Italian critic Franco Moretti has argued, for example, that literature that makes us cry operates via a special manipulation of temporality: what triggers our crying is not just the sadness or suffering of the character in the story but a very precise moment when characters in the story catch up with and realize what the audience already knows. We cry, Moretti argues, not just because the characters do, but at the precise moment when desire is finally recognized as futile. The release of tension produces tears—which become a kind of homage to a happiness that is kissed good-bye. Pathos is thus a surrender to reality, but it is a surrender that pays homage to the ideal that tried to wage war on it.[28] Moretti thus stresses a subversive, utopian component in what has often been considered a form of passive powerlessness. The fantasy of the meeting with the other that is always too late can thus be seen as a reflection of the utopian desire that it not be too late to merge again with the other who was once part of the self.

Obviously there is a great deal of work to be done to understand the form and function of these three body genres in relation to one another and in relation to their fundamental appeal as "original fantasies." And obviously the most difficult work of understanding this relation between gender, genre, fantasy, and structures of perversion will come in the attempt to relate original fantasies to historical context and specific generic history. However, one thing already seems clear: these "gross" body genres, which may seem so violent and inimical to women, cannot be dismissed as evidence of a monolithic and unchanging misogyny, as either pure sadism for male viewers or as masochism for females. Their very existence and popularity hinges upon rapid changes taking place in relations between the sexes and by rapidly changing notions of gender—what it means to be a man or a woman. To dismiss them as bad excess—whether of explicit sex, violence, or emotion, or as bad perversions, whether of masochism or sadism—is not to address their function as cultural problem solving. Genres thrive, after all, on the persistence of the problems they address; but genres thrive also in their ability to recast the nature of these problems.

Finally, as I hope this analysis of the melodrama of tears suggests, we may be wrong in our assumption that the bodies of spectators simply reproduce the sensations exhibited by bodies on the screen. Even those masochistic pleasures associated with the powerlessness of the "too late!" are not absolutely abject. Even tearjerkers do not operate to force a simple mimicry of the sensation exhibited on the screen. Powerful as the sensations of the jerk might be, we may only be beginning to understand how they are deployed in generic and gendered cultural forms.

Notes

I owe thanks to Rhona Berenstein, Leo Braudy, Chick Callenbach, Paul Fitzgerald, Mandy Harris, Brian Henderson, Jane Gaines, Marsha Kinder, Eric Rentschler, and Pauline Yu for generous advice on drafts of this essay.

1. Ann Douglas, "Soft-Porn Culture," *New Republic* 30 (August 1980): 25.

2. David Bordwell, Kristin Thompson, and Janet Staiger, *The Classical Hollywood Cinema: Film Style and Mode of Production to 1960* (New York: Columbia University Press, 1985).

3. Rick Altman, "Dickens, Griffith, and Film Theory Today," *South Atlantic Quarterly* 88, no. 2 (Spring 1989): 321–359.

4. Ibid., pp. 345–346.

5. For an excellent summary of many of the issues involved with both film melodrama and the "woman's film," see Christine Gledhill's introduction to the anthology *Home Is Where the Heart Is: Studies in Melodrama and the Woman's Film* (London: British Film Institute, 1987). For a more general inquiry into the theatrical origins of melodrama, see Peter Brooks, *The Melodramatic Imagination* (New Haven: Yale University Press, 1976). And for an extended theoretical inquiry and analysis of a body of melodramatic women's films, see Mary Ann Doane, *The Desire to Desire* (Bloomington: Indiana University Press, 1987).

6. Carol J. Clover, "Her Body, Himself: Gender in the Slasher Film," *Representations* 20 (Fall 1987): 187–228.

7. Michel Foucault, *The History of Sexuality*, vol. 1, *An Introduction*, translated by Robert Hurley (New York: Pantheon Books, 1978).

8. Doane, *The Desire to Desire*, p. 95.

9. Robin Morgan, "Theory and Practice: Pornography and Rape," in *Take Back the Night: Women on Pornography*, edited by Laura Lederer (New York: Morrow, 1980), p. 139.

10. James Twitchell, *Dreadful Pleasures: An Anatomy of Modern Horror* (New York: Oxford, 1985), p. 10.

11. Clover, "Her Body, Himself," discusses the meanings of this famous quote.

12. Laura Mulvey, "Visual Pleasure and Narrative Cinema," *Screen* 16, no. 3 (1975): 6–18.

13. Dollimore's project, along with Teresa de Lauretis's more detailed examination of the term "perversion" in Freudian psychoanalysis (in progress), will be central to any detailed attempts to understand the perverse pleasures of these gross body genres. See Jonathan Dollimore, "The Cultural Politics of Perversion: Augustine, Shakespeare, Freud, Foucault," *Genders* 8 (July 1990): 2–16.

14. See, for example, Andrea Dworkin, *Pornography: Men Possessing Women* (New York: Perigee Books, 1979), and Catherine MacKinnon, *Feminism Unmodified: Discourses on Life and Law* (Cambridge: Harvard University Press, 1987).

15. Linda Williams, "When the Woman Looks," in *Re-Vision: Essays in Feminist Film Criticism*, American Film Institute Monograph Series, edited by Mary Ann Doane, Patricia Mellencamp, and Linda Williams (Frederick, Md.: University Publications of America, 1984), pp. 83–97.

16. Clover, "Her Body, Himself," pp. 206–209.

17. Gilles Deleuze, *Masochism: An Interpretation of Coldness and Cruelty*, translated by Jean McNeil (New York: Braziller, 1971); Kaja Silverman, "Masochism and Subjectivity," *Framework* 12 (1980): 2–9, and "Masochism and Male Subjectivity," *camera obscura* 17 (1988): 31–66; and Gaylyn Studlar, *In the Realm of Pleasure: Von Sternberg, Dietrich, and the Masochistic Aesthetic* (Urbana: University of Illinois Press, 1985).

18. See my *Hard Core: Power, Pleasure, and the 'Frenzy of the Visible'* (Berkeley: University of California Press, 1989), pp. 184–228.

19. I discuss these issues at length in ibid.

20. Titles of these relatively new (post-1986) hard-core videos include *Bisexual Fantasies; Bi-Mistake; Karen's Bi-Line; Bi-Dacious; Bi-Night; Bi and Beyond: The Ultimate Fantasy; Bi and Beyond II; Bi and Beyond III: Hermaphrodites.*

21. Williams, *Hard Core*, pp. 120–152.

22. Jean Laplanche and J. B. Pontalis, "Fantasy and the Origins of Sexuality," *International Journal of Psychoanalysis* 49, no. 1 (1968): 16.

23. Ibid., p. 11.

24. Sigmund Freud, "Instincts and Their Vicissitudes," in *The Standard Edition of the Complete Psychological Works of Sigmund Freud* (London: Hogarth Press, 1957), 14: 117–140.

25. Laplanche and Pontalis, "Fantasy," p. 11.

26. Steven Marcus, *The Other Victorians: A Study of Sexuality and Pornography in Mid-Nineteenth-Century England*, rev. ed. (New York: New American Library, 1974), p. 269.

27. Steve Neale, "Melodrama and Tears," *Screen* 27, no. 6 (November–December 1986): 6–22.

28. Franco Moretti, "Kindergarten," in *Signs Taken for Wonders* (London: Verso, 1983), p. 179.

13. Questions of Genre

STEVE NEALE

This article will discuss some of the issues, concepts, and concerns arising from work on film genres published over the last decade or so. It seeks to highlight a number of questions and problems that may pinpoint some possible directions for future research. I will be particularly concerned with the constitution of generic corpuses—the extent to which they are constituted by public expectations as well as by films, and the role of theoretical terms, on the one hand, and industrial and institutional terms, on the other, in the study of genres. The concept of verisimilitude is central to an understanding of genre, as is the question of the social and cultural functions that genres perform. These, too, will be discussed. Throughout I shall stress the changing, and hence historical, nature, not just of individual genres, but of generic regimes as well.

I shall be referring to several books and articles (thus, to some extent, this piece will serve as an extended review). But at a number of key points I shall be taking my cue, explicitly or otherwise, from an article by Alan Williams entitled "Is a Radical Genre Criticism Possible?" (an article that is itself a review of Thomas Schatz's *Hollywood Genres* and, to some extent, of my own book, *Genre*).[1]

Despite, or perhaps because of, the fact that it raises so many fundamental questions, Williams's article has not been discussed as much as it deserves. In saying this, however, I should note that, insofar as I shall be concentrating here on American cinema and American genres, I shall be ignoring (or at least setting to one side) one of Williams's most important points—that " 'genre' is not exclusively or even primarily a Hollywood phenomenon" and that "we need to get out of the United States."[2] I concentrate on American cinema partly because, as Williams himself notes elsewhere in his article, there is still an enormous amount of research to be done on what is still the most powerful national cinema in the world, and partly because most of the work published on genre to date has tended overwhelmingly to concern itself with Hollywood. In order to engage with this work, it is necessary to engage with its object. However, I should like to note too that a number of the more general, conceptual points I wish to make are equally applicable to film genres in India or Japan or Italy or Britain.

EXPECTATION AND VERISIMILITUDE

There are several general, conceptual points to make at the outset. The first is that genres are not simply bodies of work or groups of films, however classified, labeled, and defined. Genres do not consist only of films: they consist also, and equally, of specific systems of expectation and hypothesis that spectators bring with them to the cinema and that interact with films themselves during the course of the viewing process. These systems provide spectators with a means of recognition and understanding. They help render films, and the elements within them, intelligible and therefore explicable. They offer a way of working out the significance of what is happening on the screen: why particular events and actions are taking place, why the characters are dressed the way they are, why they look, speak, and behave the way they do, and so on. If, for instance, a character in a film bursts into song for no reason (or no otherwise explicable reason), the spectator is likely to hypothesize that the film is a musical, a particular kind of film in which otherwise unmotivated singing is likely to occur. These systems also offer grounds for further anticipation. If a film is a musical, more singing is likely to occur, and the plot is likely to follow certain directions rather than others.

Inasmuch as this is the case, these systems of expectation and hypothesis involve a knowledge of—indeed they partly embody—various regimes of verisimilitude—various systems of plausibility, motivation, justification, and belief. *Verisimilitude* means "probable" or "likely."[3] It entails notions of propriety, of what is appropriate and therefore probable (or probable and therefore appropriate).

Regimes of verisimilitude vary from genre to genre. (Bursting into song is appropriate, therefore probable—therefore intelligible, therefore believable—in a musical. Less so in a thriller or a war film.) As such, these regimes entail rules, norms, and laws. (Singing in a musical is not just a probability; it is a necessity. It is not just likely to occur; it is bound to.) As Tzvetan Todorov has insisted, there are two broad types of verisimilitude applicable to representations: generic verisimilitude and a broader social or cultural verisimilitude. Neither equates in any direct sense to "reality" or "truth":

> If we study the discussions bequeathed us by the past, we realize that a work is said to have verisimilitude in relation to two chief kinds of norms. The first is what we call *rules of the genre*: for a work to be said to have verisimilitude, it

must conform to these rules. In certain periods, a comedy is judged "probable" only if, in the last act, the characters are discovered to be near relations. A sentimental novel will be probable if its outcome consists in the marriage of hero and heroine, if virtue is rewarded and vice punished. Verisimilitude, taken in this sense, designates the work's relation to literary discourse: more exactly, to certain of the latter's subdivisions, which form a genre.

But there exists another verisimilitude, which has been taken even more frequently for a relation with reality. Aristotle, however, has already perceived that the verisimilar is not a relation between discourse and its referent (the relation of truth), but between discourse and what readers believe is true. The relation is here established between the work and a scattered discourse that in part belongs to each of the individuals of a society but of which none may claim ownership; in other words, to *public opinion*. The latter is of course not "reality" but merely a further discourse, independent of the work.[4]

There are several points worth stressing here. The first is the extent to which, as the example of singing in the musical serves to illustrate, generic regimes of verisimilitude can ignore, sidestep, or transgress these broad social and cultural regimes.

The second is the extent to which this "transgression" of cultural verisimilitude is characteristic of Hollywood genres. This has implications for conventional notions of realism. There is, of course, always a balance in any individual genre between purely generic and broadly cultural regimes of verisimilitude. Certain genres appeal more directly and consistently to cultural verisimilitude. Gangster films, war films, and police procedural thrillers, certainly, often mark that appeal by drawing on and quoting "authentic" (and authenticating) discourses, artifacts, and texts: maps, newspaper headlines, memoirs, archival documents, and so on. But other genres, such as science fiction, Gothic horror, or slapstick comedy, make much less appeal to this kind of authenticity, and this is certainly one of the reasons why they tend to be despised, or at least misunderstood, by critics in the "quality" press. For these critics, operating under an ideology of realism, adherence to cultural verisimilitude is a necessary condition of "serious" film, television, or literature. As Todorov goes on to argue, realism as an ideology can partly be defined by its refusal to recognize the reality of its own generic status or its own adherence to a type of generic verisimilitude.

A third point to be made is that recent uses of the concept of verisimilitude in writing on genre tend to blur the distinction between generic and cultural verisimilitude, vitiating the usefulness of the term. Both Christine Gledhill and Kathryn Kane, for instance, in writing about melodrama and the war film respectively, tend to use "verisimilitude" simply as a synonym for "realism" or "authenticity."[5] This is a pity because, as both Gledhill and Kane implicitly demonstrate, melodrama and the war film are genres that often seek to blur the distinction between the cultural and the generic, and they are often particularly marked by the tensions between the different regimes.

The fourth point is that, at least in the case of Hollywood, generic regimes of verisimilitude are almost as "public," as widely known, as "public opinion" itself. It is not simply in films or in genres that the boundaries between the cultural and the generic are blurred: the two regimes merge also in public discourse, generic knowledge becoming a form of cultural knowledge, a component of "public opinion."

Fifth, and finally, it is often the generically verisimilitudinous ingredients of a film, those elements that are often least compatible with regimes of cultural verisimilitude—singing and dancing in the musical, the appearance of the monster in the horror film—that constitute its pleasure and thus attract audiences to the film in the first place. They too, therefore, tend to be "public," known, at least to some extent, in advance.

These last two remarks lead on to the next set of points, which concern the role and importance of specific institutional discourses, especially those of the press and the film industry itself, in the formation of generic expectations, in the production and circulation of generic descriptions and terms, and, therefore, in the constitution of any generic corpus.

GENRE AND INSTITUTIONAL DISCOURSE

As John Ellis has pointed out, central to the practices of the film industry is the construction of a "narrative image" for each individual film: "An idea of the film is widely circulated and promoted, an idea which can be called the 'narrative image' of the film, the cinema's anticipatory reply to the question, 'What is the film like?'"[6] The discourses of film-industry publicity and marketing play a key role in the construction of such narrative images; but important too are other institutionalized public discourses, especially those of the press and television, and the "unofficial," "word of mouth" discourses of everyday life.

Genre is, of course, an important ingredient in any film's narrative image. The indication of relevant generic characteristics is therefore one of the most important functions that advertisements, stills, reviews, and posters perform. Reviews nearly always contain terms indicative of a film's generic status, while posters usually offer verbal generic (and hyperbolic) description—"The Greatest War Picture Ever Made"—as anchorage for the generic iconography in pictorial form.

These various verbal and pictorial descriptions form what Gregory Lukow and Steven Ricci have called the cinema's "intertextual relay."[7] This relay performs an additional, generic function: not only does it define and circulate narrative images for individual films, beginning the im-

She's **ALIVE** . . .
YET DEAD!!!

She's **DEAD** . . .
YET ALIVE!!!

Doomed to be one of the "walking dead" by weird and wily witchcraft . . . her radiant blonde loveliness ravaged through the curse of vengeful voodoo!

RKO
RADIO

I walked with a ZOMBIE

with
JAMES ELLISON · FRANCES DEE · TOM CONWAY
Produced by VAL LEWTON · Directed by JACQUES TOURNEUR
SCREEN PLAY BY CURT SIODMAK AND ARDEL WRAY
BASED ON AN ORIGINAL STORY BY INEZ WALLACE

28. Lobby card: Advertising helps consolidate a genre film's narrative image.

mediate narrative process of expectation and anticipation; it also helps to define and circulate, in combination with the films themselves, what one might call "generic images," providing sets of labels, terms, and expectations that will come to characterize the genre as a whole.

This is a key point. It is one of the reasons why I agree with Lukow and Ricci on the need to take account of all the component texts in the industry's intertextual relay when it comes to studying not only films but genre and genres. And it is one of the reasons why I would disagree with Rick Altman, in *The American Film Musical*, on the limited significance he assigns to the role of industrial and journalistic discourses in establishing a generic corpus.[8] (One of the many merits of Altman's book, however, is that he devotes the best part of a chapter to this issue. Most books and articles on genre fail to discuss it at all.)

For Altman, the role of industrial and journalistic terms is crucial in establishing the presence of generic consistencies but of limited use in defining them: "The fact that a genre has previously been posited, defined, and delimited by Hollywood is taken only as *prima facie* evidence that generic levels of meaning are operative within or across a group of texts

29. Lobby card: Advertising depicts relevant generic characteristics.

roughly designated by the Hollywood term and its usage. The industrial/ journalistic term thus founds a hypothesis about the presence of meaningful activity, but does not necessarily contribute a definition or delimitation of the genre in question."[9]

The identification of an industrial/journalistic term, then, is for Altman merely the first step in a multistage process. Having established a preliminary corpus in this way, the role of the critic is next to subject the corpus to analysis, to locate a method for defining and describing the structures, functions, and systems specific to a large number of the films within it. Then the critic, using this method as a basis, reconstitutes and redefines the corpus: "Texts which correspond to a particular understanding of the genre, that is, which provide ample material for a given method of analysis, will be retained within the generic corpus. Those which are not illuminated by the method developed in step three will simply be excluded from the final corpus. In terms of the musical, this would mean admitting that there are some films which include a significant amount of diegetic music, and yet which we will refuse to identify as musicals in the strong sense which the final corpus implies."[10] Having thus established a final corpus, the critic is finally in a position to produce a history of the genre and to analyze "the way in which the genre is molded by, functions within, and in turn informs the society of which it is a part." [11]

Before explaining my disagreement with this reasoning, it is important to recognize, along with Altman, that it is not possible to write about genres without being selective, and that many of the deficiencies of a good deal of writing on genre stem from defining and selecting on the basis of preestablished and unquestioned canons of films. As Alan Williams points out, this is one of the central deficiencies of Schatz's book, in which coverage of any given genre "depends not on historical or theoretical evenhandedness but on tacitly agreed-upon landmarks. Thus the chapter on the musical covers mainly Warner Brothers/Busby Berkeley, Fred Astaire at RKO, and the Freed Unit at MGM. So where is Lubitsch and the operetta? (Maybe the latter is not a 'Musical,' but *Hollywood Genres* does not explain.) Al Jolson and the crucially important melodramatic musicals of the early sound years? Who decided that these points alone would suffice?" [12]

In contrast, Altman's book is impressively wide in its range of references and refreshingly free from established canons of taste and categorization, including not only Jolson, operetta, and Lubitsch, but also the Elvis Presley films of the fifties and sixties and films like *Grease* (Randal Kleiser, 1978) and *Flashdance* (Adrian Lyne, 1983). It is important to say, too, that I agree with Altman that journalistic and industrial labels rarely, on their own, provide a conceptual basis for the analysis of genres or for the location of generic patterns, structures, and systems, just as I agree that such analysis is vitally important.

Where I disagree, however, is on Altman's assertion that the importance of industrial/journalistic terms is restricted to the first step of generic analysis. I disagree with this because I do not believe the aim of generic analysis is the redefinition of a corpus of films. Such an aim is in the end no different, in effect if not in intention, from the highly selective categorizations of Schatz or from the worst pigeonholing inheritances of neoclassical literary theory. We can easily end up identifying the purpose of generic analysis with the rather fruitless attempt to decide which films fit, and therefore properly belong to, which genres. We can also end up constructing or perpetuating canons of films, privileging some and demoting or excluding others. (Thus even Altman, despite his broad range and the power of his method, finds himself excluding films like *Dumbo* [Ben Sharpsteen, 1941] and *Bambi* [David Hand, 1942] and nearly excluding *The Wizard of Oz* [Victor Fleming, 1939].)

Such an aim is, therefore, inherently reductive. More than that, it is in danger of curtailing the very cultural and historical analysis upon which Altman rightly insists as an additional theoretical aim. The danger lies not only in the devaluation of industrial/journalistic discourses, but in the separation of genre analysis from a number of the features that define its public circulation. These features include the fact that genres exist always *in excess* of a corpus of works; the fact that genres comprise expectations and audience knowledge as well as films; and the fact that these expectations and the knowledge they entail are public in status. As Todorov has argued (while himself tending to equate genres solely with works):

> One can always find a property common to two texts, and therefore put them together in one class. But is there any point in calling the result of such a union a "genre"? I think that it would be in accord with the current usage of the word and at the same time provide a convenient and operant notion if we agreed to call "genres" only those classes of texts that have been perceived as such in the course of history. The accounts of this perception are found most often in the discourse on genres (the metadiscursive discourse) and, in a sporadic fashion, in the texts themselves.[13]

As far as the cinema is concerned (Todorov here is writing about literature—and High Literature at that), this metadiscursive discourse is to be found in its intertextual relay. Clearly, generic expectations and knowledge do not emanate solely from the film industry and its ancillary institutions; and, clearly, individual spectators may have their own expectations, classifications, labels, and terms. But these individualized, idiosyncratic classifications play little part, if any, in the public formation and circulation of genres and generic images. In the public sphere, the institutional discourses are of central importance. Testimony to the existence of genres, and evidence of their properties, is to be found primarily there.

A distinction needs to be made, then, between those studies of genres conceived as institutionalized classes of texts and systems of expectation and those studies that use critically or theoretically constructed terms as the basis for discussing classes of films. (Studies of film noir are obvious examples of the latter.) A distinction also needs to be made between institutionally recognized subgenres, cycles, and categories (operetta and the singing Western) and theoretical or scholarly classifications (the fairy tale musical, the show musical, and the folk musical). This is not to argue that theoretical studies and classifications are somehow illegitimate. (Far from it. These examples all illustrate how productive they can be.) It is however, to insist on the pertinence of Todorov's distinction for an understanding of what it is that is being studied.

INSTITUTIONAL DISCOURSES AND GENRE HISTORY

Not only do industrial and journalistic labels and terms constitute crucial evidence for an understanding of both the industry's and the audience's generic conceptions in the present; they also offer virtually the only available evidence for a historical study of the array of genres in circulation, or of the ways in which individual films have been generically perceived at any point in time. This is important for an understanding of the ways in which both the array and the perceptions have changed.

Let me give some examples. Both "the western" and *The Great Train Robbery* (Edwin S. Porter, 1903) are firmly established in genre studies, the latter as an early, highly influential example of the former. However, in his *Dictionary of Slang and Unconventional English*, Eric Partridge dates the first colloquial use of the term *western* in anything other than an adjectival sense to around 1910. The first use of the term cited in the *Oxford English Dictionary* with reference to a film dates from 1912, occurring in a review of *The Fight at the Mill* (1912) in a July 1912 issue of the trade magazine *The Moving Picture World*. This was nine years after *The Great Train Robbery* was released.

Now it may be argued, of course, that this is merely quibbling. While the specific term *western* may not have been available to audiences in 1903, westerns themselves, in the form of dime novels, Wild West shows, paintings, illustrations, short stories, and the like (as well as one or two films), had been around for some time.[14] Thus audiences of *The Great Train Robbery*, well accustomed to these forms, would have drawn on the paradigms they provided in understanding and locating the film. Charles Musser, however, has convincingly argued that this was not the case, that the paradigms used both by the industry and its audiences were different and that it was the confluence of paradigms provided by melodrama, the chase film, the railway genre, and the crime film, rather than the western, that ensured the film's contemporary success:

> Kenneth MacGowan attributed this success . . . to the fact that the film was "the first important Western," William Everson and George Fenin find it important because it is "the blueprint for all Westerns." These, however, are retrospective readings. One reason for *The Great Train Robbery*'s popularity was its ability to incorporate so many trends, genres and strategies fundamental to the institution of cinema at that time. The film includes elements of both re-enactment of contemporary news events (the train hold-up was modeled after recently reported crimes) and refers to a well-known stage melodrama by its title. Perhaps most importantly, *The Great Train Robbery* was part of a violent crime genre which had been imported from England a few months earlier. Porter was consciously working (and cinema patrons viewing) within a framework established by Sheffield Photo's *Daring Daylight Burglary*, British Gaumont/Walter Haggar's *Desperate Poaching Affair [Affray]* and R. W. Paul's *Trailed by Bloodbounds*. . . . [Thus,] when initially released, *The Great Train Robbery* was not primarily perceived in the context of the Western. Its success did not encourage other Westerns but other films of

crime—Lubin's *Bold Bank Robbery* [Jack Frawley, 1904] Paley and Steiner's
[*Avenging a Crime; Or,*] *Burned at the Stake* [1904], and Porter's own *Capture of the Yegg Bank Robbers* [1904]. . . . It was only when the Western
genre emerged as a vital force in the nickelodeon era that *The Great Train
Robbery* was interpreted from this new perspective.[15]

Musser's argument here serves to indicate, in addition to the change in
generic status of *The Great Train Robbery,* the extent to which different
periods in the history of the American cinema have been marked by different generic systems, different "generic regimes." It is an important theoretical point that genres "do not exist by themselves; they are named and
placed within hierarchies or systems of genres, and each is defined by reference to the system and its members." [16] Furthermore, "Each era has its
own system of genres." [17] Company catalogues are a particularly useful
resource in establishing the generic regimes of the earliest years of the cinema. Their terminology and their groupings indicate the considerable differences between these regimes and the regimes of the studio era. Thus,
instead of the westerns, horror films, and war films of later years, the
Kleine Optical Company's catalogue for 1905 lists films in the following
groupings:

1. Story
   a. historical
   b. dramatic
   c. narrative
2. Comic
3. Mysterious
4. Scenic
5. Personalities [18]

Meanwhile, Biograph's "Advance Partial List" of films for sale in 1902
lists its "subject" under the following titles and headings: Comedy Views,
Sports and Pastime Views, Military Views, Railroad Views, Scenic Views,
Views of Notable Personages, Miscellaneous Views, Trick Pictures, Ma-
rine Views, Children's Pictures, Fire and Patrol Views, Pan-American Exposition Views, Vaudeville Views, and Parade Pictures.[19] (The number of
"documentary" or "actuality" categories here is, of course, indicative of
the extent to which these genres far outweighed fiction in the period prior
to 1903–1904.)

In demonstrating the degree to which genre categories and generic regimes have changed, these examples illustrate the historical character of
all genres. Genres are inherently temporal: hence, their inherent mutabil-
ity on the one hand and their inherent historicity on the other. In dis-
agreeing with Altman on the significance of institutional discourses, I now
wish to focus attention on a further aspect of that temporality.

30. *The Moving Picture World,* July 20, 1912: The first appearance of the term "western."

GENRE AS PROCESS

It may at first sight seem as though repetition and sameness are the primary hallmarks of genres, as though, therefore, genres are above all inherently static. But as Hans Robert Jauss and Ralph Cohen (and I myself) have argued, genres are, nevertheless, best understood as *processes*.[20] These processes may, for sure, be dominated by repetition, but they are also marked fundamentally by difference, variation, and change.

The processlike nature of genres manifests itself as an interaction between three levels: the level of expectation, the level of the generic corpus, and the level of the "rules" or "norms" that govern both. Each new genre film constitutes an addition to an existing generic corpus and involves a selection from the repertoire of generic elements available at any one point in time. Some elements are included; others are excluded. Indeed, some are mutually exclusive: at most points in its history, the horror film has had to characterize its monster *either* supernaturally—as in *Dracula* (Tod Browning, 1930)—*or* psychologically—as in *Psycho* (Alfred Hitchcock, 1960). In addition, each new genre film tends to extend this repertoire, either by adding a new element or by transgressing one of the old ones. Thus, for instance, *Halloween* (John Carpenter, 1979) transgressed the division between psychological and supernatural monsters, giving its monster the attributes of both. In this way the elements and conventions of a genre are always *in* play rather than being simply *re*played;[21] and any generic corpus is always being expanded.

Memories of the films within a corpus constitute one of the bases of generic expectation. So, too, does the stock of generic images produced by advertisements, posters, and the like. As both corpus and image expand and change with the appearance of new films, new advertising campaigns, and new reviews, so also what Jauss has termed the "horizon of expectation" appropriate to each genre expands and changes as well: "The relationship between the individual text and the series of texts formative of a genre presents itself as a process of the continual founding and altering of horizons. The new text evokes for the reader (or listener) the horizon of expectations and 'rules of the game' familiar to him from earlier texts, which as such can then be varied, extended, corrected, but also transformed, crossed out, or simply reproduced."[22]

This is one reason why it is so difficult to list exhaustively the characteristic components of individual genres, or to define them in anything other than the most banal or tautological terms: a western is a film set on the American western frontier; a war film is a film that represents the waging of war; a detective film is a film about the investigation of criminals and crime; and so on. More elaborate definitions always seem to throw up exceptions. Altman provides an example. He cites Jean Mitry's definition of the western as a "film whose action, situated in the American West, is consistent with the atmosphere, the values and the conditions of existence in the Far West between 1840 and 1900."[23] He then goes on to cite an exception, the "Pennsylvania western": "To most observers it seems quite clear that films like *High, Wide and Handsome* (Rouben Mamoulian, 1937), *Drums along the Mohawk* (John Ford, 1939), and *Unconquered* (Cecil B. DeMille, 1947) have definite affinities with the western. Employing familiar characters set in relationships similar to their counterparts west of the Mississippi, these films construct plots and develop a frontier structure clearly derived from decades of western novels and films. But they do it in Pennsylvania and in the wrong century."[24] *Exclusive* definitions, lists of *exclusive* characteristics, are particularly hard to produce. At what point do westerns become musicals like *Oklahoma!* (Fred Zinnemann, 1955) or *Paint Your Wagon* (Joshua Logan, 1969) or *Seven Brides for Seven Brothers* (Stanley Donen, 1954)? At what point do singing westerns become musicals? At what point do comedies with songs (like *A Night at the Opera* [Sam Wood, 1935]) become musical comedies? And so on.

These examples all, of course, do more than indicate the processlike nature of individual genres. They also indicate the extent to which individual genres not only form part of a generic regime, but also themselves change, develop, and vary by borrowing from, and overlapping with, one another. Hybrids are by no means the rarity in Hollywood many books and articles on genre in the cinema would have us believe. This is one reason why, as Marc Vernet has pointed out, "a guide to film screenings will often offer to the spectator rubrics like: western, detective film, horror film, and comedy; but also: dramatic comedy, psychological drama, or even erotic detective film."[25] Indeed, in Hollywood's classical era, as Bordwell, Staiger, and Thompson have shown, nearly all its films were hybrids insofar as they always tended to combine one type of generic plot, a romance plot, with others.[26] Moreover, it is at least arguable that many of the most apparently "pure" and stable genres, both inside and outside the cinema, initially evolved by combining elements from previously discrete and separate genres either within or across specific generic regimes. Ernest Mandel, for example, has argued that the detective genre emerged in this way by combining three such generically disparate elements: the "reverse story," developed by Godwin (*Caleb Williams,* 1794); the divination deduction technique, which originated in Persia and was introduced into modern literature by Voltaire (*Zadig*); and the *coup de théatre,* borrowed from melodrama.[27] Similarly, Richard Traubner has shown, in painstaking detail, how operetta emerged by combining the features of *opera buffa,* German *Singspiel,* and British ballad opera and how it subsequently evolved by replacing some of these features with elements of burlesque and revue; then, in America at least, these were displaced in turn, until the genre finally emerged as the "musical play" with shows (and films) like *Show Boat* (filmed in 1936 by James Whale and in 1951 by George Sidney), *Oklahoma!, Brigadoon* (filmed in 1954 by Vincente Minnelli), *Carousel* (filmed in 1956 by Henry King), *West Side Story* (filmed in 1961 by Robert Wise), and *My Fair Lady* (filmed in 1964 by George Cukor).[28]

Hence the importance of *historicizing* generic definitions and the parameters both of any single generic corpus and of any specific generic regime. For it is not that more elaborate definitions are impossible to provide, just that they are always historically relative and therefore historically specific. It is not that the processslike nature of genres renders generalizations invalid. Genre films, genres, and generic regimes are always marked by boundaries and by frameworks, which always have limits. Thus even hybrids are recognized as hybrids—combinations of specific and distinct generic components—not as genres in their own right. (This is why I would prefer not to say, as Jim Collins has recently done, that a genre text always "remakes" norms, but rather that a genre text always either reworks them, extends them, or transforms them altogether.)[29] The point, though, is that if these limits are historically specific, they can be determined only empirically, not theoretically.

GENRE HISTORY: THREE APPROACHES

There currently seem to exist three major ways in which genre history has been conceived. The first is what Jauss has called "the evolutionary schema of growth, flowering, and decay."[30] This schema is open to several objections: it is teleological; it is (for all its organic metaphors) highly mechanistic; and it treats genres in isolation from any generic regime.

Similar objections apply to a second model of evolutionary development, used by Thomas Schatz, in which genres progress toward self-conscious formalism. Here is Williams's description of Schatz's approach: "As genres change over time, and their audiences become more and more self-conscious, genres progress from transparency to opacity, 'from straightforward storytelling to self-conscious formalism' (p. 38). Not all genres complete this cycle unimpeded. Gangster Films, for example, were disrupted by the threat of censorship as were, at various points, War Films." To this Williams poses a theoretical objection: "Note that Schatz locates this shift to opacity *within individual genres,* such that a 'new' genre in the 1980s would have to go through a 'classical' stage before evolving into self-conscious formalism. It is not the filmmaking system or the social context that has changed, but the genres that have evolved. (In my opinion, this is clearly wrong.)" And here is an empirical objection:

"One can find self-conscious Westerns, such as Fairbanks' *Wild and Woolly* [John Emerson, 1917], as early as the late teens. In fact, the entire mid-to-late silent cinema seems remarkably 'formalistic,' which is possibly one reason it is wholly absent from Schatz's book." [31] (A similar point has been made at greater length, and to equally devastating effect, in an article by Tag Gallagher.) [32]

The third historical model is the one provided by the Russian formalists. [33] It has the virtue of embedding the history of individual genres within the history not just of generic formations but of wider cultural formations as well. It is perhaps best known for Tynyanov's concept of "the dominant" (with its correlative concept of genre history as the displacement of one dominant genre by another), [34] and by Shklovsky's idea that such displacements occur according to a principle known as "the canonization of the junior branch": "When the 'canonized' art forms reach an impasse, the way is paved for the infiltration of the elements of non-canonized art, which by this time have managed to evolve new artistic devices." [35] Quoting from Juri Streidter's introduction to a German anthology of Russian formalist texts, Jauss describes the formalists' conception as a whole:

> The Formalist conception of genre as a historical system of relations participates in the attempt to replace the classical notion of literary tradition—as a steady, unilinear, cumulative course—with the dynamic principle of literary *evolution*, by which they do not mean an analogy to organic growth or to Darwinian selection. For here "evolution" is supposed to characterize the phenomenon of literary "succession" "not in the sense of a continuous 'development,' but rather in the sense of a 'struggle' and 'break' with immediate predecessors through a contemporary recourse to something older."
> In the historical evolution of literature thus understood, literary genres can be grasped in the periodic alternation of the dominating role as well as in a sequence of rivalries.

In addition,

> From a diachronic perspective the historical alternation of the dominating genre manifests itself in the three steps of canonization, automation, and reshuffling. Successful genres . . . gradually lose their effective power through continual reproduction; they are forced to the periphery by new genres often arising from a "vulgar" stratum if they cannot be reanimated through a restructuring (be it through the playing up of previously suppressed themes or methods, or through the taking up of materials or the taking-over of functions from other genres). [36]

There is clearly a great deal here that is both attractive and useful. As a theory or model, it takes account of the historicity not only of genres but of specific generic regimes; it takes account of their processlike nature; and, in its insistence on the importance of an interplay between canonized and noncanonized forms of representation and between canonized and noncanonized genres, it takes account both of the transience of generic hierarchies as well as the role of hybridization in the formation and dissolution of individual genres.

In sketching the application of this model to the American cinema, one could argue, for instance, that the cinema itself arose in and as the conjunction of a variety of art forms—canonized and otherwise: from photography, through pictorial entertainments and spectacles like the diorama, the zoëtrope, and the magic lantern show, to magic itself and to the vaudeville routine. Its earliest generic regime, in America as elsewhere, was dominated by the genres associated with these forms: the moving snapshot or "view," reenacted and reconstructed news, trick films, and slapstick and gag-based comedy. Subsequent to this, there is a shift to a predominance of fiction, in particular melodrama (whether in its thrilling, mysterious, domestic, or spectacular guise) on the one hand and comedy on the other. With accompanying subdivisions and with the addition of genres like the musical, this "dominant" came to be stabilized in the era of oligopoly and studio control. Later, in a period of crisis and readjustment, "adult" drama and "epic" values—marked by, and derived principally from, the epic itself and spreading from there to the western, the war film, the musical, and even, with films like *The Great Race* (Blake Edwards, 1965) and *It's a Mad, Mad, Mad, Mad World* (Stanley Kramer, 1963), to slapstick comedy—gained a position of dominance, though by now they were beginning to jockey for position with "exploitation" genres and the "juvenilization" of Hollywood's output. Finally, more recently, the process of juvenilization has continued, with the emergence of the "teenpic" and the predominance of science fiction and horror. Meanwhile, in exemplary illustration of Shklovsky's thesis, some of these genres, in combination with serial-derived individual films like *Raiders of the Lost Ark* (Steven Spielberg, 1981) and *Romancing the Stone* (Robert Zemeckis, 1984), have been promoted from the "junior branches" of Hollywood's output to achieve hegemony within the realms of the family blockbuster.

What is particularly valuable about the formalists' model is that it neither prescribes the conditions for generic outmodedness nor specifies any single mechanism by which noncanonized forms, devices, or genres might find a place within generic regimes or assume a position of dominance within them. It allows for a variety of factors and reasons. This is especially important in the case of the cinema, where, for example, the initial predominance of actuality genres is as much a consequence of technological factors as it is of their popularity or "canonization" elsewhere in the contemporary culture and where, on the other hand, the promotion and predominance of "juvenile" genres is as much a consequence of market research, the targeting of audiences, and, in some cases, of new special-effects techniques as it is of any newfound aesthetic vitality.[37]

What is particularly striking about this historical sketch, meanwhile, is the extent to which many genres either originated in forms and institutions of entertainment other than the cinema or were (and are) circulated additionally by them. Melodrama, for example, originated on the stage. It fed from there, in a process of increasing and mutual interaction, first into written fiction and then into the cinema. All the while, in all three fields, it generated subdivisions like the crime story, the mystery, the adventure story, the romance, and domestic drama. Comedy came from vaudeville, the circus, burlesque, and the newspaper cartoon strip as well as from the "legitimate" stage and, later, from radio and television. The musical came from Broadway (and its songs from Tin Pan Alley). Cheap hardback and paperback books, meanwhile, together with both "slick" and "pulp" magazines, comic books, comic strips, and mass-produced fiction of all kinds, helped in some cases to originate, and in all cases to circulate, genres like the western, the detective story and the thriller, horror, science fiction, war, and romance. This generic fiction often appeared in series or serial format with precise generic titles and names: *Adventure Library* (1897), *The Detective Library* (1917), *Western Story Magazine* (1919), *Thrill Book* (1919), *Love Story Magazine* (1921), *Love Story Library* (1926), *War Stories* (1922), *Gangster Stories*, *The Magazine of Fantasy and Science-Fiction* (1942), *Bestseller Mysteries* (1942), *The Vault of Horror* (1950), and so on.[38]

At this point it is worth signaling the need for a great deal more research both on cross-media generic formation and circulation and, as a corollary, on the particular contributions of individual institutions and forms.[39] More research is needed, too, on the aesthetically specific transformations and adaptations that each genre undergoes in each institution and form.[40]

AESTHETICS AND IDEOLOGY

Finally, I should like to move on to discuss a set of questions about the aesthetic characteristics of mass-produced genres, their institutional functions within the cinema, and their putative social, cultural, and ideological significance.

The first point to make here is, again, a historical one. It concerns the provenance, and status, of the term "genre" itself, its applicability to the cinema, and its role in characterizing not only the cinema but mass-produced art and entertainment in general. It is a point that, once more, has usefully been focused by Williams:

Perhaps the biggest problem with genre theory or genre criticism in the field of cinema is the word *genre*. Borrowed, as a critical tool, from literary studies . . . the applicability of "genre" as a concept in film studies raises some fairly tough questions. Sample genres are held to be Westerns, Science Fiction Films, more recently Disaster Films, and so on. What do these loose groupings of works—that seem to come and go, for the most part, in ten- and twenty-year cycles—have to do with familiar literary genres such as tragedy, comedy, romance, or (to mix up the pot a bit) the epistolary novel or the prose poem?

He continues,

For the phrase "genre films," referring to a general category, we can frequently, though not always, substitute "film narrative." Perhaps *that* is the real genre. Certainly there is much more difference between *Prelude: Dog Star Man* [Stan Brakhage, 1961] and *Star Wars* than there is between the latter and *Body Heat* [Lawrence Kasdan, 1981]. It's mainly a question of terminology, of course, but I wonder if we ought to consider the principal genres as being narrative film, experimental/avant-garde film, and documentary. Surely these are the categories in film studies that have among themselves the sorts of significant differences that one can find between, say, epic and lyric poetry. If we reserve this level for the term *genre,* then film genres will by definition have the kind of staying power seen in literary genres. What we presently call film genres would then be *sub-genres.*[41]

In many ways, it seems to me, Williams is right about this. However, apart from the fact that, as he says, it is "probably too late" to change things, there is an important qualification to be made.

As Ralph Cohen has pointed out, the term *genre* is a nineteenth-century term.[42] Thus, although the concept is clearly much older, the term itself emerges precisely at the time that popular, mass-produced generic fiction is making its first appearance (its genres, incidentally, just as susceptible to Williams's strictures). At the same time also there began to emerge a distinct shift in the value placed on generic literature by High Culture artists and critics. As Terry Threadgold has explained, prior to the advent of romanticism "it was *literature* that was generic": "The rest, the 'popular culture' of political pamphlets, ballads, romances, chapbooks, was not only *not* literature, but also *not* generic; it escaped the law of genre, suffering a kind of rhetorical exclusion by inclusion in the classical distinction between high, middle, and low styles. It was seen as a kind of anarchic, free area, unconstrained by the rules of polite society and decorum, by *genre* in fact."[43]

With the emergence of new technologies, new capital, mass production, and new means of distribution (notably the railway), with the formation of a relatively large literate (or semiliterate) population (with the formation, therefore, of a market), and with the commodification of all forms of leisure and entertainment, the equation is reversed. Now it is "popular culture," mass culture, that is generic, ruled as it is by market pressures to differentiate to a limited degree in order to cater to various sectors of consumers and to repeat commercially successful patterns, ingredients, and formulas. By contrast, "true literature" is marked by self-expression, creative autonomy, and originality, and hence by a freedom from all constrictions and constraints, including those of genre.

It is at this point absolutely crucial to disentangle a number of assumptions and conflations, for this is where a great deal of "genre theory" (indeed "popular cultural theory" in general) tends to go astray. First, of course, it has to be recognized that no artist, in whatever sphere of aesthetic production, at whatever period in history, in whatever form of society, has ever been free either of aesthetic conventions and rules or of specific institutional constraints (whether he or she has reacted against them or not). Second, as Geoffrey Nowell-Smith has recently reemphasized, *all* cultural and artistic production in Western societies is now, and has been for some time, subject to capitalist conditions of production, distribution, and exchange, hence to commodification.[44] (This means, among other things, that High Cultural art, whether it still draws upon "traditional," precapitalist genres like lyric poetry or eschews both "traditional" and modern, popular genres, is still itself "generic" insofar as it is thereby still engaged in catering for a sector of the market and still involved in a form of product differentiation.)[45] The third point, therefore, is that mass-produced, popular genres have to be indeed understood within an economic context, as conditioned by specific economic imperatives and by specific economic contradictions—in particular, of course, those that operate within specific institutions and industries. That is why it is important to stress the financial advantages to the film industry of an aesthetic regime based on regulated difference, contained variety, pre-sold expectations, and the reuse of resources in labor and materials. It is also why it is important to stress the peculiar nature of films as *aesthetic* commodities demanding at least a degree of novelty and difference from one to another, and why it is necessary to explore the analogies and the distinctions between cycles and genres in the cinema, on the one hand, and models and lines in the field of nonartistic commodity production, on the other.

Failure to recognize these points results in approaches to genre that are inadequate and simplistic. It is worth specifying two such approaches here. The first is what Altman has called the "ritual" approach, exemplified again by Thomas Schatz (along with Will Wright and John Cawelti, a pioneer of this particular approach).[46] Here is Williams's summary of this approach: "The repetitive nature of genre production and consumption produces active but indirect audience participation; successful genres are 'stories the audience has isolated through its collective response.' Hence genre filmmaking can be examined as 'a form of collective cultural expression' (pp. 12–13).[47] Quite apart from the doubtful assumption that consumer decision-making can be considered a form of "cultural expression" and quite apart from the tendency of such an approach to conflate the multiplicity of reasons for consumer "choices" and a multiplicity of readings of these "choices," the ritual theory of genres is open to question on other grounds. Principal among these is that it ignores the role of institutional determinations and decisions, bypassing the industry and the sphere of production in an equation between market availability, consumer choice, consumer preference, and broader social and cultural values and beliefs. This is an equation open to challenge on its own grounds. During the studio era, for instance, westerns were regularly produced in large numbers, despite the fact that, as Garth Jowett has shown, such market research as was conducted at this time indicated that the genre was popular only with young adolescent boys and sectors of America's rural population and that is was *actively disliked* more than it was liked by the viewing population as a whole.[48]

Second, objections can also be made to what Altman calls the "ideological" approach to genre, which recognizes the capitalist nature of the film industry and the status of its films as commodities but which treats genres simply as vehicles for "capitalist" (or the "dominant") ideology.[49] This approach is open to the charges of reductivism, economism, and cultural pessimism.[50] It tends to presume, in the final analysis, that representations reflect their social and economic conditions of existence, that institutions and social formations necessarily secure their own reproduction, and, in Colin MacCabe's words, that "the meanings of texts . . . are always finally anchored in a class struggle which is not to be understood in cultural terms."[51] As both MacCabe and Geoffrey Nowell-Smith have insisted, each in his different way, "Stressing the capitalist character of modern cultural production is in itself neither optimistic nor pessimistic."[52] The ideological significance of any text—or any genre—is always to be sought in a context-specific analysis. It cannot simply be deduced from the nature of the institution responsible for its production and circulation, nor can it ever be known in advance.

Both these theories, for all their differences, suffer from the fact that they pay little attention to aesthetics—for them, form is always, and only, a wrapping for the cultural or ideological content in which they are almost exclusively interested. Insofar as they do discuss form, they tend to stress the repetitive, stereotypical aspects of genres, setting aside the differences within and between them in order to provide themselves with a stable corpus and in order to substantiate their underlying premise: that the reasons for the popularity and longevity of genres are relatively uniform, as are, aside from a few Lévi-Straussian antinomies, the genres themselves, the meanings they convey, and the culture (or ideology) that underpins them. While it may be that repetition is important, it is also true that, as we have seen, variation and difference are crucial. Equally, while it may be that Hollywood genres are in most instances best considered as subgenres of narrative film, and while these subgenres may not be marked by the kinds of apparent discursive peculiarities that tend to differentiate the narrative film from documentary or the structuralist avant-garde, there is still a great deal of scope for the investigation of specific discursive characteristics. Aside from my own attempt, in *Genre,* to explore the ways in which different genres exploit in different ways the features and characteristics of the narrative film (an attempt somewhat marred by an overschematic approach, by a lack of attention to hybridization, and, above all, by a lack of attention to history), the basis for an approach can perhaps be found in the Russian formalist idea that genres can each involve a "dominant" (or dominating) aesthetic device (or ideological element).[53]

On this basis, particular genres can be characterized not as the only genres in which given elements, devices, and features occur, but as the ones in which they are dominant, in which they play an overall organizing role.

Approaches to individual genres—and to individual genre films—that draw centrally on the notion of a generic dominant are few and far between. However, it could be argued, for example, that the epic is marked by the dominance of spectacle; that the thriller and the detective genre, especially as discussed by Dennis Porter and Kristin Thompson, are dominated by the devices of suspense, narrative digression, and hermeneutic delay;[54] and that, as the Russian formalists themselves have argued, melodrama involves the subordination of all other elements "to one overriding aesthetic goal: the calling forth of 'pure,' 'vivid' emotions."[55] In doing so, however, emphasis must again be placed on the fact that dominant elements are not necessarily exclusive elements, occurring only in the genre concerned. Clearly, spectacle, digression, suspense, and the generation of passion and emotion are properties common to all Hollywood films.

By way of conclusion, I would like to stress the need for further research, for further concrete and specific analyses, and for much more attention to genres hitherto neglected in genre studies, such as the adventure film, the war film, and the epic. In stressing this, I can do no better than to quote Williams for the last time. In his own summation, he calls for a "return to film history," for "genre studies with real historical integrity." This would mean, he says, three things: "(1) starting with a genre's 'prehistory,' its roots in other media; (2) studying all films, regardless of perceived quality; and (3) going beyond film content to study advertising, the star system, studio policy, and so on in relation to the production of films."[56] I would merely add that the scope of this investigation needs to be extended beyond individual genres to encompass specific generic regimes both inside and outside the cinema.

Notes

1. Alan Williams, "Is a Radical Genre Criticism Possible?" *Quarterly Review of Film Studies 9,* no. 2 (Spring 1984): 121–125; Thomas Schatz, *Hollywood Genres: Formulas, Filmmaking, and the Studio System* (New York: Random House, 1981); Steve Neale, *Genre* (London: BFI, 1980).

2. Williams, "Is a Radical Genre Criticism Possible?" p. 124.

3. For discussions of verisimilitude and genre, see Ben Brewster, "Film," in *Exploring Reality,* edited by Dan Cohn-Sherbok and Michael Irwin (London: Allen & Unwin, 1987), esp. pp. 147–149; Gerard Genette, "Vraisemblance et motivation," in *Figures,* vol. 3 (Paris: Seuil, 1969); and Tzvetan Todorov, "The Typology of Detective Fiction" and "An Introduction to Verisimilitude," in *The Poetics of Prose* (Ithaca: Cornell University Press, 1977), and *Introduction to Poetics* (Brighton: Harvester Press, 1981), esp. pp. 118–119.

4. Todorov, *Introduction to Poetics,* pp. 118–119.

5. Christine Gledhill, "The Melodramatic Field: An Introduction," in *Home Is Where the Heart Is: Studies in Melodrama and the Woman's Film,* edited by Christine Gledhill (London: BFI, 1987), esp. p. 9: "As a bourgeois form, melodrama is constrained by the same conditions of verisimilitude as realism. If the family melodrama speciality is generational and gender conflict, verisimilitude demands that the central issues of sexual difference and identity be 'realistically' presented." Kathryn Kane, *Visions of War: Hollywood Combat Films of World War II* (Ann Arbor: UMI Research Press, 1976), esp. p. 121: "The achievement of [*The Story of*] *G. I. Joe* [William Wellman, 1945] however is not really one of historical data providing the truth of what is portrayed. . . . Rather, its power is the result of an insistence on *verisimilitude,* the stylistic groundwork on which the authenticity props rest."

6. John Ellis, *Visible Fictions: Cinema, Television, Video* (London: Routledge, 1981), p. 30.

7. Gregory Lukow and Steve Ricci, "The 'Audience' Goes 'Public': Intertextuality, Genre, and the Responsibilities of Film Literacy," *On Film,* no. 12 (Spring 1984): 29.

8. Rick Altman, *The American Film Musical* (Bloomington and Indianapolis: Indiana University Press, 1989).

9. Ibid., p. 13.

10. Ibid., p. 14.

11. Ibid., pp. 14–15.

12. Williams, "Is a Radical Genre Criticism Possible?" p. 123.

13. Tzvetan Todorov, "The Origin of Genres," *New Literary History* 8, no. 1 (Autumn 1976): 102.

14. On the western prior to the emergence of the cinema and on all these forms,

see *The BFI Companion to the Western,* edited by Edward Buscombe (New York: Atheneum, 1988), pp. 18–22.

15. Charles Musser, "The Travel Genre in 1903–04: Moving Toward Fictional Narratives," *Iris* 2, no. 1 (1984): 56–57. The references here are to Kenneth Mac-Gowan, *Behind the Screen* (New York: Delacorte, 1965), p. 114; and George Fenin and William K. Everson, *The Western: From Silents to Cinerama* (New York: Orion Press, 1962), p. 49.

16. Ralph Cohen, "History and Genre," *New Literary History 17,* no. 2 (Winter 1986): 207.

17. Todorov, "The Origin of Genres," p. 103.

18. *Complete Illustrated Catalog of Moving Picture Machines, Stereoptikons, Slides, Films* (Chicago: Kleine Optical Company, November 1905), p. 36.

19. *Biograph Bulletins, 1896–1908,* compiled by Kemp R. Niver (Los Angeles: Locaire Research Group, 1971), pp. 59–73.

20. Cohen, "History and Genre," pp. 205–206; Hans Robert Jauss, *Towards an Aesthetic of Reception* (Brighton: Harvester Press, 1982), p. 80; Neale, *Genre,* p. 19.

21. I owe this phrase to an unpublished lecture on genre by Elizabeth Cowie.

22. Jauss, *Towards an Aesthetic,* p. 79.

23. Jean Mitry, *Dictionnaire du cinéma* (Paris: Larousse, 1963), p. 276; quoted in Altman, *American Film Musical,* p. 95.

24. Altman, *American Film Musical,* p. 96. See also Altman's discussion of the definition of the western in "A Semantic/Syntactic Approach to Film Genre," reprinted in this volume.

25. Marc Vernet, "Genre," *Film Reader* 3 (February 1978): 13.

26. David Bordwell, Janet Staiger, and Kristin Thompson, *The Classical Hollywood Cinema: Film Style and Mode of Production to 1960* (New York: Columbia University Press, 1985), pp. 16–17.

27. Ernest Mandel, *Delightful Murder: A Social History of the Crime Story* (London and Sydney: Pluto Press, 1984), p. 18.

28. Richard Traubner, *Operetta: A Theatrical History* (New York: Oxford University Press, 1989).

29. Jim Collins, *Uncommon Cultures: Popular Culture and Post-Modernism* (New York and London: Routledge, 1989), p. 46.

30. Jauss, *Towards an Aesthetic,* p. 88.

31. Williams, "Is a Radical Genre Criticism Possible?" pp. 123–124.

32. Tag Gallagher, "Shoot-Out at the Genre Corral: Problems in the 'Evolution' of the Western," *Film Genre Reader,* edited by Barry K. Grant (Austin: University of Texas Press, 1986), pp. 202–216; reprinted in this volume.

33. See, in particular, Boris Eikenbaum, "The Theory of the Formal Method," and Jury Tynyanov, "On Literary Evolution," both in *Readings in Russian Poetics: Formalist and Structuralist Views,* edited by Ladislav Matejka and Krystyna Pomorska (Ann Arbor: Michigan Slavic Publications, 1978); and Viktor Shklovsky's views as summarized both in these works and in Victor Erlich, *Russian Formalism: History-Doctrine* (New Haven and London: Yale University Press, 1981), pp. 259–260.

34. Tynyanov, "On Literary Evolution," pp. 72–73.

35. Quoted in Erlich, *Russian Formalism*, p. 260.

36. Jauss, *Towards an Aesthetic,* pp. 105–106.

37. On exploitation, juvenilization, and the emergence of the teenpic, see Thomas Doherty, *Teenagers and Teenpics: The Juvenilization of American Movies in the 1950s* (Boston: Unwin Hyman, 1988). On the role of special effects, see Steve Neale, "Hollywood Strikes Back—Special Effects in Recent American Cinema," *Screen* 21, no. 3 (1981): 101–105.

38. Dates for series titles indicate initial year of publication. On mass-produced fiction, series, and genres, see, among others, Christine Bold, *Selling the Wild West: Popular Western Fiction, 1860–1960* (Bloomington and Indianapolis: Indiana University Press, 1987); *The Pulps: Fifty Years of American Pop Culture,* edited by Tony Goodstone (New York: Chelsea House, 1970); Ron Goulart, *Great History of Comic Books* (Chicago and New York: Contemporary Books, 1986); Theodore Peterson, *Magazines in the Twentieth Century* (Urbana: University of Illinois Press, 1956); Janice A. Radway, *Reading the Romance: Women, Patriarchy and Popular Literature* (Chapel Hill: University of North Carolina Press, 1984); Quentin Reynolds, *The Fiction Factory, or From Pulp Row to Quality Street* (New York: Random House, 1955); Frank L. Schick, *The Paperbound Book in America* (New York: R. R. Bowker, 1958); and Piet Schreuders, *The Book of Paperbacks: A Visual History of the Paperback* (London: Virgin Books, 1981).

39. The only books dealing with a number of genres across a variety of institutions and forms are, so far as I am aware, John G. Cawelti, *Adventure, Mystery, and Romance* (Chicago and London: University of Chicago Press, 1976); and Robert C. Toll, *The Entertainment Machine: American Show Business in the Twentieth Century* (Oxford: Oxford University Press, 1982). Research is also needed on the institutional connections between the cinema, the theater, radio, television, and popular music, which in part enable cross-media generic circulation. For a summary and bibliography of some of the work to date, see Calvin Pryluck, "Industrialization of Entertainment in the United States," in *Current Research in Film: Audiences, Economics and Law,* vol. 2, edited by Bruce A. Austin (Norwood, N.J.: Ablex, 1986).

40. The kind of studies I have in mind are best represented, to date, by Altman's *American Film Musical,* especially his emphasis on edited alternation in constructing a "dual focus" narrative and his concepts of the "audio" and "video" dissolve, esp. pp. 16–27 and 59–89; John Mueller's *Astaire Dancing: The Musical Films* (New York: Knopf, 1985), esp. "Astaire's Use of the Camera," pp. 26–34; and Christine Saxton's *Illusions of Grandeur: The Representation of Space in the American Western* (Ann Arbor, Mich.: University Microfilms, Inc., 1988).

41. Williams, "Is a Radical Genre Criticism Possible?" pp. 121–122.

42. Cohen, "History and Genre," p. 203.

43. Terry Threadgold, "Talking about Genre: Ideologies and Incompatible Discourses," *Cultural Studies* 3, no. 1 (January 1989): 121–122.

44. Geoffrey Nowell-Smith, "Popular Culture," *New Formations,* no. 2 (Summer 1987): 79–90.

45. For a discussion of this idea in relation to the cinema, see Steve Neale, "Art Cinema as Institution," *Screen* 22, no. 1 (1981): 11–40.

46. Cawelti, *Adventure, Mystery, and Romance;* Schatz, *Hollywood Genres;* Will Wright, *Sixguns and Society: A Structural Study of the Western* (Berkeley: University of California Press, 1975).

47. Williams, "Is a Radical Genre Criticism Possible?" p. 123.

48. Garth S. Jowett, "Giving Them What They Want: Movie Audience Research before 1950," in *Current Research in Film,* vol. 1, edited by Austin.

49. Altman, *American Film Musical,* p. 94.

50. Possibly the worst example I have come across is Judith Hess Wright, "Genre Films and the Status Quo," *Jump Cut,* no. 1 (May–June 1974): 1, 16, 18; reprinted in this volume.

51. Colin MacCabe, introduction to *High Theory/Low Culture: Analysing Popular Television and Film,* edited by MacCabe (Manchester: Manchester University Press, 1986), p. 4.

52. Nowell-Smith, "Popular Culture," p. 88.

53. See Tynyanov, "On Literary Evolution."

54. Dennis Porter, *The Pursuit of Crime: Art and Ideology in Detective Fiction* (New Haven: Yale University Press, 1981); Kristin Thompson, *Breaking the Glass Armor: Neoformalist Film Analysis* (Princeton: Princeton University Press, 1988), esp. pp. 49–86.

55. Daniel Gerould, "Russian Formalist Theories of Melodrama," *Journal of American Culture* 1, no. 1 (Spring 1978): 154.

56. Williams, "Is a Radical Genre Criticism Possible?" p. 124.

14. Hybrid or Inbred: The Purity Hypothesis and Hollywood Genre History

JANET STAIGER

Two theses in recent film scholarship seem closely linked. One thesis is that films produced in Hollywood in the past forty years or so are persistently instances of genre mixing. For example, in discussing two films, *Back to the Future Part III* (Robert Zemeckis, 1990) and *Dances with Wolves* (Kevin Costner, 1990), Jim Collins writes,

> . . . they represent two divergent types of genre film that co-exist in current popular culture. One is founded on dissonance, on eclectic juxtapositions of elements that very obviously don't belong together, while the other is obsessed with recovering some sort of missing harmony, where everything works in unison. Where the former involves an ironic hybridization of pure classical genres . . . , the latter epitomizes a "new sincerity" that rejects any form of irony in its sanctimonious pursuit of lost purity.[1]

Collins notes that John Cawelti noticed this generic transformation happening as long ago as the early 1970s. What Collins hopes to contribute is a description of the 1990s films as "ironic hybridization" and "new sincerity," as well as an explanation for the trend.

The second thesis in recent scholarship is that genre studies has been handicapped by its failure to sort out just exactly what critics are doing when they think about "genre." Examples of this thesis are excellent essays by Rick Altman, Tom Gunning, and Adam Knee in a 1995 issue of *Iris*. Interestingly, it is also in the early 1970s that Andrew Tudor provides a detailed discussion of the problems of doing genre studies, just when Cawelti notices a rash of genre transformations occurring.[2]

This conjunction of theses about genre films and how to do genre studies in the 1970s and again in the 1990s might be explained in two different ways. One is that something different happens in Hollywood movies which provokes critical attention to how we categorize and define groups of films. Another—and the one I want to argue for—is that Hollywood films have never been "pure"—that is, easily arranged into categories. All that has been pure has been sincere attempts to find order among variety.

Good reasons exist to find such order. For one thing, patterns of plot structure and conventions of representation do persist throughout decades (and some plot structures and conventions predate the emergence of cinema). To suggest, as I shall, that Hollywood films have never been pure instances of genres is not to say that Hollywood films do not evince patterns. Patterns do exist. Moreover, patterns are valuable material for deviation, dialogue, and critique. Variations from patterns may occur for making a text fresh or for commentary about the issues raised within the standard pattern, and both aesthetic and ideological functions of variations make no sense without a notion of some pattern or order. Hence, although the tactics of grouping films by genre have been eclectic, grouping films can still be an important scholarly act because it may elucidate what producers and consumers of films do. That is, they see films against a hypothesized pattern based on viewing other films. The process of comparison—which requires pattern—is crucial to communication and may contribute to the enjoyment of a text.[3]

Where finding order may go awry, however, is when a subjective order visible in the present is mapped onto the past and then assumed to be the order visible in the past. This historicist fallacy is then compounded if the past pattern is assumed to be pure against a visible present that is not, that the visible present is some transformation, deterioration, or hybridization of a pure essence and origin.

To claim that films produced in "New Hollywood" (hereafter "post-Fordian Hollywood") are typified by a recombinant force is to misunderstand seriously "Old Hollywood" (hereafter "Fordian Hollywood").[4] And the cause of the historical error is our own critical apparatus that has led us to believe erroneously that Hollywood films and genres were once pure. To make this argument more than an assertion, I want in this essay to review why the "genre" purity thesis is fallacious, both theoretically and historically, and why the "hybrid" claim for post-Fordian Hollywood is a particularly pernicious characterization.

A THEORETICAL REJECTION OF THE PURITY THESIS FOR FORDIAN HOLLYWOOD

Two ways exist to argue theoretically against a purity thesis for films created during the Fordian era of Hollywood. One argument is to note that the eclectic practices and failures of prior critics of genre suggest that any attempt to find a suitable method for describing genres is doomed: if critics could have done it, they would have already. The other theoretical argument is to take a poststructuralist position that any observed pattern will invariably criticize itself. Both arguments have recently been used to discuss the activity of genre study.

The observation of eclectic practices and failures to describe genres by previous critics is the argumentation method preferred by film scholars when tackling the difficulties of hypothesizing patterns across films. Indeed, this is the strategy employed by Tudor in his 1973 analysis of the pitfalls of doing genre work. Tudor notes four methods by which critics might try to group films, and he underlines the problems for each one. These methods, and my labels for them, are as follows: (1) find a film and judge other films against the pattern and conventions in that film (the *idealist* method); (2) determine from empirical observation the necessary and sufficient characteristics to include a film in the category (the *empiricist* method); (3) make an a priori declaration of the characteristics of the group (the *a priori* method); and (4) use cultural expectations to categorize the text (the *social convention* method).

Problems with the *idealist method* include finding ways to judge among various declarations of which film is the ideal from which the pattern should be derived. For the *empiricist method,* a circularity exists. The critic cannot observe objectively, since the critic has already predetermined which films to include in the group in order to find the necessary and sufficient characteristics. The a priori method like the *idealist method* presents problems of settling debates among critics as well as operating in a predetermined fashion. Finally, the *social convention method* raises questions about how the critic finds evidence of expectations and determines cultural consensus. Moreover, for all four methods, characteristics can shift from grouping to grouping. Tudor notes that while the western is defined by "certain themes, certain typical actions, certain characteristic mannerisms," the horror film is defined by the above *and* also the "intention to horrify." [5] Tudor's reaction is to take the practical approach I have mentioned already: simply to live with the inconsistencies in method and "deficiencies" in the objects of analysis for the sake of what might be learned from textual comparison. Indeed, most film scholars know these theoretical shortcomings of genre study, and then just forge ahead anyway.

The inability of previous scholarship to find an appropriate method of genre categorizing has also been the focus of the recent essays by Gunning, Knee, and Altman. They, too, note the eclectic practices and failures associated with genre criticism. Gunning particularly stresses that the groupings created by critics assume some kind of "preexistent phenomena" that critics "articulate." [6] These phenomena may be quite at odds with the use of genre terms by individuals charged with distributing and exhibiting films, who may have much to gain by expanding the categories into which a film might fit and thus widening the appeals to various audiences. Thus, Gunning urges that scholars distinguish carefully between academic and industrial acts of genre classification.

In reviewing the sources of science fiction films of the 1950s, Knee details a variety of categories of films from which these movies drew their features. Among them are the war film of the 1940s and the postwar documentary. In fact, Knee eventually concludes that 1950s "science fiction in a sense functions both as a genre and as a mode of generic discourse, a rendering fantastic of other generic forms."[7] Such a view of the "adjectival" possibilities of genre categories has existed for some time among scholars of melodrama who argue that melodrama is less a narrative formula and more a mode of vision, inflected upon many different narrative patterns.

Altman, too, outlines contradictions in categorizing films by genre. Expanding somewhat on Gunning's list, he details four different approaches to "genres": (1) a *model,* which becomes a formula of production; (2) a *structure,* which exists as a textual system in a film; (3) an *etiquette,* which is the category used by distributors and exhibitors; and (4) a *contract,* which is an agreement with spectators on how to read a film.[8] These four approaches then produce five disparities in the critical application of genres to individual texts or groups of texts: (1) words used for genres are sometimes nouns and sometimes adjectives; (2) producers try to reproduce the norm but also deviate from it; (3) genres defined by critics are different from genres perceived by audiences; (4) genre categories are sometimes historical and sometimes trans-historical; and (5) genres defined by producers are different from genres analyzed by critics.

In all of these cases of attention to the eclectic practices and failures of critics to delineate clear, coherent, and consistent categories for films, the underlying premise is *not* that this could not be done. Rather, it is that until critics sort this out and everyone—from the authors to the distributors and exhibitors to the audiences and the critics—agrees on how to categorize films, no hope exists for genre study to function so that critics might find exemplars of the formulas, patterns, and conventions. Thus, this theoretical argument against a "purity" thesis operates from an assumption that human behavior and labeling can never be controlled in such a way that critics would know a "pure" genre or genre film.

This practical approach to arguing against critical knowledge of "pure" genre films is quite different from a poststructuralist thesis. A poststructuralist thesis would argue that every text inherently displays what it is not. A good example of this has been the argumentation against a purity thesis invoked by Thomas O. Beebee in his study of literary texts, and this method could fruitfully be applied to film studies. Like Tudor and Altman, Beebee finds four different approaches to genre: (1) as *rules,* which display the "authorial intention" in production of the text (adherence to or deviation from the conventions and patterns might occur); (2) as *species,* which is the historical and cultural lineage of a genre text; (3) as *pat-*

terns *of textual features,* which exist "in the text itself"; and (4) as *reader conventions,* which exist "in the reader."[9] Appealing to poststructuralism, Beebee suggests that every act of labeling is "always already unstable":[10] "I argue that, since a 'single' genre is only recognizable as difference, as a foregrounding against the background of its neighboring genres, every work involves more than one genre, even if only implicitly."[11] Thus, genre labeling by any of the above four approaches is "inescapable" (individuals cannot understand a text except in context with surrounding texts). Moreover, the text is inevitably impure because it cannot but be known by the context in which it exists. Beebee goes on to argue that genre texts often are in dialogue with their own definition by (fallacious) exclusion, creating moments of metatextuality and places for assessing ideological struggle.[12]

Beebee's approach to the problems of genre and notions of the "purity" of a text is most obviously familiar in poststructuralist criticism that elucidates structuring absences ("what a text cannot say but says in spite of itself"), evidences of overdetermination, and intertextual dialogues. Since poststructuralism hypothesizes this breaching of boundaries and impurity to be features of every text, then any text located as an instance of genre would also, ipso facto, breach generic boundaries and display its excluded otherness. In other words, no genre film is pure.

Both the practical argument about eclectic practices and failures and the poststructuralist argument provide theoretical reasons why critics should reject the notion that Fordian Hollywood ever produced pure examples of genre films. Why is it, then, that the sense of a "transformation" in genres or an "ironic hybridization" and a "new sincerity" exists strongly enough in the era of post-Fordian Hollywood to encourage special attention to generic instability as some new feature of the post-Fordian era?[13] Cawelti believes the trend is due to an exhaustion and inability of the underlying myths of popular genres to deal with the post–Vietnam War era. Collins explains "ironic hybridization" and "new sincerity" as attempts to master "the media-saturated landscape of contemporary culture."[14] In cases of "ironic hybridization," the films explore the plurality of genre experiences through referential dialogues with their sources. In cases of "new sincerity," the films revert nostalgically to seek a lost "authenticity."[15] Both textual strategies are methods to control a sensory experience of the "hyperconscious."[16]

Another explanation exists as to why Cawelti and Collins find generic transformations and hybridizations in post-Fordian Hollywood, and that is that they never interrogate the generic descriptions of Fordian Hollywood. As Gunning notes, the beginning of genre classification by film critics occurs in the 1940s, particularly in the writings of Robert Warshow and James Agee. Film genre study accelerates with the arrival in the universities of academic film studies and the critical methods of new criticism, structuralism, and semiotics. The descriptions of Fordian Hollywood genres upon which Cawelti and Collins rely are ones constituted by film critics observing a limited set of films produced mostly between 1930 and 1960.[17] Additionally, those founding generic descriptions display the definitional fallacies described above.

Even more significantly, the generic descriptions are produced by critical methods that *by their very methodology* offer one genre category with which to label and analyze the text. New criticism analyzes how great works overcome apparent contradictions to create a master coherence: all the parts are made to fit together by the critic or the text is demeaned as a lesser artistic work. Structuralism finds one underlying binary opposition influencing the surface. Semiotics looks for narrative patterns and transformations that also reveal primary, if perhaps contradictory, structuring paradigms.

What Cawelti and Collins do not tackle is how arbitrary and inadequate those original generic descriptions are to the original texts. Fordian Hollywood genre texts appear to be suddenly transforming in the 1970s or hybridizing in the 1990s because the generic definitions were "fixed" by critics in the 1960s using critical methods that sought coherence and purity. This "fixing" of genre definition (and of text in genre category) ignored (or sought to overcome through critical argumentation of coherence) the industrial practice by Fordian Hollywood of providing at least two plots for every movie. And it is here that I turn to historical reasons to reject the purity thesis of Fordian Hollywood genres.

A HISTORICAL JUSTIFICATION FOR THE REJECTION OF THE PURITY THESIS FOR FORDIAN HOLLYWOOD

Several fundamental economic and ideological forces influenced the normative construction of the conventions of the classical film produced by Fordian Hollywood. Among these were the needs to (1) both standardize and differentiate products, and (2) market movies to many individuals. From the 1910s, Hollywood business people assumed several types of audiences: adult and child, male and female, urban and rural. In analyzing what appealed to these various audiences, these people assumed that certain genres had greater appeals to the various subgroups. Throughout the history of Fordian Hollywood, discourse is plentiful about the varying tastes. Moreover, a movie appealing to a variety of audiences was praised as having good potential box office. Reviewers often tried to describe what the various audiences would or would not find in a film.

The Fordian Hollywood film is typified by usually having two plots— one often being a heterosexual romance. What makes this dual plot line "classical" is that the two plot lines hinge on and affect each other. The advantage of the dual plot line, I would argue, is that such a narrative structure permits appeals to multiple subgroups of taste. Moreover, the edge for one plot line being a heterosexual romance is the presumptive appeal to women consumers (whom the industry also assumed from the 1910s were major decision-makers in family entertainment choices). Finally, add to this the need to differentiate product. Combinations and rearrangements of formulas are quite simple if two conventional plot lines from different genres are merged together.

To test the thesis that Fordian Hollywood films are a mixture of multiple genres and not pure examples, I need to analyze them. However, since the theorists of genre point out how many different ways genres might be defined, I want briefly to show that no matter how I create the criteria by which genres are constructed, Fordian Hollywood movies will not stand up to the purity hypothesis. For the most part, I will make only gestures toward this proof, but I hope the evidence and argumentation will seem to have sufficient validity that common sense will take my argument to its conclusion.

For my purposes here, I will use Altman's set of the four methods for defining genres that I described previously: a *model*, a *structure*, an *etiquette*, and a *contract*. To determine etiquette and contract, I will use film reviews as a sort of explicit statement of mediation among the distributors, exhibitors, and spectators. My presumption is that film reviewers are functioning as surrogate consumers, following up on the promotion and publicity generated by the studios and affirming or denying the proposed reading strategies to counsel viewers about what they will see. Thus, the reviews are one among several sites of evidence for both etiquette and contract.

How did Fordian Hollywood construct genres as models of production? They certainly did not construct them rigorously or neatly. One way to determine how studios perceived formulas would be to examine the work areas of associate producers for studios. In 1932, Irving Thalberg's associate producers were organized as follows: Al Lewin was in charge of sophisticated stories; Bernie Hyman, animal stories; Bernie Fineman, genre pics and curios; Eddie Mannix, action films; Larry Weingarten, Marie Dressler films; Paul Bern, sex fables; and Harry Rapf, sad stories.[18]

Beyond the use of dual-plot structures and the incoherence evident in MGM's allocation of work assignments (which is typical of all the studios) is the production source of stories. Since Fordian Hollywood found purchasing novels, plays, and magazine stories economical (the story came ready-made and possibly with some indication of consumer satisfaction and advance publicity), Fordian Hollywood dealt a good deal of the time with pre-made stories that might not fit any studio-produced formula.[19]

The pre-made stories were usually reconfigured to adhere to Fordian Hollywood norms of storytelling, but their original sources outside the studio system contaminated them. Moreover, the value of innovation produced work in cycles, widely acknowledged by commentators on the Fordian Hollywood system.[20] No, the purity hypothesis most certainly would not hold up if I were to use the *model* method of defining Fordian Hollywood genres.

What about the *structure* method? Here is the method most likely to result in satisfactory findings, since the point of the structure method is to uncover underlying, nonconscious patterns that only the sensitive critic can reveal. Is Fordian Hollywood replete with examples of films that display pure examples of genres with no interference by other patterns or formulas, no hybridizing? Here is how three critics deal with apparently prototypical genres or examples of genre films:

(1) Paul Kerr, in discussing film noir, writes: "Furthermore, the 'hybrid' quality of the film noir was perhaps, at least in part, attributable to increasing studio insecurities about marketing their B product (covering all their generic options, as it were, in each and every film)."[21]

(2) Dana Polan, in discussing *In a Lonely Place* (Nicholas Ray, 1950), allocates the film to film noir, screwball comedy, and gothic romance categories.[22]

(3) Peter Wollen, discussing *Psycho* (Alfred Hitchcock, 1960) and *Marnie* (Hitchcock, 1964), declares: "[The films are] hybrids of the fairy tale with a detective story."[23]

I do not mean by these examples to suggest that no critic could ever find examples of "pure" structures of a genre. However, I would also argue that if another critic came along, that second, argumentative critic could likely make a case for contamination, influence, or degradation of the pure-case example. How to do this is neatly argued by David Bordwell in his book *Making Meaning*.[24] Recalcitrant data exist in all Fordian Hollywood films to permit critical debate and perception of other patterns and formulas: see the second plot line just to begin. Moreover, the argumentative critic could easily dispute the pure-example critic's original definition of the pattern and conventions of the genre category, as shown by the theoretical work of Altman, Gunning, and Beebee.

How easy this argumentation would be to do is evident when I turn to the *etiquette* and *contract* methods of genre definition. The routine effect of combination within Fordian Hollywood is obvious not only for apparent cases such as *Abbott and Costello Meet Frankenstein* but even for films that critics have labeled as classics in a particular genre. Take, for instance, the classic "screwball comedy," *It Happened One Night* (Frank Capra, 1934), described by contemporaneous reviewers as "a smooth blending of the various ingredients" with "a deadly enough familiarity all

31. *Abbott and Costello Meet Frankenstein:* The routine effect of genre combination within Fordian Hollywood.

through"; intertextual references include the film being called "another long distance bus story" and a "Molière comedy," while the male protagonist is "one of those crack newspaper men frequently discovered in Hollywood's spacious studios."[25] Those remarks notwithstanding, the reviewers thought the film charming but not the start of a new movie pattern.

Little Caesar (Mervyn LeRoy, 1930) is a crime movie but the "modern criminal . . . thirsts primarily for power." Thus, it is also a "Greek epic tragedy," a gangster film, and a detective movie. *The Public Enemy* (William Wellman, 1931) is a gang film, documentary drama, and comedy, but "in *detail The Public Enemy* is nothing like that most successful of gangster films [*Little Caesar*]."

Stagecoach (John Ford, 1939) is resolutely not described in *Variety* as a western (this would be a derogatory term in 1939), but instead is a "'Grand Hotel' on wheels," an "absorbing drama without the general theatrics usual to picturizations of the early west." Likewise, the *New York Times* uses "frontier melodrama" and concludes with a pun on the

32. *Stagecoach* (1939): A "*Grand Hotel* on wheels."

film director's name: "They've all done nobly by a noble horse opera, but none so nobly as its director. This is one stagecoach that's powered by a Ford."[26]

Casablanca (Michael Curtiz, 1942) will succeed because of the "variety of moods, action, suspense, comedy and drama." While it "goes heavy on the love theme," *Casablanca* also has "adventure" and "anti-Axis propaganda." "[Warner Bros.] is telling it in the high tradition of their hard-boiled romantic-adventure style" with "a top-notch thriller cast," and "they have so combined sentiment, humor and pathos with taut melo-drama and bristling intrigue that the result is a highly entertaining and even inspiring film." It is another "*Grand Hotel* picture, a human cross-roads." *Mildred Pierce* (Curtiz, 1945) is a "drama," "melodrama," "frank sex play," "mother-love" story, and, of course, a "murder-mystery."

As several of the theoreticians of Hollywood suggest, the ways to create genre categories are multiple. By all of them, except the critical method that a scholar can find a pattern within the text, I have argued that, his-torically, no justification exists to assume producers, distributors, exhib-itors, or audiences saw films as being "purely" one type of film. In the case of the structural method, both the problems with traditional critical methods of genre study and the evidence that critics have argued that genres are mixed in Fordian Hollywood cinema suggest that even the structural method of defining genre fails to locate "pure" examples of genres within Fordian Hollywood cinema. This is not to suggest that the pattern or genre is not "pure" but that Fordian Hollywood films do not provide clean examples of the critically defined genre.

THE PERNICIOUS HYBRID THESIS OF POST-FORDIAN HOLLYWOOD

In the preceding two sections, I have argued that representing Fordian Hollywood films as simple examples of films that would fit into neat, co herent genre categories is an inadequate thesis both theoretically and historically. Rather, films produced during that period were perceived by the producers and audiences to belong potentially to several categories. No one worried about this. Instead the lack of purity broadened the film's appeal in terms both of the likely audiences who might enjoy the movie and of the film's originality.

The reason, however, to expend this much effort on the problem of the purity thesis for Fordian Hollywood cinema is that the purity hypothesis is then used as the foundation upon which is built a *critical difference* for the post-Fordian Hollywood era. It is one thing to claim, as Cawelti does, that genres are transforming in the early 1970s. It is another to propose that post-Fordian cinema is typified by its hybridity.

The reasons for my complaint are twofold. One is that this proposed difference just is not the case.[27] The second reason is that the use of the term *hybrid* for post-Fordian cinema distorts and reduces the potential value that the theory of hybridity has for cultural scholars.

The notion of "hybridity" comes from botany and zoology and describes the crossbreeding of separate species.[28] An influential application of this organic concept to literature comes from Mikhail Bakhtin. What Bakhtin writes stresses the meeting of two different "styles" or "languages" derived from different cultures. He summarizes: "The novelistic hybrid is *an artistically organized system for bringing different languages in contact with one another,* a system having as its goal the illumination of one language by means of another, the carving out of a living image of another language."[29] Bakhtin particularly emphasizes that the event of hybridization permits *dialogue* between the two languages. In botany and zoology, the function of hybridization is to produce invigorated offspring by crossbreeding, but the offspring may be sterile. So too, the hybridized literary text (often a parody) may create a strong effect, but the hybrid itself does not generate a new family.

In accord with Bakhtin's original proposition, the recognition of textual hybridity has been fruitfully appropriated by postcolonial scholars to describe the outcome of cross-cultural encounters. The editors of *The Post-Colonial Studies Reader* write that an event of textual hybridity does not deny "the traditions from which [a hybrid text] springs," nor does a hybrid event signal the disappearance of the culture from which the hybrid derives.[30]

More significantly, however, a textual hybrid has effects on colonizers. Homi K. Bhabha points out that the recognition by colonizers of hybridity produced by the colonized must call into question the transparency of colonizing authority. In "Signs Taken for Wonders," Bhabha cautions,

> The discriminatory effects of the discourse of cultural colonialism, for instance, do not simply or singly refer to a "person," or to a dialectical power struggle between self and Other, or to a discrimination between mother culture and alien cultures. Produced through the strategy of disavowal, the reference of discrimination is always to the process of splitting as the condition of subjection: a discrimination between the mother culture and its bastards, the self and its doubles, where the trace of what is disavowed is not repressed but repeated as something different—a mutation, a hybrid. . . .
> . . . Hybridity is the sign of the productivity of colonial power, its shifting forces and fixities; it is the name for the strategic reversal of the process of domination through disavowal (that is, the production of discriminatory identities that secure the "pure" and original identity of authority).[31]

Bhabha's point here is clear: to recognize a hybrid forces the dominant culture to look back at itself and see its presumption of universality. Hybridity always opens up the discriminatory presumptions of purity, authenticity, and originality from which this textual hybrid is declared to be a deviation, a bastard, a corruption. Bhabha goes on to explain that "the hybrid object . . . revalues its presence by resiting it as the signifier of *Entstellung—after the intervention of difference*. It is the power of this strange metonymy of presence to so disturb the systematic (and systemic) construction of discriminatory knowledges that the cultural, once recognized as the medium of authority, becomes virtually unrecognizable."[32]

To use the notion of hybridity for the mixing of genres in post-Fordian Hollywood cinema is, thus, to pervert doubly its potential value for cultural studies. In the social and communicative sense in which Bakhtin uses the term *hybridity,* the notion ought to be reserved for truly cross-cultural encounters. I have to ask, are the breedings of genres occurring in Fordian and post-Fordian Hollywood truly cross-cultural? Truly one language speaking to another? I seriously doubt that the strands of patterns that intermix in Hollywood filmmaking are from different species. Rather, they are in the same language family of Western culture. The breeding occurring is not cross-cultural, but perhaps, and with a full sense of the derogatory implications involved, even *a case of inbreeding.*

Moreover, Bhabha's very particular political sense of hybridity suggests that when critics encounter a cross-cultural hybrid, the questions of power, of presumptive authority, purity, and origination of the dominant genre, ought to be the focus of the analysis. Unlike Bakhtin, Bhabha stresses the historical fact of an inequality of cross-cultural contacts and communications.

I cannot, of course, do more than request that critics respect the possibility that narrowing the application of theories such as textual hybridity to a specific situation has value—both descriptive and explanatory—to scholars. However, I do make the plea. Despite all the theoretical and historical problems associated with categorizing films, perhaps the most valuable critical contribution that can be made is to analyze the social, cultural, and political implications of pattern mixing. In the above theoretical discussion, none of the writers ultimately declared the project of genre criticism impossible or unworthy—only fraught with scholarly difficulties. My rejection of the hybridity thesis for post-Fordian Hollywood cinema is not a rejection of (1) the view that pattern mixing is occurring; or (2) the fact that post-Fordian Hollywood cinema is producing hybrids both internally within the United States and externally throughout the world economy of signs. Internal hybrids[33] would be examples of films created by minority or subordinated groups that use genre mixing or genre parody to dialogue with or criticize the dominant. Films by U.S. feminists, African Americans, Hispanics, independents, the avant-garde, and so forth might be good cases of internal hybrids.

Both inbreeding and hybridizing need to be studied, and genre criticism has a contribution to make toward that work. Considering the implications of how critics apply theories can help in that cultural and critical work, but distinguishing between inbreeding and hybridity throughout the history of Hollywood has scholarly potential.

Notes

1. Jim Collins, "Genericity in the Nineties: Eclectic Irony and the New Sincerity," in *Film Theory Goes to the Movies,* ed. Jim Collins, Hillary Radner, and Ava Preacher Collins (New York: Routledge, 1993), pp. 242–243.

2. Rick Altman, "Emballage réutilisable: Les produits génériques et le processus de recyclage," *Iris* 20 (Fall 1995): 13–30; Tom Gunning, "'Those Drawn with a Very Fine Camel's Hair Brush': The Origins of Film Genres," *Iris* 20 (Fall 1995): 49–61; Adam Knee, "Generic Change in the Cinema," *Iris* 20 (Fall 1995): 31–39; Andrew Tudor, *Theories of Film* (New York: Viking Press, 1973), reprinted as "Genre and Critical Methodology" in *Movies and Methods,* ed. Bill Nichols (Berkeley: University of California Press, 1976), pp. 118–126; John G. Cawelti, "*Chinatown* and Generic Transformation in Recent American Films," this volume.

3. Tudor, "Genre and Critical Methodology," pp. 119–121.

4. I reject the representation of Hollywood as "new" after World War II; rather, I see Hollywood's industrial structure, modes of production, signifying practices, and modes of reception as an intensification of monopoly capitalism. Following contemporary theorists of global capitalism, I am relabeling the period of Hollywood of 1917 to around 1960 as "Fordian Hollywood"; the Hollywood of post-1960 or so I will call "post-Fordian Hollywood" to emphasize the strong linkages to the past as well as the industry's accommodations to late monopoly capitalism. Moreover, this labeling permits the possibility of a new descriptive term for Hollywood if it moves beyond "post-Fordian" practices—which is less the case for a label such as "new." See Kevin Robins, "Reimagined Communities? European Image Spaces, Beyond Fordism," *Cultural Studies* 3, no. 2 (1989): 145–165; Arjun Appadurai, "Disjuncture and Difference in the Global Cultural Economy," *Public Culture* 2, no. 2 (Spring 1990): 1–24; and Annabelle Sreberny-Mohammadi, "The Global and the Local in International Communications," in *Mass Media and Society,* ed. James Curran and Michael Gurevitch (London: Edward Arnold, 1991), pp. 118–138.

5. Tudor, "Genre and Critical Methodology," p. 120 (emphasis in original).

6. Gunning, "'Those Drawn with a Very Fine Camel's Hair Brush,'" p. 50.

7. Knee, "Generic Change in the Cinema," p. 36.

8. Altman, "Emballage réutilisable," p. 14. This list is quite similar to Thomas O. Beebee's list, summarized below, in *The Ideology of Genre: A Comparative Study of Generic Instability* (University Park: Pennsylvania State University Press, 1994). Altman does not refer to Beebee, and I have no reason to assume influence: just the happy coincidence of intelligences.

9. Beebee, *The Ideology of Genre,* p. 3.

10. Ibid., p. 27.

11. Ibid., p. 28.

12. Ibid., pp. 12–19.

13. Cawelti, "*Chinatown* and Generic Transformation"; James Monaco, *American Film Now: The People, the Power, the Money, the Movies* (New York: New American Library, 1979); Robin Wood, "Smart-ass and Cutie-pie: Notes towards an Evaluation of Altman," *Movie,* no. 21 (Autumn 1975): 1–17. Monaco writes: "*Easy Rider,* by all accounts one of the most significant movies of the decade, was a Chase-Caper-Road-Youth-Drag-Buddy film," and in the 1970s, "the lines of definition that separate one genre from another have continued to disintegrate" (p. 56). Wood even uses the "hybrid" term: "[Robert Altman's] best films are hybrids, products of a fusion of 'European' aspirations with American genres" (p. 7). As I shall discuss below in the third section, at least Wood's use of the term *hybrid* may have justification, since he suggests an encounter between two "languages" (although whether European cinema is another "language" than Hollywood could be debated).

14. Collins, "Genericity in the Nineties," p. 243.

15. Ibid., p. 257.

16. Ibid., p. 248.

17. The lack of access to films prior to 1930 is an important cause for the problem of the limited descriptions by these critics of Hollywood genres.

18. "Metro-Goldwyn-Mayer," *Fortune* (6 December 1932), reprinted in *The American Film Industry,* ed. Tino Balio (Madison: University of Wisconsin Press, 1976), p. 260.

19. Motion Picture Producers and Distributors of America, *Film Facts 1942: 1922—20 Years of Self Government—1942* (New York: MPPDA, n.d.), p. 52.

20. William J. Fadiman, "Books into Movies," *Publishers' Weekly,* 8 September 1934, pp. 753–755.

21. Paul Kerr, "'My Name Is Joseph H Lewis,'" *Screen* 24, nos. 4–5 (July–October 1983): 52.

22. Dana Polan, *In a Lonely Place* (London: British Film Institute, 1993).

23. Peter Wollen, "Hybrid Plots in *Psycho,*" in Wollen, *Readings and Writings: Semiotic Counter-Strategies* (London: Verso, 1982), p. 37.

24. David Bordwell, *Making Meaning: Inference and Rhetoric in the Interpretation of Cinema* (Cambridge, Mass.: Harvard University Press, 1989).

25. These and the following unattributed quotations are from contemporary reviews in *Hollywood Reporter, Motion Picture Herald, New Republic, New York Times, Saturday Review, Time,* and *Variety.*

26. *Variety* and *Motion Picture Herald* would not use "western" because of that genre's association with a rural taste, but the *New Yorker* does not hesitate.

27. Or both Fordian and post-Fordian cinemas are hybridity cinemas, which is not the way I want to go. See below.

28. It can also apply to genera and family, so technically the term could be used for what we are discussing. However, see my remarks below.

29. Mikhail M. Bakhtin, *The Dialogic Imagination: Four Essays,* trans. Caryl Emerson and Michael Holquist (Austin: University of Texas Press, 1981), p. 361 (emphasis in original).

30. Bill Ashcroft, Gareth Griffiths, and Helen Tiffin, eds., *The Post-Colonial Studies Reader* (London and New York: Routledge, 1995), p. 184.

31. Homi K. Bhabha, "Signs Taken for Wonders: Questions of Ambivalence and Authority under a Tree outside Delhi, May 1817," *Critical Inquiry* 12, no. 1 (Autumn 1985): 153–154.

32. Ibid., p. 157.

33. The term *internal* implies accepting the notion of a "nation," which is a problem for theories of post-Fordian capitalism. This is an issue impossible to take to its appropriate conclusions here.

Part Two: SELECTED GENRE CRITICISM

15. The Western (Genre and Movies)

DOUGLAS PYE

The generic and individual identities of narrative works are created by a large number of elements in combination, many (all?) of which are necessary to those identities without any one or small group being sufficient to define them. In the American cinema, characteristics of the narrative tradition that run across generic boundaries contribute to our sense of what "the western" is as greatly as those features most obviously characteristic of the genre.

In an essay called "The Use of Art for the Study of Symbols," E. H. Gombrich describes a parlor game he remembers from his childhood to illuminate the process of symbol formation in the visual arts. It is also evocative in relation to genre.

> We would agree, for instance, that the person to be guessed would be a film star. . . . The task would be to guess his identity through a series of appropriate emblems or comparisons. The guesser would ask the group in the know such questions as: If he were a flower what would he be? Or what would be his emblem among animals, his style among painters? . . . You might compare each of the answers to the indices of letters and numbers on the sides of an irregular map which combine to plot a position. The psychological category of bearlike creatures sweeps along a wide zone of the metaphorical field, and so does the category of thistly characters, but the two categories are sufficiently distant to determine an area that can be further restricted by further plottings.

Later, Gombrich remarks of the categories that might be employed: "None of these, of course, can be said to have an intrinsic meaning, but they can interest through their very multiplicity and generate meaning within suitably narrow contexts." [1]

The recognition of works as belonging to a specific genre may be seen as the result of a similar process—the intersection of a range of categories, the interplay of which generates meaning within a context narrow

Note: This chapter is excerpted from a longer essay published previously.

enough for recognition of the genre to take place but wide enough to allow enormous individual variation. If the categories are thought of as involving conventions of various kinds, it is easy to see why exhaustive classification of generic elements is impossible. Given the number and possible combinations of elements within a field, the range of meanings and associations that can be generated through the constant movement of narrative and mise-en-scène will be infinite.

Within the American cinema in general, narrative traditions can be characterized in a number of ways: in terms of linearity, psychological involvement, dramatic and temporal-spatial unity, illusionism, and so on.[2] In approaching the western I want to concentrate on a limited number of conventions, some of which relate to broad tendencies of narrative (inside and outside the cinema) and others of which seem more obviously determined by the historical moment, national tradition, and local circumstances.

Certain broad tendencies of narrative can be approached through a theory of fictional modes of the kind Northrop Frye constructs in *The Anatomy of Criticism*.[3] He distinguishes five modes, defined in terms of the range and power of action of the protagonist:

1. Myth, in which the protagonist is superior in kind to other men and his environment. The hero is in fact a god.

2. Romance, in which the hero is superior in degree to other men and his environment. Here the hero is mortal, but his actions are marvelous and the laws of nature tend to be to some extent suspended.

3. The high mimetic mode, in which the protagonist is superior in degree to other men but not to his environment. The hero in this mode is a leader whose authority, passions, and power of expression are greater than ours but who is subject to social control and to the order of nature. This is the mode of tragedy and most epic.

4. The low mimetic mode, in which the protagonist is superior neither to other men nor to the natural world. He is one of us; we respond to his common humanity and demand the same canons of probability we find in our own lives. This is the mode of most realistic fiction.

5. The ironic mode, in which the protagonist is inferior in power or intelligence to ourselves, so that we have a sense of looking down on a scene of frustration or absurdity.

Frye's framework is a useful one if we bear in mind that the modes are not mutually exclusive but form points on a sliding scale, so that they can occur in various combinations in individual works. Frye also adds a further distinction that is relevant here, between tragedy and comedy. Again, these are tendencies, not exclusive categories, and can be found together with any one or more of the five modes. In tragedy the hero is isolated from his society in his fall and death, and in comedy the theme is the re-verse: the integration of the hero with his society. From the five modes and the tragedy/comedy axis, several sources of conflict within the narrative emerge as characteristic—the nature of those conflicts and their outcome contributing to the structure, theme, and mood of the work. The major sources of conflict will be between one human being and another, human beings and nature, and the human being and society—personal/heroic, elemental, and social.

Whatever validity Frye's poetics have, such distinctions are helpful in pointing to issues that must be significant in any discussion of narrative genres.[4] Although Frye's modes are unsatisfactory as final categories, for the purposes of this article, the notion of modes remains useful. Tendencies of this kind may well have a lot to do with genre recognition. At this level, literary and filmic narrative can be seen as continuous, and we may find common tendencies across a number of genres we commonly think of as distinct. Generic differences emerge from the combination of these basic tendencies and the more local conventions.

A further general, and perhaps rather obvious, point. In classical aesthetics, "levels of style" were prescribed for each major kind of literary work: a particular manner accompanied the subject matter. So, in tragedy, the fall and death of a hero would be handled in a serious and elevated style. These levels of style never completely dominated Western literature,[5] but they remained important for each succeeding classicizing movement. Since the early nineteenth century, however, and the achievement of the realist novel, levels of style have effectively broken down, with important consequences. There is no longer any necessary correlation between subject matter and the manner in which it is treated. In the terms I have already used, a fictional mode does not determine a level of style. For instance, a work may contain strong elements of Romance and yet be realized (in its setting, characterization, treatment of action) in a manner that might be called low mimetic, or realistic. This fluid relationship between mode and manner of realization, and especially between a low mimetic manner and high mimetic or romantic mode, is important for the western, the genre I intend to concentrate on.

Apart from the conventions that relate to broad tendencies of narrative are others more obviously determined by local conditions of various kinds. They might include the following:

1. *Plot.* It might be possible to identify within a genre recurring plots that carry with them associations and expectations.

2. *Other structural features.* These might relate both to mode and to plot: recurring "block" constructions, day and night, journey and rest, action and repose.

3. *Character.* Individual incarnations of both central and peripheral figures. In the western, both the distribution of identification figures and the expected hero, heroine, villain configuration. A large list of conventional types can easily be drawn up for the western, together with their most common roles in the action.

4. *Time and space.* Not just the expected temporal-spatial continuity, but recurring historical and geographical settings.

5. *Iconography.* In the western, this would include landscape, architecture, modes of transport, weapons and clothes, and even soundtrack, including recurrent sounds, voices, and kinds of speech.

6. *Themes.* Particular concerns associated with or arising from a complex of elements.

Each of these contains a wide range of possibilities—in combination, the possibilities are enormously multiplied and, with the conventions of mode and so on, the permutations are endless. The variable combination of elements within the western will therefore make each individual work unique in some respects even if it appears highly stereotyped, but it will be unique within a field plotted by the intersection of these various matrices. In terms of Gombrich's game, the field would therefore be narrow enough to register as familiar to an audience and to invoke a wide spectrum of expectations that are aroused, defined, confirmed, or surprised by the moment-to-moment conjunction of elements within each film. The number of more or less familiar elements within the total work is very large, and the movement, both on the screen and in the narrative, creates a dynamic that produces new combinations at each moment of the film.

Seen in this way, a genre will be capable of taking an enormously wide range of emphasis, depending on the interests and intentions of the individual artist. Any one or more than one element can be brought to the foreground while others may all but disappear. Plot, character, theme—each can become central. The relationship of character to the natural world may be a major issue in some westerns while in others landscape may be simply a background to the action; characters can be fully individualized, given complex or conflicting motivation, or presented schematically as morality play figures, embodiments of abstract good or evil. Part of the western's richness must be due to this potential range of emphasis and situation, but underlying this is the peculiar impurity of its inheritance, the convergence of various currents that achieve a special resonance in America.

One current that seems of particular importance is romantic narrative, in Frye's sense. In this mode, the hero is superior in degree to other men and to his environment, but he is mortal—a hero but not a god. His actions in the story tend to be marvelous—he performs wonders—and he often lives in close harmony with the natural world. When such a hero dies, it creates the sense of a spirit passing out of nature, coupled with a melancholy sense of the passing of time, the old order changing and giving way to the new. The mood that is evoked when the hero dies Frye calls "elegiac." At the other end of the scale of romance for Frye is romantic comedy, and he describes the mood corresponding to the elegiac in romantic comedy as "idyllic." In this form, the simple life of the country or frontier is idealized, and the close association with the natural world recurs in the sheep and pleasant meadows of pastoral. Interestingly, Frye identifies the western as the pastoral of modern popular literature, with cattle and ranches instead of sheep and pleasant pastures. But it is clear that the western as we know it is more complex than such a definition will allow. It seems more rewarding to think of its debt from romance as dual, with elements of the elegiac and idyllic modes.

This duality is present in Fenimore Cooper's Leatherstocking tales, the first significant fiction of the West and a formative influence on the tradition of western fiction through the nineteenth century. The five novels present an ambivalent vision of the process of westward expansion—the encroachment of civilization on the wilderness—centering on the scout and hunter, Natty Bumppo. The setting of the tales moves gradually west from New York State to the Great Plains of *The Prairie*, in which Natty, now a very old man, dies facing the setting sun. Natty is in some ways very much the hero of romance (although his social status gave Cooper difficulties): he has talents that set him apart from all other characters, and, more important, he is endowed with an infallible moral sense—he has the ability to know good from evil. Natty lives outside the settlements, which he regards with deep suspicion as corrupt and ungodly, wasteful of the goods God has provided for human use. And yet, although his values are presented as ideal, the westward expansion of society encroaches more and more on the wilderness, pushing Natty farther and farther west. His death, and in fact the tone of more than one of the tales, can be described as elegiac in Frye's sense. At the same time, Natty lives in harmony with the natural world, reading the wilderness as the book of God, so that images of perfected natural life recur in the tales, images in which the natural and moral worlds are united, as they are in Frye's idyllic mode. Characteristically, the tales end with the genteel heroes and heroines, the army officers and their ladies, the kidnapped aristocratic girls, being reintegrated into society—the movement Frye describes as characteristic of comedy—while Natty remains estranged from it, a movement into isolation that evokes the elegiac mood, the inevitable passing of an ideal order.

In Cooper, this current of romantic narrative, capable of inflection in more than one direction, meets other currents of thought associated particularly with the idea of the West and its significance for America, and this conjunction of romantic mode and complex thematic gave a basic shape to the western. It isn't necessary to do more than refer to the complex of ideas about the West that dominated so much of nineteenth-century American thought, since many of the ideas have become commonplaces in the discussion of American literature and film. But it is important to stress the variable associations of the terms "West" and "frontier." From the earliest times, these concepts could mean several things, some of them apparently contradictory. If the West was seen as a potential Eden, the garden of the world, it was also seen as the wilderness, the great American desert. The life of the frontier was both ennobling, because it was close to nature, and primitive, at the farthest remove from civilization. The Indian could be both a child of nature, primitive but innocent, and the naked savage. In Cooper, this dual vision of the Indian is a feature of most of the tales—the virtuous tribe of the Mohicans set against the unredeemable evil of the Mingoes. These very familiar oppositions of garden/desert, civilization/savagery, which are at the heart of ideas about the West, were bound up with the western from the earliest times. They were not always overt, or as important to meaning as they are in Cooper, but they are always at least latent within the material of the genre, providing the western with a unique potential for reflecting on American themes. It is also worth emphasizing the continuity of the developing images of the West in America with much older ideas and myths. So, the images of the garden connect with much earlier images—the Garden of the Hesperides and other earthly paradises to be found in the direction of the sunset—and the opposition of garden and desert can easily take up the biblical images of the Promised Land and the wilderness. Similarly, views of the Indian are at least partially formed from earlier images of the noble savage.

The western is founded, then, on a tremendously rich confluence of romantic narrative and archetypal imagery modified and localized by recent American experience—the potential source of a number of conflicting but interrelated streams of thought and imagery.

After Cooper, the thematic concern with ideas of the West is not maintained at the same level of fiction.[6] Stories of pioneers feed into existing molds of ideas and into existing romantic structures to create the story of western adventure, less concerned with American identity than with action and excitement. In dime novels, the western tale became increasingly extravagant and fantastic, although it was fed by actual events—the Indian wars, the adventures of outlaws and lawmen, the cattle drives. Actual people became the basis of heroes of dime-novel sagas in a constant process of romanticizing actuality in the service of sentimental fiction and the adventure story. The western was also taken up on the stage, becoming one form of melodrama, sometimes with famous western characters playing themselves, and in the Wild West show.

In addition to these developments, the representations of the West in American painting may well have influenced attitudes and helped to create a specifically visual repertoire of western imagery. It is difficult to locate with any precision the film western's debt to these sources, but there are several potentially interesting areas. It is plausible to suggest that landscape painters, themselves probably influenced by contemporary attitudes, should in turn have contributed to ways in which the American landscape was thought of, both in terms of its sublimity and wildness and in terms of the American mission of domesticating the wilderness.[7] Through most of the nineteenth century, there were also painters whose major interest was in recording the appearance and customs of the Indians and frontiersmen, a documentary impulse that retains an important grip on the tradition. Thus the fantastic invention of the dime novelists and their cover designers coexisted with the much more sober accuracy of painters (and photographers) interested in recording what they saw; in between these extremes were various shades of invention, distortion, and interpretation.

Frederic Remington, whose work was disseminated by *Harper's* and *Collier's* weeklies in the years between 1886 and 1909, contains in himself various impulses that indicate the range of visual responses to the West during the period.[8] Many of his drawings of Indians, hunters, and cowboy life are straightforwardly factual, but even here Remington presents a range of incidents that define life on the range for his audience. A second category is more overtly dramatic—narrative pictures with strong romantic or melodramatic feeling ("Fight over a Water Hole," "A Misdeal"). There are others that are moralistic or thematic, the equivalent of much Victorian anecdotal painting: "Solitude" (a solitary buffalo in an open, hilly landscape and near it, a single buffalo skull); "The Twilight of the Indian" (an Indian behind a plough with a fence behind him and in the background both wooden shack and tepee). It is very difficult to separate different impulses in Remington—the categories I have indicated are by no means clearly defined—and this is a crucial point about the western tradition in general: by the end of the nineteenth century, there is no possibility of disentangling the confused and conflicting impulses within the tradition.

I mentioned earlier the importance for the western of the breakdown of levels of style, the split between the mode of fiction and its manner. With the development of the film western, manner—the nature of the presented world—becomes particularly important. From early on, the western film gravitated toward exteriors and a comparative solidity and fullness in the presentation of the fictive world (something we see already in Remington and other painters). However fabulous the story, there tends to be a kind of verisimilitude of surface. We can see this if we compare the minimal setting and costumes that will convey the idea of "western town" in a musical or in a number in a TV spectacular—flats seen in silhouette only, a pair of saloon doors, and a cast wearing jeans and wide-brimmed hats—with almost any town scene in a film or TV western. Clearly, the film setting is stylized, but it has a solidity of appearance that creates a sense of reality—an inhabitable world. The "realism" reveals itself in the large level of repetition and redundancy in such a scene. Many details duplicate or double each other, providing much more than the bare minimum that would signify a western town, enough detail to convince us of the solidity of the presented world.

Obviously enough, this kind of realism is not peculiar to the western—it is a feature of most narrative genres in the American cinema. But a tension between a realism of presentation and a much greater degree of abstraction at other levels does seem characteristic of many westerns—the low mimetic realization "anchors" and gives credence to other, more abstract elements: romantic narrative structures, plots inherited from melodrama, the simple moral framework of sentimental fiction. In the last section of this essay I want to illustrate this kind of tension as one way in which the conflicting elements of the tradition contribute to the richness of the western.

In some films, this tension produces a resonance we tend to associate with symbol. The simultaneous presence of the solid surface and a high degree of abstraction elsewhere causes an oscillation of response from one level to another, an awareness that the narrative flow is not the sole source of meaning, but that it is accompanied by another dimension, intimately tied to it but supplying another kind of meaning. Neither the realism of the surface nor the underlying abstraction dominates in such a context, but a balance is achieved between the two, a relationship analogous to that between denotation and connotation in Roland Barthes.[9]

The famous dance sequence in John Ford's *My Darling Clementine* (1946) seems to me to work like this. The whole passage is something of an interlude in the main development of the narrative, contributing nothing to the revenge plot and little to the Doc Holliday interest. In fact, the episode tends to unbalance the film structurally by being so markedly different from what has gone before. Yet it is partly the reduction of narrative interest that gives the passage its particular force. The interruption of the main channel of communication has the effect of throwing others into relief, while the specific detail is maintained at a level high enough to retain the solidity of the presented world—in the acting, for instance, there is a splendid fullness and individuality.

33. *My Darling Clementine:* Wyatt Earp (Henry Fonda) and Clementine Carter (Cathy Downs) walk toward the dance.

The abstraction is present in the particularly bold conjunction of elements Ford brings together to form the central complex of the sequence: the landscape of Monument Valley, which is barren and inhospitable but beautiful, with the desert coming right to the edge of the town; the partly built church; the stars and stripes; the dance itself. All these things have associations of their own, but together they form an enormously rich associative cluster. At the simplest level we see the dedication of Tombstone's first church, one milestone in the town's growth. But the church is also a tangible sign of community identity and solidarity and of the faith of the settlers (less in religion perhaps than in their own abilities and their social future); and the flag is the emblem of their sense of national identity. These ideas are fused with the more personal human values of family and community in the dance, while the bold juxtaposition of desert and town suggests broader ideas of the conquering of the wilderness, the growth of American civilization. The abstractions invoked are given particular force and the whole scene great emotional weight by the presentation of the dance itself: the inexpert musicians, the naive enthusiasm and lack of pretension, and the homeliness of dances and dancers—the

34. The dance on the church platform (*My Darling Clementine*).

density, at this level, of circumstantial detail "grounds" the symbolized aspiration, giving it concrete form.

The sequence achieves formal completeness with the integration of Wyatt Earp (Henry Fonda) and Clementine (Cathy Downs) into the dance, and they too have both individual and representative significance, as characters within the narrative and also as representatives of East and West— Clementine the embodiment of Eastern refinement, Earp of the "natural," untutored virtues of the frontier. Their walk away from the town toward the dance is given, through their bearing and the visual presentation, a formality and dignity that inevitably suggests a couple walking down the aisle, but a couple that unites the traditional East/West opposition. The interruption of the dance as Earp and Clementine reach the floor has none of the tension or disruptive force interrupted dances take on in other Ford westerns; it is a prelude to a greater harmony, the community joining the dance around the marshal and "his lady fair"—an image that points toward the possibility of a perfected society in the West that will reconcile opposing forces in an ideal harmony.

The ideas invoked in the sequence are commonplaces of the tradition, and Ford asserts them with extraordinary economy in a kind of visual shorthand, so that both the basic image structure of the sequence and its conceptual foundation are highly abstract. But it is impossible to respond only at this denuded level of meaning. If the conceptual, symbolized meaning in a sense robs the scene of its individual life to confer a wider, representative significance on it, the concrete realization constantly reasserts its specific and detailed life in which the objects, people, movement, and music are of this moment only and refuse to be contained by any schematic framework. Response oscillates between the levels of meaning, unable to choose definitely one or the other, rather in the way Barthes describes as characteristic of myth.

Different forms of this tension, in which other elements are in the foreground, can be found in many westerns. The famous "silent" opening of *Rio Bravo* (Howard Hawks, 1959), for instance, is in its way equally abstract, without invoking themes to do with westward expansion at all. The abstraction here is in the characters and action. The main characters are readily identifiable genre types characterized in largely conventional ways: the drunk, the smiling killer, the unbending sheriff. Their presentation is so unambiguous and familiar, and the intense and violent action so compressed in time, that the sequence is almost melodramatic in effect and quite bewildering in the opening moments of the film. Because it is the opening, we rely not on a context for action established by the director during the film, but almost exclusively on genre recognition and expectation, and Hawks plays directly on our experience in his use of Dean Martin, John Wayne, and Claude Akins. His use of conventions of character and action is more than economical, although it is certainly that— it involves a kind of balancing act in which the emblematic presentation of character and the extreme compression of intense action border on the unacceptably schematic. But abstraction is in fact necessary to the sequence's functions in establishing the basic situation of the film and stating its central theme. It is precisely the abstraction that signals the scene so clearly as thematic statement. The rest of the film can be seen as developing and exploring in various forms the issue of self-respect, between the moral poles presented so boldly in the opening action. In fact, the abstraction remains within dramatically acceptable limits partly because Hawks makes his statements not in dialogue but through action that has a specific life of its own in addition to its thematic role, and partly (a related point) because the whole scene is sufficiently grounded in the detail we conventionally expect of a saloon: decor, other characters, actions, costume, and so on. But even so, there is a remarkably low level of redundancy in the sequence, as in fact throughout the film: Hawks excludes a great many familiar western elements and narrows his focus to a small group of characters in, for a western, a very restricted setting. More than any other conventions, he invokes those of character and action, excluding virtually all thematic material related to history and never activating the symbolic potential of the form as Ford does so frequently. This is interesting in relation to Hawks's earlier westerns, *Red River* (1948) and

35. Earp and Clementine are integrated into the dance (*My Darling Clementine*).

The Big Sky (1952), which involve wider "epic" and historical dimensions in which Hawks seems only marginally interested. In both films, the central concern is a very small group of characters and their relationships, but the presence of the epic material has the effect of dissipating to some extent the effectiveness of that focus. The compression of *Rio Bravo* is the result of a self-discipline based on understanding the possibilities inherent in the generic material.

Concentration on positively valued films like *My Darling Clementine* and *Rio Bravo* inevitably tends to suggest that one can ignore the vast mass of western movies and TV series that constitute the bulk of the genre. In practice, this huge number of more or less undistinguished films *is* ignored by criticism, and it is difficult to conceive of a situation in which they will ever receive detailed study. But it is important to bear in mind that these films have made possible the achievements of the recognized directors, keeping alive the conventions. The elements of the tradition are found in all westerns, of whatever quality.

For example, *The Lone Ranger* (William Witney and John English, 1938), which had a long run in the cinema and on TV as a children's series, exists at the pulp end of the western spectrum, while *The Searchers* (John Ford, 1956) is by one of the acknowledged masters of the American cinema and is arguably one of the greatest westerns ever made. It is not a juxtaposition that can be held very long, but long enough to point to common elements. *The Lone Ranger* represents the inheritance of romantic narrative in one of its simplest forms; it centers on the anonymous masked hero who possesses extraordinary powers that set him apart from ordinary men. He is virtually invulnerable—the nearest thing to a god without being immortal. He rides a horse of incredible beauty, which, like its master, has extraordinary gifts. And he is accompanied by a faithful Indian companion—a fact which draws attention to the direct line of descent from Fenimore Cooper. In fact, *The Lone Ranger* can be seen as a debased and simplified version of Cooper's tales, with the hero riding off from the settlements after each adventure, away from all human company except that of his Indian friend, retaining his emotional isolation and his celibacy. There is none of Cooper's complexity, of course, but instead a simple moral scale of polarized good and evil, with the basic terms and the hero's status never questioned.

The Searchers incorporates elements of romance that are very similar, and again the line of descent from Cooper can be fairly easily traced. One thread within the film is the idea of the solitary, invulnerable, wandering hero, Ethan Edwards (John Wayne), for whom life within the settlements is impossible. He appears from the wilderness as the story opens, and when his job is finished he returns to the desert again. In common with the hero of Frye's romantic mode, Ethan's power of action is greater than that of other men. At the same time the film is structured around a version of the romantic quest, which brings to mind the grail quest (Ethan's grail being Debbie), and is largely set in desert terrain that evokes the imagery of the Waste Land familiar from versions of the grail legend but also, through the repeated biblical allusions, the journey of the Israelites to the Promised Land and their years wandering in the wilderness. The settlers are in a sense both attempting to find a Promised Land and are still wandering in the wilderness, living in the barren landscape of Monument Valley. They are also led by an Old Testament soldier-priest in the figure of the Reverend Samuel Johnson Clayton, captain of the Texas Rangers. These elements are very powerful in *The Searchers,* but they are combined with others in such a way that they are never dominant. In particular, Ford gives great complexity to the romance structure by combining it with features more characteristic of lower modes. So, unlike the Lone Ranger, Ethan is humanized, his mortality and human needs emphasized. The aspiration to achieve autonomy and emotional isolation is held in tension with the love for his sister-in-law that binds him to the settlements, and this tension contributes to the psychic split that brings him close to madness. Again, Ethan does not possess the perfect moral sense of Cooper's Leatherstocking; in this respect, he is more like the characteristic heroes of realist fiction, only too fallible morally.

I think it is reasonable to claim that *The Searchers* consistently achieves the resonance of symbolic drama that *My Darling Clementine* achieves only in one passage, and that it does so partly as a result of the fusion of modes and impulses that are held in productive tension: romantic narrative and a version of the hero of romance with a low mimetic insistence on human needs and moral fallibility; a high level of abstraction (or unreality) in the setting—the farm set in the middle of barren desert—with a fullness of naturalistic detail in the presentation of the settlers' lives. Part of any claim for the greatness of *The Searchers* needs to be based on these tensions, which make what could have been simply a story of Indian savagery and revenge into a work that can be seen as a film about America— a symbolic representation of the American psyche—as one might discuss the Leatherstocking tales or *Moby Dick*. Ford's achievement is based on a profound understanding of his tradition. Even the comic domestic scenes, the grotesquery of sexual relationships in the film, which are often ignored or apologized for, belong to a tradition stretching back to "Rip Van Winkle," in which marriage and settlement are presented as crippling or at least inhibiting, a tradition that Leslie Fiedler has discussed at some length.[10]

Less complex than *The Searchers,* but interesting in this context, is Delmer Daves's *3:10 to Yuma* (1957). What is most frequently commented on in the film is its "realism," its evocation of an unusually barren and unromanticized West in which environment dominates people, as well as its refusal of "romantic" (in both senses) characterization. From the outset, the barren landscape suggests the bleakness of life in this West. The holdup that follows the extended shot of the stage approaching across the desert is undramatic, unclear, shrouded in dust. The iconographical profile of the hero, Evans (Van Heflin), when he appears, conflicts with expectation—he is with his two sons, dressed in functional, worn working clothes, without a gun, and he is almost immediately deprived of his horse and forced to chase his cattle on foot. The insistence on the harshness of the environment is reinforced by discussion of the drought that dominates the lives of the ranchers in the area. The hero is also unusually motivated exclusively by money—his need to raise cash to buy water for his parched ranch. This need is played on throughout, the captured outlaw Wade (Glenn Ford) tempting him with offers of more and more money if he will release him. Both towns in the film are unprepossessing, dominated by harsh sunlight and hard shadows; the inhabitants are reluctant to risk anything over the outlaw, as if the heat and drought have sapped physical and moral resolve. These elements of the film are firmly low mimetic, in terms of the relationship between the human and natural worlds and the stature of the hero (he is one of us). Daves goes even further in this direction by handcuffing Glenn Ford when he is first captured, and so effectively preventing the possibility of conventional confrontations between hero and villain.

But it is partly, perhaps, the consistency with which the low mimetic manner is maintained that begins to suggest, paradoxically, through its absence for most of the film, the existence of another dimension. Daves consistently refuses possible developments through action in favor of a concentration on the tension between Evans's desperate need for money (his motive for taking in Wade), with its accompanying sapping of moral energy, and the moral obligation to complete his undertaking in the face of Wade's bribes. The film moves toward Evans's final decision to take Wade from the hotel to the train, not as a moral obligation or a way of making the necessary money (it is going to be paid anyway) but as a completely free act. It is at this point that the suppressed dimension of the film emerges clearly with the thunder which accompanies the buildup to Evans's decision but which his wife somehow fails to hear. He takes the thunder as promising the long-needed rain but also, it seems clear, as confirmation of the rightness of his resolve. The simultaneity of moral climax and thunder signals dramatically an other than contingent relationship between the human and the natural worlds, the drought as expression of and punishment for the spiritual state of the people. Their atrophy of will and resigned selfishness stand in a necessary relationship to the blight on the land in a way that clearly evokes the wasteland of Grail legends. Evans's action ends the drought as the quester's can in legend. It is free of the considerations of money and family that have dominated him earlier—"The awful daring of a moment's surrender/Which an age of prudence can never retract." What is interesting in *3:10 to Yuma* is not the presence of this romantic dimension but its sudden revelation. Not only does the selective hearing of the characters (we hear the thunder, why can't the wife?) break with the established naturalism of the film's manner, but the climactic thunder, which is acceptable in other conventions, has such obvious dramatic and symbolic significance in this resolutely low mimetic context that the context cannot contain it. The thunder and the rain at the end assert with melodramatic force the existence of, on the whole, unprepared dimensions (the solemn sympathy of human beings and nature characteristic of romance) in a way that seems to threaten the film's unity. In other words, there seems in *3:10 to Yuma* a collision of mode and manner rather than a productive tension between them, a capitulation of sense to meaning, which makes the end of the film unfortunately glib.

These attempts to approach particular films in terms of genre are necessarily tentative. The description of tendencies within generic traditions needs finally to be based on more detailed study of the available materials. In this respect, the western is likely to remain central to genre criticism. It is unique in the accessibility of its prehistory and the continuity of its traditions, which make an accurate description of the evolution of conventions adopted by the cinema both possible and necessary. Comparative work is needed on the antecedents of other genres, the tendencies that seem to contribute to their recognition, and most especially on the ways in which modes intersect other, often more obvious conventions. Inevitably this kind of emphasis will contribute to the modification of notions of authorship in the American cinema. It may also provide materials for other approaches—accounts, for instance, of the sociological and psychological contexts of genre—which should tell us more about the social significance of popular forms and the ways in which conventions are sustained.

Notes

1. E. H. Gombrich, "The Use of Art for the Study of Symbols," in *Psychology and the Visual Arts,* edited by James Hogg (Baltimore: Penguin, 1969), pp. 149–170.

2. See, for instance, Thomas Elsaesser, "The American Cinema II: Why Hollywood," *Monogram,* no. 1 (April 1971): 4–10.

3. Northrop Frye, *Anatomy of Criticism* (Princeton: Princeton University Press, 1957). See especially the theory of fictional modes.

4. For a critique of Frye's theory of modes, see Tzvetan Todorov, *The Fantastic: A Structural Approach to a Literary Genre,* translated by Richard Howard (Cleveland and London: Case Western Reserve University Press, 1973).

5. Eric Auerbach, *Mimesis* (New York: Doubleday, 1957).

6. Henry Nash Smith traces the development of western fiction after Cooper in chapters 7 through 10 of *Virgin Land* (Cambridge, Mass.: Harvard University Press, 1950).

7. *American Frontier: Images and Myths,* catalogue of the 1974 London Exhibition of paintings of the West, July 26–Sept. 16, 1973 (New York: Whitney Museum of American Art, 1973), contains a useful introduction on this topic. Roderick Nash, *Wilderness and the American Mind,* 3d ed., revised (New Haven: Yale University Press, 1982), deals in greater detail with developing American attitudes to wilderness.

8. *Frederic Remington: 173 Drawings and Illustrations* (New York: Dover Books, 1972).

9. Roland Barthes, "Myth Today," in *Mythologies,* translated by Annette Lavers (London: Jonathan Cape, 1972).

10. Leslie Fiedler, *Return of the Vanishing American* (London: Jonathan Cape, 1968).

16. Apes and Essences: Some Sources of Significance in the American Gangster Film

EDWARD MITCHELL

Most of the study of film genres is taken up with an examination of formulas, icons, motifs—in short, the elements of repetitive patterning common to all the films that we call detective films, or westerns, or gangster films. This is as it should be. Indeed, no serious discussion of genre is possible without recourse to those elements that a particular genre film shares with others of its kind. But what concerns me at the moment is not so much those elements that give a particular film meaning within a context of other similar films. Rather, I am concerned with the patterns emerging from a culturally shared and habitual structuring of thought, the usually unexamined convictions that bestow value—in other words, the patterns that give an entire genre significance whatever the meaning of any particular film.

For the American gangster film there are three such patterns: a secularized Puritanism; the ideas and attitudes that came to be known as Social Darwinism; and the Horatio Alger myth. For the present generation, Puritanism has been reduced in meaning until it is virtually synonymous with a narrow sexual morality. But at one time it was, and in some unlabeled ways continues to be, a statement about the nature of God, the meaning of good and evil, and the nature of a person's precarious relationship to each. Briefly, Puritanism à la Calvin held that people were conceived and born in sin, helplessly depraved and without hope of redemption except for those few whom an omnipotent and omniscient God elected to save. The reasons for such salvation were totally unfathomable by the common person, but the signs of election were clear, generally manifested in increased material prosperity. Whatever their material fortunes, however, Puritans were admonished to look on them with equanimity because they were saved to, not by, virtue, and a person's primary responsibility was to attempt to avoid evil in what could be a winning game only by the "grace of God."

For our purposes, there are three chief respects in which Puritanism framed the all-important relationship between human beings and their

world. The first is condemnation: we are guilty, and nothing alters that—
"in Adam's fall we sinned all." Second, we are helpless: election, if it
comes, is an action initiated by God over which we have no influence. Finally, we are inescapably moral agents: we are born in sin, there is no neu-
trality. We cannot escape the onus of choice even if that choice is onto-
logically meaningless.

From Puritanism to Social Darwinism, at least in the subconscious convictions of a culture, is less of a leap than it might appear. Thanks to
Spencer's interpretation of Darwin, an intractable nature came to be substituted for an all-powerful God. Human beings are a product of evolution, and by a process of natural selection (which the Social Darwinists
found it convenient to translate to "survival of the fittest"), the adaptive
ends of evolution are served. In short, Social Darwinism was a determinism, a kind of naturalistic Calvinism in which human beings were sub-
jugated to their environment rather than to the will of God.[1] But the
thought that either could be influenced or altered was, as William Graham Sumner succinctly put it, "absurd," since to attempt to influence the
process of evolution was in effect to attempt to subvert a natural law. Like
Calvinism, Social Darwinism placed the individual in a passive role—at
least in theory. But in the notion of survival of the fittest lay an emphasis
on adaptability, which could be, and was, interpreted to mean that nature
favored the more dynamic, the most aggressive and intelligent (which
came to mean most cunning) of the species. Thus in practice Social Darwinism served as a rationalization for economic and geographic rapa-
ciousness while numbing moral judgment with the comforting assurance
of a slow but inevitable progress up the evolutionary ladder.

The boy hero of Horatio Alger, Jr., at first glance may appear misplaced
in company with the concepts and convictions making up Puritanism and
Social Darwinism. But like Natty Bumppo or George Babbitt, Alger's
hero lives on in the American imagination quite independently of his novelistic origins. Moreover, while the Alger novels were the most immediate
historical antecedents of the gangster film, popular myths have a way of
mixing and combining with little or no regard for history. The basic pattern of the Alger books is simple and can be found with minor variations
in each of the novels. The hero is a young lad, who, either through mis-
fortune or the machinations of relatives, has been separated from his family and deprived of his rightful inheritance. The chief task of the hero is
either to win back the family homestead for himself and his aging mother,
or, if no apparent family exists, to rise from his status as urban waif to a
position of monetary security and respectability. His chief weapons in this
struggle are the manly fortitude and traditional virtues that Alger signified by "pluck," and the continuous stream of fortuitous circumstances,

"luck," which provided occasion for the employment of that fortitude and those virtues.

For our purposes the important point is that all of Alger's plots play upon the theme of disinheritance. In Alger's fictional world, security means above anything else being confident of one's identity and of one's position in the world. Thus the retention of "home" or the securing of a comfortable middle-class job becomes a metaphor for the orderly and respectable life. Moreover, except for the conveniences of plot and the maintenance of an artificial suspense, the outcome is never in doubt. The Alger hero *is* the rightful heir, and his recognition as the long-lost son merely completes the pattern of temporary dispossession and eventual restoration. Thus the Alger hero's task is not so much to earn his success as it is to maintain his traditional values until the inevitable justification and restoration occur.

Now even this cursory review of Puritanism, Social Darwinism, and the Horatio Alger myth reveals the basis for a welter of potential conflicts and contradictions. Perhaps the weakest chink in the Puritan armor was the very remoteness of the wrathful God who ostensibly governed the Puritan's destiny. In any case, the burgeoning New England villages and towns were concrete and immediate, and the material well-being they generated became inextricably linked in the Puritan mind with moral worth. In the everyday world, therefore, hard work, perseverance, and ingenuity yielded a material wealth with palpable consequences, while the question of damnation or salvation, or at least the consequence of that question, was postponed to an eschatological future. In its turn, Social Darwinism was in many ways the rationalization generated to account for a complex, largely urbanized society riding the crest of the Industrial Revolution. Consequently, the individual guilt that could haunt the Puritan mind became detoxified in a process of evolution that tended to render value judgments irrelevant by insisting that evolution was self-justifying. However, by its mutual insistence on both the dominance of the environment and the idea of survival of the fittest, Social Darwinism reopened the door of ambivalence and ambiguity in human conduct. On the one hand a man or woman was a "product of the environment," while on the other he or she was enjoined to observe those "fittest" who not only survived but exploited that environment.

The conflict between the inevitability of passive acceptance and the demand for adaptive strategies produced anxiety, and it is precisely that anxiety which the Horatio Alger stories, at the mythic level, were designed to relieve. By adapting the encounters of a picaresque tale, Alger kept the surface of his plot busy with action, making it appear that his hero is actively struggling with the forces arrayed against him. However, by the time we reach the happy ending it is evident that Alger's hero has always been simply himself, steadfastly waiting out adversity and practicing homely virtues until he is restored to a position of identity, security, and comfort that really has always been his except for this temporary interruption. In other words, by the dexterity always practiced in the products of popular culture, Alger has managed, temporarily, to achieve an apparent synthesis among contradictory elements. While paying homage to adaptive "pluck," Alger ensures that the plot will turn on a stroke of "luck" for which the hero is prepared but not responsible. Moreover, that synthesis is further aided by a general pejoration of all consequences. Salvation, which is really due the hero anyway, is reduced to the monetarily secure, middle-class life. Evil, insofar as it is dealt with at all, is equated to greedy relatives seeking self-preferment, while punishment consistently takes the form of a pay cut.

So, what has all this to do with the issue of significance in American gangster films? First of all, more than any other film genre, gangster films are the home of the conflict between good and evil.[2] This may take the form of the well-dressed, antiseptic, technology-oriented T-men versus the malevolent, psychotic Cody Jarrett (James Cagney) in *White Heat* (Raoul Walsh, 1949). Or the good and evil elements may be mixed in a single character, such as Roy Earle (Humphrey Bogart) in *High Sierra* (Raoul Walsh, 1941). Or perhaps a director will undertake to examine and question the very basis upon which conventional notions of good and evil rest, as does Fritz Lang in *The Big Heat* (1953). But whatever its form, taint and corruption pervade the gangster film and have consequences that the characters cannot escape.

There has always been something "fated" about the main character in American gangster films. We know that no matter what happens, somehow the gangster will "get his." Although he is often dispatched by minions of the law, death comes to the gangster not as a result of a social or legal process, but because he has sinned. Occasionally we are permitted to see the effects of that sin, as in the hysterical pleading of Tony Camonte (Paul Muni) before he is machine-gunned by police in *Scarface* (Howard Hawks, 1932), or in the penultimate scene of hospital repentance before the body of Tommy Powers (James Cagney) is brutally dumped in his mother's living room by a rival gang in *The Public Enemy* (William Wellman, 1931). The law may be the instrument of the gangster's demise, but is never really the cause. Thus even in a semidocumentary like Richard Wilson's *Al Capone* (1959), Capone (Rod Steiger) is ritualistically but unauthentically stoned into bloody unconsciousness by his fellow prisoners in Alcatraz while the narrator reminds us that Capone died insane, totally debilitated by a "social disease." While it is never overtly related to

36. *The Big Heat:* Conventional notions of good and evil are questioned.

a wrathful God, justice, or at least punishment, usually in the form of an early and violent death, inevitably awaits the gangster.

Yet, while he somehow cannot succeed, the film gangster hero insidiously demands our admiration. His is a violent and hostile environment, a labyrinth of dark alleys and concrete canyons, a warren of mean streets from which danger constantly threatens. The gangster survives as long as he does against heavy odds because of his energy, cunning, and bravura. His adaptive strategies are simple and classically summed up by Tony Camonte when he regales his partner Little Boy (George Raft). Forefinger extended, thumb up, he says, "Do it first, do it yourself, and keep on doing it." Roy Earle commands our respect precisely because he will not adapt to a changing environment composed of self-serving renegade cops, unprofessional punks, and shallow, pleasure-seeking "nice" girls. Ivan Martin (Jimmy Cliff) sings "The Harder They Come, the Harder They Fall," lyrics that become ironic in *The Harder They Come* (Perry Henzell, 1973). Ivan is a "badass," temporarily but flamboyantly defying rural ignorance, the cops, exploitative capitalism—in short, every oppressive element in his environment.

Still, although the environment may mold and motivate the gangster, it never wholly determines him. Tommy Powers is more attractive than the

Putty Noses or Paddy Ryans he comes in contact with. He retains possibilities that were never theirs. Nor can one seek in the environment an explanation for Michael, Tommy's law-abiding, hard-working, middle-class brother. The pervasive corruption that defines the environment in *The Big Heat* becomes finally almost irrelevant. It is the innate depravity, the universal capacity for rage, revenge, and murder which is the motivating force in this film. And Francis Ford Coppola's *Godfather II* (1975) is most revealing in regard to the issue of environment. On the surface Michael Corleone (Al Pacino) appears to be *the* most successful adaptor. He has risen to and held power in the face of rival "families," treacherous relatives, Senate investigating committees, and changing economic and political conditions. Yet, at the film's somber close, he sits staring emptily at his vacant Reno mansion. He is utterly alone in a world depopulated by his own orders.

Following the lead of Robert Warshow, many critics have pointed to the perverted Horatio Alger pattern especially evident in early gangster films.[3] The evidence is everywhere: in the steady rise to position and power of Rico (Edward G. Robinson) in *Little Caesar* (Mervyn LeRoy, 1930); the neon sign flashing "The World Is Yours" to Tony Camonte in *Scarface;* Cody Jarrett demonically screaming "Top of the world, Ma" as a fireball of exploding gas tanks carries him into oblivion in *White Heat.* Interestingly enough, however, the traditional Alger message has always been savagely undercut in the gangster film. Uneasy in its ersatz synthesis of conflicting elements, the Horatio Alger myth seems particularly vulnerable to the chilling facts of a Depression or the sobering realities of Third World exploitation. The opening scenes of *The Harder They Come* are accompanied by Jimmy Cliff singing "You Can Get It If You Really Want." The pathetic falsity of that claim becomes ever more painfully clear as the film progresses. Ivan's will, sagacity, courage, and style, his fundamental demand for his "propers," is futile. He is a man without a home in country or city. He is ultimately borne down by the system—too much money, influence, and finally firepower—everything connoted by "the man." But mostly Ivan is defeated by his own illusions. The harder they come, the harder they *do* fall. He is not an idol of the silver screen scattering baddies before him (although he clearly identifies himself with that image), nor will the military police send out "one baaad man" to shoot it out on the empty beach.

Despite the fact that social mobility and bank-book morality are held out to and eagerly adopted by the American film gangster, he finally proves heir to nothing but calamity. What the Horatio Alger myth chiefly affirms is precisely what the American gangster film denies. The gangster *is* disinherited—permanently. Socially and financially he is a usurper.

37. *White Heat:* Cody Jarrett (James Cagney) shouts "Top of the world, Ma."

While the gangster may feel that he is restoring to himself some rightful position, status, or power, the films repeatedly reveal that nothing could be farther from the truth. While retaining most of the surface trappings of the Horatio Alger myth, the gangster film denies its meaning at the source and returns to other, and conflicting, cultural convictions—chiefly, a pervasive sense of alienation and impending doom, a punishment that cannot be escaped for a fault that cannot be irradicated.

Perhaps more recent gangster films suggest a moving away from the patterns I have been discussing. But this is true more in appearance than in reality. Martin Scorsese's *Mean Streets* (1973) seems to jettison the Horatio Alger myth. Charlie is not motivated by a desire to "get ahead" or supplant his Uncle Giovanni. His guilt and his need to aid the damaged people like Teresa and Johnny Boy overpower his desire to take over the restaurant and thus rise in the Mafiosi-dominated family business. Nor does Scorsese fall back on a simplistic environmental determinism. While he immerses us in an environment that is almost claustrophobic, Scorsese never permits the audience to use it as the basis for normative judgments.

38. *Little Caesar:* The gangster's rise . . .

39. . . . and fall: Cagney in *The Roaring Twenties*.

It is simply there, sufficient for and ignored by those who live in it. Yet calamity does come. And, ironically, it is brought about by Michael (Richard Romanus), who *does* take himself seriously, who sees himself rising
to the top in this world of punks, and who affects the expensive clothes,
big cars, and strong-arm methods that compose the traditional icons of
the gangster film. But, more important, it is the basic depravity, the capacity for evil, which ultimately surfaces in this film. Thus it is no accident that it is a parallel scene from *The Big Heat* which Uncle Giovanni
is watching on television as a wounded Charlie drags himself from a de-
molished automobile across town.

In summation, what I am suggesting is that the elements of Puritanism,
Social Darwinism, and the Horatio Alger myth are hopelessly contradictory. And it is precisely these contradictions which the American gangster
film embodies and which, because they remain unresolved in America's
collective consciousness, provide the imbalances, ambiguities, and am-
bivalences with which the gangster film abounds. However, this does not
at all imply that individual gangster films are without meaning or that the

genre lacks significance. It is exactly the contradictory attitudes toward freedom and fate; the irreconcilable conflicts regarding the sources and signs of good and evil; the simultaneous and mutually exclusive admonition to accept/wait and adapt/initiate which form at least part of the dynamics of the American mind. These same dynamics provide the bases for the significance of American gangster films.

Notes

1. For a more detailed account of the origin and influence of the ideas we call Social Darwinism, see Richard Hofstadter, *Social Darwinism in American Thought* (Philadelphia: University of Pennsylvania Press, 1944).

2. For example, consider the issue of good and evil in most westerns. While the western is considered the province of the "good guys" and the "bad guys," that conflict is seldom central to the western. More often the western hero is pursuing some private vendetta or finds himself in the "man in the middle" position, fighting to usher in a civilization which, once established, will have no place for him. For more on this issue see John Cawelti, *The Six-Gun Mystique* (Bowling Green: Bowling Green University Popular Press, [1970]).

3. Robert Warshow, "The Gangster as Tragic Hero," in *The Immediate Experience* (New York: Atheneum, 1977), pp. 127–133.

17. Notes on Film Noir

PAUL SCHRADER

In 1946 French critics, seeing the American films they had missed during the war, noticed the new mood of cynicism, pessimism, and darkness that had crept into the American cinema. The darkening stain was most evident in routine crime thrillers, but was also apparent in prestigious melodramas. The French cinéastes soon realized they had seen only the tip of the iceberg: as the years went by, Hollywood lighting grew darker, characters more corrupt, themes more fatalistic, and the tone more hopeless. By 1949 American movies were in the throes of their deepest and most creative funk. Never before had films dared to take such a harsh uncomplimentary look at American life, and they would not dare to do so again for twenty years.

Hollywood's film noir has recently become the subject of renewed interest among moviegoers and critics. The fascination that film noir holds for today's young filmgoers and film students reflects recent trends in American cinema: American movies are again taking a look at the underside of the American character, but compared to such relentlessly cynical examples of film noir as *Kiss Me Deadly* (Robert Aldrich, 1955) or *Kiss Tomorrow Goodbye* (Gordon Douglas, 1959), the newer self-hate cinema of *Easy Rider* (Dennis Hopper, 1969) and *Medium Cool* (Haskell Wexler, 1969) seems naive and romantic. As the current political mood hardens, filmgoers and filmmakers will find the film noir of the late forties increasingly attractive. The forties may be to the seventies what the thirties were to the sixties.

Film noir is equally interesting to critics. It offers writers a cache of excellent, little-known films (film noir is oddly both one of Hollywood's best periods and least known) and gives auteur-weary critics an opportunity to apply themselves to the new questions of classification and transdirectorial style. After all, what is a film noir?

Note: This chapter is excerpted from a longer essay published previously.

Film noir is not a genre, as Raymond Durgnat has helpfully pointed out over the objections of Higham and Greenberg's *Hollywood in the Forties*.[1] It is not defined, as are the western and gangster genres, by conventions of setting and conflict but rather by the more subtle qualities of tone and mood. It is a film "noir," as opposed to the possible variants of film "gray" or film "off-white." Film noir is also a specific period of film history, like German expressionism or the French New Wave. In general, film noir refers to those Hollywood films of the forties and early fifties that portrayed the world of dark, slick city streets, crime and corruption.

Film noir is an extremely unwieldy period. It harks back to many previous periods: Warner's thirties gangster films, the French "poetic realism" of Carné and Duvivier, Sternbergian melodrama, and ultimately German expressionist crime films (Lang's Mabuse cycle). Film noir can stretch at its outer limits from *The Maltese Falcon* (John Huston, 1941) to *Touch of Evil* (Orson Welles, 1958), and most every dramatic Hollywood film from 1941 to 1953 contains some noir elements. There are also foreign off-shoots of film noir, such as *The Third Man* (Carol Reed, 1949), *Breathless* (Jean-Luc Godard, 1959), and *Le Doulos* (Jean-Pierre Melville, 1963).

Almost every critic has his or her own definition of film noir, along with a personal list of film titles and dates to back it up. Personal and descriptive definitions, however, can get a bit sticky. A film of urban nightlife is not necessarily a film noir, and a film noir need not necessarily concern crime and corruption. Since film noir is defined by tone rather than genre, it is almost impossible to argue one critic's descriptive definition against another's. How many noir elements does it take to make a film noir? Rather than haggle about definitions, I would rather attempt to reduce film noir to its primary colors (all shades of black), those cultural and stylistic elements to which any definition must return.

INFLUENCES

At the risk of sounding like Arthur Knight, I would suggest that there were four influences in Hollywood in the forties that brought about the film noir. (The danger of Knight's *Liveliest Art* method is that it makes film history less a matter of structural analysis and more a case of artistic and social forces magically interacting and coalescing.) Each of the following four catalytic elements, however, can define the film noir; the distinctly noir tonality draws from each of these elements.

War and Postwar Disillusionment

The acute downer that hit the United States after the Second World War was, in fact, a delayed reaction to the thirties. All through the Depression,

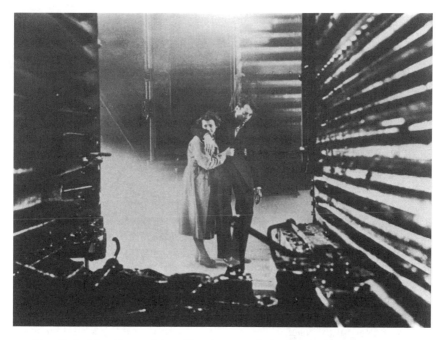

40. *You Only Live Once:* Crime films became darker in the late thirties.

movies were needed to keep people's spirits up, and, for the most part, they did. The crime films of this period were Horatio Algerish and socially conscious. Toward the end of the thirties a darker crime film began to appear (*You Only Live Once,* Fritz Lang, 1937; *The Roaring Twenties,* Raoul Walsh, 1939), and, were it not for the war, film noir would have been at full steam by the early forties.

The need to produce Allied propaganda abroad and promote patriotism at home blunted the fledgling moves toward a dark cinema, and the film noir thrashed about in the studio system, not quite able to come into full prominence. During the war the first uniquely film noir appeared in *The Maltese Falcon, The Glass Key* (Stuart Heisler, 1942), *This Gun for Hire* (Frank Tuttle, 1942), and *Laura* (Otto Preminger, 1944), but these films lacked the distinctly noir bite the end of the war would bring.

As soon as the war was over, however, American films became markedly more sardonic—and there was a boom in the crime film. For fifteen years the pressures against America's amelioristic cinema had been building up, and, given the freedom, audiences and artists were now eager to take a less optimistic view of things. The disillusionment that many soldiers, small businessmen, and housewife/factory employees felt in returning to a peacetime economy was directly mirrored in the sordidness of the urban crime film.

This immediate postwar disillusionment was directly demonstrated in films like *Cornered* (Edward Dmytryk, 1945), *The Blue Dahlia* (George Marshall, 1946), *Dead Reckoning* (John Cromwell, 1947), and *Ride the Pink Horse* (Robert Montgomery, 1947), in which a serviceman returns from the war to find his sweetheart unfaithful or dead, or his business partner cheating him, or the whole society something less than worth fighting for. The war continues, but now the antagonism turns with a new viciousness toward American society itself.

Postwar Realism

Shortly after the war, every film-producing country had a resurgence of realism. In America it first took the form of films by such producers as Louis de Rochemont (*House on 92nd Street,* Henry Hathaway, 1945; *Call Northside 777,* Hathaway, 1948) and Mark Hellinger (*The Killers,* Robert Siodmak, 1946; *Brute Force,* Jules Dassin, 1947) and directors like Hathaway and Dassin. "Every scene was filmed on the actual location depicted," the publicity for the 1947 de Rochemont–Hathaway *Kiss of Death* proudly proclaimed. Even after de Rochemont's particular "March of Time" authenticity fell from vogue, realistic exteriors remained a permanent fixture of film noir.

The realistic movement also suited America's postwar mood; the public's desire for a more honest and harsh view of America would not be satisfied by the same studio streets they had been watching for a dozen years. The postwar realistic trend succeeded in breaking film noir away from the domain of the high-class melodrama, placing it where it more properly belonged, in the streets with everyday people. In retrospect, the pre–de Rochemont film noir looks definitely tamer than the postwar realistic films. The studio look of films like *The Big Sleep* (Howard Hawks, 1946) and *The Mask of Dimitrios* (Jean Negulesco, 1944) blunts their sting, making them seem polite and conventional in contrast to their later, more realistic counterparts.

The German Expatriates

Hollywood played host to an influx of German expatriates in the twenties and thirties, and these filmmakers and technicians had, for the most part, integrated themselves into the American film establishment. Hollywood never experienced the "Germanization" some civic-minded natives feared, and there is a danger of overemphasizing the German influence in Hollywood.

But when, in the late forties, Hollywood decided to paint it black, there were no greater masters of chiaroscuro than the Germans. The influence of expressionist lighting has always been just beneath the surface of Hollywood films, and it is not surprising, in film noir, to find it bursting out into full bloom. Neither is it surprising to find a larger number of Germans and East Europeans working in film noir: Fritz Lang, Robert Siodmak, Billy Wilder, Franz Waxman, Otto Preminger, John Brahm, Anatole Litvak, Karl Freund, Max Ophüls, John Alton, Douglas Sirk, Fred Zinnemann, William Dieterle, Max Steiner, Edgar G. Ulmer, Curtis Bernhardt, Rudolph Maté.

On the surface the German expressionist influence, with its reliance on artificial studio lighting, seems incompatible with postwar realism, with its harsh unadorned exteriors; but it is the unique quality of film noir that it was able to weld seemingly contradictory elements into a uniform style. The best noir technicians simply made all the world a sound stage, directing unnatural and expressionistic lighting onto realistic settings. In films like *Union Station* (Maté, 1950), *They Live by Night* (Nicholas Ray, 1948), and *The Killers,* there is an uneasy, exhilarating combination of realism and expressionism.

Perhaps the greatest master of noir was Hungarian-born John Alton, an expressionist cinematographer who could relight Times Square at noon if necessary. No cinematographer better adapted the old expressionist techniques to the new desire for realism, and his black-and-white photography in such gritty examples of film noir as *T-Men* (Anthony Mann, 1948), *Raw Deal* (Mann, 1948), *I, the Jury* (Harry Essex, 1953), and *The Big Combo* (Joseph H Lewis, 1955) equals that of such German expressionist masters as Fritz Wagner and Karl Freund.

The Hard-Boiled Tradition

Another stylistic influence waiting in the wings was the "hard-boiled" school of writers. In the thirties, authors such as Ernest Hemingway, Dashiell Hammett, Raymond Chandler, James M. Cain, Horace McCoy, and John O'Hara created the "tough," a cynical way of acting and thinking that separated one from the world of everyday emotions—romanticism with a protective shell. The hard-boiled writers had their roots in pulp fiction or journalism, and their protagonists lived out a narcissistic, defeatist code. The hard-boiled hero was, in reality, a soft egg compared to his existential counterpart (Camus is said to have based *The Stranger* on McCoy), but he was a good deal tougher than anything American fiction had seen.

41. *The Big Combo* adapted the old expressionist techniques to the new desire for realism.

When the movies of the forties turned to the American "tough" moral understrata, the hard-boiled school was waiting with preset conventions of heroes, minor characters, plots, dialogue, and themes. Like the German expatriates, the hard-boiled writers had a style made to order for film noir; and, in turn, they influenced noir screenwriting as much as the Germans influenced noir cinematography.

The most hard-boiled of Hollywood's writers was Raymond Chandler himself, whose script of *Double Indemnity* (from a James M. Cain story) was the best written and most characteristically noir of the period. *Double Indemnity* (Billy Wilder, 1944) was the first film that played film noir for what it essentially was: small-time, unredeemed, unheroic; it made a break from the romantic noir cinema of *Mildred Pierce* (Michael Curtiz, 1945) and *The Big Sleep*. In its final stages, however, film noir adapted and then bypassed the hard-boiled school. Manic, neurotic post-1948 films such as *Kiss Tomorrow Goodbye, D.O.A.* (Maté, 1950), *Where the Sidewalk Ends* (Preminger, 1950), *White Heat* (Raoul Walsh, 1949), and *The Big Heat* (Fritz Lang, 1953) are all post–hard-boiled: the air in these regions was even too thin for old-time cynics like Chandler.

STYLISTICS

There is not yet a study of the stylistics of film noir, and the task is certainly too large to be attempted here. Like all film movements, film noir drew upon a reservoir of film techniques, and given the time one could correlate its techniques, themes, and casual elements into a stylistic schema. For the present, however, I'd like to point out some of film noir's recurring techniques.

1. The majority of scenes are lit for night. Gangsters sit in offices at midday with the shades pulled and the lights off. Ceiling lights are hung low and floor lamps are seldom more than five feet high. One always has the suspicion that if the lights were all suddenly flipped on, the characters would shriek and shrink from the scene like Count Dracula at sunrise.

2. As in German expressionism, oblique and vertical lines are preferred to horizontal. Obliquity adheres to the choreography of the city, and is in direct opposition to the horizontal American tradition of Griffith and Ford. Oblique lines tend to splinter a screen, making it restless and unstable. Light enters the dingy rooms of film noir in such odd shapes—jagged trapezoids, obtuse triangles, vertical slits—that one suspects the windows were cut out with a penknife. No character can speak authoritatively from a space that is being continually cut into ribbons of light. Anthony Mann and John Alton's *T-Men* is the most dramatic example, but far from the only one, of oblique noir choreography.

3. The actors and setting are often given equal lighting emphasis. An actor is often hidden in the realistic tableau of the city at night, and, more obviously, his face is often blacked out by shadow as he speaks. These shadow effects are unlike the famous Warner Brothers lighting of the thirties in which the central character was accentuated by a heavy shadow; in film noir, the central character is likely to be standing *in* the shadow. When the environment is given an equal or greater weight than the actor, it, of course, creates a fatalistic, hopeless mood. There is nothing the protagonists can do; the city will outlast and negate even their best efforts.

4. Compositional tension is preferred to physical action. A typical film noir would rather move the scene cinematographically around the actor than have the actor control the scene by physical action. The beating of Robert Ryan in *The Set-Up* (Robert Wise, 1949), the gunning down of Farley Granger in *They Live by Night,* the execution of the taxi driver in *The Enforcer* (Bretaigne Windust, 1951) and of Brian Donlevy in *The Big Combo* are all marked by measured pacing, restrained anger, and oppressive compositions, and seem much closer to the film noir spirit than the rat-tat-tat and screeching tires of *Scarface* (Howard Hawks, 1932) twenty years before or the violent, expressive actions of *Underworld USA* (Samuel Fuller, 1960) ten years later.

42. *T-Men:* Oblique and vertical lines splinter the screen.

5. There seems to be an almost Freudian attachment to water. The empty noir streets are almost always glistening with fresh evening rain (even in Los Angeles), and the rainfall tends to increase in direct proportion to the drama. Docks and piers are second only to alleyways as the most popular rendezvous points.

6. There is a love of romantic narration. In such films as *The Postman Always Rings Twice* (Tay Garnett, 1946), *Laura, Double Indemnity, The Lady from Shanghai* (Orson Welles, 1949), *Out of the Past* (Jacques Tourneur, 1947), and *Sunset Boulevard* (Billy Wilder, 1950), the narration creates a mood of *temps perdu:* an irretrievable past, a predetermined fate, and an all-enveloping hopelessness. In *Out of the Past* Robert Mitchum relates his history with such pathetic relish that it is obvious there is no hope for any future: one can only take pleasure in reliving a doomed past.

7. A complex chronological order is frequently used to reinforce the feelings of hopelessness and lost time. Such films as *The Enforcer, The Killers, Mildred Pierce, The Dark Past* (Maté, 1948), *Chicago Deadline* (Lewis Allen, 1949), *Out of the Past,* and *The Killing* (Stanley Kubrick, 1956) use a convoluted time sequence to immerse the viewer in a time-

disoriented but highly stylized world. The manipulation of time, whether slight or complex, is often used to reinforce a noir principle: the *how* is always more important than the *what*.

THEMES

Raymond Durgnat has delineated the themes of film noir in an excellent article in the British *Cinema* magazine,[2] and it would be foolish for me to attempt to redo his thorough work in this short space. Durgnat divides film noir into eleven thematic categories, and although one might criticize some of his specific groupings, he covers the whole gamut of noir production, thematically categorizing over 300 films. In each of Durgnat's noir themes (whether Black Widow, killers-on-the-run, *doppelgangers*), one finds that the upwardly mobile forces of the thirties have halted; frontierism has turned to paranoia and claustrophobia. The small-time gangster has now made it big and sits in the mayor's chair, the private eye has quit the police force in disgust, and the young heroine, sick of going along for the ride, is taking others for a ride.

Durgnat, however, does not touch upon what is perhaps the overriding noir theme: a passion for the past and present, but also a fear of the future. Noir heroes dread to look ahead, but instead try to survive by the day, and if unsuccessful at that, they retreat to the past. Thus film noir's techniques emphasize loss, nostalgia, lack of clear priorities, and insecurity, then submerge these self-doubts in mannerism and style. In such a world style becomes paramount; it is all that separates one from meaninglessness. Chandler described this fundamental noir theme when he described his own fictional world: "It is not a very fragrant world, but it is the world you live in, and certain writers with tough minds and a cool spirit of detachment can make very interesting patterns out of it."[3]

PHASES

Film noir can be subdivided into three broad phases. The first, the wartime period (1941–1946 approximately), was the phase of the private eye and the lone wolf, of Chandler, Hammett, and Greene, of Bogart and Bacall, Ladd and Lake, classy directors like Curtiz and Garnett, studio sets, and, in general, more talk than action. The studio look of this period was reflected in such pictures as *The Maltese Falcon, Casablanca* (Michael Curtiz, 1942), *Gaslight* (George Cukor, 1944), *This Gun for Hire, The Lodger* (Brahm, 1944), *The Woman in the Window* (Lang, 1945), *Mildred Pierce, Spellbound* (Alfred Hitchcock, 1945), *The Big Sleep, Laura, The Lost Weekend* (Wilder, 1945), *The Strange Love of Martha Ivers* (Lewis Milestone, 1946), *To Have and Have Not* (Howard Hawks,

1944), *Fallen Angel* (Preminger, 1946), *Gilda* (Charles Vidor, 1946), *Murder, My Sweet* (Dmytryk, 1944), *The Postman Always Rings Twice, Dark Waters* (André de Toth, 1944), *Scarlet Street* (Lang, 1945), *So Dark the Night* (Lewis, 1946), *The Glass Key, The Mask of Dimitrios,* and *The Dark Mirror* (Siodmak, 1946).

The Wilder/Chandler *Double Indemnity* provided a bridge to the postwar phase of film noir. The unflinching noir vision of *Double Indemnity* came as a shock in 1944, and the film was almost blocked by the combined efforts of Paramount, the Hays Office, and star Fred MacMurray. Three years later, however, *Double Indemnity*s were dropping off the studio assembly lines.

The second phase was the postwar realistic period from 1945 to 1949 (the dates overlap and so do the films; these are all approximate phases for which there are exceptions). These films tended more toward the problems of crime in the streets, political corruption, and police routine. Less romantic heroes like Richard Conte, Burt Lancaster, and Charles McGraw were more suited to this period, as were proletarian directors like Hathaway, Dassin, and Kazan. The realistic urban look of this phase is seen in such films as *The House on 92nd Street, The Killers, Raw Deal, Act of Violence* (Zinnemann, 1949), *Union Station, Kiss of Death, Johnny O'Clock* (Robert Rossen, 1947), *Force of Evil* (Abraham Polonsky, 1948), *Dead Reckoning, Ride the Pink Horse, Dark Passage* (Delmer Daves, 1947), *Cry of the City* (Siodmak, 1948), *The Set-Up, T-Men, Call Northside 777, Brute Force, The Big Clock* (John Farrow, 1948), *Thieves' Highway* (Dassin, 1949), *Ruthless* (Ulmer, 1948), *The Pitfall* (de Toth, 1948), *Boomerang!* (Elia Kazan, 1947), and *The Naked City* (Dassin, 1948).

The third and final phase of film noir, from 1949 to 1953, was the period of psychotic action and suicidal impulse. The noir hero, seemingly under the weight of ten years of despair, started to go bananas. The psychotic killer, who had in the first period been a subject worthy of study (Olivia de Havilland in *The Dark Mirror*), and in the second a fringe threat (Richard Widmark in *Kiss of Death*), now became the active protagonist (James Cagney in *Kiss Tomorrow Goodbye*). There were no excuses given for the psychopathy in *Gun Crazy* (Lewis, 1949)—it was just "crazy." James Cagney made a neurotic comeback, and his instability was matched by that of younger actors like Robert Ryan and Lee Marvin. This was the phase of the B noir film and of psychoanalytically inclined directors like Ray and Walsh. The forces of personal disintegration are in such films as *White Heat, Gun Crazy, D.O.A., Caught* (Max Ophuls, 1949), *They Live by Night, Where the Sidewalk Ends, Kiss Tomorrow Goodbye, Detective Story* (William Wyler, 1951), *In a Lonely Place* (Ray, 1950), *I, the Jury, Ace in the Hole* (Wilder, 1951), *Panic in the Streets* (Kazan,

1950), *The Big Heat, On Dangerous Ground* (Ray, 1952), and *Sunset Boulevard.*

This third phase is the cream of the film noir period. Some critics may prefer the early "gray" melodramas, others the postwar "street" films, but film noir's final phase was the most aesthetically and sociologically piercing. After ten years of steadily shedding romantic conventions, the later noir films finally got down to the root causes of the period: the loss of public honor, heroic conventions, personal integrity, and, finally, psychic stability. The third-phase films were painfully self-aware; they seemed to know they stood at the end of a long tradition based on despair and disintegration and did not shy away from that fact. The best and most characteristically noir films—*Gun Crazy, White Heat, Out of the Past, Kiss Tomorrow Goodbye, D.O.A., They Live by Night,* and *The Big Heat*—stand at the end of the period and are the results of self-awareness. The third phase is rife with end-of-the-line noir heroes: *The Big Heat* and *Where the Sidewalk Ends* are the last stops for the urban cop, *Ace in the Hole* for the newspaper man, the Victor Saville–produced Spillane series *I, the Jury, The Long Wait* (Victor Saville, 1954), and *Kiss Me Deadly* for the private eye, *Sunset Boulevard* for the Black Widow, *White Heat* and *Kiss Tomorrow Goodbye* for the gangster, *D.O.A.* for the John Doe American.

Appropriately, the masterpiece of film noir was a straggler, *Kiss Me Deadly,* produced in 1955. Its time delay gives it a sense of detachment and thoroughgoing seediness—it stands at the end of a long sleazy tradition. The private-eye hero, Mike Hammer, undergoes the final stages of degradation. He is a small-time "bedroom dick," and has no qualms about it because the world around him isn't much better. Ralph Meeker, in his best performance, plays Hammer, a midget among dwarfs. Robert Aldrich's teasing direction carries noir to its sleaziest and most perversely erotic. Hammer overturns the underworld in search of the "great whatsit," and when he finally finds it, it turns out to be—joke of jokes—an exploding atomic bomb. The inhumanity and meaninglessness of the hero are small matters in a world in which the Bomb has the final say.

By the middle fifties film noir had ground to a halt. There were a few notable stragglers—*Kiss Me Deadly,* the Lewis/Alton *The Big Combo,* and film noir's epitaph, *Touch of Evil*—but for the most part a new style of crime film had become popular.

As the rise of McCarthy and Eisenhower demonstrated, Americans were eager to see a more bourgeois view of themselves. Crime had to move to the suburbs. The criminal put on a grey flannel suit, and the footsore cop was replaced by the "mobile unit" careening down the expressway. Any attempt at social criticism had to be cloaked in ludicrous affirmations of the American way of life. Technically, television, with its demand for full lighting and close-ups, gradually undercut the German influence, and color cinematography was, of course, the final blow to the noir look.

New directors like Siegel, Fleischer, Karlson, and Fuller, and TV shows like *Dragnet, M-Squad, Lineup,* and *Highway Patrol* stepped in to create the new crime drama. This transition can be seen in Samuel Fuller's 1953 *Pickup on South Street,* a film that blends the black look with the red scare. The waterfront scenes with Richard Widmark and Jean Peters are in the best noir tradition, but a later, dynamic fight in the subway marks Fuller as a director who would be better suited to the crime school of the middle and late fifties.

Film noir was an immensely creative period—probably the most creative in Hollywood's history—at least, if this creativity is measured not by its peaks but by its median level of artistry. Picked at random, a film noir is likely to be a better made film than a randomly selected silent comedy, musical, western, and so on. (A Joseph H Lewis B film noir is better than a Lewis B western, for example.) Taken as a whole period, film noir achieved an unusually high level of artistry. Film noir seemed to bring out the best in everyone: directors, cameramen, screenwriters, actors. Again and again, a film noir will make the high point on an artist's career graph. Some directors, for example, did their best work in film noir (Stuart Heisler, Robert Siodmak, Gordon Douglas, Edward Dmytryk, John Brahm, John Cromwell, Raoul Walsh, Henry Hathaway); other directors began in film noir and, it seems to me, never regained their original heights (Otto Preminger, Rudolph Maté, Nicholas Ray, Robert Wise, Jules Dassin, Richard Fleischer, John Huston, André de Toth, and Robert Aldrich); and other directors who made great films in other molds also made great film noir (Orson Welles, Max Ophüls, Fritz Lang, Elia Kazan, Howard Hawks, Robert Rossen, Anthony Mann, Joseph Losey, Alfred Hitchcock, and Stanley Kubrick). Whether or not one agrees with this particular schema, its message is irrefutable: film noir was good for practically every director's career. (Two interesting exceptions to prove the case are King Vidor and Jean Renoir.) Film noir seems to have been a creative release for everyone involved. It gave artists a chance to work with previously forbidden themes, yet had conventions strong enough to protect the mediocre. Cinematographers were allowed to become highly mannered, and actors were sheltered by the cinematographers. It was not until years later that critics were able to distinguish between great directors and great noir directors.

Film noir's remarkable creativity makes its long-time neglect the more baffling. The French, of course, have been students of the period for some time (Borde and Chaumeton's *Panorama du film noir* was published in

1955), but American critics until recently have preferred the western, the musical, or the gangster film to the film noir.

Some of the reasons for this neglect are superficial; others strike to the heart of the noir style. For a long time film noir, with its emphasis on corruption and despair, was considered an aberration of the American character. The western, with its moral primitivism, and the gangster film, with its Horatio Alger values, were considered more American than the film noir.

This prejudice was reinforced by the fact that film noir was ideally suited to the low-budget B film, and many of the best noir films were B films. This odd sort of economic snobbery still lingers on in some critical circles: high-budget trash is considered more worthy of attention than low-budget trash, and to praise a B film is somehow to slight (often intentionally) an A film.

The fundamental reason for film noir's neglect, however, is the fact that it depends more on choreography than sociology, and American critics have always been slow on the uptake when it comes to visual style. Like its protagonists, film noir is more interested in style than theme, whereas American critics have been traditionally more interested in theme than style. American film critics have always been sociologists first and scientists second: film is important as it relates to large masses, and if a film goes awry, it is often because the theme has been somehow "violated" by the style. Film noir operates on opposite principles: the theme is hidden in the style, and bogus themes are often flaunted ("middle-class values are best") that contradict the style. Although, I believe, style determines the theme in every film, it was easier for sociological critics to discuss the themes of the western and gangster film apart from stylistic analysis than it was to do for film noir.

Not surprisingly, it was the gangster film, not the film noir, which was canonized in *The Partisan Review* in 1948 by Robert Warshow's famous essay, "The Gangster as Tragic Hero." Although Warshow could be an aesthetic as well as a sociological critic, in this case he was interested in the western and gangster film as "popular" art rather than as style. This sociological orientation blinded Warshow, as it has many subsequent critics, to an aesthetically more important development in the gangster film —film noir.

The irony of this neglect is that in retrospect the gangster films Warshow wrote about are inferior to film noir. The thirties gangster was primarily a reflection of what was happening in the country, and Warshow analyzed this. The film noir, although it was also a sociological reflection, went further than the gangster film. Toward the end film noir was engaged in a life-and-death struggle with the materials it reflected; it tried to make

America accept a moral vision of life based on style. That very contradiction—promoting style in a culture that valued themes—forced film noir into artistically invigorating twists and turns. Film noir attacked and interpreted its sociological conditions and, by the close of the noir period, created a new artistic world that went beyond a simple sociological reflection, a nightmarish world of American mannerism that was by far more a creation than a reflection.

Because film noir was first of all a style, because it worked out its conflicts visually rather than thematically, because it was aware of its own identity, it was able to create artistic solutions to sociological problems. And for these reasons films like *Kiss Me Deadly, Kiss Tomorrow Goodbye,* and *Gun Crazy* can be works of art in a way that gangster films like *Scarface, The Public Enemy,* and *Little Caesar* can never be.

Notes

1. Raymond Durgnat, "Paint It Black: The Family Tree of Film Noir," *Cinema* (U.K.), nos. 6–7 (August 1970): 49–56.
2. Ibid.
3. Raymond Chandler, "The Simple Art of Murder," in *Detective Fiction: Crime and Compromise,* edited by Dick Allen and David Chacko (New York: Harcourt Brace Jovanovich, 1974), p. 398.

18. *Chinatown* and Generic Transformation in Recent American Films

JOHN G. CAWELTI

One of the fascinating things about Roman Polanski's *Chinatown* (1974) is that it invokes in so many ways the American popular genre of the hard-boiled detective story. Most of us, I suppose, associate this tradition particularly with two films, both of which starred Humphrey Bogart: John Huston's *The Maltese Falcon* (1941) and Howard Hawks's *The Big Sleep* (1946). But these are only the two most remembered and perhaps the most memorable versions of a narrative formula that has been replicated in hundreds of novels, films, and television programs. Next to the western, the hard-boiled detective story is America's most distinctive contribution to the world's stock of action-adventure stories, our contemporaneous embodiment of the drama of heroic quest that has appeared in so many different cultures in so many different guises. Unlike the western — the heroic quest on the frontier — which can perhaps be traced back as far as the Indian captivity narratives of the late seventeenth century and certainly to Cooper's Leatherstocking saga of the early nineteenth century, the hard-boiled detective story is of quite recent origin. It developed in the twenties through the medium of short action stories in pulp magazines like the famous *Black Mask*. By 1929, Dashiell Hammett had produced in *Red Harvest* the first hard-boiled detective novel. Before retiring into literary silence in the mid-thirties, Hammett had created a basic core of hard-boiled adventure in his Continental Op stories and his novels — *The Dain Curse* (1929), *The Maltese Falcon* (1930), *The Glass Key* (1931), and *The Thin Man* (1934). In very short order, the hard-boiled detective made the transition from novel to film. *The Maltese Falcon* appeared in two film versions in the early thirties, before John Huston made the definitive version in 1941. *The Glass Key* was produced in the early thirties and in the forties; *The Thin Man* became one of the great movie successes of the later thirties, so popular that it led to a number of invented sequels. And while the hard-boiled detective flourished in film, Hammett's example was followed in novels by writers whose literary approach ranged from the subtlety and depth of Raymond Chandler and Ross Macdonald to the sensational—and bestselling—crudity of Mickey Spillane. Radio and television, too, made many series based on the figure of the hard-boiled detective and his quest for justice through the ambiguous landscape of the modern American city. If a myth can be defined as a pattern of narrative known throughout the culture and presented in many different versions by many different tellers, then the hard-boiled detective story is in that sense an important American myth.

Chinatown invokes this myth in many different ways. Its setting in Los Angeles in the 1930s is very much the archetypal "hard-boiled" setting, the place and time of Hammett's and Chandler's novels. While it is true that many hard-boiled novels and films are set in different places and times— Mickey Spillane's Mike Hammer stories in New York City, John D. Macdonald's Travis McGee saga in Florida—the California city setting of Hammett and Chandler and the approximate time of their stories, memorialized in the period furnishings, visual icons, and style of the great hard-boiled films of the 1940s, have become for us the look and the temporal-spatial aura of the hard-boiled myth. It is this aura that Polanski generates, though there is something not quite right, something disturbingly off about it. In this case, it is the color. The world of the hard-boiled myth is preeminently a world of black and white. Its ambience is that compound of angular light and shadow enmeshed in webs of fog that grew out of the visual legacy of German expressionism in drama and film, transformed into what is now usually called film noir by its adjustment to American locales and stories. Polanski carefully controls his spectrum of hue and tone in order to give it the feel of film noir, but it is nonetheless color with occasional moments of rich golden light—as in the scene in the dry riverbed. These moments of warm color often relate to scenes that are outside the usual setting or thematic content—for example, scenes in the natural landscape outside the city—which are themselves generally outside the world of the hard-boiled detective story. The invocation of many other traditional elements of the hard-boiled myth, the film noir tone and the 1930s setting cue us to expect the traditional mythical world of the private-eye hero. But the presence of color, along with increasing deviations from established patterns of plot, motive, and character, give us an eerie feeling of one myth colliding with and beginning to give way to others.

Let us begin by examining *Chinatown*'s relation to the traditional myth of the hard-boiled detective. The established narrative formula of the hard-boiled story has as its protagonist a private investigator who occupies a marginal position with respect to the official social institutions of criminal justice. The private eye is licensed by the state, but though he may be a former member of a police force or district attorney's staff, he is not now connected with such an organization. In the course of the story, he is very likely to come into conflict with representatives of the official machinery, though he may also have friends who are police officers. His position on the edge of the law is very important, because one of the central themes of the hard-boiled myth is the ambiguity between institutionalized law enforcement and true justice. The story shows us that the police and the courts are incapable of effectively protecting the innocent and bringing the guilty to appropriate justice. Only the individual of integrity who exists on the margins of society can solve the crime and bring about true justice.

The marginal character of the private-eye hero is thus crucial to his role in the myth. It is also central to his characterization. We see him not only as a figure outside the institutionalized process of law enforcement, but as the paradoxical combination of a man of character who is also a failure. The private eye is a relatively poor man who operates out of a seedy office and never seems to make very much money by his exploits; he is the most marginal sort of lower-middle-class quasi professional. Yet unlike the usual stereotype of this social class, he is a man of honor and integrity who cannot be made to give up his quest for true justice. He is a compelling American hero type, clearly related to the traditional western hero who manifests many of the same characteristics and conditions of marginality.

The story begins when the hard-boiled hero is given a mission by a client. It is typical that this initial mission is a deceptive one. Either the client is lying, as Brigid O'Shaughnessy lies to Sam Spade in *The Maltese Falcon,* or the client has been deceived and does not understand what is really at stake in giving the detective the case, as with General Sternwood in *The Big Sleep.* Often the detective is being used as a pawn in some larger plot of the client's. Whatever his initial impetus to action, the detective soon finds himself enmeshed in a very complex conspiracy involving a number of people from different spheres of society. The ratiocinative English detectives of authors like Dorothy Sayers, Agatha Christie, or Ngaio Marsh investigate crimes by examining clues, questioning witnesses, and then using their intellectual powers of insight and deduction to arrive at the solution. The hard-boiled detective investigates through movement and encounter; he collides with the web of conspiracy until he has exposed its outlines. The crime solved by the ratiocinative detective is usually that of a single individual. With this individual's means and motives for the criminal act rationally established, he or she can be turned over to the law for prosecution. But the hard-boiled detective encounters a linked series of criminal acts and responsibilities; he discovers not a single guilty individual, but a corrupt society in which wealthy and respectable people are linked with gangsters and crooked politicians. Because it is society that is corrupt, and not just a single individual, the official machinery of law enforcement is unable to bring the guilty to justice. The hard-boiled detective must decide for himself what kind of justice can be accomplished in the ambiguous urban world of modern America, and he himself must, in many instances, undertake to see this justice through. There have always been two different tendencies within the hard-boiled myth. Some writers, like Mickey Spillane and his many current followers, place their emphasis on the hero playing the role of executioner as well as detective and judge. More complex and artistic writers, like Hammett, Chandler, and Ross Macdonald, develop instead the theme of the hero's own relationship to the mythical role of lawman-outside-the-law. Their versions of the story rarely end with the detective's execution of the criminal; they prefer instead either to arrange for the criminal's self-destruction, as in Chandler's *Farewell, My Lovely,* or simply to bring about the criminal's exposure and confession, as in *The Maltese Falcon.* But this latter trend, though it has produced greater literature, is perhaps best understood as a humane avoidance of the true thrust of the myth, which is, I think, essentially toward the marginal hero becoming righteous judge and executioner, culture hero for a society that has profoundly ambiguous conflicts in choosing between its commitment to legality and its belief that only individual actions are ultimately moral and just.

One further element of the hard-boiled myth needs to be particularly noted: the role of the feminine antagonist. In almost every case, the hard-boiled hero encounters a beautiful and dangerous woman in the course of his investigations and finds himself very much drawn toward her, even to the point of falling in love. Sometimes the woman is his client, sometimes a figure in the conspiracy. In a surprising number of cases (*The Maltese Falcon, The Big Sleep, Farewell, My Lovely, I, the Jury,* and many others) the woman turns out to be the murderess and, in Spillane at least, is killed by her detective-lover. This murky treatment of the "romance" between detective and dangerous female is occasionally resolved happily, as in the Bogart-Bacall relationship at the end of the film version of *The Big Sleep* (in the novel this romantic culmination does not take place). However, such an outcome is rare. Even if the beautiful woman does not turn out to be a murderess, the detective usually separates from her at the end to return to his marginal situation, basically unchanged by what has happened to him and ready to perform more acts of justice when the occasion arises.

We can see from this brief resumé of the hard-boiled formula how close a resemblance *Chinatown* bears to it. But the film deviates increasingly from the myth until, by the end of the story, the film arrives at an ending almost contrary to that of the myth. Instead of bringing justice to a corrupt society, the detective's actions leave the basic source of corruption untouched. Instead of protecting the innocent, his investigation leads to the death of one victim and the deeper moral destruction of another. Instead of surmounting the web of conspiracy with honor and integrity intact, the detective is overwhelmed by what has happened to him.

True, the action of *Chinatown* increasingly departs from the traditional hard-boiled formula as the story progresses; however, there are, from the very beginning, a number of significant departures from the standard pattern. The choice of Jack Nicholson and Faye Dunaway as leading actors is a good instance of this. Nicholson and Dunaway have certain physical and stylistic resemblances to Bogart and Bacall, and these are obviously played up through costume, makeup, and gesture. Indeed, there is one early scene in a restaurant that is almost eerily reminiscent of the famous horse-racing interchange between Bogart and Bacall in *The Big Sleep*. But much as they echo the archetypal hard-boiled duo in a superficial way, Nicholson and Dunaway play characters who are very different. Dunaway has a neurotic fragility, an underlying quality of desperation that becomes even more apparent as her true situation is revealed. She never generates the sense of independence and courage that Bacall brought to her hard-boiled roles; her qualities of wit and sophistication—those characteristics that made Bacall such an appropriate romantic partner for the hard-boiled detective—are quickly seen to be a veneer covering depths of anguish and ambiguity. Nicholson also portrays, at least early on, a character who is not quite what he seems. His attempt to be the tough, cynical, and humorous private eye is undercut on all sides; he is terribly inept as a wit, as his attempt to tell his assistants the Chinese joke makes clear. Nor is he the tough, marginal man of professional honor he pretends to be at the beginning; actually, he is a successful small businessman who has made a good thing out of exploiting the more sordid needs of his fellow-men. One of the most deeply symbolic clichés of the traditional hard-boiled formula is the hero's refusal to do divorce business, in fact one of the primary functions of the private detective. By this choice the traditional private eye of the myth established both his personal sense of honor and his transcendent vocation, distinguishing himself from the typical private investigator. However, from the beginning of *Chinatown,* it is clear that the accumulation of evidence of marital infidelity is Jake Gittes's primary business. He is, indeed, drawn into the affairs of Noah Cross, his daughter, and her husband by a commission to document a supposedly clandestine affair between the latter and a much younger woman. The name, J. J. Gittes, which Polanski and Robert Towne, the screenwriter, chose for their protagonist, is a good indication of this aspect of his character. Think of the names of the traditional hard-boiled detectives: Sam Spade, with its implication of hardness and digging beneath the surface; Philip Marlowe, with its aura of knightliness and chivalry; Lew Archer, with its mythical overtones. Gittes, or "Gits," as Noah Cross ironically keeps pronouncing it, connotes selfishness and grasping and has, in addition, a kind of ethnic echo very different from the pure Anglo of Spade, Marlowe, and Archer.

Yet, qualified and even "antiheroic" as he is, Gittes is swept up into the traditional hard-boiled action. His initial and deceptive charge involves him in the investigation of a murder, which in turn leads him to evidence of a large-scale conspiracy involving big business, politics, crime, and the whole underlying social and environmental structure of Los Angeles. Like the traditional hard-boiled detective, Gittes begins as a marginal individual, but gradually finds himself becoming a moral agent with a mission. At the same time he becomes romantically involved with a character deeply implicated in the web of conspiracy, the mysterious widow of the man who has been murdered. By the middle of the film Gittes is determined to expose the political conspiracy that he senses beneath the surface, and also to resolve the question of the guilt or innocence of the woman to whom he has been so strongly attracted. Thus far, the situation closely resembles that of *The Maltese Falcon* and *The Big Sleep*. It is at this point, however, that the action again takes a vast departure from that of the traditional hard-boiled story. Instead of demonstrating his ability to expose and punish the guilty, Gittes steadily finds himself confronting a depth of evil and chaos so great that he is unable to control it. In relation to the social and personal depravity represented by Noah Cross and the world in which he can so successfully operate, the toughness, moral concern, and professional skill of Gittes not only seem ineffectual, but lead to ends that are the very opposite of those intended. At the end of the film, Noah Cross is free to continue his rapacious depredations on the land, the city, and the body of his own daughter-granddaughter; and the one person who might have effectively brought Cross to some form of justice—his daughter-mistress—has been destroyed. Gittes's confrontation with a depth of depravity beyond the capacity of the hard-boiled ethos of individualistic justice is, I think, the essential significance of the Chinatown motif in the film. Chinatown becomes a symbol of life's deeper moral enigmas, those unintended consequences of action that are past understanding and control. Gittes has been there before. In another case his attempts at individual moral action had led to the death of a woman he cared for. It is apparently this tragedy that motivated him to leave the police force and set up as a private investigator. Now he has been drawn back into moral action, and it is again, in Chinatown, that his attempt to live out the myth of individualistic justice collides with the power of evil and chance in the world. The result is not heroic confrontation and the triumph of justice, but tragic catastrophe and the destruction of the innocent.

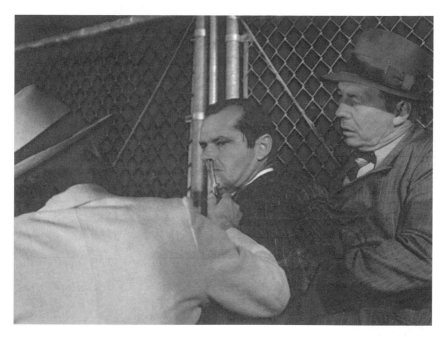

43. *Chinatown:* The antiheroic detective J. J. Gittes (Jack Nicholson) gets his nostril sliced for nosing around.

Chinatown places the hard-boiled detective story within a view of the world that is deeper and more catastrophic, more enigmatic in its evil, more sudden and inexplicable in its outbreaks of violent chance. In the end, the image of heroic, moral action embedded in the traditional private-eye myth turns out to be totally inadequate to overcome the destructive realities revealed in the course of this story. This revelation of depths beneath depths is made increasingly evident in the film's relentless movement toward Chinatown, the symbolic locus of darkness, strangeness, and catastrophe; but it also appears in the film's manipulation of action and image. The themes of water and drought, which weave through the action, not only reveal the scope of Noah Cross's conspiracy to dominate a city by manipulating its water supply, but create a texture of allusion that resonates with the mythical meanings traditionally associated with water and drought. Polanski's version of Los Angeles in the 1930s reveals the transcendent mythical world of the sterile kingdom, the dying king, and the drowned man beneath it—the world, for example, of Eliot's *The Waste Land* and before that of the cyclical myths of traditional cultures. Another of the film's motifs, its revelation of the rape-incest by which Noah Cross has fathered a daughter on his own daughter and is apparently intending to continue this method of establishing a progeny through the agency of his daughter-granddaughter, is another of the ways in which the hard-boiled myth is thrust into depths beyond itself. Though traditionally an erotically potent figure, the private eye's sexuality seems gentility itself when confronted with the potent perversity embodied in the figure of Noah Cross. Cross is reminiscent of the primal father imagined by Freud in *Totem and Taboo,* but against his overpowering sexual, political, and economic power, our hero-Oedipus in the form of J. J. Gittes proves to be tragically impotent, an impotence symbolized earlier in the film by the slashing of his nose and the large comic bandage he wears throughout much of the action.

In its manipulation of a traditional American popular myth and the revelation of the tragic inadequacy of this myth when it collides with a universe that is deeper and more enigmatic in its evil and destructive force, *Chinatown* is one of the richest and most artistically powerful instances of a type of film of which we have seen many striking instances in the last decade. It is difficult to know just what to call this type of film. On one level, it relates to the traditional literary mode of burlesque or parody in which a well-established set of conventions or a style is subjected to some form of ironic or humorous exploitation. Indeed, many of the most striking and successful films of the period have been out-and-out burlesques of traditional popular genres, such as Mel Brooks's *Blazing Saddles* (1974, westerns), his *Young Frankenstein* (1974, the Frankenstein horror cycle), and his *High Anxiety* (1977, Hitchcock's psychological suspense films). However, burlesque and parody embody a basically humorous thrust, and many of the most powerful generic variations of the last decade or so—films like *Bonnie and Clyde* (Arthur Penn, 1967), *The Wild Bunch* (Sam Peckinpah, 1968), *The Godfather* (Francis Ford Coppola, 1972), and *Nashville* (Robert Altman, 1975)—tend more toward tragedy than comedy in their overall structures. It seems odd to speak of a tragic parody or a doomed burlesque. Therefore, one is at first tempted to conclude that the connection between *Blazing Saddles* and *The Wild Bunch,* or *The Black Bird* (David Giler, 1975) and *The Long Goodbye* (Altman, 1973) is only superficial. Yet it is clear that in many of these films the line between comedy and tragedy is not so simply drawn. What, for example, of the extraordinary combination of Keystone Cops chase scenes and tragic carnage in *Bonnie and Clyde,* or the interweaving of sophomoric high jinks and terrible violence in Altman's *M*A*S*H* (1970)? This puzzling combination of humorous burlesque and high seriousness seems to be a mode of expression characteristic of our period, not only in film, but in other literary forms. It is at the root of much that is

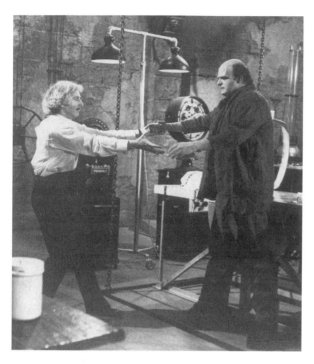

44. *Young Frankenstein:* A burlesque of the Frankenstein horror cycle.

commonly described as the literature of the absurd or of so-called black humor, and is, as well, characteristic of the style of major contemporary novelists like Thomas Pynchon. By adopting this mode, American movies have, in a sense, become a more integral part of the mainstream of postmodernist literature, just as, through their frequent allusion to the narrative conventions of American film, contemporary novelists and dramatists have created a new kind of relationship between themselves and the traditions of popular culture.

The linkage between these many different kinds of contemporary literary, dramatic, and cinematic expression is their use of the conventions of traditional popular genres. Basically, they do in different ways what Polanski does in *Chinatown:* set the elements of a conventional popular genre in an altered context, thereby making us perceive these traditional forms and images in a new way. It appears to me that we can classify the various relationships between traditional generic elements and altered contexts into four major modes.

First, there is the burlesque proper. In this mode, elements of a conventional formula or style are situated in contexts so incongruous or exaggerated that the result is laughter. There are many different ways in which this can be done. The formulaic elements can be acted out in so extreme a fashion that they come into conflict with our sense of reality, forcing us to see these aspects of plot and character as fantastic contrivances. A good example of this is the burlesque image of the gunfighter in *Cat Ballou* (Elliott Silverstein, 1965). In this film we are shown how, by putting on his gunfighter costume, a process that involves strapping himself into a corset within which he can barely move, an old drunk can become the terror of the bad guys. Or, in a closely related type of altered context, a situation that we are ordinarily accustomed to seeing in rather romanticized terms can be suddenly invested with a sense of reality. This is how the famous campfire scene in *Blazing Saddles* operates. The cowboys sit around a blazing campfire at night, a scene in which we are accustomed to hearing mournful and lyrical cowboy ballads performed by such groups as the Sons of the Pioneers. Instead we are treated to an escalating barrage of flatulence. Anyone who knows the usual effect of canned wilderness fare is likely to be delighted at this sudden exposure of the sham involved in the traditional western campfire scene. Sam Peckinpah's *Ride the High Country* (1962) offers another instance of the humorous effect of the sudden penetration of reality into a fantasy when one of his aging heroes attempts to spring gracefully into the saddle and is suddenly halted by a twinge of rheumatism.

In addition to these sudden confrontations with "reality," conventional patterns can be turned into laughter by inverting them. A good example of this is the device of turning a character who shows all the marks of a hero into a coward, or vice versa. A favorite manifestation of this in recent films and novels is what might be called the hard-boiled schlemiel, the private detective who turns out to be totally unable to solve a crime or resist villains except by accident. This type of burlesque is even more effective when the inverted presentation actually seems to bring out some latent meanings that were lurking all the time in the original convention. Mel Brooks is a particular master of this kind of burlesque. In his *Young Frankenstein*, the monster attacks Frankenstein's fiancée Elizabeth—a moment of tragic violence in the original novel—and the result is complete sexual satisfaction on both sides, something most of us had suspected all along.

These two primary techniques of burlesque, the breaking of convention by the intrusion of reality and the inversion of expected implications, have frequently appeared in the history of literature as a response to highly conventionalized genres. Just as the Greek tragedies gave rise to their burlesque counterparts in the plays of Aristophanes, the western, one of our most formally distinctive genres, has been the inspiration of parody and burlesque throughout its history from Twain and Harte's assaults on James Fenimore Cooper to Brooks's send-up of *Shane* and *High Noon*. Thus, there is nothing particularly new in the penchant toward humorous burlesque so evident in recent films. What is more striking in the films of the last decade is their use of these techniques of generic parody for ultimately serious purposes.

The second major mode of generic transformation is the cultivation of nostalgia. In this mode, traditional generic features of plot, character, setting, and style are deployed to recreate the aura of a past time. The power of nostalgia lies especially in its capacity to evoke a sense of warm reassurance by bringing before our mind's eye images from a time when things seemed more secure and full of promise and possibility. Though one can, of course, evoke nostalgia simply by viewing films of the past, a contemporary nostalgia film cannot simply duplicate the past experience, but must make us aware in some fashion of the relationship between past and present. Attempts to evoke nostalgia merely by imitating past forms, as was the case with the television series *City of Angels,* do not generally work because they seem simply obsolescent. A truly successful nostalgia film—like Henry Hathaway's *True Grit* (1969), one of the last highly popular westerns—succeeds because it set its highly traditional generic content in a slightly different context, thereby giving us both a sense of contemporaneity and of pastness. In *True Grit,* this was done in a number of ways. First of all, the central character played by Kim Darby represented an extremely contemporary image of adolescent girlhood. She was independent, aggressive, and full of initiative, a shrewd horse trader and a self-confident, insistent moralist, unlike the shy desert rose of the traditional western. John Wayne, aging and paunchy, did not attempt to cover up the ravages of the years and reaffirm without change the vigorous manhood of his earlier films. Instead, with eyepatch, unshaven face, and sagging flesh, he fully enacted his aging. Similarly, the film's images of the western landscape were in many ways deromanticized. But out of this context of contemporaneity there sprang the same old story of adventure and heroism culminating in an exuberant shoot-out that seemed to embody everybody's best dreams of Saturday matinees. The same quality of nostalgic reinvocation of the past played an even more powerful role in Peckinpah's *Ride the High Country,* in which two tired, aging, and obsolescent heroes ride again, and in Dick Richards's recent version of Raymond Chandler's *Farewell, My Lovely* (1975), where a sagging Robert Mitchum moves out of the malaise of modernity and reenacts once more the ambiguous heroic quest of the hard-boiled detective of the 1930s and 1940s.

The difference between nostalgic reincarnation of an earlier genre like *Farewell, My Lovely* and the more complex ironies of *Chinatown* and

45. John Wayne as the Ringo Kid in *Stagecoach* . . .

Robert Altman's *The Long Goodbye* is considerable. It is a difference similar to the one between *True Grit* and neowesterns like Altman's *McCabe and Mrs. Miller* (1971) or Arthur Penn's *Little Big Man* (1970). In the former case, nostalgia is the end result of the film. In the latter nostalgia is often powerfully evoked, but as a means of undercutting or ironically commenting upon the generic experience itself. This brings us to the third and, in many respects, the most powerful mode of generic transformation in recent films: the use of traditional generic structures as a means of demythologization. A film like *Chinatown* deliberately invokes the basic characteristics of a traditional genre in order to bring its audience to see that genre as the embodiment of an inadequate and destructive myth. We have seen how this process of demythologization operates in *Chinatown* by setting the traditional model of the hard-boiled detective's quest for justice and integrity over and against Polanski's sense of a universe so steeped in ambiguity, corruption, and evil that such individualistic moral enterprises are doomed by their innocent naiveté to end in tragedy and self-destruction.

46. . . . and as Rooster Cogburn in *True Grit.*

The work of Arthur Penn has also explored the ironic and tragic aspects of the myths implicit in traditional genres. His *Night Moves* (1975), a transformation of the detective story, was, like *Chinatown,* the ambiguous enactment of a reluctant quest for the truth about a series of crimes. As the detective approaches a solution to the crimes, he becomes morally and emotionally involved in the quest, making it more and more difficult for him to integrate truth, feeling, and morality. In the end, like Polanski's Jake Gittes, he is more dazed than fulfilled by the catastrophe his investigation has brought about.

In other films, such as *The Left-Handed Gun* (1958), *Bonnie and Clyde,* and *Little Big Man,* Penn created a version of the western or the gangster film in which traditional meanings were inverted, but the effect was tragic rather than humorous. In *Little Big Man,* for example, the conventional western opposition between Indians and pioneers serves as the basis of the plot, which embodies two of the most powerful of our west-

47. *Little Big Man:* Jack Crabbe (Dustin Hoffman) in his gunfighter phase.

ern myths, the Indian captivity and the massacre. However, the conventional renderings of these myths pit the humanely civilizing thrust of the pioneers against the savage ferocity and eroticism of the Indians and thereby justify the conquest of the West. Penn reverses these implications. In his film it is the Indians who are humane and civilized, while the pioneers are violent, corrupt, sexually repressed, and madly ambitious. By the end, when Custer's cavalry rides forward to attack the Indian villages, our sympathies are all with the Indians. From this perspective, the conquest of the West is demythologized from the triumph of civilization into a historical tragedy of the destruction of a rich and vital human culture.

Despite its many virtues, the film version of *Little Big Man* was less artistically successful than Thomas Berger's novel, on which it was based, primarily because as the film proceeds, Penn loses the ironic detachment that Berger successfully maintains throughout the novel. Penn's portrayal of Custer as a lunatic symbol of aggressive American imperialism is overstated, and toward the end the cinematic *Little Big Man* tends to fall back from the serious exploration of mythical meanings into melodramatic burlesque. This is an artistic problem common to films in the mode of demythologization of traditional genres. Penn was far more successful in *Bonnie and Clyde,* which will remain one of the major masterpieces of recent American film. Taking off from the traditional gangster film with its opposition between the outlaw and society, *Bonnie and Clyde* establishes a dialectic between conventional and inverted meanings that is far richer and more powerfully sustained throughout the film. In the traditional gangster film, a powerful individual, frustrated by the limitations of his lower-class origin, is driven to a life of crime. Initially the audience is inclined to sympathize and identify with this character, but as he becomes involved in criminal actions, he overreaches himself and becomes a vicious killer who must be tracked down and destroyed by the representatives of society. The underlying myth of this genre affirms the limits of individual aggression in a society that tolerates and even encourages a high degree of personal enterprise and violence. The gangster becomes a tragic figure not because he is inherently evil, but because he fails to recognize these limits. The myth assures us that society is not repressive or violent; instead it shows how criminal violence evokes its own inevitable doom.

It is this comforting myth of proper and improper violence that Penn demythologizes in *Bonnie and Clyde.* As in *Little Big Man,* meanings become inverted. Instead of representing a limit to aggression and violence, society is portrayed as its fountainhead, while the outlaw protagonists are seen as victims of society's bloodlust. Throughout the film, we are shown a society of depression and chaos that yearns for action, and projects this yearning into a vicarious excitement about the robberies and murders of the Barrow gang. Penn effectively develops this theme through his representation of the newspapers which so avidly report the gang's adventures and by the reactions of witnesses to the gang's attacks on banks. Finally, its lust for the hunt aroused, society itself takes up the pursuit in packs and posses, and, in a final ambush that set a new level in explicit screen violence, the doomed Bonnie and Clyde are shot to pieces. But the inversion of generic meanings is still more complex, for Penn refuses to make the opposition between gangster and society a simple reversal of traditional generic meanings as he does in *Little Big Man.* The protagonists of *Bonnie and Clyde* are not simply victims of society. They are themselves very much a part of the society they are attacking. They share its basic aspirations and confusions, and they yearn above all to be reintegrated with it. In many respects, their actions reflect a desperate and misconceived attempt to achieve some measure of the status, security, and sense of belonging that ought to be among the basic gifts of a society to its members.

Instead of simply reversing the meanings conventionally ascribed to the opposing forces of criminal and society in the gangster genre, *Bonnie and Clyde* expressed a more complex and dark awareness that this basic opposition was itself a mythical simplification, and showed us the deeper and more difficult irony of the twisted and inseparable fates of individuals and their society. This was in its way a recognition of that skein of ambiguous inevitability which Polanski summed up in the symbol of Chinatown and which Francis Ford Coppola developed through the fateful intertwining of individuals, "families," and society in *The Godfather.*

Though the demythologization of traditional genres has been primarily evident in the work of younger directors, it has also had some influence on the later work of some of the classic filmmakers, most noticeably perhaps in the later westerns of John Ford, particularly *The Searchers* (1956), *Cheyenne Autumn* (1964), and *The Man Who Shot Liberty Valance* (1962). Indeed, in the last-named film, Ford symbolized the conquest of the West through a story in which the territory's last major outlaw was killed in a shootout by a man destined to lead the territory into the blessings of civilization. In fact, the legend of Senator Stoddard's heroic deed was a myth, the actual shooting of Liberty Valance having been done by another man. Toward the end of the film, the newspaper editor to whom Senator Stoddard confesses the truth about his past makes the famous and ambiguous comment, "When the legend becomes a fact, print the legend." But is this an ironic comment on the falsity of legends and newspapers alike, or is it some kind of affirmation of the significance of myth in spite of its unreality? Ford was apparently inclined to the latter interpretation, for he once told Peter Bogdanovich, "We've had a lot of people who were supposed to be great heroes and you know damn well they weren't. But it's good for the country to have heroes to look up to." [1]

This brings us to a fourth and final mode of generic transformation that might be described as the affirmation of myth for its own sake. In films in this mode, a traditional genre and its myth are probed and shown to be unreal, but then the myth itself is at least partially affirmed as a reflection of authentic human aspirations and needs. This is the element that becomes dominant in Ford's later westerns, in which he seems to see the heroic ethos of the West in critical terms and becomes more and more sympathetic with the Indian victims of the westward movement. Yet, at the same time that he became more cynical about the reality of the West, he seemed to feel even more strongly the need to affirm its heroic ideals. Thus, in his powerful late film *The Searchers,* Ford turns to the old western theme of Indian captivity, portraying the mad obsessive hatred with which a white man pursues a band of Indians who have captured and adopted his niece. Yet Ford also accepted a change in the ending of the original novel, where this mad Indian-hater was finally destroyed by his obsession, in order to reaffirm at the end the heroism and self-sacrifice of this obsessive quest. *The Searchers* is a powerful and beautiful film, yet one feels uncomfortable at the end, as if the gap between Ford's sense of historical reality and his feelings about genre and myth have come into collision.

Sam Peckinpah's *The Wild Bunch,* for all its ugliness and violence, is a more coherent example of the destruction and reaffirmation of myth. Throughout the film, Peckinpah points up the gap between the conventional western's heroic struggle between pioneers and outlaws. His pioneer lawmen are despicable bounty hunters in the employ of the railroad, and they kill the guilty and the innocent indiscriminately. His outlaws are not much better; they are brutal, coarse, and quite capable of leaving a wounded comrade behind. Moreover, their type of criminal operation has become absurdly obsolescent in the early twentieth-century West of the film. In the end, Peckinpah's outlaw protagonists are drawn into a ridiculously destructive shoot-out with an entire Mexican village full of troops and are completely wiped out in the process. Yet the film also leaves us with a sense that through their hopeless action these coarse and vicious outlaws have somehow transcended themselves and become embodiments of a myth of heroism that people need in spite of the realities of their world.

While I have separated the four modes of generic transformation—humorous burlesque, evocation of nostalgia, demythologization of generic myth, and the reaffirmation of myth as myth—into separate categories in order to define them more clearly, most films that employ one of these modes are likely to use another at some point. Probably the best films based on generic transformation employ some combination of several of these modes in the service of one overriding artistic purpose; *Chinatown* uses both humorous burlesque and nostalgic evocation as a basis for its devastating exploration of the genre of the hard-boiled detective and his myth. Some directors seem to have a primary predilection for one of these modes; Brooks is primarily oriented toward burlesque, Bogdanovich toward nostalgia, Penn toward demythologization, and Peckinpah toward reaffirmation. Some directors—Robert Altman springs particularly to mind—have, in their best films, worked out a rich and fascinating dialectic between different modes of generic transformation. In films like *McCabe and Mrs. Miller, The Long Goodbye, Thieves Like Us* (1974), and *Nashville* it is quite difficult to decide at the end whether Altman is attacking or reaffirming the genre on which he has based each particular work. In fact, until the last two or three years, Altman's filmography has looked almost as if he had planned a systematic voyage through the major traditional film genres. That generic transformation has been so important a source of artistic energy to the most vital younger directors suggests that it is a central key to the current state of the American film.

There are probably many reasons for the importance of these modes of filmmaking in the last decade, but in conclusion I will comment briefly on what seem to me the most important factors involved in the proliferation of this kind of film. I think it is not primarily the competition of television. Though television has been somewhat more conservative in its use of generic transformation than film, the same modes seem to be turning up with increasing frequency in television series. Instead I would point to the tendency of genres to exhaust themselves, to our growing historical awareness of modern popular culture, and finally, to the decline of the underlying mythology on which traditional genres have been based since the late nineteenth century. Generic exhaustion is a common phenomenon in the history of culture. One can almost make out a life cycle characteristic of genres as they move from an initial period of articulation and discovery, through a phase of conscious self-awareness on the part of both creators and audiences, to a time when the generic patterns have become so well known that people become tired of their predictability. It is at this point that parodic and satiric treatments proliferate and new genres gradually arise. Our major traditional genres—the western, the detective story, the musical, the domestic comedy—have, after all, been around for a considerable period of time, and it may be that they have simply reached a point of creative exhaustion.

In our time, the awareness of the persistence of genres has been intensified by an increasing historical awareness of film. A younger generation of directors has a sense of film history quite different from many of their predecessors who, like Ford and Hawks, were involved with the art of film almost from its beginnings. Similarly, audiences have a kind of sophistication about the history of genres different from earlier film publics because of the tremendous number of past films now regularly shown on television and by college film societies.

But I am inclined to think that there is more to it than that. The present significance of generic transformation as a creative mode reflects the feeling that not only the traditional genres but the cultural myths they once embodied are no longer fully adequate to the imaginative needs of our time. It will require another essay to explain and justify this assertion, but if I may hazard a final prediction, I think we will begin to see emerging out of this period of generic transformation a new set of generic constructs more directly related to the imaginative landscape of the second half of the twentieth century. Thus, the present period of American filmmaking will seem in retrospect an important time of artistic and cultural transition. Like many transition periods, it may also turn out to be a time of the highest artistic accomplishment.

Note

1. Quoted in Jon Tuska, *The Filming of the West* (Garden City: Doubleday, 1976), p. 519.

19. Shoot-Out at the Genre Corral: Problems in the "Evolution" of the Western

TAG GALLAGHER

"The Western," writes Thomas Schatz in *Hollywood Genres,* "is without question the richest and most enduring genre of Hollywood's repertoire." [1] Without question it has been the richest and most enduring genre for genre critics as well. Certain writings on the western, however—notably works by Robert Warshow, John G. Cawelti, Philip French, Jack Nachbar, Will Wright, Frank D. McConnell, Leo Braudy, and Thomas Schatz [2]—have, it seems to me, been marred by flaws in theory and practice so similar that, despite the scholarly illumination these writers have otherwise cast upon the western, their similar flaws reflect upon genre criticism itself.

Genre criticism has tended to ignore the evidence.

"There is," writes French, "general agreement that . . . the Western has changed significantly since World War II, becoming more varied, complex, and self conscious." [3] But French, concerned mostly with post-1950 westerns, offers no supporting evidence for changes, and the other seven critics, although they concur, fail as well to defend this position. "Of course," asserts McConnell, "artistic forms evolve under their own impetus, and it was inevitable that sooner or later the Western film should have achieved the self-consciousness [of 1959]." [4] The western's "ritualistic affirmations of progress and success become more and more ambiguous and strained," claims Cawelti. [5] "In most contemporary Westerns . . . heroes are no longer necessarily heroic, the civilized no longer necessarily civilized," states Nachbar, in comparison to the past. [6] "Even the horses," sighs Warshow, "grow tired and stumble more often than they did." [7]

Probably no one makes stronger claims for the western's "evolution" than Schatz. After citing Christian Metz to the effect that westerns, from 1939 to 1959 or so, progressed, as audiences and filmmakers grew increasingly "self-conscious," from "classic" treatments, to "parody," to "contestation" (straining the conventions), to "deconstruction" (self-critiquing the conventions), Schatz draws an analogy with Henri Focillon's observation that styles in art pass through various clear stages: the *experimental,* when stylistic conventions become established; the *classical,* when they have been accepted by the public; *refinement,* when style becomes more elaborate; and *mannerist,* when style becomes self-reflective.[8] Schatz feels that genres evolve similarly to styles. Although he does not detail the evolution of the western through four phases, his perceptions of differences between later (c. post-1950) and earlier westerns resemble those of the seven other genre critics and are basically three in number: (1) the later western projects a less optimistic and more unflattering vision of the West's potential synthesis of nature and culture; (2) the western hero, once an agent of law and order, has become a renegade, a professional killer, an antihero, neurotic, psychotic, less integratable into a synthesis; (3) the later western is less simple, tidy, and naive, more ambiguous, complex, and ironic, more self-critical and into the "art of telling."

It is a curious testament to the continued vitality of the western that Warshow back in 1954 found differences between early-1950s and prewar westerns almost identical to those which critics like Schatz and company detect a quarter-century later between westerns of the 1970s and early 1950s. Perhaps older westerns, like olden times, will always strike the modern mind as less complex, less amoral, and above all less vivid—particularly when the modern mind feels it unnecessary to examine the past in any detail. Collectively, our octet of genre critics evinces only the scantiest acquaintance with 1939–1940 prewar westerns, and infinitely less acquaintance with earlier and silent westerns. "In earlier Westerns," writes Braudy, apparently referring back to 1939, "while basics of the form were being worked out"—in 1939?!—"the issues were more patterned and the individual played a more stereotyped role."[9] In any other academic discipline one would suppose that Braudy's authority for such a statement rested upon a judicious survey of the more than five thousand westerns made before World War II; in actual fact, however, there is no such authority and Braudy's phrase smacks of pure conjecture. Wright's is the most rigorous evolutionary essay, purporting to examine westerns from 1931 through 1972, but, having already excluded the first thirty-five years of western cinema, Wright then disqualifies from his study any western that has not grossed at least $4,000,000. Not surprisingly, given inflation in ticket prices from 10¢ to $4.00, of Wright's sixty-four sample films only three were made before 1939, while fifty-eight were made since the war. Wright's survey is obviously inadequate. Western buffs might further object that blockbuster westerns tend to be unrepresentative of the genre in any case—is this true?—and that Wright would have done better to have considered only westerns that grossed *under,* say, $500,000.

Every argument that evolution exists at all comes down not to evidence mustered through representative sampling but either to bald assertions or to invidious comparisons between a couple of titles—a "classic" western versus a "self-conscious" western—selected specifically to illustrate the assertion. A film is considered "classic" when it matches a critic's paradigm of the ideal western. But the paradigm is entirely arbitrary, with the result that there is some disagreement about which pictures are "classic" and which have evolved astray. Warshow, for example, is intent on showing how the 1943 *Ox-Bow Incident* (William Wellman), the 1950 *Gunfighter* (Henry King), and the 1952 *High Noon* (Fred Zinnemann) transformed the primeval western into a vehicle for social criticism, in comparison with Victor Fleming's naively archetypal 1929 *Virginian.* Thus he found an "unhealthy preoccupation with style," an "aestheticizing tendency," in *Stagecoach* (John Ford, 1939), *My Darling Clementine* (Ford, 1946), and *Shane* (George Stevens, 1954) that he felt "violat[ed] the Western form."[10] Later genre critics regard the last three pictures as "classic" and regard as "self-conscious" movies such as *The Man Who Shot Liberty Valance* (Ford, 1962), *Hour of the Gun* (John Sturges, 1967), *Chisum* (Andrew V. McLaglen, 1970), and *The Wild Bunch* (Sam Peckinpah, 1969).

In sum, while it is undoubtedly true that each age's westerns reflect each age, and that westerns of recent years, *like almost every film made,* evince sorts of violence, pornography, and cynicism that probably were not present to the same degree in the same ways during the 1940s, little evidence has been brought forward to support the theory that there has been growing "self-consciousness"—or any other sort of linear evolution—in and specific to the western. Indeed, the evidence has not even been considered. So perhaps the opposite is true.

Schatz asserts that "the earliest Westerns (many of which actually depicted then-current events) obviously were based on social and historical reality. But as the genre developed, it gradually took on its own reality."[11] This may be obvious, but is it true? Granted, *The Great Train Robbery* (Edwin S. Porter, 1902) has reference to a current event (although note that even in this case an antihero is being glorified and the use of the antihero's close-up firing, outside of the movie's diegesis, at the audience constitutes a species of self-reflexivity); but no such basis was required in 1904 and 1905, when the only historical reality in many westerns was their conventionality. The bulk of westerns in this period were—like the very first western novels—produced for European markets, mostly by European film companies, and romantic myth rather than reality, current or otherwise, was the standard. In fact, so popular were westerns during narrative cinema's formative years (1903–1911) that it may well be that, rather than the cinema having invented the western, it was the western, already long existent in popular culture, that invented the cinema.

48. *The Great Train Robbery:* The bandit fires at the audience.

Picturesque scenery, archetypal characters, dialectical story construction, long shots, close-ups, parallel editing, confrontational cross-cutting,
montaged chases—all were explicit in the western before the Lumières
cranked their first camera. By 1909, and during the next six years, there
were probably more westerns released *each* month than during the entire
decade of the 1930s. Hyperconsciousness of the genre resulted. Almost all
the observations of our octet of genre critics were commonplace in pre-
World War I writings on the western. More subtly, westerns were then divided into quite distinct subgenres, each of which was known to possess
its own specific conventions—among them, frontier dramas, Indian dramas, Civil War dramas, western comedies. Not only did the mode of exhibition (the average theater changing its bill frequently, the average
moviegoer attending several times per week) and the mode of criticism (a
host of thick weekly trade and popular magazines reviewing every new release, along with lengthy plot summaries) encourage both generic consciousness and self-consciousness, but so did the mode of production:
each "studio" was subdivided into semiautonomous troupes, so that a

core group of director, writer, cameraman, and actors worked together regularly and were expected to turn out one, sometimes two, new pictures (fifteen to sixty minutes long) each week. Instruction booklets, moreover, were available by mail order for nascent scenarists, in which all the basic plots and their many variations within each genre were carefully outlined.

Anything novel was instantly seized upon and copied voraciously. Will Wright in 1975 proposes as fresh insight "my argument . . . that within each period the structure of the [western] myth corresponds to the conceptual needs of social and self understanding required by the dominant social institutions of that period," but no one thought otherwise back in 1913. Any news event or fashion trend—labor actions, bloomers, Apaches, prohibition, female suffrage, Balkan crises, and a myriad of forgotten issues of the day—were zealously incorporated not only into westerns but into whatever other genres were currently popular, the western hero and the nature of his struggles altering accordingly.

The actual number of genres was considerably greater in these years than at any time since, and there was far more awareness of generic specificities: each new picture was labeled as belonging to a given genre by its producers and in the trade journals. Exhibitors, critics, and filmmakers grumbled constantly about the hackneyed versus the original, the stale versus the new, in character, story, and theme. No one complained in 1956 when a baddy's presence in *Rio Bravo* (Howard Hawks) is revealed when his blood drips down from the floor above; but when the same gag was used back in 1918 in Ford's *The Scarlet Drop* it was contemptuously dismissed as "old hat" by *Exhibitors' Trade Review*.

Schatz, along with his colleagues, assumes that the earliest westerns were somehow more realistic, primitive, and unself-conscious. But, quite the contrary, "realism" was a big issue in 1907 because people thought that the western was too much a parody and concerned only with its own conventions. Some years later, William S. Hart was campaigning against, and Harry Carey was spoofing, the dandy cowboy hero represented by Bronco Billy, Tom Mix, and others. Carey, in 1919, talked longingly about wanting to "Jack Londonize the Western cowboy—that is, present him as he really is in life . . . totally unlike the one we see in [movies]. He has his distinctive characteristics and they are amusing enough without exaggeration." [12] Without exaggeration, clichés are already an issue. Self-reflexivity in the early teens was often evident as well in the form of films within films: characters frequently fall asleep and dream, friends deceive friends with elaborate masquerades (put-on kidnappings and the like), Remington paintings (as in Ford's 1918 *Hell Bent*) come alive in an onlooker's fantasy—all methods of critiquing generic conventions. In fact, so familiar had western conventions become by 1913 that Universal announced its despair of ever again doing anything new, and—two years before Griffith's *The Birth of a Nation*—said it was giving up frontier, Indian, and Civil War pictures.[13]

Heroes before World War I evince many of the complex, "self-conscious" qualities Schatz and Braudy assign to the evolved western. The "double" character Braudy traces from *Jesse James* (Henry King) in 1940[14] was of course the basis of innumerable "good badmen" heroes in early Ford (most of Harry Carey's roles in 25 Ford pictures, as well as those of other directors), Anderson (Bronco Billy), Ince (William S. Hart), and others. In the remarkable series of 101-Bison westerns initiated by Thomas Ince and Francis Ford in 1912, heroes were almost routinely ambivalent, endings unresolved, and visions tragic. In fact, tragic endings were quite modish before the war, but by 1919 the weather vane had clearly shifted away from the morally daring and innovative hero. *Exhibitors' Trade Review* (November 21, 1918) sternly lectured Harry Carey for "consistently portray[ing] a rough character throughout [Ford's *Three Mounted Men*]. The only wonder of it is that anyone should attempt to heroize such a type. There may be such men in the west, but it is best on the screen to show them up as horrible examples of what a man may be." The change in audience and producer attitudes after World War I is typified, I suspect,[15] by the case of Ford's *Straight Shooting*, in which, as originally issued in 1917, the hero, a hired killer who finds his conscience in the film's course, declines to settle down with the woman who loves him and goes off into the sunset instead. When the picture was rereleased in 1925, however, its title was changed to *Straight Shootin'* (parody?), and the hero, by dint of some clumsy reediting, is made to accept marriage.[16]

It is surprising that none of our genre critics, well-armed as each of them is with battalions of analytic theory gleaned from literary studies, psychology, anthropology, communications, sociology, and political science, seems aware of the rich roles played by genre films in the years before World War I. Immense research into actual movies, or at least into surviving accounts of them, ought, one would think, to precede attempts to theorize their development. Yet the teens and preteens are not the only periods of cinema history of which our knowledge is vague and our cant deceptive. My own glance at the pre–World War I western—cursory, superficial, and undetailed as it is—nonetheless suggests strongly that, while a genre does reflect its era, no such evolutionary process as described by Metz or our octet of critics has ever occurred in which, because audiences and filmmakers demand variations, reexaminations, more complications, and stylistic embellishments, a form is first established and then elaborated upon.[17]

Quite the contrary, pictures such as *Stagecoach, Shane,* or *The Searchers* (John Ford, 1956), even *Once Upon a Time in the West* (Sergio Leone, 1968) show that audiences respond forcibly to stark apotheoses of the genre's most primeval elements—even, in the case of *Star Wars* (George Lucas, 1977), after eighty years of repetition. "Self-consciousness" is too readily assumed to have come to movies only in reaction against Hollywood's so-called "classic codes" (whose existence, never demonstrated, is at least to be questioned), while such consciousness has traditionally been considered a necessary ingredient of any mature work of art and would certainly seem to be abundant in pictures of the 1930s, where style, far from being "invisible," is so overwhelming. It is perhaps natural that people today, attuned to contemporary film styles and only vaguely acquainted with the past, should feel they are onto something new when in an ostentatiously revisionist film by Robert Altman (*McCabe and Mrs. Miller*, 1971, or *Buffalo Bill and the Indians*, 1976) they perceive references to motifs and conventions from other westerns made twenty or thirty years earlier and thus cast forcibly into a "straight man's" role for the revisionist's lampooning. But they forget that even such putatively naive classics as *Stagecoach* were similarly perceived by audiences in 1939; indeed, *Stagecoach* in particular is a virtual anthology of gags, motifs, conventions, scenes, situations, tricks, and characters drawn from past westerns, but each one pushed toward fresh intensities of mythic extremism, thus consciously revisiting not only the old West but old westerns as well, and reinterpreting at the same time these elements for modern minds.

A superficial glance at film history suggests cyclicism rather than evolution. Despair and an appetite for realism were modish before World War I, escapism and genuinely happy endings became mandatory after the war. Films were moody and depressed during the early years of the Depression, when both surrealism and realism were in fashion; then with the censorship codes of 1934 films turned escapist and during the next ten years were awesomely repressed. A demonic period after World War II precedes a mingling of optimism and anguish in the 1950s, followed by extremism and schizophrenia in the 1960s, escapism mingling with serious concern in the late 1970s and 1980s. It would be easy to cite apt examples for each period; but it would be just as easy to cite exceptions. But nothing suggests the western changed separately from film production as a whole.

Genre critics tend to be unsympathetic to the subtleties of "old" movies.

Like neo-Wagnerites who loved Mozart and Haydn only for their sweetness, "modernist"-inclined genre critics tend to love "old" movies only for their supposed naiveté. In misinterpreting these pictures—by failing to grasp the subtleties of so-called "classic" styles and the conventions of earlier decades—while yet using these pictures as the "fall guys" for invidious comparisons, these genre critics necessarily misperceive the history of the cinema.

Stagecoach (1939) and *My Darling Clementine* (1946) are among the pictures used most frequently as antipodes to the recent western, and Schatz uses these pictures within Ford's career to exemplify an alleged evolution. But how do Schatz and his colleagues regard these movies?

Nachbar, for example, begins his essay by stating that Wyatt Earp's motives are "very clear" in *My Darling Clementine*: he has "both the right and the duty to kill the Clantons [who killed Earp's two brothers and stole his cattle]. It is no surprise, then, that after the famous battle, Earp is recognized as the hero of the community and will soon be rewarded by wedding the lovely maiden from the East, Clementine Carter." In contrast, in *Hour of the Gun* (John Sturges, 1967), Wyatt "contemptuously hides under the law to satisfy his near-psychotic lust for violent revenge. Obviously between 1946 and 1967 there were some important changes in the legend of Wyatt Earp." [18]

The problem is that Nachbar misreads Earp's character as badly as he misreads *My Darling Clementine*'s plot. [19] The films of the sixties had to work harder, had to be more strident and dissonant, in order to try to express the same notions as earlier films. Eroticism, for example, has not necessarily increased along with nudity, although it may seem to have, for those incapable of getting emotionally involved with the types of people in 1930s films. Similarly, violence and ugliness do not necessarily increase as they are denuded. In the case of Ford's Wyatt Earp, charm hides a self-righteous prig, and a marshal's badge and noble sentiments hide a "near-psychotic lust for violent revenge" even from Earp himself; but this upstanding Wyatt is all the more ambivalently complex a character for the sublimation of his hypocrisy and violence. Schatz, who like Nachbar sees Wyatt as a naive archetype, describes him as a stoic, laconic militarist who uses force only when necessary and disdains Holliday's penchant for gunplay. [20] But Wyatt clearly relishes lording it over people without using his gun, and Ford is far too much of a moralist to accept Earp simply as a "redeemer" (Schatz) who has an unequivocal "right and duty to kill" (Nachbar). Wyatt, in any case, morally abdicates his "right to kill" when, just before the battle, he declines the assistance of the town mayor and parson, calling his feud with the Clantons "strictly a family affair"; he is thus left only with "duty" to kill—that is, vengeance duty. Duty, however, as a myopic, negative quality, is an obsessive theme throughout Ford's oeuvre, while the major theme of *My Darling Clementine* is wrapped around musing over whether one can ever have the right or duty to kill, whether one should "be or not be" (i.e., the staging of Shakespeare's *Hamlet* soliloquy), and the fearsome cost wreaked by vengeance:

Wyatt loses a second brother in trying to avenge the first; Chihuahua and Doc Holliday also perish amid Wyatt's efforts. Contrary to Nachbar, there is no recognition in the film of Wyatt as "hero of the community": Ford cuts directly from the battle's last death to Wyatt's solitary farewell to Clementine virtually outside of town. Nor is there any "reward" of a wedding: Wyatt has known Clementine only two days, the great love of her life has just been killed, and the forlorn feelings in the air— Wyatt must go to California and tell his father that two sons are dead— suggest he may never "pass through here again someday" (an intimation strengthened by the gone-forever "Clementine" song).[21]

The question, then, of whether heroes change in the 1960s is not as simple as some critics would have us believe. Perhaps heroes sometimes merely disappear, allowing, as they did at times during earlier decades, the fellows who play supporting roles to step to center stage. Perhaps heroes merely stop shaving. Ford's heroes, in any case, fail to act in accordance with the model Schatz proposes—that is, electing civilization in early westerns, choosing wilderness in later westerns, remaining distinct from either civilization or wilderness in still later westerns. Ford's heroes in *Three Bad Men* elect wilderness in 1926, as do the Ringo Kid in 1939, Wyatt Earp in 1946, and Cheyenne Harry in 1917. But John Wayne in *Three Godfathers* in 1948 and Ben Johnson in *Wagon Master* in 1950 choose civilization, while Ethan Edwards in *The Searchers* (1956) represents not wilderness but the purity of civilized values: he values home and family, loathes Indians, and execrates miscegenation. *The Man Who Shot Liberty Valance* shows the hero's surrender to civilization, the antihero's corruption by it.

Schatz bases much of his argument on an extended comparison between *Stagecoach* (1939) and *Liberty Valance* (1962). But to assume, as he does and as many people seem routinely to do, that *Stagecoach* proffers a more optimistic vision of synthesis between nature and civilization than does *Liberty Valance*—merely because Ringo and Dallas ride off into the sunrise to start their lives together in 1939, whereas Ranse and Hallie sadly recognize their failure at the end of their lives in 1962—is to ignore rather than perceive the conventions of the films' times.

First of all, it is never sufficiently acknowledged to what degree the much-maligned Hollywood "happy ending" during the whole Depression era, but markedly during the 1939–1941 years, is tacked onto narrative structures whose abysmally despairing logic the happy endings arbitrarily contradict. Deus ex machina conclusions patently escape the dismal messages that Mr. Smith is doomed in Washington, that the western dream has vanished completely from *Stagecoach*'s ramshackle frontier towns, that the Joad family has hopelessly disintegrated at the end of *The Grapes of Wrath* (Ford, 1940), that family and village are completely

49. *Stagecoach:* The intolerant ladies of the law and order league force the prostitute (Claire Trevor) to leave town.

destroyed at the end of *How Green Was My Valley* (Ford, 1941); even Dorothy's search for the Wizard of Oz fizzles out. What is my point? That these films, and many more, deliver the sorts of messages Schatz finds typical of evolved genres (messages questioning official ideology or generic expectations and values), but that by giving audiences tacked-on happy endings, producers provided *formal* satisfaction *plus* a telling interaction between form and message; whereas in the late 1960s and 1970s—when until *Breaking Away* (Peter Yates, 1979) it was difficult to find *any* happy ending or unneurotic film—aesthetic form was the mere maidservant of message: exactly the opposite of what Schatz contends. In short, *Stagecoach*'s vision is not optimistic merely because it has a sort of happy end tacked on.

Second, Ransom Stoddard in *Liberty Valance* spends a lifetime figuring out what everyone knows already in *Stagecoach*—that civilization is corrupting. In malodorous, dirty, sleazy Lordsburg and Tonto, full of the mean, intolerant, aggressive people inhabiting *Stagecoach,* one finds nothing of the idealism, progressivism, and enlightenment shared by virtually everyone in *Liberty Valance*'s Shinbone. As a hero, moreover,

Stagecoach's Ringo implies no solutions, no syntheses. He ignores society rather than confronting it; he is less an outlaw than oblivious, an unconscious god. Who else would nonchalantly save three bullets to kill three men? Naturally Ringo can pluck up Dallas and spirit her away to never-never land. But who of *us* resembles Ringo? How is *his* solution reason for optimism for us? We are neither outlaws, never-never land's gods, nor detachable from civilization. (In any case, far from representing a synthesis between nature and civilization, as Schatz contends, Ringo and Dallas are explicitly "saved from the blessings of civilization," as Doc tells the sheriff.) If we fantasize with Ringo, it is only because hope is more primal than reason.

My point in this section is not that I disagree with certain interpretations of certain films by certain genre critics, nor even that such interpretations *can* be questioned. My point is that in each case rich lodes of ambivalence are overlooked in order to bolster a specious argument that "classic" westerns are simple and naive. That genre critics tend to be oblivious, as I see it, to the complexities of "classic" westerns is perhaps due to a more deeply endemic flaw in their methodology.

Genre critics deal not with the phenomenon of cinema art but with a derived abstraction—narrative.

Taking the case of Ford, as Schatz does, it seems at first obvious that change has occurred over fifty years. But the more closely one looks, the less such change seems definable as an increase in self-consciousness, self-criticism, or pessimism, and the more it becomes difficult to specify *what* has changed, or even how. Granted, Ford's career closed with two blackly suicidal tragedies, *Cheyenne Autumn* (1964) and *7 Women* (1965), but are we entitled to conclude an *evolution* in his sensitivity on that account? Shakespeare, after all, ended with two happy idyllic romances, but we do not thereby conclude that he was repudiating *Hamlet* and *King Lear*, or even that his vision of life had changed. Actually, in Ford's case, his last picture would have been a comedy, *The Miracle of Merriford*, but his funding disappeared a week before shooting was to begin. And, in any case, Ford's oeuvre is arguably the most melancholic in the American cinema. Lost illusion, cynicism, tragedy, and moral trauma permeate his pictures—particularly during the decade before the war—as in *Air Mail* (1932), *Pilgrimage* (1933), *The Whole Town's Talking* (1935), *The Informer* (1935), *The Prisoner of Shark Island* (1936), *The Hurricane* (1937), *The Grapes of Wrath, Young Mr. Lincoln* (1939), and *How Green Was My Valley*. The sunny pictures of the early 1950s—*She Wore a Yellow Ribbon* (1949), *Wagon Master*, and *The Quiet Man* (1952)—are outstanding exceptions. And John Ford, finally, is the worst possible paradigm with which to attempt to illustrate the evolution of the western, for the cyclical alterations in Ford's vision and style occur regardless of the genre in which he is working. Since the "feel" and narrative structures of a given western will at any given date resemble closely those of the non-westerns, Schatz's and Braudy's arguments of some internally generated evolution specific to the western genre cannot be verified. And since the changes they note in all, not just Ford's, westerns over the decades resemble changes they do not note in all contemporaneous genres and non-genre films, their arguments tend to collapse.

Surely a great artist's powers become more acute during the artist's lifetime, at least in certain moments; but can the perturbations of soul that aestheticize great cinema be accounted for by plot twists? The human being is more than that, and so are movies. Whatever the ontology of cinematic art, it is certainly not, as Warshow describes the western, "an art form for connoisseurs, where the spectator derives his pleasure from the appreciation of minor variations within the working out of a pre-established order." [22] Really? Is my pleasure in loving a woman in my appreciation of her minor variations from other women? Do I enjoy a good dish of pasta through appreciating its variations from chop suey? Schatz apparently does: "Our ultimate goal is to discern a genre film's quality, its social and aesthetic value. To do this, we will attempt to see its relation to the various systems that inform it." [23] What of the *thing itself?* Granted, comparisons, classifications, contrasts may aid us, but is not their illumination ultimately peripheral to the work itself?

Alas. Every one of our octet of genre critics virtually equates *experience* of a movie with analytic apperception of its narrative! Everything that can be is abstracted into literature. An "icon" is catalogued, and immediately is stripped of its iconicity and transformed into a verbal symbol. "A white hat in a Western," writes Schatz, "is significant because it has come to serve a specific symbolic function within the narrative system." [24] It has, then, no significance more important than that? Apparently not. And, similarly, land and nature become "land" and "nature," abstractions from the real world photographed in the movie, abstractions reduced into the essentially verbal background symbols they become in bad O'Neill plays.

Genre criticism seems almost endemically antiphenomenological. [25] It cannot conceive the true nature of cinema. It cannot recognize that extraction of a "narrative" is distant indeed from experience of cinema, that narrative analysis of cinema, when divorced from a phenomenological approach, is virtually as irrelevant to cinematic criticism as narrative summaries of operas are to music criticism. Literary critics exalt the "idea," but they regard its actualization as a mere illustration. They concern themselves with narrative because they comprehend cinema chiefly in terms of what happens, as *becoming,* as "action." Cinema critics, on the other hand, tend to comprehend cinema more as *being*, as a world and soul experienced in an immediate now. A rose is a rose in cinema, or at least nearly so: its value lies primarily in its being a real image of a real rose; symbolic accretions are imposed subsidiarily. But a "rose" is not a rose in literature: it is primarily a sign, rich in accretions but universally abstracted from any actual rose. For these reasons, narrative is more important than character in literature, because character can be suggested only through event, whereas in cinema character is more important than narrative, because cinema gives us direct and immediate experience of another person, and an event is more the personality of the doer than the deed that is done. What is nearly impossible in literature—virtually direct experience of the world—is the essence of cinema. And thus it is that many of cinema's greatest works—among them, certain pictures of Sternberg, Ophüls, Dreyer, Ford, and Rossellini—offer little more for the grist of narrative criticism than platitudinous plots, stereotyped characters, and hackneyed dialogue. But genre criticism tends—not always, but frequently enough—to delete the sensuous from the dialectic between sensuousness and logic that creates art; in so doing, such criticism emasculates cinema of its aesthetic dimension and transforms it into an effete, conceptual vehicle. Art becomes an academic exercise, pornography or propaganda, raped of its capability, its *aesthetic* capability, to give us knowledge of ourselves and our world.

Notes

1. Thomas Schatz, *Hollywood Genres: Formulas, Filmmaking, and the Studio System* (New York: Random House, 1981), p. 45.

2. Robert Warshow, "Movie Chronicle: The Westerner," in *The Immediate Experience* (New York: Atheneum, 1979), pp. 135–154; John G. Cawelti, *The Six-Gun Mystique* (Bowling Green, Ohio: Bowling Green University Popular Press, [1970])—a more cautious essay than the author's subsequent "Reflections on the New Western Films," in *Focus on the Western*, edited by Jack Nachbar (Englewood Cliffs, N.J.: Prentice Hall, 1974), pp. 113–117; Philip French, *Westerns: Aspects of a Movie Genre* (New York: Viking Press, 1973); Jack Nachbar, "Riding Shotgun: The Scattered Formula in Contemporary Western Movies," in *Focus on the Western*, pp. 101–112; Will Wright, *Sixguns and Society: A Structural Study of the Western* (Berkeley: University of California Press, 1975); Frank D. McConnell, *The Spoken Seen* (Baltimore: Johns Hopkins University Press, 1976); and Leo Braudy, *The World in a Frame* (Garden City: Anchor Press/Doubleday, 1976). Many others have written on the western as a genre, of course, without exhibiting the flaws cited in my essay.

3. French, *Westerns*, pp. 12–13.

4. McConnell, *The Spoken Seen*, p. 158.

5. Cawelti, *Six-Gun Mystique*, p. 74.

6. Nachbar, "Riding Shotgun," pp. 102–103.

7. Warshow, "Movie Chronicle," p. 144.

8. Schatz, *Hollywood Genres*, p. 37. See Christian Metz, *Language and Cinema* (New York: Praeger, 1975), pp. 148–161, and Henri Focillon, *Life of Forms in Art* (New York: George Wittenborn, 1942), p. 10.

9. Braudy, *The World in a Frame*, p. 135.

10. Warshow, "Movie Chronicle," pp. 149–150.

11. Schatz, *Hollywood Genres*, p. 36.

12. *Moving Picture World*, March 29, 1919, p. 1768.

13. Ibid., May 10, 1913, p. 582.

14. Schatz, *Hollywood Genres*, pp. 135–139.

15. Many pictures of the teens were reissued in the twenties; one would have to compare published plot summaries. But reediting was a common occurrence, making a picture shorter or longer, depending upon the new use planned for it, and it seems reasonable to assume that story material would have been updated when possible. But the matter should be checked. Pictures made between 1929 and 1934 were frequently reedited when reissued during the next twenty years in order to conform to the more stringent censorship codes.

16. (*Universal*) *Motion Picture Weekly* of August 17, 1917, and the concurrent number of *Moving Picture World* describe the original ending. The later ending is described in (*Universal*) *Motion Picture Weekly* of January 1925. The clumsy editing may be seen in extant copies of the movie itself, all of which descend from a print from the Czech Film Archives into which new title cards have been interpolated, so that they incorrectly bear the original rather than the reissue title.

17. Schatz, *Hollywood Genres*, p. 38. See also Braudy, *The World in a Frame*, p. 179: "Change in genre occurs when the audience says, 'That's too infantile a form of what we believe. Show us something more complicated.'" Braudy offers no data to support his conjectures about what audiences say or when, nor about audiences influencing change.

18. Nachbar, "Riding Shotgun," pp. 101–102. In fact, history, not legend, had changed. The heroic portrait of Earp in Stuart N. Lake's *Wyatt Earp, Frontier Marshall* (Boston: Houghton Mifflin, 1931) had been discredited by the revisionist history in Frank Waters, *The Earp Brothers of Tombstone* (Lincoln: University of Nebraska Press, 1960), in which Earp and Holliday are revealed to have been partners in a hold-up racket who massacred the Clantons in an ambush (not a battle) and hung their bodies up in the butcher-shop window. Ford, who had based his *My Darling Clementine* on Lake's book, acknowledged the new truth three years before 1967 with a salacious version of Earp in *Cheyenne Autumn* (and with a salacious marshal in *Two Rode Together* in 1961). But since Ford had known Earp personally in the teens, he tempered his 1946 Earp with undercutting criticism.

19. Similarly, McConnell in *The Spoken Seen* misreads the nature of society and hero in *Stagecoach:* "The society of *Stagecoach* is the explicitly nomadic one of the travelers in the coach to Lordsburg . . . The Ringo Kid (John Wayne) saves the group and holds it together against danger from within and without . . ."

(p. 155). Half of *Stagecoach* occurs in the two towns; most of what we see of the voyage occurs at the two way-stations. Is this "nomadic"? The Ringo Kid does not specifically save the group or hold it together, either from within or from without; he is captured, held against his will, fails to escape only because Indians appear, and places his personal vengeance above saving the group by holding back the three bullets.

20. Schatz, *Hollywood Genres*, pp. 67–69.

21. For elaboration of these and subsequent arguments about Ford, see Tag Gallagher, *John Ford* (Berkeley: University of California Press, 1985).

22. Warshow, "Movie Chronicle," p. 146.

23. Schatz, *Hollywood Genres*, p. 21.

24. Ibid., p. 22.

25. An exposition of a phenomenological approach to cinema theory may be found in J. Dudley Andrew, *The Major Film Theories* (New York: Oxford University Press, 1976), pp. 242–254.

20. The Bug in the Rug: Notes on the Disaster Genre

MAURICE YACOWAR

Disaster films constitute a sufficiently numerous, old, and conventionalized group to be considered a genre rather than a popular cycle that comes and goes. The disaster film is quite distinct from the science fiction genre Susan Sontag discusses in "The Imagination of Disaster,"[1] though like sci-fi, the disaster film exploits the spectacular potential of the screen and nourishes the audience's fascination with the vision of massive doom.

The disaster genre is older than Griffith's *Intolerance* (1916). One might argue that the first disaster film was Méliès's happy accident whereby a jammed camera transformed an ordinary autobus into a hearse. There we have the essence of the genre: a situation of normalcy erupts into a persuasive image of death. More obvious examples could be found in Méliès's *Collision and Shipwreck at Sea* (1898), perhaps in *The Misfortunes of an Explorer* (1900) and *The Interrupted Honeymoon* (1899), but certainly in *The Eruption of Mount Pelée* (1902) and *The Catastrophe of the Balloon "Le Pax"* (1902).

THE BASIC TYPES

At least eight types of disaster film can be distinguished. Of course, there will be overlap between them and even with other genres.

Natural Attack

The most common disaster type pits a human community against a destructive form of nature. The attack may be by an animal force, such as rats—*Willard* (Daniel Mann, 1970), *Ben* (Phil Karlson, 1972). It may be ants—either normal (*The Naked Jungle,* Byron Haskin, 1954) or abnormal (*Them!,* Gordon Douglas, 1954; *Phase IV,* Saul Bass, 1975). It may be fish (*Jaws,* Steven Spielberg, 1975) or fowl (*The Birds,* Alfred Hitchcock, 1961) or amphibian (*Frogs,* George McCowan, 1972). It may be a rampage of natural monsters (*Elephant Walk,* William Dieterle, 1954) or of giant forms of natural monsters, like *King Kong* (Merian C. Cooper and Ernest B. Schoedsack, 1933), *The Giant Gila Monster* (Ray Kellogg, 1959), or *Tarantula* (Jack Arnold, 1954). Or they can be fantasy monsters, like Honda's *Godzilla* (1954). Mothra, Reptilicus, Gappa, Rodan, and the rest of the boys in that band. In *The Lost World* (Harry Hoyt, 1924) an aquatic dinosaur rips up London Bridge, as *Gorgo* was to do again for Eugène Lourié in 1961.

Or it may be an attack by the elements, as in John Ford's *The Hurricane* (1937), or in the ever-popular flood movie, such as *The Rains Came* (Clarence Brown, 1939) and *The Rains of Ranchipur* (Jean Negulesco, 1955). Volcanoes figure in *The Last Days of Pompeii* (Maggi, 1908), *Volcano* (Dieterle, 1953), and of course *Krakatoa, East of Java* (Bernard Kowalski, 1969), about the volcano Krakatoa, which is west of Java. The flood and volcano films, wherever they are set, bear the moral weight of the urban renewal sagas of Pompeii, Sodom, and Gomorrah. Mark Robson's *Earthquake* (1974) is a variation on this type.

A third type of natural attack is by an atomic mutation, as the giant ants of *Them!*, the giant grasshoppers of Bert Gordon's *The Beginning of the End* (1953), *The Cyclops* (Gordon, 1957), *The Terror Strikes* (Gordon, 1958; also called *War of the Colossal Beast*), *Kronos* (Kurt Neumann, 1957), *The Creature from the Black Lagoon* (Arnold, 1954), *The Beast from 20,000 Fathoms* (Lourié, 1953), and *It Came from beneath the Sea* (Robert Gordon, 1955). Or it may be the disaster of mutation or radioactive effect, as in *The Incredible Shrinking Man* (Arnold, 1957), *The Amazing Colossal Man* (Bert Gordon, 1957), and *The Atomic Kid* (Leslie Martinson, 1954).

In all three types, the natural disaster film dramatizes people's helplessness against the forces of nature. In the 1950s, obsession with atomic disasters showed human beings diminished by their own technology, as in the credits of *The Incredible Shrinking Man*, where the human outline dwindles as the mushroom cloud swells. The animal films typically dramatize the power of familiar, small creatures, like ants and frogs, often developing the threat out of domesticated animals, like cats and birds. In *The Birds* a complacent society is attacked by birds for no logical reason. *Willard* is an impure disaster film, for the rats' power and malice are at first released under a human's control. Generally, the animal-attack films provide a frightening reversal of the chain of being, attributing will, mind, and collective power to creatures usually considered to be safely without these qualities. At the end of *Willard*, however, the ungentle Ben sniffs smugly in close-up, ominously free of human control, dominant.

The Ship of Fools

The dangers of an isolated journey provide the most obviously allegorical disaster films, given the tradition of "the road of life." Such westerns as *Stagecoach* (John Ford, 1939) and *Hombre* (Martin Ritt, 1967) are cousins in another form, where the savagery of Indians or outlaws is the threatening disaster.

The most common travel disaster involves flying. So we have Walter Booth's *Battle in the Clouds* (1909), *No Highway in the Sky* (Henry Koster, 1951), *The High and the Mighty* (William Wellman, 1954), *Zeppelin* (Etienne Perier, 1971), *The Hindenburg* (Robert Wise, 1976), and the spawn of *Airport* (George Seaton, 1969), *Airport 75* (Jack Smight, 1975), and indeed any air films that involve massive threat of destruction without the elements of human warfare. Hawks's *Only Angels Have Wings* (1939) has elements of the disaster film, but not *Tora! Tora! Tora!* (Richard Fleischer, Toshio Masuda, and Kinji Fukasaku, 1970), which belongs in the neighboring genre of war films. The flying disasters are based on the audience's familiar sense of insecurity in flight and upon the tradition of punishment for the hubris of presuming to fly. It's even hubristic to float, as in *Titanic* (Negulesco, 1953) and *A Night to Remember* (Roy Baker, 1958). The same anxiety is addressed by the horrors of underground disaster in Gary Sherman's powerful *Death Line* (1972; in America, *Raw Meat*) and, with the modification by human malevolence, in *The Incident* (Larry Peerce, 1967) and *The Taking of Pelham One Two Three* (Joseph Sargent, 1974). Godard works round to a disaster vision in his traffic jam in *Weekend* (1967), but the fullest extension of the auto mythology into disaster is Peter Weir's *The Cars That Ate Paris* (1974).

The City Fails

Here people are most dramatically punished for placing their faith in their own works and losing sight of their maker. So their edifices must crumble about them. This type dates back to Ernest Schoedsack's *The Last Days of Pompeii* (1935), E. A. Martin's *War o' Dreams* (1915), Mary Pickford's *Waking Up the Town* (1925), Luitz Morat's *La Cité foudroyée* (1924), Lang's *Metropolis* (1926), G. W. Pabst's *Atlantis* (1932), *Earthquake,* John Guillermin's *The Towering Inferno* (1974), and so on. In *The Neptune Factor* (Daniel Petrie, 1973) an underwater lab and living experiment is threatened by giant fish and eels bred by undersea volcanoes, so both the monster and failed-city forms converge.

In this type the advances of civilization are found to be fragile and dangerous. In *The Incredible Shrinking Man* the world of commonplace ob-

50. *The Incredible Shrinking Man:* The world of commonplace objects over-whelms the hero (Grant Williams).

jects overwhelms the hero, until he resolves in mystic humility to enjoy his disappearance, his fade into the rich nothingness of God. As we learned from the coffee tin he passed, "Use less for best results." In *Invasion USA* (Alfred E. Green, 1952) and *Red Planet Mars* (Harry Horner, 1952) we enjoy visions of the cataclysmic destruction of America and Russia respectively.

The Monster

Natural and aberrant monsters were listed under the natural-attack category above. But the beast may come from the vast beyond, as in *X from Outer Space* (Kazui Nihonmatsu, 1967). Space monsters are terrifying even when they are not malevolent, as in *20 Million Miles to Earth* (1957) and *The Day the Earth Stood Still* (Robert Wise, 1951). The monster can be a vegetable (*The Day of the Triffids,* Steve Sekely, 1963; *The Thing,* Christian Nyby, 1951). It can be constructed by human beings (*Der*

Golem, Paul Wegener, 1920; *Frankenstein,* James Whale, 1931). Or it can be bacterial, as in *Shivers* (David Cronenberg, 1975). It can even be a computer, as in *Westworld* (Michael Crichton, 1974), *2001* (Stanley Kubrick, 1968), *Colossus: The Forbin Project* (Sargent, 1969). The beast can be a shapeless evil, like that in *The Quatermass Experiment* (Val Guest, 1955), *The H-Man* (Honda, 1958), *X the Unknown* (Leslie Norman, 1956), *The Blob* (Irving A. Yeaworth, 1958), and *The Green Slime* (Kinji Fukasaku, 1969). Even the destruction scenes in *The Exorcist* (William Friedkin, 1974) satisfied the appetite for disaster.

Often the monster threatens dehumanization, not death: *Shivers, Night of the Blood Beast* (Bernard Kowalski, 1958), *Attack of the Crab Monsters* (Roger Corman, 1957), *Not of This Earth* (Corman, 1957), *It Conquered the World* (Corman, 1956), *Invasion of the Body Snatchers* (Don Siegel, 1956). Often the monster is a zombie: *Night of the Living Dead* (George Romero, 1968), *Plan 9 from Outer Space* (Edward D. Wood, Jr., 1956), *The Undead* (Corman, 1956), *Plague of the Zombies* (John Gilling, 1966), and Ray Dennis Stecker's *The Incredibly Strange Creatures Who Stopped Living and Became Zombies* (1962). Humans are occupied by alien, dehumanizing forces in *Invasion of the Body Snatchers* and *The Earth Dies Screaming* (Terence Fisher, 1964). Then we have the host of vampire films. These all work as black parodies of the mystique of Christian inspiration/possession. The form shades off into the gothic horror tale in the one direction—*Nosferatu* (F. M. Murnau, 1922) and *Dracula* (Tod Browning, 1931)—and into the science fiction genre in the other—*Zombies of the Stratosphere* (Fred Brannon, 1953)—according to its iconography (settings, costumes, etc.). Large-scale destruction characterizes the films of the disaster type.

The monster is often a projection of or a metaphor for the character's psychological state. In *Forbidden Planet* (1956), Fred Wilcox's clever variation on *The Tempest,* the beast is explicitly an externalization of the human id. (The planet Altair was once the empire of the Krel, whose "mindless beast" impulses destroyed their highly technical civilization.) In *Willard* the rats express Martin's corruption but Willard's mousiness.

Survival

A respectable variety of disaster films detail the problems of survival after a disastrous journey—*Lifeboat* (Hitchcock, 1943), *Marooned* (John Sturges, 1970), *The Naked Prey* (Cornell Wilde, 1966), *Flight of the Phoenix* (Robert Aldrich, 1966), *Sands of the Kalahari* (Cy Endfield, 1965), *The Savage Is Loose* (George C. Scott, 1974)—or after the brawl is over—*Soylent Green* (Richard Fleischer, 1973), *The War Game* (Peter Watkins, 1967), *Planet of the Apes* (Franklin Schaffner, 1968), *The*

World, the Flesh and the Devil (Ranald MacDougall, 1959), *On the Beach* (Stanley Kramer, 1959), *Panic in the Year Zero* (Ray Milland, 1962), *The Omega Man* (Boris Segal, 1971), *Zero Population Growth* (Michael Campus, 1971), *Teenage Caveman* (Corman, 1958).

War

The war film becomes a disaster film when the imagery of carnage and destruction predominates over the elements of human conflict. Thus *The War Game, Fires Were Started* (Humphrey Jennings, 1943), and the destruction scenes of *Gone with the Wind* (Victor Fleming, 1939) and *Slaughterhouse Five* (George Roy Hill, 1972) could qualify. In the fifties the atomic threat provided a host of visions of the day of judgment: *The Day the Earth Stood Still, The Day the Earth Caught Fire* (Val Guest, 1962), *The Day the Sky Exploded* (Paolo Heusch, 1958), and *The Day the World Ended* (Corman, 1956).

The Historical

A separate classification should be made of disasters set in remote times, either past (*San Francisco,* W. S. Van Dyke II, 1936; *The Last Days of Pompeii; Cabiria,* Giovanni Pastrone, 1914) or future (*Planet of the Apes; When Worlds Collide,* Rudolph Maté, 1951; *War of the Worlds,* Haskin, 1953; *Things to Come,* William Cameron Menzies, 1936). The disaster film characteristically depends upon the audience's sense of contemporaneity, but these films belong by the power and centrality of their doom imagery.

The Comic

There are three types of comic disaster film. In the first type, the disaster can provide a happy ending, as in DeMille's spectaculars *Samson and Delilah* (1949) and *The Ten Commandments* (1923, 1956), assuming that one's critical perspective is not that of the Philistines or the Egyptians. Here there is a discrepancy between the destruction in the image and its constructive spirit. More recent affirmations through disaster include the balletic explosion of the house and contents at the end of Antonioni's *Zabriskie Point* (1970) and at the ending of John Boorman's *Leo the Last* (1970).

In the second type, the destruction can be extended into exuberant absurdity, as in the snowballing destruction in certain films by Laurel and Hardy, in the Mack Sennett smashups, and Stanley Kramer's *It's a Mad, Mad, Mad, Mad World* (1963). In Olsen-Johnson and in the Crosby-

51. *The Big Bus:* Full-scale parody of the trip disaster film.

Hope road films, delight is taken in the violation of the logic and integrity of the image itself. This is a comic kind of violence. Then, too, there is the comedy among the ruins that one finds in two brilliant films, Richard Lester's *The Bed-Sitting Room* (1968) and L. Q. Jones's *A Boy and His Dog* (1976). In the comic disaster film, the audience's delight in seeing familiar treasures smashed—an element in all disaster films—is freest.

The third type of disaster comedy is parody. Among the various film parodies in Woody Allen's *Everything You Always Wanted to Know about Sex* (1972), for example, is the invasion of an isolated countryside by a giant breast. "I can handle boobs," the hero confidently avers, but as usual, the monster is an externalization of the hero's own phobia/obsession/ boobishness.

A genre comes of age when its conventions are well enough known to be played for laughs in a parody. *The Big Bus* (James Frawley, 1976) is a full-scale parody of the trip disaster film. A twelve-million-dollar nuclear-powered bus is attempting to make the first nonstop journey from New York to Denver. No one, of course, asks "Why bother?" Much of the comedy involves mock heroic twists. So the hero's brawl has him wielding a broken milk carton, supported by a man with a broken candle. This sends up every bar fight ever fought on screen. In Joseph Bologna's ostracized driver the film parodies the ostracism of Richard Barthelmess in *Only Angels Have Wings*. But generally the parody is of such contemporary films as *The Hindenburg* and *Airport 75*. As Dana Andrews crashes a small plane into the jet in *Airport 75*, here a farmer rams his half-ton into the bus. The bus itself is a ludicrous demonstration of technology extended into absurdity: its self-washing mechanism and exploding tire-changer, its system of jettisoning the soda pop, its luxurious fittings in washroom, bowling alley, dining room, and pool, and the alternately fastidious and sloppy handling of radioactive matter. The details of the parody in *The Big Bus* brings us to the conventions of the genre as it is played seriously.

THE CONVENTIONS

There are numerous conventions that operate in the disaster film.

1. Except in the historical/fantasy type, there is no distancing in time, place, or costume, so the threatened society is ourselves. The disaster film aims for the impact of immediacy. So in the American film of *The War of the Worlds* the setting was changed from H. G. Wells' London to contemporary Los Angeles. When the American *No Blade of Grass* (Cornell Wilde, 1970) was set in England, it was to emphasize the tradition of culture and sophistication ("Keep up your Latin, David; it will stand you in good stead"!!) that is destroyed by the famine and anarchy.

The device of Sensurround purported to provide the physical sensation of *Earthquake*. Significantly, the first tremor felt is when a character is shown at a movie—that is, when there is a precise continuity between the threatened character's situation and the viewer's. Similarly, one of the liveliest frights in *Night of the Living Dead* is when the zombies attack the girl cowering in her automobile. The movie was made for drive-in showings, where the subjective shots here would have had heightened impact. In the horror genre, Peter Bogdanovich's *Targets* (1968) works a similar effect.

2. Given this immediacy, it is difficult to define an iconography for the disaster film as one can do for the western, the gangster film, even the musical and gothic horror. The basic imagery of the disaster film would be disaster, a general, spectacular destruction, but usually this imagery occurs only at the end, though often with brief and promising samples along the way. More than by its imagery, then, the genre is characterized by its mood of threat and dread. Thus films as different as the B space monster films and Bunuel's *The Exterminating Angel* (1962) and Bergman's *The Seventh Seal* (1957) can properly be considered disaster films.

3. The entire cross section of society is usually represented in the cast.

The effect is the sense of the entire society under threat, even the world, instead of a situation of individual danger and fate. The ads for *The Big Bus* typically presented a line of head-and-shoulder pictures of its many main characters, each labeled.

Often the stars depend upon their familiarity from previous films, rather than developing a new characterization. Plot more than character is emphasized, suspense more than character development. In *The Towering Inferno* an inherited sentiment plays around Jennifer Jones and Fred Astaire, Robert Vaughn repeats his corrupt politician from *Bullitt* (Peter Yates, 1968), and Richard Chamberlain reprises his corrupt all-American from *Petulia* (Lester, 1968), itself an ironic inversion of his Kildare. In *The Big Bus* Ruth Gordon provides both a parody of the Helen Hayes figure in *Airport* and an extension of her own salty-old lady act from *Where's Poppa?* (Carl Reiner, 1970) and *Harold and Maude* (Hal Ashby, 1972).

Similarly, in *Earthquake* the romantic legend of Ava Gardner keys us to expect that husband Charlton Heston will gravitate toward her in the crunch, particularly when his mistress is lightly accented as an alien (French Canadian Genevieve Bujold). When Marjoe Gortner's amiable grocer turns out to be a sadistic fascist, we're prepared by our knowledge of the actor's career as a duplicitous evangelist. In *Airport 75* Gloria Swanson is Gloria Swanson and Linda Blair is a poor little sick girl about to have her kidney exorcised.

4. The disaster film often dramatizes class conflict. Thus we have the racial concerns in Arch Oboler's *Five* (1951), *The World, the Flesh and the Devil,* and the tensions between John Hodiak and Tallulah in *Lifeboat.* In *The Big Bus* posh designer Lynn Redgrave allows her secret new styles to be worn as some vague part of the company's rescue scheme. A hustling businessman is common in the form, like Henry Hull's Rittenhouse in *Lifeboat* or Theodore Bikel in *Sands of the Kalahari.* Gig Young acts suspicious in *The Hindenburg* but only out of his concern for a cunning business deal. The material concerns—and our differences—of daily life are supposed to pale in the shadow of death cast off in disaster films. In *Earthquake,* the villains are the officials of the Seismology Institute who ignore the graduate student's warnings because they fear loss both of face and of a possible foundation grant.

5. Particularly in American films, gambling is a recurrent device. There is a card game in *Lifeboat,* two sharks on *The Hindenburg,* and overall much drawing of straws, flipping of coins, and poetic justice, suggesting the inscrutability of fate and the pettiness of people's attempts to alter their doom. Superstition is a fossil of piety. Life is a gamble.

6. The exception to the cross-section drama is where a family is beset by the disaster. In *The Birds, The Savage Is Loose, Frogs,* and *Food of the Gods* (Bert I. Gordon, 1976), one of the central issues is the family's re-

52. *The Birds:* The family is reluctant to admit an outsider to the intimacy of the family unit.

luctance to admit an outsider to the intimacy of the basic unit. In *Zero Population Growth* the parents at first refuse to share their parenthood with the couple who have found them out. The horrific climax in *Night of the Living Dead* is when the daughter eats the father, who had frantically kept outsiders out of the family basement. In *Lifeboat* the "family" of Americans must deal with the attempt of Germans to join them, including the German American Schmidt/Smith. Many disaster films will develop the image of an inner circle or haven being defended against invasion, with a near-sexual tinge to the entrance (in *The Birds,* the pecking through the wood and the invasion of the attic).

7. The disaster film is predicated upon the idea of isolation. No help can be expected from the outside. Further, the threatened characters are jammed together, without escape, without relief from each other. The disaster is often directed at an island community (*The Birds, Frogs*) or one isolated by its remoteness (*The Thing*) or cut off from others by the disaster (*The Towering Inferno*). Then there are all the survival films set in

remote areas. Sometimes even a connection with someone will heighten the isolation: the separated family talking ship-to-shore in *Juggernaut* (Lester, 1974) or in *The Hindenburg,* when the ostensible villain, Boeth, learns that the Gestapo has killed his girlfriend.

The isolation is an important convention of the genre. Westerns and musicals both assume strong human community. But the disaster film draws its anxiety from its conception of human beings as isolated and helpless against the dangers of their world.

8. The characters' isolation is exacerbated by the various conflicts between them. The basic point of the genre is that people must unite against calamity, that personal or social differences pale beside the assaulting forces in nature.

In *Jaws* there is a hostility between the noble savage, Quint, and the wealthy college man, Hooper, that is only briefly glossed over by their drunken camaraderie—and by their sharing of wounds! The town knows Amity in its name only. Both in *Jaws* and in *Grizzly* (William Girdler, 1976), the hero and his political superior quarrel over the danger of the animal threat. In *The Poseidon Adventure* (Ronald Neame, 1972), the rivalry between the Reverend Scott (Gene Hackman) and the policeman Rogo (Ernest Borgnine) seems like the Renaissance debate between the orders of grace and nature.

Here lies the essential relationship between the disaster film and the war film. In both, a society at odds within itself unites against a common threat. In the war film the threat is human; in the disaster film, natural or supernatural. But both genres provide the mimetic harmonizing of a shattered community. War films and disaster films seem to arrive in an alternating cycle, both performing the same general function but with significant shifts of emphasis. War films are at a peak during periods of war and express nationalist confidence. Disaster films express the triviality of human differences in the face of cosmic danger.

The politics of Vietnam did not find expression in war films, because the climate of opinion about the war was so widely and deeply divided in America; but it did emerge in the cycles of amoral cop and spy thrillers, with their ambiguous myths of militant police action on the local or international scale. The disaster cycle of the 1970s followed the slow ending of the American presence in Vietnam. The subsequent cycle of war films was possibly spurred by the fervor of the Bicentennial, but it continued the successful elements of the disaster film: suspense, spectacle, formulaic characterization, and the drama of a divided society seeking vital reconciliation.

In *The Big Bus* there is a variety of comic reconciliations. At home base Scotty gets his lover/attendant back at the end. The passionate and quarrelling couple, Sybil and Claude, fight, divorce, then are remarried. The driver is reconciled to the woman he abandoned at the altar and to the woman whose father he ate (granted, "Just one foot!").

9. The war and disaster genres share the further sense that savagery continues to underlie a pretense to civilization. Thus disasters usually breed a lawless anarchy, as Gortner personifies in *Earthquake,* or the selfishness of Ralph Meeker in *Food of the Gods,* the savagery of *No Blade of Grass;* or states of rigorous repression, as in *Zardoz* (Boorman, 1973), *1984* (Michael Anderson, 1955), and the underworld of *A Boy and His Dog.* In *Sands of the Kalahari* Theodore Bikel asks the typical question: "Look at us. Victims of civilization. Are we lost now or were we lost all those years before?" Technology leads people to disaster, by plane or ship, by their dominating creations. They build towers higher than their fire hoses can reach (*The Towering Inferno*). Often their works survive them, like the Rolls Royce abandoned on a hilltop in *No Blade of Grass,* while the sound track repeats a car commercial. People's works are dangerous, like their robots, their monsters, their transports of delight, even the earphone transistors which in *The Towering Inferno* deafen the boy to the danger around him. In *The Savage Is Loose* the father systematically rejects the paraphernalia of society: the pocket watch, the alphabet, and the guilt-edged family Bible.

And yet, there is an optimism in the genre. The center holds even when chaos has broken loose. The maniacs and fascists are in a minority in the film vision of anarchy. Gortner's fascist is quickly subdued. Order is reasserted. Even in *The Savage Is Loose,* having tried to kill his father, the lad still comes to his mother gently, like a lover, not a rapist. War is hell, but the disaster world is only an earth of brief disturbance. Pessimistic visions without relief, without hope, are rare: Watkins's *The War Game,* for example, and *No Blade of Grass.* Few films raise a disaster that cannot be survived or that does not bring out the best in the characters and our society.

10. Among the recurring character types is the specialist—the various Edmund Gwenn or Cecil Kellaway scientists or professors, or the amateur ornithologist in *The Birds,* whose knowledge provides the basic factual framework for the drama. Significantly, these specialists are almost never able to control the forces loose against them. Specialists are there to measure the force of the mystery by their impotence. For the form serves the principle of the unknowable, the superhuman, the mystery that dwarfs science.

Usually there is also someone of ominous complacency. Sometimes he is the scientist, as Carrington in *The Thing.* Or he may be a businessman/politician, like the mayor in the sharkskin grey suit in *Jaws.* "We *are* the ugly rich," Ray Milland smugly admits in *Frogs.* This confidence represents the extreme form of the security which the audience brings into the theatre for playful threatening—and perhaps the deeper need to be punished for possessing it.

11. There is rarely a religious figure in the disaster film, because faith would temper the dread, a sense of God's abiding support would nullify the suspense. In *The Big Bus* René Auberjonois plays a doubting priest who wants to date, who gloats over God's giving him the window seat, and who finally, his faith recovered, leads them all in a singsong, but a secular one. But he is not proof of a common type. He seems a specific parody of Hackman's priest in *The Poseidon Adventure,* whose religion is based on secular confidence and self-help. He learns a nonreligious kind of humility and sacrifice through the events of the film. The singing nun in *Airport 75* is safely Helen Reddy. Her song—something about your being your own best friend because no one looks after you better than you do—is strikingly oblivious of Jesus. Moreover, the film turns on the salvation from a lover from earth. God is no copilot in the current disaster film and probably never was. For only in wars, not in the upheavals of peacetime, can one claim that God is on one's side.

Instead of church figures, the form presents evangelical crackpots, like the drunken seer in *The Birds.* This coheres with the literary tradition of disaster visions, deriving out of the irregular, outcast prophets of the Old Testament, proclaiming doom and destruction for the godless pride and corruption of the human race.

12. All systems fail in the disaster. Politicians are corrupt, save the Sam Ervin type of mayor of *The Towering Inferno.* The church is usually absent, as irrelevant. The police are either absent or skeptical about anything beyond the familiar. James Whitmore in *Them!* is virtually unique as a policeman hero of a disaster film. George Kennedy is a heroic cop in *Earthquake,* but he is disillusioned with and suspended from the force.

In *War of the Worlds* the Martians attack the three basic authorities of 1950s America: church, army, and science. The courageous pastor is immediately converted into steaming ash. The army and science fail in turn to assert their powers stronger than faith. The Martians are finally vanquished by earthly bacteria ("For best results use less"!). Nature alone holds sway in the disaster world.

13. The hero is usually a layman with practical sense but without specialized knowledge. In *The Birds* Mitch the lawyer can board up a house. A black handyman is the hero of *Night of the Living Dead.* The modest sheriff saves the day in *Jaws,* when both the savvy of the savage and the knowledge of the scholar have failed. The specialist in *Grizzly,* Richard Jaeckel, dies twice, because he presumed to live in the hide of his prey. In *The Towering Inferno* Paul Newman is a specialist, an architect, but his knowledge is leavened by his rusticity. Heston plays an industrialized ex-athlete in *Earthquake,* and his achievement in *Airport 75* is acrobatic

as much as aviational. Cornell Wilde's persona in his socially conscious period reverses his old image of easy, swashbuckling triumph.

14. Almost invariably there is a romantic subplot. Romance is a vital aspect of the tension between social instinct and selfishness. So the romance is not just a matter of box-office concession (few things that traditionally work could be!). The romantic byplay dramatizes the virtue of emotionally responsive humanity.

The romance is risible in *Food of the Gods,* where the scientist is sexually aroused by Marjoe Gortner from the strain of fighting giant rats. The theme is worked out most explicitly in *The Thing,* where the hero's emotional capacity opposes him to the foolish Carrington, to whom the monster is the perfect creature: no heart, no emotions, no pleasure or pain. For the hero, the icy landscape is a garden spot, for his romantic response to the lady expresses his feeling and joy of life. The icy landscape is a projection of Carrington's soul. To Carrington, "Knowledge is greater than life," but to the hero the pleasures and vulnerabilities of the heart are more important than science. Thus the hero preserves the animal quality of the human being against the vegetable values of The Thing and Dr. Carrington. Similarly, in *The Neptune Factor* Yvette Mimieux's love for the lost Ed McGibbon causes her to cut the Neptune loose, risking everyone and everything, to recover her lost lover—and the lost laboratory. Her love opposes the unsentimental logistics of Captain Ben Gazzara.

The romance is a variation upon the primary antithesis between a selfish, fragmented society and a community impelled by other-concern. Libertinism is to be punished by disaster (Pompeii, Sodom, the opening murder in *Jaws*). In *Earthquake* Heston must die for his infidelity—and as a reward for his courage and final faithfulness, his death saves him from the long pain of a loveless marriage. The ability to love is the primary virtue of the disaster hero, promiscuity and coldness the main though opposite faults. In *The Poseidon Adventure,* Rogo's wife, Stella Stevens, is an ex-prostitute. Her early demise is ordained by the same tradition that has the saloon gal intercept the bullet intended for the white-hatted hero and that claims Heston's life in *Earthquake.*

In *The Andromeda Strain* (Robert Wise, 1970) James Olson wears a prophylactic rubber sheath to approach the infected survivors, but to save everyone he must break through his sterile invulnerability. In *The Omega Man* Heston valiantly fights off plague-riddled inferiors until he falls in love with the negress. His new susceptibility costs him his life, but he dies with a fertile and romantic gesture, passing on the serum from his blood to another.

The romantic strain is so familiar that variations can be played by implication. In *The Hindenburg* the Scott and Atherton characters, a questioning Nazi and a German resistance youth, are kindred spirits for having girlfriends. The nobility of ex-lovers Scott and Bancroft harkens back to the warmth of an earlier Germany. In *The Forbin Project* we have a romantic attachment between two computers who plot to be reunited when their political masters, the United States and Russia, break their connection. The romantic element is introduced when Colossus watches voyeuristically over Forbin's affair and pours his martinis. In *The Savage Is Loose* the romantic dilemma moves to the center of the film; the incestuous solution is but an extension of the romantic values of the genre. In *No Blade of Grass* the middle-class daughter must reject the gentleman ordinarily esteemed in her class, in favor of the coarser, rougher man, who can afford her better protection. That slight inflection of the romantic convention speaks volumes in the film.

15. Often the disasters have a contemporary significance. In *The Big Bus* there is topical comedy in Stockard Channing's blowsy parody of Liz Taylor and in the doctor's fear of a malpractice suit. Something of post-Nixon America is expressed in *Airport 75*, in the image of an airplane heading toward the mountains with a hole where its pilots used to be. Whether Gerald Ford is played by Karen Black or Charlton Heston is a matter of party politics, but Larry Storch as the press must be an Agnew invention. *The Towering Inferno* is a modern Babel, people building to the heavens without talking to those who might help them. *Earthquake* is an image of a society with its footing shaken out from under it, both personal and professional responsibilities rent asunder. Its climax of the bursting Hollywood Dam is an image of what happens when personal codes are abandoned.

In *Demons of the Swamp* (Bernard L. Kowalski, 1959; also called *The Giant Leeches*) the monster is a reasonable squid. The leeching is done by various interloping humans, a congenital poacher, and parasitic exploiters of the merchant's wife and shame. The hero is a game warden committed to preserving animal rights and property.

In *Frogs* the Crockett family is attacked by reptiles and amphibians, as if to punish them for having tampered with the balance of nature. Young Crockett starts the film by upsetting the canoe of the ecologist hero. The Crocketts may recall pioneers to us, but the animals avenge themselves against them as smug intruders. The frogs can be taken as the process of nature; thus one Crockett lady reports her aging in terms of frog-like bags under her eyes. The indictment becomes a national one when father Crockett celebrates his birthday on the Fourth of July. The film abounds in striking images: a snake in the crystal chandelier; a frog on the Old Glory birthday cake; Clint's wife devoured by a turtle ("Slow and steady . . ."); a lizard casually upsetting a canister of insecticide to asphyxiate the grandson; Crockett at the end among his now-menacing hunting trophies, covered by frogs. In one sly irony, the daughter who earlier complained that her profits were reduced by the cost of antipollution devices is lured by a butterfly into the swamp, then bled by leeches. The large close-ups of the frogs suggest they sit in judgment of human beings for their arrogant abuse of nature, with a force hitherto restrained. The film articulates the concern of the 1970s with the abuse of the environment. So does *Food of the Gods,* where nature itself provides a dangerous food that will turn small creatures into monsters, once catalyzed by human greed.

Walon Green's *The Hellstrom Chronicle* (1971) avoids the fictional form in favor of a documentary pretense, but it has the effect of a disaster film, dramatizing the smallness and vulnerability of human beings in the context of the smaller creatures of nature. Its science and pseudoscience give the film the air of newspaper factuality, as the atomic dramas seemed to have amid the red and bomb scares of the 1950s. The anxiety fostered by "Dr. Hellstrom" recalls the dislocation Gulliver suffers in going from Lilliput to Brobdignag. The film achieves that kind of reorientation of the viewer's senses.

Both *The Hellstrom Chronicle* and *Fantastic Voyage* (Richard Fleischer, 1966) were produced in the early years of the LSD phenomenon, when society was excited with prospects of revolutionary perception. So Hellstrom makes a gigantic, compelling world out of the insect close-ups. And *Fantastic Voyage* sets an adventure story in "inner space," the body providing the kind of eerie spectacle previously found in interplanetary travel. The final danger in that adventure is the explosion of the heroes into full size while still within the host body. Premature explosion is a danger that is not remote in any dream that exploits the presence of Raquel Welch.

16. Poetic justice in disaster films derives from the assumption that there is some relationship between a person's due and his or her doom. Hitchcock's *The Birds* is distinctive in not providing a cause for the birds' attack, but typical in presenting the characters as selfish, complacent figures who generally deserve to be shaken up. So do we all, or we wouldn't go to disaster films.

Specific flaws need not cause the disaster, but some inference of guilt by association may be drawn. In *San Francisco* the earthquake is not just due to the San Andreas Fault, but seems at least partly a response to the moral atmosphere in which Clark Gable could knock down priest Spencer Tracy for banning a scantily clad performance by Jeanette Macdonald.

In one respect poetic justice breaks down in disaster films. Often the good die with the evil. In *The Poseidon Adventure* prostitute, priest, and generous swimmer die alike. No logic dictates who will live and who will die in the crash of the *Hindenburg.* The mortality rate among stars and

53. *Shivers* works against the romantic conventions of the genre and the liberated sensuality of its day.

heroes is higher in the disaster film than in any of the other didactic popular genres.

THE APPLICATION

The main purpose in defining a genre is to establish a context for the approach to an individual work. David Cronenberg's *Shivers* might serve as an example of a film illuminated by the sense of the disaster genre.

Shivers opens with a media-sell voice-over, oozing with the complacency that in disaster films is doomed for downfall. It is an assured voice of brittle normalcy, selling the joys of the Starliner apartment building on an island in Montreal. The company prides itself on the apartment's self-containment. The setting is thus developed into an image of the enislement of the sensually obsessed. The facilities cater to nothing but the appetites and the image of the beautiful life. Yet the inhabitants are lonely, insular people, condemned to sad privacy until the disaster frees them for unbridled lust, a horrible parody of community and love.

The disaster is an attack of red, phallic little critters that have been bred by the mad Dr. Emil Hobbes, combining the effects of VD and aphrodisiac. To save people from having tragically lost contact with their physical nature, Hobbes would convert the world into a gigantic orgy.

The Starliner presents life as a trip, a new, exciting ultramodern exploration. The film is about the "sex trip," about the use of free sex as an escape from the ostensible stasis of the responsible and restrained life. The film works against the romantic conventions of the genre and against the liberated sensuality of its day, by making the sexual connection between people the horror, not the cure. The parasite is spread by figures representative of the current sexual liberation: a precocious nymphet, an adulterer, the old swinger with his megavitamin virility, the Swedish couple, the bachelor swingers, hetero and gay.

Cronenberg's Emil Hobbes has a connection to the real world, the philosopher Thomas Hobbes who in *Leviathan* argued the primacy of the physical nature of man and his universe. As Hobbes provided the rationale for Restoration libertinism, Cronenberg reverts to his name for his reversal, a horrific vision of our exalted libertinism. Our sensual togetherness Cronenberg makes more horrifying than the initial loneliness of his characters. The parasites appear as a cross between your standard red phallus and miniature whales, to confirm the Hobbes connection.

As so often in the genre, the monsters are only partly threats from the external world and partly projections of the characters' mental or emotional states. In this case the parasites are images of the characters' sexual compulsions. So when they attack Barbara Steele they come up from within the drainage system, through the plugged drain pipe of her tub, sexually to enter her. She had been moping around in a premasturbatory lethargy, lying open in her tub, loosening up with a large brandy, as if in unconscious hope for sexual engagement.

The hero is a young doctor (Paul Hampton) who restrains his sexual responses. He chats coolly on the phone while his nurse strips for him. The audience, both out of vicarious appetite and by its acquaintance with the conventional romance of the genre, expects and wants him to curtail his call and make love to the nurse. But Cronenberg's hero puts science and duty ahead of casual lust. That is the central moral thrust of the film.

Cronenberg makes the lusting creatures his zombies, against the tradition of the genre. His orgiasts' hyperactivity belies their void in will, soul, and sense. Cronenberg dramatizes the depersonalization of "liberated" sexuality. It is unsettling to find that the zombies are the characters fulfilling our fondest fantasies—sex unlimited by law or capacity.

The film closes with a completion of the media-sell frame. A disc jockey assures his audience that nothing dangerous has happened. While the beautiful people drive out in their performance cars to infest the world with debilitating appetite, all in the name of love and freedom, the disaster itself is hushed up by the loud confidence of the announcer.

Shivers is a powerful, unnerving film. Even its supporters are repelled by it. Much of its anxiety derives from the effective way that Cronenberg has inflected—and in some cases radically reversed—the conventions of the disaster film, the cultivated but unwritten expectations of his audience. That is one of the things that a genre is supposed to do.

Note

1. Susan Sontag, "The Imagination of Disaster," in *Against Interpretation* (New York: Delta, 1966), pp. 209–225.

21. "Surge and Splendor": A Phenomenology of the Hollywood Historical Epic

VIVIAN SOBCHACK

"And what do you *call an epic?"*
"You know, a picture that's real long and has lots of things going on."
                                                    —Dixon in In a Lonely Place

The Hollywood historical epic has been despised, if not completely ig-nored, by most "serious" scholars of American cinema and historiogra-phy.[1] Its aesthetic extravagances seen as essentially in bad taste and its historical depictions as essentially anachronistic, the genre is generally re-garded as a suspect form of both *cinematic* and *historical* representation. Indeed, for those who have been culturally trained to value asceticism, caution, and logic, there is something uncomfortably embarrassing about the historical epic's visual and aural excessiveness, about the commercial hype that surrounds its production, about its self-promotional aesthetic aura, its fuzzy and emotional content, and its spectatorial invitation to in-dulge in wantonly expansive, hyperbolic, even hysterical acts of cinema.

As a film genre, the historical epic emerged with the medium itself. First realizing its "spectacular" possibilities in Italian silent cinema, it was subsequently elaborated upon by Americans D. W. Griffith and Cecil B. DeMille, reached its apogee in Hollywood productions in the 1950s and early 1960s, and then—for complex reasons both economic and cul-tural—entered its present period of decline.[2] For those viewers who re-member the Hollywood historical epic of the 1950s and 1960s, or for those who have more recently seen the restored and rereleased *Gone with the Wind* (Victor Fleming, 1939) or *Lawrence of Arabia* (David Lean, 1962) in a theater, the genre calls up grandiose visions—those of the mod-ern period literally inflated by Cinerama, Cinemascope, and 70mm.[3] It evokes "casts of thousands" and the assertively anachronistic punctuation of its historical representation by major Hollywood stars. Playing "great" historical figures from Antony and Cleopatra to John Reed and Louise Bryant as passionate livers, lovers, and major historical agents who de-stroy and build empires (whether Roman or Red), stars both dramatize and construct Hollywood's particular idea of History—lending the past a present stature, attributing its production to select individuals (most of them Charlton Heston) and (T. E. Lawrence aside) providing the literal "embodiment of Hollywood's faith that historical events rise to the occasion of exceptional human romance."[4]

The Hollywood historical epic also makes one think of portentous calligraphy introducing us to History writ in gilt and with a capital *H*, of prologues usually beginning, as George MacDonald Fraser in *The Hollywood History of the World* remembers, with the words "In the Year of Our Lord," followed by "a concise summary of the War of the Spanish Succession, or the condition of the English peasantry in the twelfth century, or the progress of Christianity under Nero."[5] And, if the prologue was not written, its function of authorizing History was accomplished by a less literal but more sonorous—and patriarchal—"Voice of God" narration. Maps often accompanied these historicizing voices—punctuating the text; simultaneously promising the viewer epic scope, empire building, and adventure; and signaling the pastness of the past and its safe history-book distance from the present. As Fraser puts it, "In the heyday of the historicals there were few things more exciting, yet at the same time, more tranquilising in their effect on the front stalls on a Saturday afternoon than a good map, Olde Worlde for choice."[6]

The Hollywood epic also defines History as occurring to music—pervasive symphonic music underscoring every moment by overscoring it. And it evokes spectacular, fantastic costumes—particularly gold lamé ones with underwire bras. Indeed, the Hollywood epic shows us that the people—most particularly, the women—living History almost always wore extravagant clothes and spent a good deal of History changing them. Although no one in the audience is inclined to such accountancy, we are nonetheless told that Linda Darnell in *Forever Amber* (Otto Preminger, 1947) wears "eighteen evening gowns, twenty daytime dresses, three negligées, and a wedding gown as part of the effort to recreate the seventeenth century England of King Charles II." Or that *The Prodigal* (Richard Thorpe, 1955), starring Lana Turner, "had more than 4,000 costumes," with "292 costume changes for the principals alone"—one of the latter, according to MGM sources, involving apparel made for Turner "entirely of seed pearls, thousands of which were handsewn."[7]

This sartorial extravagance is fully matched by an extravagance of action and place. There are all those chariot races, all those stampedes and crowd scenes, all those charges and campaigns on land and battles at sea, all those horses and slaves and Christians and wagon trains. There is also the vastness of deserts, plains, and oceans, and the monumentality of Rome, the Pyramids, Khartoum, and Babylon. Monumental productions regularly produced historical monuments—massive Albert Speerish sets mythifying the mundane and quotidian into "imperialist" and "orientalist" fantasies of History.

54. *The Ten Commandments:* Geographical vastness in the epic.

At first, the purpose of all this hyperformalism seems significant only as a perverse and inflated display of autoerotic spectacle—that is, as cinema tumescent: institutionally full of itself, swollen with its own generative power to mobilize the vast amounts of labor and money necessary to diddle its technology to an extended and expanded orgasm of images, sounds, and profits. Thus, however seriously the historical epic presents itself to us or however pleasurably caught up we actually are as we watch it, upon reflection we find its excesses and our pleasure embarrassing— and tend to make disclaimers about our indulgence in such cinematic experience. In sum, the Hollywood historical epic seems hardly subtle or substantial enough to invite much in the way of semiological and cultural analyses from those scholars interested in exploring the nature and function of various forms of historical representation. Indeed, viewing all this extravagance and excess, one wonders how it is possible to take the genre seriously and what in the world it has to do with what we think of as "real" historical interpretation.

Nonetheless, in that it engages human beings of a certain culture at a certain time with the temporally reflexive and transcendent notion that is History, the Hollywood historical epic is as "real" and significant as any

55. *Cleopatra:* Massive Albert Speerish sets and extravagance characterize the epic mise-en-scène.

other mode of historical interpretation that human beings symbolically constitute to make sense of a human—and social—existence that temporally extends beyond the life and times of any single person. Indeed, I would suggest that the Hollywood historical epic is as central to our understanding of what we mean by the "historical" and "History" as any work of academic scholarship. Obviously, its modality is different from the latter. In contrast to the reflective, highly specialized, "disciplined" mode of representation that stands in our culture and time as the site for theoretically comprehending the opaqueness of past others, the Hollywood historical epic is prereflective, popular, and "undisciplined." As well, despite its superficial exoticism, it presumes the transparency of past others, pretheoretically apprehending their human sameness in time rather than their difference. However, in that both the work of academic scholarship and the Hollywood historical epic construct interpretive narratives formulated around and foregrounding past human events as coherent and significant, both are temporally reflexive and both respond —if in different ways and through different experiences—to the same central and philosophical question: *how to comprehend ourselves in time.*

Whereas the reticent and opaque work of academic histories is the objectification and projection of *ourselves-now* as *others-then*, the expansive and transparent work of Hollywood's epic histories seems to be the subjectification and projection of *ourselves-now* as *we-then*. However, both kinds of historicizing are cultural productions of a certain mode of temporal consciousness, and both produce their history effects for model readers and spectators through formal and narratological devices that are conventional. In sum, although academic history enjoys an institutional legitimation that the Hollywood epic doesn't, neither mode of historicizing, of creating History, is "truer" than the other. As Sande Cohen puts it in his major attack on academic historiography in *Historical Culture*: "There is no *primary* object or complex that warrants calling forth the signifier 'history.'"[8]

Thus, I want to begin this phenomenological exploration of the Hollywood historical epic not by establishing or debating definitions of the "epic" and the "historical," nor by testing the genre's "truth claims." Rather, my project here is to describe, thematize, and interpret an *experiential field* in which human beings pretheoretically construct and play out a particular—and culturally encoded—form of *temporal existence*. Since my aim is to "isolate the history effects" of the Hollywood historical epic, but to do so "as they pertain to an *audience*" and "the manufacturing of public life,"[9] my object of study is not so much the films "in themselves" as it is the rhetorical and semiological praxis surrounding the public experience of them—expressed in the prereflective or "ordinary" language used in our particular culture to delimit and describe what is commonly perceived as an "extraordinary" mode of filmic representation.[10] Phenomenological analysis of this ordinary language of experience, listening to the sense it makes to embodied subjects, may help us better understand the appeal of the Hollywood historical epic to audiences who live in specific times and particular cultures. In sum, rather than a totalizing description, the descriptions of the experiential field of the historical epic I offer here are highly qualified—meant to unpack the sense and sense making of a particular form of representation and its discourse which is *in* "history" as well as *about* it.[11]

> *It makes you realize what God could have done if He'd had the money.*
> —*Attributed to James Thurber in Fraser,* Hollywood History

The advertising rhetoric that sells the Hollywood historical epic to its American, middle-class, Caucasian, consumer audience provides us with the most blatant and compressed invocation to the genre's prereflective significance. Consider the following litany: "They Slashed and Stormed and Sinned Their Way Across Adventure's Most Violent Age!" (*The Vik-*

ings, Richard Fleischer, 1958); "An Epic Film That Sweeps Across the Horizon of Ancient Times" (*Sodom and Gomorrah,* Robert Aldrich, 1962); "The Mightiest Story of Tyranny and Temptation Ever Written—Ever Lived—Ever Produced!" (*The Silver Chalice,* Victor Saville, 1954); "The Glory That Was Egypt! The Grandeur That Was Rome!" (*Cleopatra,* DeMille, 1934); or simply, "The Power The Passion The Greatness The Glory" (*King of Kings,* DeMille, 1927).[12] This kind of exclamation, generalization, and hyperbole is not necessarily dated. Indeed, a recent ad announcing the availability of *The Last Emperor* (Bernardo Bertolucci, 1987) on videocassette reads: "Emperor. Playboy. Prisoner. Man. An Adventure Like This Comes Along Only Once in 10,000 Years." In more detail and smaller print, it gathers together nearly all the elements that somehow have come to be associated with epic and historical screen narrative: "This is the extraordinary true life story of Pu Yi. An epic adventure full of warlords and concubines, conspiracy, seduction and intrigue. In 1908 he toddled to the Imperial Dragon Throne to become China's last emperor. And the rest, as they say, is history."[13]

This is an interesting tag line, particularly for what it tells us about the relation between, on the one hand, the extraordinary plenitude of adventure, action, and detail that characterizes the "spectacular" nature of the epic film and, on the other hand, the "rest"—the something "they say" is "history."[14] This latter seems to emerge from the accumulation and sedimentation (or coming to rest) of adventure, action, and detail, and is characterized as *excess*—a cultural remainder ("the rest") left over as the effect of the already amplified spectacle we see on the screen. Indeed, there is the suggestion here that History emerges in popular consciousness not so much from any *particular accuracy* or even *specificity* of detail and event as it does from a *transcendence of accuracy and specificity* enabled by a *general* and *excessive* parade and accumulation of detail and event.

Thus, in reviews of the genre, one generally finds praise not for its historical accuracy or specificity but rather for its extravagant generality and excess—of sets, costumes, stars, and spectacle, of the money and labor that went into the making of such entertainment. One such review tells us of the 1951, 171-minute-long *Quo Vadis?* (Mervyn LeRoy): "Colossal is just one of the superlatives trumpeting the size and scope of this mammoth drama about Romans, Christians, lions, pagan rites, rituals, and Nero. Roman soldier Robert Taylor loves and pursues Christian maiden Deborah Kerr. It's Christians versus Nero and the lions in the eternal fight between good and evil. The sets, scenery, and crowd scenes are nearly overwhelming. Peter Ustinov as Nero is priceless."[15]

Conversely, another such review chides the 1971, 183-minute-long *Nicholas and Alexandra* (Franklin Schaffner) for being *too* historically particular and specific: "This is an overlong, overdetailed depiction of the events preceding the Russian Revolution until the deaths of Czar Nicholas . . . his wife . . . and family. Some of the performances are outstanding . . . and the sets and costumes are topnotch. However, the film gets mired in trying to encompass too much historical detail." [16] Apparently, then, despite the "lots of things going on in it," the phenomenological significance and discursive power of the Hollywood historical epic is not to be found in the specificity and accuracy of its historical detail. Too much specificity and accuracy, this reviewer suggests, "mires" the film—bogs it down in the concrete and disallows the emergence of something that, through generalization and extravagance, *exceeds* and *transcends* the concrete.

In a paradoxical way, the suggestion here is that the Hollywood historical epic is not so much the narrative accounting of *specific historical events* as it is the narrative construction of *general historical eventfulness*. This is perhaps why the genre is popularly conceived as such an admixture of different kinds (and not merely periods) of past events: mythic, biblical, folkloric, and quasi- or "properly" historical. Thus, Fraser can point out that Hollywood's "Ancient World" takes place in "the Egypto-Biblo-Classic era, since threads from all three were often intertwined in its productions." [17] This is precisely the kind of categorical and theoretical sloppiness scholars despise and try to clarify and clean up—and that popular audiences don't mind at all.[18] It could also be argued that this sloppiness is profoundly functional—and that it is by means of iconographic expansiveness and formal excessiveness that the Hollywood historical epic creates a field of temporality experienced as subjectively transcendent and objectively significant. The importance of the genre is not that it narrates and dramatizes historical events accurately according to the detailed stories of academic historians but rather that it opens a temporal field that creates the *general* possibility for recognizing oneself as a *historical subject* of a particular kind.[19] Thus, counter to the judgment of most film scholars and historians who have ignored or scoffed at the genre as "heavy-handed" cinema or "lightweight" history, I tend to side with the *London Times* reviewer who, attending the world premiere of *How the West Was Won* (John Ford, Henry Hathaway, and George Marshall, 1962), wrote of the historical epic: "It has a surge and splendor and extravagance not to be despised." [20]

My agreement, however, is perverse. That is, I would suggest that the Hollywood historical epic not be despised *lightly*. Indeed, rather than cursorily dismissing the "surge and splendor and extravagance" of the genre, we should recognize its excessive elements as essential to the genre's functional capacity to construct a discursive field in which American, middle-class, white (and disproportionately male) spectators/consumers could experience—not think—that particular mode of temporality which con-

56. *Intolerance:* Formal extravagance in the epic film.

stituted them as historical subjects in capitalist society before the late 1960s. To use Hayden White's characterization, the "content of the form" of the Hollywood genre is its *mimetic* and *onomatopoetic* modes of representation and rhetoric, together constituting a representational excess that yields a particular "history effect."[21] That is, the genre *formally repeats* the surge, splendor, and extravagance, the human labor and capital cost entailed by its narrative's *historical content* in both its *production process* and its *modes of representation.* Through these means, the genre *allegorically* and *carnally* inscribes on the model spectator a sense and meaning of being in time and participating in human events in a manner and at a magnitude exceeding any individual temporal construction or appropriation—and, most important, in a manner and at a magnitude that is *intelligible as excess* to lived-body subjects in a historically specific *consumer* culture. Thus, it is through this multileveled and repetitive discourse (and politics) of *excess*—not only within the movie theater and cinematic text but also without—that the Hollywood historical epic has the philosophical capacity to constitute what Maurice

Merleau-Ponty identifies as a temporal "spread staggered out in depth," a structure that creates in us a "perception of history."[22] However, although one might have philosophical justification to argue that a sense of temporal excess is universally necessary to constitute a "perception of history," it is important to emphasize that precisely what *signifies* temporal excess is not universal but culturally and historically determined. And, in the case of the Hollywood historical epic, temporal excess tends to be encoded as *empirically verifiable* and *material* excess—entailing scale, quantification, and consumption in relation to money and human labor.[23]

Consider the rhetoric of a press book memorializing the production and release in 1962 of Hollywood's first narrative film made in Cinerama: the 155-minute historical epic *How the West Was Won*.[24] The hardcover volume opens with the presidents of both MGM and Cinerama introducing us to a "new era" and a "milestone" in the "world of entertainment" through a statement that compares the transcendent magnitude of past events in American History with those of the new process of cinematic production. They write: "Never has so vast a chapter of our American heritage been seen by motion picture audiences; never has any film process encompassed such grandeur of sight and sound." They also tell us: "Thousands of creative men and women and skilled technicians combined their talents to make this motion picture a reality." This statement appears on the same double-page spread that features a panoramic shot from the film of a crowd of people with baggage ready to set out for the West, its caption reading: "They came by the thousands from everywhere, for to them the West was the promise of the future." A correlation is clearly established here between the present events of the film's production and the past events it is intended to represent. A peculiar temporal equivalence is made as well between the "new era" of entertainment ushered in by the "futuristic" technology of Cinerama and the "promise of the future" that the West held for past Americans. It is hardly surprising, then, that on the next double-page spread (a vaguely drawn map of the United States punctuated by iconic figures signaling the film's representation of events from 1839 to 1889), the legend below the film's title quotes Walt Whitman in what, in context, seems a generalized paean to the protagonists of both the "winning" of the American West and the conquest of motion picture technology: "Moving yet and never stopping, Pioneers! O Pioneers!"

With the same strategy, the book goes on to tell us "The MGM Cinerama Story." Historical adventures of epic quality, quantification of the scope and magnitude of hardships and obstacles that had to be endured and overcome, heroic perseverance, appeal to national pride—at each rhetorical turn, these elements equivalently mark both the winning of the West and the achievement of its *appropriate* cinematic representation.

The laborious struggle entailed by the film's production *formally repeats* the laborious struggle of the American pioneers—even in its direction. "Fleets of trucks" moved Cinerama's headquarters from Oyster Bay, New York, to MGM Studios in California, and a section entitled "A Monumental Production" tells us: "Filming the fully definitive story of the winning of the American West was one of the most demanding projects ever undertaken. This was never attempted before." Location experts "traveled through the historic Ohio River Valley, once a water highway to the West, and into the heart of the proud Rocky Mountains. They rode over unused paths and roads as long as four-wheeled vehicles would carry them, and by foot along trails where there were no roads. They took thousands of photographs and sent them back to the studio as often as they could get to a post office." Production notes give us endless numbers: how many buffalo, horses, extras, pairs of shoes, yards of homespun ordered from "ancient looms in India"; actual American Indian tribes participating; pounds of hay, grain, food, and crew—and how arduous all this gathering and deploying was and how long it took. All, apparently, to achieve historical accuracy, yet stressing *labor* and *quantity*: "The research alone filled 87 volumes which were cross-indexed for easier reference." The end goal is *authenticity*, a word appearing frequently throughout the text in reference to—and equating—both the filmmakers' and spectators' experience of the production as "truly" historical.[25]

In between the lengthier portions of text that equate and apotheosize both the *history of production* and the *production of history* (and imply their reversibility) are sections organized around photographs. First are "The Stars," presented by their Hollywood names—their identity as characters subordinated in smaller print underneath their pictures.[26] Next are the production stills from the film, marked by individual captions that focus on a seeming specificity of character and event. Throughout, small black-and-white engravings—"old" and "authentic" pieces from the Bettmann Archives—contrast with and complement the color photographs, serving both as their pale models and "authenticating primary documents."[27] In large and boldface type, on many of the double-page layouts, appears a suggestive and quasi-documented quotation that abridges and iconographically generalizes the specificity of the photographs, subtending the film's family romance narrative that spans three generations. Above all, the quotations lend intertextual "historical" and "literary" significance to the photos and seem selected particularly to emphasize the narrative's largess of scope and action. From William MacLeod Raine's *Guns of the Frontier* comes "The West was won by the pioneer. He blazed trails, gutted mountains, ran furrows, and planted corn on the prairies." Whitman is repeated: "Through the battle, through defeat, Moving yet and never stopping, Pioneers! O Pioneers!" Abraham Lincoln's Gettysburg Address tells us: "Now we are engaged in a great civil war, testing whether that nation, or any nation so conceived and so dedicated, can long endure." Horace Greeley is cited: "A million buffalo is a great many, but I am certain that I saw that many yesterday." And, finally, accompanying and elevating photographs of bandit attacks and "blazing gun battle," is a quote from Daniel Webster: "Those who break the great law of Heaven by shedding man's blood seldom succeed in avoiding discovery."

The press book concludes with an illustrated and quasi-technical explanation of the Cinerama process, asserting that the scope of such a form of representation begins "a new motion picture era—an age where the audience can live a real story on the screen," and this is followed by a description and critical assessment of the "glittering world premiere" of the film in London, before, among others, bejeweled British royalty.[28] At the conclusion of this "overwhelming" spectacle, we are told: "London's critics went off to seek new adjectives to describe *How the West Was Won*, predicting it would run for ten years, stating it was one of the most monumental entertainments ever conceived." In addition to *overwhelming* and *monumental*, some of these supposedly "new" adjectives included *giant, spectacular, splendiferous, rich, sprawling, star-studded*, and *immensely stirring*. The *London Daily Mirror* said the film was "a thundering, ear-splitting smasheroo of a spectacle." Praising it for showing us "not only the landmarks of America, but the famous faces of Hollywood," the *London Evening Standard* reported that the film "makes good history as well as eye-popping hyperbole."

> One can only conclude that its scale put it beyond the normal critical reach; in a way, it is rather like criticising an elephant.
>
> —Fraser, Hollywood History

I have spent some time describing the discursive field of the Hollywood historical epic for three reasons. The first has been to emphasize how easy it is to laugh at the language in which it is expressed, how entertaining to trash the naiveté and excesses of both the rhetoric and its objects and to feel superior to what seems their debased project. The second has been to foreground the complex way in which this seemingly laughable and naive kind of hyperbolic language is commonly used not only to describe but also *mimetically* to elevate the epic film into a *historical eventfulness* that exceeds its already excessive screen boundaries—accomplished by creating equivalence and reciprocity among the epic's "historic" cinematic production, its historical narrative content and histrionic form, and its "historic" reception. The third has been to provide the experiential basis for further unpacking and thematizing the "content of the form" of the genre—those structures that are the objective correlates of a certain subjective mode of temporal being and that, in the cinematic experience, mark their sense on and make their sense to an *embodied* spectator.

In this regard, Paul Ricoeur's complex observation that the existential relationship between narrativity and temporality is a "reciprocal" one is of real importance here. He tells us: "I take temporality to be the structure of existence that reaches language in narrativity and narrativity to be the language structure that has temporality as its ultimate referent."[29] I would further argue, however, that this reciprocity is possible only because narrativity as a structure of language and temporality as a structure of existence find their *common ground* in bodily being, in a *carnal reckoning* with time and space that precedes the accountancy of objective reckoning and, as Ricoeur points out, is thus "not an abstract measure" but "a *magnitude* which corresponds to our concern and to the world into which we are thrown."[30]

As Merleau-Ponty suggests, given that we are fleshly and mortal beings, both our carnal "reckoning" with time and our accountancy of it as a magnitude of human value provide the prereflective grounds for that reflective focus on temporality that we call "historical consciousness." We also come into the world both *after* and *before* other mortal beings and the actions inscribed by their lives, and a consideration of our own existence as being always in medias res directs us not only to the future of human existence but also to its past. Thus, as Merleau-Ponty puts it, "a wave of transcendence . . . springs up in the carnal opening"—that is, our bodies are imbued with the sense and meaning of time not only as the "now" that is given to us as the lives that we presently live, but also as a "then" and "when" that exceeds us but that our bodies can comprehend and to which we are substantially connected. When this immediate and pretheoretical bodily knowledge of a repeatable and shared temporality is reflected upon and made symbolically explicit, it is constituted as History—a temporality that is abstracted from the individual bodily experience of time, a temporality that becomes "a kind of acquisition, belonging henceforth not only to a particular individual's horizon but to that of all possible individuals."[31]

These phenomenological interpretations of the emergence of and relations between narrativity and temporality suggest that if the "content of the form" of the Hollywood historical epic is the *mimetic and onomatopoetic representation* of antecedent human actions, then the "theme of the form" is *temporal magnitude*—extended and elevated to its highest existential degree as intelligible within a particular cultural framework. Recognition of both the content and theme of the genre's form moves us to an apprehension of its deep structure—that is, the "form of its form." The Hollywood historical epic is a *reflexive* structure founded in *repetition*.

It seems no coincidence that of all kinds of commercial cinematic representation, the Hollywood historical epic—through repetition—calls the most explicit, reflexive, and self-authorizing attention to its own existence as a *representation*. Mentioned earlier, the most obvious example is the frequent written or spoken narrative with which the majority of historical epics begin and which later punctuate their dramatic action. Such narration not only chronologically locates the present viewer relative to a past event that, by reflexive authorial focus, is foregrounded as *retrospectively* and *now* historically significant. It also *repeats* the dramatic representation in a reflexive and reflective mode—creating an additional textual level that *temporally extends* the emplotment of the story from the past to the present and confers significance on the story from the present to the past. As Pierre Sorlin points out, "Historical films are distinguished by something we could call. . . the *double exposure* of time, with the superimposition of symbolic time on other forms of time." [32] Janet Staiger also notes the repetition entailed by such narration and so necessary to its "history effect": "Because framing information is a 'separate' text, at a distance and not part of the enclosed story, it can easily take on an authenticity in comparison to that which it embeds. Yet this voice-over of masculine authority assures (or perhaps reassures) us of the educational value of this true story—*doubling and redoubling* its claims. Thus the voice-over narrator acts . . . in a subtle way as a textual device of *compulsively repeating*, 'this is, as "I" say, a true story.'" [33]

At times, this temporal repetition is graphically introduced into the text—its often exotic calligraphic presentation both invoking "the past" in visual onomatopoetic reference to antecedent forms of writing, to "original" documents, and claiming the anonymous authority that the written word has secured in our particular culture. At times, the repetition is oral. While voice-over narration also performs the function of doubly exposing time, its authorizing power is different. The narrators entailed by the genre to establish, repeat, and elaborate upon the dramatic representation call particular and reflexive attention to their own personal (if cinematically derived) authority as a means of further authorizing and "authenticating" the dramatic material. Their offscreen voices are especially male, highly sonorous, and distinctively recognizable, marking these narrators of History as literally transcendental—significant stars of such "celestial" stature that they, like the face of God, must not be seen. John Huston, for example, narrated *The Bible* (Huston, 1966); [34] Orson Welles narrated *The Vikings;* and Spencer Tracy, whose distinctive vocal presence signifies "integrity" as well as authority, narrated *How the West Was Won*. In the aforementioned press book, Tracy's photograph as one of "The Stars" (he is wearing a cowboy hat) bears this caption: "The Narrator. Although this famous star, one of the few ever to be honored by two Academy Awards, does not appear in the film, his magnificent speaking voice has the important role of narrating the stirring drama of the winning of the West." Standing in for the institutional voice of historiography, Tracy's trusted persona lends received ideas a particular credibility, while his absence from the screen secures them a transcendental space outside the drama from which they can assert a privileged validity.[35] In sum, a significant actor retelling the story over and "above" its visible, dramatic representation gives us *two* levels of narrative, temporality, and significance—and spans the space *between*.

Most Hollywood historical epics not only repeat the narrative *within* the film through a doubling narration but also repeat that narrative *outside* the film—if within its cinematic discourse. That is, the genre often formally or literally celebrates and represents the historic struggles under which it produced itself as a *mimetic imitation* of the historical events it is dramatizing. This extratextual and elevated repetition of historical events is not only evident in such commemorative volumes as the *How the West Was Won* press book. It is also evident in television accounts of "The Making of . . . ," picture magazine coverage of production hardships, and the like—reflexive and repetitious narratives of the historical epic's own repetition of historical narrative. This extratextual repetition can itself be quite dramatic. Movie stars other than Taylor and Burton have made headlines while working on a film, but consider how the duo's illicit extratextual romance—and their magnitude as stars—mimicked the historical situation of the text in which they were imitating Cleopatra and Antony and extended the produced History of the past into the present moment of historical production. Additionally, as Fraser notes of *Cleopatra* (Joseph L. Mankiewicz), "The 1963 production by Twentieth Century-Fox became a byword for extravagance, crisis and disappointment"[36]—the troubled production history of the film popularly perceived and written about as isomorphic with the narrative shape of the popular conception of Antony and Cleopatra's emotional and political history. I don't mean to suggest here that Liz and Dick's romance was consciously planned so as formally to "repeat history" in an excess of temporality that transgressed the boundaries of the film they were making, or that *Cleopatra* was a financial disappointment on purpose. Rather, I mean to foreground how important extratextual discourse about the production of the film is to the construction of the Hollywood historical epic's temporal field. In its elevation of elements of the film's historical narrative to yet another discursive level, the genre expands and extends the temporality of "ordinary" textuality into an extensive and excessive temporality which literally transcends the film frame, the text, and the time of the spectator's immediate presence to the film in the theater.

This extension of temporality is also one of the functions, I would suggest, of casting highly recognizable stars to represent historical figures. Perhaps laughable, certainly distracting, and possibly reprehensible to those who seek in the historical epic cinema the physical anonymity of an "underdetermined" body to paradoxically signify both the physical specificity and the vagueness of half-known historical persons, stars people the represented historical past with the present. Their "overdetermined" presence in a film punctuates the representation of the past and stresses the representation as repetition, as imitation of previous events, and thus, like the narration, doubles the film's temporal dimension. Furthermore, their presence functions as a sign of *temporal transcendence*. Elizabeth Taylor outlives the end of History as it was writ by Cleopatra. Charlton Heston outlives not only El Cid but also Moses. And Peter Ustinov will perpetually be in temporal excess of Nero. Thus, stars not only exceed the representation or "re-presencing" of past historical figures to remind us that the representation is a repetition, but additionally serve to *generalize* historical specificity through their own *iconographic* presence. Stars are cast not *as* characters but *in* character—as "types" who, however physically particular and concrete, signify universal and general characteristics. Thus, while not embodying historical figures in any way that could be called "accurate" by a historian's standards, stars nonetheless contribute to an expansive, excessive, and multileveled temporality that can be experienced by the spectator as subjectively transcendent and objectively significant. Indeed, the very presence of stars in the historical epic mimetically represents not *real historical* figures but rather the *real significance* of historical figures. Stars literally lend *magnitude* to the representation.

This kind of *conceptual* mimesis—that is, the representation or imitation of a general idea rather than a specific person, event, or thing—paradoxically often takes the most *literal* and *material* form, creating at the formal level of representation what I choose to call cinematic *onomatopoeia*. Thus, as was mentioned at the beginning of this essay, the defining characteristics of the Hollywood historical epic translate the sense of temporal *magnitude* and the existential *weight* of being in historical time into visible size and scale and quantity and extravagance. Similarly, "being caught up" in and "swept along" by social events not of one's own making are translated into massive surges of movement—from buffalo stampedes to revolutions to the Exodus. The Hollywood historical epic thus constructs a "field of historicality" by mimicking the subjective sense we have of temporal excess and giving it objective and visible form—although it does so in a way that is informed by its own cultural bias and historicality. Its literalization of temporal excess is informed not only by capitalist materialism but also by the conceptual apparatus of the Enlightenment.[37] As Staiger says of historical cinema's general strategy: "The film implies that what's historical is a physical reality. It is the mise-

57. *The Ten Commandments:* The weighty presence of Charlton Heston expresses the real significance of Moses.

en-scène, the props, the costumes and the people that are historical." [38] What shall count as the historical is not merely verified but also constituted through the visible and in material evidence.

Thus, the genre also constitutes its historical field as literally and materially—onomatopoetically—extended and expanded. An excess of temporality finds its form in, or "equals," *extended duration:* films far longer than the Hollywood norm. Correlatively, an excess of space finds its form in, or "equals," *expanded space:* Cinemascope, Cinerama, Superscope, 70mm. Indeed, if one were looking for a Bakhtinian chronotope to characterize the historical epic—that is, to identify the essential and inseparable time-space relationship that generates and makes visible its particular form, action, and character—one need go no further than Cinemascope or Cinerama or Vistavision. [39]

In this regard, however our particular culture may inflect it, it is crucial to remember that our sense of historicality begins with our existence as *embodied subjects.* It is as carnal as well as cultural beings that we get caught up in time in the movie theater. Thus, there is a paradoxical, yet culturally apt, logic to the fact that most Hollywood historical epics are a great deal longer than are other films—well over the two-hour length usual for other kinds of commercial movies. It takes, for example, 222 minutes for the South to go in *Gone with the Wind*. At 180 minutes the title of the World War II epic *The Longest Day* (Ken Annakin, Andrew Marton, and Bernard Wicki, 1962) has a double resonance. *Reds* (Warren Beatty, 1981) finds 199 minutes of screen time the extravagant equal of *Ten Days That Shook the World* (Sergei Eisenstein, 1928). And Gandhi's patience must be matched by the spectator's when watching Richard Attenborough's 188-minute film of the same name (1982). On the one hand, experiencing this extraordinary cinematic duration, the spectator as a body-subject is made more presently aware than is usual of his or her bodily presence—indeed, is "condemned" to the present and physically "tested" by the length of the film's duration. On the other hand, however, *enduring* the film in the present imprints the body with a brute sense of the possibility of transcending the present, of the literal and material capacity of the human being to be tested and *to continue* and *last through* events represented as a temporal "spread staggered out in depth."[40] This writing on the body by experience, I would argue, provides the carnal and subjective grounds necessary for the constructed abstract and objective premises considered sufficient to historical reflection. However, our bodies always also exist in culture and so physiological sense cannot be amputated from sociological sense. Thus, writing on the body of the model American spectator/consumer, the Hollywood historical epic is *transcoding* the culture's emphasis on literalism and materialism into specific carnal terms, reprinting its version of History not only for posterity but also on our posteriors. This is, philosophically and carnally, a profound form of repetition.

In the context of a complex and persuasive discussion of the relations between narrativity and temporality, Ricoeur stresses *repetition* as that aspect of narratological form most responsive to and responsible for our phenomenological sense of time as "historical."[41] The repetitions of the Hollywood historical epic, then, make historical sense. This is not merely because their ostensible "content" refers to and repeats events culturally agreed upon as significant and actually or likely to have happened, but also because their formal structures, qualified by specific cultural and ideological codes, foreground, multiply, and elevate repetition. Recycling the "now" so that it gains a "past" and presages a "future" that is familiar, repetition constructs a transcendent temporal structure that overcomes the sense of an "origin" and an "end" and thereby the finitude of any particular human existence or any particular human event. It is through repetition that one may become aware of the never-ending nature of historical time and yet still sense the finite structure of one's own individual human temporality. In effect, repetition serves as a formal recirculation of signs that, when put to the service of teleological "content" such as the linear chronology of historical events, does away with chronology and teleology and institutes a sense not of individually being toward Death, but of socially being in History.[42]

However, this universal sense of "being in History" is always already qualified by the particular and contingent specificity of individual and cultural existence. Awareness of one's temporal and historical being may differ and conflict within cultures, from culture to culture, and from time to time. Thus, historical consciousness is itself historicized. There is no "History" with a transcendental, capital *H*—except in the qualified sense that the human beings who hold power in particular cultures fix and secure it as such.[43] Thus, through the "content of its form," the Hollywood historical epic sets up a transparent dialectic—one that allows its spectators a prereflective experience of the dual nature of *historicality* as both the *making* and *being* of History. The genre entails the spectator in the *carnal labor* through which filmmakers, actors, and spectators alike transform the "advent" of provisional human "gesture" into the archetypal "adventure" of the *geste* into the institutionalized "events" of History. Thus, the phenomenological experience of the Hollywood historical epic is less one of the particular, specific, and "objectively accurate" *representation of a past event* than it is of a general, concrete, and "subjectively authentic" *representation of the production of History*. Qualified, however, by their lived value and cultural and historical situation, the concepts of both "production" and "History" have particular and delimited meaning.

Many of the people you meet today, who are responsible for seeing that movies get made, have scope the width of a TV screen and a historical consciousness that extends to last year's reruns.
    —Peter O'Toole, quoted in Barra, "Incredible Shrinking Epic"

It is particularly telling that there have been so few Hollywood historical epics made for theatrical release in the 1970s and 1980s.[44] Partially as a response to television and its obvious lack of magnitude, the screen genre peaked in production and box-office receipts in the 1950s and 1960s. It is not by chance that the decline of the historical epic in the mid-1960s coincided with the transformation of Hollywood business practices. These were brought about not only by the long-term effects of antitrust suits against the major film corporations initiated in the late 1940s, which, by the mid-1960s, had finally broken their hold on production, distribution, and exhibition. Transformation of the industry also came about as part of the contemporary restructuring of corporate capitalism to multinational (or "late") capitalism, and until the industry diversified its production base by corporately allying itself with television and the music industry and became fully incorporated by less related multinational giants like Pepsi-Cola, Hollywood's economy was in turmoil. The peak period of the production of the historical epic cinema in Hollywood also coincided with a culturally homogenizing Cold War politics and entered its decline as the United States entered Vietnam and a period of mass political and social fragmentation that challenged both the myth of American colonial benevolence and national unity. Given these "coincidences," it would be fruitful to speculate on the relationship between such politics and the "political unconscious" symbolically enacted within the culturally qualified structure of cinematic "excess" I have described here as phenomenologically constructing a particular and contingent sense of "being in History." [45]

In this regard, Allen Barra, looking for explanations for "The Incredible Shrinking Epic," quotes both British critic Paul Coates and Walter Benjamin. Coates maintains: "True film epics can only be made [and properly received by audiences] at a time when a country's national myths are still believed—or, at best, at a time when a nation feels itself slipping into decline, which produces a spate of nostalgic evocations of those myths. Afterward, a period of cynicism sets in, in which the myths are presented in a revisionist manner"—resulting in, Coates says, "that curious hybrid of the last 20 years, the anti-epic." [46] Benjamin sees this revisionism less as cynicism than as an assumption of responsibility: "To articulate the past historically does not mean to recognize it 'the way it really was. . . .' It means to seize hold of a memory as it flashes up at a moment of danger. . . . In every era, the attempt must be made anew to wrest tradition away from a conformism that is about to overpower it." [47]

The era of the Hollywood historical epic, from its beginnings in the early 1900s through its decline in the 1960s, can be characterized as informed by those cultural values identified with rational humanism, with bourgeois patriarchy, with colonialism and imperialism, and with entrepreneurial and corporate capitalism. It was in the 1960s that, for a variety of reasons, these ideological values were placed in major crisis. The civil rights, youth, and women's movements; the explicit failure of U.S. political and military might in Southeast Asia and the civil war at home; the rise of foreign economic power and the emergence of multinational capitalism; the pervasive spread of electronic media throughout the entire culture and a correspondent devaluation of the mechanical and the visible labor of men and machines that the latter entails—these events not only made explicit what had theretofore been ideologically transparent but also radically challenged and transformed the dominant culture's "rational, humanist version of the subject as a unified speaking self, cohering in mind, body, and speech."[48] In its particular representation of the "production" of History, the Hollywood historical epic depended upon a celebration of rationalism, humanism, the unity of historical agents, and the progress, continuity, and coherence of a centralized "production" process availing itself of labor's surplus value to produce excessive temporality as a fixed commodity, a stable and coherent narrative: History.

In 1938 a Hollywood press release about the MGM historical epic *Marie Antoinette* (W. S. Van Dyke II) unself-consciously, indeed proudly, went public with the information that "fifty women were brought to Los Angeles from Guadalajara, Mexico, to sew on thousands of sequins and do the elaborate embroidery used on many of the 2,500 costumes."[49] Fifty Mexican women may illegally cross the border today and end up sewing costumes, but it is highly unlikely that such colonial exploitation of cheap labor would be quite so blatantly celebrated in what, in the era of the epic, functioned as a transparent repetition of historical events.

One could also argue that, on various levels, the Hollywood historical epic's *formal* construction of historical consciousness in the 1950s and early 1960s has been coopted and, by now, radically transformed by television and the miniseries, which has given us such epic equivalents as *Roots* (1977), *The Winds of War* (1983), *The Jewel in the Crown* (1984–1985), and *North and South* (1985). To some, this has caused a formal debasement of the genre—as measured by what one can expect for one's money in consumer society. (Television, after all, is perceived as "free.") Thus, Barra laments: "The audience for *War and Remembrance,* with lowered expectations, will allow old newsreel footage of air combat; an audience going to see a modern war movie would expect completely reconstructed air forces and fleets for its money." However, he notes, on the positive side, the television miniseries has "given rise to an army of technicians and production assistants"[50]—although this army, unlike its cinematic predecessors, tends to remain publicly uncelebrated as signifying an apotheosis of labor. Like the computer casing that hides the already invisible work of electronic mediation, the television miniseries transforms the extravagant labor spent in the production of History into something less visible.

The miniseries also transforms the Hollywood historical epic in a more profound way, formally altering its temporal field and thus its construction of History. Indeed, *miniseries* is a revealing nomination. It suggests that the spatial displacement from cinematic to electronic representation has changed the existential sense and terms of epic excess, and that the electronic medium's new mode of episodic and fragmented exhibition has changed the sense and terms of the expansiveness, movement, and repetitiousness of epic—and historical—time. In this regard, we might see this move and transformation of the historical epic to television as one symptom of our own cultural move into a period conceptualized less in terms of the explicit, economically extravagant displays of corporate capitalism or of the unifying imperatives of World War I, World War II, and Cold War ideology than in terms associated with the *electronic,* the *postindustrial,* and the *postmodern.* Contemporary critics have argued that our situation and practice within a culture marked by multinational capitalism, high technology of an electronic kind, and a heightened cultural awareness and consumption of images have radically altered the value and meaning of *antecedence*—and what formally constitutes its adequate representation. In the electronic era of the television and the VCR, temporality is transformed. Repetition means reruns, and one can materially and literally manipulate time to construct various versions of "history" (which no longer are weighty enough to bear a capital *H*).

Characterized negatively by what Fredric Jameson calls an "inverted millennarianism," the narratological structure of postmodern representation has a severely *weakened* existential sense of connection to both the historical past and the future, and is caught up in an intensified present— a "within-time-ness", marked by a sense of "the end of this or that" [51]— and characterized by the *fragmentation and mixture of temporal modes* in a schizophrenic manner, by *temporal pastiche,* and by nostalgic *temporal scavenging.* Certainly the miniseries—not only fragmenting its own temporal continuity across a week but also interrupting it with advertising—stands as transparent testimony to this characterization. As does the current nostalgic fascination with restoring and recycling "old" Hollywood historical epics.

On the other hand, Linda Hutcheon characterizes postmodern representation more positively.[52] It is, she insists, resolutely historical and has a *heightened* existential sense of the present's connection to the past and future. Although still using *repetition* as the content of its form, this more conscious kind of postmodern representation, unlike the Hollywood historical epic, uses it *parodically*—that is, with a critical distance that produces irony and undermines its own assertions and truth or reality claims. This postmodern representation, Hutcheon argues, fractures the totalizing power of History into a heterogeneous dialogism of histories and a heightened awareness of their inscriptions, investments, and conflicts.

At this cultural moment, then, there seems no place between these two versions of postmodern temporality for the production of the kind of historical consciousness that the Hollywood historical epic once created through its particular discourse and politics of temporal excess. As a culture, we seem to be too self-conscious, too image-conscious, and too aware of our social heterogeneity to find any but nostalgic appeal in the directed temporal force of the genre, in its creation of a prereflective sense of "being in History." Indeed, the current restoration and reissue of *Law-*

rence of Arabia and *Gone with the Wind* in first-run theaters speaks to both the present cultural impossibility of writing History in the Hollywood epic manner and—in keeping with the Jamesonian characterization of postmodernism—a popular nostalgia for the unity and fixity of Hollywood epic values that stand against mass apprehension of shifting, heterogeneous histories engaged in contestation.

In this regard, what Leslie Berlowitz says of the American tendency to construct History rather than histories is relevant to the Hollywood historical epic and its popular appeal:

> Since the 19th century the struggle over identity and origins has distinguished the political and cultural life of all major nations. This potentially dangerous struggle has been particularly problematic for Americans, who fear that they have had no past, no patriarchal traditions or customs in the European sense, no feelings of permanent rootedness and stability. Americans have often responded to this "fear" of pastlessness by making rigid assertions about the founding myths and symbols and by insisting upon the constancy of certain values which, they have argued, constitute the moral code of America. Adept leaders, from Lincoln to Reagan, have recognized this tendency and exploited it for social and political purposes.[53]

This is the stuff of which the Hollywood historical epic was made. Since the late 1960s, however, "rigid assertions" about America's "founding myths and symbols," and the "constancy of certain values" that are unified as an American "moral code," have been challenged by many Americans—most of them marginalized in relation to dominant culture but some of them speaking, if only for a short while, within the American mainstream. Indeed, Arthur Penn's *Little Big Man* (1970, 150 min.) and Robert Altman's *Nashville* (1975, 159 min.) both use the inflated and extravagant epic form to deflate the power of founding myths and symbols and show America with no moral code whatsoever. (Altman further theorizes the construction of History in his 1976 box-office flop, *Buffalo Bill and the Indians; or, Sitting Bull's History Lesson,* which runs a contained 120 minutes.) Nonetheless, since the few American mavericks making countercultural "mainstream" films in the 1970s as a response to the history lessons of Vietnam, there has been little in the way of an American cinematic critique of the dominant mode of producing History. Warren Beatty's *Reds* (200 min.), well intentioned and "leftist" as it means to be, still buys into the formal and ideological repetitions of the Hollywood genre—playing out the "great man" theory of History outside as well as within the text, with Beatty producing, coauthoring, directing, and starring as John Reed.

Thus within the last decade (nostalgically noted by Barra as the time of "The Incredible Shrinking Epic"), it is two non-Americans who most significantly contest the Hollywood historical epic by entering into specific formal and ideological dialogue with its temporal construction. In different ways associated with the differences marked by Jameson and Hutcheon's characterizations of postmodernism, both Alex Cox's *Walker* (1987) and Bernardo Bertolucci's *The Last Emperor* are explicitly aware of the rhetoric and politics of excess that informed the Hollywood genre, and both use this knowledge critically.

Made by the same director who gave us *Repo Man* (1984) and *Sid and Nancy* (1986), *Walker,* in its depiction of the leader of an army of American irregulars who invaded Nicaragua in 1855, financed by railroad magnate Cornelius Vanderbilt, stresses the schizophrenic gap between rhetoric and action and seems to illustrate the temporal mode of Jameson's version of postmodern representation. The historical content of the film's subject matter affords its only use of representational repetition—but it is a repetition that, in its retelling the contemporary intervention in Nicaragua through the representation of a previous and obscure intervention, directs us "back to the present" rather than to the past or future.[54] The content of the film's form, however, is not the multileveled and isomorphic repetition that creates the sense of excess temporality and temporal significance in the Hollywood historical epic. Rather, we have its opposite: *formal disparity* among its levels. The film is short in duration and long on the span of its narrative. Its music is contemporary *salsa,* while its costumes are historically "accurate." The same disparity and anachronism begin increasingly to encroach on the narrative's visible mise-en-scène and temporal cohesion—with *Time* magazine, modern automobiles, and even computers forcing the present into what was initially represented as the past. Clearly, *Walker* is not directed toward antecedence; indeed, if it constructs any excess of temporality, it is an excess of the existential present that very purposefully *debases* the significance of the past. As one reviewer has said, the film "keeps our attention focused not on the hollow heroics of the past but on the bloody farce of the present."[55] *Walker* is a text in which one history interrogates another.

The Last Emperor in many ways is both the saddest and most profound of contemporary attempts to deal with historical representation in epic form. Unlike *Walker,* it does use the formal repetitions of the Hollywood genre. Textually full of surge and splendor and extravagance, it also surrounded itself with extratextual discourse about its own historic, costly, and arduous production in mainland China. Nonetheless, all that repetition, all that excess temporality that accumulates and circumscribes an expansive field for "being in History" is *ironically* put to the service of a history from which both the central protagonist—and the spectator—are excluded. Contained in the Forbidden City, contained in Manchukuo, contained in Mao's reeducation camp, China's last emperor, Pu Yi, struggles to *make* History and not merely to be *of* it. All the surge and splendor and extravagance of the historical epic cinema is paradoxically centered upon a historical figure—a "great man"—who seems to have little historical agency. As spectators of this particular spectacle, we are not engaged in a temporal field that allows us prereflectively to experience the possibility of temporal transcendence but rather are left to reflect on our own *lack* of agency and our own restricted immanence in the movie theater—particularly since we, like Pu Yi, only get glimpses of the "significant" historical events we thought we were going to see. Thus, in a paradoxical and profoundly ironic reversal of temporal direction more characteristic of Hutcheon's postmodern representation than Jameson's, *The Last Emperor* gives us a historical figure who repeats, mimics, and foregrounds the antecedence and presence not of past historical agents but of the cinema *spectator*—someone who, if at all, sees History at a distance and yet nevertheless, like Pu Yi, is *presently* responsible to and accountable for its construction.

Notes

A version of this essay was presented at the Western Humanities Conference held at the University of California, Los Angeles, in October 1988. I am indebted not only to Hayden White, my colleague at the University of California, Santa Cruz, for his generous conversation on some of the issues presented here, but also to those conference participants whose astute comments helped guide my later elaborations—most particularly Robert Rosen, Michael Rogin, John Rowe, and Robert Rosenstone.

1. While Britain and Italy have always been involved in the production of historical epics and Hollywood has often engaged in international coproduction as a way of keeping costs down, nonetheless it is Hollywood—as institution, industry, and a set of narratological structures and cinematic conventions—that is primarily responsible for constructing both the epic's standard market and (at least in scale) its standard model. Thus, the term *Hollywood*, used throughout this essay, is meant to convey a conceptual framework more than a geographical one.

2. For general discussion of the reasons surrounding this decline, see Allen Barra, "The Incredible Shrinking Epic," *American Film* 14, no. 5 (March 1989): 40–45ff.

3. *Gone with the Wind*, originally released in 1939, achieved its epic scope within the traditional aspect ratio of the 1930s and 1940s (the screen's relation of height to width was 1.33 to 1), while *Lawrence of Arabia*, originally released in 1962, used wide screen.

4. David Thomson, *Warren Beatty and Desert Eyes: A Life and a Story* (New York: Doubleday, 1987), p. 409. Thomson, in relation to Beatty's epic *Reds*, is specifically referring here to *Gone with the Wind*.

5. George MacDonald Fraser, *The Hollywood History of the World: From One Million Years B.C. to Apocalypse Now* (New York: Beech Tree Books, 1988), p. xi.

6. Ibid., p. 80.

7. Edward Maeder, "The Celluloid Image: Historical Dress in Film," in *Hollywood and History: Costume Design in Film,* edited by Edward Maeder (Los Angeles: Los Angeles County Museum, 1987), pp. 11–12.

8. Sande Cohen, *Historical Culture: On the Recoding of an Academic Discipline* (Berkeley: University of California Press, 1986), p. 21; italics mine.

9. Ibid., p. 13; italics mine.

10. A parallel project exploring the significance of popular critical response to *The Return of Martin Guerre* (Daniel Vigne, 1982) insofar as it relates to "how this fictional narrative" was "secured as a tale of the historical real" can be found in Janet Staiger, "Securing the Fictional Narrative as a Tale of the Historical Real," *South Atlantic Quarterly* 88, no. 2 (Spring 1989): 393–413.

11. My phenomenological allegiance, therefore, is not to the transcendental phenomenology derived from Edmund Husserl and bent on describing eidetic essences. Rather, it is to the existential and semiological phenomenology derived from Maurice Merleau-Ponty, a phenomenology whose "reductions" are never fully final or "essential," but are always qualified by the partial vision and finitude that marks human being.

12. Elley, *Epic Film,* p. 1.

13. *TV Guide* (San Francisco Metropolitan Edition), October 1, 1988, p. A-4.

14. It is of particular and parallel interest that Staiger, in "Securing the Fictional Narrative," rhetorically "parses" a similar critical statement by Vincent Canby about *The Return of Martin Guerre:* "This is, as they say, a true story." Her focus is on the function of the "they say"—a "gesture provoking intertextuality" as she sees it, referring less to a "specific group of people" than to "a set of texts in circulation in the social formation that give authenticity to the notion that 'this' is 'a true story'" (p. 399).

15. Mick Martin and Marsha Porter, *Video Movie Guide 1988* (New York: Ballantine, 1987), p. 674.

16. Ibid., p. 644.

17. Fraser, *Hollywood History,* p. 7.

18. It is interesting to note here that Elley in *Epic Film* conservatively focuses on epics beginning with biblical history and ending with early medieval history— indeed, defining the historical epic by the historical *distance* of its temporal content from the present. Thus, epics of the American West and more contemporary historical events are considered only in passing. Written in a more nostalgic mode, Fraser's *Hollywood History* is more encompassing in its categories and more attuned to their phenomenological function. Fraser groups his discussion of the historical accuracy of Hollywood into "seven ages": "The Ancient World," "Knights and Barbarians," "Tudors and Sea-Dogs," "Romance and Royalty," "Rule, Britannia," "New World, Old West," and "The Violent Century."

19. This issue of historical generalization is taken up by Pierre Sorlin in *The Film in History: Restaging the Past* (Oxford: Basil Blackwell, 1980). He writes: "The cultural heritage of every country and every community includes dates, events and characters known to all members of that community. This common basis is what we might call the group's 'historical capital,' and it is enough to select

a few details from this for the audience to know that it is watching an historical film and to place it, at least approximately. In this way every historical film is an indicator of a country's basic historical culture, its historical capital. . . . Behind the common knowledge, we can detect what is much more important: the underlying logic of history" (pp. 20–21).

20. *Metro-Goldwyn-Mayer and Cinerama Present "How the West Was Won"* (New York: n.p., 1963), unpaginated.

21. Hayden White, *The Content of the Form: Narrative Discourse and Historical Representation* (Baltimore: Johns Hopkins University Press, 1987), pp. ix–xi.

22. Maurice Merleau-Ponty, *The Visible and the Invisible,* translated by Alphonso Lingis (Evanston, Ill.: Northwestern University Press, 1968), p. 186.

23. Although relating such material excessiveness to intertextuality as the basis of authentication of story as "history," Staiger, "Securing the Fictional Narrative," makes a comment relevant to popular critical stress on props, sets, costumes, lighting, etc.: "The *physical* world of the film has been described as authentic and consequently true; its visible world has been pointed to and fixed as specifically historical. What has been used by the film and its contextualizing discourses to authenticate its claim to be a 'true story' is, as one reviewer put it, 'a surface sheen.'" Speaking of *The Return of Martin Guerre,* Staiger goes on to disclose her "subtext": "Even if one could say that the film in some sense really did represent completely the physical or visible world of the 1500s, it would be said within an ideology that *what is visible is what is real*" (p. 401; italics mine).

24. *Metro-Goldwyn-Mayer and Cinerama Present "How the West Was Won,"* n.p.

25. It must be emphasized that *authenticity* and *accuracy* are not synonymous terms in relation to the Hollywood epic's system of equivalencies intended to generate a "history effect." This becomes particularly apparent when one turns to discussions of hairstyles or costumes such as those in Maeder's "The Celluloid Image." For example, we are told that "Max Factor supplied Twentieth Century-Fox with 4,402 period wigs 'authentic to the last curl'" (p. 69). However, this authenticity is transparently invoked in an essay specifically indicating that women's wigs in Hollywood historical epics were *never* accurate representations. Similarly, we find out that perceived authenticity of costume depends only on *partial* accuracy: "While costumes deviate from authenticity in silhouette, fabric, and other aspects, they often include extremely precise reproduction of certain key details" (p. 15).

26. This subordination of history to stardom is also noted in ibid.: "When a star was cast in a period film, the studio faced a dilemma. While it was desirable that movie goers believed the historical image presented on the screen was indeed authentic, it was economically vital that the star's image was not sacrificed to history. In looking at how Hollywood movie makers reconciled these two conflicting demands, one can see a systematic approach to the way they handled makeup and hair, combining stars' modern images with illustrations of historical accuracy" (p. 58).

27. Discussing historical authenticity and intertextuality, Staiger, "Securing the Fictional Narrative," notes the following in reference to critical responses to *Martin Guerre:*

Ten of the reviewers consider this film authentic in part because it reminds them of other representations created in the same period. Such a proposition derives from the notion that somehow Brueghel, La Tour, and Flemish paintings should be considered reasonably authentic representations of the people of the sixteenth century because of the adjacent date of their manufacture. Since we do not assume that early Egyptian paintings faithfully mimic real Egyptians, our assumption that Brueghel's or the Flemish paintings might do so must result from our pointing to other texts: discourses on art history. Brueghel is, "as they say," a "representational" painter. This film and its adjacent texts promote spectatorial activity of reference to other "authentic" texts, hoping to secure for a fictional narrative the status of being a tale of the historical real, of fixing it as a coherent representation, and a return of the bonding of the body of the past and its name. (pp. 400–401)

28. It is telling that the authority held by British royalty is called upon to "authorize" an American text about the West emphasizing "democratic" values and intending a "history effect." Given (for this country) the historical relationship between Britain and the United States, it is as appropriate as it is also superficially bizarre.

29. Paul Ricoeur, "Narrative Time," in *On Narrative,* edited by W. J. T. Mitchell (Chicago: University of Chicago Press, 1981), p. 165.

30. Ibid., p. 169; italics mine.

31. Gary Brent Madison, *The Phenomenology of Merleau-Ponty: A Search for the Limits of Consciousness* (Athens: Ohio University Press, 1981), p. 261.

32. Sorlin, *Film in History,* p. 60; italics mine. Sorlin also discusses various semiotic possibilities of narration in historical films: no asserted narrative voice; delayed narrative voice; narrative voice opening the film and then disappearing; narrative voice distributed throughout the film; double narrative voice (see pp. 53–54).

33. Staiger, "Securing the Fictional Narrative," pp. 402–403; italics mine.

34. Huston did play a part in *The Bible,* but one clearly separated from his role as godly Narrator. Indeed, his Noah provided one of the few comic performances in the only comic sequence of the film.

35. It is useful in this context to recall that *persona*—while deriving its meaning from the face mask used by actors to portray assumed characters—also secures meaning from the actor's voice: "through sound."

36. Fraser, *Hollywood History,* p. 15.

37. In this regard, my own philosophizing descriptions here enjoy no special privilege. To talk metaphorically about temporality as a "field" would not be possible or intelligible without Enlightenment philosophy. However, insofar as phenomenology was a reaction to and critique of certain tendencies of the "European sciences," it can at least be considered a mode of description that attempts to understand and redress the limitations of the latter's particular forms of "objectivism," "empiricism," "positivism," and "psychologism."

38. Staiger, "Securing the Fictional Narrative," p. 404.

39. See M. M. Bakhtin, "Forms of Time and Chronotope in the Novel," in *The

Dialogic Imagination, edited by Michael Holquist, translated by Caryl Emerson and Holquist (Austin: University of Texas Press, 1981), pp. 84–258.

40. Merleau-Ponty, *Visible and Invisible,* p. 186.

41. Ricoeur, "Narrative Time," p. 176.

42. Staiger, "Securing the Fictional Narrative," deals with the function of repetition in relation to narrative and the constitution of history by way of reference to Freud. Toward the end of her essay, she writes: "If I were to ask then, 'who needs narrative?' Freud would, I think, say, 'everyone.' The drive to narrativize the past and to secure the fictional tale as pointing to that historical real is understandable as a repetitious desire to fix, to halt and cure. It is the death instinct aligned with Eros, a signal anxiety in our time" (p. 411).

43. Summarizing Merleau-Ponty on the relation between lived temporality and historical consciousness, Gary Madison, in *The Phenomenology of Merleau-Ponty,* says: "If it can be said that *temporality* is subjectivity itself qua continuous advent of Being, it must be said that *historicity* is personal subjectivity qua reappropriation, sublimation, and reinvestment in symbols and institutions of this same upsurge of Being. What characterizes history is that it represents and is the accumulation of the transformation man effects on his existential situation; it is like the sedimentation and gathering together of man's attempts to understand himself in his carnal relation to the world and others to transform into an open and available meaning the indigenous meaning of his ... existence" (pp. 257–258).

44. Barra, ibid., makes the point that there were some epics made in the 1970s and 1980s, but most were not historical in emphasis.

45. Fredric Jameson, *The Political Unconscious: Narrative as a Socially Symbolic Act* (Ithaca: Cornell University Press, 1981).

46. Quoted in Barra, "Incredible Shrinking Epic," pp. 43–44.

47. Quoted in ibid., p. 45.

48. Staiger, "Securing the Fictional Narrative," p. 406.

49. Maeder, "Celluloid Image," pp. 34–35.

50. Barra, "Incredible Shrinking Epic," p. 42.

51. Fredric Jameson, "Postmodernism; or, the Cultural Logic of Late Capitalism," *New Left Review* 146 (July–August 1984): 53.

52. Linda Hutcheon, "Beginning to Theorize Postmodernism," *Textual Practice* 1, no. 1 (1987): 10–31; and "The Politics of Postmodernism: Parody and History," *Cultural Critique* 5 (1987): 179–207.

53. Leslie Berlowitz, Denis Donoghue, and Louis Menard, eds., *America in Theory* (New York: Oxford University Press, 1988), quoted in *Chronicle of Higher Education,* April 12, 1989, p. A-18.

54. The connection between repetition and parody emerges when we note that Elliott Abrams's assistant for Central American affairs is named William Walker. This "lattice of coincidence" (a term used by Miller in *Repo Man*) evokes a strange euphoria provoked by that sort of irrational cohesion that characterizes the Jamesonian model of postmodernism.

55. Michael S. Gant, "Filibustering Farce," *Sun* (Santa Cruz, Calif.), April 28, 1988, p. 25.

22. Children of the Light

BRUCE F. KAWIN

There are a lot of ways to play host. Many flowers provide food, comfort, and even shelter to the insects that, in exchange for the pollen they consume, carry pollen on their bodies to other flowers and thus keep the host species alive. Some plants, like some spiders, say "Come and sit in this little room which is really my belly." Dracula is the host who consumes his guest, and the parallel between him and the natural parasites is an important theme in F. W. Murnau's *Nosferatu* (1922). The question is this: What kind of host is the horror film? What does it give to the guest and what does it take? Or, to be clearer about this, what do we as audience expect it to take? Our lives, our peace, our anxiety, our afternoon, our date's self-control, our anger, our idealism? Are its threatening but beautiful figures, like Dracula's wolves, "children of the night" or of the light?

Imagine that what is coming at you is a shuffling, gruesome, unstoppable crowd of zombies; imagine that they want to eat you and that they haven't brushed their teeth since before they died. Did you make up the details of the scene you're now imagining, or borrow them from memories of George Romero's *Night of the Living Dead* (1968)? Is it safer— does it make it "all theater"—to imagine that this is a film, or does that bring the threat somehow closer and make it more frightening? In other words, does it put the horror more in the terms of your own imagination, and has your imagination begun to model itself on film? Have you accepted the horror film as an acceptable source of imagery, stuffed your attic with its particular taste in furniture? Has the part of your mind that imagines horrors adopted the perspectives and structures of the narrative horror film, and if so, is that a way of controlling the anxiety by phrasing it in terms you recognize as artificial, or is that a way of making it more frightening? And why would that make it more frightening?

Now imagine that the zombies are from Romero's film and that the film is being shown in a darkened theater. The audience is "undead," and they are enjoying the film; it makes them feel at home. They become aware of your presence. They come after you. The only light is that provided by the projector, so that the room is, in this particular case, lit by the figures of Romero's zombies. The figures closing in on you are the children of the night; the ones on the screen are the children of the light. This scene is taken, more or less, from Peter Straub's novel *Ghost Story,* a book that examines with intelligence and care the ways that horror stories—whether portrayed on film or in literature or told in serious tones around a firelit circle—can lead us into temptation and deliver us to evil. Straub presents the ghost story as a mirror in which we can find ourselves, but only if we are willing to seek what we have found there, only if we confront our desire to be lost in horror and darkness.

In a good horror story, nobody gets off easy. In a bad horror story like *The Giant Gila Monster* (Ray Kellogg, 1959) or *Friday the 13th* (Sean S. Cunningham, 1980) a lot of people get killed, but no one really cares about them; the audience's attention skips from victim to victim until it finds the survivor, the one with whom it is thrilling but safe to identify. If there turns out to be no survivor, or if the survivor is threatened again at the end of the picture, it doesn't make much difference in the basic formula. Those shock/reversal endings, modeled on the good one in *Carrie* (Brian De Palma, 1976), work only because they play off the norm, which is that there will be at least one survivor. One way to respond to this new cliché is to regard it as a cheap but fashionable negativism. Another response, which few contemporary horror films have deserved, is to entertain the possibility that this particular horror is being extended or repeated because it is deathless, that it will recur—as in the forties paradigm of the Mummy sequels or the ending of *Halloween* (John Carpenter, 1978)—and that this recurrence has some kind of point. But here we are treading on the territory of the good horror film. In any case, it is important not to be misled by the clutch of victims into thinking that a film like *Friday the 13th* deals with real pain or loss; it deals with spectacle, and is no more threatening or profound than the fifties spectacle of a downtown crowd running and screaming with a dinosaur at their heels. As Joanna Russ observed, what passes for ethics and judgment in these films can often be reduced to "Giant ants are bad/People are good." [1] Often, but not always.

A good horror film takes you down into the depths and shows you something about the landscape; it might be compared to Charon, and the horror experience to a visit to the land of the dead, with the difference that this Charon will eventually take you home, or at least drop you off at the borders of the underworld. The seeker, who is often the survivor, confronts his or her own fallibility, vulnerability, and culpability as an aspect of confronting the horror object, and either matures or dies. ("Matures" in this sense refers to the adult act of making peace with the discrepancy between self and self-image.) Both *The Turn of the Screw* and *Heart of Darkness* are straightforward literary examples of this generic imperative.

Karl Freund's *Mad Love* (1935) offers a cinematic example at its climax, where Stephen and Yvonne Orlac manage to survive only by agreeing to function in the terms in which the villain, Dr. Gogol, has cast them. Yvonne's problem is that Dr. Gogol has confused her with her image; he gets sexually excited watching her sadomasochistic performances on stage, takes a wax statue of her into his home (and plays the organ for it, imagining that his love might make it come to life, on the model of Pygmalion—though the audience is encouraged to remember the more tragic model of *The Phantom of the Opera*), and eventually attempts to control and possess her as he has controlled and possessed her image (i.e., both the statue and the image Yvonne projects, as actress, into his fantasy life). Stephen's problem is that Dr. Gogol has grafted onto his wrists the hands of a murderous knife-thrower, Rollo, and that these hands not only cannot play the piano (Stephen's forte before a railroad accident smashed his hands) but also control him, virtually forcing him to throw knives when he is angry. At the climax, Yvonne faces her statue, accidentally breaks it, and must pretend to be her statue (i.e., her image) in order to buy time and delude Dr. Gogol, whose delusion was to confuse her and her image. When Dr. Gogol decides to perfect his control of what he believes is a statue come to life and begins to strangle her while quoting poetry (Wilde's "Ballad of Reading Gaol" and Browning's "Porphyria's Lover"), Stephen and the police arrive. Stephen saves his wife by accurately throwing a knife into Dr. Gogol's back. Earlier the doctor had tried to drive Stephen mad by convincing him that he had killed his own father with a knife. That knife, which had made its way onto the police chief's desk, is the one Stephen throws into Dr. Gogol with Rollo's hands. Although it is obvious that Dr. Gogol has created the means and exact terms of his own destruction, it is less obvious but just as true that Dr. Gogol has, by those same actions, created the terms by which Yvonne and Stephen survive. They survive by accepting those aspects of themselves that reflect Dr. Gogol's influence on their lives, the ways in which the horror has changed them. It is only by becoming a knife-wielding killer that Stephen overcomes his castration crisis and is able to save his wife and himself—though he will never again become "a great pianist" (Yvonne's phrase, which she says so rapidly that it almost sounds like "penis"). It is only by becoming her image that Yvonne survives long enough to be tortured and saved for the last time. Neither of them gets off easy.

Although it might raise the specter of knee-jerk Freudian criticism to speak of a castration crisis in *Mad Love*, to notice such a crisis does not commit one to analyze it in narrowly Freudian terms. The Gestalt psychologists, under the guidance of Fritz Perls, have developed methods of exploring dream fields that appear at least as valid, in their own terms, as Freud's and that have a more natural connection with the analysis of visual structures. Social psychology, in which it is possible to speak of the lower classes as somehow "repressed," also has its relevance, and the Jungian archetypes present another framework that can be useful in sorting out recurrent figures and images in the horror film, many of which come from classical mythology for a good reason. But there is a great deal of phallic imagery in *Mad Love,* and it is fairly obvious: the pianist who cannot play, the man who has lost his hands, the man who throws only knives and pens, the man who throws his first knife at his taunting father (but does not hurt him; it is Dr. Gogol who does the killing later on). In fact, Stephen and Yvonne are setting out for a delayed honeymoon when disaster intrudes, and the implication is that they must go through a horror phase, something identified with Dr. Gogol and his "mad love," before they can settle into their marriage, which in this case is an emblem of (interrupted) sexual and social stability.

This turns out to be a relatively consistent pattern in the horror films of the twenties, thirties, and forties: a perverse or somehow unsatisfactory love triangle among the boy, the girl, and the monster; a happy coupling of the surviving couple that depends on their dealing with the monster or coming to some kind of understanding with the forces it represents (the same question is at issue in *Nosferatu,* even though the wife dies at the end); and a romantic resolution that bodes well for the society at large. ("Well" is, of course, usually defined in terms of the prevailing ideology of the culture that produces the film, but it often appears that the genre itself has a built-in ideology or at least a regularly preferred state of affairs.) Whatever relationship there is between the monster and the girl must be resolved, and this can be a matter—in the dumbest prototype—of monster steals girl, boy kills monster, girl kisses boy. In the more complex films, like *Mad Love,* John Badham's recent *Dracula* (1979), or—to pick another Freund film—*The Mummy* (1932), there is some real emotional and ethical intercourse between monster and survivor, in the course of which both are changed. Consider, for instance, the serious girl-and-werewolf relationships in George Waggner's *The Wolf Man* (1941) and John Landis's *An American Werewolf in London* (1981) or the really complex situation of the newscaster in *The Howling* (Joe Dante, 1981), who is both girl and monster and has to save/sacrifice herself.[2] In any case, this triangle is an important psychological structure, and the device of the delayed honeymoon—which carries over from *Frankenstein* (James Whale, 1931) to *The Bride of Frankenstein* (Whale, 1935), as poor Henry (Victor in the novel) only gradually gets the idea that he would do better to create life with the aid of a human female—reminds the viewer that there is something that needs to be settled before the characters can be considered healthy. Another aspect of the triangle, as in the example of Cocteau's *Beauty and the Beast* (1946), is that the boy and the monster often represent two sides of the girl's own sexual desire (i.e., of her own sexual self-image), and the implication is that she cannot choose Mr. Right without first confronting her desire for—or to be—Mr. Wrong. Essentially this is the same issue as that of Stephen Orlac's phallic crisis, because it demonstrates how the horror film functions as a mirror or series of mirrors in which aspects of the self demand to be confronted.

This confrontation is usually in the interests of the health of the protagonists, and almost any great horror film can send ripples down our understanding of the therapies of Freud, Jung, and Perls, as suggested before. In Freudian terms, it is possible to think of the horror object as an idlike force that compels attention through compulsive repetition, that often expresses itself in dream formats, complete with displacement and secondary revision (i.e., if films are like dreams, or work in similar ways with the "language" of the unconscious in a situation where the audience is as apparently passive as the dreamer, then horror films can be fruitfully compared with nightmares), and that must be unmasked if healing is to take place. In Jungian terms, the monster often plugs into our shared sense of the archetypes, and in the horror film we often indulge our nostalgia for the world of myth and magic. In a Perls framework, the monster is often a projection split off from the wholeness of the protagonist (or audience), so that health is achieved not by releasing some widely shared trauma—knee-jerk Freudianism—but by taking the projection back into oneself, in other words by deeply acknowledging the connection between the monster and the official self. A Gestalt reading of *The Wizard of Oz* (Victor Fleming, 1939), for instance, would consider how Dorothy, the dreamer, projects aspects of her personality into the figures that populate Oz, leaving the image of "Dorothy Gale from Kansas" less than whole. Part of her is the Wicked Witch and can use the ruby slippers correctly (and might even want to get rid of Toto!); part of her is the Wizard, who knows what everybody needs and knows that what they need, they already have. The Scarecrow is already smart, the Tin Woodman already sentimental, the Cowardly Lion already a parody of the military hero; thus the resolution scene, in which they come into the wholeness they unknowingly already enjoy, is an emblem of the psychological value system that underlies the film as well as of the way Dorothy dreams (and, in this dream, explains to herself the nature of her own power, a little sermon on re-owning projections that is credibly motivated by her experience of powerlessness in the prologue). In many ways this reading is just as useful as a Freudian reading of the Wicked Witch as bad mother and the Wizard as helpless or castrated father, or a Jungian reading of the

Witch and Wizard as archetypes. In many ways, the deployment of elements within the field of the artwork is the one aspect of artistic psychology most congenial to Gestalt analysis and one that might prove especially valuable in sorting out how genres are constituted. It is, in any case, extremely useful in understanding the horror love triangle, the genesis and role of the monster, and the problem of effecting a resolution between self and self-image.

Now this is only one aspect of one horror formula, and I will be advancing toward larger generalizations later, but for the moment it makes the basic point: good horror films try to be good hosts. They lead us through a structure that shows us something useful or worth understanding. Because so many of them are psychologically oriented or psychoanalyzable, what they often map out is the terrain of the unconscious, and in that connection they often deal with fantasies of brutality, sexuality, victimization, repression, and so on. (How much violence they include is irrelevant; what matters is the tone and point of that violence. In the work of Tobe Hooper, for example, I would argue that *The Texas Chainsaw Massacre* [1974], *The Funhouse* [1981], and *Poltergeist* [1983] are equally valuable films.) Because they deal with the unconscious in a larger-than-Freudian sense, they often involve some disguised journey into the Jungian territory of the land of the dead,[3] which can be thought of in terms of the lawyer's glimpses of "the other side" or "the dream time" in Peter Weir's *The Last Wave* (1977) or of the intrusion of the guardians of the dead into the bland America of the post-Freund Mummy sequels. Robin Wood, among others, has argued that repressed political and social discontent, the urge to smash the system and subvert its values, is another more or less unconscious element that the horror film temporarily liberates.[4] What science fiction films do, in contrast, is to address not the unconscious but the conscious—if not exactly the scientist in us, then certainly the part of the brain that enjoys speculating on technology, gimmicks, and the perfectible future. What bad horror films do, in contrast to both of these, is to present a spectacle for the simple purpose of causing pain in the viewer's imagination—not just scaring the hell out of us, or us into hell, but attacking and brutalizing us on a deep level. Perhaps I am making a further distinction here between a bad film and a pernicious or evil film, because a badly made horror film like *Ghost Story* (John Irvin, 1981) doesn't do much more than sadden the audience at the waste of time and talent, while a pernicious film like *Friday the 13th* or *My Bloody Valentine* (George Mihalka, 1981) fuses a bizarre and destructive connection between sexuality and bloody awful death that can be hard to shake off and teaches nothing of value, coming very close to the structures, devices, and audience appeal of the sickest and most violent pornography. Since the latter is the impression of horror films most people seem to have these days, it seems important to point out how many of the real classics of film history—*Nosferatu* and *Vampyr* (Carl Dreyer, 1932), for example—have been horror films and to sketch out what the good ones did and are still doing. I would now like to posit a distinction between horror and science fiction, in the interest of working toward a definition of horror as a genre, and go on from there to outline a pattern that is as common as that of the boy-girl-monster triangle, the remarkably consistent use of reflexive devices in the good horror film.

Stephen King has said that it is hard to imagine a more boring, profitless, and terminally academic pastime than that of discriminating between horror and science fiction.[5] It seems to me that we will never fully understand the horror film until we agree on a definition of the genre, and that the genre with which horror is most regularly confused is that of science fiction. Some people have called *The Thing (from Another World)* (directed by Christian Nyby with a good deal of input from Howard Hawks, 1951), for example, a horror film, while others list it among the greatest science fiction films ever made.[6] The difficulty—which may date back to the birth of Frankenstein's monster in a scientific laboratory—is that *The Thing* deploys elements associated with both genres; the problem is that the film will reveal different meanings and emphases according to the generic context against which it is set.

Horror is, in the first place, the older literary form, with roots in folklore, mythology, classical tragedy (e.g., *Medea* and, though this may be stretching matters, *The Bacchae*), the gothic novel, and the work of Romantics from Coleridge and Mary Shelley to Poe. Indeed, in literary terms it is fairly easy to conceptualize the difference between horror and science fiction in terms of the obvious difference between Henry James and H. G. Wells, between H. P. Lovecraft and John Campbell, Jr., or between Shirley Jackson and Arthur C. Clarke. In film, however, the lines have proved much harder to draw, and this may have something to do with the role of the BEM, or bug-eyed monster, in the pulp science fiction magazines of the thirties and forties. In most cases science fiction is cross-fertilized by imagination and scientific premise: What would happen if . . . ? What would happen if there were space travel, if cloning were practical, if time travel were voluntary and multidirectional, if there were parallel worlds, if robots could think, if a police detective could read minds, if parthenogenesis were practical? Largely because of the influence of Campbell, as editor of *Astounding,* writers were expected to back up their ifs with a reasonable amount of hard science and logical speculation. (Discussing films, Campbell said that *Destination Moon* [Irving Pichel, 1950] and *Fail-Safe* [Sidney Lumet, 1964] were good examples of science fiction, while most were "totally unrealistic fantasies"; as examples of the latter he offered *Gojira* [*Godzilla, King of the Monsters,* 1954] and *The Beast*

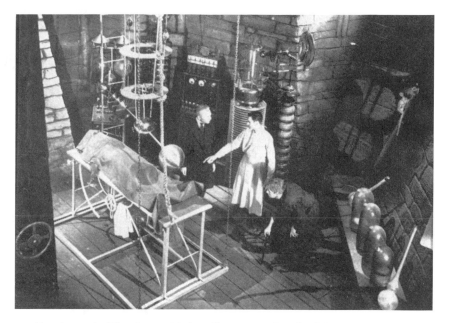

58. *Frankenstein:* The doctor (Colin Clive) at work in his lab.

from 20,000 Fathoms [Eugene Lourie, 1953].)[7] But one of the writers Campbell nurtured was A. E. Van Vogt, who perfected the tale of the space travelers who encounter the absolutely malevolent monster, and it became commonplace to refer to such pieces as science fiction, along with the horde of less original pieces in which a space voyage was hardly worth describing if it did not include some variety of extraterrestrial BEM. Science fiction provided a wide range of settings and nurturing environments for many frightening creatures, and it is out of that association of story elements that the present confusion seems to have come, particularly since the "Golden Age" pulps and the low-budget films of the fifties drew on many of the same writers and appealed to much the same audience (as the horror film of the forties shared its audience and many of its characteristic devices with the radio mystery melodrama). As a member of the fifties matinee generation and a devotee of both E. C. horror comics and the "idea literature" of the science fiction magazines, I remember going to a horror movie with the expectation of being scared—of seeing something horrible—and to a science fiction movie with the expectation of having my imagination stretched to include new possibilities, of seeing something interesting that I had probably never thought of. Spaceships

59. *Alien:* More horror than science fiction film.

meant travel to the stars; monsters meant trouble. After a while, when the market became dominated by BEM movies and hard-core science fiction purists had to wait out the hiatus between *Destination Moon* and *2001: A Space Odyssey* (Stanley Kubrick, 1968), I recall that we came to call any speculative fantasy "science fiction," while "horror films" were what the local stations played after 11:30 on Friday evenings and after the cartoons on Saturday mornings. It is probably true to say that the fifties were a decade of transition in which both genres borrowed each other's terms —*Forbidden Planet* (Fred McLeod Wilcox, 1956) is a good example of a meld—but since the genres diverged later and since it is still clear that *Friday the 13th* is not science fiction and *Close Encounters of the Third Kind* (Steven Spielberg, 1977) not horror, it seems evident that the genres remained ultimately intact and capable of definition.

Genres are determined not just by plot elements but also by *attitudes* toward plot elements. (In a recent article,[8] Rick Altman posited a very useful integration of "semantic" and "syntactic" genre strategies, taking account both of a genre's recurring terms or semantic units—e.g., horses in westerns—and the recurring ways in which those elements are deployed and interrelated—e.g., that in many westerns there is a conflict be-

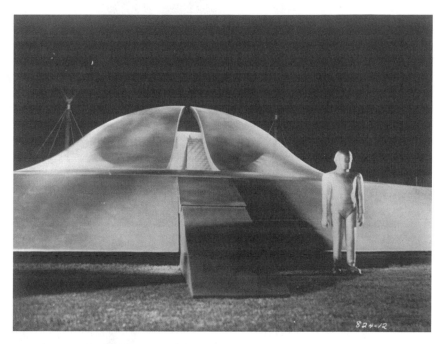

60. *The Day the Earth Stood Still:* An extraterrestrial of science fiction, not horror.

tween the semantic elements of "garden" and "desert." My use of the term "attitude" is more value-laden than his "syntactic" construct and perhaps less useful, but it is in the syntactic area that the value structures I address are generated, and we agree that the presence of certain semantic elements is inadequate to define a genre.) It not only impoverishes one's sense of these films, but also is simply inaccurate to say that "it's a horror film if it has a monster in it, a science fiction film if it has a scientist," or "it's a horror film if the monster is humanoid or an aspect of human psychology, and science fiction if the monster is a machine or the product of a machine." *Frankenstein,* for example, fits *all* of these descriptions, and so does *Alien* (Ridley Scott, 1979)—and as far as I can tell, they both are horror films even if they use elements that regularly crop up in science fiction, even if science fiction writers venerate the novel *Frankenstein,* and even if *Alien* closely follows the Van Vogt formula.

To unscramble some of this, I wrote an article for *Dreamworks* in which I suggested that *The Day the Earth Stood Still* (Robert Wise, 1951) was clearly a science fiction film while *The Thing* was clearly a horror film, although both had essentially the same plot elements—encounters between the intelligent pilots of flying saucers and a complex of military, scientific, and civilian personnel—and both were produced under similar conditions, in 1951 in American studios during the cold war. Taken together, *The Day the Earth Stood Still* and *The Thing* seemed an ideal test case:

> *The Day the Earth Stood Still* . . . is the story of a spaceman, Klaatu (Michael Rennie), who sets down his flying saucer in Washington, D.C., with the intention of putting Earth on notice: anything resembling nuclear violence will be punished by the obliteration of the planet, courtesy of a race of interstellar robot police. The spaceman has three forces to contend with: the army, which wants to destroy him; the scientists, who are willing to listen to him; and a woman (Patricia Neal) who understands and helps him. The central scientist (Sam Jaffe) is a kooky but open-minded and serious figure. Although it is suggested that earthlings understand violence better than most kinds of communication, they do respond to a nonviolent demonstration of Klaatu's power, and he does manage to deliver his message—perhaps at the expense of his life. The film's bias is in favor of open-minded communication, personal integrity, nonviolence, science, and friendship. The major villain (Hugh Marlowe) is a man who values personal fame and power more than integrity and love; he is willing to turn Klaatu over to the army, which shoots first and asks questions later—even if it means losing Neal, his fiancée.

> *The Thing (from Another World)* . . . is the story of a team of military men sent to an arctic station at the request of its scientists, to investigate what turns out to be the crash of a flying saucer. The saucer's pilot (James Arness) is a bloodsucking vegetable that is described as intelligent but spends most of its time yelling and killing and leaving evidence of plans for conquest. The minor villain is a scientist (Robert Corthwaite) who wants to communicate with the Thing rather than destroy it and who admires the alien race for its lack of sexual emotion. The Thing, however, has no interest in the scientist, and the human community (from which the scientist wishes to exclude himself), led by an efficient, hard-headed, and sexually active Captain (Kenneth Tobey), manages to electrocute the "super carrot." The film's bias is in favor of that friendly, witty, sexy, and professionally effective—Hawksian—human community, and opposed to the dark forces that lurk outside (the Thing as *Beowulf*'s Grendel). The film also relates the lack of a balanced professionalism (the scientist who becomes indifferent to the human community and whose professionalism approaches the fanatical, as opposed to the effective Captain and the klutzy but less seriously flawed reporter) to what was meant in that paranoid time by the term communism (we are all one big vegetable or zombie with each cell equally conscious).

This is how the oppositions between these two movies stack up:

1. *Army vs. scientists.* In both films the army and the scientists are in conflict with each other. The army sees the alien as a threatening invader to be defended against and, if necessary or possible, destroyed. The scientists see

the alien as a visitor with superior knowledge, to be learned from and, if possible, joined. In *The Thing* the army is right, and the scientist is an obsessive visionary who gets in the way of what obviously needs to be done. In *The Day* the scientists are right, and the army is an impulsive force that is almost responsible for the end of the world (hardly a far-fetched perspective).

2. *Violence vs. intelligence.* The Thing is nonverbal and destructive; Klaatu is articulate and would prefer to be nonviolent. The army, which meets violence with violence, is correct in *The Thing* and wrong in *The Day* because of the nature of the alien; but what I am suggesting here is that the alien has its nature because of each genre's implicit attitude toward the unknown. The curious scientist is a positive force in *The Day* and a negative force in *The Thing*, for the same reasons.

3. *Closing vs. opening.* Both horror and science fiction open our sense of the possible (mummies can live, men can turn into wolves, Martians can visit), especially in terms of community (the Creature walks among us). Most horror films are oriented toward the restoration of the status quo rather than toward any permanent opening. *The Day* is about man's opportunity to join an interstellar political system; it opens the community's boundaries and leaves them open. *The Thing* is about the expulsion of an intruder and ends with a warning to "watch the skies" in case more monsters show up; in other words, the community is opened against its will and attempts to reclose. What the horrified community has generally learned from the opening is to be on guard and that chaos can be repressed.

4. *Inhuman vs. human.* Science fiction is open to the potential value of the inhuman: one can learn from it, take a trip with it (*Close Encounters*), include it in a larger sense of what is. Horror is fascinated by transmutations between human and inhuman (wolfmen, etc.), but the inhuman characteristics decisively mandate destruction. This can be rephrased as Uncivilized vs. Civilized or as Id vs. Superego, suggesting the way a horror film allows forbidden desire to find masked expression before it is destroyed by more decisive repression. . . .

5. *Communication vs. silence.* This links most of the above. The Thing doesn't talk; Klaatu does. (Or: Romero's Living Dead are completely nonverbal, while the climax of *Close Encounters* is an exchange of languages.) What one can talk with, one can generally deal with. Communication between species is vital in *The Day*, absurd in *The Thing*. The opened community can be curious about and learn from the outsiders, while the closed community talks only among itself. Horror emphasizes the dread of knowing, the danger of curiosity, while science fiction emphasizes the danger and irresponsibility of the closed mind. Science fiction appeals to consciousness, horror to the unconscious.[9]

Horror and science fiction, then, are different because of their attitudes toward curiosity and the openness of systems, and comparable in that both tend to organize themselves around some confrontation between an unknown and a would-be knower. Where a given film includes scientists,

space travel, *and* monsters—as in *This Island Earth* (Joseph M. Newman, 1955), for instance—the important thing is to discover the dynamics of the situation, the attitude toward the question of discovery; in the
case of *This Island Earth,* such an investigation would, I think, lead to its
being identified as science fiction. In *The Fly* (Kurt Neumann, 1958), as
in *Frankenstein,* the vital elements are that the scientist and his creation
are intimately interrelated and that the white-headed fly is destroyed
rather than saved. When a scientist agrees that "there are things man is
not meant to know," it is a safe bet that one is in the realm of horror
rather than that of science. In *Forbidden Planet,* which might at first appear a nearly perfect example of genre crossover, the Krel science, the
brain booster, Robbie the Robot, and the notion of humans traveling in
a flying saucer all seem to outweigh, as genre-definitive elements, the
"monster from the id" that the father/scientist unleashes in the absence of
conscious control and that would, on its own, fit perfectly into the repertoire of the horror film. The moral of the story of the Krel monster and
the subsequent decision to destroy its planet fit explicitly into a horror
world view, but it seems important that the robot (as one aspect of Krel
science, yet built by a human) is integrated into the human crew and that
the human race is presented as being on a positive evolutionary course. It
is also significant that the scientist, by becoming conscious of his ac-
countability for the actions of his unconscious, denies the Krel monster
and releases himself and his daughter from their Oedipal nightmare. (He
cannot deny the monster without first accepting that it is *his* monster.) Ultimately *Forbidden Planet* is a "myth of human adaptability," [10] a phrase
Joanna Russ has used to characterize science fiction in contrast to fantasy
and one that is substantially in agreement with my notion of the perfectible, open community.

   Alien, on the other hand, is emphatically a horror film, if for no other
reason than because the scientist (who may well have been modeled on
the scientist played by Robert Corthwaite in *The Thing*) is a soulless robot rather than an authentic visionary and because the humans are presented as trapped between an efficient monster and a monstrously efficient military-industrial complex. The computer in *Alien,* who is called
"Mother," is addressed as "You bitch!" when she supports the company,
protects the robot, and takes her self-destruct program a bit too far; the
monster is the "son" of the "bitch." The threat behind all of these is an
organization that values military efficiency and heartless strength more
than human life and love, and in comparison with the power of that theme,
the space travel setting does not have much weight. In Robert Wise's *Star
Trek* (1979), on the other hand—which is set, like *Alien,* primarily on a
threatened spaceship—the relations between human love and curiosity
on the one hand and advanced computer technology on the other are in-

tegrated in a positive way. What begins as a story of a threat from outer space turns into a love story in which a sexual and romantic apotheosis creates a new order of being. Although most people seem to dislike Wise's film, particularly in comparison with its excellent sequels, all three *Star Treks* (like the TV series) are similar in their emphasis on humanistic values, the importance of friendship, the excitement of discovery, the mysteries opened by science, and of course the nastiness of the bad guys, whether they be Klingons or Earth-bound bureaucrats. Like *The Day the Earth Stood Still, La Jetée* (Chris Marker, 1963), and *2001*, the *Star Trek* films are useful examples of pure as well as great science fiction.

It may seem at this point as if I were arguing that science fiction is the more positive and healthful genre, but what I am really getting at is that science fiction and horror each promote growth in different ways. By appealing to the conscious, to the spirit of adventure, to the imaginative province of the medieval romance, and to the creative use of intelligent curiosity, science fiction allows us to explore our evolution and to begin the creation of the future, something it accomplishes both in cautionary tales of the dangers of technology and in adventurous celebrations of human capacity and resourcefulness. It opens the field of inquiry, the range of possible subjects, and leaves us open.

Where much science fiction is limited is in its sometimes boyish sense of adventure, its tendency to extend into some hypothetical time and place the unexamined assumptions of the present culture (e.g., the patriarchy), and its relative lack of interest in the unconscious. Where science fiction stands or falls is often in the *idea* that supports the fiction and in how far the tale is willing to follow that idea. What *The Day the Earth Stood Still* shares with Harry Bates's "Farewell to the Master" (the story on which it is based) is the idea that once human beings have passed a certain evolutionary level, it is technology that masters them; both story and movie, each in its own way, pursue this idea to logical conclusions. In the standard science fiction world of the story, which is organized around one geewhiz daring boyish reporter, the emphasis is on the robot's invention of a device that recreates beings from sound recordings and the startling discovery that Klaatu is the beloved pet of the robot, who is "the monster." In the cold-war world of the movie, which has a much more interesting human story, the relevance of this conceit is made explicit in terms of the way people are forced to learn that they must submit to the authority of the robots because they have—without knowing it—already become the servants of nuclear technology. By this ingenious twist, the Wise film offers human beings the option of mastering the atomic bomb while it extends the essence of the story's original, chilling idea. And the same often applies to horror, because what distinguishes fictions like *Frankenstein,* Matheson's *I Am Legend,* and King's *Salem's Lot* or films like *Don't Look Now* (Nicolas Roeg, 1973), *Dawn of the Dead* (George Romero, 1979), or *The Last Wave* is their pushing good ideas as far as possible.

What *The Thing* does not share with the story on which it is based (Campbell's "Who Goes There?") is an interesting idea. Even if both story and movie, in this case, explore the problem of the human community undermined by the presence of a monster, the monster in *The Thing* is fundamentally not interesting, merely a loud hulk, whereas the monster in "Who Goes There?" is a shape-shifter capable of ingesting and imitating every man and animal in the environment, a monster that threatens the notions of trust and community so seriously that Hawks and Nyby apparently felt unable to handle it (though they could well have been stopped by the problem of finding adequate special effects), with the result that they produced a movie more Hawksian than it is anything else, and as much a comedy as it is a thriller, about witty people with a less complex but still dirty job to do. It would, I think, have been a more interesting and frightening movie if the idea of Campbell's monster had been followed to its logical conclusion, as John Carpenter's remake (1982) would have been better if it had projected a more viable and engaging vision of the isolated human community.

The really scary films turn out to be those organized around a good idea, and while that may not be a scientific premise, it is often a well-struck nerve, a resonant psychological intersection, as is the case in fictions like *Heart of Darkness, The Turn of the Screw,* and *Frankenstein* and films like *The Wolf Man* (George Waggner, 1941), *Mad Love,* and *Peeping Tom* (Michael Powell, 1960). In a case like *Night of the Living Dead,* for example, the *premise* that the dead could rise and would want to eat the living is what I find scary; Romero's ghoulish imagery dramatizes that premise and would not have, on its own, the same force—a lesson that the slasher films will eventually learn.

The direction in which the horror film leads its audience—into the unconscious and through the implications of evil and of dream—can prove beneficial to the audience, and here we return to the problem of the good host. What the best horror films offer is another image of human perfectibility, and not always through the exclusion of the unconscious impulse or the lower classes (since, after all, to go to a horror film is to let the inner monster, whether psychological or social, find expression, no matter what happens at the end of the film). Sometimes what these movies offer is integration with the horror, as in the example of *Mad Love,* or reconciliation with what is valuable in the horror, as in *The Bride of Frankenstein,* or personal growth in a tragic context, as in *The Howling.* The effect of the good horror film is to show us what we are not comfortable seeing but may need to look at anyway. As a strategic aspect of its programmatic project—its intention to show us what we are comfortable ig-noring—the horror film often turns reflexive, reminding us that we are watching a movie, that we have chosen to have this nightmare experience, and that we must take responsibility for submitting to a category of illu-sion. This is, in a nutshell, the difference between *Psycho* (Alfred Hitch-cock, 1960), which implicates the audience in the voyeurism of the mad killer, and almost every mad slasher movie that pretends to pay hom-age to *Psycho* but has no interest in raising the consciousness of the au-dience and concentrates on techniques that reinforce illusion and defeat self-examination.

The first thing that happens in *Mad Love*, for instance, is that a fist smashes the glass on which the credits have been painted. This is followed by a brilliant series of image/reality fake-outs of which the most subtle is the use of Frances Drake (who plays the real Yvonne) in close shots of Yvonne's statue, which forces the audience to compare the image of Drake as Yvonne, which is supposed to be "real," and the image of Drake as the statue of Yvonne, which is supposed to be an "image"—the sort of joke that Keaton exploited so well at the end of *Sherlock Jr.* (Buster Keaton, 1924). Under the pressure of conflicting desires, Gogol's identity frag-ments into a series of mirrored self-images. For a while Gogol is the vic-tim of illusions as well as a cheerfully ruthless creator of delusions in the mind of his patient, but at the climax he is entirely unable to distinguish image from reality, which is the central feature of his madness and the twist that makes his obsessiveness interesting. But of course the point of the opening fake-outs and a number of closely related tropes throughout the film is that the audience of *Mad Love* regularly confuses image and re-ality and is, to the extent that it responds to the story and believes its il-lusions, nearly mad—and all of that is tied securely, via a series of verbal and visual allusions, to *The Cabinet of Dr. Caligari* (Robert Wiene, 1919) and its theme of the unreliability of surface impressions and the danger of a controlling illusion, whose political implications were certainly not lost on Karl Freund. (The allusion to *Dr. Caligari* is one of many; *Mad Love* anchors itself firmly in the history of the genre, making particularly good use of *The Phantom of the Opera* and—outside the genre—*The Last Laugh* [F. W. Murnau, 1924], which Freund of course photographed.)

To take a more familiar example of flagrant reflexivity in the horror film, the first line in *King Kong* (1933) is "Is this the moving picture ship?" And the finest irony in the film is that Denham starts out to make a movie, decides instead to bring the monster home (i.e., creates not film but the-ater), and is reproached by the audience—while the curtains are still closed—because they have expected to see a movie, to really "see some-thing." For *King Kong*'s audience to smile knowingly at this remark—Lady, are you going to see something, and it's not a movie, it's real!—is

61. *King Kong:* The giant gorilla is the live attraction instead of a movie.

to be brought suddenly up against the fact that *King Kong*'s audience is seeing a movie and that all this is not real. This elegant twist is supported by a labyrinth of authorially self-conscious in-jokes whereby the principal screenwriter, Ruth Rose, and her husband, Ernest B. Schoedsack, together with Merian C. Cooper, set up Ann Darrow, Jack Driscoll, and Carl Denham, respectively, as their surrogates, who are attempting to make a movie that will satisfy those who feel that adventure films ought to have a love interest—which is precisely what the filmmakers, irritated at the reception of *Chang* (1927) and *Rango* (1930), were doing in *King Kong*—all of that complicated by the fact that Rose and Schoedsack had met and fallen in love while on an expeditionary ship whose name is very like that used in *King Kong*. The audience of 1933 would not have gotten most of these jokes, though they might have remembered *Chang* and so might have been able to see themselves in the New York audience or in the images of the producers alluded to at the start, but they would certainly have been aware of the movie/theater dichotomy that informs Denham's turnaround.

These are only two examples from the thirties, and it is possible to come up with examples from virtually any decade or industry. Even a wretched knife-and-sex picture like *He Knows You're Alone* (original title, *Blood Wedding,* Armand Mastroianni, 1980) opens with a young woman being stabbed through the back of her theater seat while unwillingly watching a movie in which a young woman is threatened by a psychopathic killer. Even *Friday the 13th* plays a lot of games with dreams and the fulfillment of dreams (games that are extended and complicated in the superior Parts 2 and 3), as does *Halloween II* (Rick Rosenthal, 1981), a film that is almost entirely organized around the implications of the song that runs under the closing credits, "Mister Sandman, bring me a dream; / Make him the cutest that I've ever seen." (And then: "Please turn on your magic beam"!) My favorite example from the forties is *The Mummy's Ghost* (Reginald LeBorg, 1944), in which not even the priest can believe that "Kharis—still *lives?*"; in which a student suggests to his obsessed professor that "maybe that was a man made up as a mummy, to fool the people"; and in which a museum guard ignores an accurate preview of his own death that presents itself as a silly radio mystery. There was less of this sort of thing in the fifties, which was a bad period for self-consciousness in the first place and one in which Hollywood was particularly interested in selling illusions, but there were some reflexive elements in *House of Wax* (André de Toth, 1953), *The 5,000 Fingers of Dr. T.* (Roy Rowland, 1953), *The House on Haunted Hill* (William Castle, 1958), *The Tingler* (Castle, 1959), and *Invasion of the Body Snatchers* (Don Siegel, 1956), and it is arguable that the shift into more overt and problematic reflexivity that was announced in the great British film *Peeping Tom* and its American contemporary *Psycho* was the core of the shift into the sixties themselves. *Psycho,* of course, did not come out of nowhere, and in terms of the argument I am advancing here, it is not difficult to read *Vertigo* (Hitchcock, 1958) and to a lesser extent *Rear Window* (Hitchcock, 1954) as working with horror-film material in the genre format of the mystery; all three of these films are centrally concerned with the problem of the image and its relation to the real world, each of which is presented as a category of obsession, and in *Vertigo* and *Psycho* the figure who insists on living his dream is perceived as a destructive but fascinating force. It is these films, with Powell's *Peeping Tom,* that most prefigure the labyrinthine reflexivity of such sixties horror films as *Targets* (Peter Bogdanovich, 1968) and *Kwaidan* (Masaki Kobayashi, 1965). The seventies and early eighties have already been discussed at some length, so I would like to close with two particularly arresting reflexive images, one from Dreyer's *Vampyr* and one from De Palma's *Blow Out* (1981).

It is not necessary for a horror film to have a transcendental or even a dream element. There are horror stories that are not ghost stories and horror stories that are not psychologically oriented. There are, very

62. *Vampyr:* David Gray (Julian West) in the coffin.

broadly, three subcategories of the genre: monster stories, supernatural stories, and psychosis stories.[11] Often they overlap. The present knife-and-sex cycle is an unfortunate but apt example of the psychosis story; more fortunate examples include *Dr. Caligari, Mad Love, Peeping Tom,* and *Repulsion* (Roman Polanski, 1965). *King Kong* is a straightforward monster story, as is *Them!* (Gordon Douglas, 1954), while *Vampyr,* like *Dracula* (Tod Browning, 1931), *The Wolf Man,* and *The Mummy,* is a monster story with strong supernatural elements. *The Last Wave* is supernatural but has no monsters. The means by and ends to which consciousness is raised in the horror film depend to a certain extent on which of these subcategories is involved, and in *Vampyr* the notion of the film as dream is inseparable from its view of the night world haunted by supernatural agencies. *Vampyr* is about light and shadows, about categories of illusion and revelation, and its climax comes when the central protagonist, David Gray, gives up some of his blood and has two dreams, the first of which is an accurate warning of a forced suicide attempt and the second of which presents him to himself as trapped—dead yet sentient—in a coffin whose window first is compared to and then actually becomes the rectangle of the movie screen; this suggests to the audience that it is entombed in a dark room whose window is the image, and that the whole film is a dream or image field whole limits and dangers are only now becoming clear. In a paradoxical way, this makes the horrors real as it makes the film accountable for presenting an illusion. At the very least it makes the audience conscious of submitting to a dream field, a willing suspension of belief that results, as I have argued elsewhere,[12] in an all the more compelling trap of belief, because there is no innocent way to dismiss the artwork as an illusion once it has presented itself as being aware of being an illusion.

Blow Out, which starts as a psychosis story and turns quickly into a paranoia film[13] about the evils of Watergate, is not interested in metaphysics and has little to say about dreams or shadows, but it is much more clearly focused on the ethics of self-consciousness than either of the films on which it is modeled (*Blow-Up* [Michelangelo Antonioni, 1966] and *The Conversation* [Francis Ford Coppola, 1974]) and is in its own way as serious about the problem of knowledge and illusion as *Vertigo* or *Vampyr.* It opens with a terrible sequence from a bad horror film about a slasher in a girl's dormitory; it turns out that the protagonist of *Blow Out* is a sound engineer who needs a good scream to complete this sequence, which, we discover, he is helping to edit. Eventually he becomes involved in a complicated murder-and-politics story, falls in love with a prostitute who is entangled in that intrigue, wires her for sound so that he can save her life and capture the bad guy, and loses his entire library of sound effects when the bad guy invades his territory with a bulk eraser. What happens is that he is too late to save the woman; all he has left of her is the tape of her dying screams. In the final seconds of the film, we see the protagonist again editing the bad horror film; we realize that he has not told the authorities what he knows, because he knows that would change nothing. Then comes the moment when the girl in the bad film screams, and we recognize the scream as that of the dying prostitute. In that moment *Blow Out* becomes a real horror film, setting itself in relation to and judging the category of illusion represented by the dumb slasher movie, absolutely scaring the hell out of the audience while shifting reality gears and tackling the whole problem of action and guilt in contemporary America. This is an America disillusioned from its idealism, and therefore not realistic but helpless, and so prey to the illusion of escapism— whereas the rest of the point is of course that there is no escape from politics any more than there is a way to forget who is screaming and under what circumstances. It becomes a horror film that by critiquing its own level of illusion addresses the reality of horror—as in all great horror films, its terrible message and unpleasant imagery are meant not to destroy us but to show us something that we need to see.

Not just in film but throughout our experience of the world, vision is both an opportunity and a problem. To the extent that the world or the imagination is a darkened theater, the shadow images created by the integrated forces of projected light and masking/filtering silver—a silver that, for once, allows vampires to cast a reflection—are the children of the light. The horror film creates an opportunity for vision even as it dramatizes its dialectical partner—utter darkness, the refusal to see clearly. For even as its threatening figures advance toward the audience out of the night, the "music they make" is still the music of light, and while the image of human perfectibility that they generate may seem to have chosen odd, often monstrous terms for its expression, it is still the exploration of the human condition and the burden of knowledge to which they are dedicated. We are still on the outskirts of Eden, expelled from an easy paradise because we wanted to know the "things man is not meant to know," a knowledge that could make us like gods. Although both horror and science fiction, as genres, are dubious about the value of the apple, they are dubious in different ways. Science fiction has its challenging apple full of challenging possibilities, and horror has its dangerous apple full of destructive potential; the difference between these attitudes is the difference between the last line of The Thing—"Keep watching the skies!"—and the last line of Brainstorm (Douglas Trumbull, 1983)—"Look at the stars!" In both cases the apple will be bitten, and whether it introduces us to the world of the undead (as it did Snow White) or gives us an idea for an entirely new kind of pie, that bite will still prove nourishing.

Notes

1. Joanna Russ, "What Can a Heroine Do? or Why Women Can't Write," in Images of Women in Fiction: Feminist Perspectives, edited by Susan Koppelman Cornillon (Bowling Green, Ohio: Popular Press, 1972), p. 18. A similar observation was made by Susan Sontag in her widely reprinted essay, "The Imagination of Disaster," which first appeared in Sontag, Against Interpretation (New York: Delta, 1966), pp. 209–225, but Russ's is the better article.

2. For an extensive discussion of reflexive devices and their carefully manipulated moral implications, see Bruce Kawin, "The Funhouse and The Howling," Film Quarterly 35, no. 1 (Fall 1981): 30–32.

3. Bruce Kawin, "The Mummy's Pool," Dreamworks 1, no. 4 (Summer 1981): 291–301; reprinted in Planks of Reason: Essays on the Horror Film, edited by Barry K. Grant (Metuchen, N.J.: Scarecrow Press, 1984), pp. 3–20, and Film Theory and Criticism, 3d ed., edited by Gerald Mast and Marshall Cohen (New York: Oxford, 1985), pp. 466–481.

4. "An Introduction to the American Horror Film," in The American Nightmare, edited by Robin Wood and Richard Lippe (Toronto: Festival of Festivals, 1979), pp. 7–28; reprinted in Planks of Reason, ed. Grant, pp. 164–200.

5. Stephen King, Danse Macabre (New York: Everest House, 1981), pp. 15–17, 29–30. I think, however, that even King would be irritated if someone called Pet Sematary "science fiction."

6. See *Focus on the Horror Film,* edited by Roy Huss and T. J. Ross (Englewood Cliffs, N.J.: Prentice-Hall, 1972), p. 129, and *Focus on the Science Fiction Film,* edited by William Johnson (Englewood Cliffs, N.J.: Prentice-Hall, 1972), pp. 69, 154–156.

7. *Focus on the Science Fiction Film,* pp. 153–154.

8. Rick Altman, "A Semantic/Syntactic Approach to Film Genre," *Cinema Journal 23,* no. 3 (Spring 1984): 6–18; reprinted in this volume.

9. Kawin, "The Mummy's Pool," pp. 293–294. A point I have not had time to make here is that "Who Goes There?"—with its careful emphasis on scientifically explaining the horror—is science fiction.

10. Russ, "What Can a Heroine Do?" p. 18. See also Russ, "The Image of Women in Science Fiction," pp. 79–94. These are two of the finest essays on the subject, and I am clearly indebted to them both.

11. Huss and Ross arrived at a similar breakdown of subcategories: gothic horror, monster terror, and psychological thriller. See *Focus on the Horror Film,* pp. 1–10.

12. Bruce Kawin, *The Mind of the Novel: Reflexive Fiction and the Ineffable* (Princeton: Princeton University Press, 1982).

13. For the term "paranoia film," see Bruce Kawin, "Me Tarzan, You Junk: Violence, Sexism, and Moral Education in the Paranoia Film," *Take One 6,* no. 4 (March 1978): 29–33.

23. Monsters from the Id

MARGARET TARRATT

Few things reveal so sharply as science fiction the wishes, hopes, fears, inner stresses and tensions of an era, or define its limitations with such exactness.[1]

Most writers in English on science fiction films view them as reflections of society's anxiety about its increasing technological prowess and its responsibility to control the gigantic forces of destruction it possesses. Francis Arnold, for instance, was typical in relating the upsurge of science fiction films in the 1950s and 1960s to the existence of the Bomb and the first Sputnik.[2] It has long been a critical commonplace to deplore the introduction of the "love interest" into science fiction films. Richard Hodgens, while praising *War of the Worlds* (Byron Haskin, 1953), complained that "one unnecessary modern addition . . . was an irrelevant boy and girl theme, because [George] Pal apologized 'Audiences want it.'"[3] Penelope Houston refers cynically to "the inevitable girl" in such films.[4] The plot synopsis of *20 Million Miles to Earth* (Nathan Juran, 1957) in the *Monthly Film Bulletin*[5] omits the hero's romance, and this is no isolated example. Yet the "love interest" in science fiction films, far from being extraneous to the central concern of the works, usually forms an integral part of their structure, as certain French critics have recognized.

F. Hoda dwells with interest on the "camouflaged sensuality" of the genre,[6] pointing out that many of the situations in films of this kind could be reduced to representations of aggressive sexuality, disguised to a greater or lesser degree. Jean Loth suggested that film monsters should be regarded as embodiments of women's virginal sexual fantasies—a cross between fear and desire.[7] Raymond Lefèvre noticed the masking of sadism and eroticism by fantastic decor and poetic effects,[8] while Fereydoun Hoveyda suggested that the importance of the science fiction film lay in its tentative breakdown of certain limitations concerning the representation on the screen of love and hate and of human relationships.[9] None of these writers, however, gives any detailed illustration in support of their theses. The fullest analysis along these lines so far is in Tom Milne's study of Mamoulian's *Dr. Jekyll and Mr. Hyde* (1931),[10] but this film is not examined in a science fiction context.

Although the majority of science fiction films appear to express some kind of concern with the moral state of contemporary society, many are more directly involved with an examination of our inner nature. Curt Siodmak maintained:

> In its day, *Frankenstein,* the forerunner of a generation of admitted mumbo jumbo and lots of entertainment, was a true trail blazer, and in effect opened up Hollywood-produced motion pictures to both psychiatry and neuro-surgery. What now seems primitive in *Metropolis* or the Jekyll-Hydean cycle of werewolf pictures are simply variations on the theme which Siegfried Kra-cauer in *From Caligari to Hitler* characterised as a "deep and fearful concern with the foundations of the self." [11]

This article will argue that these films are deeply involved with the concepts of Freudian psychoanalysis and seem in many cases to derive their structure from it. They may deal with society as a whole, but they arrive at social comment through a dramatization of the individual's anxiety about his or her own repressed sexual desires, which are incompatible with the morals of civilized life. Freud described this process in "Anxiety and Instinctual Life" thus: "The commonest cause of anxiety neurosis is unconsummated excitation. Libidinal excitation is aroused but not satisfied, not employed; apprehensiveness then appears instead of this libido that has been directed from its employment . . . What is responsible for anxiety in hysteria and other neurosis is the process of repression." [12]

The battles with sinister monsters or extraterrestrial forces are an externalization of the civilized person's conflict with his or her primitive subconscious or id. Freud writes of the id in the following manner:

> We approach the Id with analogies; we call it a chaos, a cauldron full of seething excitations . . . It is filled with energy reaching it from the instincts, but it has no organization, produces no collective will, but only a striving to bring about the satisfaction of the instinctual needs subject to the observance of the pleasure principle . . . Contrary impulses exist side by side, without cancelling each other out or diminishing each other . . . No alteration in its mental processes is produced by the passage of time. Wishful impulses which have never passed beyond the id, but impressions, too, which have been sunk into the id by repression are virtually immortal; after the passage of decades they behave as if they had just occurred. They can only be recognized as belonging to the past, can only lose their importance and be deprived of their cathexis of energy when they have been made conscious by the work of analysis . . . The id, of course, knows no judgments of value; no good and evil; no morality. . . . Instinctive cathexes seeking discharge—that, in our view, is all there is in the id. [13]

Forbidden Planet (Fred McLeod Wilcox, 1956) provides an explicit, if somewhat crude, example of the id in action. The events take place several centuries in the future, when human beings have penetrated what is significantly termed "inner" as opposed to "outer" space. A party is sent

63. *Forbidden Planet:* The innocent siren Altaira (Anne Francis) and Robby the Robot.

to discover what has happened to a group who had attempted to colonize the planet Altair 420 years before. As they try to land, they are warned off by Captain Morbius (Walter Pidgeon), leader of the original expedition, who claims he is the only survivor, needs no help, and cannot be held responsible for the consequences of their landing. They are entertained by Morbius, who lives in the height of automated luxury. Unexpectedly, his daughter Altaira (Ann Francis), appears in the room, an innocent, briefly clad siren whom Morbius had been trying to keep away from the men. She shows considerable admiration for the clean-limbed heroic spacemen, who become rivals for her affection until Commander Adams (Leslie Nielsen) wins. When he kisses her, her pet tiger, which had hitherto been harmless when in her presence, no longer recognizes her and advances, snarling, until the captain is forced to shoot it. Meanwhile, in the spaceship at night a curiously sexual, heavy panting noise is heard, the ship is smashed up, and one of the men is later found torn to bits. Eventually they see and fight the monster, a leaping tigerish shape outlined in electrical sparks. Morbius, talking to the captain, explains that the planet was

64. The monster from the id appears in electrical sparks (*Forbidden Planet*).

originally the domain of the Krel, a humane and hyperintelligent species whose scientific discoveries he is able to make use of with the help of a patent brain booster. They became extinct at a time when they were on the threshold of dispensing with their physical bodies. The captain, finding the monster is immune to all weapons, decides to have a brain boost himself in order to work out a strategy against it. Returning to Morbius's house with his scientist colleague (whose IQ is considerably higher than his own), he persuades the doctor's daughter to marry him and leave with him for Earth. Dr. Morbius opposes this plan violently, declaring that he and his daughter are "joined, body and soul." Meanwhile the captain's companion, who had sneaked off to get a brain boost himself, returns to die, gasping with his last breath: "The monster is from the id."

"The id—what's that?" asks the captain. "An obsolete term once used to describe the elementary structure of the subconscious," replies Morbius. The captain, with commendable celerity, now grasps the root of the problem. The Krel, in the passion for scientific advancement, had ignored the "mindless beast" of their own subconscious, which had ultimately destroyed them. "That thing out there is you!" he accuses the doctor, indicating the monster which is once more advancing; "We are all part monsters in our subconscious—that's why we have laws and religion. You sent your secret id out, a primitive, more enraged and inflamed with each frustration. You still have the mind of a primitive." The doctor was destroying the spacemen who threaten his relationship with his daughter. In despair, Morbius recognizes the truth, turns off the electric current which animates the monster of his id and significantly addresses the captain as "Son." The word *incest* is never mentioned, but his suppressed incestuous desires are clearly implied to be at the root of all the trouble.

Forbidden Planet has aspects in common with many science fiction films. Space travel is commonly accompanied by publicly recognized sexual frustration among the all-male crew. The scientist with his total dedication to advanced knowledge is an unbalanced figure, ruthless in defense of his own research. The hero is an ordinary man with a healthy physique, leadership qualities, a controlled sexual drive, and only average intellect—a good all-rounder.

As Kingsley Amis pointed out,[14] this film has strong structural and thematic connections with Shakespeare's *Tempest*—especially in its distrust of advanced science and its influence on human beings. In *Forbidden Planet* science has advanced to a point at which it becomes the equivalent of Prospero's occult study. Morbius has entered the realm of "forbidden knowledge," both sexually and intellectually, a realm both enticing and fearful to characters such as Baron Frankenstein or Colonel Merritt in *Conquest of Space* (Byron Haskin, 1955), who dies attempting to sabotage his sacrilegious mission.

Traditionally, the idea of forbidden knowledge has had a sexual as well as an intellectual connotation stemming from the myth of Adam and Eve. Science fiction films take up this dual interpretation. With them, we return to the problems and anxieties of the Middle Ages, when people feared to inquire too closely into the elements, thought to be inhabited by evil demons. Bacon's famous challenge to the fear of natural science, in his *Advancement of Learning,* is a challenge that seems to confront the heroes of science fiction. Freud drew a parallel between the anxieties of modern man and the "demonological neurosis" of the seventeenth century: "The states of possession correspond to our neurosis, for the explanation of which we resort to psychical powers. In our eyes the demons are bad and reprehensible wishes, derivatives of instinctual impulses that have been repudiated and repressed. We merely eliminate the projection of these mental entities into the external world, which the middle ages carried out; instead we regard them as having arisen in the patient's internal life where they have their abode."[15]

One of the classics of the science fiction genre, *The Thing (from An-*

65. Male bonding in *The Thing* (1951) . . .

other World) (Christian Nyby, 1951), provides an outstanding example of the "demonological neurosis." A group of American airmen in Alaska are called in by scientists working on secret research at the North Pole. Much emphasis is laid on the freezing conditions as well as the lack of women. A radioactive craft has landed, embedding itself in the ice.

Captain Pat Hendry, in charge of rescuing the spacecraft, is subjected to a good deal of ragging about an alleged romance with the chief scientist's secretary, Nikki (Margaret Sheridan). We learn that they have spent a disastrous evening on leave together in which Hendry got drunk and made a heavy pass at her, only to wake up and find her gone back to base. This incident has become common knowledge in the camp. Hendry, to some extent ignorant of his own drunken behavior, complains about Nikki's action and is enlightened by the indignant girl: "You had moments like an octopus—I never saw so many hands in all my life." Hendry suggests that their relationship started off on the wrong footing and asks if they can begin again. Following this is the film's best sequence, in which the men attempt to extricate the spacecraft by means of explosives, but destroy it while salvaging its occupant, who is frozen into a slab of ice. On the return journey, the Thing is not shown, but a couple of dogs in the plane whine. One of the men recalls an incident in the war when he was stranded with a bomber group: "An army nurse came ashore and caused as much disturbance as this man from Mars."

66. . . . and bondage between Nikki Nicholson (Margaret Sheridan) and Captain Patrick Hendry (Kenneth Tobey).

On their arrival back at base, Hendry resists the pressure of Dr. Carrington, who wishes to be allowed to examine the creature immediately, believing it necessary to keep it alive at all costs. The captain insists on awaiting instructions and organizes a twenty-four-hour watch to be kept. In another interlude with Nikki, she declares: "You're much nicer when you're not mad" and offers to buy him a drink. "That sounds promising," he replies, "You can tie my hands if you want." In a subsequent scene we see him "bound" to a chair, discussing men and women's relationships. "If a man tries to kiss you the first time, he is a wolf. But after 1,000 drinks and 1,000 dinners he isn't?" asks Hendry. She agrees. "Can't I be untied now?" he asks. Later she kisses him and remarks that she would not have been able to be so nice to him were he untied. Finally, when her back is turned, he loosens his bonds. Nikki: "How long have you been loose?" Hendry: "Long enough!"

Later that night, the captain is told how the man on watch is terrified by the monster's hands and eyes, and there is speculation as to whether or not it is alive. The guard covers the ice with his electric blanket so he will not see it, and the creature thaws out. Observing it free, the watchman attacks it in blind panic, and in a subsequent struggle with the airmen, it escapes into the Arctic night, leaving part of its arm and hand behind. It later grows a new one. Examining the severed arm, Dr. Carrington observes that it is entirely composed of vegetable matter and concludes that on Mars, vegetables have evolved in the same way that animals evolved on earth. He also discovers a pocket of seed pollen in the palm of the hand and marvels at the Thing's method of reproduction— "No pain, pleasure, emotions or heart. How superior!" The Thing is later found to feed off blood, but in spite of this, Carrington longs to communicate with the superior intelligence, at whatever cost to human life. Again the captain resists his pressures, stressing the need for the creature to be locked up. Later, it becomes necessary to destroy it. As it seems invulnerable to firearms they attempt to burn it with kerosene, but it escapes, leaving Hendry slightly wounded in the hand, to be ministered to by Nikki. Plans are made to electrocute the Thing. Dr. Carrington steps out to save it, urging it to communicate with them on a rational basis, but is sent flying by a violent blow from the creature's arm. Once the creature has been destroyed, the men joke: "Our worries are over, whilst our captain. . . ." Taking the hint, Hendry proposes to Nikki and she accepts. Meanwhile, the newspaper reporter radios the story he has been burning to deliver: "One of the world's greatest battles has just been fought by the human race. . . ."

The plot of this film could not meaningfully be described in less detail. A parallel is drawn between Captain Hendry and the monster, most clearly through the motif of the hand. We do not need Freud to suggest the phallic significance of this limb in dream symbolism since, in this film, the hand is explicitly established as a sexual organ. In the conflicts between the captain and Nikki, his hands are his sexual weapon, and in his use of them he becomes octopuslike or monstrous. When he is bound to his chair the purpose is to put his hands out of action. While the Thing is seen lying in its ice prison, the guards are particularly frightened by his eyes and hands and by whether or not he is alive. The scientists establish not only that his hand is his sexual organ, but that it grows again when severed—a human fantasy symbolically warding off castration. In the struggle against this monster of his id, Hendry is slightly wounded in the hand, which is tended by Nikki. He undergoes a kind of emasculation that makes him acceptable to her. The struggle against the Thing draws them closer together; by conquering the Thing he wins Nikki in marriage. His facing up to the Thing and the desires of unbridled virility that it represents is a dramatization of Freud's description of the instincts of the id being overcome when brought up into the level of consciousness through analysis. As with the demonological neurosis of the seventeenth century, the instinctual impulses are externalized and dramatized. The Thing clearly represents Hendry's repressed sexual desires, the impulses of the id. We are reminded of the parallel drawn by an airman between the arrival of a single woman in the midst of an all-male military group and the arrival of the Thing among the airmen. Like the Thing, Hendry is initially "frozen." The Arctic landscape provides an objective correlative for his emotional and sexual life, repressed in the all-male disciplined environment of an isolated base. Hendry, too, has his own accidental thaw, through drink, when on leave. His subsequent instinctual predatory behavior is as unacceptable to Nikki as that of the Thing to the airmen. His renewed courtship of Nikki is subject to a joking but rigid control of the instincts symbolized by the binding of his hands. Only in this "civilized" manner can he awaken desire in her—the repeated ritual of drinks, dinner, and restrained behavior cited by Kinsey[16] as the acceptable norm. In his courtship he must fight his surging primitive instincts, a conflict we see settled in the destruction of the Thing. The manner in which he handles the military situation created by the Thing's presence is an image of the way in which he handles himself in relation to Nikki. Unlike the scientist whose greed for knowledge leads him into questionable moral paths, Hendry fears the dangers of examining the Thing. Once it is free, he hopes to control it, to keep it alive but contained. He takes up his general's cry of "Close the door," voicing the necessity to protect human beings from the extremes of nature, whether human or climatic. The Thing is found to be incompatible with human life and must consequently be destroyed, however fascinating it may be. As in Freud's description of the id, the Thing cannot respond to human reason. Hendry's wounded hand suggests the forcible taming of his aggressive sexuality that civilized society demands. The structure of this film can only be understood in a Freudian context. A number of films, some less artistically accomplished than *The Thing,* are structured in a similar manner.

One such example can be found in Nathan Juran's *20 Million Miles to Earth* (1957), in which a U.S. rocketship returning from a flight to Venus crashes into the sea off Sicily. Its one survivor, Colonel Calder (William Hopper), is tended by a zoologist's niece, Marisa (Joan Taylor). A child finds a sealed cylindrical container and sells it to the zoologist, Dr. Leonardo, who finds a glutinous jelly inside. Out of this appears to hatch a small prehistoric type of monster with a long tail. It is extremely aggressive and found to grow at an alarming rate, and eventually escapes. Recaptured and paralyzed by electric shock, it is kept in a Rome zoo for the scientists to examine, but breaks loose again during a power failure. After a spectacular fight with an elephant it is finally killed in the Colosseum. A small circle of men stand around the corpse, regarding it with expressions of regret.

This film has a number of aspects in common with *The Thing*. At the outset, Colonel Calder and Marisa have an antagonistic relationship. Her concern is for his health, while he is obsessed with the need to safeguard his cargo. The first appearance of the creature, as it struggles to free itself from its prison of jelly, follows the goodnight wish of Dr. Leonardo to his niece: "Pleasant dreams." The monster is a clear phallic symbol with its thrashing tail, its absence of internal organs, its dramatic growth, and its reawakening to activity after it has been overpowered. Significantly, the planet it comes from is Venus, also the name of the goddess of love. We are told that the atmosphere on Venus is such that humans cannot breathe and survive in it for long. Eight of the colonel's crew died from exposure to it. The colonel wishes the creature to be kept alive so that scientists may examine it to see under what conditions life could survive on Venus. We do not have to stretch the interpretation too far to recognize this as concern as to how far the aggressive male sexual urge can be liberated in a love relationship without causing injury to the civilized way of life. The threat to civilization from man's destructive urge has been voiced at the beginning of the film with the image of an exploding atomic bomb, and this idea is kept in mind at several points in the film, especially in the Roman background with its ancient crumbling ruins and the Colosseum setting for the battle with the elephant, which remind us of the fall of the Roman Empire, popularly reputed to have sprung from an era of sexual decadence.

As in *The Thing*, battles with the monster are interspersed with increasingly romantic interludes. The more committed the colonel becomes to controlling the creature, the less antagonistic is his relationship to Marisa. She is profoundly disturbed by its appearance and is at one point attacked by it when it stretches out an arm from within its cage. Like Captain Hendry in *The Thing*, Colonel Calder is wounded in the arm—again a symbolic semi-emasculation—when he tries to master it, declaring airily: "It's just a matter of controlling the beast." Once he has been wounded, his relationship with Marisa becomes milder and more romantic. He apologizes for his aggression and looks forward to a time when they can pursue their relationship in a darkened cafe at a table with a candle burning and a bottle of wine. This is a symbolic representation of intercourse, the flame of the candle symbolizing desire rather than destruction. This is made clear in a later scene, when Marisa tells the colonel of her nightmare, in which the candle in the dark cafe is burning lower and lower. Soon it will be out. "If we hurry," suggests the colonel, "perhaps we'll be in time." The situation in which they can enjoy this dreamed-of intercourse can only arise when the monster from Venus is put down, as the colonel ultimately recognizes. If it is not quickly destroyed, their romance will have burned itself out. The colonel is unusual in this kind of film in combining the role of scientist and hero. Like Dr. Carrington in *The Thing*, he wishes the monster to be scientifically examined, but, like *The Thing*, the monster has potentially destructive power that renders this too dangerous a course of action. In *The Thing*, the refrain is "Close the door." In 20 *Million Miles to Earth* it is "Shut the gate." In order to maintain the mores of civilization, some instincts must be quelled the moment they become apparent. Both films suggest the fear of the violent primitive drives of the male id. The women are almost asexual figures of Arthurian romance offering themselves to the knight once he has slain the beast.

In *The Day the Earth Stood Still* (Robert Wise, 1951), the imperfect human male, a mixture of outward politeness and inner violence, is contrasted with the refined Martian Klaatu (Michael Rennie), who comes to Earth to warn men against the violence of their lives. Significantly, the heroine's husband has been killed in a war. A gentle asexual figure, Klaatu is tended by a powerful robot named Gort, who seems to represent man's violence and even his sexuality (in the scene where he advances threateningly on the cringing heroine and carries her off to the spaceship, as F. Hoda observed).[17] Out of control, Gort's powers are dangerous. Under Klaatu's orders he is an invaluable weapon. After the girl, Helen Benson (Patricia Neal), has been in contact with Klaatu, she is unable to go through with the marriage that her jealous and selfish fiancé urges on her. As Klaatu enters his spaceship to return to Mars, she looks at him wistfully. He is a man whose "baser instincts" or id, in the figure of Gort, are held firmly under control. The film suggests a concept of an ideal man separated from his most primitive instincts, using them only as a source of energy to aid his "higher" civilized aims.

It Came from Outer Space (Jack Arnold, 1953) is another film in which a similar pattern develops with slight variations. The hero, John Putnam (Richard Carlson), a dreamer-scientist who wishes to hasten his marriage to his slightly reluctant fiancée Ellen (Barbara Rush), is the only man in his town to realize that Earth has been invaded by alien beings. The creatures begin to take over the bodies of people in the town so that they seem simultaneously to be themselves, yet not themselves; something is different. The scientist, who quickly comes to terms with the fact that they have been invaded, tries to convince the sheriff (who, as a friend of Ellen's family, opposed his marriage), but is repeatedly ridiculed and ignored. Eventually Ellen is held as a hostage. When she is seen again, her light-colored girlish summer dress has been exchanged for a black one, and she has adopted something of the air of the femme fatale. All the invaders wish to do is to mend their spaceship and take off again. A pact, sensibly made between humans and invaders by Putnam, is finally broken by the sheriff, whose overriding instinct is to attack once he has been forced to accept their existence. The creatures manage to escape, but not before they have been compelled to "show" themselves as they really are—indistinct phallic shapes with an enormous eye (a symbol of the genitals) in the middle of their heads.[18]

In this film, society, as epitomized by the sheriff, is unwilling to probe beneath the surface and refuses to believe anything that does not accord with its own "civilized" desires. Hence, the thoughtful scientist, who recognizes the strength of his own sexual desire and who sees in marriage something more than a mere social alliance, is automatically a suspect figure. The invaders assume human form because they recognize the human weakness of being unable to confront the existence of sexuality. But the existence of the genitals cannot be ignored. Even the "nice" girl Ellen is forced to reveal her innate sexuality. Putnam's dealings with the invaders suggest that some form of harmony can be established between the civilized and sexual aspects of human beings (a more sophisticated and humane view than that in the films previously discussed), but society in the form of the sheriff, made to confront its own sexual nature, can only attempt to overcome what is, in fact, a superior force.

This film, like many science fiction films, provides a good illustration of the tensions, examined by Kinsey,[19] between publicly accepted social and sexual mores and the actual sexual needs of the individual. *Forbidden Planet, The Thing, 20 Million Miles to Earth, The Day the Earth Stood Still,* and *It Came from Outer Space* are all films concerned with the clash between the public and private individual, unwilling to defy convention but disturbed by secret impulses and desires that are incompatible with the social superego to which they aspire. The legal proscription, still widespread in the United States, of all sexual relationships outside marriage, reflected in the bourgeois consciousness of right and wrong, becomes a nagging source of disquiet, particularly in *The Thing, It Came from Outer Space,* or Mamoulian's *Dr. Jekyll and Mr. Hyde.*

The conquest of the "monster of the id" is the structural raison d'être of many science fiction films. There are also some science fiction films which, while based on psychoanalytical concepts, concern themselves with a variation on this theme. A number of them deal with impotence and frigidity. This group includes such films as *Spider Woman* (Roy William Neill, 1944), *Wasp Woman* (Roger Corman, 1960), and *The Fly* (Kurt Neumann, 1958), which explore insect phobia—fear of castration and dread of the phallic mother. One of the earliest science fiction films to look at the sexual nature of woman is James Whale's *The Bride of Frankenstein* (1935). *Frankenstein* (Whale, 1931) itself provides a fairly straightforward example of the kind of film discussed earlier, which examines the tension between subconscious sexual desires and the mores of civilization. *The Bride* assumes a knowledge of the earlier film in its continued exploration of such secret desires. The film opens with a conversation between Shelley, Byron, and Mary Shelley, author of the novel *Frankenstein*. Byron professes some amazement that such a dark story could have been created by Mary, who appears a graceful feminine figure. She is undisturbed by his suggestion of the monstrous fantasies that lurk in her inner nature. Considering Byron's claim to be the "world's greatest sinner" and Shelley's to be the "world's greatest poet," Mary suggests that a simple love story would never have done for such an audience: "So why shouldn't I write of monsters?" She then offers to continue the tale, and her narration is carried over the opening shots of the fire in which the monster is thought to have met his death.

As with Hendry and the Thing, there is a close parallel relationship between Frankenstein and his monster in the Frankenstein films. Just as, at the beginning of *The Bride of Frankenstein,* the monster, thought to be dead, shows himself very much alive, so Frankenstein (Colin Clive), brought home as a corpse on his wedding night, is revived in the presence of his wife, who, incidentally, had once been warned to beware her wedding night. As with the creature in *20 Million Miles to Earth,* this reawakening process symbolizes what Freud describes as "the revival of libidinal desires after they have been quenched through being sated."[20]

The wedding night proceeds with a scene in which Frankenstein, still weakened through illness, lies alone in bed and with reawakening enthusiasm discusses the temptations of aspiring to be a creator with his wife (Valerie Hobson). She responds with shocked arguments that what he desires is "blasphemous." "We are not meant to know such things. It is the work of the Devil." They are clearly discussing the act of procreation or some form of sexual intercourse. The analogy between love and science is taken up a little later by the eminent scientist Dr. Pretorius (Ernest Thesiger)—a man booted out of the university for knowing too much: "The creation of life is enthralling," he declares, "Science, like love, has her little surprises." In his efforts to convince Frankenstein to continue his experiments in creation, he points to the Bible, quoting the exhortation to "increase and multiply." As if to underline his point he reveals some homunculi he has created, imprisoned in glass jars—a king, queen, archbishop, devil, and ballerina. The king, watched primly by the archbishop and gleefully by the devil (who is said to resemble Pretorius), makes frenzied attempts to climb out of his jar and make love to the queen. The queen remains still, chattering anxiously. The ballerina, unaware of anything, dances to one tune. As in the relationship between Frankenstein and his wife, the male is the active transgressor, attempting from sexual motives to overcome the limits set by his creator. The female adheres to the conventions, an innocent insipid performer, seeking admiration like the ballerina, issuing anxious warnings against the predatory actions of the male, like the queen.

The wedding night is disturbed by Pretorius, whose temptations to create life once more Frankenstein is unable to resist. He is symbolically separated from his wife, and in a subsequent scene she hears a noise and cries out, "Is that you, Henry?" She then turns to find that she is being menaced by the monster (Boris Karloff), who kidnaps her. Thus the connection between Frankenstein and his monster is emphasized. Pretorius and the monster insist that Frankenstein's wife will not be returned to him until he creates a mate for the monster.

Clearly, Frankenstein's primitive sexual drives are an estranging factor between himself and his wife. She speaks to her husband and is answered by a monster. His only chance of survival is to discover the secrets of her sexual nature in order to meet the needs of his own erotic impulses. The female monster he creates is played by Elsa Lanchester, significantly the same actress who plays Mary Shelley in the film's prologue. The slow, tense attempts to stimulate this corpselike figure to life eventually succeed. She seems to look to Frankenstein for reassurance, but when confronted with the monster lets out a blood-curdling scream of terror and revulsion. The dual role played by Elsa Lanchester indicates the identification that should be made between the ultracivilized Mary Shelley and the primitive world of her subconscious from which she draws her monster fantasies. Valerie Hobson, as the gracious, civilized Elizabeth, is another substitute for Mary Shelley in the film. The suggestion is that even when woman's sexuality is most strongly aroused, she can only meet the sexual male with complete frigidity. There appears to be no distinction between woman's conscious and unconscious desires. This is why Mary Shelley is undisturbed by Byron's innuendos. It is, after all, man who is the "great sinner." The point is made; the baffled monster threatens violence, and at that moment Elizabeth, escaped from the monster's prison, knocks on the door, calling to Frankenstein. The monster, about to pull the lever that will destroy the whole building and its occupants, agrees to Frankenstein's escape: "Yes, you go; [to Pretorius] you stay. We belong dead." The innate female frigidity suggested by the reaction of the female monster to the monster shows Frankenstein the impossibility of satisfying his sexual nature. It can only destroy, and he escapes thankfully with his wife, tacitly agreeing that this part of himself should be obliterated.

Much of the dialogue has a familiar ring to those acquainted with later science fiction films—the assertion of an area of knowledge forbidden to man, Biblical quotation to support argument, as in *Conquest of Space* or *Them!,* the optimistic but ill-judged comment on the monster: "it just wants someone to handle it" (cf. *The Thing* or *20 Million Miles to Earth*).

Another film that looks at the nature of woman from a man's point of view in rather different terms is *The Incredible Shrinking Man* (Jack Arnold, 1957).

In this, as in most science fiction films, the apparently casual details of the opening scene are crucially important to the film's thematic development. A couple are seen sunbathing on a boat. The man, Scott (Grant Williams), says he is thirsty and wants the woman, Louise (Randy Stuart), to fetch him some beer. She refuses until he makes a bargain with her that he will make the dinner if she does so. They then act out a scene in mock sixteenth-century dialogue, in which he calls her "wench" and orders her down to the galley in imitation of a time when man was master and woman served him—a complete contrast to their own relationship. They reveal that they have been living together for six years and decide to get married. While the woman fetches the drinks a cloud of mist appears on the horizon and rolls toward the boat, finally enveloping the man and leaving him freezing cold.

In the next scene they are shown to be married. He comments on a loss of weight, suggesting jokingly, "Maybe it's the cooking round here." A little later, when they kiss, he observes with dawning fear, "You used to have to stretch when you kissed me." As he grows rapidly smaller from day to day, he finds out that his sickness has been caused by the radioactive mist to which he had been exposed and to which the doctors and scientists can find no antidote. "I want you to start thinking about us," he says to his wife, "—about our marriage. There's limit to your obligation." A model of patience and understanding, she stands by him, tolerating his increasing bad temper. "Every day I become smaller. Every day I become more tyrannical in my domination of Louise. I don't know how she stood it. Burning inside was my desperate need for her." He starts up a friendship with a female midget his own size but abandons it when he finds he cannot stop shrinking. We see him dwarfed by a low coffee table, with Louise, enormous in the foreground. Eventually, he is to be found living for safety in a dollhouse in the living room, complaining at the noise of his wife's feet as she appears to crash down the stairs. She answers him patiently and goes out shopping, inadvertently letting the cat in as she does so. A terrifying scene follows in which the gigantic predatory animal peers through the dollhouse window and makes a grab for him with its paw. In the ensuing struggle, he escapes and falls through the stairs to the cellar, from which he is unable to escape. In his new universe, away from Louise's cooking, his main object must be to find food. He sees a piece of cheese, but it is contained in a lethal mousetrap that could well destroy him; a piece of bread lies as bait in a spider's web, and his adversary, a monstrous spider, prowls round the cellar. "I had an enemy, the most terrifying beheld by human eyes," he comments. There is an immediate cut to Louise, upstairs, preparing to leave the house. He finds a weapon for himself in a nail which in proportion to him is the size of a sword, and he decides to pit his wits against the spider. At one point, un-armed and threatened by the creature, he retrieves his weapon: "With these, I was a man again . . . I no longer felt hatred for the spider. My enemy was not a spider but every unknown terror in the world. . . . One of us had to die." He finally kills the spider in a nauseating scene in which he impales her on his nail while black drops ooze onto his shoulder. After the spider's death, "there was no thought of hunger or shrinking." Completely reconciled to his state, he turns to philosophizing about his role: "What was I, still a human being, or a man of the future?"

Fear of castration by the female is the overriding theme of this film, and we are aware of the popular myth of the dominant American woman, served by an emasculated spouse. The opening scene observes the aggressive sexual equality of modern times and looks back to the male-dominated situation it replaces. Our first image of the couple's married life is outside the house. Louise feeds the cat and prepares breakfast. His laughing fear of what her cooking may be doing to him is taken up more strongly in the cellar scenes, where food is left as bait to lure mice and flies to their destruction—an analogy of the married woman's social and sexual relationship to her husband. In the dollhouse he is reduced to the status of a toy. The giant clawing cat is a replacement for Louise. She lets it in unconsciously. Freud wrote of animal phobias: "The anxiety felt in animal phobias is . . . an affective reaction on the part of the ego in danger: and the danger which is being signalled in this way is the danger of castration. This anxiety differs in no respect from the realistic anxiety which the ego normally feels in situations of danger, except that its content remains unconscious and only becomes conscious in the form of a distortion."[21]

This film is a first-person narrative from the man's point of view. Superficially, he and his wife at first have a good relationship. Later Louise behaves "perfectly" while he feels guilt at his resentment of her. The film is clearly concerned with his fear of her influence on him within the marriage relationship, which turns him into a toy and gradually engulfs him.

In the cellar sequences, which symbolize his subconscious, his adversary comes out into the open, a female trying to trap him with food, implicitly associated with his wife in the cut mentioned above. He specifies that his real enemy is "every unknown terror in the world." By this, he means what Freud describes as fear, not merely of the mother but of the "*phallic* mother, of whom we are afraid; so that the fear of spiders expresses dread of mother-incest and horror of the female genitals."[22] Feeling "a man again" with his weapons, he impales her with his sword/penis. By confronting her sexually he proves his ability to resist her attacks and to conquer. After the fight neither the bait of food nor the fear of "shrinking," or castration, holds any power over him. He has freed himself from the constricting area of female domination and senses a new freedom for himself in the world, comforting himself that perhaps he will not be the only one to undergo this liberating experience in the future.

Don Siegel's *Invasion of the Body Snatchers* (1956) is not concerned with fears of woman but looks at a society characterized by lack of passion in every aspect. In some ways it has something in common with *It Came from Outer Space*. This film shows a silent conspiracy by which people are taken over by some curious plant life and as a result no longer feel pain, fear, or joy, merely a vegetable contentment. Miles (Kevin Mc-Carthy) and Becky (Dana Wynter) both have broken marriages behind them. Years ago at college they had been boyfriend and girlfriend but did not have sufficient courage or passion to leave to get married, as one of their friends in similar circumstances had done. Miles's conversations reveal the extent to which his interior and sex life has been dried up and destroyed by the humdrum processes of everyday life. He claims that the reason his marriage broke up was that as a doctor, "I never was there when the food was on the table"—a comment both on the empty ritualization of the institution of marriage but also, at another level, implying that his job never left him enough time to sustain the sexual relationship. Both he and Becky pay more than lip service to society's clichés about human relationships. He chaffs his pretty nurse, telling her if she were not married, hers would have been a lost cause long ago. To Becky, he suggests that a doctor's wife needs infinite patience and the understanding of an Einstein. "What about love?" she asks. "That's for the specialists," he replies. Despite their growing feeling for each other, Becky resists a sexual relationship with conventional excuses that it is madness and the whole thing is so sudden—a point that is factually untrue, as he observes. Around them, the number of zombielike creatures grows. A child rejects his mother, saying she is not his mother. She is the same as she was before but all feeling has vanished. The sickness is contagious, as more and more people conspire to place the giant pods in contact with other victims. The psychiatrists, themselves afflicted with the common illness, suggest that worry about what is going on in the world causes the alienation problems: "The trouble is inside you." In an impassioned speech, the doctor describes how he has watched humanity draining away from his patients— "People I've known all my life. Only when we have to fight to stay human do we realize how precious it is." When he argues that love cannot so easily be discounted, with those who try to infect him, they reply cynically: "You've been in love before. It doesn't last." Becky cries out that she wants his children, but she finally succumbs from exhaustion, becoming "an inhuman enemy bent on my destruction." Standing on the motorway,

67. *Them!* The labyrinthine lair of the mutated ants.

he yells at people in cars to stop and help him escape to tell the truth. They assume he is drunk or insane and pass by regardless. "You fools! You're next!" he yells. The film ends on a false note of optimism, and he is finally believed, but this is not the ending that Siegel wanted and certainly not the logical ending to the film.

All the films discussed so far have been firmly structured around coherent themes relating the tensions of sexual drives and the obligations on behavior imposed by civilized society. They are saturated with an awareness of Freudian concepts. The symbols are established from within the narrative context. There is also a large group of films in which such tensions are latent but not fully explored. The films do not appear to create their own symbolism. *Them!* (Gordon Douglas, 1954) is a good example of this. It incorporates a skeleton romance between two people working to destroy a plague of monstrous aggressive ants—mutants from radioactive fallout. Those who see the creatures view them with horror and revulsion, and there is a long scene in which the ants are pursued through the nest they have made for themselves in the city's sewers and an attempt is made to locate and destroy the central egg chamber. This labyrinthine motif might be seen as a fantasy of anal birth,[23] but the interpretation does not clarify the preoccupations of the film in any significant way. The hero of *The Projected Man* (Ian Curteis, 1966), who has himself been hurled through space to prove a scientific point to the corrupt authorities, is clearly motivated to an equal extent by jealousy of the romance between his assistants, one of them his former girlfriend (Mary Peach). Returning from the experiment with his face hideously burned and scarred, his aggression knows no bounds, and he indulges in what might appear to be a gratuitous form of sexual menace as he carries off the office secretary, who is conveniently stripped to her underwear. His horrible appearance is the visible sign of the transformation he has undergone through jealousy, yet once more, nothing is closely worked out.

The Day the Earth Caught Fire (Val Guest, 1961) interweaves the imagery of the climatic changes with the story of a developing sexual attraction—at times it is not clear whether the hero and heroine are talking about themselves or about the weather. In the face of the potential destruction of the earth by fire, their intolerant antagonism is shown to be petty and irrelevant. The reporter is brought to shake hands with his ex-wife's husband and to wish him well.

There are other science fiction films that are firmly entrenched in exploring different areas. *2001* (Stanley Kubrick, 1968), for example, is concerned with moral and metaphysical speculation combined with a delight in technical virtuosity for its own sake. A quasi documentary such as *Destination Moon* (Irving Pichel, 1950) was an attempt to give a realistic picture of what the first moon landing might involve. *Marooned* (John Sturges, 1969) takes up the question most people were asking at the time of the first moon landing. What happens to the spacemen if their apparatus fails them and they cannot get back to earth? Such films, with their masculine emphasis and concentration on the mechanics of space flight, suggest an image of man marveling at his own genitals. They do not have the social orientation of the heterosexual films.

This article has attempted to describe and analyze only one large and probably central area within the amorphous science fiction genre and to point out some of the major preoccupations in these films with the problem of reconciling the desires of the individual as both sexual animal and social being. Although the current emphasis in science fiction films seems to be toward some form of pseudoscientific "documentary," this is just a more subtle disguise for the overriding concern of the genre with "inner space" and "monsters from the id."

Notes

1. H. L. Gold, editor of *Galaxy Science Fiction*, quoted by Kingsley Amis in *New Maps of Hell* (London: Gollancz, 1961), p. 64.

2. Francis Arnold, "Out of This World," *Films and Filming* 9, no. 9 (June 1963): 14–18.

3. Richard Hodgens, "A Brief Tragical History of the Science Fiction Film," *Film Quarterly* 13 (Winter 1959): 32.

4. Penelope Houston, "Glimpses of the Moon," *Sight and Sound* 22 (April–June 1953): 187.

5. *Monthly Film Bulletin* 24, no. 290 (November 1957): 141.

6. F. Hoda, "Epouvante et science fiction," *Positif* (November–December 1954): 1–16.

7. Jean Loth, "Le Fantastique erotique ou l'orgasme qui fait peur," *Cinema '57*, July–August 1957, pp. 9–14.

8. Raymond Lefèvre, "Le Décor de la peur," *Image et Son*, no. 192 (May 1966): 31–36.

9. Fereydoun Hoveyda, "La Science-fiction à l'ère des Spoutniks," *Cahiers du Cinéma* 11, no. 80 (February 1958): 9–16.

10. Tom Milne, *Mamoulian* (London: Thames and Hudson, 1969), pp. 39–50.

11. Curt Siodmak, "Sci-Fi or Sci-Fact?" *Films and Filming* 14, no. 12 (November 1968): 64.

12. Sigmund Freud, "Anxiety and Instinctual Life," *New Introductory Lectures on Psycho-Analysis: The Standard Edition of the Complete Psychological Works of Sigmund Freud*, 24 vols., translated by James Strachey in collaboration with Anna Freud (London: Hogarth Press and the Institute of Psycho-Analysis, 1953–1974), 22:82–83. Subsequent references to Freud are from this edition.

13. Freud, "The Dissection of the Psychical Personality," 22:73–74.

14. Amis, *New Maps of Hell*, p. 30.

15. Freud, "Introduction: A Seventeenth-Century Demonological Neurosis," 19:72.

16. Alfred C. Kinsey, Wardell B. Pomeroy, and Clyde E. Martin, *Sexual Behaviour in the Human Male* (Philadelphia and London: Saunders, 1949), p. 268.

17. Hoda, "Epouvante et science fiction," pp. 1–16.

18. Freud, "The Uncanny," 17:231.

19. Kinsey, Pomeroy, and Martin, *Sexual Behaviour in the Human Male*, pp. 263–296.

20. Freud, "The Acquisition and Control of Fire," 22:191.

21. Freud, "Inhibitions, Symptoms and Anxiety," 20:126.

22. Freud, "Revision of Dream Theory," 22:24.

23. Ibid., p. 25.

24. Tales of Sound and Fury: Observations on the Family Melodrama

THOMAS ELSAESSER

Asked about the color in *Written on the Wind* (1957), Douglas Sirk replied: "Almost throughout the picture I used deep-focus lenses which have the effect of giving a harshness to the objects and a kind of enamelled, hard surface to the colours. I wanted this to bring out the inner violence, the energy of the characters which is all inside them and can't break through." It would be difficult to think of a better way of describing what this particular movie and indeed most of the best melodramas of the fifties and early sixties are about. Or, for that matter, how closely in this film style and technique are related to theme.

I want to pursue an elusive subject in two directions: first, to indicate the development of what one might call the melodramatic imagination across different artistic forms and in different epochs; second, prompted by Sirk's remark, to look for some structural and stylistic constants in one medium during one particular period (the Hollywood family melodrama between roughly 1940 and 1963) and to speculate on the cultural and psychological context that this form of melodrama so manifestly reflected and helped to articulate. Nonetheless, this isn't an historical study in any strict sense, nor a *catalogue raisonné* of names and titles, for reasons that have something to do with my general method as well as with the obvious limitations imposed on film research by the unavailability of most of the movies. Thus I lean rather heavily on half a dozen films, notably *Written on the Wind*, to develop my points. This said, it is difficult to see how references to twenty more movies would make the argument any truer. For better or worse, what I have to say should at this stage be taken to be provocative rather than proven.

HOW TO MAKE STONES WEEP

Bearing in mind that everybody has some idea of what is meant by "melodramatic" (whatever one's scruples about an exact definition), any discussion of the melodrama as a specific cinematic mode of expression has to start from its antecedents—the novel and certain types of "entertainment" drama—from which scriptwriters and directors have borrowed their models.

The first thing one notices is that the media and literary forms that have habitually embodied melodramatic situations have changed considerably in the course of history and, further, that they differ from country to country. In England it has mainly been the novel and the literary gothic where melodramatic motifs persistently crop up (though the Victorian stage, especially in the 1880s and 1890s, knew an unprecedented vogue for the melodramas of R. Buchanan and G. R. Sims, plays in which "a footbridge over a torrent breaks under the steps of the villain; a piece of wall comes down to shatter him; a boiler bursts, and blows him to smithereens").[1] In France, it is the costume drama and historical novel; in Germany, "high" drama and the ballad, as well as more popular forms like *Moritat* (street songs); finally, in Italy the opera rather than the novel reached the highest degree of sophistication in the handling of melodramatic situations.

Two currents make up the genealogy. One leads from the late medieval morality play, the popular *gestes,* and other forms of oral narrative and drama, like fairy tales and folk songs, to their romantic revival and the cult of the picturesque in Scott, Byron, Heine, and Hugo, which has its lowbrow echo in barrel-organ songs, music-hall drama, and what in Germany is known as *Bänkellied,* the latter coming to late literary honors through Brecht in his songs and musical plays, *The Threepenny Opera* or *Mahagonny.* The characteristic features for our present purposes in this tradition are not so much the emotional shock tactics and the blatant playing on the audience's known sympathies and antipathies, but rather the nonpsychological conception of the dramatis personae, who figure less as autonomous individuals than to transmit the action and link the various locales within a total constellation. In this respect, melodramas have a myth-making function, insofar as their significance lies in the structure and articulation of the action, not in any psychologically motivated correspondence with individualized experience.

Yet what particularly marks the ballad or the *Bänkellied* (i.e., narratives accompanied by music) is that the moral/moralistic pattern which furnishes the primary content (crimes of passion bloodily revenged, murderers driven mad by guilt and drowning themselves, villains snatching children from their careless mothers, servants killing their unjust masters) is overlaid not only with a proliferation of "realistic" homely detail, but also "parodied" or relativized by the heavily repetitive verse form or the mechanical up-and-down rhythms of the barrel organ, to which the voice of the singer adapts itself (consciously or not), thereby producing a vocal parallelism that has a distancing or ironic effect, to the extent of often crisscrossing the moral of the story by a "false" or unexpected emphasis. Sirk's most successful German melodrama, *Zu neuen Ufern* (*To New Shores,* 1937), makes excellent use of the street ballad to bring out the tragic irony in the courtroom scene, and the tune which Walter Brennan keeps playing on the harmonica in King Vidor's *Ruby Gentry* (1952) works in a very similar way. A variation on this is the use of fairgrounds and carousels in films like *Some Came Running* (Vincente Minnelli, 1958) and *The Tarnished Angels* (Sirk, 1957), or more self-consciously by Hitchcock in *Strangers on a Train* and *Stage Fright* (both 1951) and Welles in *Lady from Shanghai* and *The Stranger* (both 1946) to underscore the main action and at the same time "ease" the melodramatic impact by providing an ironic parallelism. Sirk uses the motif repeatedly, as, for instance, in *A Scandal in Paris* (1946) and *Take Me to Town* (1952). What such devices point to is that in the melodrama the *rhythm* of experience often establishes itself against its value (moral, intellectual).

Perhaps the current that leads more directly to the sophisticated family melodrama of the 1940s and 1950s, though, is derived from the romantic drama which had its heyday after the French Revolution and subsequently furnished many of the plots for operas, but which is itself unthinkable without the eighteenth-century sentimental novel and the emphasis put on private feelings and interiorized (puritan, pietist) codes of morality and conscience. Historically, one of the interesting facts about this tradition is that its height of popularity seems to coincide (and this remains true throughout the nineteenth century) with periods of intense social and ideological crisis. The prerevolutionary sentimental novel—Richardson's *Clarissa* or Rousseau's *Nouvelle Héloise,* for example—go out of their way to make a case for extreme forms of behavior and feeling by depicting very explicitly certain external constraints and pressures bearing upon the characters, and by showing up the quasi-totalitarian violence perpetrated by (agents of) the "system." (Lovelace tries everything, from bribing her family to hiring pimps, prostitutes, and kidnappers in order to get Clarissa to become his wife, only to have to rape her after all.) The same pattern is to be found in the bourgeois tragedies of Lessing (*Emilia Galotti,* 1768) and the early Schiller (*Kabale und Liebe,* 1776), both deriving their dramatic force from the conflict between an extreme and highly individualized form of moral idealism in the heroes (again, nonpsychological on the level of motivation) and a thoroughly corrupt yet seemingly omnipotent social class (made up of feudal princes and petty state functionaries). The melodramatic elements are clearly visible in the plots, which revolve around family relationships, star-crossed lovers, and forced marriages. The villains (often of noble birth) demonstrate their superior political and economic power invariably by sexual aggression and attempted rape, leaving the heroine no other way than to commit suicide or take poison in the company of her lover. The ideological "message" of these tragedies, as in the case of *Clarissa,* is transparent: they record the struggle of a morally and emotionally emancipated bourgeois consciousness against the remnants of feudalism. They pose the problem in political terms and concentrate on the complex interplay of ethical principles, religious-metaphysical polarities, and the idealist aspirations typical of the bourgeoisie in its militant phase, as the protagonists come to grief in a maze of economic necessities, realpolitik, family loyalties, and through the abuse of aristocratic privilege from a still divinely ordained and therefore doubly depraved absolutist authority.

Although these plays and novels, because they use the melodramatic-emotional plot only as their most rudimentary structure of meaning, belong to the more intellectually demanding forms of melodrama, the element of interiorization and personalization of what are primarily ideological conflicts, together with the metaphorical interpretation of class conflict as sexual exploitation and rape, is important in all subsequent forms of melodrama, including that of the cinema. (The latter in America, of course, is a stock theme of novels and movies with a "Southern" setting.)

Paradoxically, the French Revolution failed to produce a new form of social drama or tragedy. The restoration stage (when theaters in Paris were specially licensed to play melodramas) trivialized the form by using melodramatic plots in exotic settings and by providing escapist entertainment with little social relevance. The plays warmed up the standard motif of eighteenth-century French fiction and drama, that of innocence persecuted and virtue rewarded, and the conventions of melodrama functioned in their most barren form as the mechanics of pure suspense.

What before the revolution had served to focus on suffering and victimization—the claims of the individual in an absolutist society—was reduced to ground glass in the porridge, poisoned handkerchiefs, and last-minute rescues from the dungeon. The sudden reversals of fortune, the intrusion of chance and coincidence, had originally pointed to the arbitrary way feudal institutions could ruin the individual unprotected by civil rights and liberties. The system stood accused of greed, willfulness, and irrationality through the Christlike suffering of the pure virgin and the selfless heroism of the right-minded in the midst of court intrigues and callous indifference. Now, with the bourgeoisie triumphant, this form of drama lost its subversive charge and functioned more as a means of consolidating an as yet weak and incoherent ideological position. Whereas the prerevolutionary melodramas had often ended tragically, those of the Restoration had happy endings; they reconciled the suffering individual to his or her social position by affirming an "open" society where everything was possible. Over and over again, the victory of the "good" citizen over "evil" aristocrats, lecherous clergymen, and the even more conventional villains drawn from the lumpenproletariat was reenacted in sentimental spectacles full of tears and high moral tones. Complex social processes were simplified either by blaming the evil disposition of individuals or by manipulating the plots and engineering coincidences and other dei ex machina, such as the instant conversion of the villain, moved by the plight of his victim, or suddenly struck by divine grace on the steps of Notre Dame.

Since the overtly "conformist" strategy of such drama is quite evident, what is interesting is certainly not the plot structure, but whether the conventions allowed authors to dramatize in their episodes actual contradictions in society and genuine clashes of interests in the characters. Already during the Revolution plays such as Monvel's *Les Victimes cloîtrées* or Laya's *L'Ami des lois,* though working with very stereotyped plots, conveyed quite definite political sympathies (the second, for instance, backed the Girondist moderates in the trial of Louis XVI against the Jacobites) and were understood as such by their public.[2]

Even if the form might act to reinforce attitudes of submission, the actual working out of the scenes could nonetheless present fundamental social evils. Many of the pieces also flattered popular sympathies by giving the villains the funniest lines, just as Victorian drama playing east of Drury Lane was often enlivened by low-comedy burlesque put on as curtain-raisers and by the servants' farces during the intermission.

All this is to say that there seems a radical ambiguity attached to the melodrama, which holds even more for the film melodrama. Depending on whether the emphasis fell on the odyssey of suffering or the happy ending, on the place and context of rupture (moral conversion of the villain, unexpected appearance of a benevolent Capucine monk throwing off his pimp's disguise), that is to say, depending on what dramatic mileage was got out of the heroine's perils before the ending (and one only has to think of Sade's Justine to see what could be done with the theme of innocence unprotected), melodrama would appear to function either subversively or as escapism—categories that are always relative to the given historical and social context.[3]

In the cinema, Griffith is a good example. Using identical dramatic devices and cinematic techniques, he could create, with *Intolerance* (1916), *Way Down East* (1920), or *Broken Blossoms* (1919), if not exactly subversive, at any rate socially committed melodramas, whereas *Birth of a Nation* (1915) or *Orphans of the Storm* (1921) are classic examples of how melodramatic effects can successfully shift explicit political themes onto a personalized plane. In both cases, Griffith tailored ideological conflicts into emotionally charged family situations.

The persistence of the melodrama might indicate the ways in which popular culture has not only taken note of social crises and the fact that

68. *Orphans of the Storm:* The shifting of explicit political themes onto a personalized level.

the losers are not always those who deserve it most, but has also resolutely refused to understand social change in other than private contexts and emotional terms. In this, there is obviously a healthy distrust of intellectualization and abstract social theory—insisting that other structures of experience (those of suffering, for instance) are more in keeping with reality. But it has also meant ignorance of the properly social and political dimensions of these changes and their causality, and consequently it has encouraged increasingly escapist forms of mass entertainment.

However, this ambivalence about the "structures" of experience, endemic in the melodramatic mode, has served artists throughout the nineteenth century for the depiction of a variety of themes and social phenomena while remaining within the popular idiom. Industrialization, urbanization, and nascent entrepreneurial capitalism have found their most telling literary embodiment in a type of novel clearly indebted to the melodrama, and the national liberals in Italy during the Risorgimento, for example, saw their political aspirations reflected in Verdi's operas (as in the opening of Luchino Visconti's *Senso* [1954]). In England, Dickens, Collins, and Reade relied heavily on melodramatic plots to sharpen social conflicts and portray an urban environment where chance encounters, coincidences, and the side-by-side existence of extreme social and moral contrasts were the natural products of the very conditions of existence—crowded tenement houses, narrow streets backing up to the better residential property, and other facts of urban demography of the time. Dickens in particular uses the element of chance, the dream/waking, horror/bliss switches in *Oliver Twist* or *Tale of Two Cities,* partly to feel his way toward a portrayal of existential insecurity and moral anguish that fiction had previously not encompassed, but also to explore deep psychological phenomena for which the melodrama—as Freud was later to confirm—has supplied the dynamic motifs and the emotional-pictorial decor. What seems to me important in this form of melodrama (and one comes across a similar conception in the sophisticated Hollywood melodramas) is the emphasis Dickens places on discontinuity, on the evidence of fissures and ruptures in the fabric of experience, and the appeal to a reality of the psyche—to which the notions of sudden change, reversal, and excess lend a symbolic plausibility.

In France it is the works of Sue, Hugo, and Balzac that reflect most closely the relation of melodrama to social upheaval. Sue, for example, uses the timeworn trapdoor devices of cloak-and-dagger stage melodrama for an explicitly sensationalist, yet committed journalism. In a popular form and rendered politically palatable by the fictionalized treatment, his *Mystères de Paris* were intended to crusade on such issues as public health, prostitution, overcrowding and slum housing, sanitation, black-market racketeering, corruption in government circles, opium smoking, and gambling. Sue exploited a "reactionary" form for reformist ends, and his success, both literary and practical, proved him right. Twenty years later Victor Hugo, who had learned as much from Sue as Sue had picked up from *Nôtre-Dame de Paris,* produced with *Les Misérables* a super-melodrama spectacular that must stand as the crowning achievement of the genre in the novel. The career of Jean Valjean, from convict and galley slave to factory owner and capitalist, his fall and literal emergence from the sewers of Paris to become a somewhat unwilling activist in the 1848 revolution, is staged with the help of mistaken identities, orphans suddenly discovering their noble birth, inconvenient reappearance of people long thought dead, hair-breadth escapes and rescues, multiple disguises, long-suffering females dying of consumption or wandering for days through the streets in search of their child—and yet, through all this Hugo expresses a hallucinating vision of the anxiety, the moral confusion, the emotional demands, in short, the metaphysics of social change and urban life between the time of Waterloo and 1848. Hugo evidently wanted to bring together in a popular form subjective experiences of crises while keeping track of the grand lines of France's history, and he succeeds singularly well in reproducing the ways in which individuals with different social backgrounds, levels of awareness, and imaginations respond to objective changes in the social fabric of their lives. For this, the melodrama, with its shifts in mood, its different *tempi,* and the mixing of stylistic levels, is ideally suited: *Les Misérables,* even more so than the novels of Dickens, lets through a symbolic dimension of psychic truth, with the hero in turn representing very nearly the id, the superego, and finally the sacrificed ego of a repressed and paranoid society.

Balzac, on the other hand, uses melodramatic plots to a rather different end. Many of his novels deal with the dynamics of early capitalist economics. The good/evil dichotomy has almost disappeared, and the Manichaean conflicts have shifted away from questions of morality to the paradoxes of psychology and economics. What we see is a Schopenhauerian struggle of the will: the ruthlessness of industrial entrepreneurs and bankers; the spectacle of an uprooted, "decadent" aristocracy still holding tremendous political power; the sudden twists of fortune with no-good parasites becoming millionaires overnight (or vice versa) through speculation and the stock exchange; the antics of hangers-on, parvenus, and cynical artist-intellectuals; the demonic, spellbinding potency of money and capital; the contrasts between abysmal poverty and unheard-of affluence and waste, which characterized the "anarchic" phase of industrialization and high finance. All were experienced by Balzac as both vital and melodramatic. His work reflects this more in plot and style than through direct comment.

To sum up, these writers understood the melodrama as a form that carried its own values and already embodied its own significant content: it served as the literary equivalent of a particular historically and socially conditioned mode of experience. Even if the situations and sentiments defied all categories of verisimilitude and were totally unlike anything in real life, the structure had a truth and a life of its own, which artists could make part of their material. This meant that those who consciously adopted melodramatic techniques of presentation did not necessarily do so out of incompetence or always from a cynical distance, but, by turning a body of techniques into a stylistic principle that carried the distinct overtones of spiritual crisis, they could put the finger on the texture of their social and human material while still being free to shape this material dramatically. For there is little doubt that the whole conception of life in nineteenth-century Europe and England and especially the spiritual problems of the age were often viewed in categories we would today call melodramatic—one can see this in painting, architecture, the ornamentation of gadgets and furniture, the domestic and public mise-en-scène of events and occasions, the oratory in parliament, and the tractarian rhetoric from the pulpit as well as the more private manifestations of religious sentiment. Similarly, the timeless themes that Dostoyevsky brings up again and again in his novels—guilt, redemption, justice, innocence, freedom—are made specific and historically real not least because he was a great writer of melodramatic scenes and confrontations, and they more than anything else define that powerful irrational logic in the motivation and moral outlook of, say, Raskolnikov, Ivan Karamasov, or Kirilov. Finally, how different Kafka's novels would be if they did not contain those melodramatic family situations, pushed to the point where they reveal a dimension at once comic and tragically absurd—perhaps the existential undertow of all genuine melodrama.

PUTTING MELOS INTO DRAMA

In its dictionary sense, melodrama is a dramatic narrative in which musical accompaniment marks the emotional effects. This is still perhaps the most useful definition, because it allows melodramatic elements to be seen as constituents of a system of punctuation, giving expressive color and chromatic contrast to the story line, by orchestrating the emotional ups and downs of the intrigue. The advantage of this approach is that it formulates the problems of melodrama as problems of style and articulation.

Music in melodrama, for example, as a device among others to dramatize a given narrative, is subjective and programmatic. But because it is also a form of punctuation in the above sense, it is both functional (i.e., of structural significance) and thematic (i.e., belonging to the expressive content) in formulating certain moods—sorrow, violence, dread, suspense, happiness. The syntactic function of music has, as is well known, survived into the sound film, and the experiments conducted by Hanns Eisler and T. W. Adorno are highly instructive in this respect.[4] A more practical demonstration of the problem can be gleaned from the almost farcical account that Lillian Ross gives of Gottfried Reinhard and Dore Shary reediting John Huston's *The Red Badge of Courage* (1951) to give the narrative a smoother dramatic shape by a musical build-up to the dramatic climaxes, which is exactly what Huston had wanted to avoid when he shot it.[5]

Because it had to rely on piano accompaniment for punctuation, all silent film drama—from *True Heart Susie* (Griffith, 1919) to *Foolish Wives* (Erich von Stroheim, 1922) or *The Lodger* (Alfred Hitchcock, 1926)—is "melodramatic." It meant that directors had to develop an extremely subtle and yet precise formal language (of lighting, staging, decor, acting, closeup, montage, and camera movement), because they were deliberately looking for ways to compensate for the expressiveness, range of inflection and tonality, rhythmic emphasis, and tension normally present in the spoken word. Having had to replace that part of language which is sound, directors like Murnau, Renoir, Hitchcock, Mizoguchi, Hawks, Lang, and Sternberg achieved in their films a high degree (well recognized at the time) of plasticity in the modulation of optical planes and spatial masses, which Panofsky rightly identified as a "dynamization of space."[6]

Among less gifted directors this sensitivity in the deployment of expressive means was partly lost with the advent of direct sound, since it seemed no longer necessary in a strictly technical sense—pictures "worked" on audiences through their dialogue, and the semantic force of language drowned out and overshadowed the more sophisticated pictorial effects and architectural values. This perhaps helps to explain why some major technical innovations, such as color, wide-angle and deep-focus lenses, crane and dolly, have in fact encouraged a new form of sophisticated melodrama. Directors (quite a sizeable proportion of whom came during the 1930s from Germany, and others were clearly indebted to German expressionism and Max Reinhardt's methods of theatrical mise-en-scène) began showing a similar degree of visual culture as the masters of silent film-drama: Ophüls, Lubitsch, Sirk, Preminger, Welles, Losey, Ray, Minnelli, Cukor.

Considered as an expressive code, melodrama might therefore be described as a particular form of dramatic mise-en-scène, characterized by a dynamic use of spatial and musical categories, as opposed to intellectual or literary ones. Dramatic situations are given an orchestration that will allow for complex aesthetic patterns: indeed, orchestration is fundamental to the American cinema as a whole (being essentially a dramatic cinema, spectacular, and based on a broad appeal) because it has drawn the aesthetic consequences of having the spoken word more as an additional "melodic" dimension than as an autonomous semantic discourse. Sound, whether musical or verbal, acts first of all to give the illusion of depth to the moving image, and by helping to create the third dimension of the spectacle, dialogue becomes a scenic element, along with more directly visual means of the mise-en-scène. Anyone who has ever had the bad luck of watching a Hollywood movie dubbed into French or German will know how important diction is to the emotional resonance and dramatic continuity. Dubbing makes the best picture seem visually flat and dramatically out of sync: it destroys the flow on which the coherence of the illusionist spectacle is built.

That the plasticity of the human voice is quite consciously employed by directors for what are often thematic ends is known: Hawks trained Lauren Bacall's voice so that she could be given "male" lines in *To Have and Have Not* (1944), an effect that Sternberg anticipated when he took great care to cultivate Marlene Dietrich's diction, and it is hard to miss the psychological significance of Robert Stack's voice in *Written on the Wind*, sounding as if every word had to be painfully pumped up from the bottom of one of his oil wells.

If it is true that speech and dialogue in the American cinema lose some of their semantic importance in favor of their aspects as sound, then conversely lighting, composition, and decor increase their semantic and syntactic contribution to the aesthetic effect. They become functional and integral elements in the construction of meaning. This is the justification for giving critical importance to the mise-en-scène over intellectual content or story value. It is also the reason why the domestic melodrama in color and wide screen, as it appeared in the 1940s and 1950s, is perhaps the most highly elaborated, complex mode of cinematic signification that the American cinema has ever produced, because of the restricted scope for external action determined by the subject, and because everything, as Sirk said, happens "inside." To the "sublimation" of the action picture and the Busby Berkeley/Lloyd Bacon musical into domestic and family melodrama corresponded a sublimation of dramatic conflict into decor, color, gesture, and composition of frame, which in the best melodramas is perfectly thematized in terms of the characters' emotional and psychological predicaments.

For example, when in ordinary language we call something melodramatic, what we often mean is an exaggerated rise-and-fall pattern in human actions and emotional responses, a from-the-sublime-to-the-ridiculous movement, a foreshortening of lived time in favor of intensity—all of which produces a graph of much greater fluctuation, a quicker swing from one extreme to the other than is considered natural, realistic, or in conformity with literary standards of verisimilitude: in the novel we like to sip our pleasures rather than gulp them. But if we look at, say, Minnelli, who had adapted some of his best melodramas—*The Cobweb* (1955), *Some Came Running, Home from the Hill* (1960), *Two Weeks in Another Town* (1962), *The Four Horsemen of the Apocalypse* (1962)—from extremely long, circumstantially detailed popular novels by James Jones, Irwin Shaw, and others, it is easy to see how in the process of having to reduce seven to nine hours of reading matter to ninety-odd minutes or so, such a more violent "melodramatic" graph almost inevitably produces itself, short of the narrative becoming incoherent. Whereas in novels, especially when they are staple pulp fare, size connotes solid emotional involvement for the reader, the specific values of the cinema lie in its concentrated visual metaphors and dramatic acceleration rather than in the fictional techniques of dilation. The commercial necessity of compression (being also a formal one) is taken by Minnelli into the films themselves and developed as a theme—that of a pervasive psychological pressure on the characters. An acute sense of claustrophobia in decor and locale translates itself into a restless and yet suppressed energy surfacing sporadically in the actions and the behavior of the protagonists—a dialectic that is part of the subject of a film like *Two Weeks in Another Town*, with hysteria bubbling all the time just below the surface. The feeling that there is always more to tell than can be said leads to very consciously elliptical narratives, proceeding often by visually condensing the characters' motivation into nonessential sequences of images, seemingly lyrical interludes not advancing the plot. The shot of the Trevi fountain at the end of a complex scene where Kirk Douglas is making up his mind in *Two Weeks* is such a metaphoric condensation, and so is the silent sequence, consisting entirely of what might appear to be merely impressionistic dissolves, in the *Four Horsemen*, when Glenn Ford and Ingrid Thulin go for a ride to Versailles, but which in fact tells and foretells the whole trajectory of their relationship.

Sirk, too, often constructs his films in this way: the restlessness of *Written on the Wind* is not unconnected with the fact that he almost always cuts on movement. His visual metaphors ought to have a chapter to themselves: a yellow sportscar drawing up the gravelled driveway to stop in front of a pair of shining white doric columns outside the Hadley mansion is not only a powerful piece of American iconography, especially when taken in a plunging high-angle shot, but the contrary associations of imperial splendor and vulgar materials (polished chrome plate and stucco plaster) create a tension of correspondences and dissimilarities in the same image, which perfectly crystallizes the decadent affluence and melancholy energy that give the film its uncanny fascination. Sirk has a peculiarly vivid eye for the contrasting emotional qualities of textures and materials, and he combines them or makes them clash to very striking effect, especially when they occur in a nondramatic sequence: again in *Written on the Wind*, after the funeral of Hadley, Sr., a black servant is seen taking an oleander wreath off the front gate. A black silk ribbon gets unstuck and is blown by the wind along the concrete path. The camera follows the movement, dissolves, and dollies in on a window, where Lauren Bacall, in an oleander-green dress, is just about to disappear behind the curtains. The scene has no plot significance whatsoever. But the color parallels black/black, green/green, white concrete/white lace curtains provide an extremely strong emotional resonance in which the contrast of soft silk blown along the hard concrete is registered the more forcefully as a disquieting visual association. The desolation of the scene transfers itself onto the Bacall character, and the traditional fatalistic association of the wind reminds us of the futility implied in the movie's title.

These effects, of course, require a highly self-conscious stylist, but they are by no means rare. The fact that commercial necessities, political censorship, and the various morality codes have restricted directors in what they could tackle as a subject has entailed a different awareness of what constituted a worthwhile subject, a change in orientation from which sophisticated melodrama benefited perhaps most. Not only did they provide a defined thematic parameter, but they encouraged a conscious use of style-as-meaning, the mark of a modernist sensibility working in popular culture. To take another example from Minnelli: his theme of a character trying to construct the world in the image of an inner self, only to discover that this world has become uninhabitable because it is both frighteningly suffocating and intolerably lonely (as in *The Long, Long Trailer* [1954] and *The Cobweb*), is transformed and given social significance in the recurrent melodrama plot of the woman who, having failed to make it in the big city, comes back to the small-town home in the hope of finding her true place at last, but who is made miserable by meanmindedness and bigotry and then suffocated by the sheer weight of her none-too-glorious, still-raw-in-the-memory past (*Hilda Crane* [Philip Dunne, 1956], *Beyond the Forest* [King Vidor, 1949], *All I Desire* [Sirk, 1953]).[7] But in Minnelli, it becomes an opportunity to explore in concrete circumstances the more philosophical questions of freedom and determinism, especially as they touch the aesthetic problem of how to depict characters who are not constantly externalizing themselves into action, without thereby trapping them in an environment of ready-made symbolism.

Similarly, when Robert Stack shows Lauren Bacall her hotel suite in *Written on the Wind,* where everything from flowers and pictures on the wall to underwear, nail polish, and handbag is provided, Sirk is not only characterizing a rich man wanting to take over the woman he fancies body and soul or showing the oppressive nature of an unwanted gift. He is also making a direct comment on the Hollywood stylistic technique that "creates" a character out of the elements of the decor and that prefers actors who can provide as blank a facial surface and as little of a personality as possible.

Everyone who has at all thought about the Hollywood aesthetic wants to formulate one of its peculiar qualities: that of direct emotional involvement—whether one calls it "giving resonance to dramatic situations" or "fleshing out the cliché" or whether, more abstractly, one talks in terms of identification patterns, empathy, and catharsis. Since the American cinema, determined as it is by an ideology of the spectacle and the spectacular, is essentially dramatic (as opposed to lyrical—i.e., concerned with mood or the inner self) and not conceptual (dealing with ideas and the structures of cognition and perception), the creation or reenactment of situations that the spectator can identify with and recognize (whether this recognition is on the conscious or unconscious level is another matter) depends to a large extent on the aptness of the iconography (the "visualization") and on the quality (complexity, subtlety, ambiguity) of the orchestration for what are transindividual, popular mythological (and therefore generally considered culturally "lowbrow") experiences and plot structures. In other words, this type of cinema depends on the ways "melos" is given to "drama" by means of lighting, montage, visual rhythm, decor, style of acting, music—that is, on the ways the mise-en-scène translates character into action (not unlike the pre-Jamesian novel) and action into gesture and dynamic space (comparable to nineteenth-century opera and ballet).

This granted, there seems to be a further problem that has some bearing on the question of melodrama: although the techniques of audience orientation and the possibility of psychic projection on the part of the spectator are as much in evidence in a melodrama like *Home from the Hill* or *Splendor in the Grass* (Elia Kazan, 1961) as they are in a western or adventure picture, the difference of setting and milieu affects the dynamics of the action. In the western, especially, the assumption of "open" spaces is virtually axiomatic; it is indeed one of the constants that makes the form perennially attractive to a largely urban audience. Yet this openness becomes problematic in films that deal with potential melodrama themes and family situations. The complex father-son relationships in *The Left-Handed Gun* (Arthur Penn, 1958), the Cain-Abel themes of Mann's *Winchester 73* (1950) and *Bend of the River* (1952), the conflict of virility and mother-fixation in Jacques Tourneur's *Great Day in the Morning* (1956) and *Wichita* (1955), or the search for the mother (-country) in Fuller's *Run of the Arrow* (1957) seem to find resolution because the hero can act positively on the changing situations where and when they present themselves. In Raoul Walsh's adventure pictures, as Peter Lloyd has shown,[8] identity comes in an often paradoxical process of self-confirmation and overreaching, but always through direct action, while the momentum generated by the conflicts pushes the protagonists forward in an unrelentingly linear course.

The family melodrama, by contrast, though dealing largely with the same Oedipal themes of emotional and moral identity, more often records the failure of the protagonist to act in a way that could shape the events and influence the emotional environment, let alone change the stifling social milieu. The world is closed, and the characters are acted upon. Melodrama confers on them a negative identity through suffering, and the progressive self-immolation and disillusionment generally end in resignation: they emerge as lesser human beings for having become wise and acquiescent to the ways of the world.

The difference can be put in another way. In one case, the drama moves toward its resolution by having the central conflicts successively externalized and projected into direct action. A jail break, a bank robbery, a western chase or cavalry charge, and even a criminal investigation all lend

69. *Double Indemnity:* Walter Neff (Fred MacMurray) is lured by the femme fatale (Barbara Stanwyck).

themselves to psychologized, thematized representations of the heroes' inner dilemmas and frequently appear that way, as in Walsh's *White Heat* (1949) or *They Died with Their Boots On* (1941), Losey's *The Criminal* (1960), Preminger's *Where the Sidewalk Ends* (1950). The same is true of the melodrama in the *série noire* tradition, where the hero is edged on or blackmailed by the femme fatale—the smell of honeysuckle and death in *Double Indemnity* (Billy Wilder, 1944), *Out of the Past* (Jacques Tourneur, 1947), or *Detour* (Edgar G. Ulmer, 1946)—into a course of action that pushes him farther and farther in one direction, opening a narrowing wedge of equally ineluctible consequences that usually lead the hero to wishing his own death as the ultimate act of liberation, but where the mechanism of fate at least allows him to express his existential revolt in strong and strongly antisocial behavior.

Not so in the domestic melodrama. The social pressures are such, the frame of respectability so sharply defined, that the range of "strong" actions is limited. The tellingly impotent gesture, the social gaffe, the hysterical outburst replaces any more directly liberating or self-annihilating action, and the cathartic violence of a shoot-out or a chase becomes an

70. *Written on the Wind:* Real and metaphorical mirrors in Sirk.

inner violence, often one that the characters turn against themselves. The dramatic configuration, the pattern of the plot, makes them, regardless of attempts to break free, constantly look inward, at each other and themselves. The characters are, so to speak, each others' sole referent; there is no world outside to be acted on, no reality that could be defined or assumed unambiguously. In Sirk, of course, they are locked into a universe of real and metaphoric mirrors, but quite generally what is typical of this form of melodrama is that the characters' behavior is often pathetically at variance with the real objectives they want to achieve. A sequence of substitute actions creates a kind of vicious circle in which the close nexus of cause and effect is somehow broken and—in an often overtly Freudian sense—displaced. James Dean in *East of Eden* (Elia Kazan, 1955) thinks up a method of cold storage for lettuce, grows beans to sell to the army, falls in love with Julie Harris, not to make a pile of money and live happily with a beautiful wife, but in order to win the love of his father and oust his brother—neither of which he achieves. Although very much on the surface of Kazan's film, this is a conjunction of puritan capitalist ethic and psychoanalysis that is sufficiently pertinent to the American melodrama to remain exemplary.

The melodramas of Ray, Sirk, or Minnelli do not deal with this displacement-by-substitution directly, but by what one might call an intensified symbolization of everyday actions, the heightening of the ordinary gesture and a use of setting and decor so as to reflect the characters' fetishist fixations. Violent feelings are given vent on "over-determined" objects (James Dean kicking his father's portrait as he storms out of the house in *Rebel without a Cause* [Ray, 1955]), and aggressiveness is worked out by proxy. In such films, the plots have a quite noticeable propensity to form a circular pattern, which in Ray involves an almost geometrical variation of triangle into circle and vice versa,[9] whereas Sirk (*nomen est omen*) often suggests in his circles the possibility of a tangent detaching itself—the full-circle construction of *Written on the Wind* with its linear coda of the Hudson-Bacall relationship at the end, or even more visually apparent, the circular race around the pylons in *The Tarnished Angels* broken when Dorothy Malone's plane in the last image soars past the fatal pylon into an unlimited sky.

It is perhaps not too fanciful to suggest that the structural changes from linear externalization of action to a sublimation of dramatic values into more complex forms of symbolization, and which I take to be a central characteristic of the melodramatic tradition in the American cinema, can be followed through on a more general level where it reflects a change in the history of dramatic forms and the articulation of energy in the American cinema as a whole.

As I have tried to show in an earlier article,[10] one of the typical features of the classical Hollywood movie has been that the hero was defined dynamically, as the center of a continuous movement, often both from sequence to sequence as well as within the individual shot. Perceptually, in order to get its bearing, the eye adjusts almost automatically to whatever moves, and movement, together with sound, completes the realistic illusion. It was on the basis of sheer physical movement, for example, that the musicals of the 1930s (Lloyd Bacon's *Forty-Second Street* [1933] being perhaps the most spectacular example), the gangster movie, and the B thriller of the 1940s and early 1950s could subsist with the flimsiest of plots, an almost total absence of individual characterization, and rarely any big stars. These deficiencies were made up by focusing to the point of exaggeration on the drive, the obsession, the *idée fixe*—that is to say, by a concentration on the purely kinetic-mechanical elements of human motivation. The pattern is most evident in the gangster genre, where the single-minded pursuit of money and power is followed by the equally single-minded and peremptory pursuit of physical survival, ending in the hero's apotheosis through violent death. This curve of rise and fall—a wholly stylized and external pattern that takes on a moral significance—

can be seen in movies like *Underworld* (Josef von Sternberg, 1927), *Little Caesar* (Mervyn LeRoy, 1930), *The Roaring Twenties* (Raoul Walsh, 1939), and *The Rise and Fall of Legs Diamond* (Budd Boetticher, 1960) and depends essentially on narrative pace, though it permits interesting variations and complexities, as in Fuller's *Underworld USA* (1961). A sophisticated director, such as Hawks, has used speed of delivery and the pulsating urgency of action to comic effect (*Scarface* [1932], *Twentieth Century* [1934]) and has even applied it to films whose dramatic structure did not naturally demand such a treatment (notably *His Girl Friday* [1940]). In parentheses, Hawks's reputed stoicism is itself a dramaturgical device, whereby sentimentality and cynicism are played so close together and played so fast that the result is an emotional hot-cold shower that is apt to numb the spectator's sensibility into feeling a sustained moral charge, where there is more often simply a very skilled switchboard manipulation of the same basic voltage. I am thinking especially of films like *Only Angels Have Wings* (1939).

This unrelenting internal combustion engine of physical and psychic energy, generically exemplified by the hard-boiled, crackling aggressiveness of the screwball comedy, but which Walsh diagnosed in his Cagney heroes as psychotic (*White Heat*) and a vehicle for extreme redneck republicanism (*A Lion Is in the Streets* [1953]), shows signs of a definite slowing down in the 1950s and early 1960s, where raucous vitality and instinctual "lust for life" is deepened psychologically to intimate neuroses and adolescent or not so adolescent maladjustments of a wider social significance. Individual initiative is perceived as problematic in explicitly political terms, as in *All the King's Men* (Robert Rossen, 1949), after having previously been merely stoically and heroically antisocial, as in the film noir. The external world is more and more riddled with obstacles that oppose themselves to personal ambition and are not simply overcome by the hero's assertion of a brawny or brainy libido. In Mann's westerns the madness at the heart of the James Stewart character only occasionally breaks through an otherwise calm and controlled surface, like a strong subterranean current suddenly appearing above ground as an inhuman and yet somehow poetically apt thirst for vengeance and primitive biblical justice, where the will to survive is linked to certain old-fashioned cultural and moral values of dignity, honor, and respect. In the films of Sirk, an uncompromising, fundamentally innocent energy is gradually turned away from simple, direct fulfillment by the emergence of a conscience, a sense of guilt and responsibility, or the awareness of moral complexity, as in *Magnificent Obsession* (1954), *Sign of the Pagan* (1954), *All That Heaven Allows* (1955), and even *Interlude* (1957)—a theme that in Sirk is always interpreted in terms of cultural decadence.

WHERE FREUD LEFT HIS MARX IN THE AMERICAN HOME

There can be little doubt that the postwar popularity of the family melo-drama in Hollywood is partly connected with the fact that in those years America discovered Freud. This is not the place to analyze why the United States should have become the country in which his theories found their most enthusiastic reception anywhere or why they became such a decisive influence on American culture, but the connections of Freud with melo-drama are as complex as they are undeniable. An interesting fact, for ex-ample, is that Hollywood tackled Freudian themes in a particularly "ro-mantic" or gothic guise, through a cycle of movies inaugurated possibly by Hitchcock's first big American success, *Rebecca* (1940). Relating his Victorianism to the Crawford-Stanwyck-Davis type of "women's pic-ture," which for obvious reasons became a major studio concern during the war years and found its apotheosis in such movies as John Cromwell's *Since You Went Away* (1944) (to the Front, that is), Hitchcock infused his film, and several others, with an oblique intimation of female frigid-ity producing strange fantasies of persecution, rape, and death—masoch-istic reveries and nightmares that cast the husband into the role of the sadistic murderer. This projection of sexual anxiety and its mechanisms of displacement and transfer is translated into a whole string of movies often involving hypnosis and playing on the ambiguity and suspense of whether the wife is merely imagining it or whether her husband really does have murderous designs on her. Hitchcock's *Notorious* (1946) and *Suspicion* (1941), Minnelli's *Undercurrent* (1946), Cukor's *Gaslight* (1944), Sirk's *Sleep, My Love* (1947), Tourneur's *Experiment Perilous* (1944), and Lang's *Secret beyond the Door* (1948) all belong in this cat-egory, as does Preminger's *Whirlpool* (1949) and in a wider sense Renoir's *Woman on the Beach* (1946). What strikes one about this list is not only the high number of European émigrés entrusted with such projects, but that virtually all of the major directors of family melodramas (except Ray) in the fifties had a (usually not entirely successful) crack at the Freudian feminist melodrama in the forties.

More challenging, and difficult to prove, is the speculation that certain stylistic and structural features of the sophisticated melodrama may in-volve principles of symbolization and coding that Freud conceptualized in his analysis of dreams and later also applied in his *Psychopathology of Everyday Life*. I am thinking less of the prevalence of what Freud called "Symptomhandlungen" or "Fehlhandlungen," that is, when slips of the tongue project inner states into interpretable overt behavior. This is a way of symbolizing and signaling attitudes common to the American cinema in virtually every genre and perhaps more directly attributable to the metonymic use of detail in the realist novel rather than to any Freudian influence. However, there is a certain refinement of this in the melodrama—it becomes part of the composition of the frame, more subliminally and unobtrusively transmitted to the spectator. When Minnelli's characters find themselves in an emotionally precarious or contradictory situation, it often affects the balance of the visual composition; wine glasses, a piece of china, or a tray full of drinks emphasizes the fragility of their situation—e.g., Judy Garland over breakfast in *The Clock* (1945), Richard Widmark in *The Cobweb,* explaining himself to Gloria Grahame, or Gregory Peck trying to make his girlfriend see why he married someone else in *Designing Woman* (1957). When Robert Stack in *Written on the Wind,* standing by the window he has just opened to get some fresh air into an extremely heavy family atmosphere, hears of Lauren Bacall expecting a baby, his misery becomes eloquent by the way he squeezes himself into the frame of the half-open window, every word his wife says to him bringing torment to his lacerated soul and racked body.

Along similar lines, I have in mind the kind of condensation of motivation into metaphoric images or sequences of images mentioned earlier, the relation that exists in Freudian dream work between manifest dream material and latent dream content. Just as in dreams certain gestures and incidents mean something by their structure and sequence rather than by what they literally represent, the melodrama often works, as I have tried to show, by a displaced emphasis, by substitute acts, by parallel situations and metaphoric connections. In dreams one tends to "use" as dream material incidents and circumstances from one's waking experience during the previous day, in order to "code" them, while nevertheless keeping a kind of emotional logic going, and even condensing their images into what, during the dream at least, seems an inevitable sequence. Melodramas often use middle-class American society, its iconography, and the family experience in just this way as their manifest material, but "displace" it into quite different patterns, juxtaposing stereotyped situations in strange configurations and provoking clashes and ruptures that not only open up new associations but also redistribute the emotional energies that suspense and tensions have accumulated in disturbingly different directions. American movies, for example, often manipulate very shrewdly situations of extreme embarrassment (a blocking of emotional energy) and acts or gestures of violence (direct or indirect release) in order to create patterns of aesthetic significance that only a musical vocabulary might be able to describe accurately and for which psychoanalysis or anthropology might offer some explanation.

One of the principles involved is that of continuity and discontinuity. What Sirk has called the "rhythm of the plot" is what makes a movie hang together. This, it seems to me, is a particularly complex aspect of the sophisticated melodrama. A typical situation in 1950s American melodramas occurs where the plot builds up to an evidently catastrophic collision of counterrunning sentiments, but a string of delays gets the greatest possible effect from the clash when it does come. In Minnelli's *The Bad and the Beautiful* (1952) Lana Turner plays an alcoholic actress who has been "rescued" by producer Kirk Douglas, giving her a new start in the movies. After their premiere, flushed with success, self-confident for the first time in years, and in happy anticipation of celebrating with Douglas, with whom she has fallen in love, she drives to his home armed with a bottle of champagne. However, we already know that Douglas isn't emotionally interested in her ("I need an actress, not a wife," he later tells her) and is spending the evening with a broad in his bedroom. Turner, suspecting nothing, is met by Douglas at the foot of the stairs. At first too engrossed in herself to notice how cool he is, she is stunned when the other woman suddenly appears at the top of the stairs in Douglas's dressing gown. Her nervous breakdown is signaled by the car headlights flashing against her windshield like a barrage of footlights and arc lamps as she drives home.

Letting the emotions rise and then bringing them suddenly down with a thump is an extreme example of dramatic discontinuity, and a similar, vertiginous drop in the emotional temperature punctuates a good many melodramas—almost invariably played out against the vertical axis of a staircase.[11] In one of the most paroxysmic montage sequences that the American cinema has known, Sirk has Dorothy Malone in *Written on the Wind* dance like some doomed goddess from a Dionysian mystery while her father is collapsing on the stairs and dying from a heart attack. Again, in *Imitation of Life* (1959), John Gavin gets the brush-off from Lana Turner as they are going downstairs, and in *All I Desire* Barbara Stanwyck has to disappoint her daughter about not taking her to New York to become an actress, after the girl has rushed downstairs to tell her father the good news. Ray's use of the staircase for similar emotional effects is well known and most spectacular in *Bigger Than Life* (1956). In Henry King's *Margie* (1946), a film following rather closely Minnelli's *Meet Me in St. Louis* (1944), the heroine, Jeanne Crain, about to be taken to the graduation ball by a blind date (whom we know to be her father) since her poetry-loving bespectacled steady has caught a cold, comes tearing down from her bedroom when she hears that the French master, on whom she has a crush, has dropped in. She virtually rips the bouquet of flowers out of his hands and is overwhelmed by joy. With some embarrassment, the poor man has to explain that he is taking someone else to the ball, that he has only come to return her papers. Margie, mortified, humiliated, and cringing with shame, has just enough time to get back upstairs before she dissolves in tears.

All this may not sound terribly profound on paper, but the orchestration of such a scene can produce strong emotional effects, and the strategy of building up to a climax so as to throttle it the more abruptly is a form of dramatic reversal by which Hollywood directors have consistently criticized the streak of incurably naive moral and emotional idealism in the American psyche, first by showing it to be often indistinguishable from the grossest kind of illusion and self-delusion and then by forcing a confrontation when it is most wounding and contradictory. The emotional extremes are played off in such a way that they reveal an inherent dialectic, and the undeniable psychic energy contained in this seemingly vulnerable sentimentality is utilized to furnish its own antidote, to bring home the discontinuities in the structures of emotional experience that give a kind of realism and toughness rare if not unthinkable in the European cinema.

What makes these discontinuities in the melodrama so effective is that they occur, as it were, under pressure. Although the kinetics of the American cinema are generally directed toward creating pressure and manipulating it (as suspense, for example), the melodrama presents in some ways a special case. In the western or the thriller, suspense is generated by the linear organization of the plot and the action, together with the kind of "pressure" that spectators bring to the film by way of anticipation and a priori expectations of what they hope to see; melodrama, however, has to accommodate the latter type of pressure, as already indicated, in what amounts to a relatively closed world.

This is emphasized by the function of the decor and the symbolization of objects: the setting of the family melodrama is almost by definition the middle-class home, filled with objects, which in a film like Philip Dunne's *Hilda Crane,* typical of the genre in this respect, surround the heroine in a hierarchy of apparent order that becomes increasingly suffocating. From Father's armchair in the living room and Mother's knitting, to the upstairs bedroom, where after five years' absence dolls and teddies are still neatly arranged on the bedspread, home not only overwhelms Hilda with images of parental oppression and a repressed past (which indirectly provoke her explosive outbursts that sustain the action), it also brings out the characteristic attempt of the bourgeois household to make time stand still, immobilize life, and fix forever domestic property relations as the model of social life and a bulwark against the more disturbing sides in human nature. The theme has a particular poignancy in the many films about the victimization and enforced passivity of women—women waiting at home, standing by the window, caught in a world of objects into which they are expected to invest their feelings. Cromwell's *Since You Went Away* has a telling sequence in which Claudette Colbert, having just taken her husband to the troop train at the station, returns home to clear up after the morning's rush. Everything she looks at or touches—dressing gown, pipe, wedding picture, breakfast cup, slippers, shaving brush, the dog—re-minds her of her husband, until she cannot bear the strain and falls on her bed sobbing. The banality of the objects, combined with the repressed anxieties and emotions, forces a contrast that makes the scene almost epitomize the relation of decor to characters in the melodrama: the more the setting is filled with objects to which the plot gives symbolic signifi-cance, the more the characters are enclosed in seemingly ineluctable situ-ations. Pressure is generated by things crowding in on them, life becomes increasingly complicated because it is cluttered with obstacles and objects that invade the characters' personalities, take them over, stand for them, become more real than the human relations or emotions they were in-tended to symbolize.

It is again an instance of Hollywood stylistic devices supporting the themes or commenting on each other. Melodrama is iconographically fixed by the claustrophobic atmosphere of the bourgeois home and/or the small-town setting; its emotional pattern is that of panic and latent hys-teria, reinforced stylistically by a complex handling of space in interiors (Sirk, Ray, and Losey particularly excel in this) to the point where the world seems totally predetermined and pervaded by "meaning" and in-terpretable signs.

This marks another recurrent feature, already touched on: that of de-sire focusing on the unobtainable object. The mechanisms of displace-ment and transfer, in an enclosed field of pressure, open a highly dynamic, yet discontinuous cycle of nonfulfillment, where discontinuity creates a universe of powerfully emotional but obliquely related fixations. In melo-drama, violence, the strong action, the dynamic movement, the full artic-ulation, and the fleshed-out emotions so characteristic of the American cinema become the very signs of the characters' alienation and thus serve to formulate a devastating critique of the ideology that supports it.

Minnelli and Sirk are exceptional directors in this respect, not least be-cause they handle stories with four, five, or sometimes six characters all tied up in a single configuration, and yet give each of them an even the-matic emphasis and an independent point of view. Such skill involves a particularly "musical" gift and a very sensitive awareness of the harmo-nizing potential contained in contrasting material and the structural im-plications of different characters' motives. Films like *Home from the Hill, The Cobweb, The Tarnished Angels,* or *Written on the Wind* strike one as "objective" films, since they do not have a central hero (though there may be a gravitational pull toward one of the protagonists). Nonetheless they cohere, mainly because each of the characters' predicaments is made plausible in terms that relate to the problems of the others. The films are built architecturally, by a combination of structural tensions and articu-lated parts, and the overall design appears only retrospectively, as it were, when with the final coda of appeasement the edifice is complete and the spectator can stand back and look at the pattern. But there is, especially in the Minnelli movies, also a wholly "subjective" dimension. Because the parts are so closely organized around a central theme or dilemma, the films can be interpreted as emanating from a single consciousness, which is testing or experiencing in dramatic form the various options and possibilities flowing from an initially outlined moral or existential contradiction. In *The Cobweb* John Kerr wants both total self-expression and a defined human framework in which such freedom is meaningful, and George Hamilton in *Home from the Hill* wants to assume adult responsibilities while at the same time he rejects the standards of adulthood implied in his father's aggressive masculinity. In the latter the drama ends with a "Freudian" resolution of the father being eliminated at the very point when he has resigned himself to his loss of supremacy, but this is underpinned by a "biblical" one which fuses the mythology of Cain and Abel with that of Abraham blessing his firstborn. The interweaving of motifs is achieved by a series of parallels and contrasts. Set in the South, the story concerns the relations of a mother's boy with his tough father, played by Robert Mitchum, whose wife so resents his having a bastard son (George Peppard) that she won't sleep with him. The plot progresses through all the possible permutations of the basic situation: lawful son/natural son, sensitive George Hamilton/hypochondriac mother, tough George Peppard/tough Robert Mitchum, both boys fancy the same girl, Hamilton gets her pregnant. Peppard marries her, the girl's father turns nasty against the lawful son because of the notorious sex life of his father, etc. However, because the plot is structured as a series of mirror reflections on the theme of fathers and sons, blood ties and natural affinities, Minnelli's film is a psychoanalytical portrait of the sensitive adolescent—but placed in a definite ideological and social context. The boy's consciousness, we realize, is made up of what are external forces and circumstances, his dilemma the result of his social position as heir to his father's estate, unwanted because felt to be undeserved, and an upbringing deliberately exploited by his mother in order to get even with his father, whose own position as a Texas landowner and local big-shot forces him to compensate for his wife's frigidity by proving his virility with other women. Melodrama here becomes the vehicle for diagnosing a single individual in ideological terms and objective categories, while the blow-by-blow emotional drama creates the second level, where the subjective aspect (the immediate and necessarily unreflected experience of the characters) is left intact. The hero's identity, on the other hand, emerges as a kind of picture puzzle from the various pieces of dramatic action.

Home from the Hill is also a perfect example of the principle of substitute acts, mentioned earlier, which is Hollywood's way of portraying the dynamics of alienation. The story is sustained by pressure that is applied indirectly and by desires that always chase unattainable goals: Mitchum forces George Hamilton to "become a man" though he is temperamentally his mother's son, while Mitchum's "real" son in terms of attitudes and character is George Peppard, whom he cannot acknowledge for social reasons. Likewise, Eleanor Parker puts pressure on her son in order to get at Mitchum, and Everett Sloane (the girl's father) takes out on George Hamilton the sexual hatred he feels against Mitchum. Finally, after his daughter has become pregnant he goes to see Mitchum to put pressure on him to get his son to marry the girl, only to break down when Mitchum turns the tables and accuses him of blackmail. It is a pattern that in an even purer form appears in *Written on the Wind:* Dorothy Malone wants Rock Hudson, who wants Lauren Bacall, who wants Robert Stack, who just wants to die. *Le Ronde à l'américaine.* The point is that the melodramatic dynamism of these situations is used by both Sirk and Minnelli to make the emotional impact carry over into the very subdued, apparently neutral, sequences of images that so often round off a scene and that thereby have a strong lyrical quality.

One of the characteristic features of melodramas in general is that they concentrate on the point of view of the victim: what makes the films mentioned above exceptional is the way they manage to present *all* the characters convincingly as victims. The critique—the questions of "evil," of responsibility—is firmly placed on a social and existential level, away from the arbitrary and finally obtuse logic of private motives and individualized psychology. This is why the melodrama, at its most accomplished, seems capable of reproducing more directly than other genres the patterns of domination and exploitation existing in a given society, especially the relation between psychology, morality, and class consciousness, by emphasizing so clearly an emotional dynamic whose social correlative is a network of external forces directed oppressingly inward and with which the characters themselves unwittingly collude to become their agents. In Minnelli, Sirk, Ray, Cukor, and others, alienation is recognized as a basic condition, fate is secularized into the prison of social conformity and psychological neurosis, and the linear trajectory of self-fulfilment so potent in American ideology is twisted into the downward spiral of a self-destructive urge seemingly possessing a whole social class.

This typical masochism of melodrama, with its incessant acts of inner violation, its mechanisms of frustration and overcompensation, is perhaps brought most into the open in characters who have a drinking problem (*Written on the Wind, Hilda Crane, Days of Wine and Roses* [Blake Edwards, 1963]). Although alcoholism is too common an emblem in films and too typical of middle-class America to deserve a close thematic analysis, drink does become interesting in movies where its dynamic signifi-

71. *Written on the Wind*: Building on the metaphoric possibilities of alcohol.

cance is developed and its qualities as a visual metaphor recognized: wherever characters are seen swallowing and gulping their drinks as if they were swallowing their humiliations along with their pride, vitality and the life force have become palpably destructive, and a phony libido has turned into real anxiety. *Written on the Wind* is perhaps the movie that most consistently builds on the metaphoric possibilities of alcohol (liquidity, potency, the phallic shape of bottles). Not only is its theme an emotional drought that no amount of alcohol, oil pumped by the derricks, or petrol in fast cars and planes can mitigate, it also has Robert Stack compensate for his sexual impotence and childhood guilt feelings by hugging a bottle of raw corn every time he feels suicidal, which he proceeds to smash in disgust against the paternal mansion. In one scene, Stack makes unmistakable gestures with an empty martini bottle in the direction of his wife, and an unconsummated relationship is visually underscored when two brimful glasses remain untouched on the table, as Dorothy Malone does her best to seduce an unresponsive Rock Hudson at the family party, having previously poured her whiskey into the flower vase of her rival, Lauren Bacall.

Melodrama is often used to describe tragedy that doesn't quite come off: either because the characters think of themselves too self-consciously as tragic or because the predicament is too evidently fabricated on the level of plot and dramaturgy to carry the kind of conviction normally termed "inner necessity." In some American family melodramas inadequacy of the characters' responses to their predicament becomes itself part of the subject. In Cukor's *The Chapman Report* (1962) and Minnelli's *The Cobweb*—two movies explicitly concerned with the impact of Freudian notions on American society—the protagonists' self-understanding as well as the doctors' attempts at analysis and therapy are shown to be either tragically or comically inadequate to the situations that the characters are supposed to cope with in everyday life. Pocket-size tragic heroes and heroines, they are blindly grappling with a fate real enough to cause intense human anguish, which as the spectator can see, however, is compounded by social prejudice, ignorance, and insensitivity on top of bogus claims to scientific objectivity by the doctors. Claire Bloom's nymphomania and Jane Fonda's frigidity in the Cukor movie are seen to be two different but equally hysterical reactions to the heavy ideological pressures that American society exerts on the relations between the sexes. *The Chapman Report,* despite having apparently been cut by Darryl F. Zanuck, Jr., remains an extremely important film partly because it treats its theme both in the tragic and the comic mode without breaking apart, underlining thereby the ambiguous springs of the discrepancy between displaying intense feelings and the circumstances to which they are inadequate—usually a comic motif but tragic in its emotional implications.

Both Cukor and Minnelli, however, focus on how ideological contradictions are reflected in the characters' seemingly spontaneous behavior —the way self-pity and self-hatred alternate with a violent urge toward some form of liberating action, which inevitably fails to resolve the conflict. The characters experience as a shamefully personal stigma what the spectator (because of the parallelisms between the different episodes in *The Chapman Report* as well as the analogies in the fates of the seven principal figures of *The Cobweb*) is forced to recognize as belonging to a wider social dilemma. The poverty of the intellectual resources in some of the characters is starkly contrasted with a corresponding abundance of emotional resources, and as one sees them helplessly struggling inside their emotional prisons with no hope of realizing to what degree they are the victims of their society, one gets a clear picture of how a certain individualism reinforces social and emotional alienation, and of how the economics of the psyche are as vulnerable to manipulation and exploitation as is a person's labor.

The point is that this inadequacy has a name, relevant to the melodrama as a form: irony or pathos, which both in tragedy and melodrama is the response to the recognition of different levels of awareness. Irony privileges the spectator vis-à-vis the protagonists, for he or she registers the difference from a superior position of knowledge. Pathos results from noncommunication or silence made eloquent—people talking at cross-purposes (Lauren Bacall telling Robert Stack she's pregnant in *Written on the Wind*), a mother watching her daughter's wedding from afar (Barbara Stanwyck in *Stella Dallas* [King Vidor, 1937]), or a woman returning unnoticed to her family, watching them through the window (Barbara Stanwyck in *All I Desire*). These highly emotional situations are underplayed to present an ironic discontinuity of feeling or a qualitative difference in intensity, usually visualized in terms of spatial distance and separation.

Such archetypal melodramatic situations activate very strongly an audience's participation, for there is a desire to make up for the emotional deficiency, to impart the different awareness, which in other genres is systematically frustrated to produce suspense: the primitive desire to warn the heroine of the perils looming visibly over her in the shape of the villain's shadow. But in the more sophisticated melodramas this pathos is most acutely produced through a "liberal" mise-en-scène which balances different points of view, so that the spectator is in a position of seeing and evaluating contrasting attitudes within a given thematic framework—a framework which is the result of the total configuration and therefore inaccessible to the protagonists themselves. The spectator, say in Otto Preminger's *Daisy Kenyon* (1947) or a Nicholas Ray movie, is made aware of the slightest qualitative imbalance in a relationship and also sensitized to the tragic implications that a radical misunderstanding or a misconception of motives might have, even when this is not played out in terms of a tragic ending.

If pathos is the result of a skillfully displaced emotional emphasis, it is frequently used in melodramas to explore psychological and sexual repression, usually in conjunction with the theme of inferiority; inadequacy of response in the American cinema often has an explicitly sexual code. Male impotence and female frigidity is a subject that allows for thematization in various directions, not only to indicate the kinds of psychological anxiety and social pressures that generally make people sexually unresponsive, but as metaphors of a lack of freedom (Hitchcock's frigid heroines) or as a quasi-metaphysical "overreaching" (as in Ray's *Bigger Than Life*). In Sirk, where the theme has an exemplary status, it is treated as a problem of decadence—where intention, awareness, and yearning outstrip sexual, social, and moral performance. From the Willi Birgel character in *Zu neuen Ufern* onward, Sirk's most impressive characters are never up to the demands that their lives make on them, though some are sufficiently sensitive, alive, and intelligent to feel and know about this inadequacy of gesture and response. It gives their pathos a tragic ring, because they take on suffering and moral anguish knowingly, as the just price for having glimpsed a better world and having failed to live it. A tragic self-awareness is called upon to compensate for lost spontaneity and energy, and in films like *All I Desire* or *There's Always Tomorrow* (Sirk, 1956), where as so often, the fundamental irony is in the titles themselves, this theme which has haunted the European imagination at least since Nietzsche, is absorbed into an American small-town atmosphere, often revolving around the questions of dignity and responsibility, of how to step down, how to yield when confronted with true talent and true vitality—in short, those qualities that dignity is called upon to make up for.

In Hollywood melodrama characters made for operettas play out the human tragedies (which is how they experience the contradictions of American civilization). Small wonder they are constantly baffled and amazed, as Lana Turner is in *Imitation of Life,* about what is going on around them and within them. The tensions of seeming and being, of intention and result, register as a perplexing frustration, and an ever-increasing gap opens between the emotions and the reality they seek to reach. What strikes one as the true pathos is the very mediocrity of the human beings involved, putting such high demands upon themselves, trying to live up to an exalted vision of the human being, but instead living out the impossible contradictions that have turned the American dream into its proverbial nightmare. It makes the best American melodramas of the fifties not only critical social documents but genuine tragedies, despite or rather because of the happy ending: they record some of the agonies that have accompanied the demise of the "affirmative culture." Spawned by liberal idealism, they advocated with open, conscious irony that the remedy is to apply more of the same idealism. But even without the national disasters that were to overtake America in the late sixties, this irony, too, almost seems now to belong to a different age.

Notes

1. Pierre Marie Augustin Filon, *The English Stage,* translated by Frederic Whyte (1897; reprint Port Washington, N.Y.: Kennikat Press, 1970), p. 195. Filon also offers an interesting definition of melodrama: "When dealing with Irving, I asked the question, so often discussed, whether we go to the theatre to see a representation of life, or to forget life and seek relief from it. Melodrama solves this question and shows that both theories are right, by giving satisfaction to both desires, in that it offers the extreme of realism in scenery and language together with the most uncommon sentiments and events" (p. 196).

2. See Jean Duvignaud, *Sociologie du théâtre* (Paris: Presses Universitaires du France, 1965), 4, no. 3, "Théâtre sans révolution, révolution sans théâtre."

3. About the ideological function of nineteenth-century Victorian melodrama, see Maurice Willson Disher, *Blood and Thunder: Mid-Victorian Melodrama and Its Origins* (London: F. Muller, 1949): "Even in gaffs and saloons, melodrama so strongly insisted on the sure reward to be bestowed in this life upon the law-abiding that sociologists now see in this a Machiavellian plot to keep democracy servile to Church and State. . . . There is no parting the two strains, moral and political, in the imagination of the nineteenth-century masses. They are hopelessly entangled. Democracy shaped its own entertainments at a time when the vogue of Virtue Triumphant was at its height and they took their pattern from it. . . . Here are Virtue Triumphant's attendant errors: confusion between sacred and profane, between worldly and spiritual advancement, between self-interest and self-sacrifice" (pp. 13–14). However, it ought to be remembered that there are melodramatic traditions outside the puritan-democratic world view: Catholic countries, such as Spain and Mexico (cf. Buñuel's Mexican films) have a very strong line in melodramas, based on the themes of atonement and redemption. Japanese melodramas have been "high-brow" since the Monogatari stories of the sixteenth century, and in Mizoguchi's films (*O Haru, Shinheike Monogatari*) they reach a transcendence and stylistic sublimation rivalled only by the very best Hollywood melodramas.

4. Hanns Eisler, *Composing for Film* (London: Dobson, 1981).

5. Lilian Ross, *Picture* (London: Penguin, 1958).

6. Erwin Panofsky, "Style and Medium in the Motion Pictures," in *Film: An Anthology*, ed. Daniel Talbot (Berkeley: University of California Press, 1969), p. 18.

7. The impact of *Madame Bovary* via Willa Cather on the American cinema and the popular imagination would deserve a closer look.

8. Peter Lloyd, "Raoul Walsh," *Brighton Film Review*, no. 14 (November 1969): 9; "Raoul Walsh: The Hero," ibid., no. 15 (December 1969): 8–12; "Raoul Walsh," ibid., no. 21 (June 1970): 20–21.

9. I have not seen *A Woman's Secret* (1949) or *Born to Be Bad* (1950), either of which might include Ray in this category, and the Ida Lupino character in *On Dangerous Ground* (1952)—blind, living with a homicidal brother—is distinctly reminiscent of this masochistic strain in Hollywood feminism.

10. Thomas Elsaesser, "Nicholas Ray (Part 1)," *Brighton Film Review*, no. 19 (April 1970): 13–16; "Nicholas Ray (Part 2)," ibid., no. 20 (May 1970): 15–16.

11. As a principle of mise-en-scène the dramatic use of staircases recalls the famous *Jessner-treppe* of German theater. The thematic conjunction of family and height/depth symbolism is nicely described by Max Tessier: "Le heros ou l'héroine sont ballotés dans un véritable scenic-railway social, ou les classes sont rigoureusement compartimentées. Leur ambition est de quitter à jamais un milieu moralement dépravé, physiquement éprouvant, pour accéder au Nirvana de la grande bourgeoisie. . . . Pas de famille, pas de mélo! Pour qu'il y ait mélo il faut avant tout qu'il y ait faute, péché, transgression sociale. Or, quel est le milieu idéal pour que se développe (cette gangrène, sinon cette cellule familiale, liée à une conception hiérarchique de la société)?" (*Cinéma 71*, no. 161, p. 46).

25. Screwball Comedies: Constructing Romance, Mystifying Marriage

DAVID R. SHUMWAY

As floating signifiers go, romance has gotten around more than usual. The term has long designated several different generic categories of prose fiction as well as a particular kind of subject matter with which fiction, romance or novel, may deal. There are film genres, such as "romantic comedy," that derive their identity from their concern with love and courtship. But in film studies the term has additionally named both a self-conscious component of a Hollywood product, its love interest, and also a frequent element of the ideological effect known as narrative displacement. Romance is very often the receptacle of displacement, which is fitting for a term that has also come to be almost a synonym for illusion. But to treat romance as merely illusion or false consciousness will lead one to ignore the particular characteristics of its construction and effect. What most analyses of both literature and film have failed to acknowledge is that romance has itself been treated as an ideology by feminist writers such as Shulamith Firestone and Juliet Mitchell. While this ideology is pervasive in Hollywood films, it is perhaps most central to the screwball comedy.[1]

The most sustained analysis of screwball comedy to date is Stanley Cavell's *Pursuits of Happiness*. Despite the fact that the focus of Cavell's argument is marriage, he neglects the feminist perspective almost entirely and the significant body of feminist film study completely. This is certainly a major reason for his failure to understand the cultural work of the genre. Where Cavell goes wrong—and it is hardly a peripheral place—is his position that the screwball comedies succeed in enlightening us about marriage itself. My argument is that they do just the opposite: they mystify marriage by portraying it as the goal—but not the end—of romance. The major cultural work of these films is not the stimulation of thought about marriage, but the affirmation of marriage in the face of the threat of a growing divorce rate and liberalized divorce laws. What an analysis of screwball comedies will show is that romance functions as a specific ideology that is used by these films to mystify marriage. I hope to show

how screwball comedies typically construct the viewer as subject of their romance so that he or she must feel marriage as the thing desired. I will then consider how certain elements in the genre suggest a critique of marriage, and examine how these elements can become dominant in such films as *Adam's Rib* (George Cukor, 1949) and *Desperately Seeking Susan* (Susan Seidelman, 1985).

Cavell claims to have noticed a previously unrecognized film genre, the comedy of remarriage, which he believes begins with *It Happened One Night* (Frank Capra, 1934).[2] His central claim is that the comedy of remarriage shifts "emphasis away from the normal question of comedy, whether a young pair will get married, onto the question whether the pair will get and stay divorced, thus prompting philosophical discussions of the nature of marriage" (p. 85). Without going into the vexed issues of genre theory, Cavell does make a strong case for these films as a group that can profitably be studied together. But how can we account for the development of this new comic genre? Why did *re*marriage suddenly become a more important issue than marriage? Germaine Greer argues persuasively that Shakespearean comedy expresses a new, middle-class myth that linked romantic love and marriage.[3] This myth having become widely accepted, the comedy of remarriage is very likely a response to what was perceived as a crisis of marriage. As Elaine Tyler May puts it, "During the late nineteenth and early twentieth centuries, American marriages began to collapse at an unprecedented rate. Between 1867 and 1929, the population of the United States grew 300 percent, the number of marriages increased 400 percent, and the divorce rate rose 2000 percent. By the end of the 1920s, more than one in six marriages terminated in court."[4] If divorce had been increasing since the nineteenth century, it continued to do so in the twentieth. Between 1910 and 1940, the divorce rate nearly doubled, in spite of a slight decline in the early 1930s.[5] Debate over the causes of the crisis was carried on by moralists and scholars. These explanations ranged from women's emancipation and liberal divorce laws to the general conditions of urban life. May suggests that each of these explanations is faulty. The one that she offers in their stead is that rising expectation of personal satisfaction and happiness put an increased burden on marriage that it was unable to bear.[6] May seems unaware, however, that a version of this explanation was also articulated at the time. Several studies related the failure of marriages to expectations engendered by romance.[7] If, as Niklas Luhmann notes, this explanation remains speculative, May's analysis of divorce cases goes some way toward supporting it. And, significantly for our purposes, she suggests that Hollywood itself was in part responsible for these rising expectations. Movies and movie stars, such as Douglas Fairbanks and Mary Pickford, became identified with "an entirely new type of home."[8] While the home had traditionally been identified as an institution that demanded sacrifice and communal values, the new home was "self-contained" and "geared to personal happiness." [9] The project of the comedies of remarriage is to reaffirm this romantic view of marriage in the face of the fact of its failure. Hollywood films take up this cultural work not only out of patriarchal interest and ideology, but for the coincident reason that films that participated in this ideology were popular. A majority of the film audience doubtless found it pleasurable to be reassured about the possibilities of marriage.

It is possible, however, to make too much of the remarriage "genre." For one thing, only two of Cavell's seven comedies deal with characters who we actually see interacting as husband and wife for any length of time, and, as I will argue, one of these, *Adam's Rib*, is entirely atypical. That leaves *The Awful Truth* (Leo McCarey, 1937), which Cavell calls "the best, or deepest, of the comedies of remarriage" (p. 231) and of which he says "it is the only member of the genre in which the topic of divorce . . . [is] undisplaced," as the only pure example of the type (pp. 232–233). In the other comedies remarriage is presented only metaphorically, or, in the case of *The Philadelphia Story* (Cukor, 1940), as the conclusion to a story that takes place after the couple has been divorced. Second, each of the seven films Cavell discusses would have been identified by Hollywood as members of the genre "screwball comedy"—i.e., as being similar kinds of products. While virtually all screwball comedies are romances that end in marriage, many cannot be called comedies of remarriage. On the other hand, Cavell's comedies share the romance that characterizes other screwball comedies. This suggests that the comedy of remarriage is best considered a special case of Hollywood romance, one that applies that same set of assumptions to a new situation. Thus the comedy of remarriage, like Shakespearean comedy, works to link romantic love and marriage. In this sense, screwball comedy continues to perform cultural work that many of the most important forms of cultural production—novels, operas, poems, etc.—had been performing throughout the period of bourgeois hegemony.

While Cavell does not discuss screwball comedy, he does define the comedy of remarriage as a subgenre of the romance, and he finds a particular connection between these films and such Shakespearean romances as *The Tempest* and *The Winter's Tale*. Cavell does not define "romance," but he accepts the view that romance deals in the fantastic, that it is less realistic than the comedy of manners. He says of *The Lady Eve* (Preston Sturges, 1941), "Preston Sturges is trying to tell us that tales of romance are inherently feats of cony catching, of conning, making gulls or suckers of their audience" (p. 48). Thus Cavell is not unaware of how romance is being used in these films. As he argues at the end of his chapter on *His*

Girl Friday (Howard Hawks, 1940): "It is a premiss [*sic*] of farce that marriage kills romance. It is a project of the genre of remarriage to refuse to draw a conclusion from this premiss [*sic*] but rather to turn the tables on farce, to turn marriage itself into romance, into adventure, which for Walter and Hildy means to preserve within it something of the illicit, to find as it were a moral equivalent of the immoral" (p. 186). Cavell seems thus to contradict himself: comedies of remarriage tell us that romance is illusion and depict marriage romantically, but they can still tell us the truth about marriage. His claim that the comedy of remarriage prompts "philosophical discussions on the nature of marriage" (p. 85) is undermined by his own remarks about romance, but we are also led to wonder why, if these films are intended to prompt "philosophical discussions on the nature of marriage," they must, with two exceptions, deal with characters who are *not* married to each other.

What Cavell does not consider in *Pursuits of Happiness* is that romance is more than simple illusion and more than a genre: it is a complex and tenacious ideology. As an ideology, romance obviously bears some connection to illusion, but there is a more important connection to the genre. While this connection exists at several levels, the most fundamental is a narratological structure that Donald Maddox discovered in the *Lais* of Marie de France. This structure is triadic, including a pair of subjects and an excluded third subject that Maddox illustrates as a triangle with each member of the pair at an angle on top and the third term at the bottom. Narrative succession occurs because the excluded subject always seeks to be included in the pair. When he or she is included, this will necessarily displace someone else.[10] Before I analyze this structure as it appears in *It Happened One Night,* I want to point out its connections to other levels of the analysis of these films. The most obvious is the figural love triangle that exists in each of the comedies of remarriage and that de Rougemont has argued is an integral part of the ideology of romantic love.[11] Thus, in most romances, the narrative structure is actually represented by a triangular set of relationships between lovers, but the narrative structure is not identical with the love triangle, since other relationships—for example, father/daughter or king/court—may constitute the included pair. At a third level of activity we should note with Maddox the parallels between triadic narrative structure and Jacques Lacan's triangular illustration of an intersubjective complex successively occupied by different characters.[12] Maddox thus describes his narrative analysis as intersubjective rather than functional or actantial. But the notion of subject positioning has also been used by film theorists to describe the interpellation of the viewing subject by film.[13] The viewer or reader of a romance is typically sutured into the position of exclusion; like the odd person out in the narrative triangle, the viewer experiences a lack, and the resulting desire motivates and structures his or her attention. In romance such suturing may shift with each new revolution on the triangle.

The coincidence of narrative and figural desire is what makes romance so powerfully attractive in a narrative, and this doubtless in part explains why heterosexual romance figures as the leading line of action in the majority of Hollywood films.[14] While it would be possible to have a story about heterosexual romance that was not ideologically romantic, we know that few Hollywood products fit this description. There are a number of different accounts of romantic ideology as expressed in different cultures and artifacts.[15] The version that seems most common in Hollywood film holds "the bliss of genitality" to be the *end* of desire.[16] When the right man or woman is found and returns one's love, the subject will be satisfied, will lack no more. But romance does not focus its energy on describing this bliss. Rather, romance seeks by almost any means it can to heighten desire. For this reason there must be obstacles to the couple's union. Furthermore, other desired objects become associated with the couple such that we are enticed into not only sexual but other material kinds of desire. One reason that screwball comedies almost always involve the rich is that their world is a metaphor for the reward that romance promises of love.

The specific illusion that the screwball comedy constructs is that one can have both complete desire and complete satisfaction and that the name for this state of affairs is marriage. But the other side of the romantic economy is that satisfaction is the death of desire. Romantic tragedies such as *Tristan and Isolde* allegorize this in the literal deaths of the lovers. According to Juliet Mitchell, romance seeks an idealized object, and when that object is attained, love ceases to be romantic.[17] Marriage must be the death of romance between the members of the couple, who, if they are to continue to participate in romance, must find other partners. Hence, for the project of the screwball comedy to work, romance must occur outside of marriage, and marriage must be the end of the movie.[18]

In these terms, if screwball comedies, or comedies of remarriage, are romances, then they would be unlikely to tell us anything about marriage. I will now explore the way romance is constructed in screwball comedy by focusing on two paradigmatic examples, *It Happened One Night* and *The Philadelphia Story*. I begin with *It Happened One Night* because the triadic structure is closer to the surface and less complicated by intersecting subplots than in *The Philadelphia Story*. The film begins with both Ellen Andrews (Claudette Colbert) and Peter Warne (Clark Gable) excluded, but not involuntarily, from something: Ellen from her father and home, Peter from his boss and the newspaper. Their exile places them on the road together trying to return, Ellen to her husband and Peter to his home and presumably a job. The resulting relationship makes Ellen and her husband, King Wesley, a pair and excludes Peter, while paradoxically also constituting Ellen and Peter as a pair and excluding King. But it is Peter, not King, who is the male subject of desire in the film, and his desire for Ellen, in fact his claim on her, is announced in an outrageous double entendre, his first words to her when she has taken the seat he has fought for by pitching some bundles of newspapers out the window and jousting verbally with the bus driver: "That upon which you sit is mine." The camera makes Ellen the object of Peter's desire and ours by giving us the first tight close-up of Colbert's face. The first part of the narrative is the story of Peter's attempts to displace King Wesley, not as Ellen's husband but in her affections. It is irrelevant, of course, that Peter may not be conscious of this desire, for we as viewers are aware of it. Just when the triangle shifts is necessarily ambiguous, as it is in all adulterous situations. Of course, Peter and Ellen do not become lovers until the end of the film—when it is still not entirely clear that they are legally married—but I think we are entitled to read their "sleeping together" separated by the "walls of Jericho" as a metaphor for adultery as well as literal chastity, just as in *The Philadelphia Story* Tracy Lord can, as Cavell argues, be said metaphorically to lose her virginity with McCauley Conner, even though she was not literally a virgin and he did not actually take advantage of her. The walls of Jericho are this film's equivalent of the sword of chastity that separated voluntarily Tristan and Isolde. In fact, the paradox of adultery without sex, having been codified in the rules for courtly love, might be said to be one of the central conventions of narratives of romantic love.[19] The transgression of the marriage bond without sex serves to create adventure and intensify desire. Officially, King Wesley is excluded for the first time when Ellen trespasses on the other side of the walls to tell Peter that she loves him. When Ellen is awakened by the owners of the tourist court and discovers that Peter is gone, she calls her father, and Peter is once again excluded. The final reversal occurs when Ellen flees for the second time in the film, here from King Wesley and knowingly to Peter.

The other screwball comedies I discuss here can be understood to fit the triadic pattern also, although it is least descriptive of *Adam's Rib,* the film most about marriage and the least romantic. As I suggested earlier, the significance of the triangular or triadic structure is its figuring of the structure of desire. Not only is the viewing subject positioned in this structure, but his or her desire is mirrored by at least one other desirer. The films constitute a desiring subject whose desire is confirmed by the gaze of another gazer, even as his or her gaze threatens the prospect of our satisfaction. The subject constituted by these films is undoubtedly heterosexual, but it is not necessarily gendered as male. What distinguishes screwball

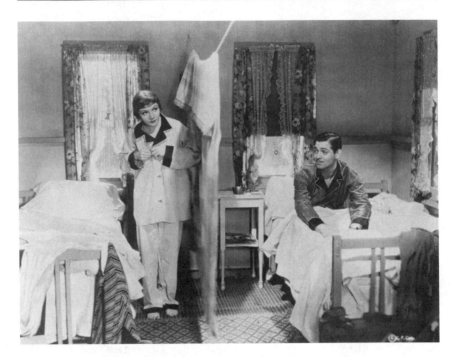

72. *It Happened One Night:* The "Walls of Jericho" between Ellen (Claudette Colbert) and Peter (Clark Gable).

comedies from dyadic narrative forms is that the woman is never merely an item of exchange between two men; she is also presented as a desiring subject. Though women in screwball comedies, as in other Hollywood films, are more often the object of the camera's voyeurism, more often presented as the object of the gaze of a male character than vice versa, men are also gazed upon. This is a formal equivalent of increased independence and importance, of the status of subject that women have in these films. While this is doubtless a progressive element, it is also a necessity for films whose topic is marriage and divorce. The belief that a woman is free to choose a mate and, if necessary, to divorce him is an important part of the ideology of bourgeois marriage. If it is the primary cultural work of comedies of remarriage to ease anxieties about divorce, then they must portray women as capable of desiring. The issue cannot be put merely in terms of a woman's presence: she must want to remarry, and her decision must be based on her attraction to as well as love for her partner. Thus it is not a coincidence that Clark Gable begins a striptease for Claudette Colbert or that it is she who first breaches the walls. But even

73. *His Girl Friday:* Casting encourages desire for the union of particular couples.

if women in screwball comedy are free subjects capable of choice, their choices are limited to the option of whether to marry one man or another.

The construction of romance as ideology in screwball comedies has to involve more, however, than the mere use of the triadic deep structure. Romance requires that we invest in the hope that a certain couple will achieve the bliss discussed earlier. In screwball comedies this is done in part by casting. We cannot imagine Rosalind Russell in love with Ralph Bellamy in *His Girl Friday*. We want her to be with Cary Grant from the moment they meet in his office at the beginning of the film. These films always tell us early on who we are supposed to root for. There is no need, for example, for *The Philadelphia Story* to open with the prologue of Dexter getting thrown out of Tracy Lord's house except to plant the seed of a wish that Cary Grant and Katharine Hepburn will get back together again.

In addition to our attraction to a Grant, a Hepburn, or a Gable, we are also invited to participate in the growth of a verbal relationship between the two. Verbal exchanges function mainly to create a sense of attraction, an "electricity" that stems first from the claim made by the man on the woman and her resistance to it. The claim may be explicit, as in Gable's double entendre, or implicit, as in *The Philadelphia Story,* in which, on the day before Tracy is to be married to Kittredge, Cary Grant returns to the Lord mansion and more or less stays there until she marries him instead. In *His Girl Friday* Grant's scheming to keep Rosalind Russell in town and at work for the newspaper serves the same purpose. The woman's response to this claim is to resist but not reject it. Tracy could, for example, simply have Dexter thrown out. The resistance by the woman to the man's claim upon her produces dialogue that is the verbal equivalent of foreplay—that is to say, teasing. I say foreplay rather than seduction because the result of the conversations is to increase desire on all sides without making the woman seem like a mere conquest. The male side of the dialogue, however, is an odd form of foreplay. Rather than speaking seductively, the males in screwball comedies typically scold, lecture, admonish, or preach. In the codes of the screwball comedy, what this tells us is that the man cares, but it also mimics rational persuasion, something that corresponds to the presumption that the woman must choose her mate.

In addition to its expression in verbal fireworks, romance is projected onto a pastoral vision of a place where the constraints and sins of civilization may be shed and innocence renewed. It may be the island of Peter Warne's dreams, the landscape of the Lord estate, or the honeymoon place to which Walter and Hildy are bound at the end of *His Girl Friday.* Romance depends not just on desire and affection but also on isolation from the claims of everyday life. It is on this point that these romantic comedies come closest to fitting the usual definition of the prose romance—as distinguished from the novel—one of the features of which is a setting far removed from everyday life: the forest, the ocean, a desert island, and the like. And yet in the Hollywood comedies I am discussing, most of the action takes place well within everyday settings. It is the purpose of each of these films to do what Cavell asserts only of *His Girl Friday:* to romanticize being at home, the everyday, even the black world. Thus we are given a vision of a world elsewhere, but not the actual experience of such a locale, since the purpose of the vision is to make us see the everyday in rose-colored hue. What distinguishes the suburbs, be they near Philadelphia or in Connecticut, is not their exotica, their isolation— though the latter is part of their attraction—but rather the luxury and the wealth they represent.

Luxury and the appeal of upper-class privilege are yet another means by which desire is heightened. As Cavell himself notes, luxury is "essentially an expression of eroticism" (p. 154). Thomas Schatz has misunderstood this when he argues that the screwball comedy, beginning with *It*

Happened One Night, is fundamentally about the overcoming of class differences. Thus, according to Schatz, if a "working-class stiff" (Peter Warne) and a "spoiled heiress" (Ellen Andrews) "can overcome their ideological disparity and finally embrace, then we should not lose faith in the traditional American ideal of a classless utopian society." [20] His definition of the genre leads Schatz to go so far as to include in it populist melodramas like *Meet John Doe* (Capra, 1941). While it seems to me that one of the ideological activities of the screwball comedy was to paper over the reality of class difference, this can hardly be seen as a "prosocial thematics," [21] for reconciliation in these films never occurs at the expense of the power and privilege of the rich. To call Peter Warne a working-class stiff is misleading since he works for a newspaper. Like the Horatio Alger hero, Warne is middle class—in education, income, and employment, if not entirely in manners—and his solid middle-class values make him appealing to Ellen's father. Yet even this degree of interclass marriage makes *It Happened One Night* an exception. More typical is *The Philadelphia Story,* which proposes and rejects intermarriage when Mike Connor proposes and is rejected by Tracy. Hildy and Walter of *His Girl Friday* are both professionals, and they are distinguished not from each other but from various less "classy" of their journalistic cohorts. *My Man Godfrey* (Gregory La Cava, 1936), one of Schatz's major examples, involves the marriage between an heiress and a forgotten man who is in fact the renegade heir, so properly bred that he can instantly succeed as her family's butler, a position he holds until his identity is revealed. Only then is he fit material for the inevitable marriage at the film's end. Like all narratives of manners, screwball comedies depend upon class differences to create, on the one hand, comedy in the form of jokes at inappropriate behavior and, on the other, romance by enhancing the appeal of the hero and heroine. Of the two, it is far more important to the demands of romance that she be rich. Working-class women do not fit well on pedestals.

The creation of desire and construction of romance are then what consume—and produce—most of the energy of screwball comedies. But do these films tell us anything about marriage? They tell us, in spite of themselves, that marriage is the instantiation of patriarchal dominance. There remains an element of dyadic narrative in many screwball comedies expressed in the frequent importance of the bride's father in spite of his extraneousness to the basic narrative structure. As artifacts of the patriarchal organization of culture, these films cannot abandon the daughter as an object of exchange between the father and husband. In both *It Happened One Night* and *The Philadelphia Story* the father has been betrayed or rejected by the daughter: in the former by Ellen's marriage to King Wesley and in the latter by Tracy's specific refusal to invite her father to her wedding and her more general refusal to be father's girl, a substitute for the mistress she has forced him to seek. In each film the concluding marriage results in a state of affairs acceptable to the father. Such approval is necessary so that the ending can be unambiguously happy.

Both *It Happened One Night* and *The Philadelphia Story* make it clear that married women must become little girls. Men, on the other hand, spend a lot of time being parental in these films.[22] The representation of this "parenting" in *It Happened One Night* includes not only "nurturing"—or preparing breakfast and offering carrots—but also the repeated reference to Ellen as a child or "brat," protecting her against external threats (the detectives, Roscoe Karns's salesman), but mainly from her own incompetence. What the journey proves to us and perhaps to Ellen herself is her own helplessness, her need for a protector like Peter. Peter Warne may be both Ellen Andrews's mother and father, but she is only his child and not a parent to him of either gender. In *The Philadelphia Story* Tracy Lord's metaphorical journey from Lord of her household to safe Haven as Dexter's wife parallels Ellen's, for Tracy also learns to lose her self-confidence and the habit of thinking for herself. She is accused by each of the significant men in the film of being unapproachable—a virgin, a goddess, one who belongs in an ivory tower—but what they are really charging is that she behaves like a man. Her high standards would be a mark of character in a male character, but they make a woman "a prig" or "a spinster." Near the end of the film, when she and Dexter will remarry, she says, "I don't know what to think anymore," and Dexter gives his approval to this lack of certainty. In another comedy of remarriage, *My Favorite Wife* (Garson Kanin, 1940), Irene Dunne declares to both her husband, Cary Grant, and the man she spent seven years with on a desert isle, Joel McCrea, that she can do fine without either of them and promptly falls into a swimming pool. Actually, however, it is less important that the woman take on any particular characteristics than that she submit to the man who will become her husband. Thus, Rosalind Russell's Hildy certainly demonstrates ability and intelligence—even a kind of professional independence—but she must submit to Walter Burns. The women give unmistakable signs of their submission. Just before her confession of love, Ellen finally does eat the carrot Peter has been trying to feed her. Tracy Lord says exactly what Dexter tells her to, just before they will remarry, and Rosalind Russell's Hildy follows Walter Burns's orders, which allows all sorts of nasty things to happen to her fiancé and his mother.

I want to emphasize, however, that the major point of these films is not to tell us that wives should be submissive if marriages are to work, because I do not believe that the films are mainly about marriage. In fact, they suggest that spunky, strong women are attractive but that their submission is required for the romance to be consummated, for marriage to take place. In this sense, they are comedies of conquest, the woman being not like one more bird taken in the hunt but like the duchy one wishes to annex. But for the marriage to occur, these films often ask us to believe that their heroines are changed utterly as a result of experiences described in the narrative. This change is often represented in a sudden reversal of the woman's repeatedly stated position or attitude, the most striking example of which, in this genre, is Tracy Lord's last-minute acceptance of Dexter. We accept the happy ending in part because of the romance that has been constructed as erotic tension seeking to be relieved in orgasm. In this sense, the ending functions as a consummation of our desire as well.

In most of the films the endings are metaphors for sexual consummation, but the ending of *The Awful Truth* is quite explicit about this. While it is true that *It Happened One Night* ends with "the walls of Jericho" being blown down, it is merely a coda. *The Awful Truth* gives us a picture of the couple's renewed attraction to each other, and ends with Jerry and Lucy Warriner (Cary Grant and Irene Dunne) in bed together (or so it is implied; we don't actually see this). This occurs only after an extended series of contrivances, first by her and then by them both. Lucy has disrupted Jerry's visit with the family of the woman he plans to marry after their divorce becomes final—at midnight that night—and then has taken him off to her Aunt Patsy's cottage in Connecticut. On the way she disables the car so that Jerry must spend the night, and when they arrive we find Lucy pretending to be surprised that Aunt Patsy is not there. This obviously sets the scene for a seduction, but it turns out to be a negotiation as well. Lucy and Jerry retire to separate but adjoining bedrooms, and Jerry first finds and then looks for reasons to cross over to her room. If we witness, as Cavell describes it, Lucy's "all but open sexual arousal, under the bedsheet" (p. 259), we also experience Jerry's response, his own desire to be in her bed. Their negotiation is an all but nonsensical exchange on the paradox of sameness and difference, but it leads to Jerry's promise that he will no longer doubt her. The film thus ends with an actual if underdeveloped reconciliation. Yet even in this film the ending radically reverses the course of events that had been expected at the beginning of the same day. When he woke up, Jerry was planning to marry someone else, but when he goes to sleep that night he finds himself remarried to Lucy.

Such reversals may seem to treat marriage ironically, as an absurd social convention. A case could be made that *The Lady Eve* does render marriage in just such terms because the couple's first marriage is an absurdity, the result of a con game. But even in this film the final reuniting of the couple wipes out the earlier failure because the man doesn't recognize her as the same woman. The endings of these films differ from those of earlier traditional comic genres—"old" and "new" comedy, to use Cavell's terms—in the enormous burden that the endings must bear.

All comic endings are resolutions, but the screwball comedies I have been discussing typically end with a complete reversal for which no plausible explanation is offered. In traditional and screwball comedy the end is achieved after obstacles are overcome. But the obstacles that lovers in traditional comedy must overcome are externally imposed, while in most screwball comedies they are primarily a function of the couple's own actions. And since these are thoroughly bourgeois comedies, there is no sense of festival accompanying the marriage. Marriage is a private matter, a fact that the invasive camera of *Spy* magazine, which records Tracy and Dexter's wedding, only serves to underline. The ending leaves the couple isolated in their own bliss; the troubles of the temporary partners they jettison never trouble them or us. As Dana Polan has argued, the ending is an "absolute point," an eternal moment "in which all contradictions are resolved under the force of a force that allows no differences, no excess."[23] In other words, there is no possibility of *post coitum triste*, but rather the explicit denial of the temporality of satisfaction. It is in this illusory eternity that marriage is rendered mystical, in spite of whichever of its realities the film has indulged earlier.

What I have argued so far is that while these "comedies of remarriage" can be made to reveal many of the conventions of marriage under patriarchy, they seek to hide these realities by constructing a romantic mystification of marriage. Marriage is presented as the natural end toward which love must inevitably tend. I now want to examine *Adam's Rib* and the recent *Desperately Seeking Susan* as films that suggest a critique of marriage and of the ideology of romance in their reversal of some of the conventions of the screwball genre.

Cavell observes of *Adam's Rib* that it is with one minor exception the only comedy of remarriage in which we see the pair at home, but he finds this merely an interesting variation and has more trouble explaining why he considers this a comedy of remarriage at all, since Adam and Amanda Bonner (Spencer Tracy and Katharine Hepburn) never get divorced. I believe these are both significant differences that demand that we treat *Adam's Rib* as a member of a different subgenre. Like another Tracy-Hepburn film, *Woman of the Year* (George Stevens, 1942), *Adam's Rib* is a screwball comedy, but it is about marriage in ways the paradigmatic films I have been discussing are not. This film is explicitly concerned with feminist issues, something that is true about the others only in the sense that they seek to defuse the threat posed by women who reject the roles imposed by patriarchy. Amanda Bonner initiates the action of *Adam's Rib* by taking the case of a woman who has wounded her husband after following him to his lover's apartment and shooting the lock off the door. Her defense of this woman is explicitly a defense of women as a class and a protest against the double standard of sexual morality that generally excuses male philandering (something that the father in *The Philadelphia Story* did explicitly). In taking the case, Amanda knows that she will have her husband as an opponent; in fact, it is his call to tell her that he has been assigned to prosecute the case that motivates Amanda to seek out and offer to defend the woman. Thus she is not only challenging gender privilege in the society at large but her husband's authority publicly in court. In winning her case, she proves to be her husband's superior as a professional, and—although not unambiguously—she also makes the case for the right of women to resist male domination.

As a result of having taken the case, Amanda and Adam quarrel, and he finally leaves. His accusation that she has no respect for the law either as it pertains to attempted murder or marriage makes it explicit that she has challenged patriarchy. Before this occurs, we have seen a marriage in which sexuality is clearly acknowledged, but we also see the husband and wife prepare dinner on the cook's night off. That is, we see a couple who are sexually related and attracted to each other, but who live lives that are not dominated by sex. We cannot mistake their relationship as one of absolute bliss. Thus the romantic element of this film remains on the margins until the end. In spite of its romantic elements, the film represents a critique of romance at several levels. For not only does the film show us the difficulties of married life, but the only real love triangle in the film, shown as a kind of prologue, is the tawdry one that results in the assault and the trial. That we do not find this triangle in the least appealing suggests that class is a decisive factor in the construction of romance. There is, however, another triangle: that formed by the Bonners and their neighbor Kip. Kip is completely extraneous to the major narrative action of the film. His only purpose is to build romance by making Amanda seem desired. Like the spurned, would-be husbands in the paradigmatic films, Kip is completely unsuitable as a mate and we cannot believe him as a threat. Nevertheless, he does attempt to woo Amanda after Adam leaves her. The second romantic element is the house in Connecticut. The romance of this location is treated ironically earlier in the film by means of home movies for which Kip provides a running commentary. At the end, however, Adam and Amanda go there to reconcile, and it is hard not to understand the place as an unambiguous retreat from the world of courts and competition. Like the other films, *Adam's Rib* ends with an unexplained change of sentiment, but this time it is the man whose feelings suddenly shift. The issue here is not that we cannot believe that Adam Bonner would change his mind and decide to stay married, but rather that the problems raised in the film about the difficulties of two genuinely adult professionals living together as equals get papered over. The narrative displaces the social conflict onto the drama of a single marriage. Furthermore, the patriarchal status quo is restored by Adam's impending election to a judgeship—where he will represent, rather than merely practice, the law. The ending makes us happy that the couple are reunited, forgetful of the problems that caused the conflict in the first place and unworried by any significant change in the patriarchal order.

Adam's Rib alters some of the conventions of the screwball comedy to produce an examination of conflict in a marriage that seems ideal, but the film nonetheless affirms marriage. This film was produced during a period when a single marriage remained the expectation of most men and women. After World War II divorce became so common that some observers began to describe the marriage system of our culture as "serial monogamy." Hollywood films could no longer treat divorce merely as something to be avoided. Too many members of the film audience had already failed to avoid it. While it took some time before Hollywood could ratify this social fact, in the 1970s and 1980s a series of films appeared that might be called comedies of remarriage in an altogether different sense, since they make as their situation the plight of the postmarried and repeatedly married. Among these films are *Choose Me* (Alan Rudolph, 1984), *Annie Hall* (Woody Allen, 1977), *Manhattan* (Allen, 1979), *Something Wild* (Jonathan Demme, 1986), *Desperately Seeking Susan,* and, most recently, *When Harry Met Sally* (Rob Reiner, 1989). The cultural work of this group of films may involve a partial critique of romance, but it also includes a reinforcing of heterosexual love as the social norm.

While many of the films I have just mentioned borrow and modify conventions of the screwball comedies of the classical period, I have chosen to focus on *Desperately Seeking Susan* here because it does so more explicitly and systematically than the others. But I have also chosen to look more carefully at this film because it seems most explicit in affirming independence and divorce as potentially positive choices. Since this film was made more than forty years after the others I have discussed here, we can assume that its director, Susan Seidelman, would have greater distance from the genre than earlier directors of screwball comedies and that she used genre conventions not (or not only) as a blueprint for the production of a popular commodity, but as a historical form to be self-consciously used as needed: transformed, parodied, played off against, and so on. However, it would be ludicrous to leave the impression that a Howard Hawks or a Preston Sturges was incapable of transforming or reversing genre conventions. In fact, these directors incorporate some significant reversals of gender roles into their screwball comedies; in *Bringing Up Baby* (Hawks, 1938) and *The Lady Eve* we find examples of weak, bumbling men being pursued by strong, competent women.[24] Likewise, but to greater effect, *Adam's Rib* alters the conventions of the genre by beginning with a strong woman but allowing her to remain strong, to defeat her

74. *Desperately Seeking Susan:* The screwball world of Susan (Madonna) invades suburbia.

husband and make him submit—if only in a charade—by crying. It is thus not the director's genius to which I appeal in trying to account for *Desperately Seeking Susan*'s reversals. Obviously, changes in American culture contributed to the possibility of these reversals. However, the director's *gender* is also a reasonable explanation for her ability to revise the conventions of screwball comedy in a way that male directors were not.

Desperately Seeking Susan picks up some potentially oppositional moments in screwball comedies and explores them further. The first of these is the possibility of life and sex outside of marriage, for although the screwball comedies set out to affirm marriage through romance, they must present an alternative to marriage in the representation of a threat to it. In other words, in representing the situation these films seek to resolve, they must acknowledge that marriage is not inevitable. In depicting women who at first are not helpless or housebound, these possibilities are made available to the viewer. Second, as I argued earlier, women in screwball comedies tend to be less the object of the camera's gaze and even occasionally the gazing subject. Thus *Desperately Seeking Susan* is not an "antiscrewball comedy" but one that acknowledges its debt to the classical films. It does this by means of several striking allusions. One is its beginning in a beauty parlor, recalling Cukor's *The Women* (1939), which featured an all-female cast. A more significant allusion is to *It Happened One Night:* Roberta and Des spend the night together in his nearly empty apartment, separated by a makeshift room divider apparently constructed of old doors. These rickety "walls of Jericho" serve the same function as the blankets did in the earlier film, but we now are able to see what it barely suggested: both man and woman sexually aroused and frustrated by the arrangement.

These references to particular screwball comedies are just the tip of the iceberg. The film may be seen as systematically reversing most of the conventions of the genre. For example, instead of beginning with an investment in marriage lost, we begin with an interest in adventure to be found. The first dialogue we hear tells us that Roberta (Rosanna Arquette) has been following a series of personal ads that feature as a headline the title of the film and that have been placed by Jim. Roberta, a bored suburban New Jersey housewife whose husband, we learn later, is having an affair, finds this desperation romantic: the film thus begins with its heroine explicitly seeking the kind of fantasy that screwball comedies typically present. What happens to Roberta eventually is that she gets amnesia and finds herself mistaken for Susan (Madonna) and living Susan's life. During this period Roberta learns that she can rely on herself and that she does not want to go back to her husband. The film ends with her involved with—not married to—Des (Aidan Quinn) but also paired with Susan as heroes who have recovered stolen antiquities.

By using the device of amnesia and mistaken identity, the film greatly complicates the typical narrative structure by proliferating the triangular relationships. In fact, one could understand this film as "coupling" almost everyone with almost everyone else at least for a brief moment. This constitutes, of course, the particular zaniness of *Desperately Seeking Susan,* but it also serves to create erotic tension by thrusting various characters together and then keeping them apart. This eroticism is sustained by visual rather than verbal pyrotechnics: the repeated use of match cuts, for example, to link Roberta's and Susan's stories. When Des and Roberta have sex for the first time—on the second night she has spent in his apartment—it serves the same function as the concluding wedding of other films, the release of erotic tension, but it is not the end of the movie. There remains a tension between Roberta's desire for Des and her identification with Susan. The final scene of the film, like that of *The Philadelphia Story* recorded in a still photograph, shows Roberta and Susan together receiving an award for the recovery of the earrings. Thus, the end of the film suggests three triangles, though it is ambiguous who is excluded by the pair of Roberta and Susan, since the other triangles include Des and Jim respectively.

If the end is ambiguous on the point, the film as a whole strongly suggests that the relationship between Roberta and Susan is its primary focus. This is represented by the match cuts that, by replacing one woman with the other who is not in the scene, disrupt expected shot/reverse shot sequences and the process of suture.[25] These match cuts are the visual representation of the two characters' identification with each other. The narrative constructs a romance—though not literally a sexual relationship—of Roberta's about Susan, a romance of identification. It is, after all, Susan whom Roberta is daydreaming about as the film opens, and it is *as* Susan that her adventures, her romance, begin. Given the lack of female identification by women in screwball comedies or other Hollywood films, Roberta's identification with Susan must be regarded as a politically significant reversal of convention.

Let me summarize *Desperately Seeking Susan*'s other major reversals of genre conventions. The film begins with marriage and ends with divorce. It opens in the suburbs, but its zone of adventure is the city. Rather than being claimed by her lover, Roberta chooses Des. In fact, Roberta is a full-fledged subject. We are sutured into her position, or Susan's, but rarely into those of the male characters. Rather than affirming the values of the middle class, the film endorses bohemian or countercultural values by Roberta's willingness to leave New Jersey and comfort for New York and excitement but relative poverty. The film deals with adultery, but this convention is also reversed because it is here explicit and undertaken by Roberta in full knowledge of what she is doing, having by this point regained her memory. Romance in the film, whether its object is Des or Susan, is used not to mystify marriage but to critique it, to show that marriage fails to live up to its billing. Thus *Desperately Seeking Susan* ends with a vision of a kind of personal liberation, one undermined to be sure by its status as a film fantasy, but one that is also made more significant by its tenuousness and ambiguity. It is a happy ending to be sure, but not one that claims a happily-ever-after.

This is not to say that *Desperately Seeking Susan* represents a full-scale critique of bourgeois or even patriarchal ideology. In affirming divorce, the film affirms individual freedom over social solidarity. Traditionally, marriage has been understood as the foundation of society or at least as a symbol for the social. It is this understanding that allows Tony Tanner to read the theme of adultery in the novel allegorically and thus to neglect the sexual politics of the topic.[26] Critique of marriage is prohibited when marriage and society are identified. We need new ways of envisioning society that do not assume the naturalness of marriage, but the best *Desperately Seeking Susan* can do is offer Roberta and Susan's relationship as a hint at such a vision. While this is a decided limitation, to dismiss Roberta's liberation because of it would be to forget that the personal is the political. It is not only the relation of marriage and society, however, that the film fails to address adequately. The film's conception of class is also impoverished. Middle-class New Jersey is contrasted not with either a genuine site of poverty and oppression or a utopian social vision, but rather with a fashionable bohemia, increasingly the focus of contemporary middle-class dreams of mobility or escape. Yet the failure to provide a critique of class politics does not negate the useful critique of sexual politics that the film gives us.

What films like *Adam's Rib* and *Desperately Seeking Susan* show us is that romance is not synonymous either with patriarchy or with false consciousness. Hence, we are entitled to speak of Roberta's relationship with Susan as both a romance and an antipatriarchal statement, and romance itself as having a utopian character in this film. This is not to deny Firestone's contention that there is an intimate connection between male culture and romance, but rather to argue that romance is a model of desiring that may, like other models, float away from the context of its production. Romance may be in one manifestation "love corrupted by . . . the sex class system," [27] but it has become a structure, a narrative chain of floating signifiers, that continues to serve the interests of patriarchy—not by any restricted connection to it but because ideological structures always tend to affirm the status quo. Screwball comedies typically construct a narrative in which the interpellated viewer experiences marriage mystified by romance, but in films such as *Desperately Seeking Susan,* romance returns to the work it may have performed in medieval culture, the suggestion of alternatives to patriarchal social practices and structures.

Notes

The number of debts I must acknowledge here seems to require Churchillian language: never has a mere essay owed so much to so many. The late Linda Singer encouraged me to take up the project in the first place and gave me insightful readings of several drafts. Others who provided helpful comments and criticism include the members of "Pittsburgh Theory," especially Jane Feuer, Lucy Fischer, Jim Kavanagh, Peggy Knapp, Brian McHale, and Dana Polan; Peter Brunette and Diane Carson, who heard the paper when it was presented at the 1986 Conference on Literature and Film at Florida State University; and, most recently, Paul Smith. The usual disclaimers apply.

    1. Scholars have had a difficult time defining screwball comedy. For discussions of this difficulty, see Wes D. Gehring, *Screwball Comedy: A Genre of Madcap Romance* (New York: Greenwood, 1986), pp. 3–12; Thomas Schatz, *Old Hollywood/New Hollywood: Ritual, Art, and Industry* (Ann Arbor: UMI, 1983), pp. 94–97, 158–163; Brian Henderson, "Romantic Comedy Today: Semi-Tough or Impossible?" in *Film Genre Reader,* edited by Barry K. Grant (Austin: Univer-

sity of Texas Press, 1986), pp. 311–313. On the other hand, James Harvey, *Romantic Comedy in Hollywood from Lubitsch to Sturges* (New York: Knopf, 1987), pp. xi–xii, simply identifies screwball comedy as romantic comedy during Hollywood's classic period. I agree in general with Harvey here, but, for my purposes, it is only necessary to note that screwball comedy is a recognizable kind of Hollywood product.

2. Stanley Cavell, *Pursuits of Happiness: The Hollywood Comedy of Remarriage* (Cambridge: Harvard University Press, 1981), p. 1; subsequent references to this work are included in the text.

3. Germaine Greer, *The Female Eunuch* (New York: McGraw Hill, 1971), p. 204.

4. Elaine Tyler May, *Great Expectations: Marriage and Divorce in Post-Victorian America* (Chicago: University of Chicago Press, 1980), p. 2.

5. Ibid., p. 167.

6. Ibid., pp. 2–7.

7. Niklas Luhmann, *Love as Passion: The Codification of Intimacy*, translated by Jeremy Gaines and Doris L. Jones (Cambridge: Harvard University Press, 1986), pp. 151, 233, n. 32. Luhmann cites studies by Ernest R. Mower (1927), Ernest W. Burgess (1926), Paul H. Landis (1936), and Francis E. Merrill (1949).

8. May, *Great Expectations*, p. 75.

9. Ibid., p. 76.

10. Donald Maddox, "Triadic Structure in the *Lais* of Marie de France," *Assays* 3 (1985): 22–29. Cf. René Girard, *Deceit, Desire, and the Novel: Self and Other in Literary Structure*, translated by Yvonne Freccero (Baltimore: Johns Hopkins University Press, 1965), pp. 1–52, where, in spite of the subtitle, triangular desire is treated as a figural element of novels rather than as proper to their narrative structure.

11. Denis de Rougemont, *Love in the Western World*, translated by Montgomery Belgion (New York: Pantheon, 1956), pp. 15–23.

12. Maddox, "Triadic Structure," pp. 31–32; Jacques Lacan, "Seminar on 'The Purloined Letter,'" *Yale French Studies* 48 (1972): 38–72.

13. For an overview and commentary on theories of suture and interpellation, see Kaja Silverman, *The Subject of Semiotics* (New York: Oxford University Press, 1983), pp. 194–236.

14. David Bordwell, Janet Staiger, and Kristin Thompson, *The Classical Hollywood Cinema: Film Style and Mode of Production to 1960* (New York: Columbia University Press, 1985), p. 16. The authors' study of an "unbiased sample" of 100 Hollywood films made between 1915 and 1960 showed 85 to have heterosexual romantic love as the leading line of action.

15. Romance as an ideology has been held to be a fundamental element of patriarchy by such theorists as Germaine Greer, *The Female Eunuch*, Juliet Mitchell, *Women: The Longest Revolution* (New York: Pantheon, 1984), and Shulamith Firestone, *The Dialectic of Sex: The Case for Feminist Revolution* (New York: Bantam, 1971), who argue that romantic love is a corruption that results from the unequal balance of power between the sexes. Mitchell, Greer, and Firestone all cite de Rougemont, although Mitchell remains closest to him in assert-

ing that romance is something that must die out once its goal is attained and that romance presupposes a fundamental connection between love and death.

16. "Bliss of genitality" is paraphrased from Eric Erikson, *Childhood and Society,* 2d ed. (New York: Norton, 1963), p. 264. Erikson argues that genitality, as the stage of true sexual maturity, is misunderstood as a permanent state of sexual bliss. Nevertheless, Erikson seems to contribute to this vision of heterosexual paradise when he calls genitality the "utopia" of his system (p. 92).

17. Mitchell, *Women,* p. 106.

18. In an article written after *Pursuits of Happiness* ("Two Cheers for Romance," in *Passionate Attachments: Thinking about Love,* edited by William Gaylin and Ethel Person [New York: Free Press, 1988], pp. 85–100), Cavell suggests that we read these endings as the beginning of an "adventure or quest" (p. 95), but he doesn't explain why the adventure of marriage is never shown in the films. In this article the relevance of the feminist critique of romance is acknowledged, but Cavell does not allow it to modify his own position. In fact, he describes "romantic marriage" as an "insulation from the larger world of politics" (pp. 90–91). While Cavell quite properly connects romantic marriage to the bourgeois constructions of "privacy" and the "personal," what he apparently cannot see is that these constructions are precisely political.

19. De Rougemont, *Love,* pp. 32–34.

20. Thomas Schatz, *Hollywood Genres: Formulas, Filmmaking, and the Studio System* (Philadelphia: Temple University Press, 1981), p. 152.

21. Ibid., p. 159.

22. Cavell makes much of Gable's being "parental" in *It Happened One Night* but fails to see any connection between being parental and patriarchy.

23. Dana Polan, "The Felicity of Ideology: Speech Acts and the 'Happy-Ending' in American Films of the Forties," *Iris* 3 (1985): 36.

24. I owe this insight to Diane Carson's unpublished paper, "A Feminist Reading of Screwball Comedy."

25. *Desperately Seeking Susan* could easily be read as an extended commentary on contemporary film theory.

26. Tony Tanner, *Adultery in the Novel: Contract and Transgression* (Baltimore: Johns Hopkins University Press, 1979).

27. Firestone, *Dialectic of Sex,* p. 146.

26. Redressing the "Natural": The Temporary Transvestite Film

CHRIS STRAAYER

Films in which characters cross-dress for sexual disguise are consistently popular with gay and lesbian audiences, despite requisite romantic endings with heterosexual couplings. Their use of comedy both creates and controls homosexual possibilities. Their visual play simultaneously challenges and supports traditional gender codes. And their paradoxical kisses—whether mistakes, jokes, or excuses—can go either way. Are these gay films? Do gay and lesbian viewers use contrary means of interpretation and identification to obtain pleasure from these films, or does the disguise already include our desires? In any case, homosexuals (and heterosexuals *alike*) keep coming back for this momentary, vicarious trespassing of society's gender boundaries—a gay fix.

This essay identifies as a genre the temporary transvestite film—a specific subset of transvestite films in which a character uses cross-dressing temporarily for purposes of necessary disguise. When contemplating the continuing popularity of films with temporary transvestism, one must consider mass-audience pleasure, which I believe is grounded in the appeasement of basic contradictions through a common fantasy of overthrowing gender constructions without challenging sexual difference. These films offer spectators a momentary, vicarious trespassing of society's accepted boundaries for gender and sexual behavior. Yet one can relax confidently in the orderly demarcations reconstituted by the films' endings. The specific conventions of the temporary transvestite narrative negotiate contradictory desires in viewers, safely providing forbidden pleasures that are corroborated by familiar visual configurations. The representation and containment of gender by clothing and other visual systems offer gender as a construction susceptible to manipulation by cross-dressing, drag, and masquerade. In films of this kind, both the text and the viewer contest gender fixity and unleash multiple identificatory processes that engage desires which, within the dominant order, might seem to be in mutual conflict.

Temporary transvestite films provide a useful site for the investigation of viewer-text interactions. As this essay demonstrates, viewer-text interactions are themselves varied and contrary. I am particularly concerned with the convergences and divergences of heterosexual and homosexual viewing experiences. In combination with a homosexual reading-against-the-grain, a genre approach allows me to investigate and denaturalize equally constructed heterosexual pleasures.

THE GENERIC SYSTEM OF THE TEMPORARY TRANSVESTITE FILM

The group of temporary transvestite films examined here presents a set of conventions that serves as a specific generic system.[1] Because the typical temporary transvestite plot occurs in several genres, it must be understood as a generic discourse operating at a multigenre intersection. This discourse, addressing a composite subject and functioning generically to alleviate contradiction through formulaic plotline, iconography, and pseudosolution, encourages bisexual eroticism and transgression of gender boundaries.[2] Its temporary transvestite play continually vacillates between the support and collapse of both heterosexuality and traditional gender roles.

Temporary transvestite films share a large number of generic elements: the narrative necessity of disguise; adoption by a character of the opposite sex's specifically gender-coded costume (and often its accessories, makeup, gestures, behaviors, and attitudes); the simultaneous believability of this disguise to the film's characters and its unbelievability to the film's audience; visual, behavioral, and narrative cues to the character's "real" sex; the transvestite character's sensitization to the plight and pleasures of the opposite sex; references to biological sex differences and the "necessary" cultural separation of the sexes; a progression toward slapstick comedy and increased physicality; heterosexual desire thwarted by the character's disguise; accusations of homosexuality regarding the disguised character; romantic encounters that are mistakenly interpreted as homosexual or heterosexual; an "unmasking" of the transvestite; and, finally, heterosexual coupling.

The Necessity for Disguise

The plot of temporary transvestite films always necessitates disguise, usually disguise as the opposite sex. Transvestism pursued as a pleasure in and of itself is outside the hermeneutic code of the main plot.[3] Although these films are often set in a context that incorporates costume (e.g., show biz), the temporary transvestism serves some need other than spectacle or

75. *Charley's Aunt* (Archie Mayo, 1941): The vacillation between supporting and collapsing traditional gender roles.

theater. Generally, this need relates to problems of access, as in the case of getting a job, or escape.

In *Queen Christina* (Rouben Mamoulian, 1933) Greta Garbo plays the title's seventeenth-century queen whose preference for male activities and practical clothes results in her being mistaken for a man as she travels incognito through the countryside. In *Sylvia Scarlett* (George Cukor, 1935) Katharine Hepburn must disguise herself as a boy, Sylvester, to travel with her father after her mother's death. In *Sullivan's Travels* (Preston Sturges, 1941) Veronica Lake disguises herself as a boy to avoid sexual harassment while accompanying a male film director on a journey to research poverty. In *Victor/Victoria* (Blake Edwards, 1982) Julie Andrews plays a singer, Victoria, who must borrow men's clothes because her dress shrinks after being rain-soaked. In this incidental transvestism, her male friend Toddy discovers a solution to Victoria's unemployment problem: Victoria should disguise herself as Victor, a very employable female impersonator. In *Yentl* (Barbra Streisand, 1983), Barbra Streisand plays a young Jewish woman in nineteenth-century eastern Europe who disguises herself as a boy, Anshel, in order to obtain a "male" education after her widower-father's death.

In *Boy! What a Girl!* (Arthur Leonard, 1947) Tim Moore plays a musician who must pretend to be a female backer, Madame, at a funding meeting. Prior to this, however, he has been "jamming" in drag with his band, an unexplained transvestism that subverts the convention of necessity. In *Abroad with Two Yanks* (Alan Dwan, 1944) Dennis O'Keefe and William Bendix play two marines who must masquerade as women to elude MPs while on furlough in Australia. In *I Was a Male War Bride* (Howard Hawks, 1949) Cary Grant plays a French captain, Henry, who masquerades as a WAC, Henrietta, to accompany his lieutenant wife on her return to the United States. In *Some Like It Hot* (Billy Wilder, 1959) Tony Curtis and Jack Lemmon play Joe/Josephine and Jerry/Daphne, two musicians who hide from the mob by working in an all-girl band. In *La Cage Aux Folles* (Edouard Molinaro, 1978) Michel Serrault plays Albin, a homosexual female impersonator who, for more practical purposes in private life, impersonates the mother of the son of his lover Renato (played by Ugo Tognazzi). The son, Laurent, wishes to marry the daughter of the Minister of Morals, who later must himself dress in drag to sneak out of Albin and Renato's disreputable nightclub. And in *Tootsie* (Sidney Pollack, 1982) Dustin Hoffman plays Michael Dorsey, an unemployed actor who disguises himself as Dorothy Michaels to get a part in a television soap opera.

Gender-Coded Behavior and Characteristics

Once in the opposite sex's costume, the transvestite often adopts the opposite sex's gestures and behaviors, either "naturally" or for parody. Similarly, gender-coded behavior and gestures are often used to remind the film audience of the character's "original" gender and also to threaten exposure in the diegetic world. For example, women characters often start slugging other characters when they are dressed as men. In trousers, Sylvester Scarlett not only slugs "his" enemies, but jumps over a ship's railing, makes "his" way through the customs crowd carrying a suitcase over "his" head, kicks "his" legs over the bed frame, climbs up a building, hangs upside down on gymnastic rings, leaps out a second-story window, and fondly tosses "his" hat in the air. Until they see her as a girl, the other characters take no notice of Sylvester/Sylvia's dirty fingernails. By contrast, when Dorothy Michaels slugs a male who tries to steal "her" cab in *Tootsie,* the incident humorously reminds the audience of "natural" maleness, as does "her" low-pitched voice in several instances.

The undermining of costume disguise by seemingly incongruous pitch

76. Cary Grant with Ann Sheridan in *I Was a Male War Bride:* The disguise as both transvestism and cross-dressing.

relies on and reinforces the conception that one's voice represents the true self. Likewise, other physical qualities such as body language and hair length receive privileged authority. Just as Josephine and Daphne find it difficult to walk in high heels in *Some Like It Hot,* Carl/Carla's male disguise in the television movie *Her Life as a Man* (Robert Ellis, 1983) requires actress Robyn Douglass to practice walking, standing, and acting like a man. In *Queen Christina,* while passing for a man, Christina is invited by the Spanish ambassador, Antonio (played by John Gilbert), to share an inn room; her masculine carriage immediately becomes feminine when she lies on their bed. Josephine and Daphne wear female wigs in *Some Like It Hot,* as do Henrietta in *I Was a Male War Bride,* Madame in *Boy! What a Girl!,* Dorothy Michaels in *Tootsie,* and Albin in *La Cage Aux Folles.* More important, the removal of these wigs, purposefully or inadvertently, always absolutely reveals the man underneath. Like Sylvia Scarlett, who must cut off her braids, Anshel's disguise in *Yentl* requires the character to cut her hair, as does Victor's in *Victor/Victoria.* Ending "his" female impersonation act with a double negative, *Victor/Victoria* collapses these generic gender conventions of short hair and removal of the wig to "expose" her (male) disguise as real.

Adequacy and Inadequacy of the Disguise

In her book on female impersonators Esther Newton distinguishes between the transvestite and the cross-dresser: the former attempts to pass as a member of the opposite sex while the latter exaggerates the opposite sex's assumed gender codes to appear obviously, inadequately disguised.[4] The male cross-dresser appears not as a woman but as a *man in woman's clothing.* Sometimes obvious male characteristics, such as a hairy chest or even a beard, contribute to a subversive and contradictory play of signification. The disguise in temporary transvestite films, then, is both transvestism and cross-dressing. Within the terms of the narrative, the disguise is sufficient to trick other characters. Therefore, I have chosen to use the term "transvestite" to describe the generic *plot* of these films. However, because the disguise is inadequate to trick the film audience, its extradiegetic operation is that of cross-dressing. This implausible image is tantamount to an extradiegetic glance at or gesture to the film audience in that it breaks the illusion of the narrative (surrogate world) and challenges that already tenuous balance—the willing suspension of disbelief.

Regardless of how unconvinced film viewers are by the transvestite's disguise, characters within the film, including the transvestite's close friends and lovers, are tricked by the simplest of gender-coded costumes. When familiar actors play these roles, it is difficult for film viewers to forget the star's profilmic sex and believe the disguise. Thus, in *Sylvia Scarlett,* it seems "natural" for Monkley (Cary Grant) to grab Sylvester (Katharine Hepburn) in a manner conventionally typical of a man pulling a woman against his body, even though Monkley believes that Sylvester is a boy.

This simultaneous diegetic adequacy and extradiegetic inadequacy of disguise provides a field in which visual language conventions are strained by the use of known actors, ideological patterns, gender clichés, and sexual stereotypes to reveal as well as disguise sex. Juxtapositions repeatedly violate the semiotic system that naturalizes sex-typed society. This play of visual signifiers keeps gender constructions shifting and produces an image of sex and gender that is often surreal. For example, in *Boy! What a Girl!,* when the sleeping Madame (cross-) dressed in a tutu is dragged away by a French suitor, the camera/audience can see boxer shorts underneath "her" skirt. Likewise, especially for 1950s audiences, the effect is quite unusual when Tony Curtis is shown wearing earrings in *Some Like It Hot.*

Cross-Gender Sensitization

Through temporary transvestism, characters in these films are sensitized to the plight of the opposite sex. Dorothy Michaels receives sexist pejoratives in *Tootsie*. Carl/Carla experiences what it is like to be feared by women when out walking one night in *Her Life as a Man*. Especially for the male character, spending time in the female gender can make him a "better person," as, for example, when Michael Dorsey "makes a better man as a woman" in *Tootsie*, or when Sugar (Marilyn Monroe) sensitizes Joe to women's feelings about male behavior with her confidential "girl talk" in *Some Like It Hot*.

For women characters, transvestism often means a taste of male privilege, which the characters commonly resist relinquishing. In the end, however, the female character usually sacrifices temporary male mobility and privilege for "permanent" heterosexual love. In *Queen Christina*, when it is suggested that Christina will die an old maid, she replies that she will "die a bachelor"—nevertheless, she later relinquishes her throne for love. When King urges Victoria to give up her successful career as a female impersonator, she responds with, "I'm my own man now"—but when her disguise as Victor is nearly uncovered, she turns over her act to Toddy and attends his performance coupled with King. This necessity to relinquish the disguise is, of course, like the prior necessity for disguise, a product of textual/generic discourse enacted through chosen paradigmatic and syntagmatic limitations. As a case in contrast, Yentl/Anshel refuses to give up her independence for marriage and instead pursues a future in America, which she hopes will not require such a choice.

Biological Authority and Increased Physicality

Temporary transvestite films generally present the futility of a character's desire to maintain the disguise indefinitely. The initial undoing of traditional gender construction is finally corrected through an emphasis on physicality and a signaling of biological sex differences. Typically the comedies become more slapstick as they progress, maximizing visual contradictions relating to gender and allowing tumultuous movement and indecorous body positionings. The comic action becomes increasingly physical, especially when the cross-dressing involves male characters. This allows not only for manly characters to "outgrow" their female disguises, but also for physical violence to be directed at male transvestites. This comedy functions as corrective humor in preparation for the eventual narrative reinstatement of rigid sex roles and heterosexuality. Physical comedy can also achieve a temporary free-for-all, which for women becomes a rebellion against the restrained body movement necessitated by female dress.

Biological sex is signaled in a variety of ways. A bathroom scene, for example, is often included to reestablish the futility of transvestism by reminding the transvestite (and the film audience) of the "fact" of two biologically distinct sexes and their cultural segregation—as if the purpose of cross-dressing was to change sex rather than gender. Like Sylvester in *Sylvia Scarlett,* Josephine and Daphne hesitate before bathroom doors in *Some Like It Hot.* Bedroom, locker-room, and dressing-room scenes can also serve this purpose, as when "her" scantily clad dressing-room mate embarrasses Dorothy Michaels in *Tootsie.* Such trespassing scenes often signal a breakdown of the privacy and safety afforded by sex-specific clothing and by the conventional segregation of the sexes.

Biology and red tape clash for comic effect during an official interview in *I Was a Male War Bride.* Because the necessary application form is written only for female war brides, Henry (Cary Grant), not yet sexually disguised, is questioned on such ridiculous topics as his pregnancy history. The comedy derives from the conversation's inappropriateness, but the scene also implies that, just as red tape is pigheadedly insistent, gender is stridently affixed to biology.

The presence of past or current heterosexual partners can also be used to signal a cross-dresser's "true" gender, much as, in other contexts, the presence of a biological child recoups a homosexual's "normalcy." At the end, the films reinforce society's heterosexual hegemony and the absolute alignment of gender, sex, and heterosexual preference; sexual desire now signals the transvestite's "true" sex.

Homosexual Appearances

Possible misinterpretations or fears of homosexual desire resulting from a character's sexual disguise often impede heterosexual pursuits in the temporary transvestite plot. When Dorothy Michaels kisses Julie in *Tootsie,* Julie thinks Dorothy is a lesbian. In *Yentl* Avigdor fears his own homosexuality until his feelings toward Anshel are "explained" when Anshel/Yentl reveals her breasts. King's heterosexual attraction toward performer Victoria turns into a repulsion of homosexuality when she pulls off her wig and reveals herself to be Victor. King's continuing attraction then turns into a compulsion to discover Victoria's "true" sex. On one level, King's compulsion epitomizes the ultimate endpoint in the hermeneutic code of temporary transvestite films—the (re)organization of gender according to heterosexual coupling. Even films such as *Some Like It Hot* and *Yentl,* which end with gender transgressions still active, also provide the requisite heterosexual closure through other characters.

77. King (James Garner) and Victor/Victoria (Julie Andrews): Disguise becomes a hindrance to heterosexual pursuit.

HETERO/HOMOSEXUAL COLLAPSE: THE PARADOXICAL BIVALENT KISS

In temporary transvestite comedies and dramas, the sexual misidentity achieved by one character's disguise as the opposite sex eventually becomes a hindrance to heterosexual pursuit. As Victor (Julie Andrews) says in *Victor/Victoria,* when he/she becomes attracted to King (James Garner), "Pretending to be a man has its disadvantages." Similarly, Tony Curtis, disguised as a woman in *Some Like It Hot,* and Katharine Hepburn, disguised as a man in *Sylvia Scarlett,* have to sneak out of their disguises to pursue their heterosexual love objects. To accomplish the obligatory love story, an "unmasking" must occur. Heterosexuality is the guardian of sexual difference. The generic problematic consists in the restrictions of gender fixity as well as the fear of sexual unfixedness. This is expressed in the following passage from Annette Kuhn's *The Power of the Image:*

> A quest to uncover the truth of the concealed body may be precisely the desire that activates a narrative of sexual disguise. When the body is confirmed as the location of an absolute difference, this desire is gratified in the pleasure offered in the resolution. If crossdressing narratives always in some measure problematise gender identity and sexual difference, then, many do so only to

confirm finally the absoluteness of both, to reassert a "natural" order of fixed gender and unitary subjectivity.[5]

Hence, those viewers who do not experience pleasure in heterosexuality, or for whom pleasurable heterosexuality does not pacify cross-gender aspirations, need to resist the traditional narrative thrust and to focus instead on potentially subversive performance and visual elements.

Cross-dressing is the manipulation of a system of codes commonly used to signify gender. But cross-dressing may also challenge gender constructions. It offers a potential for the deconstruction and radical appropriation of gender codes and conventions. The following discussion will show that temporary transvestite films can significantly challenge gender fixity via performance and visuals, even as plot evokes biology as the final determinant of sex and brings about the "proper" realignment of gender.

Temporary transvestite films often support heterosexual desire at the narrative level and challenge it at a more ambiguous visual level where other desires are suggested. Following this, the generic system of the temporary transvestite film constructs a specific configuration that achieves the intersection of gender/sex crosscurrents in an equivocal romantic event. In this generic system the conflict between a character's actual sex and the sex implied by the character's disguise and performance functions to create simultaneous heterosexual and homosexual interactions. Narrative point of view and nonnarrative spectacle collaborate through their contradictions to create a double entendre of simultaneous homosexual and heterosexual readings, identifications, and experiences in film viewers—viewers trapped within narrative and nonnarrative interpretations and by identification with a bisexed figure.

This heterosexual/homosexual event is most dramatically typified by a "paradoxical kiss" between two characters, one of whom is sexually disguised. Although the narrative promotes one interpretation of this kiss, an alternative interpretation is suggested visually to the viewer when the kiss interrupts the narrative as a spectacular pause. Whether the kiss is consciously seen and experienced as heterosexual, homosexual, or bisexual depends on several variables: whether the viewer predominantly experiences the scene through the narrative point of view, the plot, or the direct image; to what degree the costume is convincing to the viewer; whether the viewer thinks or desires with a predilection for opposition or similarity; and whether the viewer chooses to believe or disbelieve the disguise, which relates to her or his preference for certain sexual encounters available vicariously within the scene. In any case, the "sexual bivalency" carried by believable/unbelievable costume and performance allows for all of these readings.

This paradoxical bivalent kiss comes in two forms. In one, the disguise

78. *Abroad with Two Yanks:* An example of the paradoxical bivalent kiss.

implies homosexuality, but knowledge of the character's true identity offers a heterosexual reading. In the other form, the characters are actually same-sexed, but one's sexual disguise implies heterosexuality. Near the end of *Some Like It Hot,* Josephine (Tony Curtis) kisses Sugar (Marilyn Monroe). This kiss collapses actual heterosexuality with implied homosexuality. In *Sylvia Scarlett* Maudie draws a moustache on Sylvester (Katharine Hepburn), which Sylvester describes as marvelous. Maudie then kisses "him." This kiss collapses actual homosexuality and implied heterosexuality. Only after quickly but surely wrapping "his" arm around Maudie's shoulders does Sylvester withdraw. Then Sylvester protests by claiming "he" already has a girl. Both straighten up when Henry (Sylvia's father and Maudie's fiancé) walks into the room. These two examples of the paradoxical kiss are mirror images of the same equivocation. In the first, a heterosexual reading requires viewers to disregard the disguise. In the second, a heterosexual reading requires viewers to believe the disguise. Homosexual readings are also available in both kisses.

In *Her Life as a Man* the implied homosexuality of a paradoxical kiss is acknowledged within the diegesis. Carla, disguised as Carl, is saying good-bye to her husband at the airport. Their ongoing marital relationship privileges them to a kiss, but their awareness of a possible homosexual reading by onlookers prevents them from kissing. At the same time that these characters prevent a homosexual reading, the scene offers viewers a second level of identification with homosexual oppression.[6]

The gay subtext of *Her Life as a Man* becomes more explicit in the scene in which Carla's husband finds her, still disguised as Carl, in the embrace of a female co-worker. The co-worker believes Carl's disguise, so can only presume Carla's jealous husband to be a gay lover. The husband, who obviously knows Carla's real sex, can only interpret the embrace as homosexual. Whether the viewer gives primacy to Carl's disguise or to Carla's real sex, she or he is trapped in a homosexual reading of the image. To grasp the scene—and to enjoy the scene—requires that the viewer both believe and disbelieve the disguise—that is, identify with the contradictory diegetic information as understood by all three characters.

Heterosexual and homosexual readings in these paradoxical scenes are not separable. The viewer experiences both simultaneously (though perhaps unequally). Although most plots intentionally correct any homosexual "mistakes" resulting from temporary transvestism (an exception is the Jack Lemmon romance in *Some Like It Hot*), this kiss is a bisexual and bisexed moment for a viewer—whether she or he finds it pleasant, unpleasant, or both.

In the generic system of temporary transvestite films, narrative structure almost invariably leads to the (re)institutionalization of heterosexuality after progressing through some "stage" of unstable gender and ambiguous sexuality. This, of course, corresponds to a sanctioned theory of human development. However, the fact that the plot is generic strongly suggests that this process is never finished and that the generic system fulfills the viewer's desire to return again and again to a less closed situation. The generic pleasure in temporary transvestite films rests partly in their ability to speak to a composite subject rather than only to that "final" one at the end of the determining narrative progression—that is, that actual beings do not experience their differing desires as linearly ordered and separate. The multiple erotic pleasures afforded by the paradoxical kiss contest narrative destiny.

In classical Hollywood cinema the classic kiss, often at the film's end, conventionally represents sexuality. The power of this kiss derives from its dual metaphoric and metonymic function. It both stands in for sexual activity and begins it. Metonymically, it suggests a continuation of sexuality at the same time that it invites the viewer to "put it there." The metonymic power of the kiss to signal postfilm yet diegetic sex relies primarily on an assumed temporal relationship between the kiss and sex— on an understanding of the kiss as a part of sex, specifically as foreplay. The classic kiss ends the process of seduction and begins the sexual act.

This metonymic relationship is strengthened by the metaphoric power of the kiss to suggest both romance and sexuality.

Unlike the classic Hollywood kiss, the bivalent kiss rarely occurs as a final scene. Rather than providing narrative closure, it obtains closure from subsequent narration.[7] Because heterosexuality is granted continuance in temporary transvestite films and homosexuality is generally negated, stopped, and corrected by the film's temporal dimension, heterosexual and homosexual components of the paradoxical kiss have different narrative-temporal contexts that reinforce and discourage, respectively, their metonymic powers. A more aggressive action on the part of a viewer is necessary for homosexual continuance. By necessarily sustaining the homosexuality of an image that momentarily contains it, as with the paradoxical kiss, the homosexual viewer claims the image as her or his own and actively constructs an alternate narrative, however tenuous.

Narrative and Visual Levels in the Two-Shot

Annette Kuhn argues that the difference in viewers' and characters' reactions to the disguise is determined by their different narrative points of view. Cinema narrates a "view behind" that allows the film viewer to see a character's private or unposed actions. In her words, " 'True' gender is repeatedly made visible to the spectator, while the ignorance of certain of the film's characters—because unlike the spectator they are not in a position to see the truth—is constantly emphasized."[8] While in agreement about this convention, I think it is equally important to recognize that viewer disbelief is also insured extranarratively by the conventional use of an unconvincing disguise. In other words, film viewers know a disguised character's "true" sex both because of their superior point of view (the narrative "view behind") and because this "true" sex is directly readable in the visual display. While narrative construction allows film viewers to witness the transvestite's adoption of disguise and various private moments when he or she drops the pretense, even without such revealing shots provided by an omniscient camera/narrator, viewers would still know that the character is disguised. In fact, the convention of inadequate disguise relies on the image superseding narrative articulations.

It is a fear of actual cross-sex passing that necessitates the convention of inadequate disguise. Even though the disguise is supposed to be convincing within the narrative, it is not allowed to be convincing in the direct image presented to the film viewer. This would pose too great a threat to society's trust in sex and gender unity as a system to communicate and recognize sex. While the generic system of the temporary transvestite genre repeatedly addresses contradictions felt by the audience regarding gender construction, it neither solves those contradictions nor finally undoes society's rules and conventions. The continuance of the temporary transvestite genre depends on its placebo function. At the same time, this enforced use of a disguise—diegetically believable though extradiegetically unbelievable—suggests the *potential* of the disguise or image to be believable in both arenas. Finally, an inadequate disguise is not equal to no disguise—the inadequately disguised character signals both sexes simultaneously. The power of the image to question narrative determinations is accentuated by the two-shot. The two-shot binds two characters by framing them together. As opposed to the shot-reverse shot, which sutures the viewer into the interaction, the two-shot positions the viewer outside. This encourages the viewer to relate to the two characters not individually (or as one's surrogate and partner) but as an intact pair. The image of the paradoxical kiss requires the viewer to look *at* the *two* characters and binds the unconvincing disguise with narrative passing via the two-shot. The two-shot delivers the kiss as a single unit. If the viewer wants visual access to the kiss, she or he must accept this whole, this action that includes the disguise—the paradoxical kiss.

To be sure, the information discrepancy between a diegetic character and the more knowing spectator—whether because of different points of view or because of the extranarrative inadequacy of the disguise for film viewers—encourages a heterosexual *understanding* of a paradoxical kiss, which is thus explainable as a "mistake." At the same time, however, narrative identification with the character maintains the kiss as authentic—desired and felt—and instills in the spectator a desire to witness the kiss so as to vicariously experience it. The paradoxical kiss benefits from desire on the part of a character, whether that desire is due to a mistaken belief in the disguise or to an informed disregard of the disguise. Therefore, although a friendly kiss can construct bivalency via a contradiction between narrative and visual information, the kiss is most charged when romantic.

A character's belief in the disguise also charges the paradoxical kiss. When the kiss combines actual homosexuality and implied heterosexuality, as when Maudie kisses Sylvester in *Sylvia Scarlett,* the undisguised character's belief in the other's disguise allows for heterosexual desire, which then motivates and charges the kiss. When the kiss combines actual heterosexuality with implied homosexuality, as when Dorothy Michaels kisses Julie in *Tootsie,* the undisguised character's belief in the other's disguise threatens a homosexual reading. This possible misreading acts as an obstacle to the kiss, which increases desire until the kiss can no longer be delayed.

In a scene in *Yentl,* which lacks a conflict in the characters' readings of the disguise, the paradoxical kiss seems less charged despite romantic motivation. When Avigdor kisses Yentl (Barbra Streisand), Yentl is still visually coded as a boy (according to the internal rules of the film), but she has revealed herself to him as female. The fact that he no longer believes her disguise—that his lust no longer produces conflict, that there is no narrative confusion or mistake to be exploited by viewers—reduces the image's vibrancy. An earlier scene, before Avigdor learns that Yentl is a woman, provides the tension that so often accentuates the paradoxical charge. During playful wrestling, Avigdor rolls on top of Anshel, then pauses and looks at "him" romantically. The homosexual tension of this scene is both confirmed and forbidden immediately afterward when Avigdor runs away, hurriedly removes all his clothes, jumps into the water, and invites the objecting Anshel to join him. Similarly, when Anshel/Yentl's wife, Hadass, approaches "him" sexually, the homosexual reading (against contrary knowledge provided to the viewer by the narrative) is charged both by her lust and her belief in the disguise. The conflict between Hadass's and the film viewer's assignment of sex to Anshel/Yentl creates a narrative/visual double entendre. Hadass's lust can be attributed by the film viewer to her belief in the disguise or to some affinity beyond the disguise. Just as Avigdor finally understands his "unnatural" attraction to Yentl when he learns that she is a woman, so can the audience attribute a "natural" attraction to Hadass as she misunderstands Anshel's sex. Scenes such as these, which determine both actual and implied sexual interactions, in which things are not—yet perhaps are—what they seem to be, deconstruct sexual preference as much as they deconstruct gender.

Generally, the heterosexual component of a paradoxical kiss, whether actual or implied, is actively initiated, whereas the homosexual component merely results from this activity. In the kiss between Dorothy and Julie in *Tootsie*, actual heterosexual desire initiates actual heterosexuality. In the kiss between Maudie and Sylvester in *Sylvia Scarlett*, misplaced heterosexual desire initiates implied heterosexuality. Conversely, while homosexuality may be implied or actual, it is generally, within the diegesis, passively achieved. By contrast, a paradoxical kiss between Queen Christina and Ebba, her court lady (Elizabeth Young), takes on radical significance. Although heterosexuality is implied via costume, the characters know one another; a homosexual reading is available at the level of narrative. Since the queen is not a passive recipient of the lady's kiss, homosexual pleasure is represented. A heterosexual reading requires belief in the disguise on the part of the viewer against diegetic disbelief. Obviously, this kiss is a rare affirmation in the genre. Although the film's narrative later assigns heterosexuality to both women, it never really "corrects" this kiss.

The success of the paradoxical kiss, then, depends on numerous interrelating factors that eventually break down the dichotomy between the

narrative and the visual levels, including the following: romantic desire
and motivation; character coupling and viewer distancing resulting from
the two-shot; visual inadequacy of the disguise for the film viewer; viewer
disbelief of the disguise due to a superior narrative point of view; characters' belief in the disguise due to an inferior narrative point of view; viewer
identification with a character's belief in the disguise; suggestiveness of
the disguise for both character and viewer; implied potential adequacy of
sexual disguise; and the rare case of a viewer's insistent belief in the disguise, despite its inadequacy and against contrary narrative information.
Finally, Hollywood's conventional displacement of sexuality by romance
contributes greatly to the ability of the paradoxical kiss to carry a sexual
charge.

TEXTUAL SYSTEMS IN TEMPORARY TRANSVESTITE FILMS: TWO CASE STUDIES

Although the focus of temporary transvestite films on clothing and disguise insures a preponderance of theatrical codes involving costume,
makeup, and performance, these films also provide opportunities to analyze how such nonspecific codes work together with specific codes, such
as editing and cinematography, to construct powerful textual systems in
which themes, structures, and various conventions reinforce one another.[9] I have already discussed the primary relevance of cinematic construction in relation to the paradoxical kiss, particularly its reliance on
the two-shot and on simultaneous contrary viewer positionings accomplished by narrative identification and the cinematic apparatus. In this
section I will analyze particular scenes from *Some Like It Hot* and *Vic-
tor/Victoria* to demonstrate the interactions of specific and nonspecific
codes in textual systems that resonate through the films.

Some Like It Hot: Parallels, Reversals, and Alternatives

In *Some Like It Hot,* parallel editing implies a connection between two
seductions. Joe (Tony Curtis), disguised as a millionaire, is seducing Sugar
(Marilyn Monroe), by pretending to be impotent. Girls, he explains, leave
him "cold." Jerry (Jack Lemmon), disguised as Daphne, and Osgood (Joe
E. Brown), a real millionaire, are engaged in mutual seduction. Shots of
Joe and Sugar kissing are intercut with shots of Daphne and Osgood dancing, via swish pans signaling simultaneity. Sugar is trying to "warm up"
Joe; Daphne is caught "leading again." Soon Joe's toes feel barbecued,
and Daphne and Osgood are passing a rose from mouth to mouth.

This film fragment constructs two simultaneous yet different seductions. In the first, the heterosexuality between Joe and Sugar is both im-

plied and actual. In the second, the heterosexuality between Daphne and Osgood is implied and the homosexuality is actual. Jerry/Daphne's seemingly complete abandonment to the seduction, his/her enthusiastic and active participation despite knowledge of the homosexual reality, and his/her exuberant movements and seductive postures strongly underline his interaction with Osgood as homosexual. The next scene, in which "she" excitedly tells Joe that "she" and Osgood are engaged, strengthens this interpretation.

The editing pattern, which alternates between Joe and Sugar kissing and Daphne and Osgood dancing, provides a formal statement of the scene's thematic content: the availability of alternatives—in seduction, gender, and sexual preference. A number of reversals signify choice and change within this structure of alternatives. As a man, Joe seduces via passivity; disguised as a woman, Daphne's aggressiveness is seductive. Joe changes from pseudoimpotence to lucky playboy; Daphne, whose original intent is to keep Osgood busy while Joe "borrows" his yacht, falls in love. Joe pretends to be a millionaire; Daphne gets engaged to a real millionaire. Osgood gives Daphne a diamond bracelet, which Joe later steals to give to Sugar.

The pattern of parallels, reversals, and alternatives in this section of *Some Like It Hot* typifies the entire film and is echoed elsewhere in its plot, dialogue, characterizations, costumes, behaviors, editing, and configurations. For example, the gender "problem" is presented increasingly as the film progresses as just one of several possible minor problems. When Jerry/Daphne tells Joe "she's" engaged, Joe asks, "Who's the lucky girl?" Daphne answers, "I am." When Joe says "she" cannot marry Osgood, Daphne replies, "Why not? You think he's too old for me?" Finally, "she" admits there's a problem—his mother. Joe reminds Jerry/Daphne of the laws and conventions prohibiting his marriage to Osgood and insists that Jerry say he's a boy. "I'm a boy," Daphne concedes. "I wish I were dead."

In the final scene of *Some Like It Hot,* Josephine, Sugar, Osgood, and Daphne escape from the mob in a motorboat. Josephine/Joe pulls off his wig and tells Sugar he is only a saxophone player. Daphne then tells Osgood that "she" cannot marry him. When he protests, a series of alternative, minor excuses prepare for a final reversal hinged upon Daphne's generic removal of the wig. First Daphne admits that "she" is not a natural blonde. Osgood assures "her" that he doesn't mind. Then Daphne says "she" smokes, something his mother dislikes. Then Daphne admits to a terrible past and the fact that "she" cannot have children. Finally, taking off his wig, Jerry/Daphne proclaims, "I'm a man." Osgood, still smiling, simply replies, "Nobody's perfect." While gender conventions are reinstated via the heterosexual coupling of Joe and Sugar, the continued ro-

79. *Some Like It Hot:* The gender "problem" is presented as just one of several possible minor problems.

mance between Osgood and Jerry/Daphne provides an alternative to this conformity. The parallel structure of *Some Like It Hot,* enacted via plot, character, and editing, exploits the generic system of the temporary transvestite film to equally celebrate repetition and variation.

Victor/Victoria: Spectator Positioning

Victor/Victoria also exploits the temporary transvestite genre, combining authorial and generic discourses and providing much viewer pleasure in intertextual and self-reflexive twists. At the same time, the film's textual system uses cinematic codes to anchor reactionary cultural codes—particularly in its alignment of viewer pleasure with dominant ideology via privileged spectator positioning. Two determining (limiting) constructions illustrate this assertion: a kernel scene in which King spies on Victor/ Victoria bathing and discovers her real sex and a chain of performance scenes in which diegetic theater/audience events diagram the film's hermeneutic engagement with gender issues. The first employs and strengthens a privileged male gaze, the second a privileged heterosexual gaze.[10]

Victor/Victoria uses the generic bathroom scene of the temporary transvestite plot not to remind the cross-dresser of the ultimate futility of disguise (despite its diegetic effectiveness) but to naturalize and empower the reliable desire and penetrating look of heterosexuality (ostensibly challenged and reputed, respectively, in the generic diegesis). Collapsing narrative and ideological causation, King's invasion of Victor/Victoria's private space is justified both by Victor's same-sex (male) disguise and by Victoria's actual (female) sex.

This scene positions the film audience via a classic hierarchical looking pattern, the enactment of male voyeurism. Conventional male cinematic/cultural prerogative and generic biological determinism collaborate to recast the authority of a narratively adequate disguise as futile theater. If, as Kuhn argues, the narrative of sexual disguise films is activated by a desire to see the body, *Victor/Victoria* pursues this as a specifically heterosexual course. When King spies on Victor/Victoria undressing for a bath, he does so to legitimize a heterosexual pursuit and attraction, not to discover whether his pursuit is homosexual or heterosexual. Furthermore, this scene is based on a heterosexual hierarchy related to looking. Here the film viewer's point of view, although not always the same as the heterosexual male character's point of view, is in accord with it.

When King sneaks into Victoria's apartment behind a maid who is delivering towels, the camera/audience sees him darting across the hallway behind her back. This composition associates the camera/audience's look with superior knowledge. Victoria then arrives, enters the bathroom, and prepares for her bath. In the bathroom closet King simultaneously hides and spies on her. The camera/audience takes advantage of both his look and his facial reactions for vicarious sexual visual pleasure.

An interesting manipulation of the point-of-view shot facilitates this pleasuring process. Shots of King looking are intercut with shots, from his point of view, of Victoria taking off her male clothing. Every time the film viewers see King's face looking, the following shot shows them what King sees. This establishes a rhythm of alternating visual information about King and Victoria. The last shot of King does not, however, cut to what he sees. Instead the shot holds on his face while what he sees, Victoria's nude body, is represented via an audio index to offscreen visuals, sounds of water splashing as she gets into the bath. The preestablished rhythm of alternating contents facilitate the substitution of King's expression of sexual visual pleasure for the sexual image, a surrogate look for "direct" access to nudity.

This scene, as it accomplishes the quest for the uncovered body, is particularly remarkable in its reliance on both cultural and cinematic codes. Viewers know that Victoria is a woman because of the narrative view-behind, the initial inadequacy of the disguise, and the psychological-sexual-cinematic apparatus. Conventions relating to all three of these "languages" intersect in a system that curtails Victoria's gender fluidity.

Similarly, homosexuality is curtailed in *Victor/Victoria*. During the film numerous stage performances occur in which a diegetic audience serves as a surrogate for the film audience, guiding its responses to the performance according to a classic tripartite configuration. As in the spying scene, the configuration here constructs the spectator's narrative and visual pleasure via privileged positioning. Generally these internal performance scenes contain, in mixed order, several establishing shots that include both performer and diegetic audience, numerous one- and two-shots plus occasional group shots of diegetic audience members responding to the performance and many shots of the performance in which the film audience experiences/watches the performance "directly" without the onscreen presence of a diegetic audience. In this manner, the reactions of diegetic audience members suggest appropriate responses to the performance as it progresses. As the camera returns repeatedly to one or several of those audience members, their surrogate status becomes increasingly authoritative. While alternate shots ostensibly offer the performance as direct spectacle to the superior film audience, the diegetic audience functions as a mirror in which the film audience recognizes its proper responses and "through" which the film audience watches the spectacle. Furthermore, throughout *Victor/Victoria* these performance scenes parallel or accomplish certain plot developments. Consequently, the diegetic spectators (particularly those members who are main characters and are present at successive performances) guide the film audience through the entire film. As the plot progresses through its generic disruption and reinstatement of conventional gender boundaries, viewers are provided an emotional response trajectory and are encouraged to follow and experience it.

An examination of three performance scenes will demonstrate this process. In the first, Victoria impersonates a female impersonator. In the audience is Victoria's male homosexual accomplice, Toddy, who knows that the female impersonation is performance and that the "male" beneath this disguise is also an impersonation—that is, that Victoria is actually not male but female. Also in the audience is King, a gangsterlike businessman who is convinced by the female impersonation. When Victoria finishes her number, the diegetic audience claps loudly and a series of shots begins intercutting Victoria with alternating responses by these two males. Throughout this series of shots, King responds enthusiastically to Victoria's performance as well as to Victoria herself, to whom he is obviously attracted. In the last shot of Victoria in this series, she removes her wig, revealing herself as a "man," Victor. King abruptly stops clapping and responds with an expression of disbelief and disappointment.

This series of shots effectively replaces Toddy with King as "leading man." Through these characters it achieves a transition that recasts the narrative goal and attempts to realign the film audience's identifications and investments. Toddy has an economic interest in Victoria's impersonation act; King has a sexual interest in Victoria. While Toddy is invested in the believability of Victoria's disguises, King is invested in the primacy of Victoria's "true" sex. While Toddy sees female impersonation in the performance, King sees female essence. When Victoria removes her wig and King stops clapping, a new conflict is posited. Heterosexual goals replace economic needs. This scene marks both the successful accomplishment of gender disguise and the beginning of a new pursuit of the sex beneath the disguise. As the camera enters this scene with Toddy and exits it with King, the goals of the homosexual male are superseded by the conventional romance story and its heterosexual imperative.

In a later performance scene, Victoria, still passing as the female impersonator Victor, wears a tuxedo (reverse cross-dressing) during her performance. King is again in the audience, but by now he knows that Victoria is really a woman. As Victor/Victoria sings, the camera tracks 360 degrees around her, holding her face and shoulders at the center of the image. At the song's end, the filmic articulation returns to a static camera and to shot-reverse shot editing between performer and audience. The camera's lengthy movement around Victor/Victoria is marked by its difference to the filmic constructions of other performances in the film. This circling shot constructs a "filmic" pedestal for the female performer and an omnipresent point of view for the viewer, who is nonetheless transfixed by this female image. This position is aligned with the knowing and infatuated King. Then Victoria/Victor throws him a rose—an obvious reference to *Morocco* (Josef von Sternberg, 1930)—both delighting and confounding him by the private heterosexual confirmation and the public homosexual condemnation.

The final scene in *Victor/Victoria* is Toddy's performance of a female impersonation act earlier performed by Victoria. Toddy has necessarily taken over Victoria's role as female impersonator to avoid the discovery of her real (female) identity by a private investigator. Victoria, no longer disguised as Victor or impersonating "Victoria," sits in the audience with King. In contrast to Victor/Victoria's earlier performance, Toddy's performance is extremely comic and slapstick. He steps on his skirt, readjusts his "breasts," and appears too heavy to be supported by an entire group of male dancers/suitors. Despite the parallel with Victor/Victoria's earlier convincing impersonation, Toddy remains recognizable as a man in this performance—costumed rather than disguised. Furthermore, any camp power in his display of clashing gender codes is undermined by his cinematic positioning as butt of the joke rather than jokester. Toddy is laughed at and punished not only for impersonating a female with the help of costume but also for assuming a specifically female position of spectacle in relation to this contractual scheme between the male look and the apparatus. His lack of "natural" femininity suggests the impossibility of men passing as women—despite the grace of secondary male dancers in the performance—and works against other efforts in the film that posit gender as constructed. More important, heterocentric authorship has determined that Toddy will laugh along and be happy with this ending scene.

Throughout this performance and during the applause that follows it, the film cuts between shots of Toddy performing onstage and reaction shots of the diegetic audience laughing—including many shots framing King and Victoria. Because of the film's repeated use of diegetic audiences to signal key themes, transitions, and responses relating to the "problem" of gender, the laughing audience strongly directs the film audience toward a similar response. Both audiences laugh at Toddy's futile attempt at femininity. Furthermore, since Victoria and King's coming out as a heterosexual couple occurs during participation in this diegetic audience, the scene clearly calls upon the film audience to endorse the "superior position" of heterosexuality.[11]

At the conclusion of this final performance, Toddy tosses a rose to King's bodyguard, Mr. Bernstein (Alex Karras), who has earlier shared Toddy's bed. This mirrors the ending of the performance in which Victor/Victoria, in tuxedo, tosses a rose to King. Since the diegetic audience never believes Toddy's female "disguise," the homosexual actuality of this affectionate gesture supersedes any heterosexual implications of the costume inside the diegesis. This constructs a limited progressiveness in the film's treatment of "out" homosexuality. Toddy's homosexuality is accepted as long as it does not sustain successful gender-crossing. Homosexuality is permitted as long as it does not threaten a system of gender boundaries that supports the dominant heterosexual narrative.[12]

GENDER, SUBJECTIVITY, AND IDENTIFICATION

Regarding the transgression of gender boundaries—one of the primary pleasures of this genre—it can be argued that those films in which the disguise grossly fails to convince the viewer are reactionary in that the films' humor is derived from the "obvious unnaturalness" of one sex being in the other sex's clothing, and that the resultant audience laughter acts as a corrective measure for similar transgressions in actuality. The incongruity between diegetic and extradiegetic perception, this "failure of the disguise" in temporary transvestite films, is more extreme in male cross-dressing than female. This likely relates to the value western culture places on maleness and the related prohibitions against femininity in men. More convincing transvestism, as in *Tootsie* or *Her Life as a Man,* is less funny and yet more demonstrative of the cultural power of gender and the superficiality of costume. Kuhn describes the power of ideologically fixed gender:

> In ideology gender identity is not merely absolute; it also lies at the very heart of human subjectivity. Gender is what crucially defines us, so that an ungendered subject cannot, in this view, be human. The human being, in other words, is a gendered subject. And so a fixed subjectivity and a gendered subjectivity are, in ideology, one and the same . . . As a means to, even the substance of, a commutable persona, clothing as performance threatens to undercut the ideological fixity of the human subject.[13]

Thus, as a male war bride, Henry/Henrietta cannot secure a bed. Unable to be processed as either male or female, he/she spends the night walking back and forth between the men's and women's quarters, being denied entry to both. Without *one* gender, he/she effectively has *no* subjectivity.

Of course, resistant discourses, many informed by gay and lesbian theory and politics, contest this presumption that dominant ideology actually succeeds in policing subjectivity according to dichotomous gender. The rebellious effect of a drag queen depends on a disguise that appropriates and manipulates gender conventions and on the purposeful breakdown of that disguise into essentially contradictory levels of information. This leaves the viewer unsure about sexual identification and rules for sexual determination, and thereby offers the most radical conclusions. The drag element in the films discussed here exists primarily in the image rather than in the temporary transvestite narrative.

One measure of the radicalness of a temporary transvestite film is its relative ability to dismantle viewer assumptions about gender fixity and sex-role stereotypes. This can occur when the viewer is really tricked about a character's sex because of the viewer's assumptions about gender coding (i.e., when the extradiegetic effect resembles transvestism rather than cross-dressing), when the viewer is forced to accept contradictory gender signs within the same person (i.e., when cross-dressing shifts toward camp), and when the viewer is positioned within a simultaneously homosexual and heterosexual experience (i.e., the paradoxical kiss).

The transgression of boundaries relating to gender and sexuality is an experience, I would argue, that viewers routinely enjoy, not only in films about transvestism but in most films. To assert that a viewer identifies with all the major characters in a film is not to imply that all viewers experience those identifications or that film similarly or that vicarious identification with a character of the opposite sex is necessarily a homosexual activity.[14]

Although viewers may claim they "identify" with those characters who seem to be most like them, most akin to their intellectual, ethical, and experiential selves, I believe that such sympathetic identification is accompanied by more complicated empathic identification. The identificatory process engulfs not only those parts of a film that the viewer endorses but also those that she or he rejects. Repulsion indicates empathic identification as intensely as does pleasure. The film-viewing experience contains ambivalence and requires identification at all levels of the divided subject—conscious and unconscious. Analysis of the temporary transvestite genre system exposes the reductionism of binary-based theory that would assume sex-specific identification.

Without denying the participation of oppositions, we need to acknowledge other relationships that influence understanding and experience, such as those that privilege similarity, recognize continuums, and promote ambiguity and fluidity. Certainly myth works to simplify the notion of gender in ways that discourage recognition of the vast diversity that occurs, to make variance invisible. Especially in academic work, however, there must also be an attempt to "see through" myths, such as this one of two opposite and separate genders, and to acknowledge deviance as ordinary.

The privileging of binary opposition as the dominant thinking pattern naturalizes the concept of heterosexuality. However, heterosexuality is not itself a closed state. How much, we might ask, does eroticism, heterosexual or homosexual, depend on imposture and secrecy? While a disguise denies what would otherwise be obvious, an *obvious* disguise may falsely proclaim an absence. Perhaps the expansive pleasures of the temporary transvestite film depend on a shared "sneaking in" process in which both heterosexuals and homosexuals willingly self-deconstruct.

Notes

I would like to thank Nancy Fink and Ken Kirby for their helpful suggestions and assistance during the preparation of this essay.

1. Due to limitations of space, I have restricted my examples throughout this article to a minimum necessary for illustration of generic parameters (and significant departures). However, similar examples can be found regularly in most of the films discussed here.

2. Thomas Schatz, *Hollywood Genres: Formulas, Filmmaking, and the Studio System* (Philadelphia: Temple University Press, 1981), pp. 20–41. Schatz states that a "genre's fundamental impulse is to continually renegotiate the tenets of American ideology. And what is so fascinating and confounding about Hollywood genre films is their capacity to 'play it both ways,' to both criticize and reinforce the values, beliefs, and ideals of our culture within the same narrative con-

text" (p. 35). Mary Ann Doane, in *The Desire to Desire: The Women's Film of the* 1940s (Bloomington: Indiana University Press, 1987), and Edward Lowry, in "Genre and Enunciation: The Case of Horror," *Journal of Film and Video* 36, no. 2 (Spring 1984): 13–20, 72, describe a collection of films as a shared discourse directed to a particular viewer with a particular purpose.

3. Roland Barthes, *S/Z: An Essay,* translated by Richard Miller (New York: Hill and Wang, 1974), describes the hermeneutic code as "the various (formal) terms by which an enigma can be distinguished, suggested, formulated, held in suspense, and finally disclosed" (p. 19). In the temporary transvestite film the main enigma revolves around a disguise necessitated by the main plot. Other disguises that often occur in these films, such as the stage impersonations by Albin in *La Cage Aux Folles* or the playful dressing-up scenes in *Sylvia Scarlett,* influence the film's meaning via context and characterization but are not themselves part of the primary enigma to be solved in the narrative.

4. Esther Newton, *Mother Camp: Female Impersonators in America* (Chicago: University of Chicago Press, 1972), pp. 97–111.

5. Annette Kuhn, *The Power of the Image* (New York: Routledge & Kegan Paul, 1985), p. 57.

6. Gay themes may be introduced in many ways. For instance, the progression toward physical comedy discussed earlier can camouflage in-jokes for a gay audience, as in *Abroad with Two Yanks,* in which one man throws a dart into another man's ass—suggestive of gay male anal sex. (This same dart joke is "directed," possibly with more hostile intentions, at a female impersonator on stage from a member of the diegetic audience in the film *South Pacific* [Joshua Logan, 1958].)

7. A rare exception occurs in *I Was a Male War Bride.* Because the two characters are alone and know one another, the film's ending kiss, although bivalent, requires no further narrative rectification.

8. Kuhn, *Power of the Image,* p. 65.

9. Christian Metz describes the textual system as the intelligibility of the text. Constructed by the analyst from all the codes in a particular corpus (a film fragment, a film, a genre, etc.), the textual system itself has no physical existence. Metz states that "the textual system, the interpretation of each film in its uniqueness, constitutes by definition and kind of mixed site in which specific codes (codes more or less peculiar to the cinema and only the cinema) and non-specific codes (codes more or less common to various 'languages' and a state of culture) meet and combine one with another." See "Part I: The Imaginary Signifier," in *Christian Metz: The Imaginary Signifier: Psychoanalysis and the Cinema,* translated by Celia Britton et al. (Bloomington: Indiana University Press, 1982), p. 35. Metz also writes about the textual system in *Language and Cinema* (The Hague: Mouton, 1974).

10. See Laura Mulvey, "Visual Pleasure and Narrative Cinema," *Screen* 16, no. 3 (1975): 6–18.

11. For another reading of *Victor/Victoria,* see William Luhr and Peter Lehman, *Returning to the Scene: Blake Edwards* (Athens: Ohio University Press, 1989), 2: 44–68. Luhr and Lehman note that after the bathroom scene the film

moves from King's doubts about his sexual orientation to recast the "problem" as the perception of him by others as homosexual when coupled with Victor/Victoria in public. They also note that in the film's final scene, "Victoria is dressed in and almost seems attired for a funeral. She takes the 'proper' place of a woman, sitting quietly at King's side. In one shot we actually see her silently mouthing the words to the song that was once hers but which Toddy now sings. No one hears her" (p. 54).

12. Toddy's homosexual preference, though perhaps provisionally endorsed by narrative discourse via his toss of the rose, is powerfully counteracted throughout the narrative by an absence of sexuality in his characterization and actions. The film contains two scenes of Toddy in bed with men. The first, which opens the film, shows Toddy and a younger male waking up in bed together; the sexual act is already over, and the dialogue reveals that Toddy has paid for sexual services. In the second Toddy and Mr. Berstein are in bed together when Victor/Victoria enters the room. Although they are "sharing a bed," the men are dressed in pajamas, hold tea cups, and do not interact physically; they respond to Victoria more than to each other. As if to confirm the sexual blandness of their joint image, Victoria walks completely past them before their image "shocks" her. A forbidden sexuality "foregrounds" them as invisible. Neither of these scenes contains either seduction or sexual activity. Homosexuality is effectively reduced to asexuality. Between these two homosexual but asexual scenes is a scene in which King's first girlfriend, Norma (Lesley Ann Warren), flirts with Toddy. When Toddy explains that he is gay, she says that the right girl could reform him. Toddy replies that the right girl could reform her too. This scene corrects a heterosexual assumption; however, in relation to Toddy's characterization in other parts of the film, this scene can be read as one more attempt to drain Toddy of sexuality. (After all, the narrative discourse could have been written to have a male flirt with Toddy.) In general, *Victor/Victoria* combats homophobia via a tolerance that includes a *homo*sexual couple in its final gathering and closure, but reinforces homophobia via its intolerance of homo*sex*uality.

13. Kuhn, *Power of the Image*, pp. 52–53.

14. Rather, I would argue, identification with the opposite sex more often occurs through non-gender-related similarities between viewer and character. For example, although adventure in the western genre is most frequently experienced by cowboy characters, the desire for adventure is shared by male and female viewers alike. Any tendency to identify with one's own sex coexists with other identificatory needs, such as a predilection for heroism, which may weaken or strengthen that sex-specific identification.

27. Friendly Civilians: Images of Women and the Feminization of the Audience in Vietnam War Films

SUSAN JEFFORDS

Art historian John Berger once observed that in western culture generally, "a man's presence suggests what he is capable of doing to you or for you. By contrast, a woman's presence . . . defines what can and cannot be done to her."[1] This ideological dynamic operates in a particularly interesting way in U.S. films about the Vietnam War, for it identifies not only aspects of representation but also the positioning of the spectator in relation to visual culture. To explore this dynamic, I will look in this essay at how U.S. films about the Vietnam War construct representations of women.[2] Specifically, Vietnam films employ two images of women: the women "back home," remote, removed from combat, most often seen transfixed in photographs or tearfully awaiting their soldiers' return; and the characterization of the feminine—passive, fearful, manipulable, submissive—the traditional depiction of the female character, here to be applied to men as well.[3] What I want to argue in this essay is that these two images—of "women" and the "feminine"—are used not only to further the narratives of Vietnam War films, but to bring those stories "home," to impress their messages upon the audiences of Vietnam films. Most important, these images of women become the ideological matrices from which the Hollywood Vietnam theater constructs *its* image of the audience—an audience that the dominant society wishes to create as passive, manipulable, fearful, and submissive—in other words, feminine.[4] The final effect of this feminization is to defuse social and political dissent in contemporary American society.

I will discuss three films in particular, each of which presents a different aspect of the images of women: Francis Ford Coppola's *Apocalypse Now* (1979), Hal Ashby's *Coming Home* (1978), and Ted Kotcheff's *First Blood* (1982). Though there are many other Vietnam films, I choose these because of their widespread distribution and popularity.[5] The dates of these films are important, for it is a premise of this discussion that, though two of the films' narratives date to the period of the Vietnam War, all are in fact about social events occurring in the United States in the late seventies and early eighties. As Bill Nichols explains, "Cinematic narrative . . . seeks to resolve contradictions and provide models for action in the present, not the past, though it may use the past to do so." [6] Specifically, these films are directed at those who wish to enact social change through violent or radical confrontation—women, veterans, blacks, and others who, throughout the sixties and early seventies, were pressing society for recognition of their political and economic position. Vietnam films aim to "feminize" these audiences and thereby negate their social demands. In addition, recent Vietnam films use images of women and the feminine to prepare their audiences for a revisionary attitude toward the Vietnam War and military conflicts in the present.

These images of women are best established in *Apocalypse Now*. The narrative begins with Captain Willard lying on a bed in a Saigon hotel room, the blades of the rotating overhead fan evoking the most persistent emblem of the Vietnam War and its new military strategy, the helicopter. Next to his hand lies a letter written on pale blue stationery and a photograph of his wife, a graduation picture. Willard examines the photograph while his voice-over comments, "I hardly said a word to my wife 'til I said 'yes' to the divorce." With his cigarette still hanging from his lips, he burns a hole through the center of the picture, destroying his wife's image. Willard thereby severs his last ties to "home" and to the woman there who does not understand his "mission." Before he goes deep into the Vietnam jungle in search of his prey, the rebel colonel Walter E. Kurtz, Willard must cut himself off from his past, from his emotions, from his familial values. On the perilous trip upriver to Kurtz's camp those who refuse to abandon those values, those who cling to their past, will die.

"Mr. Clean," the panicky gunner on Willard's boat, receives a cassette-taped letter from his mother in the mail picked up at the last outpost, the Du Long Bridge. In it she tells him about his family, friends, and home. Suddenly, the crew is attacked by unseen riverside guerillas and Clean is killed. While his friends gather around his body, his mother's voice continues: "Do the right thing and stay out of the way of the bullets." Unable to release himself to Vietnam, Clean is killed.

In contrast, Lance, the Malibu surfer, adapts himself more and more to his surroundings, masking himself in jungle camouflage, shaping a head ornament out of native wooden arrows, and echoing the animalistic cries that reverberate throughout the jungle. He blends in with the Montagnard tribesmen of Kurtz's army, wearing only their loincloth and bathing himself in the ritual blood of the sacrificial bull. Lance is the only one to return with Willard from the "mission."

On the way upriver, Willard seals his pact with Vietnam when he responds to a soldier's wish to be back home: "Trouble is, I've been back there, and I know that it just didn't exist anymore." The first man sent on this mission, Captain Richard Colby, failed; instead of "exterminating" Kurtz, he joined his brutal army. From the camp, Colby sends a scrawled message to his wife: "I'm not coming back. . . . Sell the house. . . . Forget it." Kurtz's file is filled with pictures of his wife and son, but like Colby and Willard, he knows that he cannot go home; for them, "It didn't exist anymore." The farther they are from home, from images of women, the deeper they become enmeshed in Vietnam.

Earlier, when Chef had tried to go into the jungle to collect mangoes (he fantasizes about Raquel Welch and mangoes), he and Willard were chased back to the boat by a tiger. Chef's conclusion: "Never get off the boat." Willard agrees: "Never get off the boat. Absolutely Goddamn right. Unless you're going all the way. . . . Kurtz got off the boat." Fighting the war his own way—head-hunting, scalping, midnight murders, brutal tribal raids—Kurtz has indeed, as far as the military is concerned, "got off the boat." For this crime, he has to be "terminated, with extreme prejudice." In a war filled with its own atrocities, Kurtz, fighting with blood-thirsty success, has gone beyond the limits of accepted military behavior. But as Willard objects, "Accusing someone of murder in this war is like handing out speeding tickets at the Indy 500."

The American counterpart of the wife's photograph, the centerfold, adorns the military store at Hau Phat, the site of the Playboy Bunnies' landing in Coppola's Vietnam. Equally out of place in this jungle war, this is the other image of women in *Apocalypse Now*. The Playboy dancers are flown into the jungle by helicopter, landing on a stage surrounded by hooting soldiers and phallic columns that appear alternately and indeterminably to be missiles and lipstick. The Bunnies here embody the fantasies of American manhood, dressing as a cowboy, an Indian, and a cavalry soldier, reviving yet another era of American expansionism and imperialism, of a less troublesome war where the battles were more clearly won and the slaughters more simply patriotic. The women dance seductively with cap pistols on their hips, making love to the soldiers' M-16s while Vietnamese villagers watch from outside the barbed wire fences. The Playmates dance as they would "at home," back within the guarded confines of the Playboy clubs. What they fail to realize is that they are now in Vietnam.

In the midst of the dance, the soldiers begin to leap on to the stage and accost the dancers. They seek initially only the women's autographs, but as the soldiers surround the women, their attentions become more threatening. The dancers and their promoters have failed to see the violence that lies below the surface in these soldiers' lives, the irreverence with which they treat the boundaries of an alien American life. Accustomed to American representations of the war, these women are unable to see the reality that is Vietnam.

80. *Apocalypse Now:* The Playboy Bunnies surrounded by hooting soldiers.

Apocalypse Now captures and preserves the images of women prevalent in American culture—the angel and the whore, the mother and the
mistress, continuing its trade in the mirrored coin of American sexuality.[7]
Most important, these images are defined in relation to the masculine
point of view. But because that gaze is determined not so much by its object as by its way of seeing, the masculine gaze *creates* its images as it observes them. In her discussion of pornography—the least subtle of the
masculine gazes—Susan Griffin refers to women as the "blank screen"
onto which masculine representations are projected: "The nature of her
real being is erased, as if her cultural image had been carefully prepared
for a clear projection of an image, and she comes to stand for all that man
would deny in himself."[8] Laura Mulvey reinforces this relationship in
broader cultural terms: "Woman then stands in patriarchal culture as
signifier for the male other, bound by a symbolic order in which man can
live out his phantasies and obsessions through linguistic command by im-
posing them on the silent image of woman still tied to her place as bearer
of meaning, not maker of meaning."[9]

Griffin's use of the filmic analogy is not accidental, for this is the gaze of dominant film, projecting its images onto the spectators of patriarchal cinema, simultaneously creating images of and for that audience. To return again to Mulvey, "It is the place of the look that defines cinema. . . . Playing on the tension between film as controlling the dimension of space (changes in distance, editing), cinematic codes create a gaze, a world, and an object, thereby producing an illusion cut to the measure of desire." [10] Most important for this context is the extent to which dominant cinema appropriates that gaze for the creation, not only of the objects of cinematic illusion but of the audience as well.

Although members of the audience may identify with the male characters on the Vietnam screen, they are also being made subject to the gaze that the screen returns. They are fixed by the masculine gaze of the film in the place of the feminine—the nonparticipant, the uninitiated, the blank. As the Playboy Bunnies land at Hau Phat, the camera is centered in the audience so that we see the dancers as the soldiers see them. But as the soldiers become more violent, our camera view is shifted to a spot behind the dancers; now subjected to their vulnerability, we are attacked by the violence of Vietnam. As audience, we have been fixed by the film's gaze in the place of those who are alien to Vietnam and its masculinity. D. N. Rodowick has observed that "in the play of identity and difference in which the economy of looks is regulated by the cinematic machine, a subject is produced for this place in the imaginary which structures textual operations." [11] The production of that subject by Vietnam cinema is achieved through the process of feminization.

As Susan Griffin reminds us, "The very word 'woman' signifies all those qualities which the masculine mind splits off from itself. . . . And in the female live all the qualities the male has decided are inferior and suspect." [12] This repression of the feminine is at the heart of *Apocalypse Now* and much Vietnam literature. It is most explicitly acknowledged in Bob Biderman's recent novel, *Letters to Nanette,* in which his main character, Alan Bronstein, enlists in the army in 1963 only to discover that his company is being sent out to Vietnam. He experiences moral anxiety about going to a war that he doesn't believe in and finally plots an escape through a psychiatric discharge. The tale is told in his letters to Nanette, an amorphous, undescribed woman who is the only person to whom Bronstein can express his fears and doubts. At the close of the novel, we discover that there is no Nanette, only a name that represents a suppressed part of Bronstein's character: "I suppose that was the importance of writing, it put me in touch with another self which was in hiding [during his enlistment] but which needed to come out for air every once in a while so as not to suffocate." [13] Biderman explicitly recognizes the extent to which the military masculine denies the feminine. Unlike many other Vietnam soldiers, Bronstein is aware of his need to acknowledge that part of his character. And it is the voice of "Nanette," we are to presume, that keeps Bronstein from going to the war. It is this voice that is repressed in the Vietnam theater.

We turn now to what that theater tells its audience about the feminine as we look at one of the most popular Vietnam films, Hal Ashby's *Coming Home*. Released in the same year as Michael Cimino's *The Deer Hunter* (1978), *Coming Home* begins where Cimino's film ends, with the return of the Vietnam veteran. Touted by many as the leftist Vietnam film showing the damage that the war brought to individual lives, Morris Dickstein praises the film for "bringing the war home. For once the Hollywood left has done itself proud." [14] It is seen by others as the "feminist" Vietnam film, having a hero, Luke, who espouses feminist qualities and releases Sally Hyde from her traditional female role of military wife. But the film is finally, as James C. Wilson concludes, far less radical than it might appear: "Ostensibly about the painful process of healing the wounds of Vietnam, *Coming Home* degenerates into the soap opera love story of Luke and Sally." [15] But *Coming Home* has far more damaging consequences than this. The film denies not simply the serious issues of the Vietnam War but also the very people it is trying to defend, the Vietnam veterans.

As the film opens, Luke is angry. Frustrated by the war and his senseless paralysis, he strikes out, verbally and physically, at those who come near him. In order to protect themselves, the nurses restrain him, strapping his arms and chest to a hospital bed. Still he refuses to eat and continues his verbal assault on the hospital staff. He is uncooperative, belligerent, angry. But by the end of the film, it is Luke who is preaching nonviolence and restraint, not only to another veteran, Bob Hyde, but to an auditorium full of high school students, prospective military recruits. What has happened to break Luke's anger? What has endeared him to so many film viewers? What has made him so "feminine?"

Most obviously, he has fallen in love with a woman, Sally Hyde. It is Sally whom Luke speaks to from his hospital bed, Sally who first takes him from the hospital to her home for dinner, Sally who first makes love to him. The hospital's message is clear: as Luke becomes more passive, he is allowed more freedom, graduating from bed to gurney to wheelchair to sportscar. He moves from his single room to a multipatient ward to his own apartment. In other words, the more "feminine" he becomes, the more access to society he gains. So much so that, by the end of the film, Luke has achieved the freedom to encourage *others* to be equally nonviolent, equally passive.

The anger against the war and the government that fueled his early violence has been defused from a political to a personal one. Instead of striking out against the society that sent him to Vietnam, by the end of the film he is indicting only himself.[16] In the closing scenes when he speaks to the high school class, he talks not of the injustice of the war or the imperialism of U.S. intervention or even the destruction of Vietnamese lives and land, but of his own guilt instead. In tears he confesses, "There are lots of things that I did that I find pretty hard to live with now." His argument to the students is that he doesn't want them to feel that regret as well. The guilt for the war has been reinterpreted so as to lie in the *personal* failings of individual soldiers, not the political failings of the government. And it is femininity that is the mechanism for that reinterpretation.

I am *not* suggesting that Luke should have encouraged the young men to enlist or should have excited their passion to kill. I am trying to analyze why, when the war had been over for three years, the last troops being withdrawn in March of 1973, this film was espousing pacifism. There was no real question of these students enlisting to fight a war. As Lawrence Suid remarks, "The message came at least ten years too late."[17] Recalling Bill Nichols's insistence that cinematic narratives resolve contradictions and provide models for action *in the present, who* was this film's audience?

First and foremost, *Coming Home* was directed at the Vietnam veteran. Luke's lesson was "If you want to be reincorporated into society, if you want to 'come home,' you must be passive." Luke becomes the apostle for this message as he encourages Bob Hyde to "put the gun down" and accept, as he had, Sally's love. Rehabilitated, Luke can say (ostensibly to Bob but really to the audience), "I am not the enemy." On a larger scale, Al Auster and Leonard Quart suggest that Vietnam films of the seventies are oriented toward reviving a lost confidence in American strength and will, both social and military.[18] But for a closer ideological understanding of these films, we need to look at one of Hollywood's most recent Vietnam productions, Ted Kotcheff's *First Blood*.

Sylvester Stallone plays John Rambo, a veteran of the Green Beret special forces in Vietnam. While hiking through the northwestern mountains, he passes through the town of Hope. Upon entering the town, the sheriff, Will Teasle, tells him, "We don't want guys like you in this town." Taking him for a wanderer and a misfit, Teasle escorts him unkindly out of town. Rambo, determined not to be rerouted, reenters the town and is promptly arrested. Trying to contain him in the jail, the officers strip, shower, and shave Rambo by force. Following a flashback that returns him to a Viet Cong prisoner camp, Rambo strikes out, using his special-forces training to escape the jail. Pursued by the sheriff and his deputies into the woods, Rambo begins a war on the town, using special-forces tactics that eventually leave many injured and much of the town destroyed. Turning on the town the skills that he was taught by the military

81. John Rambo (Sylvester Stallone) in *First Blood:* The veteran must be feminized or eliminated.

in order to fight the government's war, Rambo tells them, "In there you are the law. Out here, it's me—I'll give you a war you'll never believe."

The implication of this plot is clear; Rambo is to be seen as a victim of the government's policies in Vietnam. Like Sheriff Teasle, who pushes Rambo until he responds and then hunts him when the response is violent, the government, in recruiting and training soldiers for Vietnam, pushed them to violence. As Alan Bronstein says of his military training, "They want me to be angry. They want me to be mean. They want me to be capable of murder."[19] Like Teasle, the government refuses to allow the violence to escape into the towns of America. Veterans who retain this violence and use it against the state, for whatever reason, are restrained, confined, or, as the novel *First Blood* makes explicit, eliminated. *First Blood*, in its novel and film versions, offers the two choices allowed to the veteran—to become feminized or be eliminated.[20]

In the novel Rambo's battle with Teasle is a personal contest of manhood, until finally Teasle, having shot Rambo and been shot himself, projects himself into Rambo's mind and identifies with him so much that he believes he knows what Rambo is thinking. Tracking him to a brush field with Colonel Trautman, the man who trained Rambo, Teasle "knows" that Rambo wants to die fighting. Still trying to make his best attempt at the battle, Rambo shoots Teasle and mortally wounds him. With this shot, he lies back on the ground and imagines death taking over his body: "He let it happen, went with it, erupted free through the back of his head and his skull, catapulted through the sky, through myriad spectra, onward, outward, forever dazzling, brilliant, and he thought if he kept on like this for long enough he might be wrong and see God after all." [21] But death does not simply "take over." Rambo has been shot in the head by his former mentor, Colonel Trautman. When Teasle learns this, he dies in peace. Rambo has been eliminated.

In the film version of *First Blood,* Rambo, still stalked by Teasle and Trautman, shoots Teasle and allows Trautman into the sheriff's office where he is hiding. But instead of shooting Rambo, Trautman listens to his veteran's tale. Rambo had lost all the men in his unit but one, whom he traced to this mountain region only to find that he had died of Agent Orange contamination. Alone except for Trautman, Rambo tells the colonel: "You don't just turn it off. I do what I have to do to win, but somebody can't let us win." Exhausted from his confession, Rambo falls into Trautman's arms, crying. Trautman, with his arms around Rambo, convinces him to give up the battle, and Rambo leaves the station wearing Trautman's overcoat. The movie ends here, with a freeze frame of Rambo going out into the world, while we hear the voice-over song chant for us, "It's a real war, / right outside your front door." In the film Rambo has been feminized.

In *Apocalypse Now,* Captain Willard is told that Colonel Kurtz could have been accepted back into the fold if he had reformed, but refusing to change, he had to be eliminated. *Coming Home* offers the same theme in its ending, showing Bob Hyde stripping and running into the ocean. Has he gone to be cleansed or to commit suicide? to be feminized or eliminated? This 1978 film leaves open the question that the 1982 *First Blood* answers, the question not simply of the Vietnam veterans but of dissent in general. These films re-*place* dissenters, through feminization, in their traditional role as members of the status quo, of the audience. What are the characteristics traditionally required of an American audience in dominant cinema? Silence, passivity, immobility, sensitivity, impressionability—the stereotypical qualities of the feminine. So to be replaced in that audience is to be silenced, pacified, immobilized. The ideological theater that represents the Vietnam War creates its own audience.

The Vietnam literature itself testifies to the effectiveness of this Hollywood theater.[22] Over and over again Vietnam veterans confess to Hollywood's impact on their war experience: "It was like a big movie"; "I was John Wayne in *Sands of Iwo Jima* [Allan Dwan, 1949]; I was Aldo Ray in

Battle Cry [Raoul Walsh, 1955]"; "I was seduced by W. W. II and John Wayne movies."²³ From their first day in the country, the soldiers were treated to the movie that was to be Vietnam. Jonathan Polansky, recalling his arrival in Vietnam in November of 1968 for Al Santoli's *Everything We Had*, remembers seeing *The Green Berets* (John Wayne and Ray Kellogg, 1968) his first night in Vietnam.²⁴ Soldier after soldier talks of John Wayne, wanting to take his place in the movie: "I had flash images of John Wayne films with me as the hero."²⁵ As one soldier perceives, "Everything is symbolism that you're living on."²⁶ Most recently, the Vietnam films themselves have become the mise-en-scène for new military actions, as we learn that the American soldiers going into Grenada played Wagner, reenacting the attack scenes of *Apocalypse Now*.

Interestingly, Julian Smith believes that Hollywood in some way failed the Vietnam veteran: "Today's films about veterans actually reflect the moral isolation of the combat soldier—an isolation created in part by Hollywood's reluctance to provide the kind of patriotic and emotional support for this war as for the earlier ones."²⁷ The contradiction in this reasoning reveals the real purpose of the Vietnam films. On the one hand, Smith refers to films' ability to "reflect" ongoing reality; on the other, he acknowledges Hollywood's power to shape that reality. If Smith had applied his more astute insights on Hollywood war films to his first observation, he would have concluded that those dismal pictures of veteran life, their "moral isolation," are there for a reason.

As Santoli notes, "It was apparently not uncommon for Vietnam vets to come back angry, and when some became upset, their method of coping was to become violent."²⁸ A veteran imprisoned for possession of a weapon describes the prison situation: "But coming out of orientation they put all the Vietnam vets in the worst possible situation in the prison system. *They* know that *you* know what danger is really all about. . . . They know that you'll take a chance because you already have."²⁹ Given their high level of military training, their experience in combat, and their familiarity with violence, it is no surprise that Hollywood has failed to "support" the Vietnam veterans. Instead, it needs to divert their anger, dilute it, defuse it—feminize it, or, as a last alternative, eliminate it.

The identification of a "feminine" audience is not original to Hollywood. Earlier in this century the masses were depicted by Adolf Hitler as "feminine": "The people, in an overwhelming majority, are so feminine in their nature and attitude that their activities and thoughts are motivated less by sober consideration than by feeling and sentiment." Hitler continues his argument: "Like a woman. . .who will submit to the strong man rather than dominate the weakling, thus the masses love the ruler rather than the suppliant. . . ; they often feel at a loss what to do with [freedom], and even easily feel themselves deserted." [30] This association of the passive, manipulable masses with the image of women lies at the core of much of Hollywood's Vietnam theater.

For a reason. It is not simply the violence of the Vietnam veteran that these movies wish to control—though that is their most direct goal—but the violence of other dissenting groups as well. Michael Renov describes the same pattern of feminization or elimination for Hollywood's World War II films directed at women who, as a result of the war, were moving out of more traditional spheres. For women who attempted to construct independent lives, "two possible resolutions for such activities became viable: selfhood is neutralized by romantic allegiance or marriage, or selfhood is annihilated by death." [31]

Peter Marin writes of a woman's reaction to the Vietnam veterans' situation: "I remember once describing to a woman friend . . . how it was the vets felt. 'But that's it, that's it exactly,' she said. 'That's how I felt having my abortions, after the abortions. The same sense of significance and meaning. The same sense of isolation—no one on either side of the question to understand how I felt.' " [32] And let us not forget that "more than any other war in American history, Vietnam was a class war, fought predominantly by minorities and the poor." [33] These are the implicit audiences for Vietnam theater—women, minorities, the poor, the veteran. These are the people who are warned not to get off the boat, not to leave their seats in the theater.

Vietnam films are the most explicit examples of the general attitudes of Hollywood dominant cinema, a cinema that works to "Americanize" its audience by creating viewers who will accept, internalize, and enact the images that are projected onto them by the masculine gaze of the screen. It is quite possible to subvert this cinema, but one must first invert that gaze by altering the structure of this theater, changing the ways in which we watch and are watched by the films that are attempting to shape us.

Make no mistake; Vietnam films *are* violent. But they present violence as a part of the test of the masculine, a part of the battle that is war. They do not present violence toward the state or its institutions. And if they do, the violence is soon "eliminated." As Suid observes, "However bloody and violent filmmakers have portrayed combat on the screen, the action and excitement usually have become escapist entertainment rather than creating a revulsion against war." [34] Violence in Vietnam films is generally remote, sporadic, and meaningless—even *First Blood* takes place in the deserted mountains of the Northwest—and it is always confronted through individual, personal, or psychological experience rather than in political contexts. The Vietnam audience is shown that violence exists, but this violence is apolitical and distant. The goal of feminization is to convince the audience that brutality and violence are alien to them. To do this, Vietnam theater establishes its authority by identifying the audience with the place of women—back home, away from the battles, away from the war—and then presenting the consequences of any attempt to challenge that authority. Vietnam violence cannot "come home" with the veterans, cannot be "at home" with the audience. As John Rambo tells us, "There *are* no friendly civilians."

Notes

1. John Berger, *Ways of Seeing* (New York: Viking, 1972), pp. 45–46.

2. Many Vietnamese films have been made about the "American War," such as *The Abandoned Field* (Nguyen Hong Sen, 1979); *When Mother Is Absent* (Nguyen Khanh Du, 1979); *When the Tenth Month Comes* (Dang Nhat Minh, 1984); and *White Flowers on the River* (Tran Phuong, 1989). Women in these films are generally depicted as brave warriors and strong family members.

3. Laura Mulvey suggests a similar pattern for the western: "Here two functions emerge, one celebrating integration into society through marriage, the other celebrating resistance to social standards and responsibilities . . . the sphere represented by women." "Afterthoughts on 'Visual Pleasure and Narrative Cinema' Inspired by *Duel in the Sun* (King Vidor, 1946)," *Framework*, nos. 15–17 (Summer 1981): 18. The cross-gender application of these categories is similar to Steve Neale's insistence that men can also be the objects of a masculine (i.e., voyeuristic and fetishistic) gaze. See "Masculinity as Spectacle: Reflections on Men and Mainstream Cinema," *Screen* 24, no. 6 (November–December 1983): 2–17.

4. Annette Kuhn, in her fine book *Women's Pictures: Feminism and Cinema* (Boston: Routledge & Kegan Paul, 1982), uses the term "feminine" to describe "an attribute of textual organization . . . that poses a challenge to dominant forms of relationship between texts and recipients. . . . A feminine text would in this way constitute a subversion of and challenge to a 'mainstream' text" (p. 12). Our definitions are opposed, yet complementary, as the feminization of the audience that I discuss here is an *effect* of dominant cinema, while the "feminine" reading that Kuhn proposes is a means of discovering and subverting that effect. The process that I am describing is more like that which Ann Douglas identifies in *The Feminization of American Culture* (New York: Avon, 1977), in which she sees "feminization" as a means of identifying and shaping marginal cultures, specifically those of women and the clergy in nineteenth-century America.

5. For the most complete Vietnam filmographies, see James C. Wilson, *Vietnam in Prose and Film* (Jefferson, N.C.: McFarland and Company, 1982), and Gilbert Adair, *Vietnam on Film: From "The Green Berets" to "Apocalypse Now"* (New York: Proteus, 1981).

6. Bill Nichols, *Ideology and the Image* (Bloomington: Indiana University Press, 1981), p. 76.

7. For a further discussion of these contrasting characterizations of women and their use in literary culture, see Sandra Gilbert and Susan Gubar's excellent

study, *The Madwoman in the Attic* (New Haven: Yale University Press, 1979), pp. 17–31.

8. Susan Griffin, *Pornography and Silence* (New York: Harper and Row, 1981), p. 19.

9. Laura Mulvey, "Visual Pleasure and Narrative Cinema," *Screen* 16, no. 3 (1975): 7.

10. Ibid., p. 19.

11. D. N. Rodowick, "The Difficulty of Difference," *Wide Angle* 5, no. 1 (1982): 6.

12. Susan Griffin, "The Way of All Ideology," *Signs* 7, no. 3 (1982): 630.

13. Bob Biderman, *Letters to Nanette* (San Francisco: Contemporary Literature Series, 1982), p. 243.

14. Morris Dickstein, "Bringing It All Back Home," *Partisan Review* 45, no. 4 (1978): 632.

15. Wilson, *Vietnam in Prose and Film,* p. 83. Hollywood was to repeat this pattern a few years later with the romanticized version of the Russian revolution, *Reds* (Warren Beatty, 1981).

16. As Richard Ohmann points out in relation to American literature of the sixties and seventies, contemporary society encourages individuals to see social problems as their own fault rather than that of the society at large. "The Shaping of the Canon in U.S. Fiction, 1960–1975," *Critical Inquiry* 10 (September 1983): 199–223.

17. Lawrence Suid, "Hollywood and Vietnam," *Film Comment* 15 (September 1979): 23.

18. Al Auster and Leonard Quart, "Hollywood and Vietnam: The Triumph of the Will," *Cineaste* 9 (Spring 1979): 4–9.

19. Biderman, *Letters to Nanette,* p. 28.

20. Jean-Francois Lyotard characterizes this imperative as "be operational . . . or disappear" in *The Postmodern Condition: A Report on Knowledge,* translated by Geoff Bennington and Brian Mossumi (Minneapolis: University of Minnesota Press, 1984), p. xxiv.

21. David Morrell, *First Blood* (New York: Fawcett Crest, 1972), p. 255.

22. Julian Smith's study, *Looking Away: Hollywood and Vietnam* (New York: Charles Scribner's Sons, 1975), offers a good discussion of the influence of Hollywood films on the audiences of World Wars I and II and the Korean War.

23. Mark Baker, *Nam* (New York: Berkeley Books, 1981), p. 75; Phillip Caputo, *A Rumor of War* (New York: Ballantine Books, 1977), p. 255; Baker, *Nam,* p. 15.

24. Al Santoli, *Everything We Had* (New York: Ballantine Books, 1981), p. 104.

25. Baker, *Nam,* p. 22.

26. Santoli, *Everything We Had,* p. 99.

27. Smith, *Looking Away,* p. 159.

28. Santoli, *Everything We Had,* p. 144.

29. Baker, *Nam,* pp. 280–281.

30. Adolf Hitler, *Mein Kampf* (New York: Reynal and Hitchcock, 1940), pp. 237, 56.

31. Michael Renov, "From Fetish to Subject: The Containment of Sexual Difference in Hollywood's Wartime Cinema," *Wide Angle* 5, no. 1 (1982): 22.

32. Peter Marin, "What the Vietnam Vets Can Teach Us," *Nation*, November 27, 1982, p. 24.

33. Wilson, *Vietnam in Prose and Film*, p. 4.

34. Suid, "Hollywood and Vietnam," p. 24.

28. The Self-Reflexive Musical and the Myth of Entertainment

JANE FEUER

Within the musical film the most persistent subgenre has involved kids (or adults) "getting together and putting on a show." *The Jazz Singer* (Alan Crosland, 1927) featured a show-business story, and during the talkie boom that followed (1929–1930), a large percentage of the early musicals took for their subjects the world of entertainment: Broadway, vaudeville, the Ziegfeld Follies, burlesque, night clubs, the circus, Tin Pan Alley, and, to a lesser extent, mass entertainment media in the form of radio or Hollywood itself. Warner Brothers' *Forty-Second Street* (Lloyd Bacon, 1933) precipitated a second cycle of musicals. The *Forty-Second Street* spinoffs tended to feature a narrative strategy typical of the backstage musical: musical interludes, usually in the form of rehearsal sequences detailing the maturation of the show, would be interspersed with parallel dramatic scenes detailing maturation of the off-stage love affairs. Even a radio story such as *Twenty Million Sweethearts* (Ray Enright, 1934) took its narrative structure from this paradigm. Perhaps these "art" musicals fulfilled a need for verisimilitude; perhaps the audience felt more comfortable viewing musical numbers within the context of a show than seeing fairy-tale queens and princes suddenly feel a song coming on in the royal boudoir. Whatever the explanation of its origins, the backstage pattern was always central to the genre. Incorporated into the structure of the art musical was the very type of popular entertainment represented by the musical film itself. The art musical is thus a self-referential form.

All art musicals are self-referential in this loose sense. But given such an opportunity, some musicals have exhibited a greater degree of self-consciousness than others. *Dames* (Enright, 1934) climaxes its show-within-the-film with an apology for its own mode of entertainment, appropriately entitled "Dames." Moreover, the "Dames" number resolves a narrative in which the forces of Puritanism do battle with the forces of entertainment. It is the victory of what might be termed the "prurient ethic" over the Puritan ethic that the final show celebrates within the film and that the "Dames" number celebrates within that show. In similar fashion,

82. *Forty-Second Street:* The backstage musical.

the Fred Astaire–Ginger Rogers cycle at RKO (1933–1939) began to reflect upon the legends created in its dancing stars.[1]

Shall We Dance (Mark Sandrich, 1937) culminates in a show merging popular dancing with ballet. Yet that merger consists not in an equal union but rather in the lending of youth, rhythm, and vitality to the stiff, formal, classical art of ballet. Once again, a musical film has affirmed its own value for the popular audience.

Dames and *Shall We Dance* are early examples of musicals that are *self-reflective* beyond their given self-referentiality. Historically, the art musical has evolved toward increasingly greater degrees of self-reflectivity. By the late forties and into the early fifties, a series of musicals produced by the Freed unit at MGM used the backstage format to present sustained reflections upon, and affirmations of, the musical genre itself. Three of these apologies for the musical (all scripted by Betty Comden and Adolph Green), *The Barkleys of Broadway* (Charles Walters, 1949), *Singin' in the Rain* (Stanley Donen and Gene Kelly, 1952), and *The Band Wagon* (Vincente Minnelli, 1953) involve contrasts between performances that fail to please audiences and performances that are immediately audience-pleasing.[2] Performances in these films are not restricted to onstage numbers. Multiple levels of performance and consequent multiple levels of audience combine to create a myth about musical entertainment permeating ordinary life. Through the work of these filmic texts all successful performances, both in art and in life, are condensed into the MGM musical.

To say that entertainment is "mythified" is to institute a triple play upon conventional meanings of the word "myth." Most simply, it means that entertainment is shown as having greater value than it actually does. In this sense musicals are ideological products; they are full of deceptions. As students of mythology have demonstrated, however, these deceptions are willingly suffered by the audience. In *American Vaudeville as Ritual*, Albert F. McLean attempts to explain this contradiction in his definition of myth as "a constellation of images and symbols, whether objectively real or imaginary, which brings focus and a degree of order to the psychic (largely unconscious) processes of a group or society and in so doing endows a magical potency upon the circumstances of persons involved."[3] McLean's notion of myth as "aura" occupies a pole opposite that of myth as "untruth" in constituting the myth of entertainment.

According to Claude Lévi-Strauss, the seemingly random surface structure of a myth masks contradictions that are real and therefore unresolvable.[4] Art musicals are structurally similar to myths, seeking to mediate contradictions in the nature of popular entertainment. The myth of entertainment is constituted by an oscillation between demystification and remythicization.[5] Musicals, like myths, exhibit a stratified structure. The ostensible or surface function of these musicals is to give pleasure to the audience by revealing what goes on behind the scenes in the theater or Hollywood—that is, to demystify the production of entertainment. But the films remythicize at another level that which they set out to expose. Only unsuccessful performances are demystified. The musical desires an ultimate valorization of entertainment; to destroy the aura, reduce the illusion, would be to destroy the myth of entertainment as well.[6] For the purpose of analysis, the myth of entertainment can be subdivided into three categories: the myth of spontaneity, the myth of integration, and the myth of the audience. In the films, however, the myth makes its impact through combination and repetition. Thus, a single musical number can be highly overdetermined and may be discussed under all three categories.

THE MYTH OF SPONTANEITY

Perhaps the primary positive quality associated with musical performance is its spontaneous emergence out of a joyous and responsive attitude toward life. The musical buffs' parlor game that attempts to distinguish Fred Astaire's screen persona from Gene Kelly's ignores the overriding similarities in both dancers' spontaneous stances.[7] *The Barkleys of Broadway,*

Singin' in the Rain, and *The Band Wagon* contrast the spontaneity of Astaire or Kelly with the prepackaged or calculated behavior of other performers.

In *Singin' in the Rain,* spontaneous talent distinguishes Don, Cosmo, and Kathy from Lina Lamont. Lina's laborious attempts to master basic English are followed by Don Lockwood's elocution lesson. Don and Cosmo seize upon the tongue-twister to turn the lesson into a spontaneous, anarchic dance routine, "Moses Supposes." Spontaneous self-expression through song and dance characterizes the three positive performers: Cosmo in "Make 'Em Laugh," Don in "Singin' in the Rain," and all three in "Good Mornin'," which evolves out of their collective solution to the problems of "The Dueling Cavalier."

In addition, the impression of spontaneity in these numbers stems from a type of *bricolage;* the performers make use of props at hand—curtains, movie paraphernalia, umbrellas, furniture—to create the imaginary world of the musical performance. This *bricolage,* a hallmark of the post–Gene Kelly MGM musical, creates yet another contradiction: an effect of spontaneous realism is achieved through simulation.

The Barkleys of Broadway opposes strained, artificial "serious" performances to spontaneous and natural musical comedy performances. Dinah Barkley's sparkling costume and demeanor in the title sequence with Astaire ("Swing Trot") contrasts with her subdued garb and sullen demeanor as a dramatic actress. Early in the film we see Dinah truncating her understudy's carefully calculated audition, doing a brief warm-up, and going into a perfectly executed rehearsal of a tap routine with her husband. The rehearsals of "Young Sarah" (a play about Sarah Bernhardt's *struggle* to become an actress) are quite the opposite. Josh (Astaire), the musical comedy director-performer, is always spontaneous and natural. In the parallel sequence to Dinah's labors over "Young Sarah," we see Josh doing a completed number from his new show. "Shoes with Wings On" presents musical comedy dancing as an involuntary response, like breathing. Dancing is so spontaneous for Josh that animated shoes pull him into performance. The Astaire character never changes; he is presented as an utterly seamless monument of naturalness and spontaneity. Others must adapt to his style. Dinah can succeed as a performer only in a musical setting with Josh. Even their offstage performances stem from a spontaneous responsiveness to ordinary life, as when their dance to "You'd Be Hard to Replace" evolves out of the natural movements of putting on robes.

Similar oppositions between spontaneous and canned performers structure *Singin' in the Rain* and *The Band Wagon.* Astaire's trademark, "reflex" dancing, has its counterpart in the "Gotta Dance" motif that informs Kelly's "Broadway Ballet," part of the ultimately successful film-

83. *The Band Wagon:* Dancing and the myth of spontaneity.

within-the-film. *The Band Wagon* cuts from Tony Hunter's (Astaire's) spontaneous eruption into song and dance at the penny arcade to Jeffrey Cordova in *Oedipus Rex*. The moaning sounds in the background of this production are later associated with the reactions of an audience to Cordova's laborious musical version of *Faust*. We are shown Cordova from the point of view of Tony and the Martons in the wings (almost always a demystifying camera position), as he segues from his curtain calls as Oedipus into his offstage pomposity. Although Cordova's *Oedipus* is said to be successful with audiences in the film, the extent to which it is demystified for us undercuts its status as a successful show. Cordova is characterized throughout the first half of the film by the mechanical nature of his actions and utterances. He continually gives rehearsed speeches such as the one about Bill Shakespeare's immortal lines and Bill Robinson's immortal feet. On the first day of rehearsals, Cordova tells the cast exactly what will happen to them before the show opens. Not until he dances with Astaire (and in Astaire's style) in the top hat, white tie, and tails soft-shoe number in the second "Band Wagon" does Cordova achieve true spontaneity as a performer.

Almost every spontaneous performance in *The Band Wagon* has a matched segment that parodies the lack of spontaneity of the high art world. Tony drops Gaby while attempting a lift during the rehearsal of a ballet number for the first show; later in "The Girl Hunt," a jazz ballet, he lifts her effortlessly. Tony and Gaby's relaxed offstage rehearsal of a dance to "You and the Night and the Music" literally explodes onstage at the dress rehearsal. A prepackaged orchestra rendition of "Something to Remember You By" at the official New Haven cast party dissolves into a vocal version of the same song spontaneously performed by the "kids" at the chorus party. Spontaneity thus emerges as the hallmark of a successful performance.

The myth of spontaneity operates through what we are shown of the work of production of the respective shows as well as how we are shown it. In *Singin' in the Rain,* we see the technical difficulties involved with filming and projecting "The Dueling Cavalier," including Lina's battle with the microphone and the failure of the film when its technological base is revealed to the preview audience. "The Dancing Cavalier," in contrast, springs to life effortlessly. The film shows an awareness of this opposition between the foregrounding of technology in "The Dueling Cavalier" and the invisibility of technology in "The Dancing Cavalier." "The Broadway Ballet" is presented in the context of an idea for a production number, and one of the biggest jokes in the film concerns the producer's inability to visualize what we have just been shown, elaborate and complete. Yet at many other points in *Singin' in the Rain* this awareness is masked, often in quite complex ways.[8] In "You Were Meant for Me" the exposure of the wind machine figures prominently in the demystification of romantic musical numbers. Yet in a dialogue scene outside the soundstage just prior to this number, Kathy's scarf had blown to the breeze of an invisible wind machine. Even after we are shown the tools of illusion at the beginning of the number, the camera arcs around and comes in for a tighter shot of the performing couple, thereby remasking the exposed technology and making the duet just another example of the type of number whose illusions it exposes. Demystification is countered by the reassertion of the spontaneous evolution of musical films. Perhaps the ultimate in spontaneous evolution of a musical number occurs in *The Barkleys of Broadway.* At the end of the film, the couple decides to do another musical. Josh describes a dance routine which, unlike "Young Sarah," will have *tempo,* and the couple goes into a dance, framed to the right of a curtain in their living room. As they spin, there is a dissolve to the same step as part of an elaborate production number in the new show.

In *The Band Wagon* the labor of producing the first show eclipses the performances. Never do we see a completed number from the first show. Technical or personal problems prevent the completion of every number shown in rehearsal, as when Tony walks out or when Cordova is levitated by the revolving stage. It is not because high art (ballet) and popular art (musical comedy) are inherently mutually exclusive that Cordova's show fails. After all, it is Tony's impressionist paintings that pay for the successful show. Rather, the film suggests that Cordova fails because he has been unable to render invisible the technology of production in order to achieve the effect of effortlessness by which all entertainment succeeds in winning its audience.

Of course spontaneous performances that mask their technology have been calculated, too—not for audiences within the films but for audiences *of* the film. The musical, technically the most complex type of film produced in Hollywood, paradoxically has always been the genre that attempts to give the greatest illusion of spontaneity and effortlessness. It is as if engineering were to affirm *bricolage* as the ultimate approach to scientific thought. The self-reflective musical is aware of this in attempting to promulgate the myth of spontaneity. The heavily value-laden oppositions set up in the self-reflective films promote the mode of expression of the film musical itself as spontaneous and natural rather than calculated and technological. Musical entertainment thus takes on a natural relatedness to life processes and to the lives of its audiences. Musical entertainment claims for its own all natural and joyous performances in art and in life. The myth of spontaneity operates (to borrow Lévi-Strauss's terminology) to make musical performance, which is actually part of culture, appear to be part of nature.

THE MYTH OF INTEGRATION

Earlier musicals sometimes demonstrated ambiguous attitudes toward the world of musical theater, perceiving conflicts between success on the stage and success in the performers' personal lives. In *Ziegfeld Girl* (Robert C. Leonard, 1941), Lana Turner is destroyed when she forsakes the simple life in Brooklyn for the glamour of the Follies. In *Cain and Mabel* (Lloyd Bacon, 1936), Marion Davies has to be physically dragged onto the stage after deciding to retire to a garage in Jersey with prizefighter beau Clark Gable. But the self-reflective musical asserts the integrative effect of musical performance. Successful performances are intimately bound up with success in love, with the integration of the individual into a community or a group, and even with the merger of high art with popular art.

In *Singin' in the Rain,* the success of the musical film brings about the final union of Don and Kathy. This consummation takes place on the stage at the premiere in front of a live audience and in the form of a duet. The music is carried over to a shot of the lovers embracing in front of a billboard of Don and Kathy's images. But the successful show on the billboard is no longer "The Dancing Cavalier"; it is *Singin' in the Rain,* that is, the film itself. This hall-of-mirrors effect emphasizes the unity-giving function of the musical both for the couples and audiences *in* the film and for the audience *of* the film. In *The Barkleys of Broadway,* Josh and Dinah are reunited when she realizes she wants "nothing but fun set to music," that is, the type of performance associated with the MGM musical. Gaby, in *The Band Wagon,* learns the value of popular entertainment as she learns to love Tony. "Dancing in the Dark" imitates the form of a sexual act as it merges two kinds of dancing previously set in conflict. The number combines the ballet movements associated with Gaby and her choreographer beau Paul Byrd with the ballroom dancing associated with Astaire. At the end of the film the long run of their successful show is used by Gaby as a metaphor for her relationship with Tony.

The right kind of musical performance also integrates the individual into a unified group just as the wrong kind alienates. *The Band Wagon* traces Tony's repeated movements from isolation to the joy of being part of a group. At the beginning of the film, Tony sings "By Myself" isolated by the tracking camera; as he enters the crowded terminal, the camera stops moving to frame him against the crowd, a mass that becomes an audience for Tony's antics with the Martons. The arcade sequence repeats this opening movement. Once again Tony overcomes his sense of isolation by reestablishing contact with an audience through spontaneous musical performance. The "?" machine at the arcade symbolizes the problem/solution format of the narrative. When Tony answers the question of how to make a comeback by dancing with a shoeshine man, the machine bursts open and his audience rushes to congratulate him. Another such movement occurs when, after the failure of the first show, Tony finds himself the only guest at the official cast party. "I Love Louisa" marks his renewal of contact with yet another audience—this time the common folk of the theater itself. At the end of the film, Tony moves from a reprise of "By Myself" into the final integration—a symbolic marriage to Gaby and to the rank and file of the theater. The myth of integration makes itself felt through the repetitive structure of the film.

Paralleling Tony's movement from isolation to integration and also paralleling the integration of the couple is Gaby's integration into the populist world of musical theater from the elitist world of high art. We first see Gaby in a ballet performance in which she functions as prima ballerina backed by the corps. At Cordova's, the two worlds are spatially isolated as the representatives of high art (Gabrielle and Paul) and those of popular art (Tony and the Martons) occupy separate rooms. The possibility of movement between the two worlds is stressed by the precisely parallel actions taking place in each room as well as by Cordova's role as mediator between the two rooms (worlds). Cordova prevents a terminal clash between Tony and Gaby by rushing into the neutral space of the front hall and drawing the representatives of both worlds back into his own central space.

Gabrielle begins her integration into the world of popular art through a renewal of contact with the common folk in Central Park, a process which culminates in "I Love Louisa" with Gaby serving as part of the chorus. Paul Byrd draws Gaby away from the group into an isolated space symbolic of the old world of ballet; the camera frames the couple apart from the mass. The colors of their isolated space—subdued shades of brown and white—contrast with the vibrant colors of the chorus's costumes, which have just filled the frame. In leaving this isolated space to return to the group, Gaby has taken the side of the collective effort that will produce the successful musical. "New Sun in the Sky," the first number in the new show, again finds Gaby backed up by a chorus, but this time the mood is celebratory—the bright golds and reds as well as the lyrics of the song emphasize Gaby's rebirth. Even the musical arrangement of the song, upbeat and jazzy, contrasts with the more sedate balletic arrangement we heard in that rehearsal for the Faustian *Band Wagon* in which Tony dropped Gaby. At the end of the film, Gaby expresses her feelings for Tony by speaking for the group, the chorus framed in back of her as she speaks.

Everyone knows that the musical film was a mass art produced by a tiny elite for a vast and amorphous consuming public; the self-reflective musical attempts to overcome this division through the myth of integration. It offers a vision of musical performance originating in the folk, generating love and a cooperative spirit that includes everyone in its grasp and that can conquer all obstacles. By promoting audience identification with the collectively produced shows, the myth of integration seeks to give the audience a sense of participation in the creation of the film itself. The musical film becomes a mass art that aspires to the condition of a folk art—produced and consumed by the same integrated community.

THE MYTH OF THE AUDIENCE

It follows that successful performances will be those in which the performer is sensitive to the needs of the audience and which give the audience a sense of participation in the performance. Josh Barkley berates Dinah for her participation in the performance in the subway scene because "the audience wants to cry there and you won't let them." Cordova is more concerned with the revolving stage than with delivering audience-pleasing performances; his canned speeches of solidarity with the cast are undercut by his delivering them with his back to the group, oblivious to their response. Tony Hunter, on the other hand, is willing to leave the self-enclosed world of the theater to regain contact with the folk who make up his audience. "Dancing in the Dark" is precipitated by observing ordinary people dancing in Central Park.

The insensitive performer also attempts to manipulate the audience. Cordova wants to control the timing of the curtain, the actress's exit pace, and the placing of an amber spot in *Oedipus*. Lina Lamont masks the fact that she is unable to speak for herself either onstage or onscreen.

Yet while setting up an association between success and lack of audience manipulation, the musicals themselves exert continuous control over the responses of their audiences. The film musical profits rhetorically by displacing to the theater the myth of a privileged relationship between musical entertainment and its audience. Popular theater can achieve a fluidity and immediacy in this respect that the film medium lacks. The out-of-town tryout, the interpolation of new material after each performance, the instantaneous modulation of performer-to-audience response—none of these common theatrical practices is possible for film. Hollywood had only the limited adaptations made possible by the preview system and the genre system itself, which accommodated audience response by making (or not making) other films of the same type. The backstage musical, however, manages to incorporate the immediate performer-audience relationship into films, thus gaining all the advantages of both media. Musical numbers can be shot from the point of view of a front-row theatrical spectator and then move into filmic space—combining the immediate contact of the theater with the mobility of perspective of the camera. Numbers that begin within theatrical space merge, often quite imperceptibly, into filmic space. Extended musical sequences such as "Shoes with Wings On" and "The Girl-Hunt Ballet" start within a proscenium frame and then become fully edited filmic sequences, in a tradition stemming from the early Berkeley musicals.

The Band Wagon uses this double perspective to manipulate the film audience's point of view. In "That's Entertainment," Cordova and the Martons try to convince Tony that all successful art is entertainment. The number takes place on the stage of an empty theater with the first refrain of the song shot from camera positions that approximate the point of view of a spectator *on* the stage (angles available only to the cinema). Midway through the number, at the point where Tony is convinced, the action shifts to the performing area of the stage and the point of view shifts to that of a spectator in the theater. The film audience sees, from the point of view of a theater audience, the number performed in the empty theater becoming a direct address to the film's audience. The effort to convince Tony has become an effort to convince *us*. In the reprise of "That's Entertainment" at the film's finale, the point of view shifts from over-the-

84. *Dames:* Musical numbers can be shot from filmic space.

shoulder shots to frame the performers directly in front of the camera as they ask us to celebrate once again the merging of all art into entertainment, this time in the form of the film *The Band Wagon* itself (an effect quite like that of the billboard at the end of *Singin' in the Rain*). "Make 'Em Laugh" is much more subtle in shifting point of view. Starting from a subjective shot over Don's shoulder, the number begins as an affirmation of the value of entertainment as Cosmo attempts to cheer up his friend; however, the point of view quickly shifts so that the message is addressed to the film's audience. We quickly lose track of Don's point of view, and the number never returns to it.

The use of theatrical audiences *in* the films provides a point of identification for audiences *of* the film. Even *Singin' in the Rain* emphasizes the responses of live audiences at previews and premieres. Although inserted shots of applauding audiences can be used as a trick similar to television's use of canned laughter, self-reflective musicals tend to use audiences within the film more subtly. In *The Barkleys of Broadway,* Astaire and Rogers dance "Swing Trot," a routine designed to arouse nostalgia for the famous team, under the film's titles. At the end of the number there is a cut to a side angle, and we see the couple taking a bow before a live audience. The audience in the film is there to express the adulation the number itself sought to arouse from the film's audience.

MGM musicals make use of natural, spontaneous audiences that form around offstage performances.[9] "Shine on Your Shoes" in *The Band Wagon* demonstrates Astaire's ability to adapt his dancing to any occasion and any audience as well. In "I Love Louisa" the chorus serves first as an audience for Tony and the Martons' clowning, and then participates in the dance, providing a vicarious sense of participation for the film audience. Audiences in the films suggest a contagious spirit inherent in musical performance, related to the suggestion that the MGM musical is folk art; the audience must be shown as participating in the production of entertainment.

Intertextuality and star iconography can be a means of manipulating audience response. Many of the later MGM musicals play upon the audience's memories of earlier musicals. *The Barkleys of Broadway* plays on the Astaire-Rogers legend from its first shot of the couple's feet, which echoes the title sequence of *Top Hat* (Sandrich, 1935). The couple's reunion performance to "You Can't Take That Away from Me" harks back to *Shall We Dance,* with the dance itself reminiscent of one of their old routines. Such attempts to evoke nostalgia play on the star system's desire to erase the boundaries between star persona and character, between onscreen and offscreen personalities. *The Barkleys of Broadway* thus celebrates the return of Ginger Rogers to musical comedy after a series of straight dramatic films, suggesting that the only way she can succeed with an audience is by dancing with Astaire in musicals.[10]

Other self-reflective musicals make use of audience response to songs from previous stage musicals or films. Most of the songs in *Singin' in the Rain* were written for the earliest MGM film musicals. *The Band Wagon* takes its music from stage reviews of the same period, the late twenties to early thirties. In the interim many of these songs had become standards, and the films were able to play upon the audience's familiarity with the lyric. "Dancing in the Dark," for example, is used only in instrumental arrangement, thus inviting the audience to participate by supplying the lyric. Two related practices of the Freed unit—biopics fashioned around a composer's hit songs and the purchase of a song catalog around which to construct an original musical—depended upon audience familiarity (through both filmic and nonfilmic intertexts) for their effectiveness.

CONCLUSION

Self-reflective musicals mediate a contradiction between live performance in the theater and the frozen form of cinema by implying that the MGM musical *is* theater, possessing the same immediate and active relationship to its audience. Both the myth of integration and the myth of the audience suggest that the MGM musical is really a folk art, that the audience participates in the creation of musical entertainment. The myth of integration suggests that the achievement of personal fulfillment goes hand in hand with the enjoyment of entertainment. And the myth of spontaneity suggests that the MGM musical is not artificial but rather completely natural. Performance is no longer defined as something professionals do on stage; instead, it permeates the lives of professional and nonprofessional singers and dancers. Entertainment, the myth implies, can break down the barriers between art and life.

The myth of entertainment, in its entirety, cannot be celebrated in a single text or even across three texts. Different aspects of the myth achieve prominence in different films, but the myth is carried by the genre as a whole. The notion of breaking down barriers between art and life, for example, is more prominent in Vincente Minnelli's *The Pirate* than in any of the films discussed here. It might be said that the elements of the myth of entertainment constitute a paradigm that generates the syntax of individual texts.

Ultimately, one might wonder why these films go to such lengths to justify the notion that all life should aspire to the conditions of a musical performance. That is, why expend so much effort to celebrate mythic elements the audience is likely to accept anyway? Answering this question involves an awareness both of the function of ritual and of the ritual function of the musical. All ritual involves the celebration of shared values and beliefs; the ritual function of the musical is to reaffirm and articulate the place that entertainment occupies in its audience's psychic lives. Self-reflective musicals are then able to celebrate myths created by the genre as a whole.

Yet the extremes of affirmation in *The Band Wagon* need further justification in terms of its function for MGM as well as for the popular audience. At a time when the studio could no longer be certain of the allegiance of its traditional mass audience, *The Band Wagon,* in ritual fashion, served to reaffirm the traditional relationship. For the musical was always the quintessential Hollywood product: all Hollywood films manipulated audience response, but the musical could incorporate that response into the film itself; all Hollywood films sought to be entertaining, but the musical could incorporate a myth of entertainment into its aesthetic discourse. As Thomas Elsaesser says, "The world of the musical becomes a kind of ideal image of the [film] medium itself." [11]

Nowhere is Lévi-Strauss's notion of myth more applicable to the musical than in the relationship of the genre to the studio system that produced it. Faced with declining attendance due to competition from television, the studio could suggest, through *Singin' in the Rain*, that making musicals can provide a solution to any crisis of technological change. Faced with charges of infantilism from the citadels of high art, the studio could suggest, through *The Barkleys of Broadway*, that all successful performances are musical performances. Faced with the threat of changing patterns of audience consumption, the studio could suggest, through *The Band Wagon*, that the MGM musical can adapt to any audience. *The Band Wagon* ends where *That's Entertainment* (Jack Haley, Jr., 1974) and *That's Entertainment, Part 2* (Gene Kelly, 1976) commence, in an attempt to recapture the aura of the "Golden Age" of the Freed/MGM musicals. It is not surprising that the "That's Entertainment" number from *The Band Wagon* should have been inserted into the contemporary sequences of the nostalgia compilations. For the ending of *The Band Wagon* already marked the genre's celebration of its own (and Hollywood's) economic death and ritual rebirth.

Self-reflectivity as a critical category has been associated with films, such as those of Godard, which call attention to the codes constituting their own signifying practices. The term has been applied to aesthetically or politically radical films that react against so-called classical narrative cinema by interrogating their own narrativity. Thus we tend to associate reflexivity with the notion of deconstruction within filmmaking practice. The MGM musical, however, uses reflexivity to perpetuate rather than to deconstruct the codes of the genre. Self-reflective musicals are conservative texts in every sense. MGM musicals have continued to function both in the popular consciousness and within international film culture as representatives of the Hollywood product at its best. I hope to have shown that this was the very task these texts sought to accomplish.

Notes

1. See Leo Braudy, *The World in a Frame* (New York: Anchor Press/Doubleday, 1976), pp. 143–147, for a discussion of self-consciousness in *Shall We Dance*.

2. *The Barkleys of Broadway* presents Josh and Dinah Barkley (Fred Astaire and Ginger Rogers) as the Lunts of musical comedy. Dinah leaves musical comedy to do a serious play ("Young Sarah"), and finally learns the lesson that there's no difference between serious acting and musical comedy acting. She returns to do a musical at the end of the film. *Singin' in the Rain* depicts the coming of sound to Hollywood. An early talkie that fails ("The Dueling Cavalier") is remade as a

musical that succeeds ("The Dancing Cavalier"). *The Band Wagon* also involves a second production of a show that flops (a musical version of the Faust story called "The Band Wagon") into a musical revue that succeeds (again called "The Band Wagon").

3. Albert F. McLean, *American Vaudeville as Ritual* (Lexington: University of Kentucky Press, 1965), p. 223.

4. Claude Lévi-Strauss, "The Structural Study of Myth," in *Structural Anthropology* (New York: Basic Books, 1963), p. 220. I am also indebted to Lévi-Strauss for other ideas contained in the same essay: first, that a myth works itself out through repetition in a number of texts; second, that myth works through the mediation of binary oppositions.

5. These terms are taken from Paul Ricoeur, *Freud and Philosophy* (New Haven: Yale University Press, 1970), p. 54. Ricoeur uses them to refer to two schools of hermeneutics that nevertheless constitute "a profound unity." I find them equally applicable to texts that seek to interpret themselves.

6. The inseparability of demystification from its opposite (remythicization) is best illustrated by *A Star Is Born* (George Cukor, 1954), at once the last bearer of the studio's myth of entertainment and the first of the antimusicals. Even the supposedly Brechtian antimusical *Cabaret* (Bob Fosse, 1972) merely inverts the backstage paradigm while maintaining its narrative strategy.

7. See Braudy, *The World in a Frame*, pp. 147–155, for a discussion of the function of spontaneity in the Astaire and Kelly personas.

8. See David Lusted, "Film as Industrial Product—Teaching a Reflexive Movie," *Screen Education* 16 (Autumn 1975): 26–30, for detailed examples of the mystification-demystification dynamic in *Singin' in the Rain*.

9. Other good examples of "natural audiences" in the MGM musical include "By Strauss," "I Got Rhythm," and "'S Wonderful" in *An American in Paris* (Minnelli, 1951); "Nina" in *The Pirate* (Minnelli, 1948); and "I Like Myself," Gene Kelly's dance on roller skates in *It's Always Fair Weather* (Kelly, 1955). The history of this device in the musical film may be traced from Jolson to Chevalier to Astaire to Kelly and back to Astaire, spontaneity of performance providing the link among the major male musical stars.

10. The extreme example of this phenomenon is *A Star is Born*, the signification of which depends upon the audience's knowledge of Judy Garland's offscreen life as the negation of her MGM onscreen image.

11. Thomas Elsaesser, "The American Musical," *Brighton Film Review* 15 (December 1969): 13.

29. The Black Gangster Film

MARK A. REID

In general, little attention has been given to the filmic representation of race in film genre criticism. This essay analyzes how early "race films" depict criminal life in black communities. The term "race film" refers to films with all-black casts that small independent film companies produced for the African American audience. Race films were usually exhibited in movie theaters frequented by African Americans. In this essay I provide a short interpretive history of the filmic construction of black gangsters in early race films. For the purposes of this essay, a black gangster is any individual who acquires income through extortion, burglary, gambling, pimping, and drug dealing; a black gangster film is any film whose narrative features a black gangster in a major or secondary role. I would like to suggest a few reasons for this lack of interest in racial matters in film genre studies and in previous writings on the American gangster film.

First, the subject of race and the construction of the racial subject in popular media and the social and biological sciences continues to be a shunned subject. The way in which we describe blacks resembles the problems we encounter when attempting a monolithic description of Jews, Moslems, Serbians, and Croatians. Any attempt to describe these subject identities provokes volatile disagreements among scholars and lay persons regardless of their race, ethnicity, and political hue. Nevertheless, I offer a tentative description of the representation of "race" and "blacks" in genre film. My description holds that "race" and "blacks" are ever-changing sociocultural constructions. Sometimes national boundaries and local political factors redefine what constitutes the racial and or black subject. Rather than biological and genetically assigned characteristics, "race" and "blackfolk" are sociological categories. Furthermore, the sociohistorical moment determines the contours of the representation of race. Scholars have previously avoided writing about the representation of race in genre film. Before the Rodney King–Reginald Denny era, the socioeconomic status of African Americans did not immediately affect film scholarship.

The videotaped beatings of these two Americans helped to sway media scholars to pay closer attention to the visual construction of the racial subject.

Second, recent articles that discuss the representation of race in black gangster films have narrowed their survey to discuss such trendy "gangsta rap" films as *Boyz N the Hood* (John Singleton, 1991), *New Jack City* (Mario Van Peebles, 1991), and *Juice* (Ernest Dickerson, 1992). Consequently, these scholars inadvertently suggest that there exists no history or tradition for black gangster films.

Third, and most important, the typical black gangster film shares the contemporary narrative conventions and iconography of the mainstream Hollywood gangster movie. For the most part, African American moviegoers desire the same fantasies as their white counterparts. The sole difference between the two audiences bears on the racial and sociocultural elements that construct the gangster hero(ine). Genre conventions and audience expectations demand that black gangsters perform similar feats. One then might ask, why even study the black gangster film if it is only a second-rate imitation of Hollywood fare?

Even though most imaginative portrayals of African American criminal life borrow mainstream narrative conventions and iconography, there are certain black gangster films that evoke a markedly *ethnic*-inflected difference. For instance, a particular noncriminal segment of the black community may condone certain illegal activities while certain middle-class individuals in the same community denounce them. Such a culturally marked difference in the construction of "law and order" results from *sociocultural* divisions within and without the African American community, as in any community. Such an experience, however, does *not* reflect a biological or racial fact.

This essay neither argues for a biologically determined aesthetic construction of blackness nor does it support the belief that racial experience determines the formal elements of a film practice. In outlining a short history of the black gangster film, this essay shows how the representation of race resists certain narrative conventions that support a strict definition of "law and order" and a monolithic definition of "blackness."

SOCIAL, HISTORICAL, AND ARCHIVAL PROCESSES AND FILM HISTORY

When discussing the history of black film and its political nature, analysis should take into account who produces and distributes these films. Interpretations should describe how blacks have surreptitiously controlled the financing and distribution of their films or, what is more important, how blacks avoided the disempowering effects of studio decisions and censorship board rulings. If analysis does not consider both the creative

85. *New Jack City:* The trendy "gangsta rap" film.

and the industrial aspects of black filmmaking, then research will further mask the determining factors that inhibit the production of black independent films.

The group of currently existing race films has been selected by agents of culture and commerce who have financed, distributed, or archived particular films. These agents inadvertently permit the disappearance of certain black-oriented films while they define the boundaries of what critics can discuss in their reviews of these films. Therefore, when critical attention is directed at race films, the critic must recognize the various selective processes that these films have undergone. Early black film history is a story of omissions as well as of inclusions.

BLACK GANGSTERS AND INDEPENDENT FILM

As early as 1926, Oscar Micheaux wrote and directed *Spider's Web* (1927), which documents the numbers racket, an organized form of gambling prevalent in certain urban communities. The following year, Frank Peregini directed the David Starkman screenplay *The Scar of Shame* (1927). This film describes a racially dualistic world in which socioeconomic factors create the "good black" as an assimilated, whitened Negro and the "bad nigger" as a person "true" to his or her primitive nature. *The Scar of Shame*'s depiction of black middle-class mobility supports a Manichaean view of America as a racially dualistic system. Confined to the determinants of this system, according to the narrative logic of *The Scar of Shame*, African Americans achieve socioeconomic success only if they either adopt European standards or accept their essential "bad nigger" nature. According to this dualistic system, the more unfortunate blacks must use their natural "bad nigger" ways to survive in the ghetto streets. The middle-class black in *The Scar of Shame* has somehow suppressed the essentially black gangster self to become assimilated; the black criminal in the film, however, has made good use of his or her "natural" criminal character. Thus, it is better to be true to one's black criminal genes than to assimilate and suppress one's essentially devilish and primitive nature. The film's portrayal of black criminality as biologically determined is thus flawed. In rejecting this biologically deterministic portrait, film historian Thomas Cripps, taking a slightly different view, writes,

> The picture placed the black thrust for "the finer things" against the drag of the coarse, grinding ghetto that cheats the hero of beauty and virtue. . . . The hard world of the streets makes brutes and hustlers of smart blacks with a will to live. They are the unassimilable "bad niggers" who can never leave the darkened doorways of the ghetto demimonde, but whose guile permits them to survive in cool style. Unfortunately, the picture stumbles when it asks the Negro to rise above the life of the streets because it draws a veil over the external forces that made the slum what it is. Thus the hero . . . can end his suffering only by opting for white culture and rejecting black.[1]

The narrative closure of *The Scar of Shame* reflects the cultural period of the Harlem Renaissance and the economic necessity of pleasing the white patrons of black art. During the 1920s the psychological well-being of white middle-class urbanites rested on the ability of black performers to satiate the primitivist fantasies of the paying audience. For instance, Josephine Baker, in the "banana dress" that revealed her backside, provided her white audience with the unholy juju of one of their most primitive obsessions.

Although *Harlem after Midnight* (Micheaux, 1934) developed a fuller sociocultural description of black organized crime, the film sustained the color-caste system and Manichaean moral choices found in *The Scar of Shame*. Micheaux's ability to imitate his successful white contemporaries is also apparent in *Underworld* (1937). Ten years before his 1937 lensing of *Underworld*, Paramount Studios released Joseph von Sternberg's *Underworld* (1927). Sternberg's *Underworld* is the first and perhaps one of the best examples of the classic American gangster film. Like the many other directors of gangster films who followed *Underworld*, Micheaux borrowed narrative devices from Sternberg's silent film masterpiece. Both films portray an innocent young man's ascendance through the ranks of crime, culminating with the young gangster's spiritual and physical possession of the former crime boss's girlfriend. In the classic gangster narrative, the heir of the mob boss deposes the reigning paternal order. The hero takes possession of the objects that had once validated his boss's entrepreneurial skill and sexual prowess. The objects include the former mob boss's territory, his henchmen, his material tokens of wealth, and his girlfriend. The territory of the crime family includes the gang leader's girl; the classical gangster film narrative generates patriarchal rights of succession. Micheaux's *Underworld,* however, gives a black slant to the classical gangster narrative by introducing a fictionalized history of the African Americans' post–World War I northern migration to industrialized urban centers.

Micheaux's *Underworld* borrows several gangster film elements from von Sternberg's film. For instance, Micheaux's film dramatizes the advancement of a young, college-trained black gangster who takes over a gang leader's territory, his henchmen, and his girl. This film, unlike other contemporary ganster films, dramatizes a black middle-class history that speaks to both the classical ganster narrative and the strivings of a postwar black middle-class community because it shows how a southern black college graduate moves to Chicago, falls into a life of crime, and rises through the ranks of the black-controlled crime organization. Additionally, Micheaux's narrative presents Chicago's socioeconomic conditions as a major factor in the moral decay of an educated southern black youth. In von Sternberg's film black gangsters and the black community are totally absent unless they appear as local color and background props.

BLACK GANGSTERS AND THE MAINSTREAM

In 1937 Ralph Cooper and George Randol, two African Americans, and Ben Rinaldo, a white American, organized the Cooper-Randol Production Company in Los Angeles. The same year, *Dark Manhattan* (Ralph Cooper and Harry Fraser, 1937) became the first gangster film with an all-black cast made in Hollywood.[2] The film dramatizes a man's rise in the numbers racket, his love for a nightclub singer, and his death at the hands of a rival mobster. The Cooper-Randol film company was short lived and produced only one film; Ralph Cooper left the company and established Million Dollar Productions with Harry and Leo Popkin, two white Americans. Cooper wrote and sometimes directed while the Popkin brothers financed and distributed the films.[3] Their first such collaboration was *Bargain with Bullets* (Cooper, 1937), which Cooper wrote, directed, and starred in.[4] The following year, Cooper wrote and directed *Gang*

Smashers (1938), which featured Nina Mae McKinney as a Harlem crime boss (almost ten years earlier McKinney had performed the leading role of Chick in *Hallelujah!* [King Vidor, 1929]). And the film *Gang War* (Cooper, 1939) portrayed a mobster's unsuccessful struggle for control over the jukebox machines in Harlem. *Gang War* was Cooper's last film for Million Dollar Productions.

Cooper's departure from Million Dollar Productions coincided with the Popkins' establishment of an exclusive sales distribution contract with Sack Amusement Enterprise of Dallas, Texas. Sack Amusement, from the early 1920s through the 1940s, was the leading distributor of race films because it entered into deals with production companies and theaters that catered to the African American market.[5] In Cooper's last gangster film, *Am I Guilty?* (1940), produced by Supreme Pictures, he played a naive doctor whose clinic is surreptitiously financed and controlled by a mobster. Thus, *Gang War* and *Am I Guilty?* explored the demise of a black protagonist who lost control over his business. Henry Sampson speculates that Cooper quit Million Dollar Productions because he was tired of playing gangster roles.[6] But I suspect that Cooper's last two films dramatize the ineffective power relationship he had with the Popkin brothers. Cooper was a copartner in the firm, an actor in its films, and the writer-director of several of its projects. Obviously, Cooper enjoyed some creative freedoms, but he lacked decisive control over the extent to which the company financed and distributed his creative work. One can easily conclude that because the Popkins controlled the financing, distribution, and exhibition of these films, they probably forced a too-ambitious Cooper to seek employment elsewhere.

Despite the importance of Oscar Micheaux's contribution to the development of black gangster films (he was one of the first to feature a black gangster in a major role), it was director-actor Ralph Cooper who developed the northern, urbane black gangster film, beginning with *Dark Manhattan.* This type of black gangster figured in the cycle of 1970s black action films typified by *Superfly* (Gordon Parks, Jr., 1972) and *The Black Godfather* (John Evans, 1974) and recently revived in *New Jack City.*

BLACK PERFORMERS IN ALL-BLACK-CAST AND MAINSTREAM GANGSTER FILMS

Veteran African American stage and screen performers such as Frank Wilson, Ralph Cooper, Edna Mae Harris, and Nina Mae McKinney appeared in several of the earliest all-black-cast gangster films: *Harlem after Midnight, Underworld, Dark Manhattan, Bargain with Bullets, Gang Smashers, Gang War, Paradise in Harlem* (Joseph Seiden, 1939), and *Murder on Lenox Avenue* (Arthur Dreifuss, 1941).

During the thirties, a few Hollywood crime films featured an interracial group of criminals. For example, Edward Thompson appears as a police lieutenant in *Bargain with Bullets,* a gangster in *Double Deal* (Arthur Dreifuss, 1939), a lawyer in *Am I Guilty?,* and again as a gangster in the Humphrey Bogart vehicle *The Petrified Forest* (Archie Mayo, 1936). Louise Beavers, the mammy figure in many Hollywood films, performs maternal roles in her two Million Dollar Productions race films—*Life Goes On* (William Nolte, 1938) and *Reform School* (Leo C. Popkin, 1939). The Hollywood gangster film *Bullets or Ballots* (William Keighley, 1936) features Edward G. Robinson, Humphrey Bogart, Joan Blondell, and Beavers as Madame Nellie La Fleur, the boss of a Harlem numbers racket. Since both *Bullets or Ballots* and the all-black *Gang Smashers* feature a black woman as boss of the Harlem crime world, one might easily surmise that the female mobster role was a popular novelty in films of the period.

In American crime films from the sixties to the present, black lawmen have been members of governmental policing agencies. For example, Virgil Tibbs (Sidney Poitier) of *In the Heat of the Night* (Norman Jewison, 1967) and Axel Foley (Eddie Murphy) of *Beverly Hills Cop* (Martin Brest, 1984) are police officers, while John Shaft (Richard Roundtree) of *Shaft* (Gordon Parks, Sr., 1971) is a state-licensed private detective. In black-cast gangster films of the post–civil rights period, blacks portray police officers and federal agents. Major motion pictures of the 1930s and 1940s, however, rarely featured blacks as licensed agents of the law. Many of the films of this period depict figures of lawful authority in roles as community leaders and paternal figures. A few of these race films generate established ideas of "law and order." On viewing some of these films, one can trace how different belief systems organize and police the black community. I shall discuss how two black gangster films of the 1940s, *Murder on Lenox Avenue* and *Souls of Sin* (Powell Lindsay, 1948), generate different ideas about "race" and the construction of the gangster figure. The morally upright characters tend to espouse a traditional understanding of "law and order." These agents of the law are neither officially recognized nor licensed by state institutions, as are Virgil Tibbs, Axel Foley, and John Shaft. Thus, analysis must consider how the *imagined* black community authorizes its leaders and, in turn, how leaders, or other narrative forces, rid the community of gangsters.

The community leader as unlicensed policing agent and the black gangster as innate villain reflect the conventional gangster paradigm in *Murder on Lenox Avenue.* The film illustrates how a gangster narrative incorporates a conservative view of "law and order." Pa Wilkins, the film's major protagonist, is a single parent and a respected member of the Harlem business community. Ola Wilkins, Pa's daughter, is a schoolteacher who wants to leave Harlem and help Frank, her boyfriend, educate black children in the South. Both Ola and Pa respect the principles of civic duty, personal honesty, and the value that education has for the advancement of the race. Pa, however, disapproves of Ola's plans to move to the South. He prefers that Ola remain in Harlem, forget Frank, and marry Jim Branston, his adopted son, whose deceased father was Pa's army buddy. Unknown to Pa, Jim has been sleeping with the now-pregnant daughter of Pa's cleaning lady. Branston rejects his paternal responsibility for the pregnancy because Pa has promised him Ola to wed and her trust fund when Pa dies. Rejecting her father's wishes, Ola marries Frank, and the two leave for the south. This exerts a momentary rupture of the Wilkins family.

Additionally, Pa Wilkins must rectify the financial problems that plague the Harlem Better Business League. Marshall, the league's president, has persuaded the members to buy expensive equipment on credit. Later, the members discover that the monthly loan payments are draining their cash reserves. The Harlem Better Business League is Pa's second family—a community, business family. Consequently, Pa must remedy Marshall's recklessness, and this occasions a second family rupture. Pa corrects the problem by unseating Marshall as the league's president.

Marshall, however, is unable to accept this public loss and arranges for one of his henchmen to murder Pa Wilkins. He also enlists Jim Branston, who reluctantly accepts after recognizing that Pa's death will permit the distribution of Ola's trust fund. Marshall's first attempt at murder fails. When Ola and Frank read about the attempt on Pa's life, they leave the South and rush to his aid. Ola's return reunites the Wilkins family, but Pa must still correct the financial problems that threaten the Harlem Better Business League. Finally, when gangsters make a second attempt on Pa's life, narrative forces of "law and order" prevail. Jim Branston tries to save Pa from a bullet fired by Marshall's henchman and receives the fatal shot. The police finally arrest Marshall and his gunman. The reunited Wilkins family and Pa's presidency of the Harlem Better Business League celebrate paternal order, righteousness, and Christian redemption. Jim's altruistic action and death are penance for the abandonment of his pregnant lover and her ensuing suicide. Furthermore, Jim's move to save Pa restores his loyalty to Pa Wilkins, a paternal figure of moral order. Moreover, his death permits a morally upright and civic-minded couple, Ola and Frank, to continue Pa Wilkins's work and inherit his legacy.

The film's narrative reconstitutes Pa Wilkins's private family and public responsibility, which reflects a rather patriarchal understanding of "law and order." Pa Wilkins is "father" to the Harlem Better Business League; he is "Pa" to Ola and her mate; and he is the adoptive father of Branston, the man who gave his life for the betterment of the whole community. The film's seamless moral code and narrative thus construct Pa Wilkins as an *unlicensed* policing agent.

Similar to the construction of evil in the morality play, *Murder on Lenox Avenue* does not attempt to justify or explain Marshall's criminality. His baseness is both naturalized and fixed in his handsome physiognomy, in his neat urban dress, and in his amoral determination to control his social environment. *Murder on Lenox Avenue* borrows the moral logic of the conventional gangster film and presents a simplistic image of criminality as a genetically fixed trait. Consequently, we do not know why Marshall sought a life of crime.

Another film of the 1940s attempted to dramatize why an individual might seek crime to advance his socioeconomic position. Progressive African Americans produced, wrote, and directed *Souls of Sin,* a film that portrays how daunted hopes lead one into a life of crime. Similar to Richard Wright's argument in *Native Son* (1940), *Souls of Sin* portrays how social factors, not the inherent disposition of the individual, produce criminals.

Souls of Sin dramatizes the lives of three men who live in a Harlem rooming house, each of whom has a special dream of success. Roberts, a middle-aged writer and paternal figure, has hopes of gainful employment, but publishers have consistently rejected his stories. Yet he continues typing his tales and cherishes the hope that someday some press will publish his work. He maintains an authorial distance from what he refers to as "the jungle." Dollar Bill is a well-dressed and embittered gambler who maintains a sufficient amount of self-pity. Bill's misguided pride fuels a desire to regain his former status as a neighborhood celebrity. Unable to win fame as a successful gambler, he joins a burglary gang led by Bad Boy George. As a gang member, Bill transports and sells stolen goods. Dollar Bill, like Jim Branston in *Murder on Lenox Avenue,* is a prodigal son. His social experiences in Manhattan have dehumanized him; yet, unlike Jim's disrespect for Pa Wilkins, Dollar Bill shows a sincere kindness toward his two roommates, the elderly Roberts and the youthful Alabama. Alabama, the last of the three roomers, has recently arrived from Alabama. He is a naive but promising youth. He is new to New York and therefore has not run across the professional obstacles that keep Roberts punching away at a typewriter and Bill dodging the police. Unlike Dollar Bill, a commonplace life playing music satisfies Alabama. His patience rewards him with employment playing his guitar and singing the blues, so Alabama is quick to achieve fame. The relationship of these three men resembles a motherless family in which Roberts, like Pa Wilkins, is the paternal figure and spiritual advisor.

Both *Murder on Lenox Avenue* and *Souls of Sin* reflect familial bonding in which mothers are absent. Both films portray Harlem nightclub life

86. Harlem nightclub life in *Souls of Sin*.

and feature black vaudeville acts. Yet these similarities are insignificant since *Souls of Sin* focuses on the social environment that breeds criminality in the black community. The film begins with panoramic shots of the New York skyline and a voice-over narration that links them to a bird's-eye view of busy Harlem streets. Then the narration and the camera follow a solitary individual as he walks through the windy and cold Manhattan streets. An eye-level long shot records a man briskly walking toward the camera and into the centrality of the film's visual and aural frames of reference.

The establishing shots inform us of the specific setting, New York's Harlem neighborhood. An eye-level long shot records a black man: as he grasps his thin outer clothing, as he coolly walks toward the camera, and as he disappears into a tenement building. It is easy to assume that this man wants to avoid a lurking gust of wind, to escape the socioeconomic forces that beat back his ever-so-cool movements. In a voice mixed with poetic metaphors and social determinism, the narrator informs us: "This is New York, as enchanting and imaginative as a dream. As romantic as moonlight on the ocean. As beautiful as fine sculpture. As ugly as this poverty-ridden slum. As warm and tender as a mother's love. . . . This is magnetic Manhattan. This is the story of souls lost in sin. . . . Caught in the panorama of this chaotic magnetic is one William Burton, alias Dollar Bill."

These introductory remarks generate compassion for Dollar Bill and disdain for the socioeconomic forces that lead him into a life of crime. The voice-over narrator argues for a special understanding of Harlem as "this poverty-ridden street" that caught William Burton in its chaotic web. Thus both the narrator and the film's initial documentary style construct Harlem as a social case study. The characters represent a vision of Harlem life that is consistent with the social realism of the opening establishing shots.

At the film's close, a publisher commissions Roberts to write the story of Dollar Bill's life of crime. Roberts, however, does not see the importance of glamorizing Bill's criminality. He rejects the offer but agrees to write a story about the socioeconomic forces that produce criminals like Bill. Roberts thus shares the social outlook of the voice-over narrator, the perspective that opens and closes the film.

In 1945 William Alexander, the producer of *Souls of Sin*, founded the Associated Producers of Negro Pictures, a company that produced several black-oriented documentaries and feature-length fiction films. Alexander's postwar films include *The Call of Duty* (1946) and *The Highest Tradition* (1946), documentaries about black participation in the navy and army, respectively; *Flicker Up* (1946), a musical short that features Billy Eckstine and May Lou Harris; *Love in Syncopation* (1947), a feature film, Alexander's first, that dramatizes the story of a black band and black participation in World War II; *The Fight Never Ends* (1947), a feature depicting Joe Louis as himself fighting juvenile delinquency; *That Man of Mine* (1947), starring Powell Lindsay and Ruby Dee; and a film that Alexander co-produced, *The Klansman* (Terence Young, 1974), starring Richard Burton, Lee Marvin, Lola Falana, and O. J. Simpson. Alexander's productions of the late 1940s and his collaboration with Powell Lindsay mark the end of black-controlled race-film production companies. William Alexander shared the entrepreneurial interests of Oscar Micheaux but also the social interests of Powell Lindsay, the muse of black social realism on film.

Powell Lindsay, the writer and director of *Souls of Sin*, belonged to the short-lived Negro Playwrights Company. In 1940 he directed the company's first and last production, Theodore Ward's *The Big White Fog*. Lindsay's work reflects a cultural period in which black social realism prevailed, as evidenced in the dramatic work of Theodore Ward, the fiction of Richard Wright, and the songs and speeches of Paul Robeson. A black social realist ideology was the stated purpose of the Negro Playwrights Company. One has only to read the company's brochure, *A Professional Theatre with an Idea*, to understand that Powell Lindsay and his fellow members shared the viewpoint of the narrator of *Souls of Sin* and Roberts, a fictional character but one who spoke with the authorial voice of Powell Lindsay. The brochure reads: "These new writers recognize that they live in a real society. . . . They will be writers worthy of the name, only if they remain independent of the forces which have reduced brains to a commodity, and driven weaklings and panderers to the practice of falsifying truth in order to make it conform to accepted beliefs, and the tastes of those who tend to regard the Negro people as children, or slaves placed in the world for their own exploitation or amusement."[7] *Souls of Sin* is a fitting close to the era of the black gangster film before the sixties. The film and the people who collaborated to produce it prove that black gangster films can be socially conscious and entertaining while also instructing an audience.

LITERARY SOURCES OF BLACK GANGSTER TYPES OF THE SIXTIES

Black gangster films or films depicting black criminal elements also employ familiar criminal stock types as found in African American literature. During the civil rights era, the novels of Holloway House writers Robert Beck (Iceberg Slim) and Donald Goines (Al C. Clark) created the most popular versions of black-oriented crime literature. The titles of their works create a typology of popular black criminals who appear in certain post-1960 black gangster films. Their Holloway House crime novels include such titles as Beck's *Pimp: The Story of My Life* (1967) and *Trick Baby* (1967; film version directed by Larry Yust for Universal, 1973); and Goines's *Dopefiend, The Story of a Black Junkie* (1971), *Whoreson: The Story of a Ghetto Pimp* (1972), and *Street Players* (1973).

A second group of black crime novels attracted the attention of literary scholars. These "canonical" works include Louise Meriwether's *Daddy Was a Numbers Runner* (1971), Robert Deane Pharr's *Book of Numbers* (1969; film version directed by Raymond St. Jacques for Avco-Embassy, 1973), and Chester Himes's *Cotton Comes to Harlem* (1965; film version directed by Ossie Davis for UA, 1970). Thieves, numbers runners, confidence men, drug dealers, and pimps form the gangster types who populate the post-1960s black gangster films. Individual gangsters employ professionals whose activities retain the veneer of respectability, though they may serve illegal purposes. For example, accountants, lawyers, politicians, and police officers are highly respected members of society, yet they might have business connections with organized crime.

ORGANIZED CRIME AND ITS (DIS)CONTENTS

On the other side of the tracks are the criminal elements: hoodlums, drug dealers, pimps, and members of organized crime families. Audiences, regardless of their ethnic or racial makeup, recognize the requirements of a gangster film. They are also able to agree that certain actions are criminal, although they may differ on the moral issues surrounding these acts. This divergence of opinion might reflect any given audience's identification with the gangster. Because the film industry must adhere to censorship laws and depends on approval from the broadest audience of filmgoers, movie directors imitate successful gangster formulas and avoid controversial acts that would anger local censors and mainstream audiences.

The second aspect of this genre is its thematic elements. The treatments of certain social problems sometimes reflect the differences between the gangster films made by large studios like Paramount and Warner Brothers and the black gangster films made by independent producers. This difference resembles the difference between organized crime and the random, anarchic criminal elements that exist outside a *legitimized* system of criminal production like the recent savings and loan scandal or Irangate.

Black gangster films of the late sixties present black detectives and community leaders who are uneasy with their role as agents for governmental institutions of "law and order." Black gangster films do not reflect the moral vision of all members of the black community. An audience who constantly views these films must share a similar type of visual and psychic pleasure. This audience might identify with the gangster's adventurous life, material possessions, and sexual prowess. The audience momentarily identifies with the gangster's acts of violence as he unseats his rivals and evades the law. Audiences relish his unwavering ability to garner the love of women without reciprocating. Gangster films celebrate individual fortitude and imperialistic greed. Only the gangster's capture awakens the viewer from this amoral daydream and reestablishes the monotony of the moral majority within the film's fictional framing. Until the 1960s, censors demanded that criminals be punished before the film's close. The rise of the civil rights movement, the increased use of hallucinogenic drugs, the preponderance of free love, and the condemnation of middle-class suburban values provided an opportunity for the revival of the black gangster types of the 1930s and 1940s. The black gangsters of the 1970s, however, became saturated with black consciousness, as was apparent in the street heroes Sweetback and Super Fly. The American film industry welcomed black gangster films just as the American music industry would later welcome black gangster rappers because both forms of entertainment seemed to channel raw black anger and frustration into a marketable enterprise that attracted paying customers regardless of race. The gangster protagonists of the post-1960 black film provided their public with profane and sacred fantasies.

Censorship laws and social taboos determined how gangster heroes celebrated criminality and how they died as a result in this game. Most important, it was the historical events of the new black consciousness that

87. *Shaft's Big Score* (Gordon Parks, 1972): The gangster film celebrates individual fortitude.

created certain black characters and made certain themes more appealing to the audiences of gangster films.

The film *The Godfather* (Francis Ford Coppola, 1972) exemplifies a system of "law and order" generated by ethnic and class factors, pitting working and lower class Italian-Americans against the Anglo-American managed corporations and non-Italian law officers. Similarly, *The Black Godfather*, a black-oriented remake, pits working and lower class African-Americans against established Italian-American mafiosi and Anglo-American business and law officers. Both of these films dramatize codes of criminal behavior as honorable among the working and poor. The films, however, differ in their ethnic and racial allegiances. Considering the codes of honor depicted in the two films, "law and order" are not static ideas shared between the classes. The established codes reflect a particular audience's perception of "law and order" during a particular time. The conventions of classical gangster films demand that "good guys" be authenticated by city, state, and federal agencies. Taken together, these agents of state authority are a more effective consensus and override any particular gangland family.

Sociologically speaking, gangsters are constructed within an imagined but very urban experience that occasions both moral and immoral actions. Studios, screenwriters, directors, film technicians, the sociocultural environment, and the psychological needs of the target audience produce gangster films. Because the black audience has different psychological demands and expressive traditions, gangster films made for blacks are markedly different from white-cast, studio-produced gangster films. Images of organized and well-dressed black criminals with impeccable speech, black police officers and private detectives, black middle-class professionals, and the spiritual striving of poor but proud blacks were rarely present in mainstream Hollywood films of the 1960s and 1970s.

Black gangster films imaginatively present the cultural beliefs and social experiences of its black audience during a particular time and place. From the 1960s through the 1970s, black gangster films borrowed some of their elements from mainstream gangster fare, the films commonly suggesting a conventional understanding of "law and order." Black gangster films, nonetheless, presented African American concerns, employed African American vaudeville humor, and featured black music. These remain the Afrocentric elements that continue to distinguish black-cast gangster films from their white-cast counterparts, although major studios produce both types.

THE NINETIES AND GANGSTA RAP FILMS

In John Singleton's *Boyz N the Hood* there are options beyond the over-determined social factors of racism and poverty. Yet some newer films still portray black urban gangster culture as a "bad nigger" phenomenon. Ironically, such films as Mario Van Peebles's *New Jack City* and Ernest Dickerson's *Juice* again present the "bad nigger" type as a gangster who preys on other members of the black community. If there existed a truly black essential self, would the black gangster's heroic code produce a "bad nigger" driven by unrestrained capitalistic desires? The analysis of black gangster films must transcend the narrative limitations of Manichaean constructions of "good" and "bad" blacks and describe the social construction and ideological function of particular types of black gangsters.

Earlier I stated that *The Scar of Shame* monolithically depicts the social difference between the black middle class and the black lower class in the form of a style of race. Unfortunately, there are many films that simulate essentialist racial notions about black styles and white styles. These films inadvertently create the "bad nigger" as the only appropriate outlet for a community that has limited socioeconomic resources and opportunities. Thus, criminality is defined in large part as a resistance to the alleged "assimilated" style of the black middle class. Nonetheless, black folk culture provides examples of transgressive and liberating acts by folk heroes such as Brer Rabbit and Shine, who show that compromise does not always lead to assimilation.

As *Souls of Sin* evoked a social realist style, two recent black gangster films have attempted to portray a new social realist style for young inner-city black men caught in the claws of poverty and despair. The two films, *Juice* and *Boyz N the Hood,* portray a complex array of black gangster elements that include the motifs of familial concern and community responsibility. The films work against the too-easy assumption that black middle-class style equals the suppression of the essential "bad nigger" and vice versa. Both films present violence, drug addiction, and unwed mothers, but both films resist portraying gangster life and racial assimilation as the two available forms of escape for inner-city dwellers. The gangsta rapper is the post-Negritude muse who entertains the grandchildren of Norman Mailer's White Negroes now facing early retirement. There exist legitimate ideological concerns in the recent depiction of black gangster characterizations as performed by rapper Tupac Shakur in his cinematic debut in *Juice.* This is equally true for his hyperreal-life experiences; Tupac has allegedly raped a woman in his Manhattan hotel room and has been in a gun battle with two Atlanta police officers. Many critics and the middle-aged audience see only the primitive rage of Shakur, whose father was a member of the Black Panthers during the 1960s. His portrayals of Bishop in *Juice* and Lucky in Singleton's *Poetic Justice* (1993) mirror the contained and inarticulate predicament of the protagonist in Eugene O'Neill's *The Hairy Ape.* The critics tend to ignore the source of his frustration and anger. Tupac Shakur and those who identify with him are unable to seize the televised images that reek of economic prosperity. These images claw at inner-city youths who lack educational opportunities that would provide them with jobs, money, and the veneer of middle-class respectability. When music-industry executives finance the "bad nigger" press, it helps support racist, patriarchal myths that are marketable. In the black community, these myths are often registers of the "masculine" degree of one's blackness. The bad-boy image of Shakur and other gangsta rappers expresses a raging hatred for white racism while it also placates the misogynist desires of young white patriarchs, slumming in black face. One critic calls it "The Rapper's New Rage." [8] Thereby he assists a music industry that makes a rapper black to simulate danger and then displaces him when his words are politically dangerous.

The further study of films that feature black gangsters and agents of law and order might pose some of the following questions. Is violence shown

88. *Juice:* Inner-city realities belie the middle-class imagery of mainstream representations.

to be an act of retribution or is it left unjustified? What is reprehensible about the gangster's manner of achieving his or her aspirations? How does the gangster's style conflict with established rules? Why might one audience permit violent actions while another audience might condemn them? These questions can assist us in analyzing the formal qualities of the black gangster film paradigm and its relationship both to its parallel dominant (white) form and to the historical experiences of African Americans.

Notes

This essay is an expanded version of a paper delivered at the American Museum of the Moving Image, New York, October 27, 1990.

1. Thomas Cripps, *Slow Fade to Black* (New York: Oxford University Press, 1977), p. 196.

2. Cripps, *Slow Fade to Black.* In commenting on the significance of *Dark Manhattan,* Cripps writes that the film was "the first from Hollywood" (p. 328). Also see Henry T. Sampson, *Blacks in Black and White* (Metuchen, N.J.: Scarecrow Press, 1977), p. 204.

3. Sampson, *Blacks,* p. 63.

4. Ibid.

5. Ibid., p. 67.

6. Ibid., p. 241.

7. Quoted in Doris E. Abramson, *Negro Playwrights in the American Theatre, 1925–1959* (New York: Columbia University Press, 1969), p. 92.

8. Malcolm Gladwell, "The Rapper's New Rage," *Washington Post*, December 17, 1992, sec. C, pp. 1–2.

30. Teen Films: The Cinematic Image of Youth

TIMOTHY SHARY

American cinema in the late twentieth century revealed a curious and often inconsistent cultural fascination with stories about and images of young people. Various film trends catering to young audiences had emerged over past generations, but movies in the last twenty years of the century appeared almost fixated on capturing certain youth styles and promoting certain perspectives on the celebration (or, really, survival) of adolescence. Many arguments persist as to why teenagers have been targeted by Hollywood: youth have disposable incomes which they enjoy spending on entertainment; today's children become the consumption-driven parents of tomorrow; filmmakers engage in the vicarious experiences of their own lost youth. As evidenced by the latest massive outpouring of American youth films starting in the late 1990s, and the parallel production of teen-oriented television shows, magazines, and multimedia outlets, as well as the attention paid to youth attitudes and behaviors in the wake of various scandals, crimes, and accomplishments, the imaging of contemporary youth has become indicative of our deepest social and personal concerns.

Consider, for instance, Todd Solondz's 1996 film *Welcome to the Dollhouse*. As we approach the bittersweet climax, the awkward adolescent heroine, Dawn Weiner (Heather Mattarazzo), is preparing to declare her unrequited romantic longings to an older boy at a party. Dressed in a colorful, even garish outfit, Dawn gazes at her crush until she decides that this is her moment: she stands holding her breath, fists clenched, mustering up all her energy to take this plunge, looking as if she could explode. What appears to be merely Dawn's tormented affection for a boy is in fact connected to her sexual awakening, her familial strife, her peers' approval, and her social standing, all signifying the inevitable conflict of becoming an adult. In this one image, Solondz evokes the very intensity that is the nature of growing up, and Dawn's pained expression reminds us that the stakes are high.

Dramas thrive on conflict, and the process of aging is a natural conflict familiar to all by their teenage years. While many filmgoers freely participate in screen fantasies about the possibilities of life as a secret agent or of saving a loved one from the clutches of death, most of our lives are filled with less spectacular experiences, such as how we come to be accepted by society, discover romance, have sex, gain employment, make moral decisions, and learn about the world and who we are in it. These are the experiences that most of us first encounter in our adolescence, and how we handle them largely determines how we live the rest of our lives. The gravity of adolescence thus makes for compelling drama, even if many of us would rather forget those trying years, because understanding how we learn and grow in our youth is integral to understanding who we become as adults.

Since the 1950s the American cinema, with varying waves of interest, has been relying on people under thirty to pay for movies about their daily dramas and fantasies.[1] However, there has not always been a steady output of coming-of-age stories by Hollywood, and the themes of youth films have changed considerably since the days of young Mary Pickford and Lillian Gish in the early 1900s. One of the telling dilemmas of youth films since cinema began is that while they address young people, they are not *produced* by young people, for children and teens are effectively restricted from the commercial filmmaking process. Thus, screen images of youth have always been traditionally filtered through adult perspectives. Virtually all feature films ever made about youth have been produced by filmmakers over twenty, even though many are now produced by filmmakers under thirty, and most recent youth films have become as complex and sophisticated as adult dramas, no longer content to showcase the trite frivolity of beach parties or the overwrought warfare of urban gangs and schools. Since the early 1980s a number of distinct subgenres and character types within the genre of "youth/teen/young adult" films have emerged, offering richly provocative images that question the changing concepts of youth in America.

The deep and compelling history of films about youth does more than inform us of the changing social conditions and perceptions of young people—it also gives us a special appreciation for how successive generations have endured the conflicts of claiming identity and seeking recognition for their actions. This endurance was seen most visibly in teen films after World War II as young people restively entered the Cold War era their parents created, and then again in counterculture films of the sixties, and most recently at the turn of the millennium, as youth begin to face a future that will be far more fast-paced and removed from the traditions and mores of their parents' generation. This study focuses on American youth films in the last twenty years of the twentieth century to determine how recent generations of young people have been represented in American cinema and what that representation tells us about the various phenomena that constitute the contemporary coming-of-age process. Through this examination I demonstrate not only that youth films are a legitimate genre worthy of study on their own terms, but that they are imbued with a cultural significance unique to the genre: they question our evolving identities from youth to adulthood while simultaneously shaping and maintaining those identities.

GENRE AND YOUTH

American films about teenagers have utilized different techniques and stories to represent young people within a codified system that delineates certain subgenres and character types within the "youth film" genre. Unlike other genres that are based on subject matter, the youth genre is based on the ages of the films' characters, and thus the thematic concerns of its subgenres can be seen as more directly connected to specific notions of different youth behaviors and styles. I consider the image of the American youth population within certain ranges of experience that youth are afforded, such as school, relationships, and delinquency. These experiences are essentially what define the more precise "subgenres" within the genre of youth films.

In terms of defining and analyzing the youth genre, both of Andrew Tudor's (1973) solutions to the "empiricist dilemma" can be employed: first, temporarily set aside cultural context in the definition of the genre by simply maintaining a defined and consistent limit on the genre (see "youth" described below); then, in addressing the cultural context, be explicitly aware of the fallibility of generalizing, which remains an inherent danger in observing the characteristics of a genre and extrapolating social conditions from them.[2] Since my study argues primarily from the point at which images of youth are produced—the texts of the films and not their reception within a historical reality of youth, nor their stylistic components (e.g., lighting techniques, editing patterns, use of sound)—I can only offer interpretive hypotheses about the social milieu as well as about the industrial and narrative range of the films themselves. Conditions of education, employment, and lifestyle among young people are too complex to analyze within the scope of this study, although the representation of certain youth trends or practices in films against the historical or statistical "reality" of youth conditions is considered.

One of the most conspicuous problems of genre analysis over the past generation has been the assumption by most scholars that a genre's characteristics and development can be discerned by studying only the most popular and "successful" examples of a genre, or else a random sample of its offerings. Obviously this approach presents a number of dilemmas: how the determination of "importance" is made for the sample selected, what is lost in the films not studied, and how claims about the genre may not apply to every film that can be argued to fit the genre's codes. Yet comprehensive inclusion is essentially impossible; there are simply many films that are so obscure as to be inaccessible. Inevitably, some valuation must be placed on films and styles that do warrant more extensive commentary, while others are given shorter coverage or omitted altogether. This reveals the inherently judgmental nature of generic definition in determining which films are most representative and which address youth issues "significantly," as well as how they operate within their various subgenres. I argue that most youth films fall into one of five subgenres, but not all portray youth in such a way as to lend deeper insight into the patterns and operations of the subgenres.

The difficulty of genre analysis has been examined by Janet Staiger, who claims in her critique of the "purity hypothesis" in genre study that "Hollywood films have never been 'pure'—that is, easily arranged into categories. All that has been pure has been sincere attempts to find order among variety." [3] She does, however, go on to say that these sincere attempts are in the service of understanding larger structural and representational patterns in film history, while questioning why scholars such as Tudor can point out the inconsistencies of genre study and then essentially pass over them with precise efforts to study genre films. To this day an agreement within the field on how to conduct genre studies has yet to be reached, as evidenced by the number of current texts that continue to debate the issue.[4]

That films about youth actually compose a genre has only recently been established in film studies. After the pioneering work of David Considine and a few other authors in the 1980s, two genre catalogs offered codifications for the youth genre.[5] In the first, the massive compendium *Films by Genre: 775 Categories, Styles, Trends, and Movements Defined, with a Filmography for Each* (1993), Daniel Lopez identifies the "teen movie," which has also been called the "'juve' movie," "teenage movie," "teenpic," and "youth picture." [6] He then divides the teen movie into subgenres, while cross-listing other relevant genres such as the "exploitation film," the "juvenile delinquency film," the "motorcycle movie," the "rock film," and the "youth film." Of teen movie subgenres, Lopez offers the divisions of "beach films," "high school films," "teen-violence films," and "teen comedies," which he distinguishes from "teen sex comedies." [7] His further distinction of the "youth film" appears a matter of historically specific semantics, since he cites examples only from 1967 to 1972 and claims that these films "highlighted the concerns of young people querying the Establishment, society and its values," as if films before or since this time had failed to do so as well.[8] Such a dubious category exposes the difficulty of finding accurate descriptors for generic styles and movements, since Lopez would have done better to label the Vietnam-era films to which he was referring by their thematic concerns, calling them perhaps "anti-establishment films," or placing them in a temporal subgenre such as the "Vietnam-era youth film." Nonetheless, Lopez's attempt to define and divide films about youth is still significant, for he locates teen movies as a genre unto itself, and sees the necessity of making subgeneric distinctions.

In 1995, the Library of Congress commissioned its Motion Picture/Broadcasting/Recorded Sound Division to study the cataloging of films by types, and by 1997 the group produced *The Moving Image Genre-Form Guide,* which relies on the work of archival sources (such as the *Film Literature Index* and *The American Film Institute Catalog of Feature Films*) to construct a descriptive structure for the various genres and forms of film. This guide locates one comprehensive genre it labels "youth," which comprises "fictional work portraying aspects of the trajectory through adolescence, including high school years, peer pressure, first love, beach parties, and initial attempts at adulthood, along with strains in the relationship with family."[9] The emphasis in these films is on teenage characters, and the guide thus subsumes the distinction of "teen" films within this category, moving films about characters age twelve and younger to "children," and films set in a collegiate environment to "college." These are essentially the same distinctions that I make (although I do include twelve-year-old characters) in delimiting the genre that is the youth film.

As Staiger and other authors have continued to argue, many films do not easily conform to manufactured categories: some films may simply not fit into a clear (sub)generic classification, or may cross over so many themes and styles as to defy any single (sub)generic location. This is a dilemma of which I am keenly aware, and I attempt to address it by always foregrounding the existence of youth cinema as a genre itself, which has a relatively reliable denotative frame, i.e., films in which youth appear. Then within that frame, I allow for much categorical interplay and cross-generic influence. Yet because not even all "films in which youth appear" can properly be identified as youth cinema (usually because the young characters are secondary to adult leads), the larger generic frame under which I work is still somewhat fragile in its determination of the "youth film" definition. This methodological obstacle nonetheless does not disrupt the process of understanding how youth have been represented in cinema as long as a wide range of youth images are still being studied, from both popular and unpopular films, over a long span of time, and from a variety of generic styles. It does raise the question, however, of whether a truly reliable, consistent, and complete model of genre study by social types may be an impractical goal.

What does delimit youth in this context? For the purposes of this essay, I consider the youth population to be between the ages of twelve and twenty. This represents a range of years that includes the actual teen years as well as the traditionally recognized entrance into adolescence (or at least in the United States, the beginning of middle school, or junior high school), as well as late adolescence and entry into the post–high school world.[10] However, I do not consider films that are about characters in college (who tend to be between eighteen and twenty-four years old), except for the rare cases where clearly defined adolescents attend college in the story. This is not to say that college-age characters are not youthful, but since the college genre has itself already been extensively covered in other studies, and further because the ages of college characters are often vague and are usually implied as the "early twenties," and most of all because the majority of college films do not concern the same issues about youth as do teen and high school films, analyzing these films would detract from the primary focus here on teen representation.[11]

I further delimit the genre by concentrating on feature-length films, although I do consider straight-to-video movies that achieved recognition outside of theatrical release. I do not consider films that, despite the presence of young performers or their appeal to young audiences, are not *about* the youth experience. As Thomas Doherty and other critics have argued, Hollywood "juvenilized" its films after Word War II to such an extent that virtually all movies can be said to appeal to youth.[12] Thus, I omit films that only tangentially or incidentally depict youth, since the comprehensive reach of what can be labeled "youth films" is so vast, and I concentrate only on those films that are relevant to the dominant subgenres of youth depictions since 1980.

THE STUDY OF YOUTH

Any study of cinema and youth offers an interesting historical parallel: motion pictures were invented in the 1890s, and "youth" as an area of academic research emerged less than twenty years later, in 1904, when social psychologist G. Stanley Hall wrote his pathbreaking two-volume tome *Adolescence: Its Psychology, and Its Relations to Physiology, Anthropology, Sociology, Sex, Crime, Religion, and Education,* which is often credited with inaugurating the serious study of youth.[13] That the proliferation of cinema and the founding of youth studies coincide within the same historical generation may not be indicative of a cause-and-effect relationship; however, the relationship between cinema and youth is significant. The twentieth century produced a series of "moral panics" around young people and social behavior, and the cinema has been a perennial source of those panics, not only due to its function as a social gathering place, but more so in generating concerns about the ways that popular media influence youth.[14]

Of course children and teenagers existed before the twentieth century began, but the social perception of the preadult population was considerably different before the early 1900s, and certainly before the industrial revolution. Many girls and boys left school at preteen ages in the nineteenth century and started families soon thereafter, often entering the labor force in their early teen years or younger. As the modern era took hold, certain researchers like Hall (and later Havighurst, Piaget, Winnicott, Erikson, and Anna Freud) began recognizing a distinct age of specialized development between childhood and adulthood that had been initially described through characteristics of sexual development and was then later examined as a more complex sociopsychological manifestation of cultural and internal conflict.[15] This age of development was adolescence, and its study by researchers (including Keniston, who even divided adolescence from youth) and its progressive acceptance by society during the twentieth century resulted in a new notion of youth, if only to distinguish a crucial transitional period during the teen years between childhood and adulthood.[16]

Until the 1960s the study of youth remained largely a discipline within the behavioral sciences as researchers studied the changing attitudes and "pathologies" of youth during the various cycles of twentieth-century life. Then in the sixties, certain global political events brought about a visible change in the activities of young people, not the least of which were the escalating war in southeast Asia and the student revolts in France in 1968. These events led to new research on youth within the growing field of cultural studies in Britain, which eagerly considered how the youth uprisings of that era could be representative of previously repressed or diffused class, gender, and race conflicts.[17] By the 1980s, as the Reagan/Thatcher era brought about a series of new moral panics based on the vision of the New Right, the trend in youth research shifted back toward studies of youth "pathologies" (e.g., teen pregnancy, unemployment, crime), yet still employing a cultural studies method.[18] Regardless of how youth studies have focused on deviance and development (psychology) and/or resistance and economics (politics), one aspect of youth studies has been undoubtedly clear since the 1980s: youth culture is not homogeneous.

The 1980s became a time of distinct change in youth studies as the trajectories of sociology, history, and cultural studies merged over concerns about renewed conservative attitudes which were largely vilifying youth.[19] These concerns were legitimate given conditions of the time; however, these conditions were not necessarily being *visibly* addressed in the American cinema at this time. Most Hollywood films about youth in the 1980s relied upon formulae that exploited youth issues, especially sexual development, while gradually revealing an increasing tension and confusion about the role of youth in this era. By the early nineties, in the wake of the Reagan and Thatcher years and the patriotic swell of the Gulf War, teens in American films had been entirely reconfigured, if not often obscured, as increasing emphasis fell on portraits of the post-teen "twenty-something" generation, now labeled "Generation X" after Douglas Coupland's 1991 novel.[20] "Youth" by the end of the twentieth century thus covered a wider age range than ever before, spanning the first year of post-elementary education (the age of twelve) to the first few years after college (or, considering that the majority of young people do not complete college, at least the mid-twenties).[21]

This perception had already been supported in various studies, many of which argued that "youth" has been reconfigured as a specialized and crucial age group for American commercial marketing, and pointed out how certain youth attitudes—notably cynicism and narcissism—have been amplified and abused by advertisers, businesses, and even politicians.[22] Most recently, a psychosociological interest in studying youth conditions has emerged following Mary Pipher's very successful *Reviving Ophelia: Saving the Selves of Adolescent Girls* (1994), which chronicles the tales of a wide range of troubled teenage girls facing negative body images, difficult familial conditions, and confusing romantic and social experiences.[23] More than any generation since the 1960s, today's teens are the subjects of intensive media examination; more than any generation ever before, they are the objects of outright media exploitation.

YOUTH IN FILM HISTORY

Young people have always been a concern in American film history, both in terms of their images onscreen and their reception of films as an audience. In the earliest days of cinema there did not exist a distinct youth genre, nor for that matter much of an agreed social sense of what constituted youth. Children in the early twentieth century often left school by the age of fourteen to begin jobs (only 6.4 percent of young Americans completed high school in 1900), and many were married and having children by eighteen, a condition which kept the state of "youth" limited to just a few years between childhood and adulthood.[24] The reception of movies at that time was also affected by social fears about their corruptive potential, especially as they could influence children. Many moral guardians preached about the dangers of exposing children to typically adult-oriented dramas, and, rather than make films that specifically catered to a young audience, the vulnerable new movie industry tended to side with concerns over propriety.[25] By the 1920s, Hollywood formed the Hays Office and began formal evaluations and restrictions on the moral content of American films, and despite a choice few popular films that featured young characters of the time—Lillian Gish in *Broken Blossoms* (D. W. Griffith, 1919), Mary Pickford in *Pollyanna* (Paul Powell, 1920), Jackie Coogan in *The Kid* (Charlie Chaplin, 1921), Baby Peggy in *Captain January* (Edward Cline, 1924)—the industry took a clear position on youth films by the thirties: children were either preadolescent (such as Shirley Temple or the kids in *Our Gang*) or were developed into early adulthood (such as in the Andy Hardy series starring Mickey Rooney, or the old-before-their-time Dead End Kids). In either case, young people certainly did not have onscreen discussions about otherwise typical developmental issues like sexuality, drug or alcohol use, or family dysfunction.

The notable youth films that followed in the years after the Great Depression tended to be optimistic and endearing fables starring the likes of Deanna Durbin, Judy Garland, and/or Mickey Rooney, but these films were still directed at and most often seen by an adult audience or by a family audience. Hollywood studios promoted these small troupes of young stars (also including Frankie Darro, Bonita Granville, Freddie Bartholomew, Dickie Moore, and Joyce Reynolds), who came to represent the contemporary ideals, if not the realistic conditions, of youth. Then with the resolution of World War II, a distinct population in America began to emerge: the teenager.

Gradually the age between childhood and adulthood came to be codified, debated, celebrated, and, perhaps most significantly, elongated.[26] More young people stayed in school and, with the arrival of postwar prosperity, more began attending college. Other factors contributed to the burgeoning presence of the teenager in the fifties: the greater availability of automobiles, which allowed youth to travel and thus achieve a certain independence; the recovering economy, which gave many teens extra money for entertainment outside the home; the popular reception of rock 'n' roll, which clearly flew in the face of previous musical standards; and the influence of television, which, while giving all Americans a new common entertainment medium, also kept more adults at home.

In terms of the film industry, two landmark legal cases set the stage for the eventual proliferation of young adult fare. The "Paramount Case" was handed down by the Supreme Court in 1948 and soon thereafter began the process of divesting major movie studios from the theaters they owned, giving rise to more small independent studios that would take advantage of their increased theatrical access by catering to niche audiences like teenagers. Then the important "Miracle Decision" by the Supreme Court in 1952 brought certain First Amendment protections to films,

89. *Rebel without a Cause* (1955): The teen angst of James Dean.

thereby opening the door for depicting a wider range of moral issues on-screen, which attracted young people to theaters where they could view more "adult" dramas than were available on television.[27]

However, Hollywood studios did not suddenly bank on hedonistic teen roles in the early 1950s: their process of introducing the postwar teenager was careful if not apprehensive, as they gradually exaggerated the ephebi-phobia—fear of teenagers—that was seeping into popular culture and politics. After a few notable "clean teen" performances in the 1940s by Jeanne Crain in *Margie* (Henry King, 1946), Jane Powell in *A Date with Judy* (Richard Thorpe, 1948), and Elizabeth Taylor in *Little Women* (Mervyn LeRoy, 1949), the fifties teen performer was embodied in the archetypal James Dean, whose performance in *Rebel without a Cause* (Nicholas Ray, 1955) is probably the most influential demonstration of pure teen angst in American cinema. Of course, Marlon Brando had al-ready showcased the young rebel image when he made *The Wild One* (Laszlo Benedek, 1953), but Dean's affected demeanor was more endur-ing. Hollywood then continued to mold other performers into troubled youth, as in the milder but still afflicted roles of Natalie Wood in *Rebel, Marjorie Morningstar* (Irving Rapper, 1958), and *West Side Story* (Robert Wise and Jerome Robbins, 1961); John Saxon in *Rock, Pretty Baby* (Richard Bartlett, 1956), *The Unguarded Moment* (Harry Keller, 1956), and *The Restless Years* (Helmut Käutner, 1958); and Brandon de Wilde in *Blue Denim* (Philip Dunne, 1959), *All Fall Down* (John Frankenheimer, 1962), and *Hud* (Martin Ritt, 1963).

Perhaps a more notable trend than the emergence of these new young performers was the film industry's active confrontation with the conditions of youth. *Rebel* showcased the high school outcast who couldn't fit in, while also considering alcoholism, family dynamics, basic crime, and, in more concealed terms, homosexuality; *The Blackboard Jungle* (Richard Brooks, 1955) dramatized the potentially violent conditions of urban high schools and tangentially introduced rock music to American cinema, giving rise to teen "rock movies" that would become a subgenre thereafter; and *Peyton Place* (Mark Robson, 1957) and *Splendor in the Grass* (Elia Kazan, 1961) demonstrated the supposed dangers of teenage sexuality. Each of these films dealt with issues important to young adults, but now that Hollywood was finally making films about the difficulty of being young, a reactionary movement began, in binary form: films were made that avoided or toned down the dilemmas of youth for the sake of celebrating its carefree aspects, or films were made to further capitalize on and inflame the dangers of teen delinquency and decadence. This was a phenomenon recognized by Richard Staehling in his 1969 early analysis of teen films, as he divided the mild from the wild: "To the majority of Americans, confronted with news of gang wars, Elvis, and drag racing, there were only two kinds of kids: the good ones and the bad ones." [28]

Despite this divide, movie studios (especially American International Pictures) catered to both ends of the teen spectrum. The cheery end of that spectrum was exemplified by a wave of inane beach films by the sixties, many featuring Frankie Avalon and Annette Funicello after their well-attended *Beach Party* (William Asher, 1963), as well as the popular *Gidget* series (Paul Wendkos, 1959, and two sequels before the 1965 TV show). Meanwhile, studios also promoted a lesser-seen but nonetheless conspicuous output of darker youth exploitation films, a genre that emerged as early as 1936 with *Reefer Madness* (Louis Gasnier) and was carried on by *City across the River* (Maxwell Shane, 1949) and sustained in such productions as *Teenage Devil Dolls* (Bamlet Lawrence Price Jr., 1952), *Teenage Crime Wave* (Fred Sears, 1955), *High School Confidential!* (Jack Arnold, 1958), *This Rebel Breed* (Richard Bare and William Rowland, 1960), *Teenage Strangler* (Ben Parker, 1964), and *The Wild Angels* (Roger Corman, 1966).[29] To this day, the movie industry still has a reductive tendency to polarize teens in terms of their moods, morals,

90. Annette Funicello and Frankie Avalon starred in a series of inane beach films in the 1960s (publicity photo).

and ideas, thereby making their experiences more extremely dramatic while denying the more neutral and natural aspects of teens' complex daily lives.

By the early 1970s, after the implementation of the Motion Picture Association of America's ratings system in 1968 and the national suffrage of eighteen-year-olds in 1971, not to mention the young ages at which boys were being drafted to fight in Vietnam, American youth began to have a different sense of their identity than that which had been provided for them in so many of the happier, hipper sixties films. The dark and more rebellious aspects of youth that had emerged in the fifties teen films continued in counterculture productions like *Wild in the Streets* (Barry Shear, 1968), *Easy Rider* (Dennis Hopper, 1969), *Getting Straight* (Richard Rush, 1970), *R.P.M.* (Stanley Kramer, 1970), and *The Strawberry Statement* (Stuart Hagmann, 1970). As was the case with films of the previous generation, most of these movies were not about adolescents but rather young adults, just leaving high school or in college. In fact, Hollywood virtually abandoned its practice of promoting teenage performers in the sixties and certainly had very few to account for in the seventies (the three prominent exceptions were Jodie Foster, Tatum O'Neal, and Robby Benson).

After the dearth of teen stars and films in the 1970s, Hollywood could have maintained its lower output of youth films in the eighties, but instead the industry concentrated more on young adult dramas than ever before. The most likely factor contributing to this was the emergence of another icon of youth independence, the shopping mall. The mall became a scene of teen congregation where arcades and food courts replaced the pool halls and soda fountains of the past. Furthermore, since the seventies, following the dramatic decline of American movie theaters, Hollywood had come to rely on the centralization of multiple theaters in large retail centers to increase the number of screen venues and to offer moviegoers greater variety and convenience. Thus the multiplex was born. With the relocation of most movie theaters into or near shopping malls in the 1980s, the need to cater to the young audiences who frequented those malls became apparent to Hollywood, and those audiences formed the first generation of multiplex moviegoers.

THE MULTIPLEX GENERATION

The clearest result of the multiplex movement was a voluminous outpouring of films directed toward and featuring teens, but in order to avoid an inevitable homogenization of the teen genre, Hollywood revised its fifties formula by intensifying the narrative range of youth films through placing teenage characters in previously established genres with more dramatic impact (gory horror, dance musicals, sex comedies), and as a result, a new variety of character types grew out of this generic expansion. Given the categorical choices offered by the multiplex theater, teens in the eighties were then able to go to the mall and select the particular youth movie experience that appealed to them most, and Hollywood tried to keep up with changing teen interests and styles to ensure ongoing profits. This led to evolving efforts by the film industry to maintain the youth market through further generic expansions and revisions; more significant for the audience, teens were then exposed to a wider range of characters and situations that directly addressed their current social conditions, even if many of the films that did so clearly had puerile provocation as their motive. Unlike in the fifties, when screen teens were steered down relatively rigid righteous paths, in the eighties teens witnessed a complexity of moral choices and personal options on which the multiplex movies thrived. This gave teenage movie audiences at the end of the twentieth century a greater sense of presence in popular media, a deeper potential to be influenced by the films they saw, and a wider range of options from which they could construct and compare their senses of themselves.

The late seventies suggested the teen trends to come, as the popularity of such films as John Travolta's *Saturday Night Fever* (John Badham, 1977) and *Grease* (Randal Kleiser, 1978)—both of which combined music, sex (or the repression thereof), and style—created a segue to the more dynamic stories that young audiences would soon demand. A handful of other films truly inaugurated new cycles: two 1978 American films, the low-budget sensation *Halloween* (John Carpenter) and the college farce *Animal House* (John Landis), as well as two unassuming Canadian films, *Meatballs* (Ivan Reitman, 1979) and *Porky's* (Bob Clark, 1981). These were the starting guns of the new youth subgenres of the eighties. *Animal House, Meatballs,* and *Porky's* were raucous comedies featuring goofy and/or hormonal youth pursuing pleasure at, respectively, college, summer camp, and a fifties-era high school. Their success spawned numerous imitations over the next few years which featured desperate variations on this storyline, with such suggestive titles as *Goin' All the Way* (Robert Freedman, 1981), *The Last American Virgin* (Boaz Davidson, 1982), *Losin' It* (Curtis Hanson, 1983), *Getting It On* (William Olsen, 1983), *The First Turn-On* (Michael Herz and Lloyd Kaufman, 1983), *Screwballs* (Rafal Zielinski, 1984), *The Joy of Sex* (Martha Coolidge, 1984), and *The Wild Life* (Art Linson, 1984). The new abundance of teen sexuality onscreen also coincided with an increasing awareness that the age of first intercourse was dropping for American youth, and the few earlier films that solemnly featured teens losing their virginity—for instance, *Rich Kids* (Robert M. Young, 1979), *The Blue Lagoon* (Kleiser, 1980), *Endlesslove* (Franco Zeffirelli, 1981)—faded into the new appeal of carnal comedies about the plight of sexual pursuits.[30] At the same time, *Halloween* and similar films like *Friday the 13th* (Sean S. Cunningham, 1980) and *Slumber Party Massacre* (Amy Jones, 1982) were capitalizing on the reactionary aspect of teen sexuality, slaughtering wholesale those youth who deigned to cross the threshold of sexual awareness, even though these films usually hinged on a major suspension of realism. The early eighties then marked the beginning of a new era in American youth movie production with the release of numerous popular teen horror films in 1981 and of *Fast Times at Ridgemont High* (Amy Heckerling, 1982), which was the first commercially successful hybrid of the contemporary sex, school, and delinquency elements.

By the early eighties, there were six major approaches to youth cinema offered by Hollywood, most revised from past trends in the genre: the horror film, the science fiction film, the sex comedy, the romantic melodrama, the juvenile delinquent drama, and the school picture, which often borrowed generic elements from the rest. Of these approaches, the horror film tended to offer the highest grosses (literally and figuratively) and often showed the least knowledge of true youth conditions. Many of these films were runaway successes in the early eighties and may have been responsible for bringing a new image of youth to American cinema, however incomplete that image was. Within the youth horror subgenre, graphic depictions of sex and violence had come to be expected, and such previous taboos as the depiction of "underage" nudity were broached. The eighties youth horror subgenre (represented by its three most successful franchises, *Halloween, Friday the 13th,* and *A Nightmare on Elm Street* [Wes Craven, 1984]) not only depicted teens as sexually active but as morally culpable for their explorations of sexuality, paying with their lives for their indiscretions. The youth horror film soon reached beyond its most popular "slasher" style and considered the influences on youth of such forces as the supernatural (*Christine* [John Carpenter, 1983], *Society* [Brian Yuzna, 1991], *The Rage: Carrie 2* [Katt Shea, 1999]), the occult (*Night of the Demons* [Kevin Tenney, 1987], *Mirror, Mirror* [Marina Sargenti, 1990], *The Craft* [Andrew Fleming, 1996]), the militaristic (*Return of the Living Dead* [Dan O'Bannon, 1985], *The Blob* [Chuck Russell, 1988], *Body Snatchers* [Abel Ferrara, 1993]), and even rock 'n' roll (*Trick or Treat* [Charles Martin Smith, 1986], *The Gate* [Tibor Tikács, 1987], *Black Roses* [John Fasano, 1988]). These films thereby brought attention to teen sexuality and morality, and other issues, by the most dramatic means possible.

Society offers an explicit examination of teens' sexual and moral torment within the horror subgenre. Billy (Billy Warlock) is a high school senior who gradually realizes that his wealthy family is involved in a spooky local cult, which practices a vile means of eliminating the poor members of their community by erotically sucking out their internal organs at perverse parties. Billy is of course shocked by this, and even more terrified after learning that since he is not one of the "pure" elites, he's next on their list of victims. He must then fight his way through the mutating members of the society, including his libidinous parents and sister, yielding a complex commentary on incestuous, oedipal, and homoerotic tensions for teens. *Society* also works as a parable of youthful alienation during the transition to adulthood, and its haunting vision of the "accepted" upper class speaks to a youthful sense of rebellion against elite social customs.

The science fiction teen film represents the smallest subgenre, but its presence is nonetheless crucial to understanding the industry's treatment of adult and youth difference. The youth science fiction film had early stirrings in *E.T.: The Extra-Terrestrial* (Steven Spielberg, 1982) but came into its own in 1983 with *WarGames* (John Badham) and then continued with further nuclear-era projects like *Real Genius* (Martha Coolidge, 1985) and *The Manhattan Project* (Marshall Brickman, 1986). Two distinct styles emerged in the eighties: films dealing with "science," such as

Zapped! (Robert Rosenthal, 1982), *Weird Science* (John Hughes, 1985), and *SpaceCamp* (Harry Winer, 1986), and films focusing on computer and/or video technology, including *The Last Starfighter* (Nick Castle, 1984), *Explorers* (Joe Dante, 1985), and *Defense Play* (Monte Markham, 1988). Youth science fiction films then went into a clear decline as the Cold War came to a close, and even films featuring youth using computers and video games, such as *Arcade* (Albert Pyun, 1993), *Brainscan* (John Flynn, 1994), and *Evolver* (Mark Rosman, 1995), were primarily relegated to smaller studios by the nineties, suggesting that Hollywood was aware of changing cultural conditions for youth using technologies of power but chose not to celebrate this liberating potential. Of course, many adults have serious concerns about children's access to technology, and so despite the ever-increasing interest that youth have in computers, games, and gizmos, the continuing paucity of films about these topics may indicate a tacit dissension by Hollywood toward making teen-oriented science fiction. However, teens' own disinterest in these stories also signals a curious dissension, since the few recent films that have been made in this mold have all been met with scant attention. Despite heavy promotional campaigns, box-office returns for *Hackers* (Iain Softley, 1995, $7.5 million), *October Sky* (Joe Johnston, 1999, $32.4 million), and *Clockstoppers* (Jonathan Frakes, 2002, $37 million) have been less than astronomical.

Hackers reveals much of the fascination and failure that teen science fiction films have faced. The story focuses on Dade (Jonny Lee Miller) and his teenage troupe of computer enthusiasts, who stumble upon an evil corporation's plot to embezzle money and create a massive pollution problem, which they set out to disrupt through their productive computer hacking. Yet oddly enough, despite the film's abundance of tech talk, the narrative would have you believe that being a good hacker is simply a matter of fast typing and hard keypunching. Within a video game format that is unlike any *real* computer system of the nineties, the teens use their cyber-acrobatic flair in a climactic montage of aggressive physical moves that celebrates their success. The film is certainly a kinetic ride, but perhaps its overwrought attempt to portray the mercurial young computer culture demonstrates the difficulty recent films have had in addressing youths' access to computers. The film's image of computer youth in the nineties is the same as that of the thrill-seekers of past generations, only now their toys can literally change the world. Given the film's high exposure but small audience, this may be a level of responsibility that, while powerful, teens do not yet want to accept.

The sex comedy and romantic melodrama companion each other, for despite the often gratuitous content of many of these films, both subgenres consider the trial by fire that is the discovery of young lust and love. All youth love films can be categorized by identifying the obstacle to the protagonists' romance, and teen films have featured those obstacles accordingly: class in *Valley Girl* (Martha Coolidge, 1983), *Reckless* (James Foley, 1984), and *Can't Buy Me Love* (Steve Rash, 1987); age in *Blame It on Rio* (Stanley Donen, 1984), *Man in the Moon* (Robert Mulligan, 1991), and *Boys* (Stacy Cochran, 1996); popularity in *Sixteen Candles* (Hughes, 1984), *Trojan War* (George Huang, 1997), and *A Walk to Remember* (Adam Shankman, 2002); race in *China Girl* (Abel Ferrara, 1987), *Bleeding Hearts* (Gregory Hines, 1995), and *Save the Last Dance* (Thomas Carter, 2001); and, more recently, homosexual preference in *Totally Fucked Up* (Gregg Araki, 1994), *All over Me* (Alex Sichel, 1996), and *Edge of Seventeen* (David Moreton, 1999). Of course, the obstacle most commonly portrayed, going back to the days of Shakespeare's *Romeo and Juliet,* has been the familial conflict, which has factored in the star-crossed romances of *Endlesslove, Say Anything . . .* (Cameron Crowe, 1989), *Fear* (Foley, 1996), and *The Virgin Suicides* (Sofia Coppola, 2000).

Say Anything . . . is one of the most celebrated youth love stories of the past generation, and its familial conflict is, as in so many films, an actual catalyst for the union of the young lovers. After Lloyd (John Cusack) and Diane (Ione Skye) begin a promising relationship, she breaks up with him under her father's pressure to put her studies before their love. But once Diane realizes that her father has been stealing money from the nursing home he runs, she returns to Lloyd and devotes herself to him again. The final scene of *Say Anything . . .* is one of the special moments in youth love films where the teen characters are happily united and facing a promising future together: on a plane waiting to leave for England, Lloyd holds the nervous Diane's hand and reassures her that they will be safe, even if they cannot see where they are going. This ending leaves open a certain ambiguity and tension about their destiny, and thus the film is not merely about the morality of devotion—Lloyd's is righteous while Diane's father's is selfish—but about the risks and rewards of romantic patience and loyalty.

Meanwhile, by the early eighties the depiction of teens' sexual pursuits had become primarily ribald and explicit, as in *Private Lessons* (Alan Myerson, 1981), *Fast Times at Ridgemont High* (Amy Heckerling, 1982), *Risky Business* (Paul Brickman, 1983), and *Hollywood Hot Tubs* (Chuck Vincent, 1984). Then, in the mid-eighties, a distinct shift took place toward more serious and sensitive representations of teen relationships, particularly in the films written by John Hughes, such as *Pretty in Pink* (Howard Deutch, 1986) and *Some Kind of Wonderful* (Deutch, 1987). Certainly one of the reasons for this shift was the increasing public awareness that AIDS was a threat to teens, resulting in an informal but consistent moratorium on the newly flowered "losing virginity" plotline that lasted for nearly a decade from the mid-eighties. When teenage sexual practice began to reemerge in mid-nineties films, the industry again re-

acted in its bipolar way, and in the summer of 1995 offered films that both
brutally maligned teen sex (*Kids,* Larry Clark) or made it into a chaste
joke (*Clueless,* Heckerling). By the end of the decade, teenage sexual practice had at least become more realistically visible again, and was now
more complex, as witnessed in such diverse productions as *Manny and
Lo* (Lisa Krueger, 1996), *Wild Things* (John McNaughton, 1997), *The
Opposite of Sex* (Don Roos, 1998), *American Pie* (Paul Weitz, 1999), and
Coming Soon (Colette Burson, 1999).

In fact, *Coming Soon* represents a potentially promising turning point
in cinematic depictions of teenage sexuality. Written and directed by
women, the film depicts the adventures of Stream (Bonnie Root) and her
two girlfriends as they seek not the loss of their virginity but the attainment of their first orgasms. The girls realize that what they thought they
knew about sex was based on misconceptions and often patriarchal mis-
information, and Stream actively seeks out a more satisfying sex life, first
with a conceited boyfriend, then on her own, and finally with a guy who
has her interests in mind. Meanwhile, the film offers other possible trajectories for her friends, as one realizes she is a lesbian, and the other admits her sexual confusion despite her abundant sexual activity. Yet due to
the film's extolling of young women's sexual satisfaction, it garnered an
NC-17 rating in its initial release, leading to considerable distribution
problems. The male-centric *American Pie* became a huge hit after being
reedited from its NC-17 to an R that same year; the more sensitive *Coming Soon,* without the support of a major studio, faded to video, where
few teens saw its healthy gender inversion of the sex quest plot.

The output of juvenile delinquent dramas has been the most voluminous of youth films, although their attention to contemporary realism is
much debated, since they offer a rich appreciation for the aggressive expressions which teens most crave and parents most fear. A clear range of
immorality can be studied across this subgenre, from the harmless mis-
chief that youth enact in daily life, as in *Ferris Bueller's Day Off* (Hughes,
1986), *Don't Tell Mom the Babysitter's Dead* (Stephen Herek, 1991),
and *Snow Day* (Chris Koch, 2000), to the life-threatening criminality of
distraught teens in films like *Class of 1984* (Mark Lester, 1982), *River's
Edge* (Tim Hunter, 1987), and *American History X* (Tony Kaye, 1998).
Some of the specific delinquent styles that fall within this spectrum include the "deviant dancing" film, in which youth rebel through their choreography, as in *Beat Street* (Stan Lathan, 1984), *Dirty Dancing* (Emile
Ardolino, 1987), and *Lambada* (Joel Silberg, 1990); the "wilderness survival" film, in which youth fight nature's elements to prove themselves,
as in *Lord of the Flies* (Harry Hook, 1990), *A Far Off Place* (Mikael Sa-
lomon, 1993), and *Alaska* (Fraser Heston, 1996); the "tough girl" story
featuring angry young women expressing their gender oppression, such as

Fun (Rafal Zielinski, 1994), *Foxfire* (Annette Haywood-Carter, 1996), and *Girlfight* (Karyn Kusama, 2000); and the African-American crime drama of the early nineties, a successful and influential trend that brought an invigorating tension to youth films but nonetheless faded in the mid-nineties after the declining successes of *Boyz N the Hood* (John Singleton, 1991), *Menace II Society* (Albert and Allen Hughes, 1993), and *Clockers* (Spike Lee, 1995).

Foxfire is indicative of the sincere and yet aggressive depiction of young delinquents. Four high school seniors are joined by a runaway girl named Legs (Angelina Jolie), who inspires them to begin a latent feminist movement at their school when they confront a sexually harassing teacher. After the girls are suspended for their actions and form a small commune in an abandoned house, their protest feels real and powerful, and their sense of liberation is palpable. Yet the narrative soon becomes increasingly dependent on the girls' unusual displays of difference, such as breaking into the school, drinking whiskey, and smoking dope, while unfortunately revealing little more about them as characters. Legs remains their kindred spirit, but she is a necessary cipher, since the film suggests that these girls have been longing to break free and simply needed a vague shove to do so. The film is not ambiguous in its bold message to girls—they should unite and stand up for themselves—while the conventions of delinquency depictions burden the film with celebrating the entertainment of rebellion and minimizing the otherwise fulfilling discovery of personal and political convictions.

School films are probably the most foundational subgenre of youth films, yet they often consider teenage identities quite separately from other subgenres. In most school films, the educational setting becomes an elaborate domain for youth issues, featuring a variety of youth culture styles and types, as best represented by *The Breakfast Club* (Hughes, 1985). Five character roles played out in that film—the nerd, the jock, the rebel, the popular girl, and the delinquent—are the roles most commonly seen in all school films, exhibiting the impulse of smart students to transform (*Lucas* [David Seltzer, 1986], *Angus* [Patrick Read Johnson, 1995], *She's All That* [Robert Iscove, 1999]), the impact of delinquents on school order (*My Bodyguard* [Tony Bill, 1980], *The Principal* [Christopher Cain, 1987], *187* [Kevin Reynolds, 1997]), the threat of conformity to rebels (*The Chocolate War* [Keith Gordon, 1988], *Pump Up the Volume* [Allan Moyle, 1990], *10 Things I Hate about You* [Gil Junger, 1999]), the depiction of sensitive athletes (*Vision Quest* [Harold Becker, 1985], *Only the Strong* [Sheldon Lettich, 1993], *Remember the Titans* [Boaz Yakin, 2000]), and the effects of popularity on teen girls (*Can't Buy Me Love, Clueless, Election* [Alexander Payne, 1999]). The cycles in school films are thus best revealed through tracing the characters that embody those

91. *The Breakfast Club* (1985): Left to right: the delinquent, the rebel, the jock, the popular girl, and the nerd.

cycles, from the nerd and delinquent outcasts of *Class Act* (Randall Miller, 1991) to the tormented clique queens of *Heathers* (Michael Lehmann, 1989) to the jock heroes of *Varsity Blues* (Brian Robbins, 1999).

The satirical *Heathers* exploded many of the past traditions of school movies in its examination of teenage popularity. Jason Dean (Christian Slater), a.k.a. "JD" (his name not far from its 1950s James Dean inspiration, and his initials reminding us that he is indeed a juvenile delinquent), becomes the boyfriend of Veronica (Winona Ryder) just as she is staging a revolt against "the most powerful clique in the school," of which she is a member along with a trio of her fellow rich friends who are all named Heather. Veronica is initially impressed with JD's open contempt for their school's social structure, which she shares in more concealed ways, until he lures her into a series of murder-suicides that the deluded students reframe as positive acts of resistance. Along the way, *Heathers* points accusations at all elements of the secondary educational system for why such strife exists among adolescents, placing responsibility on teachers and administrators who are sorely out of touch with their students, parents who are self-absorbed and as immature as their children, and the students themselves, who succumb too easily to the pressures of acceptance. JD's extreme efforts to gain individuality yield a psychotic inability to accept others and result in his own eventual suicide, whereas Veronica finds a way to manifest her rebellion more effectively, disrupting the school's oppressive caste system and exposing, however briefly, the inability of high school to provide social acceptance at all.

CONCLUSION

These subgenres remained in place in American cinema through the end of the twentieth century and, with the ironic exception of the now-dormant science fiction film, they still form the frame in which youth films are made and marketed in the early twenty-first century, even as a number of the particular styles within the subgenres fade or change. In general terms, after the boom of the early eighties, the output of successful American youth films began to decline by the late eighties, as the "Brat Pack" of popular teen stars in the mid-eighties (e.g., Molly Ringwald, Rob Lowe, Emilio Estevez, Ally Sheedy, Judd Nelson) began taking adult roles and Hollywood moved away from the limited market of teen stories. Many little-seen youth films did continue to be made at this time, and while many were quite good, most were by small studios and had restricted release. With the exception of a few notable films focusing on African American teens in criminal settings, this marginalizing effect continued until the mid-nineties, when Hollywood began to cultivate a revived interest in youth films, partially due to the recycling pattern of most film genres, but also in an effort to lure youth back to theaters and away from the proliferation of new teen-oriented Internet sites and cable TV channels.

By the mid-nineties, the latest expansion of youth movie production emerged, especially in the wake of highly successful and/or provocative youth films such as *The Brady Bunch Movie* (Betty Thomas, 1995), *Kids, Dangerous Minds* (John N. Smith, 1995), *Powder* (Victor Salva, 1995), *William Shakespeare's Romeo + Juliet* (Baz Luhrmann, 1996), *Scream* (Wes Craven, 1996), *Foxfire*, and *Girls Town* (Jim McKay, 1996). The new Hollywood strategy worked: by 1997, the national teenager demographic tracking organization Teen Research Unlimited announced that teens labeled "going to the movies" the most popular "in" activity, ahead of (in descending order) using the Internet, dating, partying, sports, and shopping.[31] (Since most movie studios are now owned by a handful of corporations that also own vast Internet and television outlets, the industry's appeal to youth may have formed into a more diffuse effort to maintain constant media consumption rather than any medium-specific loyalty.) In fact, just as they saved Hollywood profits in the early eighties, youth movies of the late nineties offered a much-needed boost to a previously sluggish film industry, with relatively low-budget productions such as *Can't Hardly Wait* (Harry Elfont and Deborah Kaplan, 1998), *Halloween H₂O* (Steve Miner, 1998), *The Faculty* (Robert Rodriguez, 1998), *Varsity Blues, Go* (Doug Liman, 1999), and *Never Been Kissed* (Raja Gosnell, 1999), each yielding tidy revenues—not to mention the hugely budgeted and overwhelmingly successful *Titanic* (James Cameron, 1997), a film that owed much of its profit to a youth audience captivated by the film's teen romance. Various media outlets began covering the escalating interest in teen culture, which was apparent not only at the multiplex but in television shows such as *Party of Five, Buffy the Vampire Slayer, 7th Heaven, Moesha,* and the relatively huge hit *Dawson's Creek* (developed by *Scream* screenwriter Kevin Williamson), and which thus had a synergistic effect in increasing the output of teen roles in the cinema.[32]

The youth population at the turn of the millennium was clearly witness to a new wave of films that catered to their interests and explored their images, both through familiar formats based on titillation and tumult, as in *Cruel Intentions* (Roger Kumble, 1999), *Josie and the Pussycats* (Elfont and Kaplan, 2001), and *Spider-Man* (Sam Raimi, 2002), and through freshly intelligent and diverse approaches of films like *Getting to Know You* (Lisanne Skyler, 1999), *George Washington* (David Gordon Green, 2000), and *Ghost World* (Terry Zwigoff, 2001). All such films were and will continue to be influenced by and built upon the evolution of cinematic youth representations in previous generations. Movie studios and their related media outlets will continue capitalizing on youth interests with the goal of boosting corporate profits, but they will need to maintain a timely and informed sense of youth conditions in order to be successful. With youth gaining greater access to media technology, we may even see the emergence of popular films *made* by teens about teens.[33] The question remains if the new teen films of the twenty-first century will continue the problematic yet popular tradition of pushing their characters to the extreme limits of moral and social acceptability, or if they will continue the project of certain recent films in thoughtfully and effectively examining the realistic conditions and positive energies of teenagers.

NOTES

1. See Thomas Doherty, *Teenagers and Teenpics: The Juvenilization of American Movies in the 1950s* (Boston: Unwin Hyman, 1988), pp. 1–16; rev. and expanded ed., Philadelphia: Temple University Press, 2002.

2. Andrew Tudor, "Genre," in *Theories of Film* (New York: Viking Press, 1973), p. 136. Reprinted in this volume.

3. Janet Staiger, "Hybrid or Inbred: The Purity Hypothesis and Hollywood Genre History," *Film Criticism* 22, no. 1 (Fall 1997): 6. Reprinted in this volume.

4. The newest texts on film genre include Torben Grodal, *Moving Pictures: A New Theory of Film Genres, Feelings, and Cognition* (New York: Oxford University Press, 1997); *Refiguring American Film Genres: History and Theory*, ed. Nick Browne (Berkeley: University of California Press, 1998); Rick Altman, *Film/Genre* (London: British Film Institute, 1999); Steve Neale, *Genre and Hollywood* (New York and London: Routledge, 2000); and *Film Genre 2000: New Critical Essays*, ed. Wheeler Winston Dixon (Albany: State University Press of New York, 2000).

5. David M. Considine, *The Cinema of Adolescence* (Jefferson, N.C.: McFarland, 1985). In addition to this and the subsequent books by Doherty and Lewis mentioned above and below, other significant studies of youth in cinema include: Kathy Merlock Jackson, *Images of Children in American Film: A Sociocultural Analysis* (Metuchen, N.J.: Scarecrow Press, 1986); Timothy Shary, "The Teen Film and Its Methods of Study," *Journal of Popular Film and Television* 25, no. 1 (Spring 1997): 38–45; Wheeler Winston Dixon, "'Fighting and Violence and Everything, That's Always Cool': Teen Films in the 1990s," in *Film Genre 2000*, pp. 125–142; and Steve Neale, "Teenpics," in *Genre and Hollywood*, pp. 118–125. The two most recent comprehensive studies of teens in films are Jonathan Bernstein, *Pretty in Pink: The Golden Age of Teenage Movies* (New York: St. Martin's Griffin, 1997), and my *Generation Multiplex: The Image of Youth in Contemporary American Cinema* (Austin: University of Texas Press, 2002).

6. Daniel Lopez, *Films by Genre: 775 Categories, Styles, Trends, and Movements Defined, with a Filmography for Each* (Jefferson, N.C.: McFarland and Company, 1993), p. 331.

7. Ibid., p. 332.

8. Ibid., p. 390.

9. *The Moving Image Genre-Form Guide*, compiled by Brian Taves (Chair), Judi Hoffman, and Karen Lund, Library of Congress Motion Picture/Broadcasting/Recorded Sound Division report, February 12, 1997, p. 60. My thanks to Brian Taves for providing me with this report.

10. This is the same age range that David Considine analyzed in his work on adolescents in film, as well as that used by Mark Thomas McGee and R. J. Robertson in their study of juvenile delinquency in movies, *The J.D. Films: Juvenile Delinquency in the Movies* (Jefferson, N.C.: McFarland, 1982).

11. See Wiley Lee Umphlett, *The Movies Go to College: Hollywood and the World of the College-Life Film* (Rutherford, N.J.: Fairleigh Dickinson University

Press, 1984), and David Hinton, *Celluloid Ivy: Higher Education in the Movies, 1960–1990* (Metuchen, N.J.: Scarecrow Press, 1994).

12. Further evidence of this can be found in Michael Barson and Steven Heller, *Teenage Confidential: An Illustrated History of the American Teen* (San Francisco: Chronicle Books, 1998).

13. G. Stanley Hall, *Adolescence: Its Psychology, and Its Relations to Physiology, Anthropology, Sociology, Sex, Crime, Religion, and Education* (New York: D. Appleton & Company, 1904). Scholars who credit Hall with some variety of "discovering" adolescence are Johan Fornas, "Youth, Culture, and Modernity," in *Youth Culture in Late Modernity*, ed. Johan Fornas and Goran Bolin (London: Sage, 1995), p. 5; Christine Griffin, *Representations of Youth: The Study of Youth and Adolescence in Britain and America* (Cambridge, U.K.: Polity Press, 1993), p. 11; and John R. Gillis, *Youth and History: Tradition and Change in European Age Relations, 1770–Present* (New York: Academic Press, 1981), p. 118.

14. Griffin, *Representations of Youth*, pp. 18–26.

15. See Robert Havighurst, *Developmental Tasks and Education* (New York: Longman, 1948); Jean Piaget (with Barbel Inhelder), *The Growth of Logical Thinking* (New York: Basic Books, 1958); Erik Erikson, *The Challenge of Youth* (Garden City, New York: Anchor Books, 1963) and *Identity, Youth, and Crisis* (New York: W. W. Norton, 1968); D. W. Winnicott, *The Child, the Family, and the Outside World* (Baltimore, Md.: Penguin, 1964) and *Playing and Reality* (New York: Tavistock, 1971); Anna Freud (with Joseph Goldstein and Albert Solnit), *Beyond the Best Interests of the Child* (New York: Free Press, 1979); and Peter Heller, *A Child Analysis with Anna Freud* (Madison, Conn.: International Universities Press, 1990).

16. Kenneth Keniston, *Youth and Dissent* (New York: Harcourt, Brace, Jovanovich, 1960).

17. See Stuart Hall and Tony Jefferson, eds., *Resistance through Rituals: Youth Subcultures in Post-war Britain* (London: Hutchinson, 1976); Dick Hebdige, *Subculture: The Meaning of Style* (London: Methuen, 1979) and *Hiding in the Light* (London: Methuen, 1993); and Angela McRobbie, *Feminism and Youth Culture: From "Jackie" to "Just Seventeen"* (London: Macmillan, 1991).

18. See Griffin, *Representations of Youth*, pp. 196–214. For examples of the "pathology" approach, see Geoffrey Pearson, *Hooligan: A History of Respectable Fears* (New York: Schocken Books, 1983), and Jon Lewis, *The Road to Romance and Ruin: Teen Films and Youth Culture* (New York and London: Routledge, 1992). More recent teen studies include Grace Palladino, *Teenagers: An American History* (New York: Basic Books, 1996), and Lucy Rollin, *Twentieth-Century Teen Culture by the Decades: A Reference Guide* (Westport, Conn.: Greenwood Press, 1999).

19. William S. Loiry, *The Impact of Youth: A History of Children and Youth with Recommendations for the Future* (Sarasota, Fla.: Loiry Publishing House, 1984), pp. 223–245.

20. Douglas Coupland, *Generation X: Tales for an Accelerated Culture* (New York: St. Martin's Press, 1991).

21. This elongation of youth, or more specifically the delay of adulthood, is dis-

cussed in broader social terms in Marcia Mogelonsky, "The Rocky Road to Adulthood," *American Demographics* 18, no. 5 (May 1996): 26–35, 56.

22. See Susan Littwin, *The Postponed Generation: Why America's Grown-Up Kids Are Growing Up Later* (New York: Morrow, 1986), and Karen Ritchie, *Marketing to Generation X* (New York: Lexington Books, 1995). Barbara Schneider and David Stevenson have conducted an extensive longitudinal study that questions the Generation X notion of youth in *The Ambitious Generation: America's Teenagers, Motivated but Directionless* (New Haven: Yale University Press, 2000).

23. Mary Pipher, *Reviving Ophelia: Saving the Selves of Adolescent Girls* (New York: Ballantine, 1994). Also see Sara Shandler, *Ophelia Speaks: Adolescent Girls Write about Their Search for Self* (New York: Harper Perennial, 1999); William Pollack, *Real Boys: Rescuing Our Sons from the Myths of Boyhood* (New York: Owl Books, 1999); and Rachel Simmons, *Odd Girl Out: The Hidden Culture of Aggression in Girls* (New York: Harcourt Brace, 2002).

24. Kenneth Keniston, "Youth: A 'New' Stage of Life," in *Youth and Culture: A Human-Development Approach,* ed. Hazel V. Kraemer (Monterey, Calif.: Brooks/Cole Publishing, 1974), p. 103.

25. A classic example of the moral concerns raised about children's exposure to movies in the early twentieth century is Jane Addams's "The House of Dreams" from her book *The Spirit of Youth and the City Streets* (1909), reprinted in *The Movies in Our Midst: Documents in the Cultural History of Film in America,* ed. Gerald Mast (Chicago: University of Chicago Press, 1982), pp. 72–78. A plethora of studies claiming the negative influence of movies on children then appeared throughout the twenties and thirties, including the infamous Payne Fund studies, although rarely did these analyses consider the image of youth presented in film, being more concerned with how youth could emulate supposedly immoral behaviors of adults onscreen. See Garth S. Jowett, Ian C. Jarvie, and Kathryn H. Fuller, eds., *Children and the Movies: Media Influence and the Payne Fund Controversy* (New York: Cambridge University Press, 1996).

26. See Loiry, *The Impact of Youth,* p. 135; and Griffin, *Representations of Youth,* pp. 18–23.

27. The actual Paramount ruling can be found in *United States v. Paramount Pictures, Inc.,* 334 U.S. 131, 166 (1948). The "Miracle Decision" is *Burstyn v. Wilson,* 343 U.S. 495 (1952).

28. Richard Staehling, "From *Rock around the Clock* to *The Trip:* The Truth about Teen Movies," *Rolling Stone,* Dec. 27, 1969; reprinted in *Kings of the Bs: Working within the Hollywood System,* ed. Todd McCarthy and Charles Flynn (New York: Dutton, 1975), p. 230.

29. For an account of these films, see Alan Betrock, *The I Was a Teenage Juvenile Delinquent Rock 'n' Roll Horror Beach Party Movie Book: A Complete Guide to the Teen Exploitation Film, 1954–1969* (New York: St. Martin's Press, 1986).

30. See Geoffrey T. Holtz, *Welcome to the Jungle: The Why Behind "Generation X"* (New York: St. Martin's Griffin, 1995), pp. 69–70.

31. Janet Weeks, "Hollywood is Seeing Teen," *USA Today,* December 22,

1997, p. D1. See also "Media Taps into Zit-geist," by Leonard Klady and Dan Cox, *Variety*, February 22–28, 1999, p. 1, in which Klady provides a "Teen Screen Time Line" from 1955 to 1998 that testifies to the decline in teen films during the late eighties—he mentions no "key events in the life of juve pics" from 1984 to 1992, the longest gap in the forty-three years he covers. This supposedly fallow period nonetheless contained such significant films as *The Breakfast Club, Dirty Dancing, Say Anything . . . , Heathers,* and *Boyz N the Hood.*

32. Chris Nashawaty, "The New Teen Age," *Entertainment Weekly,* November 14, 1997, pp. 24–35. See also Mark Singer, "Youth," *Sight and Sound* 8, no. 5 (June 1998): 5–7; Josh Young, "They're All That," *Entertainment Weekly,* March 12, 1999, pp. 20–29; and Kay Dickinson, "Pop, Speed, and the 'MTV Aesthetic' in Recent Teen Films," *Scope* (2001), online at <http//www.nottingham.ac.uk/film/journal/articles/pop-speed-and-mtv.htm>.

33. A very small number of feature films directed by teens have thus far found their way to theatrical or video release, only one of which, *Straight out of Brooklyn* (1991) by Matty Rich, garnered any wide attention. However, Harmony Korine was still a teen when he wrote the moneymaking *Kids,* and as this book goes to press, the film *Purgatory House* is scheduled to go into release, written by and starring fourteen-year-old Celeste Davis. Mary Kearney's work on youth filmmaking has been promising in its suggestion that we may soon witness the evolution of popular films written and directed by teens, perhaps even features; her book *Producing Girls: Female Youth as Media Producers* is forthcoming.

31. Global Noir: Genre Film in the Age of Transnationalism

DAVID DESSER

"What works in New York also works in Brussels, Hong Kong and Tokyo," said former Citicorp CEO John Reed in a discussion of global consumerism.[1] An examination of crime films of recent years similarly reveals that what works in Hollywood also works in Brussels, Hong Kong, and Tokyo, not to mention London, Paris, and Seoul. Sometimes termed "neo-noir," crime films of the last two decades produced in global cities for global markets reveal startling similarities of style, theme, and characterization. Basic genre theory tells us that if something works, commercial cinema will make it again and again, but basic genre theory arose to account for nationally specific genres. Neo-noir, or what I am calling global noir, is a transnational genre, with examples appearing literally across the globe. This essay will examine global noir from the point of view of transnational filmmaking, cross-cultural influences, and the idea of global culture. Issues to be discussed include transnational capital and cultural flows, worldwide film distribution, and the creation of a global culture that can produce and consume films as from a single, formerly "national" source. One particularly important question to ask is, if classic film noir was said to respond to then-contemporary issues in American culture and society, can we account for the transnational "neo-noir" or global noir in terms of contemporary issues in global culture and society?

NOIR AND THE POSTCLASSICAL CINEMA

Film noir is a notoriously difficult genre to classify and define. In semiotic terms, it appears to be a signifier without a true signified, a sign without a referent. Unlike, say, the musical, the western, and the horror film, classical Hollywood had no genre which it called "film noir." It was defined retrospectively by film critics (in France), thus making it a "critical" genre at best and not an industrial or popular genre. Films in the noir canon (however it is defined) were at the time of their production generally understood as crime films, or thrillers, or detective stories. Even as a retrospective genre it is open to various terminology, such as Frank Krutnik's all-encompassing "criminal-adventure thriller."[2] Despite its ambiguous status as a genre, it has a critical currency and a contemporary understanding. Notes Steve Neale, ". . . as a result of the growing ubiquity of the term, and as a result of the fashion for producing films which draw on its image, film noir has a generic status it originally did not possess in the past."[3] In other words, *film noir* is now a term available for use by critics, scholars, and, most important, audiences, at least those of a certain sophistication.

As noir came to be named, defined, and debated, postclassical Hollywood filmmakers began to use the noir canon, often by returning to the literary sources of film noir—Raymond Chandler, in particular, but also Dashiell Hammett, James M. Cain, David Goodis, Patricia Highsmith, and Jim Thompson, among others. Interestingly, if film noir was thought to be subversive in its classical mode, subversions of noir appeared to be even more subversive in their postclassical appearance, as in *The Long Goodbye* (Robert Altman, 1973) and *Chinatown* (Roman Polanski, 1974).[4] By the 1980s, remaking classic noirs (*The Postman Always Rings Twice* [Bob Rafelson, 1981], *D.O.A.* [Rocky Morton and Annabel Jankel, 1988], and *Against All Odds* [Taylor Hackford, 1984], an updating of *Out of the Past* [Jacques Tourneur, 1947]), or otherwise deliberately recalling noir (Lawrence Kasdan's *Body Heat* [1981] is a gloss on noir much the way his *Silverado* [1985] is a gloss on the western) had become commonplace. By the 1990s, this tendency had become so noticeable that critics categorized a new group of noirs as "neo-noir," with some critics including all postclassical noir in this category, and others limiting it to a group of films appearing in the nineties. Thus J. P. Telotte links *King of New York* (Abel Ferrara, 1990), *Bad Lieutenant* (Ferrara, 1992), *Romeo Is Bleeding* (Peter Medak, 1993), and *Pulp Fiction* (Quentin Tarantino, 1994) to each other as a group in a lengthy discussion of *Reservoir Dogs* (Tarantino, 1992). That these five films were directed by only three directors should be noted; nevertheless, this is a significant list of films, considering both the box-office mastery of the Tarantino efforts and the controversy over those directed by Abel Ferrara. Alternately, Manohla Dargis names *One False Move* (Carl Franklin, 1991) and *Guncrazy* (Tamara Davis, 1992) along with *Romeo Is Bleeding* and *Reservoir Dogs* in his definition of neo-noir, which he calls a new "pulp" cinema.[5] The point here, then, is not to debate the existence of noir as a genre, but rather, to note that noir has entered the consciousness, so to speak, of filmmakers, film critics, and film audiences to such an extent that a neo- or post-noir is possible to identify and discuss.

As these comments suggest, the canon of neo-noir has tended to include mostly Anglo-American films. It seems to have been defined retrospec-

92. *Reservoir Dogs:* An influential example of neo-noir.

tively, much like noir itself, but also rather more immediately, as is typical of our postmodern moment, especially for a genre often said to be
postmodernist. Thus by the mid-nineties it was possible to understand
that a new noir or neo-noir had arisen and to claim membership for such
films as *After Dark, My Sweet* (James Foley, 1990), *The Grifters* (Stephen
Frears, 1990), *Basic Instinct* (Paul Verhoeven, 1992), *Final Analysis* (Phil
Joanou, 1992), and *Night and the City* (Irwin Winkler, 1992) along with
those films named above, especially *One False Move, Reservoir Dogs,*
and *Romeo Is Bleeding.*[6] That 1992 seems to have been something of a
watershed year (at least six films, to which one might also add the far less
well known *Laws of Gravity* [Nick Gomez, 1992]) might be worth exploring at some later date. Meanwhile, it is sufficient to note a good deal
of critical unanimity around the notion of neo-noir and the centrality of
these films to its canon.[7] The one exception to the strictly Anglo-American canon of neo-noir seems to be John Woo's *Hard-Boiled* (also 1992).

   With the success of *Pulp Fiction,* neo-noir extended itself later into the
nineties, with *Pulp Fiction,* as such, becoming the standard of generic
definition. Films in its immediate wake are almost too numerous to mention, but surely *Things to Do in Denver When You're Dead* (Gary Fleder,
1995), *2 Days in the Valley* (John Herzfeld, 1996), and *Lock, Stock and*

Two Smoking Barrels (Guy Ritchie, 1998) would immediately spring to mind, as might *The Usual Suspects* (Bryan Singer, 1995), *Suicide Kings* (Peter O'Fallon, 1997), and *The Limey* (Steven Soderbergh, 1999).[8] But it is at this time, post-1994, that we need to extend the neo-noir canon to include what I am calling global noir. For the success of *Pulp Fiction* not only influenced a British brand of noir, but extended the noir vision virtually around the world.

The presence of a kind of noir across the globe has been noted by James Naremore in his claim that noir has been apparent in Japanese cinema since the Second World War, as, for instance, in the art cinema of Akira Kurosawa, with films such as *The Bad Sleep Well* (1960) and *High and Low* (1963). It has been apparent, too, in Japanese "pop cinema," such as the films of Seijun Suzuki (*Tokyo Drifter*, 1966; *Branded to Kill*, 1967), whose work Naremore describes as "bizarrely styled movies about prostitutes and contract killers, somewhat comparable to the tabloid thrillers of Samuel Fuller."[9] But that's the extent of the discussion of noir in the Japanese cinema. Similarly, Hong Kong cinema rates merely a paragraph in Naremore's book. Here the references are to Wong Kar-wai's *Chungking Express* (1995), which is "inflected by the French New Wave's fascination with noir," and John Woo's *The Killer* (1989), which synthesizes "generic conventions from Hollywood thrillers . . . with over-the-top flourishes from martial arts movies and Far Eastern musicals."[10] This tension between recognizing a kind of noir in Asia while disavowing any "Asian" particularity in noir—Kurosawa makes "art" noir; Suzuki is like Sam Fuller; Wong's film is a variation on French New Wave; Woo derives his structures from Hollywood—is one which denies us the ability to see noir's reach beyond merely a few isolated examples.

For we might add to this ever-growing list of neo-noir films such films as *Score* (Muroga Atsushi, 1995), *Shark Skin Man and Peach Hip Girl* (Ishii Katsuhito, 1998), *Adrenaline Drive* (Yaguchi Shinobu, 1999), and *City of Lost Souls* (Miike Takashi, 2000) from Japan; from Hong Kong we would have to add *Full Alert* (Ringo Lam, 1997), *Sleepless Town* (Lee Chi-ngai, 1998), and, arguably, dozens of others (including the immediate origins of global noir, as we will see below). Similarly, *Amores Perros* (Alejandro Gonzalez Inarritu, 2001) from Mexico, France's *Total Western* (Eric Rochant, 2000), and Korea's *Nowhere to Hide* (Lee Myung-see, 1999) would need to be added, along with Britain's *Snatch* (Guy Ritchie, 2000) and *Sexy Beast* (Jonathan Glazer, 2000).[11] James Naremore would have us add films like *Foreign Land* (Walter Salles and Daniela Thomas, 1995), a Brazilian-Portuguese co-production, and *Deep Crimson* (1997), from Mexico's still overlooked master, Arturo Ripstein.[12] These films all betray the influences of *Pulp Fiction, Reservoir Dogs,* and *True Romance* (Tony Scott, 1993) in their plots of heists-gone-bad, male camaraderie, trust and betrayal, criminal couples on the run, extreme moments of violence, dark humor, and the importance of coincidence—all features, as we will see shortly, that are the hallmarks of neo-noir and its global offshoots.

What we have in the immediate year of 1992 and in the subsequent *Pulp Fiction* and its imitators is, if not a genre, then certainly a "cycle." A cycle is clearly defined by Steve Neale as "a group of films made within a specific and limited time-span and founded, for the most part, on the characteristics of individual commercial successes."[13] The success of *Reservoir Dogs, Pulp Fiction,* and *The Usual Suspects* is not to be doubted, though interestingly many of the U.S. imitators of these films fared far less well: *Things to Do in Denver When You're Dead* and *2 Days in the Valley* were hardly impressive commercial performers despite the strong cast of the former and the generally admiring reviews of the latter. The British films have all been cult hits with more than respectable box office for imports; the same is true of *Amores Perros.* The relatively wide distribution of these foreign films in the North American market speaks to the reasonable popularity of the neo-noir cycle, even if, perhaps surprisingly, none of the Hollywood films save *Basic Instinct* and *Pulp Fiction* would qualify as a blockbuster. The Asian films listed above are far less well known, but the fact that *Score, Adrenaline Drive, Sleepless Town,* and *Nowhere to Hide* are available in North America through mainstream distribution sources on VHS or DVD speaks to the transnational character of global noir.

A GENEALOGY OF GLOBAL NOIR

To some extent, film noir has always been a global genre or mode. Hollywood's tendency to import film talents made American cinema something like a global cinema in any case. American culture by the twenties was multicultural to a tremendous extent, with "newer" Americans dominating the cinematic landscape—Eastern European Jews, Irish, and Italians, especially. The ravages of World War I increased the immigration of film talent to Hollywood, at the same time enabling Hollywood to begin to dominate European and Asian markets. Noir was particularly global in its dimensions. Derived in part from German Expressionism of the 1920s, from which it gets its Rembrandt lighting and its paranoia and anxiety, and from French poetic realism, which gave noir its sense of foreboding fatality (mainly through the use of the flashback structure) and, of course, the femme fatale, noir was always somehow more European than Hollywood. Both German and French directors seeking escape from the political nightmare of Europe in the thirties continued Hollywood's global outreach and had a significant impact on the globalization of Hollywood itself. Thus, that neo-noir or global noir manifests a circulation of imagery and influence across national boundaries is hardly surprising and very much in keeping with noir's origins.

The hybridity of neo-noir and the international dimensions of global noir seem to derive from what has been called postclassical or New Hollywood. Thus, the common wisdom has it that

> . . . New Hollywood can be distinguished from the old by the hybridity of its genres and films. Most argue in addition that this hybridity is governed by the multi-media synergies characteristic of the New Hollywood, by the mixing and recycling of new and old and low art and high art media products in the modern (or post-modern) world, and by the propensity for allusion and pastiche that is said to characterize contemporary artistic production.[14]

But, as just explained, noir was always a genre characterized by hybridity (mixing American pulp fiction with German and French cinematic sources and styles), and so neo-noir need not surprise us by its use of allusion and pastiche or its hybrid nature. In addition, as Neale points out, ". . . allusion, pastiche and hybridity are not the same thing, nor are they as extensive or as exclusive to New Hollywood as is sometimes implied."[15] Janet Staiger, though not referencing Neale, makes very much the same point about genre and notions of hybridity: ". . . Hollywood films have never been 'pure'—that is, easily arranged into categories. All that has been pure has been sincere attempts to find order among variety."[16] Similarly, Staiger finds much continuity between classical and New Hollywood, though she prefers the terms *Fordian* and *post-Fordian* Hollywood. The main point, however, is that we need not debate the existence of film noir, its purity, or its hybridity, but rather admit that both filmmakers and film consumers have acknowledged a kind of "noir" and that this noir has a global dimension and impact. Perhaps it is time, that is, not to move beyond notions of genre and hybridity, but to move beyond notions of "Hollywood."

There are three strands of neo-noir, only two of which, it seems to me, very much fit into global noir, but only one of which will concern me here to any extent. Space does not permit a full analysis of two of these strands, and what I will identify as the third strand seems much more widespread and interestingly intertextual. The first strand, which seems to me not a part of global noir, but very much in the mixture of Anglo-American neo-noir, might be called "The Stranger and the Femme Fatale." Such films concern men who wander into situations where they come across a woman to whom they are immediately and fatally attracted. Such films in this mode are most clearly derived from or reminiscent of classic noir such as *Double Indemnity* (Billy Wilder, 1944) and *The Postman Always Rings Twice* (Tay Garnett, 1946). Indeed, *Double Indemnity* forms the basis of a film like *Body Heat,* and *The Postman Always Rings Twice,* as mentioned above, was overtly remade. Such neo-noirs as *After Dark, My Sweet, Romeo Is Bleeding, Red Rock West* (John Dahl, 1992), *The Last Seduction* (Dahl, 1994), and *U-Turn* (Oliver Stone, 1997) seem the fundamental films in this subcycle of neo-noir. Derived not only from classic noir, but also often from the pulp novels which both inspired and were contemporary with classic noir, these films raise the stakes of their sexual display and, as B. Ruby Rich observes, oddly empower but simultaneously demonize these duplicitous women far more than does classic noir.[17] For various culturally specific reasons this subcycle of neo-noir, where the wiles of a femme fatale drive a weak man to murder, has not been much in evidence outside of the Hollywood context. The sexual display, for instance, would little fit into the Hong Kong cinema, whose mainstream films are, given their often graphic violent content, rather tame in their sexual content. Alternatively, we might understand this strand of neo-noir as particularly American or European (or at least French), as witness the critical acclaim meted out at the 2001 Cannes Film Festival for David Lynch's *Mulholland Drive* and Joel and Ethan Coen's *The Man Who Wasn't There*—the latter a virtual compendium of classic noir images, bits, and characters.

A more globally oriented subcycle of neo-noir is what I would like to call "the couple on the run." The neo-noir paradigm for this mode is *True Romance.* Though it was made at the height of the astonishing neo-noir cycle (one year after the watershed of 1992), critics have surprisingly left it off the list of neo-noir. Written by Quentin Tarantino and starring many of the soon-to-be-icons of neo-noir (Christopher Walken, Dennis Hopper, Gary Oldman, Samuel L. Jackson, even Patricia Arquette and Brad Pitt, perhaps), *True Romance* makes no secret of its cinematic predecessors in the kind of self-consciousness and pastiche that are hallmarks of Tarantino, if not of all neo-noir. These films, which also include *Kalifornia* (Dominic Sena, 1993) and *Natural Born Killers* (Oliver Stone, 1994; script by Tarantino), focus on a newly formed couple on the run from gangsters, the law, or both. Their cinematic precursors are films like Nicholas Ray's *They Live by Night* (1949), *Bonnie and Clyde* (Arthur Penn, 1967), and Robert Altman's gloss on both, *Thieves Like Us* (1974). Terrence Malick's *Badlands* (1975), with its high quotient of violence and its particularly piquant understanding of the youthful nature of its protagonists, and thus its subsequent cult appeal, is undoubtedly the touchstone of this strand. *Adrenaline Drive, Sleepless Town,* and *City of Lost Souls* are among the Asian variations on this cycle, though others could be mentioned, particularly *Hysteric* (2000), a Japanese derivation from *Badlands* and *Natural Born Killers,* though for some the couple lacks even the remotest sense of decency or audience sympathy. Given Tarantino's avowed and obvious

93. *True Romance:* The "couple on the run" cycle of neo-noir (Christian Slater and Patricia Arquette).

interest in and influence by the French New Wave, Godard in particular, one could also claim that films like *A bout de souffle* (1959) and *Band of Outsiders* (1964, from whose French title, *Bande à part*, Tarantino named his production company), along with Truffaut's *Shoot the Piano Player* (1961), are also the global precursors to this subcycle of global noir. Yet we would be remiss if we did not acknowledge the *nouvelle vague*'s debts to classic American noir and French noir of the fifties, especially the films of Jean-Pierre Melville. Thus, given the hyperbole and pastiche of the New Wave films, one could claim, again, that neo-noir was somehow always already "postmodern."

The third strand of neo-noir, which I would like to call the "heist gone bad" film, is also perhaps the most globally oriented of global noir. Its immediate cinematic inauguration may be found in *Reservoir Dogs,* with

One False Move preceding it at its moment of origin. And it is this sub-genre or cycle within neo/global noir where we find the greatest number of films and the most interesting of them, including *Pulp Fiction; Things to Do in Denver When You're Dead; 2 Days in the Valley; The Usual Suspects; Suicide Kings; Lock, Stock and Two Smoking Barrels; Score; Shark Skin Man and Peach Hip Girl; Full Alert; Amores Perros;* and *Nowhere to Hide,* among many others. More lately, Hollywood has turned to big-budget variations as well: *The Score* (Frank Oz, 2001), *Ocean's Eleven* (Steven Soderbergh, 2001), and *Heist* (David Mamet, 2001). Most of these films are characterized by the predominantly all-male group of criminals involved in the planning and aftermath of a heist or crime caper, which invariably goes wrong due to internal deceit or betrayal or outside forces aligned against the protagonists. Critics have pointed to Stanley Kubrick's *The Killing* (1956, cowritten by Jim Thompson) as the clearest precursor to Tarantino's *Reservoir Dogs,* along with *The Asphalt Jungle* (John Huston, 1950, itself an obvious and crucial precursor to Kubrick's film, relying on the same star, Sterling Hayden, and the same basic premise). Jean-Pierre Melville's *Bob le flambeur* (1955) is also a clear precursor with its suited heroes and narrow ties. Yet the most direct and immediate precursor to *Reservoir Dogs* is the Hong Kong film *City on Fire* (Ringo Lam, 1987). Indeed, some few years after its release (after the success of *Pulp Fiction,* in fact), it was "discovered" that Tarantino had "ripped off" the plot of *City on Fire* (undercover cop infiltrates a gang of jewel thieves and becomes friends with one of the gang members) without crediting it as a source. That Hong Kong had for years "reworked" Hollywood films in title and/or plot was one element in Tarantino's defense: turnabout is fair play.[18] In fact, Tarantino borrowed what is perhaps the most famous set piece in *Reservoir Dogs,* a three-way standoff with raised guns, directly from *City on Fire,* adding ammunition to the charge of "rip-off." But all is fair in film as well as in love and war, and it is this originary moment in *City on Fire* to which we now turn.

CITIES ON FIRE

I want to claim that *City on Fire* is the direct precursor to *Reservoir Dogs,* which is itself the originary moment of the "heist-gone-bad" cycle of neo-noir. Obviously, as just mentioned, *Reservoir Dogs* owes something (a good deal, in fact) to *The Asphalt Jungle* and *The Killing.* Yet there is a period of thirty-six years between Kubrick's film and Tarantino's derivation, whereas there is only a half-decade between Tarantino's effort and Lam's Hong Kong precursor. As is well known, Tarantino's film education came through his work as a clerk in a video store, where he could experience the cinematic past as well as global cinema's more current offerings. The point is not whether Tarantino saw *City on Fire* on video (which he did), thus leading to the direct inspiration for *Reservoir Dogs,* or whether and when he saw *The Asphalt Jungle* and *The Killing.* Rather, the point is to note that American neo-noir in the period between 1956 and 1992 was not given to reworking heist or caper films. The American noir that immediately precedes neo-noir—seventies and eighties films like *The Long Goodbye, Chinatown, Body Heat,* and *Against All Odds*—is derived from the hard-boiled tradition of noir featuring a private investigator and the femme fatale, or the stranger and the deadly dame. Thus in inaugurating a new cycle of noir, a neo-noir which would have global dimensions and impact, Tarantino was himself drawing upon a film that already existed in the global marketplace, Hong Kong's *City on Fire.*

This is not the place to rehearse what should already be well known: that Hong Kong cinema was heavily dependent on transnational distribution; that the territory itself, though highly geared toward films, particularly its own, could hardly support a world-class cinema; and that, thus, overseas markets (Taiwan and southeast Asia, especially, but also Korea, Japan, and diasporic Chinese communities in the West) were necessary to its survival and success. Similarly, Hong Kong's borrowings in its Golden Age of the 1960s–1970s included a substantial importation of talent and structures from Japan and a strong reliance on Hollywood modes and genres. Thus, by the 1980s, Hong Kong provided Hollywood with stiff competition in Asian and African markets and was something like a "global cinema" along the lines of Hollywood itself. It was only until recently that, unlike in most film-consuming nations or localities, Hong Kong films performed better in Hong Kong than did Hollywood films.[19]

Critics have perhaps offered too much regarding Hong Kong's derivations from Hollywood, French, and Japanese cinema and too little regarding the specifically local context and content of many of Hong Kong's finest films. *City on Fire,* for instance, was produced in the wake of the phenomenal success of John Woo's *A Better Tomorrow* (1986). *A Better Tomorrow* set the tone, literally, for the Hong Kong police/gangster thrillers that would bring worldwide fame to John Woo as well as Ringo Lam and add the police thriller to the martial arts film as Hong Kong's global contributions to genre cinema. Loosely based on *Story of a Discharged Prisoner,* a very famous Cantonese-dialect film of 1967 by influential director Patrick Lung Kong, *A Better Tomorrow* also shows the direct influence of *Le Samourai* (1967), Melville's Japanese-inspired, ultra-hip story of a lone hitman, especially in the film's lighting and the costuming of Mark (Chow Yun-fat).[20] Woo has stated his own sense of how he has been influenced by earlier films and filmmakers: "Melville dealt a great deal with themes of friendship and honor. The characters will give their lives for their friends. Kurosawa gets into great moral arguments in his films . . ." [21] Clearly, too, Woo draws on the kind of male camaraderie and potential disruption of the all-male group represented by women that is seen most particularly in the films of Howard Hawks. Alternately, however, perceptive critics like Lisa Odham Stokes and Michael Hoover are at pains to demonstrate that much of the value system in Woo's films derives from traditional Chinese culture, including Confucianism. The influence on Woo of martial arts master Chang Cheh is also highlighted, Woo himself claiming, "I learned a lot [from Chang]. I learned how to manage action scenes." [22]

Given the nature of Hong Kong film production practices, alluded to earlier, it is no effort to see *City on Fire* as the direct result of the tremendous success of *A Better Tomorrow*. Filmed over a scant six weeks shortly after the release of Woo's films, with only thirty actual shooting days, *City on Fire* was written and directed by Ringo Lam to provide an overt social critique of Hong Kong perhaps lacking in Woo's more stylized effort. [23] Thus Lam, utilizing the same star as Woo (Chow Yun-fat), helped drive a genre very much in the making. Moreover, in addition to refining a genre, sometimes called the "heroic bloodshed" cycle, both *A Better Tomorrow* and *City on Fire* have been linked to the overall anxiety provoked in Hong Kong by the 1984 Joint Sino-British Declaration, which promised the handover, or return, of Hong Kong to the mainland in 1997. The point here is not to reproduce any of the now-lengthy criticism of Hong Kong cinema, which reads much of its post-1984 output in the light of "crisis" or of a "déjà disparu," a culture already disappearing due to pressures of colonialism and postcolonialism and the threat of the mainland's takeover, but rather to note the specificity of Hong Kong cinema, its local concerns marking its cinematic particularities. [24] Stokes and Hoover, for instance, note that "violent street crime in Hong Kong, including intentional homicide, assault, rape, robbery and theft, escalated between 1981 and 1986 . . ." [25] Thus, for all the influences and confluences apparent in mid-eighties Hong Kong heroic bloodshed films, local concerns, whether the impending handover to the mainland or increased fears of rising crime, have just as much salience for the genre as the impact of the film language and techniques of gangster movie mavens from Jean-Pierre Melville to Martin Scorsese, western mavericks like Sergio Leone and Sam Peckinpah, the samurai epics of Akira Kurosawa, and the yakuza movies of Takakura Ken in developing style and enhancing characterization and themes. [26]

CINEPHILIA

James Naremore notes, "Noir in the late twentieth century spreads across virtually every national boundary and every form of communication, including museum retrospectives, college courses, parodies, remakes, summertime blockbusters, mass-market paperbacks, experimental literature and painting, made-for-TV films . . . and soft-core 'erotic thrillers' that go directly to video stores."[27] He is alluding to the transmission of culture across a variety of national and cultural contexts and across various media, a situation that has led to a wide-ranging intertextual relay where the body of films, classic noir, is the referent, which then circulates across the new body of films, neo-noir, which then circulates in the global marketplace of Hollywood distribution, video-tape exchanges (fan-based, pirated, or legally distributed), and the ubiquitous availability in Asia of the inexpensive, often-pirated, VCD format (Video Compact Disc). This not only allows filmmakers a chance to experience a variety of cinematic offerings, but allows them, too, to recognize that their audience can participate in this intertextual loop. Whether or not, then, films grow out of a specific cultural context—something claimed, controversially or questionably, for classic noir or, as I have just done, for Hong Kong neo-noir —films certainly grow out of a specifically cinematic context, what I would like to call cinephilia. Here we might recall Janet Staiger's perceptive comments regarding intertextuality: "Research on intertextuality has focused on types of intertextuality, but little work has been accomplished on the functions of intertextuality for the reader or why a reader might be primed or cued to take up a particular function."[28] Thus, critics, in coming to terms with neo-noir, cite *Reservoir Dogs* and *Pulp Fiction* as often as or more often than they cite the specific national or timely origins of many neo-noirs. But fans, too, process these films along intertextual lines. Note, for instance, this discussion of *Shark Skin Man and Peach Hip Girl*:

> Based on a Japanese Manga . . . it's basically a road movie . . . If you're a fan of the films of Luc Besson, Tarantino, Boyle, et al. (the *Trainspotting* crew), the Coens, John Woo, Ringo Lam, and Tsui Hark, then you have GOT to see this movie. . . . Tarantino was in the audience when I saw this movie, and when [director] Ishii answered questions at the end of the film, and someone asked him who influenced him, he grinned at QT [Quentin Tarantino], and said . . . something like "I think you know the answer to that."[29]

A specific genre—the road movie—is being invoked, as well as a host of filmmakers whom the writer believes to be relevant to this film and who can act as referents by way of recommending it to potential fans. Moreover, the director is allowed to claim his inspiration, which, as we will see shortly for this film, is undeniable.

The same thing is no less true for *Score*, another Japanese film claimed in this circulation of neo- or global noir. Writes someone on the Internet Movie Database: "*Score* is a derivative Japanese crime film, borrowing liberally from, among others, *Hard-Boiled* [Woo, 1992], *Hard Target*

[Woo, 1993], *Reservoir Dogs, Trespass* [Walter Hill, 1992], *Natural Born Killers* and *The Getaway* [Sam Peckinpah, 1972]." This, however, is hardly a damning critique, as the writer goes on to say that the film is nevertheless very much enjoyable along the lines of "the grade-B crime films that Hollywood (and Hong Kong) used to produce on a regular basis." [30] This latter is a very interesting comment, for it links global noir in a film circuit reminiscent of more localized production—B-movies from the classic era of noir and Hong Kong's even lower-budget films intended strictly for specialized, regional consumption. Too, this Japanese film is claimed as the successor of both Hong Kong (*Hard-Boiled*) and Hollywood moviemaking, including an already hybridized production, *Hard Target,* Hong Kong director John Woo's first American film. Some of the intertextual references of *Score* are hardly the province of the specialized cinephiliac. After all, one of the characters fancies himself as Doc Holliday and sees the gang of jewel thieves as the Clanton gang at the OK Corral. Naming one of the gang members "Tequila," Chow Yun-fat's character in *Hard-Boiled,* is admittedly closer to fan-boy mode, while the hero's name, "Chance," seems the most intertextually allusive of all. The name of John Wayne's character in *Rio Bravo* (1959), with its OK Corral–like final shootout, "Chance" is also very much characteristic of the narrative and thematic proclivities of neo- and global noir, with their skewed chronologies, multiple storylines, and coincidental, chance, and arbitrary encounters linking the timelines and narrative threads.

The impulse toward cinephilia—that is, the ability and necessity of acknowledging the intertextual chain of references, borrowings, and reworkings—may be at the heart of global noir. For it involves filmmakers and film audiences in a circuit of acknowledgments—the ability of filmmakers to make references and their confidence in the audience's recognition of them. One such intertextual chain that requires this kind of acknowledgment can be clearly shown by the use and subsequent reuse of one particular sequence across three separate films, moving from Hong Kong to Hollywood to Japan.

Arguably the finest moment in Quentin Tarantino's *Reservoir Dogs* is the three-way, guns-drawn standoff between Mr. White (Harvey Keitel), Joe Cabot (Lawrence Tierney), and Nice Guy Eddie (Chris Penn), as Mr. Orange (Tim Roth) lies bleeding to death on the floor of the warehouse. It is an extraordinary moment, perhaps recalling the three-way gunfight in Sergio Leone's operatic *The Good, the Bad, and the Ugly* (1967), but given its modern-day context and the unusual nature of the scene, it works to create far more tension and seems far more original. Yet it is derived, almost in its entirety, from Ringo Lam's *City on Fire.* For not only does Lam's film similarly feature a three-way standoff—Fu (Danny

94. Tony Leung and Chow Yun-fat (r.) in *Hard-Boiled*: Global noir from Hong Kong.

Lee) points his gun at the Triad boss (Fong Yau), who is pointing his gun at Ko Chow (Chow Yun-fat), only to have a gun pointed at him by the second in command—but it is motivated by the same plot point, the boss's (correct) belief in both films that Mr. Orange and Ko, respectively, are undercover cops. Still, it is the visualization of this scene that is most striking and most memorable. These two scenes do not end the same way: in *Reservoir Dogs* Mr. Orange manages to squeeze off a shot at Nice Guy Eddie as Mr. White kills Joe, while in *City on Fire* the standoff is interrupted by the arrival of the police outside. The different endings may be instructive as to the cultural differences between Hong Kong and the United States—the latter more nihilistic and interior—while also attesting to the creativity of Tarantino, whose film is quite different in structure and approach. But it is the visualization of this particular scene which concerns me here, for it is taken up very much as is in Japan's *Shark Skin Man and Peach Hip Girl*. At that film's climax we again see a three-way standoff interrupted and brought to a head by a fourth party (as Mr. Orange and the police may be said to be in Tarantino's and Lam's films). Tanuki points a gun at Samehada's head, while Samehada has one leveled at Tanuki's crotch. Toshiko arrives and points a gun at Tanuki, who is then seen holding a knife to Toshiko's neck. To this standoff is added the hitman who has been more or less pursuing Samehada. This three/ four-way standoff is allowed to stand onscreen for some moments—in order, I take it, that we may appreciate its derivation from *City on Fire* and *Reservoir Dogs*. Yet it ends differently from the other two films, as Tanuki, Samehada, and the hitman all die in simultaneous gunfire, while Toshiko survives unhurt.

Is this repeated use of a multicharacter standoff merely a case of homage, as we might understand numerous obvious allusions in contemporary cinema to the cinematic past? Or is something more significant, if not necessarily profound, at work here? First of all, *City on Fire* was hardly a film classic by the time *Reservoir Dogs* was made, while *Reservoir Dogs* maintains more the status of cult than classic for *Shark Skin Man* and its fan base. Thus we might say that the films reuse what is current, what is specifically of the moment, perhaps available more to the specialized, the cult, than the better-known classics being alluded to in contemporary mainstream cinema. Similarly, these moments of overt reworking come in the context of generic play, since more is at work across these films than that one moment of repetition. For these are all films about heists, about trust and betrayal, about male camaraderie, and all feature competing or multiple storylines and, in the case of the two later films, rely on skewed chronology to tell their interlocking tales.

ADRENALINE DRIVING

It is tempting and entirely possible to understand global noir along traditional generic lines of similar plots, themes, characters, and settings—heists-gone-wrong, male camaraderie, loyalty and betrayal, young lovers on the run. But here I wish to suggest that these links, however useful, are less significant than the style, narrative and cinematic, of the films. Of greatest import are the multiple storylines, skewed chronologies, chance encounters that seem to underscore the presence of fate or destiny (or the power of coincidence, however improbable), and a shocking moment of violence, often at the start, which seems to set things in motion. In particular, a car crash is often the preferred mode or vehicle, so to speak, for inaugurating the skewed chronology and interlocking storylines.

City on Fire certainly introduces the convention of interlocking storylines, along with the plot of the heist-gone-wrong and the themes of male camaraderie, loyalty, and betrayal, to the emergent global noir. Though perhaps somewhat confusing to first-time viewers, the plot of *City on Fire* is reasonably straightforward and reasonably chronological, while the two interlocking storylines are clearly linked by the presence of Ko Chow, who (eventually) moves between the two realms of cops and crooks. Similarly, the basic plot of *Reservoir Dogs* is straightforward, the aftermath of a heist gone badly awry, while it, too, relies on its undercover cop to link its two storylines. In fact, there is far less focus on the *policier* aspects of the tale and far more on the criminal side. But *Reservoir Dogs* introduces the skewed chronology that many films to follow will favor, and it is *Pulp Fiction,* two years later, which finalizes the genre's combined use of multiple storylines, skewed chronology, and chance encounters.

In *Pulp Fiction,* the basic storyline of Jules (Samuel L. Jackson) and Vincent (John Travolta) is both separate and related to the storyline of Bruce Willis's Butch the boxer and his connection to Ving Rhames's Marsellus. Butch has a separate storyline with Marsellus (especially the absurd *Texas Chainsaw Massacre*–like homophobic nightmare) and a storyline of his own (particularly the lengthy flashback sequence with Christopher Walken's Captain Koons). The intersection of Jules and Vincent with Honey Bunny (Amanda Plummer) and Pumpkin (Tim Roth), the heroin overdose sequence, and Harvey Keitel's "cleaner" role revolving around yet another, different, storyline are in some sense tangential to what might otherwise be the story of two enforcers on the trail of a boxer who has welshed on a deal. With so many competing storylines, it is arguable that *Pulp Fiction* has completely decentered its narrative line and thus may very well be the most radical of the global noirs in this respect, though films like *Snatch* (is the heist or the boxing match the major narrative line?) and *Amores Perros* (with three distinct, though complexly interlocking stories) may also be fundamentally decentered.

The decentered narrative is not, then, simply a question of competing narrative lines, but of their often-surprising interlocking nature. Many films, after all, have multiple storylines, some of which are kept quite separate, related only by theme. Indeed, we can trace this device at least as far back as D. W. Griffith's *Intolerance* (1916). Similarly, multiple storylines which we know will converge later in a single locale are also common, as in *Dinner at Eight* (George Cukor, 1933), while multiple storylines that converge within a single locale which comprises the film's entire setting, such as *Grand Hotel* (Edmund Goulding, 1932), are not uncommon either.[31] The use of multiple storylines converging in a single locale provides the structure and thematic interest in the disaster film, where dissimilar characters with separate melodramatic concerns and singular narrative lines are joined in adversity in films like *Airport* (George Seaton, 1969), *The Poseidon Adventure* (Ronald Neame, 1972), *The Towering Inferno* (John Guillerman, 1974), and *When Time Ran Out* (James Goldstone, 1980). The difference is that global noir insists on the unrelated nature of these multiple characters. Chance, fate, or coincidence rules: a gang escaping a heist is seen by a criminal couple on the run (*Score*); a young woman running away from an abusive uncle meets up with a gangster running away from the gang he has betrayed (*Shark Skin Man and Peach Hip Girl*); two losers trying to avoid a crooked boxing promoter intersect with two other losers trying to engage in a big-time jewel theft (*Snatch*); a model in a troubled relationship drives on a street in Mexico

City only to be struck by a speeding car driven by two men trying to avoid a confrontation with crooked dogfight promoters, an accident witnessed by a hitman scoping out a case (*Amores Perros*); a woman driving a car whose brakes have been tampered with in an effort to kill her fiancé accidentally kills a nurse on her way to bring dinner to a wounded gangster in the Hong Kong film *Esprit d'amour* (William Chang, 2000). And in bringing 100,000 Deutschmarks to her careless boyfriend, Lola intersects the lives of many people along the way, changing them irrevocably in that brief instant in Tom Tykwer's *Run Lola Run* (Germany, 1998).

That many of these chance meetings, these fateful encounters, occur in or through cars, is perhaps not a coincidence either. On the shoulder of the highway, the outlaw couple sees the jewel gang driving by in *Score*; a car crash brings Samehada and Toshiko together in *Shark Skin Man*; the car crash in *Esprit d'amour* ties its three stories together, as does the even more violent crash in *Amores Perros*. The getaway car driven by the incompetent Tyrone blocks the doors of the van, thus trapping Franky Four Fingers inside and setting the confusing plot in motion in *Snatch*, while the later car accident that seems to kill Boris the Blade helps bring it to a climax. The two crashes and the near-miss in the three retellings of *Run Lola Run* signify the working of fate and coincidence in perhaps the clearest fashion. It is the automobile that best represents the post-industrial landscape of global noir, the atomization of the individual, and the imbrication of global capital in individual lives. And that these films all revolve around money—needing it, making it, stealing it—is also no coincidence.

The postindustrial landscape of globalization and the postmodern condition of the globalized individual are best represented by that city most clearly associated with the postindustrial and the postmodern, that city of cars and coincidence, of dreams and nightmares, Los Angeles. And a film that wonderfully exemplifies the multiple storylines and chance intersections of global noir, and which uses the automobile for a shocking accident that sets things in motion, is Robert Altman's *Short Cuts* (1993), made at the height of the newly emergent neo-noir. It is *Short Cuts* that may be seen as the transition between the fractured narrative of *Reservoir Dogs* and the multiple and coincidental storylines of *Pulp Fiction*. Based on separate short stories by Raymond Carver (a writer who very much grows out of the hard-boiled tradition of Raymond Chandler and, especially, Jim Thompson), *Short Cuts* blends its stories via a helicopter which links the locations and chance meetings and family ties of the characters, but the pivotal events are put in motion when Doreen's (Lily Tomlin) car accidentally strikes the Finnigan boy. We get stories, then, of the Finnigans, of Doreen and her husband, of their daughter, of the doctor treating the little boy, and so on. Los Angeles was already the site of classic noir (*Double Indemnity*) and the early films of neo-noir (*The Long Good-bye, Chinatown*) and becomes so again with *Short Cuts, True Romance, Pulp Fiction, 2 Days in the Valley,* and *The Limey.* By virtue of its association with Hollywood, its atomized neighborhoods and individuals, its ever-changing landscape ("there is no there there"), Los Angeles is the global city par excellence.

But is there an interchangeability of global cities? The Japanese film *Score* wants to convince us that it is set in the United States when actually it was filmed in the Philippines. The transnational characters in and of *City of Lost Souls,* a Japanese-Brazilian protagonist and his Chinese girl-friend, make their way from Brazil to Japan. Triads and yakuza populate *Sleepless Town,* while Hong Kong is the crossroads for the entire world, it seems, in *Chungking Express.* The director who best recognizes the transnational character of contemporary culture and cinema, and who did much to impact the style and theme of global noir, is Jim Jarmusch, whose *Night on Earth* (1991) acknowledges the interchangeability of global cities (Los Angeles, New York, Paris, Rome, Helsinki) and the concept of the simultaneity of far-flung events. Perhaps in our search for the sources of global noir, Jim Jarmusch can stand at the base. His *Stranger Than Paradise* (1984) focuses on Eastern European immigrants to the United States, told in a style derived from Ozu; Roberto Benigni is some-how implicated in the coincidental events and chance meetings in *Down by Law* (1986). *Ghost Dog* (1999) finds *Rashomon* (Akira Kurosawa, 1950) and samurai culture alive and well in a postmodern ghetto located somewhere, anywhere, in the "Industrial State." Interlocking stories, chance encounters, the retelling of simultaneous events through skewed chronology—all come together in Jarmusch's *Mystery Train* (1989), with the Italian, Japanese, and African-American characters somehow converging in a most archetypically American city of pop and kitsch, Elvis Presley's Memphis. A gunshot, not a car crash, links the tales, but otherwise this deft combination of melodrama and film noir clearly anticipates the explosion of neo-noir just a few years later.

CONCLUSION

Arjun Appadurai's conception of "mediascape" is highly suggestive of the ways and means by which a global film genre (or genres) has arisen. He writes:

> Mediascapes refers both to the distribution of the electronic capabilities to produce and disseminate information (newspapers, magazines, television stations, and film-production studios) . . . and to the images of the world created by these media. . . . What is most important about these mediascapes is that they provide (especially in their television, film, and cassette forms) large and

complex repertoires of images, narratives and ethnoscapes [landscapes of people] to viewers throughout the world.[32]

Thus a mediascape not only links divergent peoples and cultures, but enables diverse cultures to be assimilated alongside and in conjunction with more strictly local or regional ideas, images, and ideologies.

There is no doubt that Hollywood's ability to disperse its cinema internationally accounts for the impact of *Reservoir Dogs* and *Pulp Fiction* on global noir, despite its immediate beginnings in Hong Kong. But this should not blind us to the influence of Hong Kong on Hollywood cinema, or to the influence of Hong Kong cinema on the rest of world cinema. Arguably, for instance, Hong Kong cinema has had greater influence on the still hugely popular Bollywood cinema than Hollywood cinema has, and it certainly has proven as influential on Korean cinema as has Hollywood, if not more so. As well, the influence of Japanese manga and anime on Hong Kong cinema should not be overlooked, nor should their impact on U.S. television and comic books.

The transnational flow of capital has not only meant the transnational flow of culture, but also the transnational flow of people. Multiculturalism is hardly unique to the United States; global cities like London, Paris, Tokyo, Seoul, Hong Kong, and Mexico City are fully as populated by multinationals as they are by multinational corporations. A global culture, especially of young people, conversant with postmodern technologies, including videocassette, DVD, VCD, computers, and the Internet, feels at home anywhere, especially perhaps in the world of digital and cyber media. Multiple storylines, the simultaneity of events forever skewing chronology and linearity, and chance encounters are, after all, not only the very core of global noir, but the very stuff of the hypertext that is digital and cyber technologies. Is global noir, then, the future of cinema, and is the future here?

Notes

1. Quoted in Lisa Odham Stokes and Michael Hoover, *City on Fire: Hong Kong Cinema* (London and New York: Verso, 1999), p. 303.

2. Quoted in J. P. Telotte, "Fatal Capers: Strategy and Enigma in Film Noir," *Journal of Popular Film and Television* 23, no. 4 (Winter 1996): 163.

3. Steve Neale, *Genre and Hollywood* (London and New York: Routledge, 2000), p. 3.

4. See John G. Cawelti, "*Chinatown* and Generic Transformation in Recent American Films," in this volume.

5. Manohla Dargis, "Pulp Instincts," in *Action/Spectacle Cinema: A Sight and Sound Reader,* ed. José Arroyo (London: British Film Institute, 2000), p. 117.

6. I use the term *Anglo-American* to reflect the fact that British directors made *The Grifters* and *Romeo Is Bleeding* (Stephen Frears and Peter Medak, respectively), and that the latter stars British actor Gary Oldman. This anticipates the entry into neo-noir of British films per se and also the use of American stars in largely British-made films. It also anticipates the hybrid nature of filmmaking in the neo-noir mode when Hong Kong directors, especially John Woo, work in Hollywood and bring their action directors and stunt coordinators along with them. I have in mind, for instance, *Face/Off* (1997).

7. These titles are drawn from their appearance in a handful of essays reprinted in Arroyo, ed., *Action/Spectacle Cinema*, pp. 117–141.

8. Whether *The Usual Suspects*, for instance, could have been influenced by *Pulp Fiction* is unlikely. The point is that it was often linked to Tarantino's film in reviews and participated in the craze that gave life to films more clearly like *Pulp Fiction*. In fact, *Suspects* was also often compared to *Reservoir Dogs*, a film which it more obviously and importantly resembles.

9. James Naremore, *More Than Night: Film Noir and Its Contexts* (Berkeley and Los Angeles: University of California Press, 1998), pp. 227–228.

10. Ibid., p. 228.

11. It is not some intuitive sense upon which I am relying to link these films as neo-noir before I have reasonably defined it. Rather, such films are linked already in the public discourse. For example, the *San Francisco Examiner* compares *Nowhere to Hide* to *Reservoir Dogs, Run Lola Run,* the films of John Woo, and, interestingly, Sergio Leone's westerns (see <http://www.examiner.com/style/default.jsp?story=art.nowhere12290>). The same newspaper calls *Amores Perros* "*Pulp Fiction* Mexican Style" <http://www.examiner.com/ex_files/default.jsp?story=X13AMORES>. Similarly, J. Hoberman in the *Village Voice* says of *Amores Perros*, "*Reservoir Dogs* might be a translation title" <http://www.villagevoice.com/issues/0113/hoberman.php>. And Shelly Kraicer says of *Sleepless Town*, "It is a hybrid in many ways: a Lee Chi-ngai magical romance grafted onto a baroque neo-noir" <http://www.Chinesecinemas.org/sleeplesstown.html>.

12. Naremore, *More Than Night*, p. 239.

13. Neale, *Genre and Hollywood*, p. 9.

14. Ibid., p. 248.

15. Ibid.

16. Janet Staiger, "Hybrid or Inbred: The Purity Hypothesis and Hollywood Genre History," in *Perverse Spectators: The Practices of Film Reception* (New York and London: New York University Press, 2000), p. 62. Reprinted in this volume.

17. B. Ruby Rich, "Dumb Lugs and Femme Fatales," in Arroyo, ed., *Action/Spectacle Cinema*, pp. 132–134.

18. It is, of course, crucial to note that production practices in Hong Kong necessitate that films be made quickly and cheaply. Thus they need to capitalize on any current trend, whether by quickly reworking a Hollywood hit or by quickly producing a sequel to a Hong Kong hit. For example, *God of Gamblers* (Wong Jing) was a huge hit in 1989 and gave rise to three quick sequels, a spin-off, and a prequel between 1990 and 1996. The *Young and Dangerous* series is even more

———. "Stars and Genre." In *Stardom: Industry of Desire,* edited by Christine Gledhill, pp. 198–206. London and New York: Routledge, 1991.

Browne, Nick, ed. *Refiguring American Film Genres: History and Theory.* Berkeley: University of California Press, 1998.

Brunsdon, Charlotte. "Pedagogies of the Feminine: Feminist Teaching and Women's Genres." *Screen* 32, no. 4 (Winter 1991): 364–381.

Burgoyne, Robert. "Enunciation and Generic Address." *Quarterly Review of Film Studies* 10, no. 2 (Spring 1985): 135–142.

Bywater, Tim, and Thomas Sobchack. *Introduction to Film Criticism: Major Critical Approaches to Narrative Film.* New York: Longman, 1989.

Cavell, Stanley. "Types; Cycles or Genres." Chap. 5 in *The World Viewed: Reflections on the Ontology of Film.* New York: Viking, 1971.

Cawelti, John. *Adventure, Mystery, and Romance: Formula Stories as Art and Popular Culture.* Chicago: University of Chicago Press, 1976.

———. "The Concept of Formula in the Study of Popular Culture." *Journal of Popular Culture* 3, no. 3 (Winter 1969): 381–390.

———. "The Question of Popular Genres." *Journal of Popular Film and Television* 13, no. 2 (Summer 1985): 55–61.

Collins, Jim. *Uncommon Cultures: Popular Culture and Post-Modernism,* part 4. New York and London: Routledge, 1989.

Collins, Richard. "Genre: A Reply to Ed Buscombe." *Screen* 11, nos. 4–5 (August–September 1970): 66–75.

Cook, Pam, and Mieke Bernink, eds. *The Cinema Book,* 2d ed. London: British Film Institute, 1999.

Corrigan, Timothy. *A Cinema without Walls: Movies and Culture after Vietnam.* New Brunswick, N.J.: Rutgers University Press, 1991. Chap. 5, "Genre, Gender, and Hysteria," pp. 137–160.

Crafton, Donald. "Genre and Technology in 1909." *Journal of Popular Film and Television* 13, no. 4 (Winter 1986): 166–170.

Creed, Barbara. "From Here to Modernity: Feminism and Postmodernism." *Screen* 28, no. 2 (1987): 47–67.

Deinstfrey, Harris. "Hitch Your Genre to a Star." *Film Culture* 34 (Fall 1964): 35–37.

Dooley, Roger. *From Scarface to Scarlett: American Films in the 1930s.* New York: Harcourt Brace Jovanovich, 1981.

Easthope, Antony. "Notes on Genre." *Screen Education,* nos. 32–33 (Autumn–Winter 1979–1980): 39–44.

Eberwein, Robert T. "Genre and the Writerly Text." *Journal of Popular Film and Television* 13, no. 2 (Summer 1985): 62–68.

Eidsvik, Charles. *Cineliteracy: Film among the Arts.* New York: Random House, 1978.

Eisele, John C. "The Wild East: Deconstructing the Language of Genre in the Hollywood Eastern." *Cinema Journal* 41, no. 4 (Summer 2002): 68–94.

Frye, Northrop. *Anatomy of Criticism: Four Essays.* New York: Atheneum, 1970.

Gehring, Wes D., ed. *Handbook of American Film Genres.* New York: Greenwood Press, 1988.

Grant, Barry K. "Impressionism and Ideology: The State of Recent Film Genre Criticism." *Canadian Review of American Studies* 14, no. 1 (Spring 1983): 107–118.

———. "Tradition and the Individual Talent: Poetry in the Genre Film." In *Narrative Strategies: Original Essays in Film and Prose Fiction,* edited by Syndy M. Conger and Janice R. Welsch, pp. 93–103. Macomb: Western Illinois University Press, 1981.

———, ed. *Film Genre: Theory and Criticism.* Metuchen, N.J.: Scarecrow Press, 1977.

Harris, Kenneth Marc. "American Film Genres and Non-American Films: A Case Study of *Utu.*" *Cinema Journal* 29, no. 2 (Winter 1990): 36–59.

Hutchings, Peter. "Genre Theory and Criticism." In *Approaches to Popular Film,* edited by Joanne Hollows and Mark Jancovich, pp. 59–77. Manchester and New York: Manchester University Press, 1995.

Kaminsky, Stuart M. *American Film Genres: Approaches to a Critical Theory of Popular Film.* Dayton, Ohio: Pflaum, 1974.

Knight, Deborah. "Making Sense of Genre." *Film and Philosophy* 2 (1995): 58–73.

Kolker, Robert P. "Film Genre: A Dialogue—The Eighties." *Post Script* 1, no. 3 (1982): 30–32.

Landrum, Larry N. "Recent Work in Genre." *Journal of Popular Film and Television* 13, no. 3 (Fall 1985): 151–158.

Larsen, Ernest. "The Law of Genre and How to Break It." *Independent* (November 1988): 14–18.

Lehman, Peter, et al. "American Film Genre: An Interview with John Cawelti." *Wide Angle* 2, no. 2 (1978): 50–57.

Lopez, Daniel. *Films by Genre: 775 Categories, Styles, Trends and Movements Defined, with a Filmography for Each.* Jefferson, N.C.: McFarland, 1993.

Lukow, Gregory, and Steven Ricci. "The 'Audience' Goes 'Public': Intertextuality, Genre, and the Responsibilities of Film Literacy." *On Film,* no. 12 (Spring 1984): 28–36.

McConnell, Frank D. *The Spoken Seen: Film and the Romantic Imagination,* chap. 5, "Legends and History: The Problem of Film Genre." Baltimore and London: Johns Hopkins University Press, 1975.

Maltby, Richard, and Ian Craven. *Hollywood Cinema.* Cambridge, Mass.: Blackwell, 1995.

Mast, Gerald, and Marshall Cohen. "Film Genres." In *Film Genre and Criticism,* 3d ed., edited by Gerald Mast and Marshall Cohen. New York: Oxford, 1985.

Mayer, Geoff. "Formula and Genre, Myths and Patterns." *Australian Journal of Screen Theory* 4 (1978): 59–65.

Morrison, Susan. "The Ideological Consequences of Gender on Genre." *CineAction,* nos. 13–14 (August 1988): 41–45.

Neale, Stephen. *Genre.* London: British Film Institute, 1980.

———. *Genre and Hollywood.* New York and London: Routledge, 2000.

Petlewski, Paul. "Complication of Narrative in the Genre Film." *Film Criticism* 4, no. 1 (Fall 1979): 18–24.

Poague, Leland A. "The Problem of Film Genre: A Mentalistic Approach." *Literature/Film Quarterly* 6, no. 2 (Spring 1978): 152–161.

Porter, Vincent. "Between Structure and History: Genre in Popular British Cinema." *Journal of Popular British Cinema*, no. 1 (1998): 25–36.

Reed, Joseph W. *American Scenarios: The Uses of Film Genre.* Middletown, Conn.: Wesleyan University Press, 1989.

Ross, Andrew. "Families, Film Genres, and Technological Environments." *East-West Film Journal* 4, no. 1 (December 1989): 6–25.

Ryall, Tom. "British Cinema and Genre." *Journal of Popular British Cinema*, no. 1 (1998): 18–24.

———. "Genre and Hollywood." In *The Oxford Guide to Film Studies,* edited by John Hill and Pamela Church Gibson, pp. 327–341. New York: Oxford University Press, 1998.

———. "The Notion of Genre." *Screen* 11, no. 2 (March–April 1970): 22–32.

Schatz, Thomas. *Hollywood Genres: Formulas, Filmmaking, and the Studio System.* New York: Random House, 1981.

———. "New Directions in Film Genre Study (A Reply to Charles F. Altman)." In *Film: Historical-Theoretical Speculations: The 1977 Film Studies Annual,* part 2, pp. 44–52. Pleasantville, N.Y.: Redgrave, 1977.

———. *Old Hollywood/New Hollywood.* Ann Arbor: UMI Research Press, 1982.

Schiff, Stephen. "The Respectable Experience." *Film Comment* 18, no. 2 (1982): 34–36.

Selig, Michael. "The Mirror Metaphor: Reflections on the History of Hollywood Film Genres." *Film Reader,* no. 6, pp. 133–143. Evanston, Ill.: Northwestern University, 1985.

Slotkin, Richard. "The Continuity of Forms: Myth and Genre in Warner Brothers' *The Charge of the Light Brigade.*" *Representations,* no. 29 (Winter 1990): 1–23.

———. "Prologue to a Study of Myth and Genre in American Movies." *Prospects: The Annual of American Cultural Studies,* vol. 9, edited by Jack Salzman, pp. 407–432. Cambridge and New York: Cambridge University Press, 1984.

Small, Edward S. "Literary and Film Genres: Toward a Taxonomy of Film." *Literature/Film Quarterly* 7, no. 4 (1979): 209–219.

Sobchack, Thomas, and Vivian C. Sobchack. *An Introduction to Film,* chap. 4, "Genre Films." Boston: Little, Brown, 1980.

Sobchack, Vivian. "Genre Film: Myth, Ritual, and Sociodrama." In *Film/Culture: Explorations of Cinema in Its Social Context,* edited by Sari Thomas, pp. 147–165. Metuchen, N.J.: Scarecrow Press, 1982.

Solomon, Stanley J. *Beyond Formula: American Film Genres.* New York: Harcourt Brace Jovanovich, 1976.

Tudor, Andrew. *Theories of Film,* chap. 5, "Critical Method: Auteur and Genre." New York: Viking, 1974.

Turner, Graeme. *Film as Social Practice.* London and New York: Routledge, 1988.

———. "The Genres Are American: Australian Narrative, Australian Film, and the Problems of Genre." *Literature/Film Quarterly* 21, no. 2 (1993): 102–111.

Vernet, Marc. "Genre." *Film Reader,* no. 3 (1978): 13–17.

Williams, Alan. "Is a Radical Genre Criticism Possible?" *Quarterly Review of Film Studies* 9, no. 2 (Spring 1984): 121–125.

Yacowar, Maurice. "Recent Popular Genre Movies: Awash and Aware." *Journal of Popular Film* 4, no. 4 (1975): 297–305.

ACTION FILMS, ADVENTURE FILMS

Anderson, Aaron. "Action in Motion: Kinesthesia in Martial Arts Films." *Jump Cut,* no. 42 (1998): 1–11.

Anderson, J. L. "Japanese Swordfighters and American Gunfighters." *Cinema Journal* 12, no. 2 (Spring 1973): 1–21. Reprinted in *Cinema Examined: Selections from Cinema Journal,* edited by Richard Dyer MacCann and Jack C. Ellis, pp. 84–104. New York: Dutton, 1982.

Arroyo, José, ed. *Action/Spectacle Cinema: A Sight and Sound Reader.* London: British Film Institute, 2000.

Browne, Jeffrey A. "Gender and the Action Heroine: Hardbodies and the Point of No Return." *Cinema Journal* 35, no. 3 (Spring 1996): 52–71.

Cameron, Ian. *Adventure in the Movies.* London: Studio Vista, 1973.

Cawelti, John G. *Adventure, Mystery, and Romance: Formula Stories as Art and Popular Culture.* Chicago: University of Chicago Press, 1976.

Cline, William C. *In the Nick of Time: Motion Picture Sound Serials.* Jefferson, N.C.: McFarland, 1984.

Coe, Andrew. "Slugfests del Sur." *Film Comment* 23, no. 4 (July–August 1987): 27–28, 30. [Mexican wrestling films]

Fury, David. *Kings of the Jungle: An Illustrated Reference to Tarzan on Screen and Television.* Jefferson, N.C.: McFarland, 1994.

Gallagher, Mark. "I Married Rambo: Spectacle and Melodrama in the Hollywood Action Film." In *Mythologies of Violence in Postmodern Media,* edited by Christopher Sharrett, pp. 199–225. Detroit: Wayne State University Press, 1999.

Gow, Gordon. "Swashbucklers." *Films and Filming* 11 (January 1972): 34–41.

Harmon, Jim, and Donald F. Glut. *The Great Movie Serials: Their Sound and Fury.* Garden City, N.Y.: Doubleday, 1972.

Hogue, Peter. "Legion of the Lost Genre." *Film Comment* 28, no. 4 (July–August 1992): 40–51. [aviation films]

Jeffords, Susan. *Hard Bodies: Hollywood Masculinity in the Reagan Era.* New Brunswick, N.J.: Rutgers University Press, 1994.

Jones, Roy. "Swashbuckling Adventure Films." *Filmmaking* 9 (February 1972): 42–44.

Kaminsky, Stuart. "The Samurai Film and the Western." *Journal of Popular Film* 1, no. 4 (1972): 312–324. Revised as "Comparative Forms: The Samurai Film and the Western," in *American Film Genres: Approaches to a Critical Theory of Popular Film,* chap. 3. Dayton, Ohio: Pflaum, 1974.

King, Neal. *Heroes in Hard Times: Cop Action Movies in the U.S.* Philadelphia: Temple University Press, 1999.

Lahue, Kalton C. *Continued Next Week: A History of the Moving Picture Serial.* Norman: University of Oklahoma Press, 1964.

Marchetti, Gina. "Action Adventure as Ideology." In *Cultural Politics in Contemporary America,* edited by Ian Angus and Sut Jully, pp. 182–197. New York: Routledge, 1989.

Meyers, Richard, et al. *Martial Arts Movies from Bruce Lee to the Ninjas.* Secaucus, N.J.: Citadel, 1985.

Nottridge, Rhoda. *Adventure Films.* New York: Crestwood House, 1992.

Palmer, Bill, Karen Palmer, and Rick Meyers. *The Encyclopedia of Martial Arts Movies.* Metuchen, N.J.: Scarecrow Press, 1995.

Parish, James Robert. *Pirates and Seafaring Swashbucklers on the Hollywood Screen.* Jefferson, N.C.: McFarland, 1995.

Parish, James Robert, and George H. Hill. *Black Action Films: Plots, Critiques, Cast, and Credits for 235 Theatrical and Made-for-Television Releases.* Jefferson, N.C.: McFarland, 1989.

Parish, James Robert, and Don E. Stanke. *The Swashbucklers.* New Rochelle, N.Y.: Arlington House, 1976.

Pfeil, Fred. "From Pillar to Postmodern: Race, Class, and Gender in the Male Rampage Film." In *The New American Cinema,* edited by Jon Lewis, pp. 147–186. Durham and London: Duke University Press, 1998.

Richards, Jeffrey. "The Swashbuckling Revival." *Focus on Film,* no. 27 (Summer 1977): 7–29.

———. *Swordsmen of the Screen.* London: Routledge and Kegan Paul, 1977.

Schubart, Rikke. "Passion and Acceleration: Generic Change in the Action Film." In *Violence and American Cinema,* edited by J. David Slocum, pp. 192–207. New York and London: Routledge, 2001.

Silver, Alain. *The Samurai Film.* New York: Overlook Press, 1985.

Sobchack, Thomas. "The Adventure Film." In *Handbook of American Film Genres,* edited by Wes D. Gehring, pp. 9–24. New York: Greenwood Press, 1988.

Sotto, Agustin L. "Notes on the Filipino Action Film." *East-West Film Journal* 1, no. 2 (June 1987): 1–14.

Stedman, Raymond William. *The Serials: Suspense and Drama by Installment,* 2d ed. Norman: University of Oklahoma Press, 1977.

Tado, Michitaro. "The Destiny of Samurai Films." *East-West Film Journal* 1, no. 1 (December 1986): 48–58.

Tasker, Yvonne. *Spectacular Bodies: Gender, Genre, and the Action Cinema.* New York and London: Routledge, 1993.

Taves, Brian. *The Romance of Adventure: The Genre of Historical Adventure Movies.* Jackson: University Press of Mississippi, 1993.

Thomas, Tony. *The Great Adventure Films.* Secaucus, N.J.: Citadel Press, 1976.

Zhang Zhen. "Bodies in the Air: The Magic of Science and the Fate of the Early 'Martial Arts' Films in China." *Post Script* 20, nos. 2–3 (Winter/Spring–Summer 2001): 43–60.

BIOPICS

Anderson, Carolyn. "Biographical Film." In *Handbook of American Film Genres,* edited by Wes D. Gehring, pp. 331–351. New York: Greenwood Press, 1988.

Custen, George F. *Bio/Pics: How Hollywood Constructed Public History.* New Brunswick, N.J.: Rutgers University Press, 1992.

———. "The Mechanical Life in the Age of Human Reproduction: American Biopics, 1961–1980." *Biography* 23, no. 1 (Winter 2000): 127–159.

Elsaesser, Thomas. "Film History and Social History: The Dieterle/Warner Brothers Bio-Pic." *Wide Angle* 8, no. 2 (1986): 15–31.

COMEDY FILMS

Agee, James. "Comedy's Greatest Era." In *Agee on Film,* vol. 1, pp. 1–20. New York: Grosset and Dunlap, 1967. Reprinted in *Film: An Anthology,* edited by Daniel Talbot, pp. 130–147. Berkeley and Los Angeles: University of California Press, 1967. *Awake in the Dark,* edited by David Denby, pp. 230–248. New York: Vintage, 1977. *Film Theory and Criticism,* 2d ed., edited by Gerald Mast and Marshall Cohen, pp. 535–558. New York: Oxford, 1979.

Babington, Bruce, and Peter William Evans. *Affairs to Remember: The Hollywood Comedy of the Sexes.* Manchester: Manchester University Press, 1989.

Balio, Tino, ed. *History of the American Cinema,* vol. 5, *Grand Design: Hollywood as a Modern Business Enterprise, 1930–1939,* pp. 256–280. New York: Charles Scribner's Sons, 1993.

Beach, Christopher. *Class, Language, and American Film Comedy.* New York: Cambridge University Press, 2002.

Belton, John. *American Cinema/American Culture.* New York: McGraw-Hill, 1994.

Bergman, Andrew. *We're in the Money.* New York: Harper and Row, 1972. Rev. ed., Chicago: Elephant, 1992.

Byrge, Duane Paul. "Screwball Comedy." *East-West Film Journal* 2, no. 1 (December 1987): 17–25.

Byrge, Duane Paul, and Robert Milton Miller. *The Screwball Comedy Films: A History and Filmography, 1934–1942.* Jefferson, N.C.: McFarland, 1991.

Byron, Stuart, and Elizabeth Weis, eds. *Movie Comedy.* New York: Penguin, 1977.

Callenbach, Ernest. "The Comic Ecstasy." *Films in Review* 5, no. 1 (January 1954): 24–26.

Cavell, Stanley. "Leopards in Connecticut." *Georgia Review* 30, no. 2 (Summer 1976): 233–262.

———. *Pursuits of Happiness: The Hollywood Comedy of Remarriage.* Cambridge: Harvard University Press, 1981.

———. "Pursuits of Happiness: A Reading of *The Lady Eve.*" *New Literary History* 10 (1979): 581–601.

———. "Two Cheers for Romance." In *Passionate Attachments: Thinking about Love,* edited by William Gaylin and Ethel Person, pp. 85–100. New York: Free Press, 1988.

Clipper, Lawrence J. "Archetypal Figures in Early Film Comedy." *Western Humanities Review* 28, no. 4 (Autumn 1974): 355–366.

Cott, Jeremy. "The Limits of Silent Comedy." *Literature/Film Quarterly* 3, no. 2 (Spring 1975): 99–107.

Dervin, Daniel. "Primal Conditions and Conventions: The Genres of Comedy and Science Fiction." *Film/Psychology Review* 4, no. 1 (1980): 115–147.

Durgnat, Raymond. *The Crazy Mirror: Hollywood Comedy and the American Image*. New York: Delta, 1972.

Dyer, Peter John. "They Liked to Break the Rules." *Films and Filming* 6, no. 1 (October 1959): 12–14, 38–39.

Eaton, Mick. "Laughter in the Dark." *Screen* 22, no. 2 (1981): 21–28.

Eberwein, Robert. "Comedy and the Film within a Film." *Wide Angle* 3, no. 2 (1979): 12–17.

Evans, Peter William, and Celestino Deleyto, eds. *Terms of Endearment: Hollywood Romantic Comedy of the 1980s and 1990s*. Edinburgh: Edinburgh University Press, 1998.

Everson, William K. "Screwball Comedy: A Reappraisal." *Films in Review* 34, no. 10 (1983): 578–584.

Eyles, Allen. *American Comedy since Sound*. New York: A. S. Barnes, 1973.

———. "Uncle Sam's Funny Bone." *Films and Filming* 9, no. 6 (March 1963): 45–49.

Geduld, Carolyn, and Harry Geduld. "From Kops to Robbers: Transformation of Archetypal Figures in the American Cinema of the 20's and 30's." *Journal of Popular Culture* 1, no. 2 (1967–1968): 389–394.

Gehring, Wes D. *American Dark Comedy: Beyond Satire*. Westport, Conn.: Greenwood Press, 1996.

———. *Handbook of American Film Genres*. New York: Greenwood Press, 1988.

———. "McCarey vs. Capra: A Guide to American Film Comedy of the 30's." *Journal of Popular Film and Television* 7, no. 1 (1978): 67–84.

———. *Screwball Comedy: A Genre of Madcap Romance*. Westport, Conn.: Greenwood Press, 1986.

———. "Screwball Comedy: An Overview." *Journal of Popular Film and Television* 13, no. 4 (Winter 1986): 178–185.

Geller, Jeffrey L., and Richard Vela. "Happiness through Insanity: The Function of Outrageousness in Screwball Comedy." *Film and Philosophy* 4 (1997): 58–65.

Gilliatt, Penelope. *To Wit: A Lifetime of Comedy*. New York: Charles Scribner's Sons, 1990.

Glassman, Marc, and Judy Wolfe. "The Studio with the Team Spirit: A Look at Ealing Comedies." *CineAction*, no. 9 (Summer 1987): 41–46.

Glitre, Kathrina. "The Same, but Different: The Awful Truth about Marriage, Remarriage, and Screwball Comedy." *CineAction*, no. 54 (2001): 3–11.

Grant, Barry K. "Film Comedy of the Thirties and the American Comic Tradition." *West Virginia University Philological Papers* 26 (August 1980): 21–29.

Green, Ian. "Ealing: In the Comedy Frame." In *British Cinema History*, edited by James Curran and Vincent Porter, pp. 294–302. London: Weidenfeld and Nicolson, 1983.

Harvey, James. *Romantic Comedy in Hollywood from Lubitsch to Sturges.* New York: Knopf, 1987.

Henderson, Brian. "Romantic Comedy Today: *Semi-Tough* or Impossible?" *Film Quarterly* 31, no. 4 (Summer 1978): 11–23. Revised in *Film Genre Reader*, edited by Barry Keith Grant, pp. 309–328. Austin: University of Texas Press, 1986.

Higham, Charles, and Joel Greenberg. *Hollywood in the Forties.* New York: A. S. Barnes, 1968.

Horton, Andrew S., ed. *Comedy/Cinema/Theory.* Berkeley: University of California Press, 1991.

———. *Inside Soviet Film Comedy: Laughing with a Lash.* New York: Cambridge University Press, 1993.

———. *Laughing Out Loud: Writing the Comedy-Centered Screenplay.* Berkeley and Los Angeles: University of California Press, 2000.

———. *Writing the Character-Centered Screenplay.* Berkeley and Los Angeles: University of California Press, 1994.

Jenkins, Henry, III. "The Amazing Push-Me/Pull-You Text: Cognitive Processing, Narrational Play, and the Comic Film." *Wide Angle* 8, nos. 3–4 (1986): 35–44.

———. "'Fifi Was My Mother's Name!': Anarchistic Comedy, the Vaudeville Aesthetic, and *Diplomaniacs.*" *Velvet Light Trap*, no. 26 (Fall 1990): 3–27.

———. *What Made Pistachio Nuts? Early Sound Comedy and the Vaudeville Aesthetic.* New York: Columbia University Press, 1993.

Johnson, Ian. "Have the British a Sense of Humour?" *Films and Filming* 9, no. 6 (March 1963): 48–53.

Kaminsky, Stuart M. *American Film Genres: Approaches to a Critical Theory of Popular Film,* chap. 9. Dayton, Ohio: Pflaum, 1974.

Karnick, Kristine Brunovska, and Henry Jenkins, eds. *Classical Hollywood Comedy.* New York and London: Routledge/American Film Institute, 1994.

Keane, Marian. "The Authority of Connection in Stanley Cavell's Pursuits of Happiness." *Journal of Popular Film and Television* 13, no. 3 (Fall 1985): 139–150.

Kehr, David. "Funny Peculiar." *Film Comment* 18, no. 4 (1982): 9–11, 13–16.

Kendall, Elizabeth. *The Runaway Bride: Hollywood Romantic Comedy of the 1930's.* New York: Alfred A. Knopf, 1990. Reprint, New York: Anchor Doubleday, 1991.

Kerr, Walter. *The Silent Clowns.* New York: Knopf, 1975.

Knight, Arthur. "The Two-Reel Comedy—Its Rise and Fall." *Penguin Film Review* no. 9 (London: Penguin, 1949): 39–46.

Kracauer, Siegfried. "Silent Film Comedy." *Sight and Sound* 21 (August–September 1951): 31–32.

Kramer, Peter. "'Clean, Dependable Slapstick': Comic Violence and the Emergence of Classical Hollywood Cinema." In *Violence and American Cinema*, edited by J. David Slocum, pp. 103–116. New York and London: Routledge, 2001.

Krutnik, Frank. "The Clown-Prints of Comedy." *Screen* 25, nos. 4–5 (July–October 1984): 50–59.

————. "The Faint Aroma of Performing Seals: The 'Nervous' Romance and the Comedy of the Sexes." *Velvet Light Trap*, no. 26 (Fall 1990): 57–72.

Lahue, Kalton C. *World of Laughter: The Motion Picture Comedy Short, 1910–1930*. Norman: University of Oklahoma Press, 1972.

Lamm, Robert. "'Can We Laugh at God?': Apocalyptic Comedy in Film." *Journal of Popular Film and Television* 19, no. 2 (Summer 1991): 81–90.

Landy, Marcia. *British Genres: Cinema and Society, 1930–1960*. Princeton: Princeton University Press, 1991.

Langman, Larry. *Encyclopedia of American Film Comedy*. New York: Garland, 1987.

Leach, Jim. "The Screwball Comedy." In *Film Genre: Theory and Criticism,* edited by Barry K. Grant, pp. 75–89. Metuchen, N.J.: Scarecrow Press, 1977.

McCaffrey, Donald W. "The Evolution of the Chase in the Silent Screen Comedy." *Cinema Journal* 4 (1964): 1–8.

————. "Four Great Comedians of the Silent Cinema." In *The American Cinema,* 3d ed., edited by Donald E. Staples, pp. 101–115. Washington, D.C.: United States Information Agency, 1991.

————. *The Golden Age of Sound Comedy: Comic Films and the Comedians of the Thirties*. South Brunswick, N.J.: A. S. Barnes, 1973.

MacCann, Richard Dyer, ed. *The Silent Comedians*. Metuchen, N.J.: Scarecrow Press, 1993.

Maltin, Leonard. *The Great Movie Comedians*. New York: Crown/Harmony Books, 1982.

————. *Movie Comedy Teams*. New York: New American Library, 1970.

Mast, Gerald. *The Comic Mind: Comedy and the Movies*. Indianapolis and New York: Bobbs-Merrill, 1973. 2d ed., Chicago: University of Chicago Press, 1979.

Matthews, Nicole. *Comic Politics: Gender in Hollywood Comedy after the New Right*. Manchester, U.K.: Manchester University Press, 2001.

Miller, Blair. *American Silent Film Comedies: An Illustrated Encyclopedia of Persons, Studios, and Terminology*. Jefferson, N.C.: McFarland, 1995.

Monaco, James. *American Film Now*. New York: New American Library, 1979.

Montgomery, John. *Comedy Films, 1894–1954*. London: George Allen and Unwin, 1968.

Murphy, Robert. *Sixties British Cinema*, chap. 10. London: British Film Institute, 1992.

Neale, Steve. "The Big Romance or Something Wild? Romantic Comedy Today." *Screen* 33, no. 3 (Autumn 1992): 284–299.

————. "Psychoanalysis and Comedy." *Screen* 22, no. 2 (1981): 29–43.

Neale, Steve, and Frank Krutnik. *Popular Film and Television Comedy*. New York and London: Routledge, 1990.

Nelson, T. G. A. *An Introduction to Comedy in Literature, Drama, and Cinema*. New York: Oxford, 1990.

Okuda, Ted, with Edward Watz. *The Columbia Shorts: Two-Reel Hollywood Film Comedies, 1933–1958*. Jefferson, N.C.: McFarland, 1987.

Palmer, Jerry. *The Logic of the Absurd: On Film and Television Comedy*. Chicago: University of Illinois Press, 1988.

Paul, William. "Bill Murray, King of Animal Comedy: Reaganite Comedy in a Kinder, Gentler Nation." *Film Criticism* 13, no. 1 (Fall 1988): 4–19.

———. *Laughing Screaming: Modern Hollywood Horror and Comedy*. New York: Columbia University Press, 1994.

———. "The Rise and Fall of Animal Comedy." *Velvet Light Trap*, no. 26 (Fall 1990): 73–86.

Poague, Leland. "Cavell and the Fantasy of Criticism: Shakespearean Comedy and Ball of Fire." *CineAction*, no. 9 (Summer 1987): 47–55.

Porter, Vincent. "The Hegemonic Turn: Film Comedies in 1950s Britain." *Journal of Popular British Cinema*, no. 4 (2001): 81–94.

Reed, Joseph W. *American Scenarios: The Uses of Film Genre*. Middletown, Conn.: Wesleyan University Press, 1989.

Reid, Mark A. *Redefining Black Film*. Berkeley: University of California Press, 1993.

Robinson, David. *The Great Funnies: A History of Film Comedy*. New York: Dutton, 1969.

———. "The Italian Comedy." *Sight and Sound* 55, no. 2 (Spring 1986): 105–112.

Sarris, Andrew. "The Sex Comedy without Sex." *American Film* 3, no. 5 (March 1978): 8–15.

Schatz, Thomas. *Hollywood Genres: Formulas, Filmmaking, and the Studio System*. New York: Random House, 1981.

Seidman, Steve. *Comedian Comedy: A Tradition in the Hollywood Film*. Ann Arbor: UMI Research Press, 1981.

Sennett, Ted. *Lunatics and Lovers: The Golden Age of Hollywood Comedy*. New York: Limelight, 1985.

Siegel, Scott, and Barbara Siegel. *American Film Comedy: From Abbott and Costello to Jerry Zucker*. New York: Prentice-Hall, 1994.

Sikov, Ed. *Laughing Hysterically: American Screen Comedy of the 1950s*. New York: Columbia University Press, 1995.

———. *Screwball: Hollywood's Madcap Romantic Comedies*. New York: Crown, 1989.

Sklar, Robert. "Chaos, Magic, Physical Genius, and the Art of Silent Comedy." *Movie-Made America*, chap. 7. New York: Random House, 1975.

Surfin, Mark. "The Silent World of Slapstick (1912–1916)." *Film Culture* 2, no. 4 (1956): 21–22.

Sutton, David. *A Chorus of Raspberries: British Film Comedy, 1929–1939*. Exeter, U.K.: Exeter University Press, 2000.

Turk, Edward Baron. "Comedy and Psychoanalysis: The Verbal Component." *Philosophy and Rhetoric* 12, no. 2 (1979): 95–113.

Walker, Mark. *Vietnam Veteran Films*. Metuchen, N.J.: Scarecrow Press, 1991.

Weales, Gerald. *Canned Goods as Caviar: American Film Comedy of the 1930s*. Chicago: University of Chicago Press, 1985.

Winokur, Mark. *American Laughter: Immigrants, Ethnicity, and 1930s Hollywood Film Comedy*. New York: St. Martin's Press, 1996.

Wood, Robin. "The American Family Comedy: From *Meet Me in St. Louis* to *The Texas Chainsaw Massacre*." *Wide Angle* 3, no. 2 (1979): 5–11.

CRIME FILMS

Alloway, Lawrence. *Violent America: The Movies, 1946–1964.* New York: Museum of Modern Art, 1971.

Ames, Christopher. "Restoring the Black Man's Lethal Weapon: Race and Sexuality in Contemporary Cop Films." *Journal of Popular Film and Television* 20, no. 3 (Fall 1992): 52–60.

Balio, Tino, ed. *History of the American Cinema,* vol. 5, *Grand Design: Hollywood as a Modern Business Enterprise, 1930–1939,* pp. 280–298. New York: Charles Scribner's Sons, 1993.

Baxter, John. "Something More Than Night." *Film Journal* 2, no. 4 (1975): 4–9.

Bordwell, David. *Narration in the Fiction Film,* chap. 5. Madison: University of Wisconsin Press, 1985.

Brown, Jeffrey A. "Bullets, Buddies, and Bad Guys: The 'Action-Cop' Genre." *Journal of Popular Film and Television* 21, no. 2 (Summer 1993): 79–87.

Cameron, Ian. *A Pictorial History of Crime Films.* London: Hamlyn, 1975.

Cawelti, John G. *Adventure, Mystery, and Romance: Formula Stories as Art and Popular Culture.* Chicago: University of Chicago Press, 1976.

Chabrol, Claude. "Evolution of the Thriller [Policier]." *CAHIERS DU CINÉMA: The 1950s: Neorealism, Hollywood, New Wave,* edited by Jim Hillier, pp. 158–164. Cambridge: Harvard University Press, 1985.

Chibnall, Steve, and Robert Murphy, eds. *British Crime Cinema.* New York and London: Routledge, 1999.

Clarens, Carlos. *Crime Movies: An Illustrated History.* New York: Norton, 1980. Rev. ed., Cambridge, Mass.: Da Capo, 1997.

———. "Hooverville West: The Hollywood G-Man, 1934–1945." *Film Comment* 13, no. 3 (May–June 1977): 10–16.

Clay, Andrew. "When the Gangs Came to Britain: The Postwar British Crime Film." *Journal of Popular British Cinema,* no. 1 (1988): 76–86.

Clayton, Henry, Jr. "Crime Films and Social Criticism." *Films in Review* 2, no. 5 (1951): 31–35.

Cobley, Paul. *The American Thriller: Generic Innovation and Social Change in the 1970s.* New York: Palgrave, 2001.

Cocchiarelli, Joseph J. *Screen Sleuths: A Filmography.* Hamden, Conn.: Garland, 1991.

Connor, Edward. "The Mystery Film." *Films in Review* 5, no. 3 (March 1954): 120–123.

Conquest, John. *Trouble Is Their Business: Private Eyes in Fiction, Film, and Television, 1927–1988.* New York: Garland, 1989.

Cook, Pam, and Mieke Bernink, eds. *The Cinema Book.* 2d ed. London: British Film Institute, 1999.

Cooper, Stephen. "Sex/Knowledge/Power in the Detective Genre." *Film Quarterly* 42, no. 3 (Spring 1989): 23–31.

Crowther, Bruce. *Captured on Film: The Prison Movie.* London: Batsford, 1989.

Cutts, John. "Oriental Eye." *Films and Filming* 3, no. 11 (August 1957): 16.

Davis, Brian. *The Thriller.* New York: Dutton, 1973.

Deming, Barbara. *Running Away from Myself*. New York: Grossman, 1969.

Douglass, Wayne J. "The Criminal Psychopath as Hollywood Hero." *Journal of Popular Film and Television* 8, no. 4 (Winter 1981): 30–39.

Durgnat, Raymond. "Spies and Ideologies." *Cinema* (U.K.), no. 2 (March 1969): 5–13.

Everson, William K. *The Detective in Film*. Secaucus, N.J.: Citadel Press, 1972.

French, Philip. "Cops." *Sight and Sound* 43, no. 2 (Spring 1974): 113–115.

Fuller, Graham. "Right Villains." *Film Comment* 26, no. 5 (September–October 1990): 47–48, 51–52.

Gilmour, Heather. "Different Except in a Different Way: Marriage, Divorce, and Gender in the Hollywood Comedy of Remarriage." *Journal of Film and Video* 50, no. 2 (Summer 1998): 26–39.

Godfrey, Lionel. "Martinis without Olives." *Films and Filming* 14, no. 7 (April 1968): 10–14.

Gow, Gordon. *Suspense in the Cinema*. Cranbury, N.J.: A. S. Barnes, 1968.

Grace, Harry A. "A Taxonomy of American Crime Film Themes." *Journal of Social Psychology* 42 (August 1955): 129–136.

Gregory, Charles. "Knight without Meaning? Marlowe on the Screen." *Sight and Sound* 42, no. 3 (Summer 1973): 155–159.

Hammond, Laurence. *Thriller Movies*. Secaucus, N.J.: Derbibooks, 1975.

Haralovich, Mary Beth. "Sherlock Holmes: Genre and Industrial Practice." *Journal of the University Film Association* 31, no. 2 (Spring 1979): 53–57.

Haydock, Ron. *Deerstalker: Holmes and Watson on Screen*. Metuchen, N.J.: Scarecrow Press, 1978.

Henry, Clayton R., Jr. "Crime Films and Social Criticism." *Films in Review* 2, no. 5 (1951): 31–34.

Higgins, George V. "The Private Eye as Illegal Hero." *Esquire* 77, no. 6 (December 1972): 348, 350–351.

Houston, Penelope. "The Private Eye." *Sight and Sound* 26, no. 1 (1956): 22–23, 55.

Jarvie, I. C. *Movies and Society*. New York: Basic Books, 1970.

Kinder, Marsha. "The Return of the Outlaw Couple." *Film Quarterly* 27, no. 4 (Summer 1974): 2–10.

King, Neal. *Heroes in Hard Times: Cop Action Movies in the U.S.* Philadelphia: Temple University Press, 1999.

Landy, Marcia. *British Genres: Cinema and Society, 1930–1960*. Princeton: Princeton University Press, 1991.

Langman, Larry, and David Ebner. *Encyclopedia of American Spy Films*. New York: Garland, 1991.

———. *A Guide to American Crime Films of the Thirties*. Westport, Conn.: Greenwood Press, 1995.

Leitch, Tom. *Crime Films*. New York and Cambridge: Cambridge University Press, 2002.

Le Sueur, Mark. "The Private Eye: Second 'Golden Age.'" *Journal of Popular Film and Television* 7, no. 2 (1979): 181–189.

McConnell, Frank D. *The Spoken Seen: Film and the Romantic Imagination*, chap. 5. Baltimore and London: Johns Hopkins University Press, 1975.

Mayer, Geoff. "Formula and Genre, Myths and Patterns." *Australian Journal of Screen Theory* 4 (1978): 59–65. [prison films]

Miller, Don. "Private Eyes: From Sam Spade to J. J. Gittes." *Focus on Film,* no. 22 (Autumn 1975): 15–35.

Morey, Anne. "'The Judge Called Me an Accessory': Women's Prison Films, 1950–1962." *Journal of Popular Film and Television* 23, no. 2 (Summer 1995): 80–87.

Murphy, Robert. "Riff-Raff: British Cinema and the Underworld." In *All Our Yesterdays: 90 Years of British Cinema,* edited by Charles Barr, pp. 286–305. London: British Film Institute, 1986.

———. *Sixties British Cinema,* chap. 9. London: British Film Institute, 1992.

Neale, Steve. *Genre and Hollywood.* New York and London: Routledge, 2000.

Oliver, Bill. "*The Long Goodbye* and *Chinatown:* Debunking the Private Eye Tradition." *Literature/Film Quarterly* 3, no. 3 (Summer 1975): 240–248.

Parish, James Robert. *Famous Movie Detectives.* Metuchen, N.J.: Scarecrow Press, 1979.

———. *Famous Movie Detectives II.* Metuchen, N.J.: Scarecrow Press, 1991.

———. *The Great Cop Pictures.* Metuchen, N.J.: Scarecrow Press, 1990.

———. *Prison Pictures from Hollywood: Plots, Critiques, Casts, and Credits for 293 Theatrical and Made-for-Television Releases.* Jefferson, N.C.: McFarland, 1991.

Parish, James Robert, and Michael R. Pitts. *The Great Detective Pictures.* Metuchen, N.J.: Scarecrow Press, 1990.

———. *The Great Spy Pictures.* Metuchen, N.J.: Scarecrow Press, 1974.

———. *The Great Spy Pictures II.* Metuchen, N.J.: Scarecrow Press, 1986.

Park, William. "The Police State." *Journal of Popular Film and Television* 6, no. 3 (Fall 1978): 229–237.

Pitts, Michael R. *Famous Movie Detectives III.* Lanham, Md.: Scarecrow Press, 2000.

Rafter, Nicole Hahn. *Shots in the Mirror: Crime Films and Society.* New York: Oxford University Press, 2000.

Reck, Tom S. "Come Out of the Shower and Come Out Clean." *Commonweal* 26 (September 1969): 588–591.

Reed, Joseph W. *American Scenarios: The Uses of Film Genre.* Middletown, Conn.: Wesleyan University Press, 1989.

Reiner, Robert. "Keystone to Kojak: The Hollywood Cop." In *Cinema, Politics, and Society in America,* edited by Philip Davies and Brian Neve, pp. 195–220. New York: St. Martin's Press, 1981.

Reynolds, William, and Elizabeth Trembley. *It's a Print! Detective Fiction from Page to Screen.* Bowling Green, Ohio: Popular Press, 1994.

Roffman, Peter, and Jim Purdy. *The Hollywood Social Problem Film: Madness, Despair, and Politics from the Depression to the Fifties.* Bloomington: Indiana University Press, 1981.

Rubinstein, Lenny. *The Great Spy Films.* Secaucus, N.J.: Citadel Press, 1979.

———. "The Politics of Spy Films." *Cineaste* 9, no. 3 (Spring 1979): 16–21.

Ryan, Michael, and Douglas Kellner. *Camera Politica: The Politics and Ideology of Contemporary Hollywood Film*. Bloomington and Indianapolis: Indiana University Press, 1988.

Schatz, Thomas. *Hollywood Genres: Formulas, Filmmaking, and the Studio System*. New York: Random House, 1981.

Shadoian, Jack. *Dreams and Dead Ends: The American Gangster/Crime Film*. Cambridge: MIT Press, 1977.

Skene Melvin, David, and Ann Skene Melvin, comps. *Crime, Detective, Espionage, Mystery, and Thriller Fiction and Film: A Comprehensive Bibliography of Critical Writing through 1979*. Westport, Conn.: Greenwood Press, 1980.

Sobchack, Thomas. "New York Street Gangs or the Warriors of My Mind." *Journal of Popular Film and Television* 10, no. 2 (Summer 1982): 77–85.

Solomon, Stanley J. *Beyond Formula: American Film Genres*. New York: Harcourt Brace Jovanovich, 1976.

Springhall, John. "Censoring Hollywood: Youth, Moral Panic, and Crime/Gangster Movies of the 1930s." *Journal of Popular Culture* 32, no. 3 (Winter 1998): 135–154.

Telotte, J. P. "The Detective as Dreamer: The Case of *The Lady in the Lake*." *Journal of Popular Film and Television* 12, no. 1 (Spring 1984): 4–15.

Thomson, David. *America in the Dark: Hollywood and the Gift of Unreality*, chap. 6. New York: William Morrow, 1977.

Thomson, H. Douglas. "Detective Films." *Sight and Sound* 4, no. 13 (Spring 1935): 10–11.

Tuska, Jon. *The Detective in Hollywood*. New York: Doubleday, 1978.

———. *In Manors and Alleys: A Casebook on the American Detective Film*. New York: Greenwood Press, 1988.

Tyler, Parker. *The Hollywood Hallucination*, chap. 5. New York: Simon and Schuster, 1970.

Van Wert, William. "Philip Marlowe: Hardboiled to Softboiled to Poached." *Jump Cut*, no. 3 (1974): 10–13.

Vincendeau, Ginette. "France 1945–65 and Hollywood: The *Policier* as International Text." *Screen* 33, no. 1 (Spring 1992): 50–80.

Walker, Mark. *Vietnam Veteran Films*. Metuchen, N.J.: Scarecrow Press, 1991.

Waller, Gregory A. "Mike Hammer and the Detective Film of the 1980s." *Journal of Popular Film and Television* 13, no. 3 (Fall 1985): 109–125.

Wilkins, Mike. "Jailbirds, among Others." *Film Comment* 22, no. 4 (July–August 1986): 62–69. [girls-in-gangs films]

Wollen, Peter. "Riff Raff Realism." *Sight and Sound* 8, no. 4 (April 1998): 18–22.

CULT MOVIES

Corrigan, Timothy. "Film and the Culture of Cult." *Wide Angle* 8, nos. 3–4 (1986): 91–99. Revised and reprinted in *Beyond All Reason: The Cult Film Experience*, edited by J. P. Telotte, pp. 26–37. Austin: University of Texas Press, 1991.

Eco, Umberto. "*Casablanca*: Cult Movies and Intertextual Collage." *Sub-Stance* 14, no. 2 (1985): 3–12.

French, Karl, and Philip French. *Cult Movies.* New York: Watson-Guptill, 2000.

Hoberman, J. *Midnight Movies.* New York: Harper, 1983.

Hoberman, J., and Jonathan Rosenbaum. "Curse of the Cult People." *Film Comment* 27, no. 1 (January–February 1991): 18–21.

Mendik, Xavier, and Graeme Harper, eds. *Unruly Pleasures: The Cult Film and Its Critics.* Surrey, U.K.: Fab Press, 2000.

Peary, Danny. *Cult Movies: The Classics, the Sleepers, the Weird, and the Wonderful.* New York: Delta, 1981.

———. *Cult Movies 2: Fifty More of the Classics, the Sleepers, the Weird, and the Wonderful.* New York: Dell, 1983.

———. *Cult Movies 3: Fifty More of the Classics, the Sleepers, the Weird, and the Wonderful.* New York: Fireside Books/Simon and Schuster, 1988.

Samuels, Stuart. *Midnight Movies.* New York: Collier, 1983.

Studlar, Gaylyn. "Midnight S/Excess: Cult Configurations of 'Femininity' and the Perverse." *Journal of Popular Film and Television* 17, no. 1 (Spring 1989): 2–14. Reprinted in *Beyond All Reason: The Cult Film Experience,* edited by J. P. Telotte, pp. 138–155. Austin: University of Texas Press, 1991.

Telotte, J. P. "Casablanca and the Larcenous Cult Film." *Michigan Quarterly Review* 26, no. 2 (Spring 1987): 357–368. Revised and reprinted in *Beyond All Reason: The Cult Film Experience,* edited by Telotte, pp. 43–54. Austin: University of Texas Press, 1991.

———, ed. *Beyond All Reason: The Cult Film Experience.* Austin: University of Texas Press, 1991.

DISASTER FILMS

Annan, David. *Catastrophe: The End of the Cinema?* New York: Bounty Books, 1975.

Kaplan, Fred. "Riches from Ruins." *Jump Cut,* no. 6 (March–April 1975): 3–4.

Keane, Stephen. *Disaster Movies: The Cinema of Catastrophe.* London: Wallflower Press, 2001.

Rosen, David N. "Drugged Popcorn." *Jump Cut,* no. 8 (August–September 1975): 19–20.

Ryan, Michael, and Douglas Kellner. *Camera Politica: The Politics and Ideology of Contemporary Hollywood Film.* Bloomington and Indianapolis: Indiana University Press, 1988.

Wood, Michael. *America in the Movies,* chap. 8. New York: Delta, 1975. Reprint, New York: Columbia University Press, 1989.

EPIC FILMS

Babington, Bruce, and Peter William Evans. *Biblical Epics.* Manchester: Manchester University Press, 1993.

Barra, Allen. "The Incredible Shrinking Epic." *American Film* 14, no. 5 (1989): 40–45, 60.

Baxter, John. *Hollywood in the Sixties.* New York: Barnes, 1972.

Cameron, Ian. *Adventure in the Cinema.* London: Studio Vista, 1973.

Campbell, Richard H., and Michael R. Pitts. *The Bible on Film: A Checklist, 1897–1980.* Metuchen, N.J.: Scarecrow Press, 1981.

Carey, John. *Spectacular: The Story of Epic Films.* Secaucus, N.J.: Castle Books, 1974.

Dickstein, Morris. "Time Bandits." *American Film* 8, no. 1 (October 1982): 39–43.

Durgnat, Raymond. "Epic, Epic, Epic, Epic, Epic." *Films and Filming* 10, no. 3 (December 1963): 9–12. Reprinted in *Film Genre: Theory and Criticism,* edited by Barry K. Grant, pp. 108–117. Metuchen, N.J.: Scarecrow Press, 1977.

Dyer, Peter John. "Some Mighty Spectacles." *Films and Filming* 4, no. 5 (February 1958): 13–15, 34.

Elley, Derek. *The Epic Film: Myth and History.* London: Routledge and Kegan Paul, 1984.

Everson, William K. "Film Spectacles." *Films in Review* 5 (November 1954): 459–471.

Forshey, Gerald E. *American Religious and Biblical Spectaculars.* Westport, Conn.: Praeger, 1992.

Hirsch, Foster. *The Hollywood Epic.* New York: A. S. Barnes, 1978.

Hunt, Leon. "What Are Big Boys Made Of? *Spartacus, El Cid,* and the Male Epic." In *You Tarzan: Masculinity, Movies and Men,* edited by Pat Kirkham and Janet Thumim, pp. 65–83. London: Lawrence and Wishart, 1993.

Mace, Nigel. "British Historical Epics in the Second World War." In *Britain and the Cinema in the Second World War,* edited by Philip M. Taylor, pp. 101–120. New York: St. Martin's Press, 1988.

Munn, Mike. *The Stories behind the Scenes of the Great Film Epics.* Watford, U.K.: Illustrated Publications/Argus Books, 1982.

Neale, Steve. *Genre and Hollywood.* New York and London: Routledge, 2000.

Reed, Joseph W. *American Scenarios: The Uses of Film Genre.* Middletown, Conn.: Wesleyan University Press, 1989.

Richards, Jeffrey. *Swordsmen on the Screen.* London: Routledge and Kegan Paul, 1980.

Robinson, David. "Spectacle." *Sight and Sound* 25, no. 1 (Summer 1955): 22–27, 55–56.

Slotkin, Richard. "The Continuity of Forms: Myth and Genre in Warner Brothers' *The Charge of the Light Brigade.*" *Representations,* no. 29 (Winter 1990): 1–23.

Smith, Gary A. *Epic Films: Casts, Credits, and Commentary on Over 250 Historical Spectacle Movies.* Jefferson, N.C.: McFarland, 1991.

Solomon, John. *The Ancient World in the Cinema.* Cranbury, N.J.: Barnes, 1978.

Whitehall, Richard. "Days of Strife and Nights of Orgy." *Films and Filming* 9, no. 6 (March 1963): 8–14.

Wood, Michael. *America in the Movies,* chap. 8. New York: Delta, 1975.

EXPLOITATION FILMS

Benshoff, Harry M. "The Short-Lived Life of the Hollywood LSD Film." *Velvet Light Trap,* no. 47 (Spring 2001): 29–44.

Betrock, Alan. *The I Was a Teenage Juvenile Delinquent Rock 'n' Roll Horror Beach Party Movie Book: A Complete Guide to the Teen Exploitation Film, 1954–1969.* New York: St. Martin's Press, 1986.

Brottman, Mikita. "Carnivalizing the Taboo—The Mondo Film and the Open Body." *CineAction,* no. 38 (1995): 25–37.

Clark, Randall. *At a Theater or Drive-in Near You: The History, Culture, and Politics of the American Exploitation Film.* New York: Garland, 1995.

Conrich, Ian. "Forgotten Cinema: The British Style of Sexploitation." *Journal of Popular British Cinema* no. 1 (1998): 87–100.

Cook, Pam. "Exploitation Films and Feminism." *Screen* 17, no. 2 (1976): 122–127.

Cross, Robin. *The Big Book of B Movies.* New York: St. Martin's Press, 1981.

Feaster, Felicia, and Bret Wood. *Forbidden Fruit: The Golden Age of the Exploitation Film.* Baltimore: Midnight Marquee, 1999.

Fischer, Craig. "*Beyond the Valley of the Dolls* and the Exploitation Genre." *Velvet Light Trap,* no. 30 (Fall 1992): 18–34.

McCarthy, Charles, and Todd Flynn, eds. *Kings of the Bs: Working within the Hollywood System.* New York: Dutton, 1975.

McClelland, Doug. *The Golden Age of B Movies.* Nashville: Charter House, 1978.

Miller, Don. "The American B Film." *Focus on Film,* no. 5 (Winter 1970): 31–32.

———. *B Movies.* New York: Ballantine Books, 1987.

Morton, Jim. "Rebels of the Road: The Biker Film." In *Lost Highways: An Illustrated History of Road Movies,* edited by Jack Sargeant and Stephanie Watson, pp. 56–66. London: Creation Books, 1999.

Newitz, Annalee. "What Makes Things Cheesy? Satire, Multinationalism, and B-Movies." *Social Text* 63 (2000): 59–82.

Quarles, Mike. *Down and Dirty: Hollywood's Exploitation Filmmakers and Their Movies.* Jefferson, N.C.: McFarland, 1993.

Samuels, Stuart. *Midnight Movies.* New York: Collier, 1983.

Schaefer, Eric. "*Bold! Daring! Shocking! True!*": A History of Exploitation Films, 1919–1959.* Durham and London: Duke University Press, 1999.

———. "Of Hygiene and Hollywood: Origins of the Exploitation Film." *Velvet Light Trap,* no. 30 (Fall 1992): 34–47.

Sconce, Jeffrey. "Trashing the Academy: Taste, Excess, and an Emerging Politics of Cinematic Style." *Screen* 36, no. 4 (Winter 1995): 371–393.

Taves, Brian. "The B Film: Hollywood's Other Half." In *History of the American Cinema,* vol. 5, *Grand Design: Hollywood as a Modern Business Enterprise, 1930–1939,* edited by Tino Balio, pp. 313–350. New York: Charles Scribner's Sons, 1993.

FILM NOIR

Arthur, Paul. "Murder's Tongue: Identity, Death, and the City in Film Noir." In *Violence and American Cinema,* edited by J. David Slocum, pp. 153–155. New York: Routledge, 2001.

Belton, John. *American Cinema/American Culture.* New York: McGraw-Hill, 1994.

Boozer, Jack. "The Lethal Femme Fatale in the Noir Tradition." *Journal of Film and Video* 51, nos. 3–4 (Fall 1999–Winter 2000): 20–35.

Borde, Raymond, and Etienne Chaumeton. "The Sources of Film Noir." *Film Reader,* no. 3 (1978): 58–66.

Bordwell, David, Janet Staiger, and Kristin Thompson. *The Classical Hollywood Cinema: Film Style and Mode of Production to 1960.* New York: Columbia University Press, 1985.

Bryan, Geraint. "Nowhere to Run: Pulp Noir on the Road." In *Lost Highways: An Illustrated History of Road Movies,* edited by Jack Sargeant and Stephanie Watson, pp. 44–54. London: Creation Books, 1999.

Buchsbaum, Jonathan. "Tame Wolves and Phony Claims: Paranoia and Film Noir." *Persistence of Vision,* nos. 3–4 (Summer 1986): 35–47.

Buss, Robin. *French Film Noir.* New York: Marion Boyers, 1994.

Cameron, Ian, ed. *The Movie Book of Film Noir.* New York: Continuum, 1992.

Christopher, Nicholas. *Somewhere in the Night: Film Noir and the American City.* New York: Free Press, 1997.

Cohen, Mitchell S. "Villains and Victims." *Film Comment* 10, no. 6 (November–December 1974): 27–29.

Cook, Pam, and Mieke Bernink, eds. *The Cinema Book,* 2d ed. London: British Film Institute, 1999.

Copjec, Joan, ed. *Shades of Noir.* London: Verso, 1993.

Cozarinsky, Edgardo. "American Film Noir." *Cinema: A Critical Dictionary,* edited by Richard Roud, pp. 57–64. New York: Viking Press, 1980.

Crowther, Bruce. *Film Noir: Reflections in a Dark Mirror.* London: Columbus Books, 1989.

Damico, James. "Film Noir: A Modest Proposal." *Film Reader,* no. 3 (1978): 48–57.

Dick, Bernard F. "Columbia Dark Ladies and the Femmes Fatales of Film Noir." *Literature/Film Quarterly* 23, no. 3 (1995): 155–162.

Doll, Susan, and Greg Faller. "*Blade Runner* and Genre: Film Noir and Science Fiction." *Literature/Film Quarterly* 14, no. 2 (1986): 89–100.

Durgnat, Raymond. "The Family Tree of Film Noir." *Film Comment* 10, no. 6 (November–December 1974): 6–7.

———. "Paint It Black: The Family Tree of Film Noir." *Cinema* (U.K.), nos. 6–7 (1970): 49–56.

Dyer, Richard. "Homosexuality and Film Noir." *Jump Cut,* no. 16 (1977): 18–21.

Elsaesser, Thomas. "A German Ancestry to Film Noir?—Film History and Its Imaginary." *Iris* 21 (1996): 129–144.

Ewing, Dale E., Jr. "Film Noir: Style and Content." *Journal of Popular Film and Television* 16, no. 2 (Summer 1988): 61–69.

Farber, Stephen. "Violence and the Bitch Goddess." *Film Comment* 10, no. 6 (November–December 1974): 8–11.

Flinn, Tom. "*The Big Heat* and *The Big Combo:* Rogue Cops and Mink-Coated Girls." *Velvet Light Trap* 11 (1974): 23–28.

Gorman, Edward, and Lee Server, eds. *The Big Book of Noir.* New York: Carroll and Graf, 1998.

Gross, Larry. "Film après Noir." *Film Comment* 12, no. 4 (July–August 1976): 44–49.

Higham, Charles, and Joel Greenberg. *Hollywood in the Forties.* Cranbury, N.J.: A. S. Barnes, 1968.

Hirsch, Foster. *The Dark Side of the Screen: Film Noir.* San Diego: A. S. Barnes, 1981.

———. *Detours and Lost Highways: A Map of Neo-Noir.* New York: Limelight, 1999.

House, Rebecca. "Night of the Soul: American Film Noir." *Studies in Popular Culture* 9, no. 1 (1986): 61–83.

Jameson, Richard T. "Son of Noir." *Film Comment* 10, no. 6 (November–December 1974): 30–33.

Kaplan, E. Ann, ed. *Women in Film Noir.* London: British Film Institute, 1978. Rev. ed., 1980.

Karimi, A. M. *Toward a Definition of the American Film Noir (1941–1949).* New York: Arno Press, 1976.

Kemp, Philip. "From the Nightmare Factory: HUAC and the Politics of Noir." *Sight and Sound* 55, no. 4 (Autumn 1986): 266–270.

Kerr, Paul. "Out of What Past? Notes on the B Film Noir." *Screen Education,* nos. 32–33 (Autumn–Winter 1979–80): 45–65. Reprinted in *The Hollywood Film Industry,* edited by Kerr, pp. 220–244. London and New York: Routledge and Kegan Paul, 1986.

Krutnik, Frank. "Desire, Transgression, and James M. Cain: Fiction into Film Noir." *Screen* 23, no. 1 (1982): 31–44.

———. *In a Lonely Street: Film Noir, Genre, and Masculinity.* London and New York: Routledge, 1991.

Leigh, Danny. "Get Smarter." *Sight and Sound* 10, no. 6 (June 2000): 22–25.

Liebman, Nina C. "The Family Spree of Film Noir." *Journal of Popular Film and Television* 16, no. 4 (Winter 1989): 168–184.

Lyons, Arthur. *Death on the Cheap: The Lost B Movies of Film Noir.* Cambridge, Mass.: Da Capo Press, 2000.

Lyons, Donald. "Detours." *Film Comment* 27, no. 4 (July–August 1991): 2–3.

McLean, Adrienne L. "'It's Only That I Do What I Love and Love What I Do': Film Noir and the Musical Woman." *Cinema Journal* 35, no. 1 (Fall 1993): 3–16.

Maltby, Richard. "Film Noir: The Politics of the Maladjusted Text." *Journal of American Studies* 18, no. 1 (1984): 49–71.

Marling, William. "On the Relation between American *Roman Noir* and *Film Noir.*" *Literature/Film Quarterly* 21, no. 3 (1993): 178–193.

Martin, Richard. *Mean Streets and Raging Bulls: The Legacy of Film Noir in Contemporary Cinema.* Lanham, Md.: Scarecrow Press, 1997.

Maxfield, James F. *The Fatal Woman: Sources of Male Anxiety in American Film Noir, 1941–1991.* Madison: Farleigh Dickinson University Press, 1996.

Meyer, David. *A Girl and a Gun: The Complete Guide to Film Noir on Video.* New York: Avon, 1998.

Miller, Laurence. "Evidence for a British Film Noir Cycle." *Film Criticism* 16, nos. 1–2 (Fall–Winter 1991–1992): 42–51.

Morrison, Susan. "The (Ideo)logical Consequences of Gender on Genre." *Cine-Action,* nos. 13–14 (August 1988): 41–45.

Muller, Eddie. *Dark City: The Lost World of Film Noir.* New York: St. Martin's Griffin, 1998.

Munby, Jonathan. *Public Enemies, Public Heroes: Screening the Gangster from* LITTLE CAESAR *to* TOUCH OF EVIL. Chicago: University of Chicago Press, 1999.

Murphet, Julian. "Noir and the Racial Unconscious." *Screen* 39, no. 1 (Spring 1998): 22–35.

Nachbar, Jack. "Film Noir." In *Handbook of American Film Genres,* edited by Wes D. Gehring, pp. 65–84. New York: Greenwood Press, 1988.

Naremore, James. *More Than Night: Film Noir in Its Contexts.* Berkeley: University of California Press, 1998.

Neale, Steve. *Genre and Hollywood,* chap. 4. New York and London: Routledge, 2000.

Neve, Brian. *Film and Politics in America: A Social Tradition.* London and New York: Routledge, 1992.

O'Brien, Charles. "Film Noir in France: Before the Liberation." *Iris* 21 (1996): 7–20.

Orr, John. *Cinema and Modernity,* chap. 8. Oxford: Polity Press, 1993.

Osteen, Mark. "The Big Secret: Film Noir and Nuclear Fear." *Journal of Popular Film and Television* 22, no. 2 (Summer 1994): 79–90.

Ottoson, Robert. *A Reference Guide to the American Film Noir: 1940–1958.* Metuchen, N.J.: Scarecrow Press, 1981.

Palmer, R. Barton. "Film Noir and the Genre Continuum: Process, Product, and *The Big Clock.*" *Persistence of Vision,* nos. 3–4 (Summer 1986): 51–60.

———. *Hollywood's Dark Cinema: The American Film Noir.* New York: Twayne, 1994.

———. *Perspectives on Film Noir.* New York: G. K. Hall, 1996.

Place, J. A., and L. S. Peterson. "Some Visual Motifs of Film Noir." *Film Comment* 10, no. 1 (January–February 1974): 30–32. Reprinted in *Movies and Methods,* edited by Bill Nichols, pp. 325–338. Berkeley: University of California Press, 1976.

Polan, Dana. *Power and Paranoia: History, Narrative, and the American Cinema, 1940–1950.* New York: Columbia University Press, 1986.

Porfirio, Robert G. "No Way Out: Existential Motifs in the Film Noir." *Sight and Sound* 45, no. 4 (Autumn 1976): 212–217.

Rabinowitz, Paula. "Domestic Labor: Film Noir, Proletarian Literature, and Black Women's Fiction." *Modern Fiction Studies* 47, no. 1 (Spring 2001): 229–254.

Ray, Robert B. *A Certain Tendency of the Hollywood Cinema, 1930–1980.* Princeton: Princeton University Press, 1985.

Richardson, Carl. *Autopsy: An Element of Realism in Film Noir.* Metuchen, N.J.: Scarecrow Press, 1992.

Schultheiss, John. "The Noir Artist." *Films in Review* 40, no. 1 (January 1989): 33–35.

Selby, Spencer. *Dark City: The Film Noir.* Jefferson, N.C.: McFarland, 1984.

Shadoian, Jack. *Dreams and Dead Ends: The American Gangster/Crime Film,* chap. 2. Cambridge: MIT Press, 1977.

Silver, Alain, and Elizabeth Ward, eds. *Film Noir: An Encyclopedic Reference to the American Style.* Woodstock, N.Y.: Overlook Press, 1979.

Silver, Alain, and James Ursini, eds. *Film Noir Reader.* New York: Limelight, 1996.

———. *Film Noir Reader 2.* New York: Limelight, 1999.

Smith, Murray. "Film Noir, the Female Gothic, and *Deception.*" *Wide Angle* 10, no. 1 (1988): 62–75.

Sobchack, Vivian. "Lounge Time: Postwar Crises and the Chronotope of Film Noir." In *Refiguring American Film Genres: History and Theory,* edited by Nick Browne, pp. 129–170. Berkeley: University of California Press, 1998.

Stephens, Michael L. *Film Noir: A Comprehensive, Illustrated Reference to Movies, Terms, and Persons.* Jefferson, N.C.: McFarland, 1994.

Telotte, J. P. "The Big Clock of Film Noir." *Film Criticism* 14, no. 2 (Winter 1989–1990): 1–11.

———. "A Consuming Passion: Food and Film Noir." *Georgia Review* 39, no. 2 (Summer 1985): 397–410.

———. "Film Noir at Columbia: Fashion and Innovation." In *Columbia Pictures: Portrait of a Studio,* edited by Bernard F. Dick, pp. 106–117. Lexington: University Press of Kentucky, 1992.

———. "Film Noir and the Dangers of Discourse." *Quarterly Review of Film Studies* 9, no. 2 (Spring 1984): 101–112. Reprinted in *Voices in the Dark: The Narrative Patterns of Film Noir.* Urbana: University of Illinois Press, 1989.

———. "Film Noir and the Double Indemnity of Discourse." *Genre* 18, no. 1 (Spring 1985): 57–73.

———. "Outside the System: The Documentary Voice of Film Noir." *New Orleans Review* 14, no. 2 (Summer 1987): 55–63. Reprinted in *Voices in the Dark: The Narrative Patterns of Film Noir.* Urbana: University of Illinois Press, 1989.

———. "Seeing in a *Dark Passage.*" *Film Criticism* 9, no. 2 (Winter 1984–1985): 15–27.

———. "Self-Portrait: Painting and the Film Noir." *Smithsonian Studies in American Art* 3, no. 1 (Spring 1989): 3–17.

———. "Siodmak's Phantom Women and Noir Narrative." *Film Criticism* 11, no. 3 (Spring 1987): 1–10.

———. "Talk and Trouble: *Kiss Me Deadly*'s Apocalyptic Discourse." *Journal of Popular Film and Television* 13, no. 2 (Summer 1985): 69–79. Reprinted in *Voices in the Dark: The Narrative Patterns of Film Noir.* Urbana: University of Illinois Press, 1989.

———. *Voices in the Dark: The Narrative Patterns of Film Noir.* Urbana: University of Illinois Press, 1989.

Thomas, Deborah. "Film Noir: How Hollywood Deals with the Deviant Male." *CineAction,* nos. 13–14 (August 1988): 18–28.

Turim, Maureen. *Flashbacks in Film: Memory and History.* New York and London: Routledge, 1989.

Tuska, Jon. *Dark Cinema: American Film Noir in Cultural Perspective.* Westport, Conn.: Greenwood Press, 1984.

Vernet, Marc. "The Filmic Transaction: On the Openings of Film Noirs." *Velvet Light Trap,* no. 20 (Summer 1983): 2–9.

Wager, Jans. *Dangerous Dames: Women and Representation in the Weimar Street Film and Film Noir.* Athens: Ohio University Press, 2000.

Whitney, John S. "A Filmography of Film Noir." *Journal of Popular Film* 5, nos. 3–4 (1976): 321–371.

Wood, Michael. *America in the Movies,* chap. 5. New York: Delta, 1975. Reprint, New York: Columbia University Press, 1989.

Wood, Nancy. "Women in Film Noir." *Ciné-Tracts* 2, no. 2 (Spring 1979): 74–79.

Younger, Richard. "Song in Contemporary Film Noir." *Films in Review* 45, nos. 7–8 (July–August 1994): 48–51.

GANGSTER FILMS

Alloway, Lawrence. *Violent America: The Movies, 1946–1964.* New York: Museum of Modern Art, 1971.

Andrew, Geoff. *Hollywood Gangsters.* New York: Gallery Books, 1985.

Baxter, John. *The Gangster Film.* New York: A. S. Barnes, 1970.

Bergman, Andrew. *We're in the Money.* New York: Harper and Row, 1972. Rev. ed., Chicago: Elephant, 1992.

Bookbinder, Robert. *Classics of the Gangster Film.* Secaucus, N.J.: Citadel Press, 1993.

Cook, Pam, and Mieke Bernink, eds. *The Cinema Book,* 2d ed. London: British Film Institute, 1999.

Gabree, John. *Gangsters: From LITTLE CAESAR to THE GODFATHER.* New York: Galahad Books, 1973.

Hardy, Phil. *Gangsters.* London: Aurum, 1998.

Hennelly, Mark M., Jr. "American Nightmare: The Underworld in Film." *Journal of Popular Film* 6, no. 3 (1978): 240–261.

Karpf, Stephen L. "The Gangster Film." In *The American Cinema,* 3d ed., edited by Donald E. Staples, pp. 235–245. Washington, D.C.: United States Information Agency, 1991.

———. *The Gangster Film: Emergence, Variation, and Decay of a Genre, 1930–1940.* New York: Arno Press, 1973.

McArthur, Colin. *Underworld U.S.A.* New York: Viking, 1972.

McCarty, John. *Hollywood Gangland: The Movies' Love Affair with the Mob.* New York: St. Martin's Press, 1993.

Maltby, Richard. "The Spectacle of Criminality." In *Violence and American Cinema,* edited by J. David Slocum, pp. 117–152. New York and London: Routledge, 2001.

Munby, Jonathan. *Public Enemies, Public Heroes: Screening the Gangster from LITTLE CAESAR to TOUCH OF EVIL.* Chicago: University of Chicago Press, 1999.

Parish, James R., and Michael R. Pitts. *The Great Gangster Pictures.* Metuchen, N.J.: Scarecrow Press, 1976.

————. *The Great Gangster Pictures II*. Metuchen, N.J.: Scarecrow Press, 1987.

Peary, Gerald. "Notes on Early Gangster Comedy." *Velvet Light Trap,* no. 3 (Winter 1971–1972): 16–18.

Phillips, Mike. "Chic and Beyond." *Sight and Sound* 6, no. 8 (August 1996): 16–18.

Raeburn, John. "The Gangster Film." In *Handbook of American Film Genres,* edited by Wes D. Gehring, pp. 47–63. New York: Greenwood Press, 1988.

Roffman, Peter, and Jim Purdy. *The Hollywood Social Problem Film: Madness, Despair, and Politics from the Depression to the Fifties.* Bloomington: Indiana University Press, 1992.

Rosow, Eugene. *Born to Lose: The Gangster Film in America.* New York: Oxford University Press, 1978.

Roulston, Helen H. "Opera in Gangster Movies: From Capone to Coppola." *Journal of Popular Culture* 32, no. 1 (Summer 1998): 99–111.

Sacks, Arthur. "An Analysis of the Gangster Movies of the Early Thirties." *Velvet Light Trap,* no. 1 (June 1971): 5–11, 32.

Sarris, Andrew. "Big Funerals: The Hollywood Gangster, 1927–1933." *Film Comment* 13, no. 3 (May–June 1977): 6–9.

Schatz, Thomas. *Hollywood Genres: Formulas, Filmmaking, and the Studio System.* New York: Random House, 1981.

Shadoian, Jack. *Dreams and Dead Ends: The American Gangster/Crime Film.* Cambridge: MIT Press, 1977.

Simmons, Garner. "The Generic Origins of the Bandit-Gangster Sub-Genre in the American Cinema." *Film Reader,* no. 3 (1978): 67–79.

Solomon, Stanley J. *Beyond Formula: American Film Genres.* New York: Harcourt Brace Jovanovich, 1976.

Springhall, John. "Censoring Hollywood: Youth, Moral Panic, and Crime/Gangster Movies of the 1930s." *Journal of Popular Culture* 32, no. 3 (Winter 1998): 135–154.

Stephens, Michael L. *Gangster Films: A Comprehensive, Illustrated Reference to People, Films, and Terms.* Jefferson, N.C.: McFarland, 1996.

Thomson, David. *America in the Dark: Hollywood and the Gift of Unreality,* chap. 6. New York: William Morrow, 1977.

Tudor, Andrew. *Image and Influence: Studies in the Sociology of Film.* London: George Allen and Unwin, 1974.

Walker, Mark. *Vietnam Veteran Films.* Metuchen, N.J.: Scarecrow Press, 1991.

Warner, Alan. "Gangster Heroes." *Films and Filming* 18, no. 2 (November 1971): 16–25.

Warshow, Robert. "The Gangster as Tragic Hero." In *The Immediate Experience,* pp. 127–133. New York: Atheneum, 1970.

Whitehall, Richard. "Crime, Inc.: A Three-Part Dossier on the American Gangster Film." Part 1: "Rackets and Mobs in American Gangster Films," *Films and Filming* 10, no. 4 (January 1964): 7–12. Part 2: "G-Men and Gangsters," *Films and Filming* 10, no. 5 (February 1964): 17–22. Part 3: "Public Enemies," *Films and Filming* 10, no. 6 (March 1964): 39–44.

Winokur, Mark. "The African-American Voice in the Nouvelle Gangster Film." *Velvet Light Trap,* no. 35 (Spring 1995): 19–32.

————. "Eating Children Is Wrong." *Sight and Sound* 1, no. 7 (November 1991): 10–13.

HORROR FILMS

Armstrong, Michael. "Some Like It Chilled." 4 pts. *Films and Filming* 17, no. 5 (February 1971): 28–34; 17, no. 6 (March 1971): 32–37; 17, no. 7 (April 1971): 37–42; 17, no. 8 (May 1971): 77–82.

Arnzen, Michael A. "Who's Laughing Now? The Postmodern Splatter Film." *Journal of Popular Film and Television* 21, no. 4 (Winter 1994): 176–184.

Aylesworth, Thomas G. *Monsters from the Movies*. Philadelphia and New York: J. B. Lippincott, 1972.

Badley, Linda. *Film, Horror, and the Body Fantastic*. Westport, Conn.: Greenwood Press, 1995.

Balio, Tino, ed. *History of the American Cinema*, vol. 5, *Grand Design: Hollywood as a Modern Business Enterprise, 1930–1939*, pp. 298–310. New York: Charles Scribner's Sons, 1993.

Barron, Neil. *Fantasy and Horror: A Cultural and Historical Guide to Literature, Illustration, Film, TV, Radio, and the Internet*. Lanham, Md.: Scarecrow Press, 1999.

Benshoff, Harry. "Blaxploitation Horror Films: Generic Reappropriation or Reinscription?" *Cinema Journal* 39, no. 2 (Winter 2000): 31–50.

————. *Monsters in the Closet: Homosexuality and the Horror Film*. Manchester: Manchester University Press, 1997.

Benton, Robert J. "The Return of the Projected: Some Thoughts on Paranoia and a Recent Trend in Horror Films." *Psychoanalytic Review* 82, no. 6 (1995): 903–931.

Bernstein, Rhona. *Attack of the Leading Ladies: Gender, Sexuality, and Spectatorship in Classic Horror Cinema*. New York: Columbia University Press, 1996.

————. "Mommie Dearest: *Aliens, Rosemary's Baby*, and Mothering." *Journal of Popular Culture* 24, no. 2 (Fall 1990): 55–73.

Borst, Ronald V. *Graven Images: The Best of Horror, Fantasy, and Science Fiction Film Art*. New York: Grove Press, 1992.

Boss, Pete. "Vile Bodies and Bad Medicine." *Screen* 27, no. 1 (January–February 1986): 14–24.

Brophy, Philip. "Horrality—The Textuality of Contemporary Horror Films." *Screen* 27, no. 1 (January–February 1986): 2–13.

Brosnan, John. *The Horror People*. New York: New American Library, 1977.

Brunas, Michael, John Brunas, and Tom Weaver. *Universal Horrors: The Studio's Classic Films, 1931–1946*. Jefferson, N.C.: McFarland, 1990.

Brustein, Robert. "Reflections on Horror Movies." *Partisan Review* 25, no. 2 (Spring 1958): 288–296.

Burke, Frank. "'We All Go a Little Mad Sometimes, Haven't You?' Alterity and Self-Other Mirroring in Horror Film and Criticism." *Journal of the Fantastic in the Arts* 2, no. 4 (1990): 74–94.

Butler, Ivan. *Horror in the Cinema*. New York: A. S. Barnes, 1970.

Carroll, Noel. "Horror and Humor." *Journal of Aesthetics and Art Criticism* 57, no. 2 (1999): 145–160.

———. "The Nature of Horror." *Journal of Aesthetics and Art Criticism* 46, no. 1 (1987): 51–59.

———. "Nightmare and the Horror Film: The Symbolic Biology of Fantastic Beings." *Film Quarterly* 34, no. 3 (Spring 1981): 16–25. Reprinted in *The Anxious Subject: Nightmares and Daydreams in Literature and Film,* edited by Moshe Lazar, pp. 91–105. Malibu, Calif.: Undena, 1983.

———. *The Philosophy of Horror; Or, Paradoxes of the Heart.* New York and London: Routledge, 1990.

Clarens, Carlos. *An Illustrated History of the Horror Film.* New York: Capricorn Books, 1968.

Clements, William M. "The Interstitial Ogre: The Structure of Horror in Expressive Culture." *South Atlantic Quarterly* 86, no. 1 (Winter 1987): 34–43.

Clover, Carol J. "Her Body, Himself: Gender in the Slasher Film." *Representations,* no. 20 (Fall 1987): 187–228. Reprinted in *Misogyny, Misandry, and Misanthropy,* edited by R. Howard Bloch and Frances Ferguson, pp. 187–228. Berkeley: University of California Press, 1989. *Fantasy and the Cinema,* edited by James Donald, pp. 91–133. London: British Film Institute, 1989. *Gender, Language, and Myth: Essays on Popular Narrative,* edited by Glenwood Irons, pp. 252–302. Toronto: University of Toronto Press, 1992. *The Dread of Difference: Gender and the Horror Film,* edited by Barry Keith Grant, pp. 66–113. Austin: University of Texas Press, 1996.

———. "High and Low: The Transformation of the Rape-Revenge Movie." *Sight and Sound* 2, no. 1 (May 1992): 16–18. Reprinted in *Women and Film: A Sight and Sound Reader,* edited by Pam Cook and Philip Dodd, pp. 76–85. Philadelphia: Temple University Press, 1993.

———. *Men, Women, and Chain Saws: Gender in the Modern Horror Film.* Princeton: Princeton University Press, 1992.

Coates, Paul. *The Gorgon's Gaze: German Cinema, Expressionism, and the Image of Horror.* Cambridge: Cambridge University Press, 1991.

Cook, Pam, and Mieke Bernink, eds. *The Cinema Book,* 2d ed. London: British Film Institute, 1999.

Cowie, Susan D., and Tom Johnson. *The Mummy in Fact, Fiction, and Film.* Jefferson, N.C.: McFarland, 2002.

Crane, Jonathan Lake. *Terror and Everyday Life: Singular Moments in the History of the Horror Film.* Thousand Oaks, Calif.: Sage Publications, 1994.

Creed, Barbara. "From Here to Modernity: Feminism and Postmodernism." *Screen* 28, no. 2 (1987): 47–67.

———. "Horror and the Monstrous-Feminine: An Imaginary Abjection." *Screen* 27, no. 1 (1986): 44–70. Reprinted in *Fantasy and the Cinema,* edited by James Donald, pp. 63–89. London: British Film Institute, 1989. *The Dread of Difference: Gender and the Horror Film,* edited by Barry Keith Grant, pp. 35–65. Austin: University of Texas Press, 1996.

———. *The Monstrous-Feminine: Film, Feminism, Psychoanalysis.* London: Routledge, 1993.

Crutchfield, Susan. "Touching Scenes and Finishing Touches: Blindness in the

Slasher Film." In *Mythologies of Violence in Postmodern Media,* pp. 275–299. Detroit: Wayne State University Press, 1999.

Cruz, Omayra, and Ray Guines. "Asphalt Veins: On and Off the Road with the Vampire." In *Lost Highways: An Illustrated History of Road Movies,* edited by Jack Sargeant and Stephanie Watson, pp. 130–146. London: Creation Books, 1999.

Dadoun, Roger. "Fetishism in the Horror Film." *Enclitic* 1, no. 2 (1979): 39–63. Reprinted in *Fantasy and the Cinema,* edited by James Donald, pp. 39–61. London: British Film Institute, 1989.

Daniels, Les. *Living in Fear: A History of Horror in the Mass Media.* New York: Charles Scribner's Sons, 1975.

Davis, Brian. "The *Psycho* Syndrome." In *The Thriller.* London and New York: Studio Vista/Dutton, 1973.

Dendle, Peter. *The Zombie Movie Encyclopedia.* Jefferson, N.C.: McFarland, 2001.

Derry, Charles. "The Horror of Personality." *Cinéfantastique* 3, no. 3 (Fall 1974): 15–19.

Dickstein, Morris. "The Aesthetics of Fright." *American Film* 5, no. 10 (September 1980): 32–37, 56–59. Reprinted in *Planks of Reason: Essays on the Horror Film,* edited by Barry K. Grant, pp. 65–78. Metuchen, N.J.: Scarecrow Press, 1984.

Dika, Vera. *Games of Terror: HALLOWEEN, FRIDAY THE 13TH, and the Films of the Stalker Cycle.* Rutherford, N.J.: Farleigh Dickinson University Press, 1990.

Dillard, R. H. W. "Even a Man Who Is Pure at Heart: Poetry and Danger in the Horror Film." In *Man and the Movies,* edited by W. R. Robinson, pp. 60–69. Baltimore: Penguin, 1967.

———. *Horror Films.* New York: Monarch Press, 1976.

Doherty, Thomas. *Teenagers and Teenpics: The Juvenilization of American Movies in the 1950s.* Boston: Unwin Hyman, 1988.

Donald, James, ed. *Fantasy and the Cinema.* London: British Film Institute, 1989.

Douglas, Drake. *Horror.* New York: Macmillan, 1966.

Draper, Ellen. "Zombie Women When the Gaze Is Male." *Wide Angle* 10, no. 3 (1988): 52–62.

Dyer, Peter John. "All Manner of Fantasies." *Films and Filming* 4, no. 9 (June 1958): 13–15, 34–35.

———. "The Roots of Horror." In *International Film Annual,* no. 3, edited by William Whitebair, pp. 60–69. New York: Taplinger, 1959.

———. "Some Nights of Horror." *Films and Filming* 4, no. 10 (July 1958): 13–15, 34–35.

Dyson, Jeremy. *Bright Darkness: The Lost Art of the Supernatural Horror Film.* New York: Continuum, 1977.

Ebert, Roger. "Why Audiences Aren't Safe Anymore." *American Film* 6, no. 5 (March 1981): 54–56.

Eisner, Lotte. *The Haunted Screen.* Berkeley: University of California Press, 1973.

Ellison, Harlan. "Three Faces of Fear." *Cinema* (U.S.) 3, no. 2 (March 1966): 4–8, 13–14.

Elsaesser, Thomas. "Social Mobility and the Fantastic: German Silent Cinema."

Wide Angle 5, no. 2 (1982): 14–25. Revised and reprinted in *Fantasy and the Cinema,* edited by James Donald, pp. 23–38. London: British Film Institute, 1989.

Erens, Patricia. "*The Seduction:* The Pornographic Impulse in Slasher Films." *Jump Cut,* no. 32 (1987): 53–55, 52.

Evans, Walter. "Monster Movies and Rites of Initiation." *Journal of Popular Film* 4, no. 2 (1975): 124–142.

———. "Monster Movies: A Sexual Theory." *Journal of Popular Film* 2, no. 4 (Fall 1973): 353–365. Reprinted in *Planks of Reason: Essays on the Horror Film,* edited by Barry K. Grant, pp. 53–64. Metuchen, N.J.: Scarecrow Press, 1984.

Everson, William K. *Classics of the Horror Film.* Secaucus, N.J.: Citadel Press, 1974.

———. "A Family Tree of Monsters." *Film Culture* 1, no. 1 (January 1955): 24–30.

———. "Horror Films." *Films in Review* 5, no. 1 (January 1954): 12–23.

———. *More Classics of the Horror Film.* Secaucus, N.J.: Citadel, 1986.

Fell, John. "Melogenre." *North Dakota Quarterly* 51, no. 3 (Summer 1983): 100–110.

Figenshy, Tom. "Screams of a Summer Night." *Film Comment* 15, no. 5 (September–October 1979): 49–53.

Fischer, Dennis. *Horror Film Directors, 1931–1990.* Jefferson, N.C.: McFarland, 1991.

Fisher, David. "The Angel, the Devil, and the Space Traveller." *Sight and Sound* 23, no. 3 (January–March 1954): 155–157.

Flynn, John L. *Cinematic Vampires: The Living Dead on Film and Television, from THE DEVIL'S CASTLE to BRAM STOKER'S DRACULA.* Jefferson, N.C.: McFarland, 1992.

Fox, Julian. "The Golden Age of Terror." 5 parts: *Films and Filming* 22, no. 9 (June 1976): 16–23; 22, no. 10 (July 1976): 18–24; 22, no. 11 (August 1976): 20–24; 22, no. 12 (September 1976): 20–25; 23, no. 1 (October 1976): 18–25.

Frank, Alan. *The Horror Film Handbook.* Totowa, N.J.: Barnes and Noble, 1982.

———. *Horror Movies: Tales of Terror in the Cinema.* London: Octopus, 1974.

Fraser, John. "Watching Horror Movies." *Michigan Quarterly Review* 29, no. 1 (Winter 1990): 39–54.

Freeland, Cynthia. *The Naked and the Undead: Evil and the Appeal of Horror.* Boulder: Westview Press, 1999.

Galbraith, Stuart, IV. *Japanese Science Fiction, Fantasy, and Horror Films: A Critical Analysis and Filmography of 103 Features Released in the United States, 1950–1992.* Jefferson, N.C.: McFarland, 1994.

Gelder, Ken. *Reading the Vampire.* New York and London: Routledge, 1994.

———, ed. *The Horror Reader.* New York and London: Routledge, 2000.

Gifford, Denis. *Movie Monsters.* New York: Dutton, 1967.

———. *A Pictorial History of Horror Movies.* New York: Hamlyn, 1973.

Glut, Donald F. *Classic Movie Monsters.* Metuchen, N.J.: Scarecrow Press, 1978.

———. *The Frankenstein Catalogue.* Jefferson, N.C.: McFarland, 1984.

Grant, Barry Keith. "Rich and Strange: The Yuppie Horror Film." *Journal of Film and Video* 48, nos. 1–2 (Spring–Summer 1996): 4–16. Reprinted in *Contemporary Hollywood Cinema,* edited by Steve Neale and Murray Smith, pp. 280–293. New York and London: Routledge, 1998.

———. "Taking Back *The Night of the Living Dead:* George Romero, Feminism, and the Horror Film." *Wide Angle* 14, no. 1 (January 1992): 64–75. Reprinted in *The Dread of Difference: Gender and the Horror Film,* edited by Grant, pp. 200–212. Austin: University of Texas Press, 1996.

———, ed. *The Dread of Difference: Gender and the Horror Film.* Austin: University of Texas Press, 1996.

———, ed. *Planks of Reason: Essays on the Horror Film.* Metuchen, N.J.: Scarecrow Press, 1984.

Greenberg, Harvey R. "The Fractures of Desire: Psychoanalytic Notes on *Alien* and the Contemporary 'Cruel' Horror Film." *Psychoanalytic Review* 70, no. 2 (1983): 241–267.

———. *The Movies on Your Mind.* New York: Saturday Review Press/Dutton, 1975.

Guerrero, Edward. "AIDS as Monster in Science Fiction and Horror Cinema." *Journal of Popular Film and Television* 18, no. 3 (Fall 1990): 86–93.

———. *Framing Blackness: The African American Image in Film,* chap. 2. Philadelphia: Temple University Press, 1993.

Halberstam, Judith. *Skin Shows: Gothic Horror and the Technology of Monsters.* Durham, N.C.: Duke University Press, 1995.

Halliwell, Leslie. "The Baron, the Count, and Their Ghoul Friends." 2 pts. *Films and Filming* 15, no. 9 (June 1969): 13–16; 15, no. 10 (July 1969): 12–16.

———. *The Dead That Walk: Dracula, Frankenstein, the Mummy, and Other Favorite Movie Monsters.* New York: Continuum, 1988.

Hanke, Ken. *A Critical Guide to Horror Film Series.* Hamden, Conn.: Garland, 1991.

Hardy, Phil, ed. *The Encyclopedia of Horror Films.* New York: Harper and Row, 1986.

Hawkins, Joan. *Cutting-Edge: Art-Horror and the Horrific Avant-Garde.* Minneapolis: University of Minnesota Press, 2000.

Heldreth, Leonard G. "The Beast Within: Sexuality and Metamorphosis in Horror Films." In *Eros in the Mind's Eye,* edited by Donald Palumbo, pp. 117–125. New York: Greenwood Press, 1986.

Helfield, Gillian. "Mirror, Mirror on the Wall: Parent and Psycho as One in the 90's." *CineAction,* no. 30 (Winter 1992): 63–67.

Hendershot, Cyndy. "Vampire and Replicant: The One-Sex Body in a Two-Sex World." *Science Fiction Studies,* no. 67 (November 1995): 373–398.

Higham, Charles, and Joel Greenberg. *Hollywood in the Forties.* New York: A. S. Barnes, 1968.

Hill, Derek. "Horror." *Sight and Sound* 28, no. 1 (Winter 1958–1959): 6–11.

Hogan, David J. *Dark Romance: Sex and Death in the Horror Film.* Jefferson, N.C.: McFarland, 1986.

Hollinger, Karen. "The Monster as Woman: Two Generations of Cat People." *Film Criticism* 13, no. 2 (Winter 1989): 36–46. Reprinted in *The Dread of Dif-*

ference: Gender and the Horror Film, edited by Barry Keith Grant, pp. 296–308. Austin: University of Texas Press, 1998.

Holte, James Craig. "A Century of Draculas." *Journal of the Fantastic in the Arts* 10, no. 2 (1999): 109–115.

———. "Not All Fangs Are Phallic: Female Film Vampires." *Journal of the Fantastic in the Arts* 10, no. 2 (1999): 163–173.

Hunt, Leon. "Pleasure and Excess: Vincent Price and the Horror Film." *Movie,* no. 36 (2000): 80–96.

———. "A (Sadistic) Night at the *Opera:* Notes on the Italian Horror Film." *Velvet Light Trap,* no. 30 (Fall 1992): 65–75.

Huss, Roy, and T. J. Ross, eds. *Focus on the Horror Film.* Englewood Cliffs, N.J.: Prentice-Hall, 1972.

Hutchings, Peter. *Hammer and Beyond: The British Horror Film.* Manchester: Manchester University Press, 1993.

———. "Masculinity and the Horror Film." *You Tarzan: Masculinity, Movies, and Men,* edited by Pat Kirkham and Janet Thumim, pp. 84–94. London: Lawrence and Wishart, 1993.

Hutchinson, Tom. *Horror and Fantasy in the Cinema.* London: Studio Vista, 1974.

Jancovich, Mark. *Horror.* London: Batsford, 1992.

———. *Rational Fears: The American Horror Genre in the 1950s.* Manchester: Manchester University Press, 1996.

Jensen, Paul M. *The Men Who Made the Movies.* New York: Twayne, 1996.

Jones, E. Michael. *Monsters from the Id: The Rise of Horror in Film and Fiction.* Dallas: Spence, 2000.

Kaminsky, Stuart. *American Film Genres: Approaches to a Critical Theory of Popular Film,* chap. 7. Dayton, Ohio: Pflaum, 1974.

Kane, Joe. "Beauties, Beasts, and Male Chauvinist Monsters." *Take One* 4, no. 4 (March–April 1973): 8–10.

Kapsis, Robert E. "Dressed to Kill." *American Film* 7, no. 5 (1982): 52–56.

Kawin, Bruce. "The Mummy's Pool." *Dreamworks* 1, no. 4 (Summer 1981): 291–301. Reprinted in *Planks of Reason: Essays on the Horror Film,* edited by Barry Keith Grant, pp. 3–20. Metuchen, N.J.: Scarecrow Press, 1984. *Film Theory and Criticism,* edited by Gerald Mast, Marshall Cohen, and Leo Braudy, pp. 549–560. New York: Oxford University Press, 1992.

Kendrick, Walter. *The Thrill of Fear: 250 Years of Scary Entertainment.* New York: Grove Press, 1991.

Kennedy, Harlan. "Things That Go Howl in the Id." *Film Comment* 18, no. 2 (March–April 1982): 37–39.

King, Cynthia. "What's So Funny? Humor in Horror Films." *Creative Screenwriting* 7, no. 4 (2000): 47–53.

King, Stephen. *Danse Macabre.* New York: Everett House, 1981.

Kinnard, Roy. *Horror in Silent Films: A Filmography, 1896–1929.* Jefferson, N.C.: McFarland, 1995.

Kovacs, Lee. *The Haunted Screen: Ghosts in Literature and Film.* Jefferson, N.C.: McFarland, 1999.

Krasniewicz, Louie. "Cinematic Gifts: The Moral and Social Exchange of Bodies in Horror Films." In *Tattoo, Torture, Mutilation, and Adornment: The Denat-*

uralization of the Body in Culture and Text, edited by Frances E. Mascia-Lees and Patricia Sharpe, pp. 30–47. New York: SUNY Press, 1992.

Landy, Marcia. *British Genres: Cinema and Society, 1930–1960.* Princeton: Princeton University Press, 1991.

Lavery, David. "The Horror Film and the Horror of Film." *Film Criticism* 7, no. 1 (Fall 1982): 47–55.

Lazar, Moshe, ed. *The Anxious Subject: Nightmares and Daydreams in Literature and Film.* Malibu, Calif.: Undena, 1983.

Lee, Walt, ed. *Reference Guide to Fantastic Films: Science Fiction, Fantasy, and Horror.* 3 vols. Los Angeles: Chelsea-Lee Books, 1972.

Lenne, Gérard. "Monster and Victim: Women in the Horror Film." In *Sexual Stratagems,* edited by Patricia Erens, pp. 31–40. New York: Horizon Press, 1979.

Lentz, Harris, III. *Science Fiction, Horror, and Fantasy Film and Television Credits.* 2 vols. Jefferson, N.C.: McFarland, 1983.

———. *Science Fiction, Horror and Fantasy Film and Television Credits Supplement: Through 1987.* Jefferson, N.C.: McFarland, 1989.

London, Rose. *Zombie: The Living Dead.* New York: Bounty Books, 1976.

Losano, Wayne A. "The Vampire Rises Again in Films of the Seventies." *Film Journal* 2, no. 2 (1973): 60–62.

Lowry, Edward. "Genre and Enunciation: The Case of Horror." *Journal of Film and Video* 36, no. 2 (1984): 13–20, 72.

Lucanio, Patrick. *Them or Us: Archetypal Interpretations of Fifties Alien Invasion Films.* Bloomington and Indianapolis: Indiana University Press, 1987.

McCallum, Lawrence. *Italian Horror Films of the 1960s: A Critical Catalogue of 62 Chillers.* Jefferson, N.C.: McFarland, 1998.

McCarty, John. *John McCarty's Splatter Movie Guide,* vol. 2. New York: St. Martin's Press, 1992.

———. *The Modern Horror Film.* New York: Citadel Press, 1990.

———. *Psychos: Ninety Years of Mad Movies, Maniacs, and Murderous Deeds.* New York: Carol Publishing Group, 1986.

———. *Splatter Movies.* New York: St. Martin's Press, 1984.

McConnell, Frank. "Rough Beasts Slouching: A Note on Horror Movies." *Kenyon Review* 128 (1970): 109–120.

McIntosh, David. "Howling at the Machine: A Bed-Time Story." *CineAction,* no. 10 (Fall 1987): 60–64.

Manchel, Frank. *Terrors of the Screen.* Englewood Cliffs, N.J.: Prentice-Hall, 1970.

Mank, Gregory W. *It's Alive! The Classic Cinema Saga of Frankenstein.* San Diego: A. S. Barnes, 1981.

Maxford, Howard. *The A–Z of Horror Films.* Bloomington: Indiana University Press, 1996.

Modleski, Tania. "The Terror of Pleasure: The Contemporary Horror Film and Postmodern Theory." University of Wisconsin at Milwaukee, Center for Twentieth-Century Studies, Working Paper, no. 8 (Fall 1984). Reprinted in *Studies in Entertainment,* edited by Tania Modleski, pp. 155–166. Bloomington and Indianapolis: Indiana University Press, 1986.

Monaco, James. "Aaaiieeaaraggh! Horror Movies." *Sight and Sound* 49, no. 2 (Spring 1980): 80–81.

Moretti, Franco. "Dialectic of Fear." In *Signs Taken for Wonders,* pp. 83–106. London: Verso, 1983.

Murphy, Robert. *Sixties British Cinema,* chap. 8. London: British Film Institute, 1992.

Naha, Ed. *Horrors from Screen to Scream.* New York: Avon, 1975.

Neale, Steve. *Genre and Hollywood.* New York and London: Routledge, 2000.

Neuendorf, Kimberly A., and Glenn G. Sparks. "Predicting Emotional Responses to Horror Films from Cue-Specific Affect." *Communications Quarterly* 36, no. 1 (Winter 1988): 16–27.

Newman, Kim. *Nightmare Movies: A Guide to Contemporary Horror Films.* New York: Harmony Books, 1988.

Nicholls, Peter. *The World of Fantastic Films: An Illustrated Survey.* New York: Dodd, Mead, 1984.

Oliver, Mary Beth. "Adolescents' Enjoyment of Graphic Horror." *Communication Research* 20, no. 1 (1993): 30–50.

Pannill, Linda. "The Woman Artist as Creature and Creator." *Journal of Popular Culture* 16, no. 2 (Fall 1982): 26–29.

Pattison, Barrie. *The Seal of Dracula.* New York: Bounty Books, 1975.

Pendo, Stephen. "Universal's Golden Age of Horror." *Films in Review* 26, no. 3 (March 1975): 155–161.

Peters, Nancy Joyce. "Backyard Bombs and Invisible Rays: Horror Movies on Television." *Cultural Correspondence,* nos. 10–11 (Fall 1979): 39–42.

Pinedo, Isabel. "Recreational Terror: Postmodern Elements of the Contemporary Horror Film." *Journal of Film and Video* 48, nos. 1–2 (Spring–Summer 1996): 17–31.

Pirie, David. *A Heritage of Horror: The English Gothic Cinema, 1946–1972.* London: Gordon Fraser, 1973.

———. *The Vampire Cinema.* New York: Crescent, 1977.

Pitts, Michael R. *Horror Film Stars.* Jefferson, N.C.: McFarland, 1981. 2d ed., 1991.

Polan, Dana. *Power and Paranoia: History, Narrative, and the American Cinema, 1940–1950.* New York: Columbia University Press, 1986.

Prawer, S. S. *Caligari's Children: The Film as a Tale of Terror.* New York: Oxford University Press, 1980.

Prince, Stephen. "Dread, Taboo, and *The Thing:* Toward a Social Theory of the Horror Film." *Wide Angle* 10, no. 3 (1988): 19–29.

Rasmussen, Randy. *Children of the Night: The Six Archetypal Characters of Classic Horror Films.* Jefferson, N.C.: McFarland, 1998.

Reed, Joseph W. *American Scenarios: The Uses of Film Genre.* Middletown, Conn.: Wesleyan University Press, 1989.

Riccardo, Martin V. *Vampires Unearthed: The Vampire and Dracula Bibliography of Books, Articles, Movies, Records, and Other Material.* New York: Garland, 1983.

Rockett, Will H. *Devouring Whirlwind: Terror and Transcendence in the Cinema of Cruelty.* New York: Greenwood Press, 1988.

———. "The Door Ajar: Structure and Convention in Horror Films That Would Terrify." *Journal of Popular Film and Television* 10, no. 3 (Fall 1982): 130–136.

———. "Landscape and Manscape: Reflection and Distortion in Horror Films." *Post Script* 3, no. 1 (Fall 1983): 19–34.

Russell, David J. "Monster Roundup: Reintegrating the Horror Genre." In *Refiguring American Film Genres: History and Theory,* edited by Nick Browne, pp. 233–254. Berkeley: University of California Press, 1998.

Russell, Sharon. "The Witch in Film." *Film Reader,* no. 3 (1978): 80–89. Reprinted in *Planks of Reason: Essays on the Horror Film,* edited by Barry K. Grant, pp. 113–125. Metuchen, N.J.: Scarecrow Press, 1984.

Ryan, Michael, and Douglas Kellner. *Camera Politica: The Politics and Ideology of Contemporary Hollywood Film.* Bloomington and Indianapolis: Indiana University Press, 1988.

Sanjek, David. "Fans' Notes: The Horror Film Fanzine." *Literature/Film Quarterly* 18, no. 3 (1990): 150–159.

———. "Twilight of the Monsters: The English Horror Film, 1968–1975." *Film Criticism* 16, nos. 1–2 (Fall–Winter 1991–1992): 111–126. Reprinted in *Re-Viewing British Cinema, 1900–1992: Essays and Interviews,* edited by Wheeler Winston Dixon, pp. 195–209. Albany: State University of New York Press, 1994.

Saunders, Michael William. *Imps of the Perverse: Gay Monsters in Film.* Westport, Conn.: Praeger, 1998.

Schecter, Harold. *The Bosom Serpent: Folklore and Popular Art.* Iowa City: University of Iowa Press, 1988. Chap. 2, "The Bloody Chamber: Terror Tales, Fairy Tales, and Taboo." Reprinted in *Gender, Language, and Myth: Essays on Popular Narrative,* edited by Glenwood Irons, pp. 233–251. Toronto: University of Toronto Press, 1992.

Schlobin, Roger. "Children of a Darker God: A Taxonomy of Deep Horror Fiction and Film and Their Mass Popularity." *Journal of the Fantastic in the Arts* 1, no. 1 (1988): 49–58.

Schneider, Steven Jay. "Kevin Williamson and the Rise of the Neo-Stalker." *Post Script* 19, no. 2 (Winter–Spring 2000): 73–87.

———. "Uncanny Realism and the Decline of the Modern Horror Film." *Paradoxa* 3, nos. 3–4 (1997): 417–428.

Schoell, William. *Stay Out of the Shower: Twenty-Five Years of Shocker Films Beginning with PSYCHO.* New York: Dembner, 1985.

Sconce, Jeffrey. "Spectacles of Death: Identification, Reflexivity, and Contemporary Horror." *Film Theory Goes to the Movies,* edited by Jim Collins, Hilary Radner, and Ava Preacher Collins, pp. 103–119. New York and London: Routledge, 1993.

Senn, Bryan. *Golden Horrors: An Illustrated Critical Filmography of Terror Cinema, 1931–1939.* Jefferson, N.C.: McFarland, 1996.

Senn, Bryan, and John Johnson. *Fantastic Subject Guide: A Topical Index to*

2,500 Horror, Science Fiction, and Fantasy Films. Jefferson, N.C.: McFarland, 1992.

Sevastakis, Michael. *Songs of Love and Death: The Classical American Horror Film of the 1930s.* Westport, Conn.: Greenwood Press, 1993.

Silver, Alain, and James Ursini. *The Vampire Film: From NOSFERATU to BRAM STOKER'S DRACULA.* New York: Limelight, 1993.

Skal, David J. *The Monster Show: A Cultural History of Horror.* New York: Norton, 1994.

Smith, Gary A. *Uneasy Dreams: The Golden Age of British Horror Films, 1956–1976.* Jefferson, N.C.: McFarland, 2000.

Sobchack, Vivian. "Child/Alien/Father: Patriarchal Crisis and Generic Exchange." *camera obscura,* no. 15 (1986): 7–34. Reprinted in *American Horrors: Essays on the Modern American Horror Film,* edited by Gregory A. Waller, pp. 175–194. Urbana and Chicago: University of Illinois Press, 1987.

Solomon, Stanley J. *Beyond Formula: American Film Genres.* New York: Harcourt Brace Jovanovich, 1976.

Stanbrook, Alan. "Invasion of the Purple People Eaters." *Sight and Sound* 60, no. 1 (Winter 1990–1991): 48–50.

Steiger, Brad. *Monsters, Maidens, and Mayhem: A Pictorial History of Horror Film Monsters.* New York: Merit, 1965.

Stephens, Bob. "Dark Horizon: The Landscape of Horror Noir." *Films in Review* 48, nos. 1–2 (January–February 1996): 18–26.

Sullivan, Jack, ed. *The Penguin Encyclopedia of Horror and the Supernatural.* New York: Viking, 1986.

Taubin, Amy. "Killing Men." *Sight and Sound* 1, no. 1 (May 1991): 14–18.

Telotte, J. P. "The Doubles of Fantasy and the Space of Desire." *Film Criticism* 6, no. 1 (Fall 1982): 56–68. Reprinted in *Film Criticism* 11, nos. 1–2 (Fall–Winter 1987): 43–55.

———. *Dreams of Darkness: Fantasy and the Films of Val Lewton.* Urbana: University of Illinois Press, 1985.

———. "Faith and Idolatry in the Horror Film." *Literature/Film Quarterly* 8, no. 3 (1980): 143–155. Reprinted in *Planks of Reason: Essays on the Horror Film,* edited by Barry K. Grant, pp. 21–37. Metuchen, N.J.: Scarecrow Press, 1984.

———. "Through a Pumpkin's Eye: The Reflexive Nature of Horror." *Literature/Film Quarterly* 10, no. 3 (1982): 139–149. Reprinted in *American Horrors: Essays on the Modern American Horror Film,* edited by Gregory A. Waller, pp. 114–129. Urbana and Chicago: University of Illinois Press, 1987.

Tietchen, Todd F. "Samplers and Copycats: The Cultural Implications of the Postmodern Slasher in Contemporary American Film." *Journal of Popular Film and Television* 26, no. 3 (Fall 1998): 98–107.

Trencansky, Sarah. "Final Girls and Terrible Youth: Transgression in 1980s Slasher Horror." *Journal of Popular Film and Television* 29, no. 2 (Summer 2001): 63–73.

Tropp, Martin. *Mary Shelley's Monster.* Boston: Houghton Mifflin, 1976.

Tudor, Andrew. *Image and Influence: Studies in the Sociology of Film.* London: George Allen and Unwin, 1974.

————. *Monsters and Mad Scientists: A Cultural History of the Horror Movie.* London: Basil Blackwell, 1989.

————. "Why Horror? The Peculiar Pleasures of a Popular Genre." *Creative Screenwriting* 11, no. 3 (1997): 443–463.

Turner, George E., and Michael H. Price. *Forgotten Horrors: Early Talkie Chillers from Poverty Row.* South Brunswick, N.J., and New York: A. S. Barnes, 1979.

Twitchell, James B. *Dreadful Pleasures: An Anatomy of Modern Horror.* New York: Oxford University Press, 1985.

————. "*Frankenstein* and the Anatomy of Horror." *Georgia Review* 37, no. 1 (1983): 44–78.

————. *Preposterous Violence: Fables of Aggression in Modern Culture.* New York: Oxford University Press, 1989.

————. "A Psychoanalysis of the Vampire Myth." *American Imago* 37 (1980): 83–92.

Tyler, Parker. "Supernaturalism in the Movies." *Theater Arts* 29, no. 6 (June 1945): 362–369.

Urbano, Cosimo. "Projections, Suspense, and Anxiety: The Modern Horror Film and Its Effects." *Psychoanalytic Review* 85, no. 6 (1998): 889–908.

Ursini, James, and Alain Silver. *The Vampire Film.* New York: A. S. Barnes; London: Tantivy, 1975. Rev. ed., New York: Limelight, 1993.

Vale, V., and Andrea Juno. *Incredibly Strange Films.* San Francisco: V/Search Publications, 1986.

Walker, Mark. *Vietnam Veteran Films.* Metuchen, N.J.: Scarecrow Press, 1991.

Waller, Gregory A. *The Living and the Undead: From Stoker's DRACULA to Romero's DAWN OF THE DEAD.* Urbana: University of Illinois Press, 1986.

————, ed. *American Horrors: Essays on the Modern American Horror Film.* Urbana and Chicago: University of Illinois Press, 1987.

Warren, Bill. *Set Visits: Interviews with 32 Horror and Science Fiction Filmmakers.* Jefferson, N.C.: McFarland, 1997.

Weaver, James B., III, and Ron Tamborini, eds. *Horror Films: Current Research in Audience Preferences and Reactions.* Mahwah, N.J.: Laurence Erlbaum Associates, 1995.

Weaver, Tom. *Interviews with B Science Fiction and Horror Movie Makers: Writers, Producers, Directors, Actors, Moguls, and Makeup.* Jefferson, N.C.: McFarland, 1988.

————. *It Came from Weaver Five: Interviews with 20 Zany, Glib, and Earnest Moviemakers in the SF and Horror Traditions of the Thirties, Forties, Fifties, and Sixties.* Jefferson, N.C.: McFarland, 1996.

————. *I Was a Monster Movie Maker: Conversations with 22 SF and Horror Filmmakers.* Jefferson, N.C.: McFarland, 2001.

————. *Poverty Row Horrors! Monogram, PRC, and Republic Horror Films of the Forties.* Jefferson, N.C.: McFarland, 1993.

————. *Science Fiction Stars and Horror Heroes: Interviews with Actors, Directors, Producers, and Writers of the 1940s through 1960s.* Jefferson, N.C.: McFarland, 1991.

————. *They Fought in the Creature Features: Interviews with 23 Classic Horror, Science Fiction, and Serial Stars.* Jefferson, N.C.: McFarland, 1995.

Wells, Paul. *The Horror Genre: From Beelzebub to Blair Witch.* London: Wallflower Press, 2001.

Welsh, Jim, and John Tibetts. "Visions of Dracula." *American Classic Screen* 5, no. 1 (November–December 1980): 12–16.

White, Dennis L. "The Poetics of Horror: More Than Meets the Eye." *Cinema Journal* 10, no. 2 (Spring 1971): 1–18. Reprinted in *Film Genre: Theory and Criticism,* edited by Barry K. Grant, pp. 124–144. Metuchen, N.J.: Scarecrow Press, 1977. *Cinema Examined: Selections from CINEMA JOURNAL,* edited by Richard Dyer MacCann and Jack C. Ellis, pp. 251–268. New York: Dutton, 1982.

Wiater, Stanley. *Dark Visions: Conversations with the Masters of the Horror Film.* New York: Avon, 1992.

Williams, Linda. "When the Woman Looks." In *Re-Vision: Essays in Feminist Film Criticism,* edited by Mary Ann Doane and Linda Williams, pp. 83–99. Frederick, Md.: University Publications, 1983. Reprinted in *The Dread of Difference: Gender and the Horror Film,* edited by Barry Keith Grant, pp. 15–34. Austin: University of Texas Press, 1996.

Williams, Linda Ruth. "A Virus Is Only Doing Its Job." *Sight and Sound* 3, no. 5 (May 1993): 31–33.

Williams, Tony. "American Cinema in the 70's: Family Horror." *Movie,* nos. 27–28 (1981): 117–126.

————. *Hearths of Darkness: The Family in the American Horror Film.* Rutherford, N.J.: Fairleigh Dickinson University Press, 1996.

————. "Horror in the Family." *Focus on Film,* no. 36 (October 1980): 14–20.

Willis, Don. *Horror and Science Fiction Films: A Checklist.* Metuchen, N.J.: Scarecrow Press, 1972.

————. *Horror and Science Fiction Films II.* Metuchen, N.J.: Scarecrow Press, 1982.

————. *Horror and Science Fiction Films III.* Metuchen, N.J.: Scarecrow Press, 1984.

————. *Horror and Science Fiction Films IV (1984–1993).* Lanham, Md.: Scarecrow Press, 1997.

Wolf, Leonard. *Horror: A Connoisseur's Guide to Literature and Film.* New York and Oxford: Facts on File, 1989.

Wood, Gerald C. "Horror Film." In *Handbook of American Film Genres,* edited by Wes D. Gehring, pp. 211–228. New York: Greenwood Press, 1988.

Wood, Robin. "The American Family Comedy: From *Meet Me in St. Louis* to *The Texas Chainsaw Massacre.*" *Wide Angle* 3, no. 2 (1979): 5–11.

————. "Beauty Bests the Beast." *American Film* 8, no. 10 (September 1983): 63–65. Reprinted as "Returning the Look: *Eyes of a Stranger*" in *American Horrors,* edited by Gregory A. Waller, pp. 79–85. Urbana and Chicago: University of Illinois Press, 1987.

————. "Burying the Undead: The Use and Obsolescence of Count Dracula." *Mosaic* 16, nos. 1–2 (1983): 175–187. Reprinted in *The Dread of Difference:*

Gender and the Horror Film, edited by Barry Keith Grant, pp. 364–378. Austin: University of Texas Press, 1996.

———. "Return of the Repressed." *Film Comment* 14, no. 4 (July–August 1978): 25–32. Reprinted in *Planks of Reason: Essays on the Horror Film,* edited by Barry K. Grant, pp. 164–200. Metuchen, N.J.: Scarecrow Press, 1984.

Wood, Robin, and Richard Lippe, eds. *The American Nightmare: Essays on the Horror Film.* Toronto: Festival of Festivals, 1979.

Worland, Rick. "OWI Meets the Monsters: Hollywood Horror Films and War Propaganda, 1942–1945." *Cinema Journal* 37, no. 1 (Fall 1997): 47–65.

Wright, Gene. *Horrorshows.* New York: Facts on File, 1986.

Zimmerman, Bonnie. "Lesbian Vampires." *Jump Cut,* nos. 24–25 (1981): 23–24. Reprinted in *Planks of Reason: Essays on the Horror Film,* edited by Barry K. Grant, pp. 153–163. Metuchen, N.J.: Scarecrow Press, 1984. *The Dread of Difference: Gender in the Horror Film,* edited by Barry Keith Grant, pp. 379–387. Austin: University of Texas Press, 1996.

MELODRAMA

Abel, Richard. *French Cinema: The First Wave, 1915–1929.* Princeton: Princeton University Press, 1984.

Aspinall, Sue, and Robert Murphy, eds. *Gainsborough Melodrama.* London: British Film Institute, 1983.

Balio, Tino, ed. *History of the American Cinema,* vol. 5, *Grand Design: Hollywood as a Modern Business Enterprise, 1930–1939,* pp. 235–255. New York: Charles Scribner's Sons, 1993.

Barton, Sabrina. "Female Investigation and Male Performativity in the Woman's Psychothriller." In *The New American Cinema,* edited by Jon Lewis, pp. 187–216. Durham and London: Duke University Press, 1998.

Basinger, Jeanine. "When Women Wept." *American Film* 12, no. 10 (September 1977): 52–57.

———. *A Woman's View: How Hollywood Spoke to Women, 1930–1960.* New York: Knopf, 1993.

Belton, John. *American Cinema/American Culture.* New York: McGraw-Hill, 1994.

Borde, Raymond, and Etienne Chaumeton. "The Sources of Film Noir." *Film Reader,* no. 3 (1978): 58–66.

Bordwell, David. *Narration in the Fiction Film,* chap. 5. Madison: University of Wisconsin Press, 1985.

Bourget, Jean-Loup. "Faces of the American Melodrama: Joan Crawford." *Film Reader,* no. 3 (1978): 24–34. Reprinted in *Imitations of Life,* edited by Marcia Landy, pp. 429–439. Detroit: Wayne State University Press, 1991.

———. "Romantic Drama of the Forties: An Analysis." *Film Comment* 10, no. 1 (January–February 1974): 46–51.

Bratton, Jacky, Jim Cook, and Christine Gledhill, eds. *Melodrama: Stage, Picture,*

Screen. London and Bloomington: British Film Institute/Indiana University Press, 1995.

Byers, Jackie. *All That Hollywood Allows: Re-Reading Gender in 1950s Melodrama.* Chapel Hill and London: University of North Carolina Press, 1991.

Cook, Pam, and Mieke Bernink, eds. *The Cinema Book,* 2d ed. London: British Film Institute, 1999.

Creed, Barbara. "The Position of Women in Hollywood Melodrama." *Australian Journal of Screen Theory* 4 (1978): 27–31.

Cunningham, Stuart. "The 'Force-Field' of Melodrama." *Quarterly Review of Film Studies* 6, no. 4 (Fall 1981): 345–364.

———. "Stock Shock and Schlock." *Enclitic* 5, no. 2–6, no. 1 (Fall 1981–Spring 1982): 166–171.

Dermody, Susan. "Melodrama as It (Dis)appears in Australian Film." *East-West Film Journal* 5, no. 1 (January 1991): 82–106.

Doane, Mary Ann. "*Caught* and *Rebecca:* The Inscription of Femininity as Absence." *Enclitic* 5, no. 2–6, no. 1 (Fall 1981–Spring 1982): 75–89. Revised in *The Desire to Desire: The Woman's Film of the 1940s.* Bloomington and Indianapolis: Indiana University Press, 1987.

———. "The Clinical Eye: Medical Discourses in the 'Woman's Film' of the 1940s." *Poetics Today* 6, nos. 1–2 (1985): 205–227.

———. *The Desire to Desire: The Woman's Film of the 1940s.* Bloomington and Indianapolis: Indiana University Press, 1987.

———. "Melodrama, Temporality, Recognition: American and Russian Silent Cinema." *East-West Film Journal* 4, no. 2 (June 1990): 69–89.

———. "The 'Woman's Film': Possession and Address." In *Re-Vision: Essays in Feminist Film Criticism,* edited by Mary Ann Doane, Patricia Mellencamp, and Linda Williams, pp. 67–82. Frederick, Md.: University Publications, 1983. Revised in Doane, *The Desire to Desire: The Woman's Film of the 1940s.* Bloomington and Indianapolis: Indiana University Press, 1987. Reprinted in *Home Is Where the Heart Is,* edited by Christine Gledhill, pp. 70–74. London: British Film Institute, 1987.

Durgnat, Raymond. "Ways of Melodrama." *Sight and Sound* 21, no. 1 (August–September 1951): 34–40. Reprinted in *Imitations of Life,* edited by Marcia Landy, pp. 135–147. Detroit: Wayne State University Press, 1991.

Ehrenstein, David. "Melodrama and the New Woman." *Film Comment* 14, no. 5 (September–October 1978): 59–62.

Everson, William K. "British Melodrama." *Films in Review* 37, no. 11 (November 1986): 524–529.

Fell, John. "Melodrama, Movies, and Genre." In *Melodrama,* edited by Daniel Gerould, pp. 187–195. New York: New York Literary Forum, 1980.

Fischer, Lucy. *Shot/Countershot: Film Tradition and Women's Cinema.* Princeton, N.J.: Princeton University Press, 1989.

———. "Two-Faced Women: The 'Double' in Women's Melodrama of the 1940s." *Cinema Journal* 23, no. 1 (Fall 1983): 24–43.

Fletcher, John. "Melodrama—An Introduction." *Screen* 29, no. 3 (Summer 1988): 2–12.

———. "Versions of Masquerade." *Screen* 29, no. 3 (Summer 1988): 43–70.

Flinn, Caryl. "The 'Problem' of Femininity in Theories of Film Music." *Screen* 27, no. 6 (Winter 1986): 56–72.

Gaines, Jane. "*Scar of Shame:* Skin Color and Caste in Black Silent Melodrama." *Cinema Journal* 26, no. 4 (Summer 1987): 3–21. Reprinted in *Imitations of Life,* edited by Marcia Landy, pp. 331–348. Detroit: Wayne State University Press, 1991.

Gerould, Daniel. "Russian Formalist Theories of Melodrama." *Journal of American Culture* 1, no. 1 (1978): 156–168. Reprinted in *Imitations of Life,* edited by Marcia Landy, pp. 118–134. Detroit: Wayne State University Press, 1991.

Gledhill, Christine. "Signs of Melodrama." In *Stardom: Industry of Desire,* edited by Gledhill, pp. 207–229. London and New York: Routledge, 1991.

———, ed. *Home Is Where the Heart Is: Studies in Melodrama and the Woman's Film.* London: British Film Institute, 1987.

Greene, Naomi. "Coppola, Cimino: The Operatics of History." *Film Quarterly* 38, no. 2 (Winter 1984–1985): 28–37. Reprinted in *Imitations of Life,* edited by Marcia Landy, pp. 388–397. Detroit: Wayne State University Press, 1991.

Gretton, Viveca, and Tom Orman. "Regarding Men: Disease and Affliction in Contemporary Male Melodrama." *CineAction,* nos. 26–27 (Winter 1992): 114–120.

Hamilton, Annette. "Family Dramas: Film and Modernity in Thailand." *Screen* 33, no. 3 (Autumn 1992): 259–273.

Haskell, Molly. "The Woman's Film." In *From Reverence to Rape: The Treatment of Women in the Movies.* Baltimore: Penguin, 1974. 2d ed., Chicago: University of Chicago Press, 1987.

Hollinger, Karen. "Listening to the Female Voice in the Woman's Film." *Film Criticism* 16, no. 3 (Spring 1992): 34–52.

Horrigan, Bill. "An Afterword to Jean-Loup Bourget's Article ['Faces of the American Melodrama: Joan Crawford']." *Film Reader,* no. 3 (1978): 35–39.

Jacobs, Lea. "The Woman's Picture and the Poetics of Melodrama." *camera obscura,* no. 31 (January–May 1993): 121–147.

Jayamanne, Laleen. "Sri Lankan Family Melodrama: A Cinema of Primitive Attractions." *Screen* 33, no. 2 (Summer 1992): 145–153.

Kaplan, E. Ann. "Classical Hollywood Film and Melodrama." In *The Oxford Guide to Film Studies,* edited by John Hill and Pamela Church Gibson, pp. 272–288. New York: Oxford University Press, 1988.

———. "Melodrama/Subjectivity/Ideology: The Relevance of Western Melodrama Theories to Recent Chinese Cinema." *East-West Film Journal* 5, no. 1 (January 1991): 6–27.

———. *Motherhood and Representation: The Mother in Popular Culture and Melodrama.* New York: Routledge, 1992.

———. "Theories of Melodrama: A Feminist Perspective." *Women and Performance: A Journal of Feminist Theory* 1, no. 1 (1983): 40–48.

Kehr, Dave. "The New Male Melodrama." *American Film* 8, no. 6 (1983): 42–47.

Kleinhans, Chuck. "Notes on Melodrama and the Family under Capitalism." *Film Reader,* no. 3 (1978): 40–47. Reprinted in *Imitations of Life,* edited by Marcia Landy, pp. 197–204. Detroit: Wayne State University Press, 1991.

Klinger, Barbara. "'Cinema/Ideology/Criticism' Revisited: The Progressive Text." *Screen* 25, no. 1 (January–February 1984): 30–44.

Kuhn, Annette. "Women's Genres." *Screen* 25, no. 1 (January–February 1984): 18–28. Reprinted in *Home Is Where the Heart Is,* edited by Christine Gledhill, pp. 339–349. London: British Film Institute, 1987.

Landy, Marcia. *British Genres: Cinema and Society, 1930–1960.* Princeton: Princeton University Press, 1991.

———, ed. *Imitations of Life.* Detroit: Wayne State University Press, 1991.

Lang, Robert. *American Film Melodrama: Griffith, Vidor, Minnelli.* Princeton, N.J.: Princeton University Press, 1989.

Lipkin, Steven N. "Melodrama." In *Handbook of American Film Genres,* edited by Wes D. Gehring, pp. 285–302. New York: Greenwood Press, 1988.

Lippe, Richard. "Melodrama in the Seventies." *Movie,* nos. 29–30 (1982): 122–127.

Lopez, Ana. "The Melodrama in Latin America: Films, *Telenovelas,* and the Currency of a Popular Form." *Wide Angle* 7, no. 3 (1985): 4–13. Reprinted in *Imitations of Life,* edited by Marcia Landy, pp. 596–606. Detroit: Wayne State University Press, 1991.

Margolis, Harriet. "Contemporary Women's Films: A Fictional Genre?" *Film Criticism* 13, no. 2 (1989): 47–60.

Merritt, Russell. "Melodrama: Postmortem for a Phantom Genre." *Wide Angle* 5, no. 3 (1983): 24–31.

Modleski, Tania. "Time and Desire in the Woman's Film." *Cinema Journal* 23, no. 3 (Spring 1984): 19–30. Reprinted in *Home Is Where the Heart Is,* edited by Christine Gledhill, pp. 326–338. London: British Film Institute, 1987. *Film Theory and Criticism,* 4th ed., edited by Gerald Mast, Marshall Cohen, and Leo Braudy, pp. 536–548. New York: Oxford University Press, 1992.

Morse, David. "Aspects of Melodrama." *Monogram,* no. 4 (1972): 16–17.

Mulvey, Laura. "Douglas Sirk and Melodrama." *Australian Journal of Screen Theory,* no. 3 (1977): 26–30.

———. "Melodrama in and out of the House." *High Theory/Low Culture: Analysing Popular Television and Film,* edited by Colin MacCabe, pp. 80–100. New York: St. Martin's Press, 1986. Reprinted in Mulvey, *Visual and Other Pleasures,* pp. 63–80. Bloomington and Indianapolis: Indiana University Press, 1989.

———. "Notes on Sirk and Melodrama." *Movie* 25 (Winter 1977–1978): 53–56. Reprinted in *Home Is Where the Heart Is,* edited by Christine Gledhill, pp. 75–79. London: British Film Institute, 1987. Mulvey, *Visual and Other Pleasures,* pp. 39–44. Bloomington and Indianapolis: Indiana University Press, 1989.

Neale, Steve. *Genre and Hollywood.* New York and London: Routledge, 2000.

———. "Melodrama and Tears." *Screen* 27, no. 6 (November–December 1986): 6–22.

———. "Melo Talk: On the Meaning and Use of the Term 'Melodrama' in the American Trade Press." *Velvet Light Trap,* no. 32 (Fall 1993): 66–89.

Ning, Ma. "Symbolic Representation and Symbolic Violence: Chinese Family

Melodrama of the Early 1980s." *East-West Film Journal* 4, no. 1 (December 1989): 79–112.

Nowell-Smith, Geoffrey. "Minnelli and Melodrama." *Screen* 18, no. 2 (Summer 1977): 113–118. Reprinted in *Movies and Methods,* vol. 2, edited by Bill Nichols, pp. 190–194. Berkeley: University of California Press, 1985. *Home Is Where the Heart Is,* edited by Christine Gledhill, pp. 70–74. London: British Film Institute, 1987. *Imitations of Life,* edited by Marcia Landy, pp. 268–274. Detroit: Wayne State University Press, 1991.

Petro, Patrice. *Joyless Streets: Women and Melodramatic Representation in Weimar Germany.* Princeton, N.J.: Princeton University Press, 1989.

Pollock, Griselda. "Report on the Weekend School." *Screen* 18, no. 2 (Summer 1977): 105–113. Reprinted in *Imitations of Life,* edited by Marcia Landy, pp. 275–282. Detroit: Wayne State University Press, 1991.

Reed, Joseph W. *American Scenarios: The Uses of Film Genre.* Middletown, Conn.: Wesleyan University Press, 1989.

Roberts, Susan. "Melodramatic Performance Signs." *Framework,* nos. 32–33 (1986): 68–75.

Rodowick, D. N. "Madness, Authority, and Ideology: The Domestic Melodrama of the 1950s." *Velvet Light Trap,* no. 19 (1982): 40–45. Reprinted in *Home Is Where the Heart Is,* edited by Christine Gledhill, pp. 268–280. London: British Film Institute, 1987. *Imitations of Life,* edited by Marcia Landy, pp. 237–247. Detroit: Wayne State University Press, 1991.

Russell, Catherine. "'Overcoming Modernity': Gender and the Pathos of History in Japanese Film Melodrama." *camera obscura,* no. 35 (May 1995): 131–157.

Schatz, Thomas. *Hollywood Genres: Formulas, Filmmaking, and the Studio System.* New York: Random House, 1981.

Schlupmann, Heide. "Melodrama and Social Drama in the Early German Cinema." *camera obscura,* no. 22 (January 1990): 73–129.

Seiter, Ellen. "Men, Sex, and Money in Recent Family Melodramas." *Journal of the University Film and Video Association* 35, no. 1 (1983): 17–37. Reprinted in *Imitations of Life,* edited by Marcia Landy, pp. 525–537. Detroit: Wayne State University Press, 1991.

Sen, Krishna. "The Politics of Melodrama in Indonesian Cinema." *East-West Film Journal* 5, no. 1 (January 1991): 67–81.

Singer, Ben. "Female Power in the Serial-Queen Melodrama: The Etiology of an Anomaly." *camera obscura,* no. 22 (January 1990): 91–129.

———. *Melodrama and Modernity.* New York: Columbia University Press, 2001.

Smith, Murray. "Film Noir, the Female Gothic, and *Deception.*" *Wide Angle* 10, no. 1 (1988): 62–75.

Thomson, David. *America in the Dark: Hollywood and the Gift of Unreality,* chap. 7. New York: William Morrow, 1977.

Turim, Maureen. *Flashbacks in Film: Memory and History.* New York and London: Routledge, 1989.

———. "Psyches, Ideologies, and Melodrama: The United States and Japan." *East-West Film Journal* 5, no. 1 (January 1991): 118–143.

Viviani, Christian. "Who Is without Sin? The Maternal Melodrama in American

Film, 1930–1939." *Wide Angle* 4, no. 2 (1980): 4–17. Reprinted in *Imitations of Life,* edited by Marcia Landy, pp. 168–182. Detroit: Wayne State University Press, 1991.

Waldman, Diane. "'At Last I Can Tell It to Someone!': Feminine Point of View and Subjectivity in the Gothic Romance Film of the 1940s." *Cinema Journal* 23, no. 2 (Winter 1984): 28–40.

Walker, Mark. *Vietnam Veteran Films.* Metuchen, N.J.: Scarecrow Press, 1991.

Walker, Michael. "Melodrama and the American Cinema." *Movie,* nos. 29–30 (1982): 2–38.

White, Mimi. "Representing Romance: Reading/Writing/Fantasy and the 'Liberated' Heroine of Recent Hollywood Films." *Cinema Journal* 28, no. 3 (Spring 1989): 41–56.

Willeman, Paul. "Negotiating the Transition to Capitalism: The Case of *Andaz.*" *East-West Film Journal* 5, no. 1 (January 1991): 57–66.

Williams, Linda. "Melodrama Revised." In *Refiguring American Film Genres: History and Theory,* edited by Nick Browne, pp. 42–88. Berkeley: University of California Press, 1998.

———. "'Something Else beside a Mother': *Stella Dallas* and the Maternal Melodrama." *Cinema Journal* 24, no. 1 (Fall 1984): 2–27. Reprinted in *Home Is Where the Heart Is,* edited by Christine Gledhill, pp. 299–325. London: British Film Institute, 1987. *Issues in Feminist Film Criticism,* edited by Patricia Erens, pp. 137–162. Bloomington and Indianapolis: Indiana University Press, 1990. *Imitations of Life,* edited by Marcia Landy, pp. 307–330. Detroit: Wayne State University Press, 1991.

Woodward, Katherine S. "European Anti-Melodrama: Godard, Truffaut, and Fassbinder." *Post Script* 3, no. 2 (Winter 1984): 34–47. Reprinted in *Imitations of Life,* edited by Marcia Landy, pp. 586–595. Detroit: Wayne State University Press, 1991.

Yoshimoto, Mitsuhiro. "Melodrama, Postmodernism, and the Japanese Cinema." *East-West Film Journal* 5, no. 1 (January 1991): 28–55.

MUSICAL FILMS

Allen, Blaine. "Music Cinema, Music Video, Music Television." *Film Quarterly* 43, no. 3 (Spring 1990): 2–14.

Altman, Charles F. "The American Film Musical: Paradigmatic Structure and Mediatory Function." *Wide Angle* 2, no. 2 (1978): 10–17. Reprinted in *Genre: The Musical,* edited by Rick Altman, pp. 197–207. London: Routledge and Kegan Paul, 1980.

Altman, Rick. *The American Film Musical.* Bloomington: Indiana University Press, 1987.

———, ed. *Genre: The Musical.* London: Routledge and Kegan Paul, 1980.

Babington, Bruce, and Peter William Evans. *Blue Skies and Silver Linings: Aspects of the Hollywood Musical.* Dover, N.H.: Manchester University Press, 1985.

Bach, Steven. "The Hollywood Idiom: Give Me That Old Soft Shoe." *Arts Magazine,* no. 42 (December 1967–January 1968): 15–16.

Balio, Tino, ed. *History of the American Cinema*, vol. 5, *Grand Design: Hollywood as a Modern Business Enterprise, 1930–1939*, pp. 211–235. New York: Charles Scribner's Sons, 1993.

Barrios, Richard. *A Song in the Dark: The Birth of the Musical Film*. New York: Oxford University Press, 1995.

Belton, John. "The Backstage Musical." *Movie*, no. 24 (Spring 1977): 36–43.

Bergman, Andrew. *We're in the Money*. New York: Harper and Row, 1972. Rev. ed., Chicago: Elephant, 1992.

Bradley, Edwin M. *The First Hollywood Musicals: A Critical Filmography of 171 Features, 1927 through 1932*. Jefferson, N.C.: McFarland, 1996.

Cohen, Daniel. *Musicals*. Greenwich, Conn.: Bison Books, 1984.

Collins, James M. "The Musical." In *Handbook of American Film Genres*, edited by Wes D. Gehring, pp. 269–284. New York: Greenwood Press, 1988.

Conway, Mary T. "Spectatorship in Lesbian Porn: The Woman's Woman's Film." *Wide Angle* 19, no. 3 (1997): 91–113.

Cook, Pam, and Mieke Bernink, eds. *The Cinema Book*, 2d ed. London: British Film Institute, 1999.

Creekmur, Corey K. "The Space of Recording: The Production of Popular Music as Spectacle." *Wide Angle* 10, no. 2 (1988): 32–40.

Croce, Arlene. *The Fred Astaire and Ginger Rogers Book*. New York: Vintage Books, 1972.

Cutts, John. "Bye-Bye Musicals." *Films and Filming* 10, no. 2 (November 1963): 42–45.

Delamater, Jerome. *Dance in the Hollywood Musical*. Ann Arbor: UMI Research Press, 1981.

———. "Performing Arts: The Musical." In Stuart Kaminsky, *American Film Genres: Approaches to a Critical Theory of Popular Film*. Dayton, Ohio: Pflaum, 1974.

Doherty, Thomas. *Teenagers and Teenpics: The Juvenilization of American Movies in the 1950s*. Boston: Unwin Hyman, 1988.

Dowdy, Andrew. *The Films of the Fifties: The American State of Mind*. New York: Morrow, 1975.

Druxman, Michael B. *The Musical from Broadway to Hollywood*. New York: Barnes, 1980.

Dyer, Richard. "Entertainment and Utopia." *Movie*, no. 24 (Spring 1977): 36–43. Reprinted in *Genre: The Musical*, edited by Rick Altman, pp. 175–189. London: Routledge and Kegan Paul, 1980. *Movies and Methods*, vol. 2, edited by Bill Nichols, pp. 220–232. Berkeley: University of California Press, 1985.

Ehrenstein, David, and Bill Reed. *Rock on Film*. New York: Delilah Books, 1982.

Feuer, Jane. *The Hollywood Musical*. Bloomington: Indiana University Press, 1982. 2d edition, 1993.

———. "Hollywood Musicals: Mass Art as Folk Art." *Jump Cut*, no. 23 (1980): 23–25. Reprinted in *Jump Cut: Hollywood, Politics, and Counter Cinema*, edited by Peter Steven, pp. 52–63. Toronto: Between the Lines, 1985.

Fischer, Lucy. "Shall We Dance? Feminist Cinema Remakes the Musical." *Film Criticism* 13, no. 2 (Winter 1989): 7–17.

————. *Shot/Countershot: Film Tradition and Women's Cinema.* Princeton, N.J.: Princeton University Press, 1989.

Fordin, Hugh. *The World of Entertainment: Hollywood's Greatest Musicals.* New York: Avon, 1975. Reprinted as *The Movies' Greatest Musicals: Produced in Hollywood, USA, by the Freed Unit.* New York: Ungar, 1984.

Giles, Dennis. "Show-Making." *Movie,* no. 24 (Spring 1977): 14–25. Reprinted in *Genre: The Musical,* edited by Rick Altman, pp. 85–101. London: Routledge and Kegan Paul, 1980.

Godfrey, Lionel. "A Heretic's Look at Musicals." *Films and Filming* 13, no. 6 (March 1967): 5–10.

Grant, Barry K. "The Classic Hollywood Musical and the 'Problem' of Rock 'n' Roll." *Journal of Popular Film and Television* 13, no. 4 (Winter 1986): 195–205.

————. "Film Musicals." In *Facts behind the Songs: A Handbook of American Popular Music,* edited by Marvin Paymer, pp. 102–105. New York and London: Garland Press, 1993.

Green, Stanley. *Encyclopedia of the Musical Film.* New York: Oxford, 1981.

Hanson, Cynthia A. "The Hollywood Musical Biopic and the Regressive Performer." *Wide Angle* 10, no. 2 (1988): 15–23.

Hay, James. "Dancing and Deconstructing the American Dream." *Quarterly Review of Film Studies* 10, no. 2 (Spring 1985): 97–117.

Hemming, Roy. *The Melody Lingers On: The Great Songwriters and Their Movie Musicals.* New York: Newmarket Press, 1986.

Henderson, Brian. "Musical Comedy of Empire." *Film Quarterly* 35, no. 2 (Winter 1981–1982): 2–16.

Higham, Charles, and Joel Greenberg. *Hollywood in the Forties.* New York: A. S. Barnes, 1968.

Hirschhorn, Clive. *The Hollywood Musical.* New York: Crown, 1981.

Hischak, Thomas S. *The American Musical Film Song Encyclopedia.* Westport, Conn.: Greenwood Press, 1999.

Jablonski, Edward. "Filmusicals." *Films in Review* 6, no. 2 (February 1955): 56–69.

Jarvie, I. C. *Movies and Society.* New York: Basic Books, 1970.

Kaplan, E. Ann. *Rocking around the Clock: Music Television, Postmodernism, and Consumer Culture.* New York and London: Routledge, 1987.

Kehr, David. "Can't Stop the Musicals." *American Film* 9, no. 7 (May 1984): 32–37.

Kobol, John. *Gotta Sing Gotta Dance: A Pictorial History of Film Musicals.* London: Hamlyn, 1972.

Kreuger, Miles, ed. *The Movie Musical from Vitaphone to 42ND STREET, as Reported in a Great Fan Magazine.* New York: Dover, 1975.

Licata, Sal. "From Plymouth Rock to Hollywood in Song and Dance: Yankee Mythology in the Film Musical." *Film and History* 4, no. 1 (February 1974): 1–3.

Lippe, Richard. "*New York, New York* and the Hollywood Musical." *Movie,* nos. 31–32 (Winter 1986): 95–100.

Lockhart, Freda Bruce. "The Seven Ages of the Musical." In *International Film Annual,* no. 1, edited by Campbell Dixon, pp. 107–115. London: John Calder, 1957.

McGee, Mark Thomas. *The Rock and Roll Movie Encyclopedia of the 1950s.* Jefferson, N.C.: McFarland, 1990.

McGilligan, Patrick, and Mark Rowland. "Reelin' and Rockin': The Role of Rock in the Movies." *American Film* 15, no. 12 (September 1990): 28–31.

McVay, Douglas. *The Film Musical.* New York: A. S. Barnes, 1967.

Marcus, Greil. "Rock Films." In *The Rolling Stone Illustrated History of Rock & Roll,* edited by Jim Miller, pp. 390–400. New York: Random House/Rolling Stone Press, 1980.

Marsh, Dave. "Schlock around the Rock." *Film Comment* 14, no. 4 (July–August 1978): 7–13.

Marshall, Bill, and Robyn Stillwell, eds. *Musicals: Hollywood and Beyond.* Portland and Exeter, U.K.: Intellect Books, 2000.

Mast, Gerald. *Can't Help Singin': The American Musical on Stage and Screen.* New York: Overlook Press, 1987.

Mellencamp, Patricia. "Spectacle and Spectator: Looking through the American Musical Comedy." *Ciné-Tracts,* no. 2 (Summer 1977): 27–35. Reprinted in *Explorations in Film Theory: Selected Essays from CINÉ-TRACTS,* edited by Ron Burnett, pp. 3–14. Bloomington and Indianapolis: Indiana University Press, 1991.

Mordden, Ethan. *The Hollywood Musical.* New York: St. Martin's Press, 1980.

Mueller, John. *Astaire Dancing: The Musical Films.* New York: Knopf, 1985.

Murphy, Robert. *Sixties British Cinema,* chap. 6. London: British Film Institute, 1992.

Newton, Douglas. "Poetry in Fast and Musical Motion." *Sight and Sound* 22, no. 1 (July–September 1952): 35–37.

Oechiogrosso, Peter. "Reelin' and Rockin'." *American Film* 9, no. 6 (April 1984): 44–50.

Pally, Marcia. "Dancing for Their Lives." *Film Comment* 20, no. 6 (November–December 1984): 51–55.

Pantasios, Anastasia J. "Rock Music and Film." *Mise-en-Scène,* no. 1 (n.d.): 42–47.

Parish, James Robert, and Michael R. Pitts. *The Great Hollywood Musical Pictures.* Metuchen, N.J.: Scarecrow Press, 1992.

Patrick, Robert, and William Haislip. "'Thank Heaven for Little Girls': An Examination of the Male Chauvinist Musical." *Cineaste* 6, no. 1 (1973): 22–25.

Pechter, William S. "Movie Musicals." *Commentary* 53, no. 5 (May 1972): 77–81.

Ray, Robert B. *A Certain Tendency of the Hollywood Cinema, 1930–1980.* Princeton: Princeton University Press, 1985.

Reed, Joseph W. *American Scenarios: The Uses of Film Genre.* Middletown, Conn.: Wesleyan University Press, 1989.

Rickey, Carrie. "Let Yourself Go!" *Film Comment* 18, no. 2 (March–April 1982): 43–47.

Romanowski, William D., and R. Serge Denisoff. "Money for Nothin' and the Charts for Free: Rock and the Movies." *Journal of Popular Culture* 21, no. 3 (Winter 1987): 63–78.

Romney, Jonathan, and Adrian Wootton. *Celluloid Jukebox: Popular Music and the Movies since the 1950s.* London: British Film Institute, 1995.

Roth, Mark. "Some Warners Musicals and the Spirit of the New Deal." *Velvet Light Trap,* no. 17 (Winter 1977): 1–7. Reprinted in *Genre: The Musical,* edited by Rick Altman, pp. 57–69. London: Routledge and Kegan Paul, 1980.

Roth, Martin. "Women in Hollywood Musicals: Pulling the Plug on Lina Lamont." *Jump Cut,* no. 35 (1990): 59–65.

Ryan, Michael, and Douglas Kellner. *Camera Politica: The Politics and Ideology of Contemporary Hollywood Film.* Bloomington and Indianapolis: Indiana University Press, 1988.

Schatz, Thomas. *Hollywood Genres: Formula, Filmmaking, and the Studio System.* New York: Random House, 1981.

Scheurer, Timothy E. "The Aesthetics of Form and Convention in the Movie Musical." *Journal of Popular Film* 3, no. 4 (Fall 1974): 307–324. Reprinted in *Film Genre: Theory and Criticism,* edited by Barry K. Grant, pp. 145–159. Metuchen, N.J.: Scarecrow Press, 1977.

———. "I'll Sing You a Thousand Love Songs: A Selected Filmography of the Musical Film." *Journal of Popular Film and Television* 8, no. 1 (Spring 1980): 61–67.

Sennett, Ted. *Hollywood Musicals.* New York: Abrams, 1981.

Shipman, David. "The MGM Musical." In *The Story of Cinema,* pp. 660–680. New York: St. Martin's Press, 1982.

Shout, John D. "The Film Musical and the Legacy of Show Business." *Journal of Popular Film and Television* 10, no. 1 (1982): 23–26.

Sidney, George. "The Three Ages of the Musical." *Films and Filming* 14, no. 9 (June 1968): 4–9.

Siefirt, Marsha. "Image, Music, Voice: Song Dubbing in Hollywood Musicals." *Journal of Communication* 45, no. 2 (Spring 1995): 44–64.

Smoodin, Eric. "Creativity in the Hollywood Musical." *New Orleans Review* 16, no. 1 (Spring 1989): 79–87.

Solomon, Stanley J. *Beyond Formula: American Film Genres.* New York: Harcourt Brace Jovanovich, 1976.

Spence, Kenneth C. "Jazz Digest." *Film Comment* 24, no. 6 (November–December 1988): 38–43.

Spiegel, Ellen. "Fred and Ginger Meet Van Nest Polglase." *Velvet Light Trap,* no. 10 (Fall 1973): 17–22.

Springer, John. *All Talking! All Singing! All Dancing! A Pictorial History of the Movie Musical.* New York: Citadel Press, 1966.

Stern, Lee Edward. *The Movie Musical.* New York: Pyramid, 1974.

Taylor, John Russell, and Arthur Jackson. *The Hollywood Musical.* New York: McGraw-Hill, 1971.

Telotte, J. P. "A 'Golddigger' Aesthetic: The Depression Musical." *Post Script* 1, no. 1 (Fall 1981): 18–24.

————. "Ideology and the Kelly-Donen Musicals." *Film Criticism* 8, no. 3 (Spring 1984): 36–46.

————. "The Movie Musical and What We 'Ain't Heard' Yet." *Genre* 14 (1981): 505–520.

————. "Narrative Strategy in the Astaire-Rogers Films." *Journal of Popular Film and Television* 8, no. 3 (Fall 1980): 15–24.

————. "Scorsese's *Last Waltz* and the Concert Genre." *Film Criticism* 4, no. 2 (Winter 1980): 9–20.

————. "Self and Society: Vincente Minnelli and Musical Formula." *Journal of Popular Film and Television* 9, no. 4 (Winter 1982): 181–193.

————. "A Sober Celebration: Song and Dance in the 'New' Musical." *Journal of Popular Film and Television* 8, no. 1 (Spring 1980): 2–14.

Tinkcom, Matthew. "Working Like a Homosexual: Camp Visual Codes and the Labor of Gay Subjects in the MGM Freed Unit." *Cinema Journal* 35, no. 2 (Winter 1996): 24–42.

Turk, Edward Baron. "Deriding the Voice of Jeanette MacDonald: Notes on Psychoanalysis and the American Film Musical." *camera obscura*, nos. 25–26 (1991): 225–249.

Vaughan, David. "Dance in the Cinema." *Sequence*, no. 6 (Winter 1948–1949): 6–13.

White, Armond. "Half of a Note: Rock's Rebellion." *Film Comment* 24, no. 6 (November–December 1988): 32–36.

Wiener, Thomas. "The Rise and Fall of the Rock Film." 2 pts. *American Film* 1, no. 2 (November 1975): 25–29; 1, no. 3 (December 1975): 58–63.

Wills, Nadine. "'110 Percent Woman': The Crotch Shot in the Hollywood Musical." *Screen* 42, no. 2 (Summer 2001): 121–141.

Wolfe, Charles. "What's Entertainment? Recent Writing on the Film Musical." *Quarterly Review of Film Studies* 10, no. 2 (Spring 1985): 143–152.

Woll, Allen L. *The Hollywood Musical Goes to War.* Chicago: Nelson-Hall, 1983.

————. *Songs from the Hollywood Musical Comedies, 1927 to the Present.* New York: Garland, 1975.

Wood, Michael. *America in the Movies*, Chap 7. New York: Delta, 1975. Reprint, New York: Columbia University Press, 1989.

Wood, Robin. "Never Never Change, Always Gonna Dance." *Film Comment* 15, no. 5 (September–October 1979): 29–31.

PORNOGRAPHIC FILMS

Atkins, Thomas, ed. *Movies and Sexuality.* Hollins College, Va.: Film Journal, 1973.

Bazin, André. "Marginal Notes on Eroticism in the Cinema." In *What Is Cinema?* vol. 2, pp. 169–175. Berkeley: University of California Press, 1871.

Blake, Roger. *The Porno Movies.* Cleveland: Original Century Books, 1970.

Botto, Louis. "They Shoot Dirty Movies, Don't They?" *Look*, November 3, 1970, pp. 56–57, 59–60.

Buckley, Peter. "A Dirty Movie Is a Dirty Movie Is a Dirty Movie." *Films and Filming* 18, no. 11 (August 1972): 24–29.

Chappell, Fred. "Twenty-six Propositions about Skin-Flicks." In *Man and the Movies,* edited by W. R. Robinson, pp. 53–59. Baltimore: Penguin, 1967.

Corliss, Richard. "Cinema Sex: From *The Kiss* to *Deep Throat.*" *Film Comment* 9, no. 1 (January–February 1973): 4–5.

Day, Gary, and Clive Bloom, eds. *Perspectives on Pornography: Sexuality in Film and Literature.* New York: St. Martin's, 1988.

Di Lauro, Al, and Gerald Rabkin. *Dirty Movies: An Illustrated History of the Stag Film, 1915–1970.* New York: Chelsea House, 1976.

Dowdy, Andrew. *The Films of the Fifties: The American State of Mind.* New York: Morrow, 1975.

Durgnat, Raymond. *Eros in the Cinema.* London: Calder and Boyars, 1966.

———. "Eroticism in Cinema." 8 pts. *Films and Filming* 8, no. 1 (October 1961)–8, no. 8 (May 1962).

Dyer, Richard. "Male Gay Porn: Coming to Terms." *Jump Cut,* no. 30 (1985): 27–29.

Ellis, John. "Photography/Pornography/Art/Pornography." *Screen* 21, no. 1 (Spring 1980): 81–108.

Frank, Sam. *Sex in the Movies.* New York: Citadel, 1989.

Georgakas, Dan. "Porno Power." *Cineaste* 6, no. 4 (1974): 13–15.

Gibson, Pamela Church, and Roma Gibson, eds. *Dirty Looks: Women, Pornography, Power.* London: British Film Institute, 1993.

Hansen, Christian, Catherine Needham, and Bill Nichols. "Skin Flicks: Pornography, Ethnography, and the Discourses of Power." *Discourse* 11, no. 2 (Spring–Summer 1989): 65–79. Revised in Nichols, Bill. *Representing Reality: Issues and Concepts in Documentary,* chap. 8. Bloomington and Indianapolis: Indiana University Press, 1991.

Hanson, Gillian. *Original Skin: Nudity and Sex in Cinema and Theatre.* London: Tom Stacy, 1970.

Heard, Colin. "Sexploitation." *Films and Filming* 15, no. 11 (August 1969): 24–29.

Hoffman, Frank A. "Prolegomena to a Study of Traditional Elements in the Erotic Film." *Journal of American Folklore* 78 (April–June 1965): 143–148.

Johnson, Eithne. "Excess and Ecstasy: Constructing Female Pleasure in Porn Movies." *Velvet Light Trap,* no. 32 (Fall 1993): 30–49.

Kaplan, E. Ann. "Pornography and/as Representation." *Enclitic* 9, nos. 1–2 (1987): 8–18.

Knight, Arthur, and Hollis Alpert. "The History of Sex in Cinema." 20 pts. *Playboy* 12, no. 4 (April 1965)–16, no. 1 (January 1969).

Koch, Gertrude. "On Pornographic Cinema: The Body's Shadowy Realm," translated by Jan-Christopher Horak. *Jump Cut,* no. 35 (1990): 17–29.

Kurti, Laszlo. "Dirty Movies—Dirty Minds: The Social Construction of X-Rated Films." *Journal of Popular Culture* 17, no. 2 (Fall 1983): 187–192.

McDonough, Jimmy. "Sexposed." *Film Comment* 22, no. 4 (July–August 1986): 53–54, 56–61.

McGillivray, David. *Doing Rude Things: History of the British Sex Film 1957–1981*. London: Sun Tavern Fields, 1992.

Northland, John. "Porno Films: An In-Depth Report." *Take One* 4, no. 4 (March–April 1973): 11–17.

Paul, William. "Emerging Paradoxes of the New Porn." *Village Voice*, June 3, 1971, pp. 63, 73.

Prince, Stephen. "The Pornographic Image and the Practice of Film Theory." *Cinema Journal* 27, no. 2 (Winter 1988): 27–39.

Rhode, Eric. "Sensuality in the Cinema." *Sight and Sound* 30, no. 2 (Spring 1961): 93–95.

Robinson, David. "When Is a Dirty Film . . . ?" *Sight and Sound* 41, no. 1 (Winter 1971–1972): 28–30.

Rollin, Roger B. "Triple X: Erotic Movies and Their Audience." *Journal of Popular Film and Television* 10, no. 1 (1982): 2–21.

Rostler, William. *Contemporary Erotic Cinema*. New York: Penthouse/Ballantine, 1973.

Sarris, Andrew. "Reflections on the New Porn." *Village Voice*, September 1, 1975, pp. 71–72.

Schaefer, Eric. "Gauging a Revolution: 16mm Film and the Rise of the Pornographic Feature." *Cinema Journal* 41, no. 3 (Spring 2002): 3–26.

Shipman, David. *Caught in the Act: Sex and Eroticism in the Movies*. North Pomfret, Vt.: Hamish Hamilton, 1985.

Slade, Joseph W. "The Porn Market and Porn Formulas: The Feature Film of the Seventies." *Journal of Popular Film* 6, no. 2 (1977): 168–186.

———. *Pornography and Sexual Representation: A Reference Guide*. Westport, Conn.: Greenwood Press, 2000.

Sontag, Susan. "The Pornographic Imagination." In *Styles of Radical Will*. New York: Delta, 1969.

Turan, Kenneth, and Stephen F. Zito. *Sinema: American Pornographic Films and the People Who Make Them*. New York: New American Library, 1975.

Tyler, Parker. *Screening the Sexes: Homosexuality in the Movies*. New York: Doubleday, 1973.

Vogel, Amos. *Film as a Subversive Art*. New York: Random House, 1974.

Walker, Alexander. *Sex in the Movies*. Baltimore: Penguin, 1968.

Waller, Gregory A. "Auto-Erotica: Some Notes on Comic Softcore Films for the Drive-In Circuit." *Journal of Popular Culture* 17, no. 2 (Fall 1983): 135–141.

Waugh, Tom. *Hard to Imagine: Gay Male Eroticism in Photography and Film from Their Beginnings to Stonewall*. New York: Columbia University Press, 1996.

———. "Hard to Imagine: Gay Erotic Cinema in the Postwar Era." *CineAction*, no. 10 (Fall 1987): 65–72.

———. "Homosociality in the Classical American Stag Film: Off-Screen, On-Screen." *Sexualities* 4, no. 3 (2001): 275–291.

———. "Men's Pornography: Gay vs. Straight." *Jump Cut*, no. 30 (1985): 30–35.

Williams, Linda. "Fetishism and the Visual Pleasure of Hard Core: Marx, Freud, and the 'Money Shot.'" *Quarterly Review of Film and Video* 11, no. 2 (1989): 23–42.

———. "Film Body: An Implantation of Perversions." *Ciné-Tracts* 3, no. 4 (Winter 1981): 19–35. Reprinted in *Narrative, Apparatus, Ideology: A Film Theory Reader,* edited by Philip Rosen, pp. 507–534. New York: Columbia University Press, 1986. *Explorations in Film Theory: Selected Essays from CINÉ-TRACTS,* edited by Ron Burnett, pp. 46–71. Bloomington and Indianapolis: Indiana University Press, 1991.

———. *Hard-Core: Power, Pleasure, and the "Frenzy of the Visible."* Berkeley: University of California Press, 1989.

———. "Power, Pleasure, and Perversion: Sadomasochistic Film Pornography." *Representations,* no. 27 (Summer 1989): 37–65.

Wortley, Richard. *Erotic Movies.* London: Roxby, 1975.

Youngblood, Gene. "Flamingo Hours." *Take One* 5, no. 10 (July–August 1977): 50–51.

ROAD MOVIES

Cohan, Steven, and Ina Rae Hark, eds. *The Road Movie Book.* New York and London: Routledge, 1997.

Dargis, Manohla. "Road to Freedom." *Sight and Sound* 1, no. 3 (July 1991): 14–18.

Eyerman, Ron, and Orvad Löfaren. "Romancing the Road: Road Movies and Images of Mobility." *Theory, Culture, and Society* 12, no. 1 (February 1995): 53–79.

Kinder, Marsha. "The Return of the Outlaw Couple." *Film Quarterly* 27, no. 4 (Summer 1974): 2–10.

Laderman, David. *Driving Visions: Exploring the Road Movie.* Austin: University of Texas Press, 2002.

———. "What a Trip! The Road Film and American Culture." *Journal of Film and Video* 48, nos. 1–2 (Spring–Summer 1996): 41–57.

Sargeant, Jack, and Stephanie Watson, eds. *Lost Highways: An Illustrated History of Road Movies.* London: Creation Books, 1999.

SCIENCE FICTION FILMS

Amelio, Ralph J., ed. *Hal in the Classroom: Science Fiction Films.* Dayton, Ohio: Pflaum, 1974.

Anderson, Craig. *Science Fiction Films of the Seventies.* Jefferson, N.C.: McFarland, 1985.

Annas, Pamela. "Science Fiction Film Criticism in the U.S." *Science Fiction Studies* 7, no. 3 (1980): 323–329.

Arnold, Francis. "Out of This World." *Films and Filming* 9, no. 9 (June 1963): 14–18.

Atkins, Thomas, ed. *Science Fiction Films.* New York: Monarch Press, 1976.

Baxter, John. *Science Fiction in the Cinema.* New York: Paperback Library, 1970.

Beard, John. "Science Fiction Films of the Eighties: *Fin de siècle* before Its Time." *Journal of Popular Culture* 32, no. 1 (Summer 1998): 1–13.

Benson, Michael. *Vintage Science Fiction Films: The Pioneers, 1896–1949.* Jefferson, N.C.: McFarland, 1985.

Berg, Charles Ramirez. "Immigrants, Aliens, and Extraterrestrials: Science Fiction's Alien 'Other' as (among Other Things) New Hispanic Imagery." *Cine-Action,* no. 18 (1989): 3–17.

Bergstrom, Janet. "Androids and Androgyny." *camera obscura,* no. 15 (1986): 37–64. Reprinted in *Close Encounters: Film, Feminism, and Science Fiction,* edited by Constance Penley, et al., pp. 33–60. Minneapolis and Oxford: University of Minnesota Press, 1991.

Biskind, Peter. "War of the Worlds." *American Film* 9, no. 3 (1983): 36–42.

Booker, M. Keith. *Monsters, Mushroom Clouds, and the Cold War: American Science Fiction and the Roots of Postmodernism, 1946–1964.* Westport, Conn.: Greenwood Press, 2001.

Brain, Bonnie. "Saviors and Scientists: Extraterrestrials in Recent Science Fiction Films." *Et Cetera: A Review of General Semantics* 40, no. 2 (1983): 218–229.

Broderick, Mick. *Nuclear Movies: A Filmography.* Northcote, Australia: Post-Modem, 1988.

Brosnan, John. *Future Tense: The Cinema of Science Fiction.* New York: St. Martin's Press, 1978.

Brustein, Robert. "Reflections on Horror Movies." *Partisan Review* 25, no. 2 (Spring 1958): 288–296.

Byers, Thomas B. "Commodity Futures: Corporate State and Personal Style in Three Recent Science-Fiction Movies." *Science Fiction Studies,* no. 43 (November 1987): 326–339.

———. "Kissing Becky: Masculine Fears and Misogynist Moments in Science Fiction Films." *Arizona Quarterly* 45, no. 3 (Autumn 1989): 77–95.

Carter, Steven. "Avatars of the Turtles." *Journal of Popular Film and Television* 18, no. 3 (Fall 1990): 94–102.

Cartmell, Deborah, I. Q. Hunter, Heidi Kaye, and Imelda Whelchan, eds. *Alien Identities: Exploring Difference in Film and Fiction.* London: Pluto Press, 1999.

Chappell, Fred. "The Science Fiction Film Image." *Film Journal* 2, no. 3 (1974): 8–13.

Clarke, Frederick S. "Lords of the Deep." *Cinéfantastique* 19, no. 4 (May 1989): 13, 57.

Clarke, Jaimie. "Space Invaders: Speculations on the Politics of Postmodern Space in Recent Science Fiction Films." *CineAction,* no. 51 (February 2000): 10–16.

Creed, Barbara. "From Here to Modernity: Feminism and Postmodernism." *Screen* 28, no. 2 (1987): 47–67.

Dean, Joan F. "Between *2001* and *Star Wars*." *Journal of Popular Film and Television* 7, no. 1 (1978): 32–41.

Denne, John D. "Society and the Monster." *December* 9, nos. 2–3 (1967): 180–183.

Dervin, Daniel. "Primal Conditions and Conventions: The Genres of Comedy and Science Fiction." *Film/Psychology Review* 4, no. 1 (1980): 115–147.

Doherty, Thomas. *Teenagers and Teenpics: The Juvenilization of American Movies in the 1950s.* Boston: Unwin Hyman, 1988.

———. "Video, Science Fiction, and the Cinema of Surveillance." *Journal of the Fantastic in the Arts* 2, no. 2 (1989): 69–79.

Doll, Susan, and Greg Faller. "*Blade Runner* and Genre: Film Noir and Science Fiction." *Literature/Film Quarterly* 14, no. 2 (1986): 89–100.

Dowdy, Andrew. *The Films of the Fifties: The American State of Mind.* New York: Morrow, 1975.

Edelson, Edward. *Visions of Tomorrow: Great Science Fiction from the Movies.* New York: Doubleday, 1975.

Evans, Walter. "Monster Movies: A Sexual Theory." *Journal of Popular Film* 3, no. 1 (Winter 1974): 31–38. Reprinted in *Planks of Reason: Essays on the Horror Film,* edited by Barry K. Grant, pp. 53–64. Metuchen, N.J.: Scarecrow Press, 1984.

Evermore, Welch. *Cult Science Fiction Films: From THE AMAZING COLOSSAL MAN to YOG: THE MONSTER FROM SPACE.* Secaucus, N.J.: Birch Lane Press/ Carol Publishing, 1995.

Farber, Stephen. "The End of the World, Take 1." *American Film* 8, no. 1 (October 1982): 61–63.

Fischer, Dennis. *Science Fiction Film Directors, 1895–1998.* Jefferson, N.C.: McFarland, 2000.

Fitting, Peter. "Count Me Out/In: Post-Apocalyptic Visions in Recent Science Fiction Film." *CineAction,* no. 11 (December 1987): 42–51.

Frank, Alan. *The Science Fiction and Fantasy Film Handbook.* Totowa, N.J.: Barnes and Noble, 1983.

Franklin, H. Bruce. "Don't Look Where We're Going: Visions of the Future in Science Fiction Films, 1970–1982." *Science Fiction Studies* 10, no. 1 (1983): 70–80. Reprinted in *Shadows of the Magic Lamp: Fantasy and Science Fiction in Film,* edited by George Slusser and Eric S. Rabkin, pp. 73–85. Carbondale and Edwardsville: Southern Illinois University Press, 1985. Reprinted as "Visions of the Future in Science Fiction Films" in *Alien Zone: Cultural Theory and Contemporary Science Fiction Cinema,* edited by Annette Kuhn, pp. 19–31. London and New York: Verso, 1990.

———. "Future Imperfect." *American Film* 8, no. 5 (1983): 46–49, 75–76.

Galbraith, Stuart, IV. *Japanese Science Fiction, Fantasy, and Horror Films: A Critical Analysis and Filmography of 103 Features Released in the United States, 1950–1992.* Jefferson, N.C.: McFarland, 1994.

Geduld, Harry M. "Return to Méliès: Reflections on the Science Fiction Film." *Humanist* 27, no. 6 (November–December 1968): 23–24, 28.

George, Susan A. "Not Exactly 'Of Woman Born': Procreation and Creation in Recent Science Fiction Films." *Journal of Popular Film and Television* 28, no. 4 (Winter 2001): 177–183.

Gifford, Denis. *Movie Monsters.* New York: Dutton, 1969.

———. *Science Fiction Films.* New York: Dutton, 1971.

Glass, Fred. "The 'New Bad Future': *Robocop* and 1980's Sci-Fi Films." *Science as Culture,* no. 5 (1989): 7–49.

———. "Totally Recalling Arnold: Sex and Violence in the New Bad Future." *Film Quarterly* 44, no. 1 (Fall 1990): 2–13.

Glassy, Mark C. *The Biology of Science Fiction Cinema.* Jefferson, N.C.: McFarland, 2001.

Glut, Donald F. *Classic Movie Monsters.* Metuchen, N.J.: Scarecrow Press, 1978.

———. *The Frankenstein Catalog.* Jefferson, N.C.: McFarland, 1984.

Goldberg, Lee, Randy Lofficier, Jean-Marc Lofficier, and William Rabkin. *Science Fiction Filmmaking in the 1980s: Interviews with Actors, Directors, Producers, and Writers.* Jefferson, N.C.: McFarland, 1995.

Gordon, Andrew. "Science Fiction Film Criticism: The Postmodern Always Rings Twice." *Science Fiction Studies,* no. 43 (November 1987): 386–391.

———. "You'll Never Get Out of Bedford Falls: The Inescapable Family in American Science Fiction and Fantasy Films." *Journal of Popular Film and Television* 20, no. 2 (Summer 1992): 2–8.

Gow, Gordon. "The Non Humans." *Films and Filming* 20, no. 12 (September 1974): 59–62.

Grant, Barry K. "*Invaders from Mars* and Science Fiction in the Age of Reagan." *Cineaction,* no. 8 (Spring 1987): 77–83.

———. "Looking Upwards: H. G. Wells, Science Fiction, and the Cinema." *Literature/Film Quarterly* 14, no. 3 (1986): 154–163. Revised as "Looking Upwards: Reason and the Visible in Science Fiction Film." In *Gender, Language and Myth: Essays in Popular Narrative,* edited by Glenwood Irons, pp. 185–207. Toronto: University of Toronto Press, 1992.

Greenberg, Harvey R. *The Movies on Your Mind.* New York: Saturday Review Press/Dutton, 1975.

Guerrero, Edward. "AIDS as Monster in Science Fiction and Horror Cinema." *Journal of Popular Film and Television* 18, no. 3 (Fall 1990): 86–93.

———. *Framing Blackness: The African American Image in Film,* chap. 2. Philadelphia: Temple University Press, 1993.

Gunn, James. "The Tinsel Screen: Science Fiction and the Movies." In *Teaching Science Fiction: Education for Tomorrow,* edited by Jack Williamson, pp. 205–218. Philadelphia: Owlswick Press, 1980.

Hall, Peter C., and Richard D. Erlich. "Beyond Topeka and Thunderdome: Variations on the Comic-Romance Pattern in Recent SF Film." *Science Fiction Studies,* no. 43 (November 1987): 316–325.

Hardy, Phil. *Science Fiction: The Complete Film Sourcebook.* New York: Morrow, 1984.

Hauser, Frank. "Science Fiction Films." *International Film Annual,* vol. 2, edited by William Whitebair, pp. 87–90. New York: Doubleday, 1958.

Hendershot, Cyndy. "The Invaded Body: Paranoia and Anxiety in *Invaders from Mars, It Came from Outer Space,* and *Invasion of the Body Snatchers.*" *Extrapolation* 39, no. 1 (Spring 1998): 26–39.

Hodgens, Richard. "A Brief and Tragical History of the Science Fiction Film." *Film Quarterly* 13, no. 2 (Winter 1959): 30–39.

Holston, Kim R., and Tom Winchester. *Science Fiction, Fantasy, and Horror Film*

Sequels, Series, and Remakes: An Illustrated Filmography, with Plot Synopses and Critical Commentary. Jefferson, N.C.: McFarland, 1997.

Houston, Penelope. "Glimpses of the Moon." *Sight and Sound* 22, no. 2 (April–June 1953): 185–188.

Hunter, I. Q. *British Science Fiction Cinema.* New York and London: Routledge, 1999.

Hurley, Neil P. *Towards a Film Humanism,* chap. 10. New York: Delta, 1970.

Huss, Roy, and T. J. Ross, eds. *Focus on the Horror Film.* Englewood Cliffs, N.J.: Prentice-Hall, 1972.

Hutchinson, Tom. *Horror and Fantasy in the Cinema.* London: Studio Vista, 1974.

Jackson, Kevin. "The Good, the Bad, and the Ugly." *Sight and Sound* 2, no. 3 (July 1992): 11–12.

Jameson, Fredric. "SF Novels/SF Film." *Science Fiction Studies,* no. 22 (November 1980): 319–322.

Johnson, William, ed. *Focus on the Science Fiction Film.* Englewood Cliffs, N.J.: Prentice-Hall, 1972.

Jurkiewicz, Kenneth. "Technology in the Void: Politics and Science in Four Contemporary Space Movies." *New Orleans Review* 9, no. 1 (1982): 16–20.

Kaminsky, Stuart M. *American Film Genres: Approaches to a Critical Theory of Popular Film,* chap. 7. Dayton, Ohio: Pflaum, 1974.

Kane, Joe. "Nuclear Films." *Take One* 2, no. 6 (1969): 9–11.

King, Geoff, and Tanya Krzywinska. *Science Fiction Cinema: From Outerspace to Cyberspace.* London: Wallflower Press, 2001.

Kinnard, Roy. *Science Fiction Serials: A Critical Filmography of the 31 Hard SF Cliffhangers.* Jefferson, N.C.: McFarland, 1998.

Kuhn, Annette. "Border Crossing." *Sight and Sound* 2, no. 3 (July 1992): 13.

———, ed. *Alien Zone: Cultural Theory and Contemporary Science Fiction Cinema.* London and New York: Verso, 1990.

———. *Alien Zone II: The Spaces of Science Fiction Cinema.* New York and London: Verso, 1999.

Landon, Brooks. *The Aesthetics of Ambivalence: Rethinking Science Fiction Film in the Age of Electronic (Re)Production.* Westport, Conn.: Greenwood Press, 1992.

———. "From Trickery to Discovery: Trajectories of Science Fiction Film." *Journal of the Fantastic in the Arts* 2, no. 2 (1989): 3–9.

———. "Rethinking Science Fiction Film in the Age of Electronic (Re)Production: On a Clear Day You Can See the Horizon of Invisibility." *Post Script* 10, no. 1 (Fall 1990): 60–71.

Landrum, Larry. "A Checklist of Materials about Science Fiction Films of the 1950s: A Bibliography." *Journal of Popular Film* 1, no. 1 (Winter 1972): 61–63.

Landy, Marcia. *British Genres: Cinema and Society, 1930–1960.* Princeton: Princeton University Press, 1991.

———. *Film, Politics, and Gramsci,* chap. 8. Minneapolis: University of Minnesota Press, 1994.

Lee, Walt. *Reference Guide to Fantastic Films: Science Fiction, Fantasy, and Horror.* 3 vols. Los Angeles: Chelsea-Lee Books, 1972.

Lentz, Harris, III. *Science Fiction, Horror, and Fantasy Film and Television Credits,* 2d ed., 3 vols. Jefferson, N.C.: McFarland, 2001.

———. *Science Fiction, Horror, and Fantasy Film and Television Credits Supplement: Through 1987.* Jefferson, N.C.: McFarland, 1989.

Lowentrout, Peter M. "The Meta-Aesthetic of Popular Science Fiction Film." *Extrapolation* 29, no. 4 (1988): 349–364.

Lucanio, Patrick. *Them or Us: Archetypal Interpretations of Fifties Alien Invasion Films.* Bloomington and Indianapolis: Indiana University Press, 1987.

McLarty, Lianne. "Alien/Nation: Invasions, Abductions, and the Politics of Identity." In *Mythologies of Violence in Postmodern Media,* edited by Christopher Sharrett, pp. 245–359. Detroit: Wayne State University Press, 1999.

Matheson, T. J. "Marcuse, Ellul, and the Science Fiction Film: Negative Responses to Technology." *Science Fiction Studies,* no. 61 (November 1992): 326–339.

Mathieu, Philippe. "Science Fiction Film: The Genealogical Jungle." *Extrapolation* 38, no. 2 (1997): 127–134.

Menville, Douglas. *A Historical and Critical Survey of the Science Fiction Film.* New York: Arno Press, 1975.

Meyers, Richard. *SF-2: The Great Science Fiction Films.* Secaucus, N.J.: Citadel Press, 1984.

Murphy, Brian. "Monster Movies: They Came from beneath the Fifties." *Journal of Popular Film* 1, no. 1 (Winter 1972): 31–44.

Murphy, Robert. *Sixties British Cinema,* chap. 8. London: British Film Institute, 1992.

Nagl, Manfred. "The Science Fiction Film in Historical Perspective." *Science Fiction Studies,* no. 31 (November 1983): 262–277.

Naha, Ed. *Horror from Screen to Scream.* New York: Avon, 1975.

Noriega, Chon. "Godzilla and the Japanese Nightmare: When *Them!* Is Us." *Cinema Journal* 27, no. 1 (Fall 1987): 63–77.

Ohlin, Peter. "Science Fiction Film Criticism and the Debris of Postmodernism." *Science Fiction Studies,* no. 55 (November 1991): 411–419.

Parish, James Robert, and Michael R. Pitts. *The Great Science Fiction Pictures.* Metuchen, N.J.: Scarecrow Press, 1977.

———. *The Great Science Fiction Pictures II.* Metuchen, N.J.: Scarecrow Press, 1990.

Peary, Danny, ed. *Screen Flights/Screen Fantasies: The Future According to Science Fiction Cinema.* Garden City: Doubleday, 1984.

Penley, Constance. "Time Travel, Primal Scene, and the Critical Dystopia." *camera obscura,* no. 15 (1986): 67–84. Reprinted in Penley, *The Future of an Illusion: Film, Feminism, and Psychoanalysis,* pp. 121–139. Minneapolis: University of Minnesota Press, 1989. *Fantasy and the Cinema,* edited by James Donald, pp. 197–212. London: British Film Institute, 1989. *Close Encounters: Film, Feminism, and Science Fiction,* edited by Penley et al., pp. 63–80. Minneapolis and Oxford: University of Minnesota Press, 1991.

Penley, Constance, Elizabeth Lyon, Lynn Spigel, and Janet Bergstrom, eds. *Close Encounters: Film, Feminism, and Science Fiction.* Minneapolis and Oxford: University of Minnesota Press, 1991.

Pierson, Michele. "CGI Effects in Hollywood Science Fiction Cinema, 1989–1995: The Wonder Years." *Screen* 40, no. 2 (Summer 1999): 158–176.

Pohl, Frederik, and Frederik Pohl IV. *Science Fiction Studies in Film.* New York: Ace, 1981.

Rogers, Ivor A. "Extrapolative Cinema." *Arts in Society* 6 (Summer–Fall 1969): 287–291.

Roth, Lane. "The Rejection of Rationalism in Recent Science Fiction Films." *Philosophy in Context* 2 (1981): 44–55.

————. "*Vraisemblance* and the Western Setting in Contemporary Science Fiction Film." *Literature/Film Quarterly* 13, no. 3 (1985): 180–186.

Rovin, Jeff. *A Pictorial History of Science Fiction Films.* Secaucus, N.J.: Citadel Press, 1975.

Rubin, Martin. "Genre and Technology: Variant Attitudes in Science Fiction Film and Literature." *Persistence of Vision,* nos. 3–4 (Summer 1986): 95–110.

Ruppersberg, Hugh. "The Alien Messiah in Recent Science Fiction Films." *Journal of Popular Film and Television* 14, no. 4 (1987): 159–166. Reprinted as "The Alien Messiah" in *Alien Zone: Cultural Theory and Contemporary Science Fiction Cinema,* edited by Annette Kuhn, pp. 32–38. London and New York: Verso, 1990.

Ruppert, Peter. "*Blade Runner:* The Utopian Dialectics of Science Fiction Films." *Cineaste* 17, no. 2 (1989): 8–13.

Rushing, Janice Hocker, and Thomas S. Frentz. *Projecting the Shadow: The Cyborg Hero in American Film.* Chicago: University of Chicago Press, 1995.

Ryan, Michael, and Douglas Kellner. *Camera Politica: The Politics and Ideology of Contemporary Hollywood Film.* Bloomington and Indianapolis: Indiana University Press, 1988.

Samuels, Stuart. "The Age of Conspiracy and Conformity." *American History/American Film,* edited by J. E. O'Connor and M. Jackson, pp. 203–217. New York: Ungar, 1979.

Schecter, Harold. *The Bosom Serpent: Folklore and Popular Art.* Iowa City: University of Iowa Press, 1988.

Schelde, Per. *Androids, Humanoids, and Other Science Fiction Monsters: Science and Soul in Science Fiction Films.* New York: New York University Press, 1993.

Senn, Bryan, and John Johnson. *Fantastic Subject Guide: A Topical Index to 2,500 Horror, Science Fiction, and Fantasy Films.* Jefferson, N.C.: McFarland, 1992.

Shaheen, Jack G., ed. *Nuclear War Films.* Carbondale: Southern Illinois University Press, 1978.

Shapiro, Benjamin. "Universal Truths: Cultural Myths and Generic Adaptation in 1950s Science Fiction Films." *Journal of Popular Film and Television* 18, no. 3 (Fall 1990): 103–111.

Sheen, Erica. "'I'm Not *in* the Business: I *Am* the Business': Women at Work in Hollywood Science Fiction." *Where No Man Has Gone Before: Women and Science Fiction,* edited by Lucie Armitt, pp. 139–161. London and New York: Routledge, 1991.

Slusser, George E., and Eric S. Rabkin, eds. *Shadows of the Magic Lamp: Fantasy and Science Fiction in Film.* Carbondale: Southern Illinois University Press, 1985.

Sobchack, Vivian. "The Alien Landscape of the Planet Earth." *Film Journal* 2, no. 3 (1974): 16–21.

———. "Child/Alien/Father: Patriarchal Crisis and Generic Exchange." *camera obscura,* no. 15 (1986): 7–34. Reprinted in *American Horrors: Essays on the Modern American Horror Film,* edited by Gregory A. Waller, pp. 175–194. Urbana and Chicago: University of Illinois Press, 1987. *Close Encounters: Film, Feminism, and Science Fiction,* edited by Constance Penley et al., pp. 3–30. Minneapolis and Oxford: University of Minnesota Press, 1991.

———. "Cities on the Edge of Time: The Urban Science Fiction Film." *East-West Film Journal* 3, no. 1 (December 1988): 4–19.

———. *The Limits of Infinity: The American Science Fiction Film.* South Brunswick, N.J., and London: Barnes/Yoseloff, 1980. Revised as *Screening Space: The American Science Fiction Film.* New York: Ungar, 1987.

———. "Science Fiction." In *Handbook of American Film Genres,* edited by Wes D. Gehring, pp. 229–247. New York: Greenwood Press, 1991.

Solomon, Stanley J. *Beyond Formula: American Film Genres.* New York: Harcourt Brace Jovanovich, 1976.

Sontag, Susan. "The Imagination of Disaster." In *Against Interpretation,* pp. 209–225. New York: Delta, 1966. Reprinted in *Awake in the Dark,* edited by David Denby, pp. 263–278. New York: Vintage, 1977. *Film Theory and Criticism,* 2d ed., edited by Gerald Mast and Marshall Cohen, pp. 488–504. New York: Oxford, 1979.

Springer, Claudia. *Electronic Eros: Bodies and Desire in the Postindustrial Age.* Austin: University of Texas Press, 1996.

———. "The Pleasure of the Interface." *Screen* 32, no. 3 (Autumn 1991): 303–323.

Staiger, Janet. "Future Noir: Contemporary Representations of Visionary Cities." *East-West Film Journal* 3, no. 1 (December 1988): 20–44.

Stanbury, C. M. "Monsters in the Movies: A Mythology of the Absurd." *December* 10, no. 1 (1968): 74–76.

Steinbrunner, Chris, and Bert Goldblatt. *Cinema of the Fantastic.* New York: Saturday Review Press, 1972.

Stern, Michael. "Making Culture into Nature: Or Who Put the 'Special' into 'Special Effects'?" *Science Fiction Studies* 7, no. 3 (1980): 263–269. Reprinted as "Making Culture into Nature" in *Alien Zone: Cultural Theory and Contemporary Science Fiction Cinema,* edited by Annette Kuhn, pp. 32–38. London and New York: Verso, 1990.

Stevens, Bob. "United Artists Sci-Fi Matinee." *Films in Review* 46, nos. 9–10 (November–December 1995): 54–60.

Stewart, Garrett. "The Photographic Ontology of Science Fiction Film." *Iris,* no. 25 (1998): 99–132.

Telotte, J. P. "The Doubles of Fantasy and the Space of Desire." *Film Criticism* 6, no. 1 (Fall 1982): 56–68. Reprinted in *Film Criticism* 11, nos. 1–2 (Fall–Winter 1987): 43–55.

———. "Human Artifice and the Science Fiction Film." *Film Quarterly* 36, no. 3 (Spring 1983): 44–51.

———. "In the Realm of Revealing: The Technological Double in the Contemporary Science Fiction Film." *Journal of the Fantastic in the Arts* 6, nos. 2–3 (1994): 234–252.

———. "The Machine: Consciousness and the Science Fiction Film." *Western Humanities Review* 42, no. 3 (Autumn 1988): 249–258.

———. *Replications: A Robotic History of the Science Fiction Film.* Urbana and Chicago: University of Illinois Press, 1995.

———. *Science Fiction Film.* New York: Cambridge University Press, 2001.

———. "Science Fiction in Double Focus: *Forbidden Planet.*" *Film Criticism* 13, no. 3 (Spring 1989): 25–36.

———. "The Tremulous Public Body: Robots, Change, and the Science Fiction Film." *Journal of Popular Film and Television* 19, no. 1 (Spring 1991): 14–23.

———. "*The World of Tomorrow* and the 'Secret Goal' of Science Fiction." *Journal of Film and Video* 45, no. 1 (Spring 1993): 27–39.

Thomas, Susan. "Between the Boys and Their Toys: The Science Fiction Film." In *Where No Man Has Gone Before: Women and Science Fiction,* edited by Lucie Armitt, pp. 109–122. London and New York: Routledge, 1991.

Torry, Robert. "Apocalypse Then: Benefits of the Bomb in Fifties Science Fiction Films." *Cinema Journal* 31, no. 1 (Fall 1991): 7–21.

Wachhorst, Wyn. "Time Travel Romance on Film: Archetypes and Structures." *Extrapolation* 25, no. 4 (Winter 1984): 340–359.

Warren, Bill. *Keep Watching the Skies! American Science Fiction Movies of the Fifties.* vol. 1, 1950–1957; vol. 2, 1958–1962. Jefferson, N.C.: McFarland, 1982, 1985.

———. *Set Visits: Interviews with 32 Horror and Science Fiction Filmmakers.* Jefferson, N.C.: McFarland, 1997.

Weaver, Tom. *Interviews with B Science Fiction and Horror Movie Makers: Writers, Producers, Directors, Actors, Moguls, and Makeup.* Jefferson, N.C.: McFarland, 1988.

———. *It Came from Weaver Five: Interviews with 20 Zany, Glib, and Earnest Moviemakers in the SF and Horror Traditions of the Thirties, Forties, Fifties, and Sixties.* Jefferson, N.C.: McFarland, 1996.

———. *I Was a Monster Movie Maker: Conversations with 22 SF and Horror Filmmakers.* Jefferson, N.C.: McFarland, 2001.

———. *Science Fiction and Fantasy Film Flashbacks: Conversations with 24 Actors, Writers, Producers, and Directors from the Golden Age.* Jefferson, N.C.: McFarland, 1998.

———. *Science Fiction Stars and Horror Heroes: Interviews with Actors, Directors, Producers, and Writers of the 1940s through 1960s.* Jefferson, N.C.: McFarland, 1991.

———. *They Fought in the Creature Features: Interviews with 23 Classic Horror, Science Fiction, and Serial Stars.* Jefferson, N.C.: McFarland, 1995.

Wells, Paul. "The Invisible Man: Shrinking Masculinity in the 1950s Science Fiction B Movie." *You Tarzan: Masculinity, Movies, and Men,* edited by Pat Kirkham and Janet Thumim, pp. 181–199. London: Lawrence and Wishart, 1993.

Wharton, Lewis. "Godzilla to Latitude Zero: The Cycle of the Technological Monster." *Journal of Popular Film* 3, no. 1 (Winter 1974): 31–38.

Wiener, Diane R. "Representing Pre-Millennial Tensions: Hollywood's Gendered Invasion Narratives." *CineAction,* no. 51 (February 2000): 17–22.

Williams, Linda Ruth, et al. "Movie Nightmares." *Sight and Sound* 3, no. 5 (May 1993): 30–35.

Williams, Tony. "Close Encounters of the Authoritarian Kind." *Wide Angle* 5, no. 4 (1983): 22–29.

Willis, Don. *Horror and Science Fiction Films: A Checklist.* Metuchen, N.J.: Scarecrow Press, 1972.

———. *Horror and Science Fiction Films II.* Metuchen, N.J.: Scarecrow Press, 1977.

———. *Horror and Science Fiction Films III.* Metuchen, N.J.: Scarecrow Press, 1984.

———. *Horror and Science Fiction Films IV (1984–1993).* Lanham, Md.: Scarecrow Press, 1997.

Wingrove, David. *Science Fiction Source Book.* London: Longman, 1985.

Wright, Bruce L. *Yesterday's Tomorrows: The Golden Age of Science Fiction Movie Posters.* Lanham, Md.: Taylor, 1993.

SPORTS FILMS

Ardolino, Frank. "Ceremonics of Innocence and Experience in *Bull Durham, Field of Dreams,* and *Eight Men Out.*" *Journal of Popular Film and Television* 18, no. 2 (Summer 1990): 43–51.

Bergan, Ronald. *Sports in the Movies.* London and New York: Proteus Books, 1982.

Di Piero, Thomas. "Angels in the (Out)Field of Vision." *camera obscura,* nos. 40–41 (1999): 201–225.

Farber, Manny. "The Fight Films." In *Movies,* pp. 64–67. New York: Stonehill, 1976. Originally published as *Negative Space.* London: Studio Vista, 1971.

Fuller, Linda K. "The Baseball Movie Genre: At Bat or Struck Out?" *Play and Culture* 3, no. 1 (February 1990): 64–74.

Good, Howard. *Diamonds in the Dark: America, Baseball, and the Movies.* Lanham, Md.: Scarecrow Press, 1996.

Gretton, Viveca. "You Could Look It Up: Notes toward a Reading of Baseball, History, and Ideology in the Dominant Cinema." *CineAction,* nos. 21–22 (November 1990): 70–75.

Grindon, Leger. "Body and Soul: The Structure of Meaning in the Boxing Film Genre." *Cinema Journal* 35, no. 4 (Summer 1996): 54–69.

———. "Getting into Shape: Classic Conventions Make Their Move into the Boxing Film, 1937–1940." *Journal of Sport and Social Issues* 22, no. 4 (1998): 360–372.

Jahiel, Edwin. "The Ring and the Lens: Films on Boxing." *Film Society Review* (September 1996): 26–28.

Noverr, Douglas A. "The Coach and the Athlete in Football Sports Films." *Beyond the Stars: Stock Characters in American Popular Film,* edited by Paul

Loukides and Linda K. Fuller, pp. 120–130. Bowling Green, Ohio: Popular Press, 1990.

Sayre, Nora. " 'Win This One for the Gipper!' and Other Reasons Why Sports Movies Miss the Point." *Village Voice,* December 1, 1975, pp. 30–32, 35, 37. Reprinted in *Film Genre: Theory and Criticism,* edited by Barry K. Grant, pp. 182–194. Metuchen, N.J.: Scarecrow Press, 1977.

Sobchack, Vivian. "Baseball in the Post-American Cinema, or Life in the Minor Leagues." *East-West Film Journal* 7, no. 1 (January 1993): 1–23.

Spears, Jack. "Baseball on the Screen." *Films in Review* 19, no. 4 (April 1968): 198–217.

Streible, Dan. "A History of the Boxing Film, 1894–1915: Social Control and Social Reform in the Progressive Era." *Film History* 3, no. 3 (1989): 235–257.

Thomson, David. "Playing for Real." *Sight and Sound* 6, no. 9 (September 1996): 13–15.

Williams, Tony. " 'I Could've Been a Contender': The Boxing Movie's Generic Instability." *Quarterly Review of Film and Video* 18, no. 3 (2001): 305–319.

Zucker, Harvey Marc, and Lawrence J. Babich. *Sports Films: A Complete Reference.* Jefferson, N.C.: McFarland, 1987.

TEENPICS

Benton, Michael, Mark Dolan, and Rebecca Zisch. "Teen Films: An Annotated Bibliography." *Journal of Popular Film and Television* 25, no. 2 (Summer 1997): 83–88.

Bernstein, Jonathan. *Pretty in Pink: The Golden Age of Teenage Movies.* New York: St. Martin's Griffin, 1997.

Betrock, Alan. *The I Was a Teenage Juvenile Delinquent Rock 'n' Roll Horror Beach Party Movie Book: A Complete Guide to the Teen Exploitation Film, 1954–1969.* New York: St. Martin's Press, 1986.

Dixon, Winston Wheeler. " 'Fighting and Violence and Everything, That's Always Cool' ": Teen Films in the 1990s." In *Film Genre 2000,* edited by Winston Wheeler Dixon, pp. 125–141. New York: State University of New York Press, 2000.

Doherty, Thomas. "American Teenagers and Teenpics, 1955–1957: A Study of Exploitation Filmmaking." In *Current Research in Film: Audiences, Economics, and Law,* vol. 2, edited by Bruce A. Austin, pp. 47–61. Norwood, N.J.: Ablex, 1986.

———. *Teenagers and Teenpics: The Juvenilization of American Movies in the 1950s.* Boston: Unwin Hyman, 1988.

Goldstein, Ruth M., and Edith Zornow. *The Screen Image of Youth: Movies about Children and Adolescents.* Metuchen, N.J.: Scarecrow Press, 1980.

Jackson, Merlock. *Images of Children in American Film: A Sociocultural Analysis.* Metuchen, N.J.: Scarecrow Press, 1986.

Leitch, Thomas M. "The World According to Teenpics." *Literature/Film Quarterly* 20, no. 1 (1992): 43–47.

Lewis, Jon. *The Road to Romance and Ruin: Teen Films and Youth Culture.* New York and London: Routledge, 1992.

Morris, Gary. "Beyond the Beach: Social and Formal Aspects of AIP's *Beach Party Movies*." *Journal of Popular Film and Television* 21, no. 1 (Spring 1993): 2–11.

Morton, Jim. "Beach Party Films." *RE/Search* 10 (1986): 146–147.

Neale, Steve. *Genre and Hollywood*. New York and London: Routledge, 2000.

Pevere, Geoff. "Rebel without a Chance: Cycles of Rebellion and Suppression in Canadian Teen Movies." *CineAction*, no. 12 (Spring 1988): 44–48.

Pomerance, Murray, and John Sakeris, eds. *Pictures of a Generation on Hold: Selected Papers*. Toronto: Media Studies Working Group, 1996.

Pomerance, Murray, and Frances Gateward, eds. *Snips, Snails, and Puppy Dog Tails: The Cinemas of Boyhood*. Detroit: Wayne State University Press, 2004.

————. *Sugar and Spice: The Cinemas of Girlhood*. Detroit: Wayne State University Press, 2002.

Rapping, Elayne. "Hollywood's Youth Culture Films." *Cineaste* 16, nos. 1–2 (1987–1988): 14–19.

Rutsky, R. L. "Surfing the Other: Ideology on the Beach." *Film Quarterly* 52, no. 4 (Summer 1999): 12–23.

Scheiner, Georgeanne. *Signifying Female Adolescence: Film Representations and Fans, 1920–1950*. Westport, Conn.: Praeger, 2000.

Shary, Timothy. "Angry Young Women: The Emergence of the 'Tough Girl' Image in American Teen Films." *Post Script* 19, no. 2 (Winter–Spring 2000): 49–61.

————. *Generation Multiplex: The Image of Youth in Contemporary American Cinema*. Austin: University of Texas Press, 2002.

————. "The Teen Film and Its Methods of Study." *Journal of Popular Film and Television* 25, no. 1 (Spring 1997): 38–45.

Speed, Lesley. "Moving on Up: Education in Black American Youth Films." *Journal of Popular Film and Television* 29, no. 2 (Summer 2001): 82–91.

White, Armond. "Kidpix." *Film Comment* 21, no. 4 (August 1985): 9–16.

Wood, Robin. "Party Time, or Can't Hardly Wait for That American Pie." *CineAction*, no. 58 (June 2002): 2–10.

Zacharek, Stephanie. "There's Something about Teenage Comedy. . . ." *Sight and Sound* 9, no. 12 (December 1999): 62–64.

THRILLERS

Cobley, Paul. *The American Thriller: Generic Innovation and Social Change in the 1970s*. New York: Palgrave, 2001.

Davis, Brian. *The Thriller: The Suspense Film from 1946*. London: Studio Vista; New York: Dutton, 1973.

Derry, Charles D. *The Suspense Thriller: Films in the Shadow of Alfred Hitchcock*. Jefferson, N.C.: McFarland, 1988.

Dickstein, Morris. "Beyond Good and Evil: The Morality of Thrillers." *American Film* 6, no. 9 (July–August 1981): 49–52, 67–69.

Dorfman, Richard. "Conspiracy City." *Journal of Popular Film and Television* 7, no. 4 (1980): 434–456.

Eberwein, Robert. "The Erotic Thriller." *Post Script* 17, no. 3 (Summer 1998): 25–33.

Gow, Gordon. *Suspense in the Cinema*. New York: Castle Books, 1968.

Hammond, Lawrence. *Thriller Movies: Classic Films of Suspense and Mystery.* London: Octopus Books, 1974.

Keesey, Doug. "They Kill for Love: Defining the Erotic Thriller as a Genre." *Cine-Action,* no. 56 (2001): 54–66.

McCarty, John. *Thrillers: Seven Decades of Classic Film Suspense.* Secaucus, N.J.: Citadel, 1992.

Rubin, Martin. *Thrillers.* New York and Cambridge: Cambridge University Press, 1999.

WAR FILMS

Adair, Gilbert. *Hollywood's Vietnam: From THE GREEN BERETS to APOCALYPSE NOW.* New York: Proteus, 1981.

Anderegg, Michael, ed. *Inventing Vietnam: Film and Television Constructions of the U.S.-Vietnam War.* Philadelphia: Temple University Press, 1991.

Auferhide, Pat. "Vietnam: Good Soldiers." In *Seeing through Movies,* edited by Mark Crispen Miller, pp. 81–111. New York: Pantheon, 1990.

Auster, Albert, and Leonard Quart. "Hollywood and Vietnam: The Triumph of the Will." *Cineaste* 9, no. 3 (Spring 1979): 4–9.

———. *How the War Was Remembered: Hollywood and Vietnam.* New York: Praeger, 1988.

Basinger, Jeanine. *The World War Two Combat Film: Anatomy of a Genre.* New York: Columbia University Press, 1986.

Belmans, Jacques. "Cinema and Man at War." *Film Society Review* 7, no. 6 (February 1972): 22–37.

Belton, John. *American Cinema/American Culture.* New York: McGraw-Hill, 1994.

Boehringer, Kathe. "Banality Now." *Australian Journal of Screen Theory,* no. 8 (1980): 89–95.

Broderick, Mick. *Nuclear Movies: A Filmography.* Northcote, Australia: Post-Modem, 1988.

Butler, Ivan. *The War Film.* New York: A. S. Barnes, 1974.

Chambers, James Whiteclay, II, and David Culbert. *World War II, Film and History.* New York: Oxford University Press, 1997.

Corrigan, Timothy. *A Cinema without Walls: Movies and Culture after Vietnam.* New Brunswick, N.J.: Rutgers University Press, 1991.

Coultass, Clive. *Images for Battle.* Cranbury, N.J.: University of Delaware Press, 1989.

Curley, Stephen J., and Frank J. Wetta. "War Film Bibliography." *Journal of Popular Film and Television* 18, no. 2 (Summer 1990): 72–79.

Deming, Barbara. *Running Away from Myself.* New York: Grossman, 1969.

Devine, Jeremy M. *Vietnam at 24 Frames a Second: A Critical and Thematic Analysis of over 350 Films about the Vietnam War.* Jefferson, N.C.: McFarland, 1995.

Dick, Bernard F. *The Star-Spangled Screen: The American World War Two Film.* Lexington: University Press of Kentucky, 1985.

Dittmar, Linda, and Gene Michaud, eds. *From Hanoi to Hollywood: The Viet-*

nam War in American Film. New Brunswick, N.J.: Rutgers University Press, 1991.

Doherty, Thomas. "Full Metal Genre: Stanley Kubrick's Vietnam Combat Movie." *Film Quarterly* 42, no. 2 (Winter 1988–1989): 25–30.

———. *Projections of War: Hollywood, American Culture, and World War II*, rev. ed. New York: Columbia University Press, 1999.

Dolan, Edward F., Jr. *Hollywood Goes to War*. New York: W. H. Smith, 1985.

Donald, Ralph R. "Anti-War Themes in Narrative War Films: Soldiers' Experiences as Social Comment." *Studies in Popular Culture* 13, no. 2 (1991): 77–92.

———. "Masculinity and Machismo in Hollywood's War Films." In *Men, Masculinity, and the Media,* edited by Steve Craig, pp. 124–136. Newbury Park, Calif.: Sage, 1992.

Dowling, John. "Nuclear War and Disarmament—Selected Film/Video List." *Sightlines* 15, no. 3 (1982): 19–21.

Dworkin, Martin S. "Clean Germans and Dirty Politics." *Film Comment* 3, no. 1 (Winter 1965): 36–41.

Farber, Manny. "Movies in Wartime." *New Republic,* January 3, 1944, pp. 16–20.

Fyne, Robert. "The Unsung Heroes of World War II." *Literature/Film Quarterly* 7, no. 2 (1979): 148–154.

Garland, Brock. *War Movies: The Complete Viewer's Guide*. New York: Facts on File, 1987.

Giglio, Ernest. *Here's Looking at You: Hollywood, Film, and Politics*, Chaps. 8–9. New York: Peter Lang, 2000.

Gillett, John. "Westfront 1957." *Sight and Sound* 27, no. 3 (Winter 1957–1958): 122–127.

Gilman, Owen, and Lorrie Smith, eds. *America Rediscovered: Critical Essays on Literature and Films of the Vietnam War*. Hamden, Conn.: Garland, 1990.

Grossman, Edward. "Bloody Popcorn." *Harper's,* December 1970, pp. 32–40.

Guy, Rory. "Hollywood Goes to War." *Cinema* (U.S.) 3, no. 2 (March 1966): 22–29.

Higham, Charles, and Joel Greenberg. *Hollywood in the Forties*. New York: Barnes, 1968.

Hughes, Robert, ed. *Film, Book 2: Films of Peace and War*. New York: Grove Press, 1962.

Hurd, Geoff, ed. *National Fictions: World War Two in British Film and Television*. London: British Film Institute, 1984.

Hyams, Joe. *War Films*. New York: W. H. Smith, 1984.

Isaacs, Hermine Rich. "Shadows of War on the Silver Screen." *Theatre Arts* 26, no. 11 (November 1942): 689–696.

Isenberg, Michael T. "An Ambiguous Pacifism: A Retrospective on World War I Films, 1930–1938." *Journal of Popular Film* 4, no. 2 (1975): 98–115.

———. *War on Film: The American Cinema and World War I*. Rutherford, N.J.: Fairleigh Dickinson University Press, 1981.

Jacobs, Lewis. "World War II and the American Film." *Cinema Journal* 7 (Winter 1967–1968): 1–21. Reprinted in *Film Culture,* no. 47 (Summer 1969): 28–42.

Jeavons, Clyde. *A Pictorial History of War Films*. Secaucus, N.J.: Citadel Press, 1974.

————. "Why They Fought." *The Movie* (U.K.), no. 22 (1980): 438–440.

Jeffords, Susan. "Masculinity as Excess in Vietnam Films: The Father/Son Dynamic of American Culture." *Genre* 21 (Winter 1988): 487–515.

————. "The New Vietnam Films: Is the Movie Over?" *Journal of Popular Film and Television* 13, no. 4 (Winter 1986): 186–194.

————. *The Remasculinization of America: Gender and the Vietnam War.* Bloomington: Indiana University Press, 1989.

Jones, Dorothy B. "War Films Made in Hollywood, 1942–1944." *Hollywood Quarterly* 1, no. 1 (October 1945): 1–19.

Jones, Ken D., and Arthur F. McClure. *Hollywood at War: The American Motion Picture and World War II.* New York: A. S. Barnes, 1973.

Jowett, Garth. *Film: The Democratic Art,* chap. 12. Boston: Little, Brown, 1976.

Kagan, Norman. *The War Film.* New York: Pyramid, 1974.

Kane, Kathryn. *Visions of War: The Hollywood Combat Films of World War Two.* Ann Arbor: UMI Research Press, 1982.

————. "The World War II Combat Film." In *Handbook of American Film Genres,* edited by Wes D. Gehring, pp. 85–102. New York: Greenwood Press, 1988.

Kelly, Andrew. *Cinema and the Great War.* London and New York: Routledge, 1997.

King, Larry. "The Battle of Popcorn Bay." *Harper's,* May 1967, pp. 50–54.

Kinney, Judy Lee. "The Mythical Method: Fictionalizing the Vietnam War." *Wide Angle* 7, no. 4 (1985): 35–40.

Kopps, Clayton R., and Gregory D. Black. *Hollywood Goes to War: How Politics, Profits, and Propaganda Shaped World War II Movies.* New York: Free Press, 1987. Reprint, Berkeley and Los Angeles: University of California Press, 1990.

Kozloff, Max, William Johnson, and Richard Corliss. "Shooting at Wars: Three Views." *Film Quarterly* 21, no. 2 (Winter 1967–1968): 27–36.

Kuiper, John B. "Civil War Films: A Quantitative Description of a Genre." *Journal of the Society of Cinematologists* 5 (1965): 81–89.

Landrum, Larry M., and Christine Eynon. "World War II in the Movies: A Selected Bibliography of Sources." *Journal of Popular Film* 1, no. 2 (Spring 1972): 147–153.

Landy, Marcia. *British Genres: Cinema and Society, 1930–1960.* Princeton, N.J.: Princeton University Press, 1991.

Langman, Larry, and Edgar Borg. *Encyclopedia of American War Films.* New York: Garland, 1989.

Lewis, Leon, and William David Sherman. *The Landscape of Contemporary Cinema.* Buffalo: Buffalo Spectrum Press, 1967.

Lingeman, Richard R. "Will This Picture Help Win the War?" In *Don't You Know There's a War On? The American Home Front, 1941–1945.* New York: Putnam, 1970.

McClure, Arthur F. "Hollywood at War: The American Motion Picture and World War II, 1939–1945." *Journal of Popular Film* 1, no. 2 (Spring 1972): 123–135.

McGregor, Gaile. "Cultural Studies and Social Change: The War Film as Men's Magic, and Other Fictions about Fictions." *Canadian Journal of Sociology* 18, no. 3 (1993): 271–302.

Madsen, Axel. "Vietnam and the Movies." *Cinema* (U.S.) 4, no. 1 (Spring 1968): 10–13.

Malo, Jean-Jacques, and Tony Williams, eds. *Vietnam War Films*. Jefferson, N.C.: McFarland, 1994.

Manchel, Frank. "A Representative Genre of the Film." *Film Study: A Resource Guide,* chap. 2. Rutherford, N.J.: Fairleigh Dickinson University Press, 1973.

Mann, Klauss. "What's Wrong with Anti-Nazi Films?" *Decision* 2, no. 2 (August 1941): 27–35.

Manvell, Roger. *Films and the Second World War*. New York: Delta, 1976.

Mariani, John. "Let's Not Be Beastly to the Nazis." *Film Comment* 15, no. 1 (January–February 1979): 49–53.

Martin, Andrew. "Vietnam and Melodramatic Representation." *East-West Film Journal* 4, no. 2 (June 1990): 54–68.

Mast, Gerald, ed. *The Movies in Our Midst,* part 6. Chicago: University of Chicago Press, 1982.

Modleski, Tania. "A Father Is Being Beaten: Male Feminism and the War Film." *Discourse* 10, no. 2 (Spring–Summer 1988): 62–77.

Morella, Joe, et al. *The Films of World War II*. Secaucus, N.J.: Citadel Press, 1975.

Mulay, James J., et al. *War Movies*. Evanston, Ill.: CineBooks, 1989.

Neale, Steve. "Aspects of Ideology and Narrative Form in the American War Film." *Screen* 32, no. 2 (Summer 1991): 35–57.

———. *Genre and Hollywood*. New York and London: Routledge, 2000.

Newsinger, John. "'Do You Walk the Walk?': Aspects of Masculinity in Some Vietnam War Films." In *You Tarzan: Masculinity, Movies, and Men,* edited by Pat Kirkham and Janet Thumim, pp. 126–136. London: Lawrence and Wishart, 1993.

Norden, Martin F. "The Disabled Vietnam Veteran in Hollywood Films." *Journal of Popular Film and Television* 13, no. 1 (Spring 1985): 16–23.

Parish, James Robert. *The Great Combat Pictures: Twentieth-Century Warfare on the Screen*. Metuchen, N.J.: Scarecrow Press, 1990.

Perlmutter, Tom. *War Movies*. Secaucus, N.J.: Castle, 1974.

Polan, Dana. *Power and Paranoia: History, Narrative, and the American Cinema, 1940–1950*. New York: Columbia University Press, 1986.

Pym, John. "A Bullet in the Head: Vietnam Remembered." *Sight and Sound* 48, no. 2 (Spring 1979): 82–83, 115.

Quart, Leonard, and Albert Auster. "The Wounded Vet in Postwar Film." *Social Policy* 13 (Fall 1982): 24–31.

Ray, Robert B. *A Certain Tendency of the Hollywood Cinema, 1930–1980*. Princeton: Princeton University Press, 1985.

Reed, Joseph W. *American Scenarios: The Uses of Film Genre*. Middletown, Conn.: Wesleyan University Press, 1989.

Rist, Peter. "Standard Hollywood Fare: The World War II Combat Film Revisited." *CineAction,* no. 12 (Spring 1988): 23–26.

Rowe, John Carlos, and Richard Berg, eds. *The Vietnam War and American Culture*. New York: Columbia University Press, 1991.

Rubin, Steven Jay. *Combat Films: American Realism, 1945–1970*. Jefferson, N.C.: McFarland, 1981.

Ryan, Michael, and Douglas Kellner. *Camera Politica: The Politics and Ideology of Contemporary Hollywood Film*. Bloomington and Indianapolis: Indiana University Press, 1988.

Schatz, Thomas. "World War II and the Hollywood 'War Film.'" In *Refiguring American Film Genres: History and Theory*, edited by Nick Browne, pp. 89–128. Berkeley: University of California Press, 1998.

Schecter, Harold, and Jonna G. Semeiks. "*Rambo, Platoon,* and the American Frontier Myth." *Journal of Popular Culture* 24, no. 4 (Spring 1991): 17–25.

Searle, William J., ed. *Search and Clear: Critical Response to Selected Literature and Films of the Vietnam War*. Bowling Green, Ohio: Popular Press, 1988.

Selig, Michael. "Genre, Gender, and the Discourse of War: The A/historical and Vietnam Films." *Screen* 34, no. 1 (Spring 1993): 1–18.

Shain, Russell Earl. *An Analysis of Motion Pictures about War Released by the American Film Industry, 1930–1970*. New York: Arno Press, 1976.

Shindler, Colin. *Hollywood Goes to War: Films and American Society, 1939–1952*. London: Routledge and Kegan Paul, 1979.

Shull, Michael S., and David Edward Wilt. *Hollywood War Films, 1937–1945: An Exhaustive Filmography of American Feature-Length Motion Pictures Relating to World War II*. Jefferson, N.C.: McFarland, 1996.

Skogsberg, Bertil. *Wings on the Screen: A Pictorial History of Air Movies*. San Diego: A. S. Barnes, 1981.

Smith, Julian. *Looking Away: Hollywood and Vietnam*. New York: Charles Scribner's Sons, 1975.

Soderbergh, Peter A. "*Aux Armes!* The Rise of the Hollywood War Film, 1916–1930." *South Atlantic Quarterly* 65, no. 4 (Autumn 1966): 509–522.

Solomon, Stanley J. *Beyond Formula: American Film Genres*. New York: Harcourt Brace Jovanovich, 1976.

Spears, Jack. *The Civil War on the Screen and Other Essays*. South Brunswick, N.J.: A. S. Barnes, 1972.

———. "World War I on the Screen." 2 pts. *Films in Review* 17, no. 5 (May 1966): 274–292; no. 6 (June–July 1966): 347–365.

Springer, Claudia. "Antiwar Film as Spectacle: Contradictions of the Combat Sequence." *Genre* 21, no. 4 (Winter 1989): 479–486.

———. "Rebellious Sons in Vietnam Combat Films: A Response." *Genre* 21, no. 4 (Winter 1989): 517–522.

Studlar, Gaylyn, and David Desser. "Never Having to Say You're Sorry: *Rambo's* Rewriting of the Vietnam War." *Film Quarterly* 42, no. 1 (Fall 1988): 9–16. Reprinted in *From Hanoi to Hollywood: The Vietnam War in American Film*, edited by Linda Dittmar and Gene Michaud, pp. 101–112. New Brunswick: Rutgers University Press, 1991.

Suid, Lawrence. *Guts and Glory: Great American War Movies*. Reading, Mass.: Addison-Wesley, 1978.

———. "Hollywood and Vietnam." *Film Comment* 15, no. 5 (September–October 1979): 20–25.

———. "The Pentagon and Hollywood." In *American History/American Film,* edited by J. E. O'Connor and M. Jackson, pp. 219–236. New York: Ungar, 1979.

Traube, Elizabeth G. "Redeeming Images: The Wild Man Comes Home." *Persistence of Vision,* nos. 3–4 (Summer 1986): 71–94.

Tyler, Parker. "The Waxworks of War." In *Magic and Myth in the Movies,* pp. 132–147. New York: Simon and Schuster, 1947.

Virilio, Paul. *War and Cinema: The Logistics of Perception,* translated by Patrick Camiller. London and New York: Verso, 1989.

Walker, Mark. *Vietnam Veteran Films.* Metuchen, N.J.: Scarecrow Press, 1991.

Wetta, Frank J., and Stephen J. Curley. *Celluloid Wars: A Guide to Film and the American Experience of War.* Westport, Conn.: Greenwood Press, 1992.

Whillock, David Everett. "Defining the Fictive American Vietnam War Film: In Search of a Genre." *Literature/Film Quarterly* 16, no. 4 (1988): 244–250.

Whitehall, Richard. "One . . . Two . . . Three." *Films and Filming* 10, no. 11 (August 1964): 7–12.

Wilson, James C. *Vietnam in Prose and Film.* Jefferson, N.C.: McFarland, 1982.

Zinser, William. *Seen Any Good Movies Lately?* chap. 13. New York: Doubleday, 1958.

WESTERN FILMS

Adams, Lee, and Buck Rainey. *Shoot 'Em Up: The Complete Reference Guide to Westerns of the Sound Era.* New Rochelle, N.Y.: Arlington House, 1978.

Alloway, Lawrence. *Violent America: The Movies, 1946–1964.* New York: Museum of Modern Art, 1971.

Anderson, J. L. "Japanese Swordfighters and American Gunfighters." *Cinema Journal* 12, no. 2 (Spring 1973): 1–21. Reprinted in *Cinema Examined: Selections from* CINEMA JOURNAL, edited by Richard Dyer MacCann and Jack C. Ellis, pp. 84–104. New York: Dutton, 1982.

Anderson, Robert. "The Role of the Western Film Genre in Industry Competition, 1907–1911." *Journal of the University Film Association* 31, no. 2 (Spring 1979): 19–26.

Anez, Nicholas. "Westerns." 2 pts. *Films in Review* 45, nos. 7–8 (July–August 1994): 176–184; 46, nos. 1–2 (January–February 1995): 12–21.

Aquila, Richard, ed. *Wanted Dead or Alive: The American West in Popular Culture.* Urbana and Chicago: University of Illinois Press, 1996.

Armes, Roy. "The Western as a Film Genre." In *Film and Reality.* Baltimore: Penguin, 1975.

Austen, David. "Continental Westerns." *Films and Filming* 17, no. 10 (July 1971): 36–42.

Baker, Bob, et al. "ABC of the Western." *Kinema,* no. 3 (August 1971): 20–34.

Bataille, Gretchen M., and Bob Hicks. "American Indians in Popular Films." In *Beyond the Stars: Stock Characters in American Popular Film,* edited by Paul

Loukides and Linda K. Fuller, pp. 9–22. Bowling Green, Ohio: Bowling Green State University Press, 1990.

Bataille, Gretchen M., and Charles L. P. Silet. "Bibliography: Additions to the Indian in American Film." *Journal of Popular Film and Television* 8, no. 1 (Spring 1980): 50–53.

———. "A Checklist of Published Materials on Popular Images of the Indian in American Film." *Journal of Popular Film and Television* 5, no. 2 (1976): 171–182.

———. *The Pretend Indians: Images of Native Americans in the Movies.* Ames: University of Iowa Press, 1980.

Bazin, André. "The Evolution of the Western." In *What Is Cinema?* vol. 2, pp. 149–157. Berkeley: University of California Press, 1971. Reprinted in *Movies and Methods,* edited by Bill Nichols, pp. 150–157. Berkeley: University of California Press, 1976. *The Western Reader,* edited by Jim Kitses and Gregg Rickman, pp. 49–56. New York: Limelight, 1998.

———. "The Western, or the American Film *par excellence.*" In *What Is Cinema?* vol. 2, pp. 140–148. Berkeley: University of California Press, 1971.

Beale, L. "The American Way West." *Films and Filming* 18, no. 7 (April 1972): 24–30.

Blount, Trevor. "Violence in the Western." *Kinema,* no. 3 (August 1971): 14–19.

Bluestone, George. "The Changing Cowboy: From Dime Novel to Dollar Film." *Western Humanities Review* 14 (Summer 1960): 331–337.

Blumenberg, Richard. "The Evolution and Shape of the American Western." *Wide Angle* 1, no. 1 (Spring 1976): 39–49.

Boatright, Moody C. "The Formula in Cowboy Fiction and Drama." *Western Folklore* 28, no. 2 (April 1969): 136–145.

Brauer, Ralph. "Who Are Those Guys? The Movie Western during the TV Era." *Journal of Popular Film* 2, no. 4 (Fall 1973): 389–404. Reprinted in *Focus on the Western,* edited by Jack Nachbar, pp. 118–128. Englewood Cliffs, N.J.: Prentice-Hall, 1974.

Brauer, Ralph, and Donna Brauer. *The Horse, the Gun, and the Piece of Property: Changing Images of the TV Western.* Bowling Green, Ohio: Popular Press, 1975.

Buscombe, Edward. "End of the Trail?" *Sight and Sound* 57, no. 4 (Autumn 1988): 243–245.

———. "Painting the Legend: Frederic Remington and the Western." *Cinema Journal* 23, no. 4 (Summer 1984): 12–27.

———, ed. *The BFI Companion to the Western.* New York: Atheneum, 1990.

Buscombe, Edward, and Roberta Pearson, eds. *Back in the Saddle Again: New Essays on the Western.* London: British Film Institute, 1998.

Calder, Jenni. *There Must Be a Lone Ranger.* London: Hamish Hamilton, 1974.

Cameron, Ian, and Douglas Pye, eds. *The Movie Book of Westerns.* New York: Continuum, 1996.

Cawelti, John G. *Adventure, Mystery, and Romance: Formula Stories as Art and Popular Culture.* Chicago: University of Chicago Press, 1976.

———. "Cowboys, Indians, Outlaws: The West in Myth and Fantasy." *American West* 1 (Spring 1964): 28–35, 77–79.

———. "The Gunfighter and Society: Good Guys, Bad Guys, Deviates, and Compulsives—A View of the Adult Western." *American West* 5, no. 2 (March 1968): 30–35, 76–78.

———. "Prolegomena to the Western." *Studies in Public Communication,* no. 4 (Autumn 1962): 57–70.

———. "Reflections on the New Western Films." *University of Chicago Magazine,* January–February 1973, pp. 25–32.

———. *The Six-Gun Mystique.* Bowling Green, Ohio: Popular Press, 1985.

———. *The Six-Gun Mystique Sequel.* Bowling Green, Ohio: Popular Press, 1999.

———. "Zane Grey and W. S. Hart: The Romantic Western of the 1920s." *Velvet Light Trap,* no. 12 (Spring 1974): 6–10.

Clapham, Walter C. *Western Movies.* London: Octopus, 1974.

Collins, Richard. "Genre: A Reply to Ed Buscombe." *Screen* 11, nos. 4–5 (August–September 1970): 66–75. Reprinted in *Movies and Methods,* edited by Bill Nichols, pp. 157–163. Berkeley: University of California Press, 1976.

Cook, Pam, and Mieke Bernink, eds. *The Cinema Book,* 2d ed. London: British Film Institute, 1999.

Corkin, Stanley. "Cowboys and Free Markets: Post–World War II Westerns and the U.S. Hegemony." *Cinema Journal* 39, no. 3 (Spring 2000): 66–91.

Cowie, Peter. "The Growth of the Western." In *International Film Guide, 1966,* edited by Peter Cowie, pp. 39–43. New York: Barnes, 1966.

Coyne, Michael. *The Crowded Prairie: American National Identity in the Hollywood Western.* London: I. B. Taurus, 1998.

Dowell, Pat. "The Mythology of the Western: Hollywood Perspectives on Gender and Race in the Nineties." *Cineaste* 21, nos. 1–2 (February 1995): 6–10.

Durer, C. S., et al., eds. *American Renaissance and American West,* part 4. Laramie: University of Wyoming, 1982.

Durgnat, Raymond, and Scott Simmon. "Six Creeds That Won the Western." *Film Comment* 16, no. 5 (September–October 1980): 61–70. Reprinted in *The Western Reader,* edited by Jim Kitses and Gregg Rickman, pp. 69–83. New York: Limelight, 1998.

Elkin, Frederick. "The Psychological Appeal of the Hollywood Western." *Journal of Educational Sociology* 24, no. 2 (October 1950): 72–86.

Essleman, Kathryn C. "When the Cowboy Stopped Kissing His Horse." *Journal of Popular Culture* 6, no. 2 (Fall 1972): 337–349.

Etulain, Richard. "Origins of the Western." *Journal of Popular Culture* 5, no. 4 (Spring 1972): 799–805. Reprinted in *Focus on the Western,* edited by Jack Nachbar, pp. 19–24. Englewood Cliffs, N.J.: Prentice-Hall, 1974.

Etulain, Richard, and Michael T. Marsden, eds. "The Popular Western." *Journal of Popular Culture* 7, no. 3 (Winter 1973): 645–751.

Everson, William K. *A Pictorial History of the Western Film.* New York: Citadel Press, 1967.

Eyles, Allen. *The Western: An Illustrated Guide.* New York: A. S. Barnes, 1967.

Fagen, Herb. *White Hats and Silver Spurs: Interviews with 24 Stars of Film and Television Westerns of the Thirties through the Sixties.* Jefferson, N.C.: McFarland, 1996.

Fenin, George N. "The Western—Old and New." *Film Culture* 2, no. 2 (1956): 7–10.

Fenin, George N., and William K. Everson. *The Western from Silents to Cinerama.* New York: Orion Press, 1962.

———. *The Western: From Silents to the Seventies.* New York: Bonanza Books, 1973.

Fitzgerald, Michael G., and Boyd Magers. *Ladies of the Western: Interviews with 51 More Actresses from the Silent Era to the Television Westerns of the 1950s and 1960s.* Jefferson, N.C.: McFarland, 2002.

Folsom, James K. "'Western' Themes and Western Films." *Western American Literature* 2, no. 3 (Fall 1967): 195–203.

Fore, Steve. "The Same Old Others: The Western, *Lonesome Dove,* and the Lingering Difficulty of Difference." *Velvet Light Trap,* no. 27 (Spring 1991): 49–62.

Franklin, Eliza. "Westerns, First and Lasting." *Quarterly of Film, Television, and Radio* 7, no. 2 (Winter 1952): 109–115.

Frayling, Christopher. "The American Western and American Society." *Cinema, Politics, and Society in America,* edited by Philip Davies and Brian Neve, pp. 136–162. New York: St. Martin's Press, 1981.

———. *Spaghetti Westerns.* London: Routledge and Kegan Paul, 1981.

French, Philip. "The Indian in the Western Movie." *Arts in America* 60, no. 4 (July–August 1972): 32–39.

———. *Westerns.* New York: Viking, 1974.

Friar, Ralph, and Natasha Friar. *The Only Good Indian . . . : The Hollywood Gospel.* New York: Drama Book Specialists, 1972.

Garfield, Brian. *Western Films: A Complete Guide.* New York: Rawson Associates, 1982. Rev. ed., New York: Da Capo, 1988.

Garrett, Greg. "The American West and the American Western." *Journal of American Culture* 14, no. 2 (Summer 1991): 99–106.

Godfrey, Lionel. "A Heretic's View of Westerns." *Films and Filming* 13, no. 8 (May 1967): 14–20.

Graham, Don. "A Short History of Texas in the Movies: An Overview." *Literature/Film Quarterly* 14, no. 2 (1986): 71–81.

Hanfling, Barrie. *Westerns and the Trail of Tradition: A Year-by-Year History, 1929–1962.* Jefferson, N.C.: McFarland, 2001.

Hardy, Phil. *The Western: The Complete Film Sourcebook.* New York: Morrow, 1983.

Harshman, Frederick M. "The Western." *Films in Review* 41, nos. 11–12 (1990): 534–537.

Hitt, Jim. *The American West from Fiction (1823–1976) into Film (1909–1986).* Jefferson, N.C.: McFarland, 1990.

Hoffmann, Henryk. *"A" Western Filmmakers: A Biographical Dictionary of Writers, Directors, Cinematographers, Composers, Actors, and Actresses.* Jefferson, N.C.: McFarland, 2000.

Holland, Ted. *B Western Actors Encyclopedia: Facts, Photos and Filmographies for More Than 250 Familiar Faces.* Jefferson, N.C.: McFarland, 1989.

Homans, Peter. "Puritanism Revisited: An Analysis of the Contemporary Screen-

Image Western." *Studies in Public Communication,* no. 3 (Summer 1961): 73–84. Reprinted in *Focus on the Western,* edited by Jack Nachbar, pp. 84–92. Englewood Cliffs, N.J.: Prentice-Hall, 1974.

Horwitz, James. *They Went Thataway.* New York: Dutton, 1976.

Jarvie, I. C. *Movies and Society.* New York: Basic Books, 1970.

Jones, Daryl E. "The Earliest Western Films." *Journal of Popular Film and Television* 8, no. 2 (1980): 42–46.

Kaminsky, Stuart M. "Once upon a Time in Italy: The Italian Western beyond Leone." *Velvet Light Trap,* no. 12 (Spring 1974): 31–33. Reprinted in *Graphic Violence on the Screen,* edited by Thomas R. Atkins, pp. 47–67. New York: Monarch Press, 1976.

———. "The Samurai Film and the Western." *Journal of Popular Film* 1, no. 4 (1972): 312–324. Revised as "Comparative Forms: The Samurai Film and the Western." In *American Film Genres: Approaches to a Critical Theory of Popular Film,* chap. 3. Dayton, Ohio: Pflaum, 1974.

Kitchen, Lawrence. "Decline of the Western." *Listener* 14 (July 1966): 54–57.

Kitses, Jim. *Horizons West.* Bloomington and London: Indiana University Press, 1970.

———. "The Western." *The American Cinema,* 3d ed., edited by Donald E. Staples, pp. 313–329. Washington, D.C.: United States Information Agency, 1991.

Kitses, Jim, and Gregg Rickman, eds. *The Western Reader.* New York: Limelight, 1998.

Knies, Donald V. "The Aging Hero in the Changing West." *West Virginia University Philological Papers* 26 (August 1980): 66–73.

Lackman, Ron. *Women of the Western Frontier in Fact, Fiction, and Film.* Jefferson, N.C.: McFarland, 1997.

Landy, Marcia. *Italian Film,* chap. 5. New York and Cambridge: Cambridge University Press, 2000.

Langman, Larry. *A Guide to Silent Westerns.* Westport, Conn.: Greenwood Press, 1992.

Larkins, Robert. "Hollywood and the Indian." *Focus on Film,* no. 2 (March–April 1970): 44–53.

Lenihan, John H. *Showdown: Confronting Modern America in the Western Film.* Chicago: University of Chicago Press, 1980.

Lentz, Harris M., III. *Western and Frontier Film and Television Credits, 1903–1995.* Jefferson, N.C.: McFarland, 1996.

Levitan, Jacqueline. "The Western: Any Good Roles for Feminists?" *Film Reader,* no. 5 (1982): 95–108.

Lovell, Alan. "The Western." *Screen Education,* no. 41 (September–October 1967): 92–103. Reprinted in *Movies and Methods,* edited by Bill Nichols, pp. 164–175. Berkeley: University of California Press, 1976.

Loy, R. Philip. *Westerns and American Culture, 1930–1955.* Jefferson, N.C.: McFarland, 2001.

MacArthur, Colin. "The Roots of the Western." *Cinema* (U.K.), no. 4 (October 1969): 11–13.

McDonald, Archie P., ed. *Shooting Stars: Heroes and Heroines of Western Film.* Bloomington: Indiana University Press, 1987.

McMahan, Alison. "Eastern Westerns: Early French Constructions of American Identity." *Quarterly Review of Film and Video* 18, no. 3 (2001): 295–303.

McMurtry, Larry. "Cowboys, Movies, Myths, and Cadillacs: Realism in the Western." In *Man and the Movies,* edited by W. R. Robinson. Baltimore: Penguin, 1967.

McReynolds, Douglas A. "Alive and Well: Western Myth in Western Movies." *Literature/Film Quarterly* 26, no. 1 (1998): 319–335.

Magers, Boyd, and Michael G. Fitzgerald. *Western Women: Interviews with 50 Leading Ladies of Movie and Television Westerns from the 1930s to the 1960s.* Jefferson, N.C.: McFarland, 1999.

Markfield, Wallace. "The Inauthentic Western." *American Mercury* 75 (September 1952): 82–86.

Maynard, Richard A., ed. *The American West on Film: Myth and Reality.* Rochelle Park, N.J.: Hayden, 1974.

Mitchell, Charles Reed, and Frank Scheide. "The Reformation of the Good Badman." *Velvet Light Trap,* no. 12 (Spring 1974): 11–14.

Mitchell, Lee Clark. "Violence in the Film Western." In *Violence and American Cinema,* edited by J. David Slocum, pp. 176–191. New York and London: Routledge, 2001.

———. *Westerns: Making the Man in Fiction and Film.* Chicago and London: University of Chicago Press, 1996.

Nachbar, Jack. "A Checklist of Published Materials on Western Movies." *Journal of Popular Film* 2, no. 4 (Fall 1973): 411–428.

———. "Riding Shotgun: The Scattered Formula in Contemporary Western Movies." *Film Journal* 2, no. 3 (September 1973). Reprinted in *Focus on the Western,* edited by Nachbar, pp. 101–112. Englewood Cliffs, N.J.: Prentice-Hall, 1974.

———. "Seventy Years on the Trail: A Selected Chronology of the Western Movie." *Journal of Popular Film* 2, no. 1 (Winter 1973): 75–83.

———. *Western Films: An Annotated Critical Bibliography.* New York: Garland, 1975.

———, ed. *Focus on the Western.* Englewood Cliffs, N.J.: Prentice-Hall, 1974.

Nachbar, Jack, et al. *Western Films 2: An Annotated Critical Bibliography from 1974 to 1987.* New York: Garland, 1988.

Nussbaum, Martin. "Sociological Symbolism of the 'Adult Western.'" *Social Forces* 39, no. 1 (October 1960): 25–28.

O'Connor, John E. *The Hollywood Indian: Stereotypes of Native Americans in Films.* Trenton: New Jersey State Museum, 1980.

Oshana, Maryann. "Native American Women in Westerns: Reality and Myth." *Film Reader,* no. 5 (1982): 125–131.

Palmer, R. Barton. "A Masculinist Reading of Two Western Films: *High Noon* and *Rio Grande*." *Journal of Popular Film and Television* 12, no. 4 (Winter 1984–1985): 156–162.

Parish, James R. *Great Western Stars.* New York: Grosset and Dunlop, 1976.

Parish, James R., and Michael R. Pitts. *The Great Western Pictures II.* Metuchen, N.J.: Scarecrow Press, 1988.

Parkinson, Michael, and Clyde Jeavons. *A Pictorial History of Westerns.* London: Hamlyn, 1972.

Parks, Rita. *The Western Hero in Film and Television: Mass Media Mythology.* Ann Arbor: UMI Research Press, 1982.

Peary, Gerald. "Selected Sound Westerns and Their Novel Sources." *Velvet Light Trap,* no. 12 (Spring 1974): 11–14.

Pilkington, William T., and Don Graham, eds. *Western Movies.* Albuquerque: University of New Mexico Press, 1979.

Pitts, Michael R. *Western Movies: A TV and Video Guide to 4200 Genre Films.* Jefferson, N.C.: McFarland, 1986.

Podheiser, Linda. "Pep on the Range or Douglas Fairbanks and the World War I Era Western." *Journal of Popular Film and Television* 11, no. 3 (Fall 1983): 122–130.

Pye, Douglas. "Genre and History: *Fort Apache* and *The Man Who Shot Liberty Valance.*" *Movie* (U.K.), no. 25 (Winter 1977–1978): 1–11.

———. "Genre and Movies." *Movie* (U.K.), no. 20 (Spring 1975): 29–43.

Rainey, Buck. *The Reel Cowboy: Essays on the Myth in Movies and Literature.* Jefferson, N.C.: McFarland, 1996.

———. *Saddle Aces of the Cinema.* San Diego: A. S. Barnes, 1980.

———. *The Shoot-Em-Ups Ride Again: A Supplement to Shoot-Em-Ups.* Metuchen, N.J.: Scarecrow Press, 1990.

———. *Sweethearts of the Sage: Biographies and Filmographies of 258 Actresses Appearing in Western Movies.* Jefferson, N.C.: McFarland, 1992.

———. *Western Gunslingers in Fact and on Film: Hollywood's Famous Lawmen and Outlaws.* Jefferson, N.C.: McFarland, 1997.

Ramonet, Ignacio. "Italian Westerns as Political Parables." *Cineaste* 15, no. 1 (1986): 30–35.

Ray, Robert B. *A Certain Tendency of the Hollywood Cinema, 1930–1980.* Princeton: Princeton University Press, 1985.

Reed, Joseph W. *American Scenarios: The Uses of Film Genre.* Middletown, Conn.: Wesleyan University Press, 1989.

Reed, Toby, and R. J. Thompson. "The Six-Gun Simulacrum: New Metaphors for an Old Genre." *Film Criticism* 20, no. 3 (Spring 1996): 52–68.

Reitinger, Douglas W. "Too Long in the Wasteland: Visions of the American West in Film, 1980–1990." *Film and History* 26, nos. 1–4 (1996): 20–29.

Ross, T. J. "Fantasy and Form in the Western: From Hart to Peckinpah." *December* 12, no. 1 (Fall 1970): 158–169.

Rothel, David. *The Singing Cowboys.* South Brunswick, N.J., and New York: A. S. Barnes, 1978.

Ryall, Tom. "The Notion of Genre." *Screen* 11, no. 2 (March–April 1970): 22–32.

Ryan, Michael, and Douglas Kellner. *Camera Politica: The Politics and Ideology of Contemporary Hollywood Film.* Bloomington and Indianapolis: Indiana University Press, 1988.

Sarf, Wayne Michael. *God Bless You, Buffalo Bill: A Layman's Guide to History and the Western Film*. Rutherford, N.J.: Fairleigh Dickinson University Press, 1983.

Sarris, Andrew. "Death of the Gunfighters." *Film Comment* 18, no. 2 (1982): 40–42.

Saunders, John. *The Western Genre: From Lordsburg to Big Whiskey*. London: Wallflower Press, 2001.

Schatz, Thomas. *Hollywood Genres: Formulas, Filmmaking, and the Studio System*. New York: Random House, 1981.

———. "The Western." In *Handbook of American Film Genres*, edited by Wes D. Gehring, pp. 25–46. New York: Greenwood Press, 1988.

Schein, Harry. "The Olympian Cowboy." *American Scholar* 24 (Summer 1955): 309–320.

Schneider, Tassilo. "Finding a New *Heimat* in the Wild West: Karl May and the German Western of the 1960s." *Journal of Film and Video* 47, nos. 1–3 (Spring–Fall 1995): 67–81.

Self, Robert T. "Ritual Patterns in Western Film and Fiction." In *Narrative Strategies: Original Essays in Film and Prose Fiction*, edited by Syndy M. Conger and Janice R. Welsch, pp. 105–114. Macomb: Western Illinois University Press, 1980.

Silet, Charles L. P., and Gretchen M. Bataille. "The Indian in the Film: A Critical Survey." *Quarterly Review of Film Studies* 2 (February 1977): 56–74.

Silver, Charles. *The Western Film*. New York: Pyramid Books, 1976.

Skerry, Philip J. "Pursuing the Posse." *Journal of Popular Film and Television* 14, no. 1 (Spring 1986): 14–22.

———. "The Western Film: A Sense of an Ending." *New Orleans Review* 17, no. 3 (1990): 13–17.

Slotkin, Richard. *Gunfighter Nation: The Myth of the Frontier in Twentieth-Century America*. New York: Atheneum, 1992.

———. "Prologue to a Study of Myth and Genre in American Movies." In *Prospects: The Annual of American Cultural Studies*, no. 9, edited by Jack Salzman, pp. 407–432. Cambridge and New York: Cambridge University Press, 1984.

Solomon, Stanley J. *Beyond Formula: American Film Genres*. New York: Harcourt Brace Jovanovich, 1976.

Spears, Jack. "The Indian on the Screen." *Films in Review* 10 (January 1959): 18–35.

Staig, Lawrence, and Tony Williams. *Italian Westerns: The Opera of Violence*. London: Lorrimer, 1975.

Stanfield, Peter. *Hollywood, Westerns, and the 1930s: The Lost Trail*. Exeter: University of Exeter Press, 2001.

———. *Horse Opera: The Strange History of the 1930s Singing Cowboy*. Urbana and Chicago: University of Illinois Press, 2002.

———. "The Western, 1909–1914: A Cast of Villains." *Film History* 1, no. 2 (1987): 97–112.

Stedman, Raymond William. *Shadows of the Indian*. Norman: University of Oklahoma Press, 1986.

Tatum, Stephen. "The Western Film Critic as 'Shootist.'" *Journal of Popular Film and Television* 11, no. 3 (Fall 1983): 114–121.

Telotte, J. P. "A Fate Worse than Death: Racism, Transgression, and Westerns." *Journal of Popular Film and Television* 26, no. 3 (Fall 1998): 120–127.

Thompson, Anne. "Beyond the Pale Riders." *Film Comment* 28, no. 4 (July–August 1992): 52–54.

Thomson, David. "Better Best Westerns." *Film Comment* 26, no. 2 (March–April 1990): 5–8, 10–13.

Tompkins, Jane. "Language and Landscape: An Ontology for the Western." *Artforum* 28, no. 6 (February 1990): 94–99.

———. "West of Everything." *South Atlantic Quarterly* 86, no. 4 (Fall 1987): 357–377. Reprinted in *Gender, Genre, and Narrative Pleasure,* edited by Derek Longhurst, pp. 10–30. London: Unwin Hyman, 1989. *Gender, Language and Myth: Essays on Popular Narrative,* edited by Glenwood Irons, pp. 103–123. Toronto: University of Toronto Press, 1992.

———. *West of Everything: The Inner Life of the Western.* New York: Oxford University Press, 1992.

Tudor, Andrew. *Image and Influence: Studies in the Sociology of Film.* London: George Allen and Unwin, 1974.

Tuska, Jon. *The American West in Film: Critical Approaches to the Western.* New York: Greenwood Press, 1985.

Tuska, Jon, and Nicki Pierarski. *The Frontier Experience: A Reader's Guide to the Life and Literature of the American West.* Jefferson, N.C.: McFarland, 1984.

Vallance, Tom (also credited to Eric Warman). *Westerns: A Preview Special.* London: Golden Pleasure Books, 1964.

Wallington, Mike. "The Italian Western: A Concordance." *Cinema* (U.K.), nos. 6–7 (August 1970): 31–34.

Warshow, Robert. "Movie Chronicle: The Westerner." In *The Immediate Experience,* pp. 35–54. New York: Atheneum, 1971. Reprinted in *Film: An Anthology,* edited by Daniel Talbot, pp. 148–162. Berkeley and Los Angeles: University of California Press, 1967. *Focus on the Western,* edited by Jack Nachbar, pp. 45–46. Englewood Cliffs, N.J.: Prentice-Hall, 1974. *Awake in the Dark,* edited by David Denby, pp. 248–263. New York: Vintage, 1977. *Film Theory and Criticism,* 4th ed., edited by Gerald Mast, Marshall Cohen, and Leo Braudy, pp. 453–466. New York: Oxford, 1992. *The Western Reader,* edited by Jim Kitses and Gregg Rickman, pp. 35–47. New York: Limelight, 1998.

Watson, Stephanie. "From Riding to Driving: Once upon a Time in the West." In *Lost Highways: An Illustrated History of Road Movies,* edited by Jack Sargeant and Stephanie Watson, pp. 22–37. London: Creation Press, 1999.

Weisser, Thomas. *Spaghetti Westerns—The Good, the Bad, and the Violent: A Comprehensive Illustrated Filmography of 558 Eurowesterns and Their Personnel, 1961–1977.* Jefferson, N.C.: McFarland, 1992.

Whitehall, Richard. "The Heroes Are Tired." *Film Quarterly* 20, no. 2 (Winter 1966–1967): 12–24.

Willett, Ralph. "The American Western: Myth and Anti-Myth." *Journal of Popular Culture* 4, no. 2 (Fall 1970): 455–463.

Williams, John. "The Western: Definitions of a Myth." *Nation,* November 18, 1961, pp. 402–406. Reprinted in *The Popular Arts: A Critical Reader,* edited by Irving and Harriet A. Deer, pp. 98–111. New York: Scribner's, 1967.

Wright, Will. *Sixguns and Society: A Structural Study of the Western.* Berkeley: University of California Press, 1976.

Yoggy, Gary A., ed. *Back in the Saddle: Essays on Western Film and Television Actors.* Jefferson, N.C.: McFarland, 1998.

Notes on Contributors

RICK ALTMAN is Professor of Cinema and Comparative Literature at the University of Iowa. He is the author of *The American Film Musical* (1987) and *Film/Genre* (1999) and the editor of *Cinema/Sound* (1980), *Genre: The Musical* (1981), and *Sound Theory/Sound Practice* (1992).

JEAN-LOUP BOURGET has published several books on American film, including *Le Mélodrame Hollywoodien* (1985). From 1973 to 1981 he was French cultural attaché in London, Chicago, New York, and Barcelona. He teaches English and film at the University of Toulouse.

EDWARD BUSCOMBE is the editor of *The BFI Companion to the Western* (1988) and the author of *Stagecoach* (1992) and *The Searchers* (2000), both in the BFI Film Classics Series. He has published in such journals as *Screen, Cinema Journal*, and *Sight and Sound,* and has taught widely in the United Kingdom and the United States, most recently at Hollins University, Virginia.

JOHN G. CAWELTI was Professor of English at the University of Kentucky at Lexington. He is the author of *Apostles of the Self-Made Man* (1968), *The Six-Gun Mystique* (1970, rev. ed. 1985), and *Adventure, Mystery, and Romance: Formula Stories in Art and Popular Culture* (1976).

RICHARD DE CORDOVA taught film and television studies at DePaul University in Chicago and is the author of *Picture Personalities: The Emergence of the Star System in America* (1990).

DAVID DESSER is Professor of Cinema Studies at the University of Illinois. He has published widely on aspects of American, Japanese, and Hong Kong cinema. His books include *The Samurai Films of Akira Kurosawa* (1983), *Eros Plus Massacre: An Introduction to the Japanese New*

Wave Cinema (1988), and the coedited anthologies *The Cinema of Hong Kong: History, Arts, Identity* and *Hollywood Goes Shopping*. He is the former book review editor of *Film Quarterly* and a former editor of *Cinema Journal*. In 2002–2003, he was Scholar in Residence at Hong Kong Baptist University.

THOMAS ELSAESSER is Professor of Art and Culture at the University of Amsterdam and Chair of Research in Film and Television. Among his books as author and editor are *New German Cinema: A History* (1989), *Early Cinema: Space Frame Narrative* (1990), *Writing for the Medium: Television in Transition* (1994), *A Second Life: German Cinema's First Decades* (1996), *Fassbinder's Germany: History, Identity, Subject* (1996), *Cinema Futures: Cain, Abel, or Cable* (1998), *The BFI Companion to German Cinema* (1999), *Weimar Cinema and After* (2000), *Metropolis* (2000), and, with Warren Buckland, *Studying Contemporary American Film* (2002).

JANE FEUER teaches film, television, and cultural studies in the English Department at the University of Pittsburgh. She is the author of *The Hollywood Musical* (2d rev. ed., 1993) and has written numerous articles on television.

TAG GALLAGHER is the author of *John Ford: The Man and His Films* (1986) and *The Adventures of Roberto Rossellini* (1998). He has published auteur studies in such journals as *Sight and Sound, Cinémathèque, Cahiers du Cinéma, Film Comment,* and *Artforum,* and at the *Screening the Past* website, http://www.latrobe.edu.au/screeningthepast

SUSAN JEFFORDS is Director of Women's Studies and Professor of English at the University of Washington. She is the author of *The Remasculinization of America: Gender and the Vietnam War* (1989) and *Hard Bodies: Hollywood Masculinity in the Reagan Era* (1993) and coeditor of *Seeing through the Media: The Persian Gulf War* (1994).

BRUCE KAWIN is Professor of English and Film Studies at the University of Colorado at Boulder. He has written three books on Faulkner's screenplays (*Faulkner and Film*, 1977; *To Have and Have Not*, 1980; and *Faulkner's MGM Screenplays*, 1982), three on narrative theory (*Telling It Again and Again: Repetition in Literature and Film*, 1972; *Mindscreen: Bergman, Godard, and First-Person Film*, 1978; and *The Mind of the Novel: Reflexive Fiction and the Ineffable*, 1982), and two textbooks (*How Movies Work*, 1987, and a revised version of the late Gerald Mast's *A Short History of the Movies*, 1992). He is also a poet and screenwriter.

BARBARA KLINGER is Associate Professor and Director of Film and Media in the Department of Communication and Culture at Indiana University in Bloomington and the author of *Melodrama and Meaning: History, Culture, and the Films of Douglas Sirk* (1994). Her work has appeared in such journals as *Screen, camera obscura, Cinema Journal, Wide Angle,* and *Velvet Light Trap.*

EDWARD MITCHELL has taught English at the University of Ohio in Athens, Ohio. He is currently district agent for Northwestern Mutual Life Insurance in Illinois.

STEVE NEALE is Research Professor in Film, Media, and Communication Studies at Sheffield Hallam University in England. He is the author of *Genre* (1980) and *Genre and Hollywood* (2000), coauthor (with Frank Krutnik) of *Popular Film and Television Comedy* (1990), and editor of *Genre and Contemporary Hollywood* (2002) and, with Murray Smith, of *Contemporary Hollywood Cinema* (1998).

DOUGLAS PYE is Senior Lecturer in Film and Head of the School of Arts and Communication Design at the University of Reading. He coedited *The Movie Book of the Western* (with Ian Cameron) and is editor of a forthcoming anthology on Fritz Lang to be published by Cameron and Hollis in the United Kingdom.

MARK A. REID is Associate Professor of English and African American Studies at the University of Florida at Gainesville. His publications include *Redefining Black Film* (1993), *PostNegritude Visual and Literary Culture* (1997), and *Spike Lee's DO THE RIGHT THING* (1997).

THOMAS SCHATZ teaches film at the University of Texas at Austin. He is the author of *Hollywood Genres: Formulas, Filmmaking, and the Studio System* (1981) and *The Genius of the System: Hollywood Filmmaking in the Studio Era* (1988).

PAUL SCHRADER is the former editor of *Cinema* (U.S.) and the author of *Transcendental Style in Film: Ozu, Bresson, Dreyer* (1972). He is also a noted screenwriter (*The Yakuza,* 1974; *Taxi Driver,* 1976; *Rolling Thunder,* 1977; *The Last Temptation of Christ,* 1988; *Bringing Out the Dead,* 1999) and director (*Blue Collar,* 1978; *Hard Core,* 1980; *American Gigolo,* 1980; *Cat People,* 1982; *Mishima,* 1985; *Patty Hearst,* 1988; *The Comfort of Strangers,* 1990; *Light Sleeper,* 1992; *Affliction,* 1997; *Forever Mine,* 2001; and *Auto-Focus,* 2002).

TIMOTHY SHARY is Assistant Professor of Screen Studies at Clark University in Worcester, Massachusetts. He is the author of *Generation Multiplex: The Image of Youth in Contemporary American Cinema* (2002), and his work on teen films has been published in *Journal of Popular Film and Television, Post Script, Journal of Film and Video,* and elsewhere.

DAVID R. SHUMWAY is Professor of English and Literary and Cultural Studies and Director of the Center for Cultural Analysis at Carnegie Mellon University. He is the author of *Michel Foucault* (1989), *Creating American Civilization: A Genealogy of American Literature as an Academic Discipline* (1994), and *Modern Love: Romance, Intimacy, and the Marriage Crisis* (2003).

THOMAS SOBCHACK is Emeritus Professor of Film Studies at the University of Utah. He is the coauthor (with Vivian Sobchack) of *An Introduction to Film* (1980) and (with Tim Bywater) of *Introduction to Film Criticism* (1989). His articles have appeared in such journals as *Literature/Film Quarterly* and *Journal of Popular Film and Television* and in several anthologies.

VIVIAN SOBCHACK is Associate Dean and Professor of Film and Television Studies at the UCLA School of Theatre, Film, and Television. She is the author of *Screening Space: The American Science Fiction Film* (1987), *The Address of the Eye: A Phenomenology of Film Experience* (1993), and numerous essays in such journals as *Quarterly Review of Film and Video, camera obscura, Post Script, Film Quarterly, Representations,* and *Artforum.* She is also the coauthor (with Thomas Sobchack) of *An Introduction to Film* (1980).

JANET STAIGER teaches cultural, gender, and media studies at the University of Texas at Austin. Her books are *The Classical Hollywood Cinema: Film Style and Mode of Production* (1980, with David Bordwell and Kristin Thompson), *Interpreting Films: Studies in the Historical Reception of American Cinema* (1992), *Bad Women: Regulating Sexuality in Early American Cinema, 1907–1915* (1995), *Perverse Spectators: The Practices of Film Reception* (2000), and *Blockbuster TV: Must-See Sitcoms in the Network Era* (2000). She directs the university's Center for Women's Studies and is the William P. Hobby Centennial Professor in Communication.

CHRIS STRAAYER is Associate Professor and chair of the Department of Cinema Studies at New York University and the author of *Deviant Eyes/*

Deviant Bodies: Gay, Lesbian, and Queer Discourse in Film and Video (1996).

MARGARET TARRATT has served on the lecture panel of the British Film Institute. Her essay on Luchino Visconti's *The Damned* appeared in *Screen*.

ANDREW TUDOR is Reader in Sociology at the University of York in England. He is the author of *Theories of Film* (1973), *Image and Influence: Studies in the Sociology of Film* (1974), *Monsters and Mad Scientists: A Cultural History of the Horror Movie* (1989), and *Decoding Culture: Theory and Method in Cultural Studies* (1999).

LINDA WILLIAMS is Professor of Film Studies and Rhetoric at the University of California, Berkeley, and director of the Program in Film Studies. She is the author of *Hard Core: Power, Pleasure, and the Frenzy of the Visible* (1981), *Figures of Desire: A Theory and Analysis of Surrealist Film* (1989), and *Playing the Race Card: Melodramas of Black and White, from Uncle Tom to O. J. Simpson* (2001), and the editor of *Re-Vision: Essays in Feminist Film Criticism* (1984, with Mary Ann Doane and Patricia Mellencamp), *Viewing Positions* (1993), and *Reinventing Film Studies* (2000, with Christine Gledhill).

ROBIN WOOD is the author of *Hitchcock's Films* (1965), *Howard Hawks* (1968), *Ingmar Bergman* (1969), *Arthur Penn* (1969), *Claude Chabrol* (with Michael Walker, 1970), *Personal Views* (1976), *Hollywood from Vietnam to Reagan* (1985), *Sexual Politics and Narrative Film: Hollywood and Beyond* (1996), and *Wings of the Dove* (2000). He is a founding member of the *CineAction* editorial collective.

JUDITH HESS WRIGHT was Professor of Marketing in the School of Business at Sonoma State University in California, where she also taught literature, film, and folklore.

MAURICE YACOWAR teaches Film Studies at the University of Calgary, Alberta, Canada. He is the author of *Hitchcock's British Films* (1977), *Tennessee Williams and Film* (1977), *Loser Take All: The Comic Art of Woody Allen* (1979), *Method in Madness: The Comic Art of Mel Brooks* (1981), *The Films of Paul Morrissey* (1993), and *The Sopranos on the Couch: Analyzing Television's Best Series* (2002), as well as the novel *The Bold Testament* (2000).

Index

Boldface page numbers indicate photographs.